SO-DVG-558

CRIMINAL JUSTICE 96/97

Twentieth Edition

Editor

John J. Sullivan
Mercy College, Dobbs Ferry, New York

John J. Sullivan, professor and former chair of the Department of Law, Criminal Justice, and Safety Administration at Mercy College, received his B.S. in 1949 from Manhattan College and his J.D. in 1956 from St. John's Law School. He was formerly captain and director of the Legal Division of the New York City Police Department.

Editor

Joseph L. Victor
Mercy College, Dobbs Ferry, New York

Joseph L. Victor is professor and chairman of the Department of Law, Criminal Justice, and Safety Administration at Mercy College. Professor Victor has extensive field experience in criminal justice agencies, counseling, and administering human service programs. He earned his B.A. and M.A. at Seton Hall University, and his Doctorate of Education at Fairleigh Dickinson University.

Annual Editions

A Library of Information from the Public Press

Cover illustration by Mike Eagle

**Dushkin Publishing Group/
Brown & Benchmark Publishers
Sluice Dock, Guilford, Connecticut 06437**

The Annual Editions Series

Annual Editions is a series of over 65 volumes designed to provide the reader with convenient, low-cost access to a wide range of current, carefully selected articles from some of the most important magazines, newspapers, and journals published today. Annual Editions are updated on an annual basis through a continuous monitoring of over 300 periodical sources. All Annual Editions have a number of features designed to make them particularly useful, including topic guides, annotated tables of contents, unit overviews, and indexes. For the teacher using Annual Editions in the classroom, an Instructor's Resource Guide with test questions is available for each volume.

VOLUMES AVAILABLE

Abnormal Psychology
Africa
Aging
American Foreign Policy
American Government
American History, Pre-Civil War
American History, Post-Civil War
American Public Policy
Anthropology
Archaeology
Biopsychology
Business Ethics
Child Growth and Development
China
Comparative Politics
Computers in Education
Computers in Society
Criminal Justice
Developing World
Deviant Behavior
Drugs, Society, and Behavior
Dying, Death, and Bereavement
Early Childhood Education
Economics
Educating Exceptional Children
Education
Educational Psychology
Environment
Geography
Global Issues
Health
Human Development
Human Resources
Human Sexuality

India and South Asia
International Business
Japan and the Pacific Rim
Latin America
Life Management
Macroeconomics
Management
Marketing
Marriage and Family
Mass Media
Microeconomics
Middle East and the Islamic World
Multicultural Education
Nutrition
Personal Growth and Behavior
Physical Anthropology
Psychology
Public Administration
Race and Ethnic Relations
Russia, the Eurasian Republics,
    and Central/Eastern Europe
Social Problems
Sociology
State and Local Government
Urban Society
Western Civilization,
    Pre-Reformation
Western Civilization,
    Post-Reformation
Western Europe
World History, Pre-Modern
World History, Modern
World Politics

Cataloging in Publication Data
Main entry under title: Annual Editions: Criminal Justice. 1996/97.
    1. Criminal Justice, Administration of—United States—Periodicals. I. Sullivan, John J.,
comp. II. Victor, Joseph L., *comp.* III. Title: Criminal justice.
HV 8138.A67   364.973.05   77–640116
ISBN 0–697–31706–4

Twentieth Edition

Printed in the United States of America

Printed on Recycled Paper

To the Reader

In publishing ANNUAL EDITIONS we recognize the enormous role played by the magazines, newspapers, and journals of the *public press* in providing current, first-rate educational information in a broad spectrum of interest areas. Within the articles, the best scientists, practitioners, researchers, and commentators draw issues into new perspective as accepted theories and viewpoints are called into account by new events, recent discoveries change old facts, and fresh debate breaks out over important controversies. Many of the articles resulting from this enormous editorial effort are appropriate for students, researchers, and professionals seeking accurate, current material to help bridge the gap between principles and theories and the real world. These articles, however, become more useful for study when those of lasting value are carefully *collected, organized, indexed,* and *reproduced* in a *low-cost format,* which provides easy and permanent access when the material is needed. That is the role played by ANNUAL EDITIONS. Under the direction of each volume's *Editor,* who is an expert in the subject area, and with the guidance of an *Advisory Board,* we seek each year to provide in each ANNUAL EDITION a current, well-balanced, carefully selected collection of the best of the public press for your study and enjoyment.

We think you'll find this volume useful, and we hope you'll take a moment to let us know what you think.

During the 1970s, criminal justice emerged as an appealing, vital, and unique academic discipline. It emphasizes the professional development of students who plan careers in the field and attracts those who want to know more about a complex social problem and how this country deals with it. Criminal justice incorporates a vast range of knowledge from a number of specialties, including law, history, and the behavioral and social sciences. Each specialty contributes to our fuller understanding of criminal behavior and of society's attitudes toward deviance.

In view of the fact that the criminal justice system is in a constant state of flux, and because the study of criminal justice covers such a broad spectrum, today's students must be aware of a variety of subjects and topics. Standard textbooks and traditional anthologies cannot keep pace with the changes as quickly as they occur. In fact, many such sources are already out of date the day they are published. *Annual Editions: Criminal Justice 96/97* strives to maintain currency in matters of concern by providing up-to-date commentaries, articles, reports, and statistics from the most recent literature in the criminal justice field.

This volume contains units concerning crime and justice in America, victimology, the police, the judicial system, juvenile justice, and punishment and corrections. The articles in these units were selected because they are informative as well as provocative. The selections are timely and useful in their treatment of ethics, punishment, juveniles, courts, and other related topics.

Included in this volume are a number of features designed to be useful to students, researchers, and professionals in the criminal justice field. These include a *topic guide* for locating articles on specific subjects; the *table of contents abstracts,* which summarize each article and feature key concepts in bold italics; and a comprehensive *bibliography, glossary,* and *index.* In addition, each unit is preceded by an *overview* that provides a background for informed reading of the articles, emphasizes critical issues, and presents challenge questions.

We would like to know what you think of the selections contained in this edition. Please fill out the postage-paid *article rating form* on the last page and let us know your opinions. We change or retain many of the articles based on the comments we receive from you, the user. Help us to improve this anthology—annually.

John J. Sullivan

Joseph L. Victor
Editors

Contents

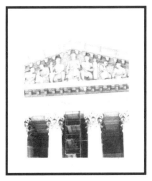

Unit
1

Crime and Justice in America

Eight selections focus on the overall structure of the criminal justice system in the United States. The current scope of crime in America is reviewed, and topics such as criminal behavior, drugs, and organized crime are discussed.

The concepts in bold italics are developed in the article. For further expansion please refer to the Topic Guide, the Index, and the Glossary.

Unit 2

Victimology

Seven articles discuss the impact of crime on the victim. Topics include the rights of crime victims and the consequences of family violence and rape.

The concepts in bold italics are developed in the article. For further expansion please refer to the Topic Guide, the Index, and the Glossary.

Unit

3

The Police

Six selections examine the role of the police officer. Some of the topics discussed include the stress of police work, utilization of policewomen, and ethical policing.

Unit 4

The Judicial System

Six selections discuss the process by which the accused are moved through the judicial system. Prosecutors, courts, the jury process, and judicial ethics are reviewed.

Unit 5

Juvenile Justice

Six selections review the juvenile justice system. The topics include effective ways to respond to violent juvenile crime, juvenile detention, and children in gangs.

The concepts in bold italics are developed in the article. For further expansion please refer to the Topic Guide, the Index, and the Glossary.

Unit 6

Punishment and Corrections

Twelve selections focus on the current state of America's
penal system and the effects of sentencing, probation,
overcrowding, and capital punishment on criminals.

The concepts in bold italics are developed in the article. For further expansion please refer to the Topic Guide, the Index, and the Glossary.

The concepts in bold italics are developed in the article. For further expansion please refer to the Topic Guide, the Index, and the Glossary.

Charts and Graphs

The concepts in bold italics are developed in the article. For further expansion please refer to the Topic Guide, the Index, and the Glossary.

Topic Guide

This topic guide suggests how the selections in this book relate to topics of traditional concern to students and professionals involved with the study of criminal justice. It is useful for locating articles that relate to each other for reading and research. The guide is arranged alphabetically according to topic. Articles may, of course, treat topics that do not appear in the topic guide. In turn, entries in the topic guide do not necessarily constitute a comprehensive listing of all the contents of each selection.

TOPIC AREA	TREATED IN	TOPIC AREA	TREATED IN
AIDS	37. HIV in Prisons and Jails	**Crime**	1. Overview of the Criminal Justice System 3. What to Do about Crime 5. How Much Crime Is There? 6. Moral Credibility and Crime
Attorneys	22. Abuse of Power in the Prosecutor's Office 23. Trials of the Public Defender 25. Trial for Our Times 27. Jury Consultants	**Crime Victims**	*See* Victimology
Battered Families	11. Protecting Our Seniors 12. Stopping Terrorism at Home 13. Responding to Domestic Violence against Women 15. Computer Technology Comes to the Aid of Crime Victims	**Criminal Justice**	1. Overview of the Criminal Justice System 6. Moral Credibility and Crime 22. Abuse of Power in the Prosecutor's Office 23. Trials of the Public Defender
Bias	8. Color Blinded? 21. Thin White Line 25. Trial for Our times	**Death Penalty**	42. Bringing God to Death Row 43. Anger and Ambivalence 44. Death Row, U.S.A. 45. 'This Man Has Expired'
Brutality	20. Crooked Blue Line	**Defense Counsel**	23. Trials of the Public Defender 25. Trial for Our Times 26. Justice English Style
Children	*See* Juveniles		
Civilian Review Boards	19. Professor Carl Klockars	**Delinquency**	*See* Juveniles
Community Policing	3. What to Do about Crime 16. Police and the Quest for Professionalism 18. Officers from Rural, Suburban, and Urban Jurisdictions Share Views 19. Professor Carl Klockars	**Discrimination**	8. Color Blinded? 17. Police Work from a Woman's Viewpoint 21. Thin White Line
		Elder Abuse	11. Protecting Our Seniors
		Ethics	6. Moral Credibility and Crime 22. Abuse of Power in the Prosecutor's Office 24. Suspect Confessions
Constitutional Rights	23. Trials of the Public Defender 24. Suspect Confessions	**Family Violence**	11. Protecting Our Seniors 12. Stopping Terrorism at Home 13. Responding to Domestic Violence against Women
Consultants	27. Jury Consultants		
Corrections	34. Probation's First 100 Years 35. Doing Soft Time 36. Punishment and Prevention 37. HIV in Prisons and Jails 38. More in U.S. Are in Prisons 39. Privatizing America's Prisons 40. Crime Takes on a Feminine Face	**Fear of Crime**	10. True Crime
		Force	19. Professor Carl Klockars 20. Crooked Blue Line
		Gangs	7. Russian Organized Crime
Courts	22. Abuse of Power in the Prosecutor's Office 23. Trials of the Public Defender 24. Suspect Confessions 25. Trial for Our Times 26. Justice English Style 27. Jury Consultants 28. Rethinking the Sanctioning Function in Juvenile Court	**Gender**	17. Police Work from a Woman's Perspective
		HIV	37. HIV in Prisons and Jails
		Judges	25. Trial for Our Times 30. Judge Hayden's Family Values

Crime and Justice in America

The "Trial of the Century," the O. J. Simpson case, is over, the verdict is in, and its impact on the criminal justice system will be felt for a long time. The case raised issues concerning racism, jury nullification, police ineptitude, and the whole judicial process. Some of these issues are discussed in this and subsequent units of this reader.

Opening this unit, the essay "An Overview of the Criminal Justice System" charts the flow of events in the administration of criminal justice. Calls for action to help stem the flow of crime are discussed in "What to Do about Crime." James Wilson offers some controversial suggestions, such as expanding police powers to stop and frisk.

In "Moral Credibility and Crime: Why People Obey the Law," it is argued that there must be some "moral credibility" within the criminal justice system if we are to expect more compliance with the law.

The report "The Real Problems in American Justice" declares that the criminal justice system is in crisis from "cops to courts to prison." Several areas of concern are listed. In "How Much Crime Is There?" Michael Hedges catalogs reasons for the increase in violent crime.

Organized crime seems to be taking on a new face (or new faces), and the essay "The Decline of the American Mafia" reflects on the waning influence of the old Mafia and the emergence of new groups. Among these new groups, Russian gangsters are a concern worldwide, as discussed in "Russian Organized Crime—A Worldwide Problem."

The final unit article, "Color Blinded? Race Seems to Play an Increasing Role in Many Jury Verdicts," deals with the issue of racism in jury deliberations.

Looking Ahead: Challenge Questions

Discuss whether or not there is racism in the jury room.

Why should (or should not) the police be given more power to stop and search people on the streets?

What indications are there of gangs from foreign countries operating in your community?

What can be done to control violence?

An Overview of the Criminal Justice System

The response to crime is a complex process that involves citizens as well as many agencies, levels, and branches of government

The private sector initiates the response to crime

This first response may come from any part of the private sector: individuals, families, neighborhood associations, business, industry, agriculture, educational institutions, the news media, or any other private service to the public.

It involves crime prevention as well as participation in the criminal justice process once a crime has been committed. Private crime prevention is more than providing private security or burglar alarms or participating in neighborhood watch. It also includes a commitment to stop criminal behavior by not engaging in it or condoning it when it is committed by others.

Citizens take part directly in the criminal justice process by reporting crime to the police, by being a reliable participant (for example, witness, juror) in a criminal proceeding, and by accepting the disposition of the system as just or reasonable. As voters and taxpayers, citizens also participate in criminal justice through the policymaking process that affects how the criminal justice process operates, the resources available to it, and its goals and objectives. At every stage of the process, from the original formulation of objectives to the decision about where to locate jails and prisons and to the reintegration of inmates into society, the private sector has a role to play. Without such involvement, the criminal justice process cannot serve the citizens it is intended to protect.

The government responds to crime through the criminal justice system

We apprehend, try, and punish offenders by means of a loose confederation of agencies at all levels of government. Our American system of justice has evolved from the English

What is the sequence of events in the criminal justice system?

Entry into the system **Prosecution and pretrial services**

Note: This chart gives a simplified view of caseflow through the criminal justice system. Procedures vary among jurisdictions. The weights of the lines are not intended to show the actual size of caseloads.

common law into a complex series of procedures and decisions. There is no single criminal justice system in this country. We have many systems that are similar, but individually unique.

Criminal cases may be handled differently in different jurisdictions, but court

decisions based on the due process guarantees of the U.S. Constitution require that specific steps be taken in the administration of criminal justice.

The description of the criminal and juvenile justice systems that follows portrays the most common sequence of events

From the *Report to the Nation on Crime and Justice,* March 1988, pp. 56-60. Reprinted by permission of the U.S. Department of Justice, Bureau of Justice Statistics.

in the response to serious criminal behavior.

Entry into the system

The justice system does not respond to most crime because so much crime is not discovered or reported to the police. Law enforcement agencies learn about crime from the reports of citizens, from discovery by a police officer in the field, or from investigative and intelligence work.

Once a law enforcement agency has established that a crime has been com-

Prosecution and pretrial services

After an arrest, law enforcement agencies present information about the case and about the accused to the prosecutor, who will decide if formal charges will be filed with the court. If no charges are filed, the accused must be released. The prosecutor can also drop charges after making efforts to prosecute (*nolle prosequi*).

A suspect charged with a crime must be taken before a judge or magistrate

nation of guilt and assessment of a penalty may also occur at this stage.

In some jurisdictions, a pretrial-release decision is made at the initial appearance, but this decision may occur at other hearings or may be changed at another time during the process. Pretrial release and bail were traditionally intended to ensure appearance at trial. However, many jurisdictions permit pretrial detention of defendants accused of serious offenses and deemed to be dangerous to prevent them from committing crimes in the pretrial period. The court may decide to release the accused on his/her own recognizance, into the custody of a third party, on the promise of satisfying certain conditions, or after the posting of a financial bond.

In many jurisdictions, the initial appearance may be followed by a preliminary hearing. The main function of this hearing is to discover if there is probable cause to believe that the accused committed a known crime within the jurisdiction of the court. If the judge does not find probable cause, the case is dismissed; however, if the judge or magistrate finds probable cause for such a belief, or the accused waives his or her right to a preliminary hearing, the case may be bound over to a grand jury.

A *grand jury* hears evidence against the accused presented by the prosecutor and decides if there is sufficient evidence to cause the accused to be brought to trial. If the grand jury finds sufficient evidence, it submits to the court an indictment (a written statement of the essential facts of the offense charged against the accused). Where the grand jury system is used, the grand jury may also investigate criminal activity generally and issue indictments called grand jury originals that initiate criminal cases.

Misdemeanor cases and some felony cases proceed by the issuance of an *information* (a formal, written accusation submitted to the court by a prosecutor) *In some jurisdictions*, indictments *may be* required in felony cases. However, the accused may choose to waive a grand jury indictment and, instead, accept service of an information for the crime.

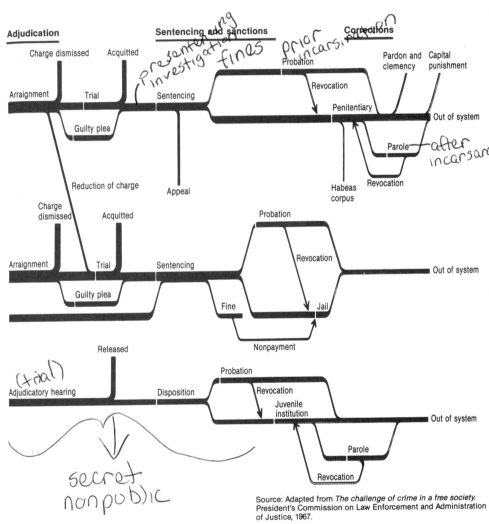

Source: Adapted from *The challenge of crime in a free society.* President's Commission on Law Enforcement and Administration of Justice, 1967.

Adjudication

Once an indictment or information has been filed with the trial court, the accused is scheduled for arraignment. At the arraignment, the accused is informed of the charges, advised of the

mitted, a suspect must be identified and apprehended for the case to proceed through the system. Sometimes, a suspect is apprehended at the scene; however, identification of a suspect sometimes requires an extensive investigation. Often, no one is identified or apprehended.

without unnecessary delay. At the initial appearance, the judge or magistrate informs the accused of the charges and decides whether there is probable cause to detain the accused person. Often, the defense counsel is also assigned at the initial appearance. If the offense is not very serious, the determi-

1. CRIME AND JUSTICE IN AMERICA

rights of criminal defendants, and asked to enter a plea to the charges. Sometimes, a plea of guilty is the result of negotiations between the prosecutor and the defendant, with the defendant entering a guilty plea in expectation of reduced charges or a lenient sentence.

If the accused pleads guilty or pleads *nolo contendere* (accepts penalty without admitting guilt), the judge may accept or reject the plea. If the plea is accepted, no trial is held and the offender is sentenced at this proceeding or at a later date. The plea may be rejected if, for example, the judge believes that the accused may have been coerced. If this occurs, the case may proceed to trial.

If the accused pleads not guilty or not guilty by reason of insanity, a date is set for the trial. A person accused of a serious crime is guaranteed a trial by jury. However, the accused may ask for a bench trial where the judge, rather than a jury, serves as the finder of fact. In both instances the prosecution and defense present evidence by questioning witnesses while the judge decides on issues of law. The trial results in acquittal or conviction on the original charges or on lesser included offenses.

After the trial a defendant may request appellate review of the conviction or sentence. In many criminal cases, appeals of a conviction are a matter of right; all States with the death penalty provide for automatic appeal of cases involving a death sentence. However, under some circumstances and in some jurisdictions, appeals may be subject to the discretion of the appellate court and may be granted only on acceptance of a defendant's petition for a *writ of certiorari*. Prisoners may also appeal their sentences through civil rights petitions and writs of habeas corpus where they claim unlawful detention.

Sentencing and sanctions

After a guilty verdict or guilty plea, sentence is imposed. In most cases the judge decides on the sentence, but in some States, the sentence is decided by the jury, particularly for capital offenses such as murder.

In arriving at an appropriate sentence, a sentencing hearing may be held at which evidence of aggravating or mitigating circumstances will be considered. In assessing the circumstances surrounding a convicted person's criminal behavior, courts often rely on presentence investigations by probation

agencies or other designated authorities. Courts may also consider victim impact statements.

The sentencing choices that may be available to judges and juries include one or more of the following:
- the death penalty
- incarceration in a prison, jail, or other confinement facility
- probation—allowing the convicted person to remain at liberty but subject to certain conditions and restrictions
- fines—primarily applied as penalties in minor offenses
- restitution—which requires the offender to provide financial compensation to the victim.

In many States, State law mandates that persons convicted of certain types of offenses serve a prison term.

Most States permit the judge to set the sentence length within certain limits, but some States have determinate sentencing laws that stipulate a specific sentence length, which must be served and cannot be altered by a parole board.

Corrections

Offenders sentenced to incarceration usually serve time in a local jail or a State prison. Offenders sentenced to less than 1 year generally go to jail; those sentenced to more than 1 year go to prison. Persons admitted to a State prison system may be held in prisons with varying levels of custody or in a community correctional facility.

A prisoner may become eligible for parole after serving a specific part of his or her sentence. Parole is the conditional release of a prisoner before the prisoner's full sentence has been served. The decision to grant parole is made by an authority such as a parole board, which has power to grant or revoke parole or to discharge a parolee altogether. The way parole decisions are made varies widely among jurisdictions.

Offenders may also be required to serve out their full sentences prior to release (expiration of term). Those sentenced under determinate sentencing laws can be released only after they have served their full sentence (mandatory release) less any "goodtime" received while in prison. Inmates get such credits against their sentences automatically or by earning it through participation in programs.

If an offender has an outstanding charge or sentence in another State, a

detainer is used to ensure that when released from prison he or she will be transferred to the other State.

If released by a parole board decision or by mandatory release, the releasee will be under the supervision of a parole officer in the community for the balance of his or her unexpired sentence. This supervision is governed by specific conditions of release, and the releasee may be returned to prison for violations of such conditions.

The juvenile justice system

The processing of juvenile offenders is not entirely dissimilar to adult criminal processing, but there are crucial differences in the procedures. Many juveniles are referred to juvenile courts by law enforcement officers, but many others are referred by school officials, social services agencies, neighbors, and even parents, for behavior or conditions that are determined to require intervention by the formal system for social control.

When juveniles are referred to the juvenile courts, their *intake* departments, or prosecuting attorneys, determine whether sufficient grounds exist to warrant filing a petition that requests an *adjudicatory hearing* or a request to transfer jurisdiction to criminal court. In some States and at the Federal level prosecutors under certain circumstances may file criminal charges against juveniles directly in criminal courts.

The court with jurisdiction over juvenile matters may reject the petition or the juveniles may be diverted to other agencies or programs in lieu of further court processing. Examples of diversion programs include individual or group counseling or referral to educational and recreational programs.

If a petition for an adjudicatory hearing is accepted, the juvenile may be brought before a court quite unlike the court with jurisdiction over adult offenders. In disposing of cases juvenile courts usually have far more discretion than adult courts. In addition to such options as probation, commitment to correctional institutions, restitution, or fines, State laws grant juvenile courts the power to order removal of children from their homes to foster homes or treatment facilities. Juvenile courts also may order participation in special programs aimed at shoplifting prevention, drug counseling, or driver education. They also may order referral to criminal court for trial as adults.

Despite the considerable discretion associated with juvenile court proceedings, juveniles are afforded many of the due-process safeguards associated with adult criminal trials. Sixteen States permit the use of juries in juvenile courts; however, in light of the U.S. Supreme Court's holding that juries are not essential to juvenile hearings, most States do not make provisions for juries in juvenile courts.

The response to crime is founded in the intergovernmental structure of the United States

Under our form of government, each State and the Federal Government has its own criminal justice system. All systems must respect the rights of individuals set forth in court interpretation of the U.S. Constitution and defined in case law.

State constitutions and laws define the criminal justice system within each State and delegate the authority and responsibility for criminal justice to various jurisdictions, officials, and institutions. State laws also define criminal behavior and groups of children or acts under jurisdiction of the juvenile courts.

Municipalities and counties further define their criminal justice systems through local ordinances that proscribe additional illegal behavior and establish the local agencies responsible for criminal justice processing that were not established by the State.

Congress also has established a criminal justice system at the Federal level to respond to Federal crimes such as bank robbery, kidnaping, and transporting stolen goods across State lines.

The response to crime is mainly a State and local function

Very few crimes are under exclusive Federal jurisdiction. The responsibility to respond to most crime rests with the State and local governments. Police protection is primarily a function of cities and towns. Corrections is primarily a function of State governments. More than three-fifths of all justice personnel are employed at the local level.

	Percent of criminal justice employment by level of government		
	Local	State	Federal
Police	77%	15%	8%
Judicial (courts only)	60	32	8
Prosecution and legal services	58	26	17
Public defense	47	50	3
Corrections	35	61	4
Total	62%	31%	8%

Source: *Justice expenditure and employment, 1985,* BJS Bulletin, March 1987.

Discretion is exercised throughout the criminal justice system

Discretion is "an authority conferred by law to act in certain conditions or situations in accordance with an official's or an official agency's own considered judgment and conscience." Discretion is exercised throughout the government. It is a part of decisionmaking in all government systems from mental health to education, as well as criminal justice.

Concerning crime and justice, legislative bodies have recognized that they cannot anticipate the range of circumstances surrounding each crime, anticipate local mores, and enact laws that clearly encompass all conduct that is criminal and all that is not. Therefore, persons charged with the day-to-day response to crime are expected to exercise their own judgment within *limits* set by law. Basically, they must decide—

• whether to take action

• where the situation fits in the scheme of law, rules, and precedent
• which official response is appropriate.

To ensure that discretion is exercised responsibly, government authority is often delegated to professionals. Professionalism requires a minimum level of training and orientation, which guides officials in making decisions. The professionalism of policing discussed later in this chapter is due largely to the desire to ensure the proper exercise of police discretion.

The limits of discretion vary from State to State and locality to locality. For example, some State judges have wide discretion in the type of sentence they may impose. In recent years other States have sought to limit the judges' discretion in sentencing by passing mandatory sentencing laws that require prison sentences for certain offenses.

Who exercises discretion?

These criminal justice officials...	...must often decide whether or not or how to—
Police	Enforce specific laws Investigate specific crimes Search people, vicinities, buildings Arrest or detain people
Prosecutors	File charges or petitions for adjudication Seek indictments Drop cases Reduce charges
Judges or magistrates	Set bail or conditions for release Accept pleas Determine delinquency Dismiss charges Impose sentence Revoke probation
Correctional officials	Assign to type of correctional facility Award privileges Punish for disciplinary infractions
Paroling authority	Determine date and conditions of parole Revoke parole

1. CRIME AND JUSTICE IN AMERICA

More than one agency has jurisdiction over some criminal events

The response to most criminal actions is usually begun by local police who react to violation of State law. If a suspect is apprehended, he or she is prosecuted locally and may be confined in a local jail or State prison. In such cases, only one agency has jurisdiction at each stage in the process.

However, some criminal events because of their characteristics and location may come under the jurisdiction of more than one agency. For example, such overlapping occurs within States when local police, county sheriffs, and State police are all empowered to enforce State laws on State highways.

Congress has provided for Federal jurisdiction over crimes that—
• materially affect interstate commerce
• occur on Federal land
• involve large and probably interstate criminal organizations or conspiracies
• are offenses of national importance, such as the assassination of the President.

Bank robbery and many drug offenses are examples of crimes for which the States and the Federal Government both have jurisdiction. In cases of dual jurisdiction, an investigation and a prosecution may be undertaken by all authorized agencies, but only one level of government usually pursues a case. For example, a study of FBI bank robbery investigations during 1978 and 1979 found that of those cases cleared—

• 36% were solved by the FBI alone
• 25% were solved by a joint effort of the FBI and State and local police
• 40% were solved by the State and local police acting alone.

In response to dual jurisdiction and to promote more effective coordination, Law Enforcement Coordinating Committees have been established throughout the country and include all relevant Federal and local agencies.

Within States the response to crime also varies from one locality to another

The response differs because of statutory and structural differences and differences in how discretion is exercised. Local criminal justice policies and programs change in response to local attitudes and needs. For example, the prosecutor in one locality may concentrate on particular types of offenses that plague the local community while the prosecutor in another locality may concentrate on career criminals.

The response to crime also varies on a case-by-case basis

No two cases are exactly alike. At each stage of the criminal justice process officials must make decisions that take into account the varying factors of each case. Two similar cases may have very different results because of various factors, including differences in witness cooperation and physical evidence, the availability of resources to investigate and prosecute the case, the quality of the lawyers involved, and the age and prior criminal history of the suspects.

Differences in local laws, agencies, resources, standards, and procedures result in varying responses in each jurisdiction

The outcomes of arrests for serious cases vary among the States as shown by Offender-based Transaction Statistics from nine States:

	% of arrests for serious crimes that result in...		
	Prose-cution	Convic-tion	Incarcer-ation
Virginia	100%	61%	55%
Nebraska	99	68	39
New York	97	67	31
Utah	97	79	9
Virgin Islands	95	55	35
Minnesota	89	69	48
Pennsylvania	85	56	24
California	78	61	45
Ohio	77	50	21

Source: Disaggregated data used in *Tracking offenders: White-collar crime*, BJS Special Report, November 1986.

Some of this variation can be explained by differences among States. For example, the degree of discretion in deciding whether to prosecute differs from State to State; some States do not allow any police or prosecutor discretion; others allow police discretion but not prosecutor discretion and vice versa.

The real problems in American justice

A system in crisis from cops to courts to prisons

The criminal justice system was low on Americans' list of esteemed institutions long before the O. J. Simpson case became a national obsession. A recent survey by *U.S. News* found only 8 percent with a "great deal" of confidence in the courts, and the public routinely complains of excessive costs and delays, as well as laxity in sentencing.

Clearly, the system is broken in fundamental ways: Each year, 4.3 million violent crimes are committed, but barely more than 200,000 people are convicted of felonies, and a little over half end up going to prison for more than a year. Here's a rundown of the major flaws:

1. Police solve too few crimes. Law enforcers never have had it easy, but their modern success rate is staggeringly low. Only 24 percent of robberies and 13 percent of burglaries are cleared by an arrest. Homicide clearance rates are down from 86 percent in 1970 to 66 percent in 1993. Fewer witnesses are willing to testify against today's armed teens. A larger witness-protection program would help.

But the biggest problem is manpower. Some help is on the way as up to 100,000 community-patrol officers are hired under last year's federal anticrime law. And shootings already are falling in some New York City precincts, where more police are returning to the beat to deal with both serious crimes and low-level offenses. But critics warn that local patrols take away from investigative units.

2. Sleuths lose vital evidence. Harried police officers inadvertently contaminate key items. Crime laboratories, which do everything from alcohol testing to DNA analysis, can compound the problem. Historically, they have been a low priority for public funds. Technicians often receive scant training, and, until recently, few of the nation's 358 labs worked under any quality control. But quality is improving, and new technologies are spreading. An Automated Fingerprint Identification System helps police at more than 80 agencies match fingerprints found at crime scenes to those in a national database. The system registers "hits" in more than 10 percent of cases. One area where quality remains suspect: the system of coroners and medical examiners. One reason is that only a few areas employ doctors trained to investigate unnatural deaths.

3. Dangerous suspects commit crimes while awaiting trials on other charges. Defendants have a legal right to be considered for release before trial, and nearly two thirds of those charged with serious crimes—including one fourth of accused murderers—are allowed out on the street while awaiting trial. While most of them stay out of trouble, a disturbingly high 1 out of 3 either is rearrested, fails to appear in court on time or commits some infraction that results in a bail revocation.

This year, Republicans in the House approved a "jail, not bail" bill that would allow states to spend new federal prison money to build local jails for pretrial inmates. Experts like D. Alan Henry of the Pretrial Services Resource Center complain that such "solutions" will only worsen the system's unfairness: Many of those who can afford to post bail will do so—regardless of how serious their crimes—while poor suspects will remain stuck behind bars.

4. Prosecutors make bargains with too many criminals. In 9 cases out of 10, no trial ever is held. The defendants accept plea bargains that let them plead guilty, usually to just a few of the charges. Critics argue that to move cases along, prosecutors too readily abandon charges that could bring tougher penalties. Although that does happen, just as common is overcharging—filing counts of dubious provability to pressure defendants.

A few places have moved to curb abuses. The most prominent example is Alaska, which banned plea bargaining in 1975. A study by the federal State Justice Institute found that the policy has improved the screening of cases and contributed to longer prison terms. However, researchers found that in some areas, bargaining over pleas has been replaced by bargaining over the charges filed.

5. Criminal cases take too long. The interval between arrest and sentencing averages 274 days nationwide for murders and 172 days for violent crimes generally. The length of the few cases that go to trial is less of a problem. The National Center for State Courts reports that trials average about 11 hours, much shorter than the time it took for single witnesses to testify in the Simpson extravaganza. Murder trials typically last one to two weeks, depending on the circumstances. California trials tend to take longer.

Still, "we can do a lot better" at expediting cases once they reach court, says Barry Mahoney of the Denver-based Justice Management Institute. Mahoney's group and others offer trial-management training to judges, but probably fewer than 10 percent nationwide have taken it. A bigger problem: There aren't enough judges to juggle all witnesses, defendants and lawyers that come to court.

6. The jury system is flawed. It took 11 weeks to choose 12 jurors and 12 alternates in the Simpson trial. Then, the jury was forced to live in a hotel for nine months under guard, which frayed nerves and cost taxpayers more than $2.5 million. The jury process is so cumbersome, says Joseph DiGenova, former federal prosecutor in Washington, D.C., that "procedures instituted a century or two ago . . . are not adequate today."

Ideas abound to simplify jury service. Some reformers urge curtailing the elaborate process of allowing prosecution and defense to eliminate potential jurors, often on the advice of expensive consultants who analyze candidates for expected biases. Once the trial is underway, a few states, including Arizona, are experimenting with permitting jurors to ask questions of witnesses. California prosecutors, noting that 14 percent of Los Angeles County trials end with a hung jury, are pressing the state legislature to allow less-than-unanimous jury verdicts—which Oregon and Louisiana already do.

7. Trials are consumed more with tactics than truth. Many believe that defense lawyers search not for truth but for "preventing evidence of a defendant's guilt

A PORTRAIT OF JUSTICE?

An estimated 4.37 million violent crimes are committed each year (including murder, rape, robbery and aggravated assault), but only a tiny fraction of criminals are put behind bars.

One figure equals 10,000

ANNUAL VIOLENT CRIMES
4.37 million

VIOLENT CRIMES REPORTED TO POLICE
1.85 million

Note: These data are the latest available. Annual violent crimes and violent crimes reported to police include multiple crimes per defendant.

CONVICTIONS FOR VIOLENT CRIMES
213,100

VIOLENT CONVICTS SENT TO PRISON/JAIL
153,730

VIOLENT CONVICTS PUT ON PROBATION
59,370

USN&WR–Basic data: U.S. Dept. of Justice

from reaching the jury," says James Wootton of the Safe Streets Alliance, an anticrime group based in Washington, D.C. Conservatives in Congress are trying to blunt the "exclusionary rule," which prevents illegally obtained evidence from being used in trials. They would allow such evidence if it was provably gathered in good faith. Others would go further. Law Prof. Joseph Grano of Wayne State University advocates that defense lawyers be required to ask their clients whether they committed the crime and to encourage the guilty to accept responsibility.

But defense lawyers will resist basic changes. "It's been a long time since I went to court looking for the truth," concedes Raymond Brown, a prominent Newark defense attorney. He says a proper role of the defense is forcing prosecutors to prove guilt.

8. Suspects get inadequate legal aid. Simpson is spending millions on a "dream team" defense. The reality for most criminal suspects is that they are fortunate to get much attention at all from overworked public defenders or court-appointed attorneys. Most such advocates are competent: They achieve roughly the same results as high-priced attorneys The problem is that there are too many cases and too little time. Experts say full-time defense lawyers should handle at most 150 felony cases each year. The actual number in many

areas is much higher: Defenders in southwest Florida are assigned some 300 cases and up to 50 appeals a year.

Although a system of public defenders is in place, its resources are limited and declining. Congress, for example, is on the verge of eliminating federal funding for a network of centers that help defenders prepare cases of candidates for the death penalty. Critics say the centers help give attorneys ammunition to prolong cases unnecessarily; supporters respond that better sorting of the evidence can actually expedite trials and prevent needless appeals—not to mention helping ensure that innocent persons are not executed or put in prison for life.

9. Some criminals strike over and over. A few criminals commit a disproportionate amount of violence, but identifying and incapacitating them has proved impossible. Limits on prison space and an inability to predict recidivists mean that nearly 6 of every 10 serious offenders are not sentenced to prison. More than 4 in 10 are arrested within three years for another serious crime. Of those who serve time, most are paroled before serving 40 percent of their time.

Several states are moving to abolish parole, and others are clamping down on early releases. Pennsylvania has slowed releases of violent offenders to a trickle. In South Carolina, retired naval officer Jim Grego founded Citizens Against Violent Crime 11 years ago when his daughter was seriously wounded in an assault by a twice-paroled felon. Now that the group has lobbied for tougher standards, the state paroles 25 to 30 percent of applicants compared with 75 percent a decade ago. Meanwhile, many states are beefing up habit-

ARRESTS FOR VIOLENT CRIMES
754,110

ual-offender laws, often by requiring life sentences for those who commit two or three violent offenses.

But get-tough measures can backfire. Some states that have eliminated parole have seen costs soar as prison populations explode. And in California, the "three strikes and you're out" law requiring life terms for third-time offenders is causing more defendants to demand trials, thus clogging the courts. "The real crisis in L.A. County is the impact of three strikes," says presiding trial Judge James Bascue.

10. The justice system is insensitive to the public, particularly crime victims. Except for their court testimony, victims tradi-tionally have been shut out when penalties are assessed. This view is changing, albeit slowly. A growing crime-victims movement has succeeded in recognizing victim rights in most states, at least on paper. The challenge is giving those rights real meaning. Victims are campaigning for "restorative justice," a program to involve them more in the sentencing process. In many cases, that means requiring convicts to provide victims restitution for losses or encouraging assailants to face their victims.

Some courts, traditionally remote institutions, are acting to improve public relations. Connecticut indoctrinates its court employees in "total quality management," partly to help citizens seeking information about cases.

Many justice reforms require an infusion of tax money. "The public gets the justice system it pays for," says Donald Rebovich of the National District Attorneys Association. Other changes would necessitate fundamental rewriting of criminal law—something that has proved remarkably resistant to reform. Defense lawyers argue that the system generally works well, even if it results at times in a criminal's going free. So it's reasonable to expect that long after the Simpson case is over, the justice system will lurch along—and so will the public's frustration and outrage.

TED GEST WITH DORIAN FRIEDMAN
AND TIMOTHY M. ITO

What To Do About Crime

James Q. Wilson

Few of the major problems facing American society today are entirely new, but in recent years most of them have either taken new forms or reached new levels of urgency. To make matters more difficult, in many cases the solutions formerly relied upon have proved to be ineffective, leaving us so frustrated that we seize desperately on proposals which promise much but deliver little.

In the hope of bringing greater clarity to the understanding of these problems, and of framing workable solutions and policies, we are inaugurating this new series of articles. Like James Q. Wilson's below, each subsequent piece in the series will begin with a reexamination of a particular issue by a writer who has lived with and studied it for a long time and who will then proceed to suggest "What To Do About" it. Among those already scheduled for publication in the coming months are Charles Murray and Richard J. Herrnstein on welfare; Gertrude Himmelfarb on the universities; William J. Bennett on our children; Robert H. Bork on the First Amendment; and Richard Pipes on Russia.

JAMES Q. WILSON, *professor of management and public policy at UCLA, is the author of many books and articles on crime, including* Thinking about Crime; Varieties of Police Behavior; *and* Crime and Human Nature *(written with Richard J. Herrnstein). He is also the editor of* Crime and Public Policy *and co-editor, with Joan Petersilia, of* Crime *(from ICS Press).*

WHEN the United States experienced the great increase in crime that began in the early 1960's and continued through the 1970's, most Americans were inclined to attribute it to conditions unique to this country. Many conservatives blamed it on judicial restraints on the police, the abandonment of capital punishment, and the mollycoddling of offenders; many liberals blamed it on poverty, racism, and the rise of violent television programs. Europeans, to the extent they noticed at all, referred to it, sadly or patronizingly, as the "American" problem, a product of our disorderly society, weak state, corrupt police, or imperfect welfare system.

Now, 30 years later, any serious discussion of crime must begin with the fact that, except for homicide, most industrialized nations have crime rates that resemble those in the United States. All the world is coming to look like America. In 1981, the burglary rate in Great Britain was much less than that in the United States; within six years the two rates were the same; today, British homes are more likely to be burgled than American ones. In 1980, the rate at which automobiles were stolen was lower in France than in the United States; today, the reverse is true. By 1984, the burglary rate in the Netherlands was nearly twice that in the United States. In Australia and Sweden certain forms of theft are more common than they are here. While property-crime rates were declining during most of the 1980's in the United States, they were rising elsewhere.[1]

America, it is true, continues to lead the industrialized world in murders. There can be little doubt that part of this lead is to be explained by the greater availability of handguns here. Arguments that once might have been settled with insults or punches are today more likely to be settled by shootings. But guns are not the whole story. Big American cities have had more homicides than comparable European ones for almost as long as anyone can find records. New York and Philadelphia have been more murderous than London since the early part of the 19th century. This country has had a violent history; with respect to murder, that seems likely to remain the case.

But except for homicide, things have been getting better in the United States for over a decade. Since 1980, robbery rates (as reported in victim surveys) have declined by 15 percent. And even with regard to homicide, there is relatively good news: in 1990, the rate at which adults killed one another was no higher than it was in 1980, and in many cities it was considerably lower.

This is as it was supposed to be. Starting

---

[1] These comparisons depend on official police statistics. There are of course errors in such data. But essentially the same pattern emerges from comparing nations on the basis of victimization surveys.

around 1980, two things happened that ought to have reduced most forms of crime. The first was the passing into middle age of the postwar baby boom. By 1990, there were 1.5 million fewer boys between the ages of fifteen and nineteen than there had been in 1980, a drop that meant that this youthful fraction of the population fell from 9.3 percent to 7.2 percent of the total.

In addition, the great increase in the size of the prison population, caused in part by the growing willingness of judges to send offenders to jail, meant that the dramatic reductions in the costs of crime to the criminal that occurred in the 1960's and 1970's were slowly (and very partially) being reversed. Until around 1985, this reversal involved almost exclusively real criminals and parole violators; it was not until after 1985 that more than a small part of the growth in prison populations was made up of drug offenders.

Because of the combined effect of fewer young people on the street and more offenders in prison, many scholars, myself included, predicted a continuing drop in crime rates throughout the 1980's and into the early 1990's. We were almost right: crime rates did decline. But suddenly, starting around 1985, even as adult homicide rates were remaining stable or dropping, *youthful* homicide rates shot up.

Alfred Blumstein of Carnegie-Mellon University has estimated that the rate at which young males, ages fourteen to seventeen, kill people has gone up significantly for whites and incredibly for blacks. Between 1985 and 1992, the homicide rate for young white males went up by about 50 percent but for young black males it *tripled*.

The public perception that today's crime problem is different from and more serious than that of earlier decades is thus quite correct. Youngsters are shooting at people at a far higher rate than at any time in recent history. Since young people are more likely than adults to kill strangers (as opposed to lovers or spouses), the risk to innocent bystanders has gone up. There may be some comfort to be had in the fact that youthful homicides are only a small fraction of all killings, but given their randomness, it is not much solace.

THE United States, then, does not have *a* crime problem, it has at least two. Our high (though now slightly declining) rates of property crime reflect a profound, worldwide cultural change: prosperity, freedom, and mobility have emancipated people almost everywhere from those ancient bonds of custom, family, and village that once held in check both some of our better and many of our worst impulses. The power of the state has been weakened, the status of children elevated, and the opportunity for adventure expanded; as a consequence, we have experienced an explosion of artistic creativity, entrepreneurial zeal, political experimentation—

and criminal activity. A global economy has integrated the markets for clothes, music, automobiles—and drugs.

There are only two restraints on behavior—morality, enforced by individual conscience or social rebuke, and law, enforced by the police and the courts. If society is to maintain a behavioral equilibrium, any decline in the former must be matched by a rise in the latter (or vice versa). If familial and traditional restraints on wrongful behavior are eroded, it becomes necessary to increase the legal restraints. But the enlarged spirit of freedom and the heightened suspicion of the state have made it difficult or impossible to use the criminal-justice system to achieve what custom and morality once produced.

This is the modern dilemma, and it may be an insoluble one, at least for the West. The Islamic cultures of the Middle East and the Confucian cultures of the Far East believe that they have a solution. It involves allowing enough liberty for economic progress (albeit under general state direction) while reserving to the state, and its allied religion, nearly unfettered power over personal conduct. It is too soon to tell whether this formula—best exemplified by the prosperous but puritanical city-state of Singapore—will, in the long run, be able to achieve both reproducible affluence and intense social control.

Our other crime problem has to do with the kind of felonies we have: high levels of violence, especially youthful violence, often occurring as part of urban gang life, produced disproportionately by a large, alienated, and self-destructive underclass. This part of the crime problem, though not uniquely American, is more important here than in any other industrialized nation. Britons, Germans, and Swedes are upset about the insecurity of their property and uncertain about what response to make to its theft, but if Americans only had to worry about their homes being burgled and their autos stolen, I doubt that crime would be the national obsession it has now become.

Crime, we should recall, was not a major issue in the 1984 presidential election and had only begun to be one in the 1988 contest; by 1992, it was challenging the economy as a popular concern and today it dominates all other matters. The reason, I think, is that Americans believe something fundamental has changed in our patterns of crime. They are right. Though we were unhappy about having our property put at risk, we adapted with the aid of locks, alarms, and security guards. But we are terrified by the prospect of innocent people being gunned down at random, without warning and almost without motive, by youngsters who afterward show us the blank, unremorseful faces of seemingly feral, presocial beings.

Criminology has learned a great deal about who these people are. In studies both here and abroad it has been established that about 6 percent of the boys of a given age will commit half or more of all the serious crime produced by all boys of that age. Allowing for measurement errors, it is remarkable how consistent this formula is—6 percent causes 50 percent. It is roughly true in places as different as Philadelphia, London, Copenhagen, and Orange County, California.

We also have learned a lot about the characteristics of the 6 percent. They tend to have criminal parents, to live in cold or discordant families (or pseudo-families), to have a low verbal-intelligence quotient and to do poorly in school, to be emotionally cold and temperamentally impulsive, to abuse alcohol and drugs at the earliest opportunity, and to reside in poor, disorderly communities. They begin their misconduct at an early age, often by the time they are in the third grade.

These characteristics tend to be found not only among the criminals who get caught (and who might, owing to bad luck, be an unrepresentative sample of all high-rate offenders), but among those who do not get caught but reveal their behavior on questionnaires. And the same traits can be identified in advance among groups of randomly selected youngsters, long before they commit any serious crimes—not with enough precision to predict which individuals will commit crimes, but with enough accuracy to be a fair depiction of the group as a whole.[2]

Here a puzzle arises: if 6 percent of the males causes so large a fraction of our collective misery, and if young males are less numerous than once was the case, why are crime rates high and rising? The answer, I conjecture, is that the traits of the 6 percent put them at high risk for whatever criminogenic forces operate in society. As the costs of crime decline or the benefits increase; as drugs and guns become more available; as the glorification of violence becomes more commonplace; as families and neighborhoods lose some of their restraining power—as all these things happen, almost all of us will change our ways to some degree. For the most law-abiding among us, the change will be quite modest: a few more tools stolen from our employer, a few more traffic lights run when no police officer is watching, a few more experiments with fashionable drugs, and a few more business deals on which we cheat. But for the least law-abiding among us, the change will be dramatic: they will get drunk daily instead of just on Saturday night, try PCP or crack instead of marijuana, join gangs instead of marauding in pairs, and buy automatic weapons instead of making zip guns.

A metaphor: when children play the schoolyard game of crack-the-whip, the child at the head of the line scarcely moves but the child at the far end, racing to keep his footing, often stumbles and falls, hurled to the ground by the cumulative force of many smaller movements back along the line. When a changing culture escalates criminality, the at-risk boys are at the end of the line, and the conditions of American urban life—guns, drugs, automobiles, disorganized neighborhoods—make the line very long and the ground underfoot rough and treacherous.

Much is said these days about preventing or deterring crime, but it is important to understand exactly what we are up against when we try. Prevention, if it can be made to work at all, must start very early in life, perhaps as early as the first two or three years, and given the odds it faces—childhood impulsivity, low verbal facility, incompetent parenting, disorderly neighborhoods—it must also be massive in scope. Deterrence, if it can be made to work better (for surely it already works to some degree), must be applied close to the moment of the wrongful act or else the present-orientedness of the youthful would-be offender will discount the threat so much that the promise of even a small gain will outweigh its large but deferred costs.

In this country, however, and in most Western nations, we have profound misgivings about doing anything that would give prevention or deterrence a chance to make a large difference. The family is sacrosanct; the family-preservation movement is strong; the state is a clumsy alternative. "Crime-prevention" programs, therefore, usually take the form of creating summer jobs for adolescents, worrying about the unemployment rate, or (as in the proposed 1994 crime bill) funding midnight basketball leagues. There may be something to be said for all these efforts, but crime prevention is not one of them. The typical high-rate offender is well launched on his career before he becomes a teenager or has ever encountered the labor market; he may like basketball, but who pays for the lights and the ball is a matter of supreme indifference to him.

Prompt deterrence has much to recommend it: the folk wisdom that swift and certain punishment is more effective than severe penalties is almost surely correct. But the greater the swiftness and certainty, the less attention paid to the procedural safeguards essential to establishing guilt. As a result, despite their good instincts for the right answers, most Americans, frustrated by the restraints (many wise, some foolish) on swiftness and certainty, vote for proposals to increase severity: if the penalty is 10 years, let us make it 20 or 30; if the penalty is life imprisonment, let us make it death; if the penalty is jail, let us make it caning.

---

[2] Female high-rate offenders are *much* less common than male ones. But to the extent they exist, they display most of these traits.

Yet the more draconian the sentence, the less (on the average) the chance of its being imposed; plea bargains see to that. And the most draconian sentences will, of necessity, tend to fall on adult offenders nearing the end of their criminal careers and not on the young ones who are in their criminally most productive years. (The peak ages of criminality are between sixteen and eighteen; the average age of prison inmates is ten years older.) I say "of necessity" because almost every judge will give first-, second-, or even third-time offenders a break, reserving the heaviest sentences for those men who have finally exhausted judicial patience or optimism.

Laws that say "three strikes and you're out" are an effort to change this, but they suffer from an inherent contradiction. If they are carefully drawn so as to target only the most serious offenders, they will probably have a minimal impact on the crime rate; but if they are broadly drawn so as to make a big impact on the crime rate, they will catch many petty repeat offenders who few of us think really deserve life imprisonment.

Prevention and deterrence, albeit hard to augment, at least are plausible strategies. Not so with many of the other favorite nostrums, like reducing the amount of violence on television. Televised violence may have some impact on criminality, but I know of few scholars who think the effect is very large. And to achieve even a small difference we might have to turn the clock back to the kind of programming we had around 1945, because the few studies that correlate programming with the rise in violent crime find the biggest changes occurred between that year and 1974. Another favorite, boot camp, makes good copy, but so far no one has shown that it reduces the rate at which the former inmates commit crimes.

Then, of course, there is gun control. Guns are almost certainly contributors to the lethality of American violence, but there is no politically or legally feasible way to reduce the stock of guns now in private possession to the point where their availability to criminals would be much affected. And even if there were, law-abiding people would lose a means of protecting themselves long before criminals lost a means of attacking them.

As for rehabilitating juvenile offenders, it has some merit, but there are rather few success stories. Individually, the best (and best-evaluated) programs have minimal, if any, effects; collectively, the best estimate of the crime-reduction value of these programs is quite modest, something on the order of 5 or 10 percent.[3]

W HAT, then, is to be done? Let us begin with policing, since law-enforcement officers are that part of the criminal-justice system which is closest to the situations where criminal activity is likely to occur.

It is now widely accepted that, however important it is for officers to drive around waiting for 911 calls summoning their help, doing that is not enough. As a supplement to such a reactive strategy—comprised of random preventive patrol and the investigation of crimes that have already occurred—many leaders and students of law enforcement now urge the police to be "proactive": to identify, with the aid of citizen groups, problems that can be solved so as to prevent criminality, and not only to respond to it. This is often called community-based policing; it seems to entail something more than feel-good meetings with honest citizens, but something less than allowing neighborhoods to assume control of the police function.

The new strategy might better be called problem-oriented policing. It requires the police to engage in *directed*, not random, patrol. The goal of that direction should be to reduce, in a manner consistent with fundamental liberties, the opportunity for high-risk persons to do those things that increase the likelihood of their victimizing others.

For example, the police might stop and pat down persons whom they reasonably suspect may be carrying illegal guns.[4] The Supreme Court has upheld such frisks when an officer observes "unusual conduct" leading him to conclude that "criminal activity may be afoot" on the part of a person who may be "armed and dangerous." This is all rather vague, but it can be clarified in two ways.

First, statutes can be enacted that make certain persons, on the basis of their past conduct and present legal status, subject to pat-downs for weapons. The statutes can, as is now the case in several states, make all probationers and parolees subject to nonconsensual searches for weapons as a condition of their remaining on probation or parole. Since three-fourths of all convicted offenders (and a large fraction of all felons) are in the community rather than in prison, there are on any given day over three million criminals on the streets under correctional supervision. Many are likely to become recidivists. Keeping them from carrying weapons will materially reduce the chances that they will rob or kill. The courts might also declare certain dangerous street gangs to be continuing criminal enterprises, membership in which constitutes grounds for police frisks.

---

[3] Many individual programs involve so few subjects that a good evaluation will reveal no positive effect even if one occurs. By a technique called meta-analysis, scores of individual studies can be pooled into one mega-evaluation; because there are now hundreds or thousands of subjects, even small gains can be identified. The best of these meta-analyses, such as the one by Mark Lipsey, suggest modest positive effects.

[4] I made a fuller argument along these lines in "Just Take Away Their Guns," in the *New York Times Magazine*, March 20, 1994.

Second, since I first proposed such a strategy, I have learned that there are efforts under way in public and private research laboratories to develop technologies that will permit the police to detect from a distance persons who are carrying concealed weapons on the streets. Should these efforts bear fruit, they will provide the police with the grounds for stopping, questioning, and patting down even persons not on probation or parole or obviously in gangs.

Whether or not the technology works, the police can also offer immediate cash rewards to people who provide information about individuals illegally carrying weapons. Spending $100 on each good tip will have a bigger impact on dangerous gun use than will the same amount spent on another popular nostrum—buying back guns from law-abiding people.[5] Getting illegal firearms off the streets will require that the police be motivated to do all of these things. But if the legal, technological, and motivational issues can be resolved, our streets can be made safer even without sending many more people to prison.

THE same directed-patrol strategy might help keep known offenders drug-free. Most persons jailed in big cities are found to have been using illegal drugs within the day or two preceding their arrest. When convicted, some are given probation on condition that they enter drug-treatment programs; others are sent to prisons where (if they are lucky) drug-treatment programs operate. But in many cities the enforcement of such probation conditions is casual or nonexistent; in many states, parolees are released back into drug-infested communities with little effort to ensure that they participate in whatever treatment programs are to be found there.

Almost everyone agrees that more treatment programs should exist. But what many advocates overlook is that the key to success is steadfast participation and many, probably most, offenders have no incentive to be steadfast. To cope with this, patrol officers could enforce random drug tests on probationers and parolees on their beats; failing to take a test when ordered, or failing the test when taken, should be grounds for immediate revocation of probation or parole, at least for a brief period of confinement.

The goal of this tactic is not simply to keep offenders drug-free (and thereby lessen their incentive to steal the money needed to buy drugs and reduce their likelihood of committing crimes because they are on a drug high); it is also to diminish the demand for drugs generally and thus the size of the drug market.

Lest the reader embrace this idea too quickly, let me add that as yet we have no good reason to think that it will reduce the crime rate by very much. Something akin to this strategy, albeit one using probation instead of police officers, has been tried under the name of "intensive-supervision programs" (ISP), involving a panoply of drug tests, house arrests, frequent surveillance, and careful records. By means of a set of randomized experiments carried out in fourteen cities, Joan Petersilia and Susan Turner, both then at RAND, compared the rearrest rates of offenders assigned to ISP with those of offenders in ordinary probation. There was no difference.

Still, this study does not settle the matter. For one thing, since the ISP participants were under much closer surveillance than the regular probationers, the former were bound to be caught breaking the law more frequently than the latter. It is thus possible that a higher fraction of the crimes committed by the ISP than of the control group were detected and resulted in a return to prison, which would mean, if true, a net gain in public safety. For another thing, "intensive" supervision was in many cases not all that intensive—in five cities, contacts with the probationers only took place about once a week, and for all cities drug tests occurred, on average, about once a month. Finally, there is some indication that participation in treatment programs was associated with lower recidivism rates.

Both anti-gun and anti-drug police patrols will, if performed systematically, require big changes in police and court procedures and a significant increase in the resources devoted to both, at least in the short run. (ISP is not cheap, and it will become even more expensive if it is done in a truly intensive fashion.) Most officers have at present no incentive to search for guns or enforce drug tests; many jurisdictions, owing to crowded dockets or overcrowded jails, are lax about enforcing the conditions of probation or parole. The result is that the one group of high-risk people over which society already has the legal right to exercise substantial control is often out of control, "supervised," if at all, by means of brief monthly interviews with overworked probation or parole officers. Another promising tactic is to enforce truancy and curfew laws. This arises from the fact that much crime is opportunistic: idle boys, usually in small groups, sometimes find irresistible the opportunity to steal or the challenge to fight. Deterring present-oriented youngsters who want to appear fearless in the eyes of their comrades while indulging their thrill-seeking natures is a tall order. While it is possible to deter the crimes they commit by a credible threat of prompt sanctions, it is easier to reduce the chances for risky group idleness in the first place.

---

[5] In Charleston, South Carolina, the police pay a reward to anyone identifying a student carrying a weapon to school or to some school event. Because many boys carry guns to school in order to display or brag about them, the motive to carry disappears once any display alerts a potential informer.

In Charleston, South Carolina, for example, Chief Reuben Greenberg instructed his officers to return all school-age children to the schools from which they were truant and to return all youngsters violating an evening-curfew agreement to their parents. As a result, groups of school-age children were no longer to be found hanging out in the shopping malls or wandering the streets late at night.

There has been no careful evaluation of these efforts in Charleston (or, so far as I am aware, in any other big city), but the rough figures are impressive—the Charleston crime rate in 1991 was about 25 percent lower than the rate in South Carolina's other principal cities and, for most offenses (including burglaries and larcenies), lower than what that city reported twenty years earlier.

All these tactics have in common putting the police, as the criminologist Lawrence Sherman of the University of Maryland phrases it, where the "hot spots" are. Most people need no police attention except for a response to their calls for help. A small fraction of people (and places) need constant attention. Thus, in Minneapolis, *all* of the robberies during one year occurred at just 2 percent of the city's addresses. To capitalize on this fact, the Minneapolis police began devoting extra patrol attention, in brief but frequent bursts of activity, to those locations known to be trouble spots. Robbery rates evidently fell by as much as 20 percent and public disturbances by even more.

Some of the worst hot spots are outdoor drug markets. Because of either limited resources, a fear of potential corruption, or a desire to catch only the drug kingpins, the police in some cities (including, from time to time, New York) neglect street-corner dealing. By doing so, they get the worst of all worlds.

The public, seeing the police ignore drug dealing that is in plain view, assumes that they are corrupt whether or not they are. The drug kingpins, who are hard to catch and are easily replaced by rival smugglers, find that their essential retail distribution system remains intact. Casual or first-time drug users, who might not use at all if access to supplies were difficult, find access to be effortless and so increase their consumption. People who might remain in treatment programs if drugs were hard to get drop out upon learning that they are easy to get. Interdicting without merely displacing drug markets is difficult but not impossible, though it requires motivation which some departments lack and resources which many do not have.

The sheer number of police on the streets of a city probably has only a weak, if any, relationship with the crime rate; what the police do is more important than how many there are, at least above some minimum level. Nevertheless, patrols directed at hot spots, loitering truants, late-night wanderers, probationers, parolees, and possible gun carriers, all in addition to routine investigative activities, will require more officers in many cities. Between 1977 and 1987, the number of police officers declined in a third of the 50 largest cities and fell relative to population in many more. Just how far behind police resources have lagged can be gauged from this fact: in 1950 there was one violent crime reported for every police officer; in 1980 there were three violent crimes reported for every officer.

I HAVE said little so far about penal policy, in part because I wish to focus attention on those things that are likely to have the largest and most immediate impact on the quality of urban life. But given the vast gulf between what the public believes and what many experts argue should be our penal policy, a few comments are essential.

The public wants more people sent away for longer sentences; many (probably most) criminologists think we use prison too much and at too great a cost and that this excessive use has had little beneficial effect on the crime rate. My views are much closer to those of the public, though I think the average person exaggerates the faults of the present system and the gains of some alternative (such as "three strikes and you're out").

The expert view, as it is expressed in countless op-ed essays, often goes like this: "We have been arresting more and more people and giving them longer and longer sentences, producing no decrease in crime but huge increases in prison populations. As a result, we have become the most punitive nation on earth."

Scarcely a phrase in those sentences is accurate. The probability of being arrested for a given crime is lower today than it was in 1974. The amount of time served in state prison has been declining more or less steadily since the 1940's. Taking all crimes together, time served fell from 25 months in 1945 to 13 months in 1984. Only for rape are prisoners serving as much time today as they did in the 40's.

The net effect of lower arrest rates and shorter effective sentences is that the cost to the adult perpetrator of the average burglary fell from 50 days in 1960 to 15 days in 1980. That is to say, the chances of being caught and convicted, multiplied by the median time served if imprisoned, was in 1980 less than a third of what it had been in 1960.[6]

---

[6] I take these cost calculations from Mark Kleiman, *et al.*, "Imprisonment-to-Offense Ratios," Working Paper 89-06-02 of the Program in Criminal Justice Policy and Management at the Kennedy School of Government, Harvard University (August 5, 1988).

Beginning around 1980, the costs of crime to the criminal began to inch up again—the result, chiefly, of an increase in the proportion of convicted persons who were given prison terms. By 1986, the "price" of a given burglary had risen to 21 days. Also beginning around 1980, as I noted at the outset, the crime rate began to decline.

It would be foolhardy to explain this drop in crime by the rise in imprisonment rates; many other factors, such as the aging of the population and the self-protective measures of potential victims, were also at work. Only a controlled experiment (for example, randomly allocating prison terms for a given crime among the states) could hope to untangle the causal patterns, and happily the Constitution makes such experiments unlikely.

Yet it is worth noting that nations with different penal policies have experienced different crime rates. According to David Farrington of Cambridge University, property-crime rates rose in England and Sweden at a time when both the imprisonment rate and time served fell substantially, while property-crime rates declined in the United States at a time when the imprisonment rate (but not time served) was increasing.

Though one cannot measure the effect of prison on crime with any accuracy, it certainly has some effects. By 1986, there were 55,000 more robbers in prison than there had been in 1974. Assume that each imprisoned robber would commit five such offenses per year if free on the street. This means that in 1986 there were 275,000 fewer robberies in America than there would have been had these 55,000 men been left on the street.

Nor, finally, does America use prison to a degree that vastly exceeds what is found in any other civilized nation. Compare the chance of going to prison in England and the United States if one is convicted of a given crime. According to Farrington, your chances were higher in England if you were found guilty of a rape, higher in America if you were convicted of an assault or a burglary, and about the same if you were convicted of a homicide or a robbery. Once in prison, you would serve a longer time in this country than in England for almost all offenses save murder.

James Lynch of American University has reached similar conclusions from his comparative study of criminal-justice policies. His data show that the chances of going to prison and the time served for homicide and robbery are roughly the same in the United States, Canada, and England.

Of late, drugs have changed American penal practice. In 1982, only about 8 percent of state-prison inmates were serving time on drug convictions. In 1987, that started to increase sharply; by 1994, over 60 percent of all federal and about 25 percent of all state prisoners were there on drug charges. In some states, such as New York, the percentage was even higher.

This change can be attributed largely to the advent of crack cocaine. Whereas snorted cocaine powder was expensive, crack was cheap; whereas the former was distributed through networks catering to elite tastes, the latter was mass-marketed on street corners. People were rightly fearful of what crack was doing to their children and demanded action; as a result, crack dealers started going to prison in record numbers.

Unfortunately, these penalties do not have the same incapacitative effect as sentences for robbery. A robber taken off the street is not replaced by a new robber who has suddenly found a market niche, but a drug dealer sent away is replaced by a new one because an opportunity has opened up.

We are left, then, with the problem of reducing the demand for drugs, and that in turn requires either prevention programs on a scale heretofore unimagined or treatment programs with a level of effectiveness heretofore unachieved. Any big gains in prevention and treatment will probably have to await further basic research into the biochemistry of addiction and the development of effective and attractive drug antagonists that reduce the appeal of cocaine and similar substances.[7]

In the meantime, it is necessary either to build much more prison space, find some other way of disciplining drug offenders, or both. There is very little to be gained, I think, from shortening the terms of existing non-drug inmates in order to free up more prison space. Except for a few elderly, nonviolent offenders serving very long terms, there are real risks associated with shortening the terms of the typical inmate.

Scholars disagree about the magnitude of those risks, but the best studies, such as the one of Wisconsin inmates done by John DiIulio of Princeton, suggest that the annual costs to society in crime committed by an offender on the street are probably twice the costs of putting him in a cell. That ratio will vary from state to state because states differ in what proportion of convicted persons is imprisoned—some states dip deeper down into the pool of convictees, thereby imprisoning some with minor criminal habits.

But I caution the reader to understand that there are no easy prison solutions to crime, even if we build the additional space. The state-prison population more than doubled between 1980 and 1990, yet the victimization rate for robbery fell by only 23 percent. Even if we assign all of that gain

---

[7] I anticipate that at this point some readers will call for legalizing or decriminalizing drugs as the "solution" to the problem. Before telling me this, I hope they will read what I wrote on that subject in the February 1990 issue of COMMENTARY. I have not changed my mind.

to the increased deterrent and incapacitative effect of prison, which is implausible, the improvement is not vast. Of course, it is possible that the victimization rate would have risen, perhaps by a large amount, instead of falling if we had not increased the number of inmates. But we shall never know.

Recall my discussion of the decline in the costs of crime to the criminal, measured by the number of days in prison that result, on average, from the commission of a given crime. That cost is vastly lower today than in the 1950's. But much of the decline (and since 1974, nearly all of it) is the result of a drop in the probability of being arrested for a crime, not in the probability of being imprisoned once arrested.

Anyone who has followed my writings on crime knows that I have defended the use of prison both to deter crime and incapacitate criminals. I continue to defend it. But we must recognize two facts. First, even modest additional reductions in crime, comparable to the ones achieved in the early 1980's, will require vast increases in correctional costs and encounter bitter judicial resistance to mandatory sentencing laws. Second, America's most troubling crime problem—the increasingly violent behavior of disaffected and impulsive youth—may be especially hard to control by means of marginal and delayed increases in the probability of punishment.

Possibly one can make larger gains by turning our attention to the unexplored area of juvenile justice. Juvenile (or family) courts deal with young people just starting their criminal careers and with chronic offenders when they are often at their peak years of offending. We know rather little about how these courts work or with what effect. There are few, if any, careful studies of what happens, a result in part of scholarly neglect and in part of the practice in some states of shrouding juvenile records and proceedings in secrecy. Some studies, such as one by the *Los Angeles Times* of juvenile justice in California, suggest that young people found guilty of a serious crime are given sentences tougher than those meted out to adults.[8] This finding is so counter to popular beliefs and the testimony of many big-city juvenile-court judges that some caution is required in interpreting it.

There are two problems. The first lies in defining the universe of people to whom sanctions are applied. In some states, such as California, it may well be the case that a juvenile *found guilty of a serious offense* is punished with greater rigor than an adult, but many juveniles whose behavior ought to be taken seriously (because they show signs of being part of the 6 percent) are released by the police or probation officers before ever seeing a judge. And in some states, such as New York, juveniles charged with having committed certain crimes, including serious ones like illegally carrying a loaded gun or committing an as-

sault, may not be fingerprinted. Since persons with a prior record are usually given longer sentences than those without one, the failure to fingerprint can mean that the court has no way of knowing whether the John Smith standing before it is the same John Smith who was arrested four times for assault and so ought to be sent away, or a different John Smith whose clean record entitles him to probation.

The second problem arises from the definition of a "severe" penalty. In California, a juvenile found guilty of murder does indeed serve a longer sentence than an adult convicted of the same offense—60 months for the former, 41 months for the latter. Many people will be puzzled by a newspaper account that defines five years in prison for murder as a "severe" sentence, and angered to learn that an adult serves less than four years for such a crime.

The key, unanswered question is whether prompt and more effective early intervention would stop high-rate delinquents from becoming high-rate criminals at a time when their offenses were not yet too serious. Perhaps early and swift, though not necessarily severe, sanctions could deter some budding hoodlums, but we have no evidence of that as yet.

F OR as long as I can remember, the debate over crime has been between those who wished to rely on the criminal-justice system and those who wished to attack the root causes of crime. I have always been in the former group because what its opponents depicted as "root causes"—unemployment, racism, poor housing, too little schooling, a lack of self-esteem—turned out, on close examination, not to be major causes of crime at all.

Of late, however, there has been a shift in the debate. Increasingly those who want to attack root causes have begun to point to real ones—temperament, early family experiences, and neighborhood effects. The sketch I gave earlier of the typical high-rate young offender suggests that these factors are indeed at the root of crime. The problem now is to decide whether any can be changed by plan and at an acceptable price in money and personal freedom.

If we are to do this, we must confront the fact that the critical years of a child's life are ages one to ten, with perhaps the most important being the earliest years. During those years, some children are put gravely at risk by some combination of heritable traits, prenatal insults (maternal drug and alcohol abuse or poor diet), weak parent-child attachment, poor supervision, and disorderly family environment.

---

[8] "A Nation's Children in Lock-up," *Los Angeles Times,* August 22, 1993.

If we knew with reasonable confidence which children were most seriously at risk, we might intervene with some precision to supply either medical therapy or parent training or (in extreme cases) to remove the child to a better home. But given our present knowledge, precision is impossible, and so we must proceed carefully, relying, except in the most extreme cases, on persuasion and incentives.

We do, however, know enough about the early causes of conduct disorder and later delinquency to know that the more risk factors exist (such as parental criminality and poor supervision), the greater the peril to the child. It follows that programs aimed at just one or a few factors are not likely to be successful; the children most at risk are those who require the most wide-ranging and fundamental changes in their life circumstances. The goal of these changes is, as Travis Hirschi of the University of Arizona has put it, to teach self-control.

Hirokazu Yoshikawa of New York University has recently summarized what we have learned about programs that attempt to make large and lasting changes in a child's prospects for improved conduct, better school behavior, and lessened delinquency. Four such programs in particular seemed valuable—the Perry Preschool Project in Ypsilanti, Michigan; the Parent-Child Development Center in Houston, Texas; the Family Development Research Project in Syracuse, New York; and the Yale Child Welfare Project in New Haven, Connecticut.

All these programs had certain features in common. They dealt with low-income, often minority, families; they intervened during the first five years of a child's life and continued for between two and five years; they combined parent training with preschool education for the child; and they involved extensive home visits. All were evaluated fairly carefully, with the follow-ups lasting for at least five years, in two cases for at least ten, and in one case for fourteen. The programs produced (depending on the project) less fighting, impulsivity, disobedience, restlessness, cheating, and delinquency. In short, they improved self-control.

They were experimental programs, which means that it is hard to be confident that trying the same thing on a bigger scale in many places will produce the same effects. A large number of well-trained and highly motivated caseworkers dealt with a relatively small number of families, with the workers knowing that their efforts were being evaluated. Moreover, the programs operated in the late 1970's or early 1980's before the advent of crack cocaine or the rise of the more lethal neighborhood gangs. A national program mounted under current conditions might or might not have the same result as the experimental efforts.

Try telling that to lawmakers. What happens when politicians encounter experimental successes is amply revealed by the history of Head Start: they expanded the program quickly without assuring quality, and stripped it down to the part that was the most popular, least expensive, and easiest to run, namely, preschool education. Absent from much of Head Start are the high teacher-to-child case loads, the extensive home visits, and the elaborate parent training—the very things that probably account for much of the success of the four experimental programs.

IN THIS country we tend to separate programs designed to help children from those that benefit their parents. The former are called "child development," the latter "welfare reform." This is a great mistake. Everything we know about long-term welfare recipients indicates that their children are at risk for the very problems that child-helping programs later try to correct.

The evidence from a variety of studies is quite clear: even if we hold income and ethnicity constant, children (and especially boys) raised by a single mother are more likely than those raised by two parents to have difficulty in school, get in trouble with the law, and experience emotional and physical problems.[9] Producing illegitimate children is not an "alternative life-style" or simply an imprudent action; it is a curse. Making mothers work will not end the curse; under current proposals, it will not even save money.

The absurdity of divorcing the welfare problem from the child-development problem becomes evident as soon as we think seriously about what we want to achieve. Smaller welfare expenditures? Well, yes, but not if it hurts children. More young mothers working? Probably not; young mothers ought to raise their young children, and work interferes with that unless *two* parents can solve some difficult and expensive problems.

What we really want is *fewer illegitimate children*, because such children, by being born out of wedlock are, except in unusual cases, being given early admission to the underclass. And failing that, we want the children born to single (and typically young and poor) mothers to have a chance at a decent life.

Letting teenage girls set up their own households at public expense neither discourages illegitimacy nor serves the child's best interests. If they do set up their own homes, then to reach those with the fewest parenting skills and the most difficult children will require the kind of expensive and intensive home visits and family-support programs characteristic of the four successful experiments mentioned earlier.

---

[9] I summarize this evidence in "The Family-Values Debate," COMMENTARY, April 1993.

One alternative is to tell a girl who applies for welfare that she can only receive it on condition that she live either in the home of *two* competent parents (her own if she comes from an intact family) or in a group home where competent supervision and parent training will be provided by adults unrelated to her. Such homes would be privately managed but publicly funded by pooling welfare checks, food stamps, and housing allowances.

A model for such a group home (albeit one run without public funds) is the St. Martin de Porres House of Hope on the south side of Chicago, founded by two nuns for homeless young women, especially those with drug-abuse problems. The goals of the home are clear: accept personal responsibility for your lives and learn to care for your children. And these goals, in turn, require the girls to follow rules, stay in school, obey a curfew, and avoid alcohol and drugs. Those are the rules that ought to govern a group home for young welfare mothers.

Group homes funded by pooled welfare benefits would make the task of parent training much easier and provide the kind of structured, consistent, and nurturant environment that children need. A few cases might be too difficult for these homes, and for such children, boarding schools— once common in American cities for disadvantaged children, but now almost extinct—might be revived.

Group homes also make it easier to supply quality medical care to young mothers and their children. Such care has taken on added importance in recent years with discovery of the lasting damage that can be done to a child's prospects from being born prematurely and with a very low birth weight, having a mother who has abused drugs or alcohol, or being exposed to certain dangerous metals. Lead poisoning is now widely acknowledged to be a source of cognitive and behavioral impairment; of late, elevated levels of manganese have been linked to high levels of violence.[10] These are all treatable conditions; in the case of a manganese imbalance, easily treatable.

MY FOCUS on changing behavior will annoy some readers. For them the problem is poverty and the worst feature of single-parent families is that they are inordinately poor. Even to refer to a behavioral or cultural problem is to "stigmatize" people.

Indeed it is. Wrong behavior—neglectful, immature, or incompetent parenting; the production of out-of-wedlock babies—*ought* to be stigmatized. There are many poor men of all races who do not abandon the women they have impregnated, and many poor women of all races who avoid drugs and do a good job of raising their children. If we fail to stigmatize those who give way to temptation, we withdraw the rewards from those who resist them. This becomes all the

more important when entire communities, and not just isolated households, are dominated by a culture of fatherless boys preying on innocent persons and exploiting immature girls.

We need not merely stigmatize, however. We can try harder to move children out of those communities, either by drawing them into safe group homes or facilitating (through rent supplements and housing vouchers) the relocation of them and their parents to neighborhoods with intact social structures and an ethos of family values.

Much of our uniquely American crime problem (as opposed to the worldwide problem of general thievery) arises, not from the failings of individuals but from the concentration in disorderly neighborhoods of people at risk of failing. That concentration is partly the result of prosperity and freedom (functioning families long ago seized the opportunity to move out to the periphery), partly the result of racism (it is harder for some groups to move than for others), and partly the result of politics (elected officials do not wish to see settled constituencies broken up).

I SERIOUSLY doubt that this country has the will to address either of its two crime problems, save by acts of individual self-protection. We could in theory make justice swifter and more certain, but we will not accept the restrictions on liberty and the weakening of procedural safeguards that this would entail. We could vastly improve the way in which our streets are policed, but some of us will not pay for it and the rest of us will not tolerate it. We could alter the way in which at-risk children experience the first few years of life, but the opponents of this—welfare-rights activists, family preservationists, budget cutters, and assorted ideologues—are numerous and the bureaucratic problems enormous.

Unable or unwilling to do such things, we take refuge in substitutes: we debate the death penalty, we wring our hands over television, we lobby to keep prisons from being built in our neighborhoods, and we fall briefly in love with trendy nostrums that seem to cost little and promise much.

Much of our ambivalence is on display in the 1994 federal crime bill. To satisfy the tough-minded, the list of federal offenses for which the death penalty can be imposed has been greatly enlarged, but there is little reason to think that executions, as they work in this country (which is to say, after much delay and only on a few offenders), have any effect on the crime rate and no reason to think that executing more federal prisoners (who account, at best, for a tiny fraction of all homicides) will reduce the murder rate. To

---

[10] It is not clear why manganese has this effect, but we know that it diminishes the availability of a precursor of serotonin, a neurotransmitter, and low levels of serotonin are now strongly linked to violent and impulsive behavior.

satisfy the tender-minded, several billion dollars are earmarked for prevention programs, but there is as yet very little hard evidence that any of these will actually prevent crime.

In adding more police officers, the bill may make some difference—but only if the additional personnel are imaginatively deployed. And Washington will pay only part of the cost initially and none of it after six years, which means that any city getting new officers will either have to raise its own taxes to keep them on the force or accept the political heat that will arise from turning down "free" cops. Many states also desperately need additional prison space; the federal funds allocated by the bill for their construction will be welcomed, provided that states are willing to meet the conditions set for access to such funds.

Meanwhile, just beyond the horizon, there lurks a cloud that the winds will soon bring over us. The population will start getting younger again. By the end of this decade there will be a million more people between the ages of fourteen and seventeen than there are now. Half of this extra million will be male. Six percent of them will become high-rate, repeat offenders—30,000 more muggers, killers, and thieves than we have now.

Get ready.

The Decline of the American Mafia

Peter Reuter

Peter Reuter is a professor in the School of Public Affairs and the Department of Criminology at the University of Maryland.

The American Mafia emerged during Prohibition as the wealthier and more violent successor to local city gangs involved in prostitution and gambling. It is thus a contemporary of the Soviet Union, another long-standing problem for the United States government. Coincidentally, the Mafia and Soviet Union have ceased to be significant strategic adversaries at almost the same time. The Mafia is almost extinguished now as a major actor in the United States' criminal world. And, to extend the comparison with the Soviet Union perhaps beyond its fair limits, the Mafia's decline is the result of both its conservatism and of federal government actions.

Initially, the American Mafia was a prominent supplier of bootlegged liquor. That required good connections with the local police department and political machines. Paying off the local beat cop provided a speakeasy, with its conspicuous and regular flow of traffic, little effective protection. Instead, it was necessary to guard against any cop who might be on that beat; the efficient solution was buying the whole department, if it was for sale. In many cities it was. Frequently, that also meant connections with urban political machines. While Al Capone's control of Chicago (though some scholars question Capone's Mafia membership) in the 1920s is the most notorious instance, almost 50 years later the Mayor of Newark, New Jersey, Hugh Addonizio, retained strong connections to the local Mafia family. Elliot Ness and the federal revenuers, frequently less honest than legend, were a nuisance but not a major one.

At the same time, the Mafia acquired control of many unions, largely through direct intimidation of members. By 1929, when John Landesco did his classic study of organized crime in Chicago, he could already list a dozen local industries that the Mafia dominated through the unions. Prices were fixed and/or territories were allocated, with the threat of union strikes or picketing of customers as the enforcement mechanism. The Depression, which created a demand for cartel-organizing services later met by various New Deal agencies, such as the Reconstruction Financing Administration, added a few more industries (e.g., fur manufacturing) to the Mafia list, particularly in New York.

By the 1960s, the Mafia had mostly shifted from direct provision of illegal services, like bookmaking and loansharking, to selling services to bookmakers, loansharks, and other criminal entrepreneurs. The organization's reputation for being able to deliver on threats was good enough that it could, in effect, sell these entrepreneurs contract insurance and dispute-settlement services. A bookmaker could insure himself against extortion by other gangsters or customer welching by making regular payments to some Mafioso. The organizational reputation, painstakingly and bloodily acquired earlier, was now the principal asset.

LOSING TO THE COMPETITION

The evidence of the Mafia's decline is partly of the "dog didn't bark" variety. A Senate committee has a hearing on international fraud and organized crime, and the American Mafia goes unmentioned. The Department of Justice lists its principal targets for drug enforcement, and Mafia leaders don't make the cut. The New York City Police Department has yet another major corruption scandal, and none of the events involve the Mafia. A major numbers banker in New York, "Spanish Raymond" Marquez, who paid 5 percent of his profits to the Mafia in the 1960s, now pays only $300 per week.

There are a few more direct indicia as well. At least one family, based in Cleveland, has effectively disbanded. The *New York Times*, long the newspaper of record for Mafia events, now lists the membership of the five major New York families as only 1,200, down from 3,000 in the early 1970s. The DeCavalcante family of New Jersey, admittedly a weaker family even then, now has only 10 members, scarcely enough to fill a good-sized dining table, let alone an organization chart of the type so dramatically displayed by the FBI at numerous Senate hearings.

The Mafia has failed to maintain control of the New York heroin market and has been a marginal player in the cocaine business everywhere. Mexican-source heroin became available when the heroin market first expanded in the early 1970s, and the Mafia was never able to prevent its distribution in New York City, the home of perhaps one-third of the nation's heroin addicts. Its earlier control of the market had apparently rested on its domination of the New York docks, through the longshoremen's union as well as its connections with southern European processors. Mexican imports evaded that bottleneck. By the late 1980s, the traditional circuitous route for Southeast Asian heroin, through Sicily, southern Italy, or France, had primarily been replaced by direct importation, via the West coast, by Chinese and Vietnamese entrepreneurs. The Mafia proved helpless to deal with any of these incursions on its traditional territories.

Asian drug distributors have major advantages as heroin importers and domestic wholesalers. In the source countries for heroin, they can more cheaply ascertain the credibility and capacities of producers and exporters, as well as the corruptibility of local officials and transportation executives. Chinese gangs are better partners for Kun Sa, the long-standing leader in the Burmese/Thai opium trade, historically connected with remnants of the Kuo Min Tang army from pre-1949 China.

In the United States, these gangs have better natural cover. Even creative and entrepreneurial drug-enforcement organizations have had difficulty developing informants and intelligence about Asian distributors. Few agents speak the relevant languages, and even fewer are of Asian origin. It is difficult to blend into the community, which, reflecting its recent immigration and cultural distinctiveness, is generally distrustful of police agencies.

In contrast, the Mafia is familiar territory to enforcement agencies, with its membership and affiliate lists updated as often at FBI headquarters as at John Gotti's Ravenite Social Club hangout. Indeed, there have been occasions in which, as was true for the U.S. Communist Party in the 1950s, FBI undercover agents seem to be as significant in some families as were the members themselves. The communities in which the Mafia recruits and operates are well known to police and provide comfortable terrain for undercover operations; language is not much of a problem anymore.

The Mafia's failure to play a role in the cocaine market is particularly striking. Most reasonable estimates suggest that this constitutes the largest single illegal market, in terms of gross sales, in recent times and perhaps ever. Credible estimates of U.S. revenues are approximately $40 billion, with as much as $10 billion going to higher-level distributors. No list of the major players has ever included any senior Mafiosi. The failure of the Mafia to participate directly in this market is partly explained by the very high legal risks associated with drug trafficking (a reason offered for the often-broken rule, immortalized in the movie *The Godfather*, for staying away from heroin), but more interesting is the Mafia's failure to serve as the source of dispute-settlement, enforcement, or financing services.

Several factors may explain the Mafia's inability to provide services to cocaine dealers. Colombian drug-dealing organizations have developed their own general reputation for violence. Indeed, the Colombians are known for their unwillingness to follow even the moderately restrictive rules of Mafia murders, e.g., that wives and children are exempt. That probably reflects a shorter planning horizon (the leaders will go back to Colombia once rich) and a belief that the criminal justice system will not punish them. The historical experience in Colombia itself since 1950 could account for that; the criminal-justice system there has been highly vulnerable to intimidation and corruption, and Colombia has experienced extraordinary levels of political and other violence over the last 40 years.

The Mafia has also suffered a major loss from its racketeering activities in legal markets. The election of a Teamsters reform slate, headed by Ron Carey, capped a decades-long battle with the U.S. Department of Justice. During that time, four teamster presidents (Dave Beck, Jimmy Hoffa, Roy Williams, and Jackie Presser) were indicted and/or convicted of corrupt activities in connection with the Mafia, particularly the Chicago and Kansas City families. The Mafia's long-standing role in Las Vegas casinos, originally arising from the pariah-like nature of the industry itself, had come to center on its ability to direct the Central States Teamsters pension funds to compliant casino operators. The shift to trusteeships of that fund, again after a remarkably long battle with the Justice Department, greatly reduced the capital available to the Mafia.

Deregulation of the trucking industry, which curtailed the bargaining power of the Teamsters, also played a major role in lowering the value of racketeer control of the union. Trucking companies now had to compete with each other, as well as with other modes of transport, and could no longer pass on wage increases in regulated prices.

The most poignant indicator of decline is evidenced by recent court pleadings. Twelve Philadelphia Mafiosi have asked for public-defender representation, and prosecutors believe that they may indeed be poor enough to justify the request. Even the bar specializing in defense of Mafiosi has apparently hit hard times:

"Lawyers who once made a steady diet of this type of work are having to diversify," said a prominent local defense lawyer.

SOURCES OF DECLINE

Some have suggested that the decline is largely the result of the "Americanization" of the Mafia—the demise of old values of loyalty to the fictive family and the increasing greed and self-centeredness of members. A less colorful, but more plausible, explanation may be found in a combination of three factors.

The altered structure of urban politics and policing. As already stated, the principal original asset of the Mafia, built during the Prohibition era, was its connection to urban political machines. Mayors in Boston, Kansas City, New York, and Philadelphia were all credibly associated with their local Mafia families between 1950 and 1980. Those connections helped the Mafia develop property rights to centralized police corruption. As Thomas Schelling argued in these pages 28 years ago, the Mafia's ability to control illegal markets may have rested largely on its ability to use the monopoly power of the police.* The Mafia was, in effect, the collector for corrupt politicians and police, with the limits of the franchise dictated by political resistance in the populace.

By 1970, urban machines were largely gone; Chicago was an important exception into the 1980s. Cities are now mostly governed by much broader coalitions, with strong federal involvement in local government financing. Local corruption, the original justification for passage in 1970 of the Organized Crime Control Act, is now much less systemic. The flight of white ethnic communities to the suburbs and the growth of strong urban black political organizations has also contributed to the decline. Though *The Godfather* movies depicted corrupt, whiskey-guzzling Irish police overcoming their contempt for wine-sloshing Sicilians and making deals with the Mafia, the traditional relationship between blacks and the Mafia has not encouraged the development of trust. For a long time, the Mafia pushed around black gambling operators, and the memory remains.

Local police agencies have become more professional, and the growth of large federal law-enforcement agencies, with concurrent jurisdiction and strong interest in making corruption cases, has inhibited the development of long-term corrupt relationships between Mafiosi and police. Before 1960, the local police effectively had a monopoly of law enforcement aimed at illegal markets; paying off the Miami Police Department was enough to provide total protection of bookmaking there in the 1950s. Federal and state agencies

---

The Public Interest, Number 7, Spring 1967.

might have jurisdiction, for example, under the Harrison Act (drugs) or the Mann Act (prostitution), but these agencies were small and timid. The famous Harry Anslinger, an aggressive proselytizer for tough drug enforcement and the head of the predecessor to DEA, had assembled a force of no more than 300 agents when he retired in 1962.

Now, the local police can sell, at best, very partial protection, since state and federal agencies can all make cases against loansharks, drug dealers, or extortionists. To make matters worse for would-be sellers of local protective services, offering up your local protector is one of the few ways for criminals to get relief from long federal sentences. The market for local police corruption has certainly not disappeared, but it is much less systemic than in previous decades. What the recent Mollen Commission inquiry in New York City uncovered was a group of entrepreneurial police who stole drugs from dealers when they had the chance but then had to sell the stuff themselves. There was no criminal organization able and willing to take advantage of their corruption to develop control of some area or market.

LEGAL EAGLES AND STUMBLING FELONS

Better federal enforcement. The FBI got out of pretentious pinstripes and into badly cut leisure suits in the late 1970s. Long-term undercover investigations, which Hoover had always rejected because of the difficulty of controlling the agents, became frequent. One of the first (UniRac, for "union racketeering") snared Anthony Scotto, a highly visible figure in the waterfront industry with close ties to the New York State political system and, as it turned out, a member in good standing of the Gambino family; that membership was scarcely surprising since he had married the daughter of Anthony Anastasia, of Murder, Inc., fame.

Federal prosecutors became much more sophisticated in their use of the Racketeer Influenced and Corrupt Organizations (RICO) and the Continuing Criminal Enterprise (CCE) statutes. Instead of convicting dons for running gambling enterprises, which was the outcome of many investigations in the early 1970s, RICO allowed them to bring cases with more significant and substantive crimes. John Gotti, the putative Godfather, was sentenced for his involvement in a homicide. The list of charges on which the heads of the five New York families were convicted in 1986 (the "Commission" case, in which, for the first time, the defendants admitted that the Mafia existed and was directed by a commission of the leaders) included three murders.

The federal judiciary, with guidelines in hand, delivered long sentences. For example, taking the *Times* listing as definitive, each of the leaders of the five families in New York in 1985 has received a sentence of at least 15 years; most of them and their principal deputies are in prison for life sentences without parole.

The price of loyalty, the much-vaunted "omerta," has thus become a lot higher. Members who might serve three years rather than inform changed their minds when 15-year terms became common. John Gotti is serving a life sentence because Salvatore Gravano, his longtime deputy and an admitted participant in 19 murders, chose to testify and turn an expected life sentence into a more reasonable five years. The federal government now reports over 100 Mafiosi in its witness protection program, compared to just a handful 10 years ago.

Not surprisingly, the increasing incidence of informants has begun to destroy the families from within; by early 1993, 11 Lucchese family members had been killed in an internal struggle. As Ronald Goldstock, longtime director of the New York State Organized Crime Task Force, commented in 1993: "The fate of anyone who assumes a leadership position in a [Mafia] family is a life prison sentence or assassination by a rival."

Incompetence. The Mafia has continued to recruit from among uneducated, tough felons and requires that they commit serious and brutal crimes to gain admission. This is not a very effective method for finding the best and the brightest of criminal talent, particularly when the shrinking pool of young Italian-immigrant labor has much better legitimate opportunities than in the past. Whereas in the period from 1900 to 1909 over one million Italian males under the age of 45 migrated to the United States, for the 1960s the figure was only 80,000.

Inevitably, some older leaders lost their edge. Mark Haller, the leading historian of American organized crime, reports that Harry Riccibone, a senior member of the Bruno group, was accused by one of his associates of turning into a "philanthropist" because of his unwillingness to act aggressively against his debtors. The current leader of the Genovese family, Vincent Gigante, may be mentally impaired, though some maintain that this is a ruse on his part to ensure that he cannot be tried.

The leaders may be decisive, they may be shrewd at determining when to use force, but they are not strategic in their thinking. Colombian drug distributors are less sophisticated than suggested by highly stylized accounts, such as novelist Tom Clancy's *Clear and Present Danger*, but they do seem to have acquired a few contemporary business practices, particularly with respect to financial services. The American Mafia languishes in suspicion of such sophistication, with nary a computer in sight.

THE FUTURE OF ORGANIZED CRIME

This is not to say that organized crime has disappeared from American cities. New ethnic gangs, mostly from East Asia, have become wealthy through their control of large-scale illicit drug-distribution systems. Chinese and Vietnamese importers have come to dominate the importation of drugs into New York and Los Angeles; they are sufficiently competent at these activities that the price of imported heroin has simply collapsed, from $2,000 per gram in 1980 to less than $500 per gram in 1992.

They are also effective extortionists of their own communities. Chinese gangs have long been able to intimidate small businesses in traditional Chinatowns; the expansion of these communities, with new migration and economic mobility, does not seem to have reduced that capacity. Like their predecessor migrant populations, Asians have been unwilling to go to alien police to deal with indigenous intimidation. Police departments have made only modest recruiting efforts in Asian communities, with little success.

Yet, these gangs have not been able to diversify, as the Mafia did, into control of mainstream political and social institutions outside of those communities. The leading Chinese triads lack the name recognition of Mafia families in the non-Asian community. Asians are only just now producing their first generation of prominent local politicians, reflecting, in many cases, the lack of an active political tradition in their own nations. The path to success of the Mafia in American urban politics does not seem to be the path that the Asian gangs will follow.

But will the Colombian gangs, fed by the vast revenues from cocaine trafficking, take on Mafia-like capabilities? So far, they have not exhibited the same entrepreneurial capacities as their 1920s counterparts and have not branched out into other activities in this country. This contrasts with their supplier organizations in Colombia, which have greatly broadened the base of their legal and illegal activities. The critical difference is probably the role of systemic corruption. In Colombia, their success has been built on the purchase of broad political influence, in addition to the intimidation of law enforcement. That influence permitted the Medellin principals to invest with impunity in agricultural land; the scenes of the baronial country homes of smugglers in *Clear and Present Danger* are allegedly close to the truth.

In this country, that same kind of systemic protection has not been available. The leaders have not built connections to political machines or developed any other institutional base for expanded operations. Gambling operators and bootleggers in earlier eras were public figures, with broad reputations that were important assets in many phases of their business. Drug dealers, in contrast, are rewarded for discretion. Moreover, major drug dealers do not need to have traditional retail businesses, but only have to make very occasional deals in varying locations; consequently, they do not need the same kind of long-term police protection.

The reduced power of unions, a concomitant of the decline in American manufacturing, also makes it difficult for new groups to acquire broad criminal powers. Thus, the list of racketeer-dominated industries has not expanded in the last 65 years. Indeed, I would argue that it was a list of low-technology industries with poorly educated workforces that have mostly disappeared.

BRING BACK THE GODFATHER?

A nostalgia for the Mafia has already emerged in this country. It is associated with a remembrance of orderly illegal markets, when bootleggers and bookmakers only shot each other and understood the dangers of killing the innocent. Alan Block, a Pennsylvania State University historian, estimates that only about 190 gangland murders occurred in New York during the 1930s, a mere bagatelle when compared with the hundreds generated annually by drug markets through the 1980s and 1990s. Unless we want to reinstall systemic, local police corruption and have police intimately involved in the regulation of the business, the Mafia would not be able to do much about the retailing end, where almost all the violence occurs.

Another component of the nostalgia is for the simplicity of having one monolithic enemy, particularly one whose leaders often displayed a certain panache and whose lineages were well known. Alas, to conclude with the Soviet analogy, we will now have to live with the more complicated world of many less well-known gangs. The FBI, like the CIA, must develop the capacity to track the activities of lots of groups, many as meaningless to the American public as the leaders of Azerbaijan. We may be better off dealing with a foe less capable of undermining government, but we will inevitably pay less attention to the struggle, and the agencies themselves will miss the public attention that goes with catching stars.

How Much Crime Is There?

Violent crime has risen dramatically compared to
30 years ago, particularly in the cities.

MICHAEL HEDGES

Michael Hedges is a national
reporter for the Washington Times.

Each person's chances of being set upon by violent thugs and robbed, killed, or raped grow each year. The number of Americans altering their behavior—avoiding night activities, eschewing automated teller machines, staying away from downtown areas even if it means missing a play, ballet, or basketball game—is at an all-time high, according to behavioral experts.

Some statistics, such as the murder rate in Washington, D.C., bear out the apprehension with which people face the world. The brutality of crime increases almost exponentially each decade, so that what once horrified us we now accept as sadly routine.

"The climate is changing," says Dennis Martin, a former police chief who is president of the National Association of Chiefs of Police. "We are working on a comprehensive study with Columbia University that shows our attitudes have clearly changed. We have become almost desensitized to crime and violence."

In a study involving 374 mayors or municipal executives from cities with populations over 10,000, the National League of Cities found a growing sense of unease among those living in urban or suburban areas.

For 1993, more than 4 in 10 felt violent crime had worsened in their city in the past year. Another 5 in 10 thought the number of gangs involved in criminal activity had grown. Only 2 in 10 thought violent crime had lessened, and fewer than 1 in 10 believed their cities were less at risk from gangs.

The increase in the number of civic officials who admitted their crime was worsening was greater than in any other year in the past decade.

The study Martin worked on contains an analysis of how college students respond to violent imagery. "The reaction to violence by young people today is significantly different than it was in 1960," he says.

Martin echoes the sentiments of other current and former law enforcement officials as he catalogs reasons why.

Early release of criminals. "One thing we are finding is that when someone is arrested for burglary today, he has committed between 40 and 100 previous crimes," says Martin. "That makes effective law enforcement impossible."

Proliferation of plea bargaining. "Offenses are being bargained down because of prosecutors' work loads and lack of jail space, until the punishment bears no resemblance to the crime," says Martin. "What you too often see is a violent criminal accepting a plea to a nonviolent offense, so he gets paroled quickly. The next time he's arrested he doesn't have a prior history as a violent felon, so he gets another deal."

Lack of values and education. "Four out of five people convicted of serious crimes never finished high school," he says. "If a person has been physically abused by his parents, his chances of being a criminal double."

Breakdown in respect for authority. "The way people view authority figures has changed remarkably since the early 1960s," says Martin. "Our figures show the number of assaults each year on police officers has risen 846 percent since 1960."

That is the stark view of what is happening: A system that can't catch and hold criminals or protect the innocent is being confronted with a rising tide of increasingly violent youths who have failed to learn, either from their families or society, how to behave. But does this situation lead to well-advised caution or panic? Are our perceptions of crime and the average person's safety accurate?

Law enforcement experts at every level—as well as the blizzard of statistics put together by the U.S. Justice Department, state agencies, and others—indicate the answers depend on who you are, where you live, and how you live your life.

Dewey Stokes, president of the National Fraternal Order of Police, says, "The heinous crimes the news media are attracted to have come to the forefront. Sometimes it seems to me there is almost a sense of one-upmanship among these violent psychopaths."

All agree that there is far too much crime in America, more than in other civilized nations. But the sense that the country is under siege by criminals, which has mushroomed since the 1970s, may be an exaggeration. The perception is fueled by media ability to put us on the scene of violence and, ironically, by improvements in the way police investigate and document crime.

To illustrate, think back to the mid-1970s, a time many might view as an age of innocence compared to today. In fact, your chances of being robbed or burglarized were greater in 1976 than in 1992, according to statistics compiled by the Justice Department. By the early 1980s, some categories of violent crime, such as rape, had peaked.

The percentage of households in the United States experiencing any kind of crime dropped from 32 to 26 percent from the mid-1970s to 1992. But the story is different if you move the time frame backward: Violent crime has risen dramatically compared to 30 years ago.

In 1960, the chances of being murdered or a victim of intentional manslaughter were 5 in 100,000 for Americans. The chances of being raped were 10 per 100,000 and of being assaulted about 86 per 100,000. In 1991, these figures had risen to almost 9 murders or manslaughters, 42 rapes, and 433 aggravated assaults per 100,000. The overall chances of being in a violent crime have risen about 600 percent since 1960, from 161 to 758 per 100,000.

"There is a decrease in some categories, such as house and business burglaries," says Stokes. "In some areas, there has been a drop in armed robberies.

"But what you are seeing is an increase in violent crime and

Personal and household crimes

	1976	1981	1986	1991
Personal crime				
Crimes of violence				
Number	5,599	6,582	5,515	6,424
Rate	32.6	35.3	28.1	31.3
Rape				
Number	145	178	130	173
Rate	0.8	1.0	0.7	0.8
Robbery				
Number	1,111	1,381	1,009	1,145
Rate	6.5	7.4	5.1	5.6
Assault				
Number	4,344	5,024	4,376	5,105
Rate	25.3	27.0	22.3	24.9
Aggravated assault				
Number	1,695	1,796	1,543	1,609
Rate	9.9	9.6	7.9	7.8
Simple Assault				
Number	2,648	3,228	2,833	3,497
Rate	15.4	17.3	14.4	17.0
Crimes of theft				
Number	16,519	15,863	13,235	12,533
Rate	96.1	85.1	67.5	61.0
Personal larceny with contact:				
Number	497	605	536	482
Rate	2.9	3.3	2.7	2.3
Personal larceny without contact:				
Number	16,022	15,235	12,699	12,050
Rate	93.2	81.9	64.7	58.7
Total population age 12 and older	171,901	186,336	196,160	205,345
Household crime				
Household burglary				
Number	6,663	7,394	5,557	5,138
Rate	88.9	87.9	61.5	53.1
Household larceny				
Number	9,301	10,176	8,455	8,524
Rate	124.1	121.0	93.5	88.0
Motor vehicle theft				
Number	1,235	1,439	1,356	2,112
Rate	16.5	17.1	15.0	21.8
Total number of housholds (in thousands)	74,956	84,095	90,395	96,839

SOURCE: U.S. DEPARTMENT OF JUSTICE, BUREAU OF JUSTICE STATISTICS, 1992

drug crimes in some areas where it becomes a high-profile phenomenon," he says. "For example, there have been increases in rape reports around major universities. In some suburban areas drug gangs have moved in seeking new markets, and there has been an accompanying surge in all the associated crimes: murders, robberies, drug arrests." The spread of drug-peddling organizations from cities to suburban areas has contributed to many Americans' feeling that nobody is safe.

Stokes, who monitors crime from all over the country, says it has become much more common for police in rural and suburban areas to end up in a shootout with a drug criminal.

"These drug dealers are not afraid of apprehension, because they understand that the way the system is set up they won't have to do more than 10 to 35 percent of the time they are given," he says. "We call these groups gangs like they were a bunch of teenagers banding together to defend their turf. What we should call them is organized crime. They are groups of criminals between 14 and 35 years old organized to make money by setting up criminal operations."

Safest places

Based on an array of statistics and information from law enforcement officers nationwide, Stokes has compiled a list of places he would still rate as safe.

"There aren't too many in the northeast quadrant," he says. "There used to be a few in Maryland, deep in South Carolina. Right now I'd say most of Wyoming and Idaho, quite a bit of the Dakotas. Colorado used to be safe, but Denver is not anymore, and there are problems in Fort Collins."

In other words, areas of low population density in the Far West. "When there is a more sparsely populated area, people depend on each other more. There is a better sense of community, and they are more wary of strangers," he says.

But the perception that the West is more crime free than elsewhere doesn't stand up under statistical analysis. According to the comprehensive Justice Department figures, one's chances of being a victim of any crime are highest in the West.

Those figures measure the number of households in which one or more people are victimized by any crime, no matter how petty, in a given year. By region, the 1992 numbers were 18 percent for the Northeast, 20.9 percent for the Midwest, 23.4 percent for the South, and 28.5 percent for the West.

The numbers of those falling prey to a "serious violent crime"—

as the Justice Department characterizes a rape, robbery, or aggravated assault—are much smaller but show a similar breakdown by region: Northeast 4.7 percent, Midwest 6.3 percent, South 7.2 percent, and West 9.1 percent.

The FBI publishes a state-by-state crime analysis each year that also includes the District of Columbia. That analysis for 1992 shows that Washington, D.C., was by far the most dangerous spot, at least when compared with states, where rural, suburban, and urban populations coexist.

The FBI Uniform Crime Reporting Program estimates crimes in various categories per 100,000 inhabitants. Its broadest index contains three categories:

● A total crime index, which measures the sum of all murders, manslaughter, forcible rape, robbery, aggravated assault, burglary, larceny, and car theft.

● A violent crime index, which counts murder, rape, armed robbery, and assault.

● Property crimes, including burglary, theft, nonviolent robbery, and car theft.

The FBI figures indicate that 10,768 out of every 100,000 inhabitants of Washington, D.C., were crime victims in 1992. North Dakota had the lowest overall crime rate by this measure, 2,793 per 100,000.

"That is accurate but some-

Percentage of Crimes by Region

Region	Population	Crime Index total	Violent crime	Property crime	Murder and non-negligent man-slaughter	Forcible rape	Robbery	Aggra-vated assault	Burglary	Larceny-theft	Motor vehicle theft
United States Total ...	100.0	100.0	100.0	100.0	100.0	100.0	100.0	100.0	100.0	100.0	100.0
Northeastern States ...	20.2	17.7	20.1	17.3	17.3	13.8	26.1	16.9	16.3	16.3	24.4
Midwestern States ...	23.9	21.3	19.9	21.5	19.1	25.7	19.5	19.5	19.8	22.8	18.4
Southern States ...	34.5	37.5	36.3	37.7	42.6	36.9	31.8	38.9	41.2	37.5	31.5
Western States ...	21.4	23.5	23.8	23.5	21.1	23.6	22.6	24.6	22.7	23.4	25.7

Violent crimes are offenses of murder, forcible rape, robbery, and aggravated assault. Property crimes are offenses of burglary, larceny-theft and motor vehicle theft. Because of rounding, percentages may not add to totals.

SOURCE: U.S. DEPARTMENT OF JUSTICE, BUREAU OF JUSTICE STATISTICS, 1992

what misleading," says a federal law enforcement expert. "Washington is probably more accurately compared to Houston, New York, Los Angeles, or Chicago, other major urban centers."

Washington also had the highest figures for violent crime. At 2,453 crimes per 100,000 inhabitants, Washington was more than twice as violent as the next most afflicted area, Florida, which had 1,184 reported acts of violence for every 100,000. California, New York, and Illinois all had violent crime rates of 1,000 per 100,000 or more. North Dakota was the least violent place, with 65 violent crimes per 100,000. Next was Vermont, with 117.

New Hampshire, South Dakota, West Virginia, Maine, Montana, Utah, Idaho, Iowa, Wisconsin, Wyoming, and Hawaii had violent crime rates of about 300 or less per 100,000.

For property crime, again, Washington, D.C., was the worst place to live, with 8,315 such offenses per 100,000 inhabitants. Florida and Texas were second and third, with 7,363 and 6,979 per 100,000. Arizona, which had a moderate rate for violent crime, is fourth in terms of frequency of property crimes, with 6,735 per 100,000.

Kentucky, South Dakota, North Dakota, New Hampshire, West Virginia, Pennsylvania, Montana, Maine, Vermont, Iowa, Idaho, and Mississippi had property crime rates under 4,000 per 100,000 inhabitants.

The Justice Department put together a list of populated areas that were low in crime. The five safest moderately populated areas in America in 1992 were Wheeling, West Virginia; Beaver County, Pennsylvania (northeast of Pittsburgh); Cumberland, Maryland; St. Cloud, Minnesota; and Johnstown, Pennsylvania. But the places Americans feel safe are in danger of disappearing, if not in fact, then in the minds of citizens.

With grim regularity, reports are issued documenting another aspect of a violent world. That information is digested and regurgitated by the media, adding another aspect to the perception of fear.

In January, for example, a survey conducted by the Justice Department's Bureau of Justice Statistics found that approximately 2.5 million of the nation's 107 million females 12 years old and older were raped, robbed, or assaulted in a typical year, or were the victim of a threat or an

It has become much more common for police in rural and suburban areas to end up in a shootout with a criminal.

attempt to commit such a crime.

Nearly a third, 28 percent, of those making the assaults or threats were the women's husbands or boyfriends. Another 40 percent were relatives or acquaintances. The survey tended to argue against the image of the shadowy stranger as rapist and put the onus on those the women knew and loved.

Violent crime has been building for years and is now regarded by many Americans as the country's greatest problem. As such it promises to be a political cause célèbre through the 1996 elections and beyond.

MORAL CREDIBILITY AND CRIME

WHY PEOPLE OBEY THE LAW

PAUL H. ROBINSON

Mr. Robinson is a professor at Northwestern University School of Law.

We are in a panic over crime. Legislators compete with one another to propose the toughest anti-crime legislation. The $30 billion federal anti-crime bill got strong support in the midst of a deficit-reduction drive. In the states "three strikes and you're out" proposals are trumped by "two strikes" proposals.

Clearheaded commentators point out that the panic is unjustified: crime rates have not in fact increased recently, they correctly note. But a complete description of our situation includes two other important pieces of information. First, one reason that crime has not increased recently is that we have altered the way we live in order to avoid it. We no longer go out at night. We no longer let our children walk to a friend's house to play. We install locks, carry Mace, and readily pay more for apartment buildings with security. In 1980 private expenditures on security were $20 billion—considerably more than the $14 billion of public spending in the same category. By 1990 annual private expenditures for security had risen to $52 billion. The rate of crime has stabilized because we increasingly diminish the quality of our lives to avoid it. The injury of crime escalates even where its incidence does not.

The other important fact is that crime *has* dramatically increased over the longer term, albeit in increments sufficiently small that no single reported increase has justified panic. In 1955 forty-six robberies occurred annually per 100,000 in the population; today the rate is more than 270—a sixfold increase. Rape rates have more than tripled. Murder per capita has more than doubled. The aggravated-assault rate has increased more than sixfold. Overall, taking into account both urban and rural areas, the major crime rate is more than four times what it was four decades ago.

Perhaps the current panic is born not of new data but of realized frustration—reminding us of the monkey who works methodically to free himself from a trap and goes berserk only when he realizes he can't escape. Frustration, not crime, has boiled over.

To many, our situation is intolerable. Five years ago, before the current panic, 82 percent of those polled in one study believed that crime was getting worse; 34 percent felt "truly desperate" about rising crime.

WHAT WE HAVE TRIED

The steady worsening of the crime problem is not the result of inattention; rather, it has occurred despite out best efforts to halt it. In the 1950s we thought we could best stop crime by not just imprisoning criminals but rehabilitating them. Today we would call it attacking the root cause of the problem: offenders have a disease; we will treat it. The logic of the rehabilitative model dictated that sentences for all felonies be indeterminate—from one day to life, depending on the treatment needed and how the offender responded. But Robert Martinson, a sociologist, concluded in his 1974 survey article "What Works?," in *The Public Interest,* "I am bound to say that these data, involving over two hundred studies and hundreds of thousands of individuals as they do, are the best available and give us very little reason to hope that we have in fact found a sure way of reducing recidivism through rehabilitation."

Deterrence became popular as an alternative. Potential offenders would be dissuaded from committing offenses by the threat of serious penalties. The greater the threatened penalty (the longer the prison term), the greater the disincentive. The high cost of imprisonment would normally put a natural limit on the severity of the deterrent threat, but the threat could be made dramatic without courting fiscal crisis if longer sentences than would actually be served were publicly imposed. The idea was that the deterrent benefit would be fully realized at the moment of public imposition, and that offenders could later be quietly released by parole boards (conveniently left over from the rehabilitation approach). Typical was the federal system, in which offenders could be eligible for release immediately, and which generally required release after serving a third of the sentence.

But in our open society the shell game was soon seen for what it was. The public came to understand that a twenty-year sentence really meant a maximum of seven years and often much less. To counteract this discounting of sentences, judges imposed ever greater sentences, sometimes of hundreds of years. But this only increased public skepticism, because the potential discount also increased; even a sentence many times as long as the human life-span could end in release after a few years if the parole board so chose. Many states are following the lead of the federal system, which recently shifted to "real-time" sentencing, under which offenders must serve at least 85 percent of the term imposed. With time, sentencing will regain credibility.

DETERRENCE   But does imprisonment deter crime? Deterrence requires that potential offenders think about the consequences of their actions, as many fail to do. More important, deterrence requires that those who do think about the consequences see some real risk that they will be caught and punished—a risk that must outweigh the benefits they expect from the crime. Unfortunately for deterrence, potential offenders think that the threat of capture and punishment applies to others but not to them. Unlike the other guy, *they* will avoid detection by taking the necessary precautions. Thus even those who might think about the consequences of their actions do not think that the threat of punishment applies to them.

But even if most offenders thought the threat did apply to them, what would be the nature of the threat they faced? An astounding number of serious offenses are never reported to the police (for example, 21 percent of rapes and 40 percent of burglaries), out of embarrassment, out or fear of reprisal, or in the belief that the police are impotent to do anything. For the offenses reported, clearance rates (the rates at which the police identify and arrest suspects) have been dropping steadily for decades. The nationwide clearance rate for homicide, which was 93 percent in 1955, has steadily declined to 67 percent. That for rape has declined from 79 to 52 percent, and that for burglary from 32 to 14 percent.

And, as our realistic potential offender knows, being arrested is a far cry from being punished. The overall conviction rate among those arrested for the most serious offenses is 30 percent. Fewer than half of those convicted of a felony are sentenced to prison. Finally, the median time served by those actually sentenced to state prison ranges from 5.5 years for murder to 2.2 years for kidnapping to 1.4 years for arson.

The cumulative effect of the many escape hatches from punishment leaves a deterrent threat that looks like this: Homicide offers a less than 45 percent chance of being caught, convicted, and imprisoned, rape a 12 percent chance, robbery a four percent chance. Assault, burglary, larceny, and motor-vehicle theft are each a hundred-to-one shot. Our potential offender may not be cowed by these threats. These statistics also explain why longer prison terms can have only a limited effect in deterring crime: if a robber faces a mere four percent chance of going to prison, why should it matter to him whether the likely sentence is two years or ten years?

Our fallback crime-control policy has increasingly been to keep in prison those offenders we think may commit another crime. We know this works (at least to protect the public—victimization of other prisoners is another matter). Unfortunately, we are no better at predicting future dangerousness than we are at rehabilitating. In a monograph published by the National Institute of Mental Health, John Monahan, a psychologist, summarizes studies indicating that we are wrong about two out of every three people predicted to commit a serious offense. In other words, as many as two thirds of the prisoners detained for dangerousness are detained needlessly. Besides its obvious unfairness, this approach makes the incapacitation strategy wildly expensive. And even at its best, the value of incapacitating dangerous offenders is limited to avoiding further offenses while the person is in prison. It does nothing to avoid offenses after imprisonment.

This is a truly depressing picture. Is this the future of mankind: ever increasing numbers of people in prison? Can't we do something to prevent people from committing crimes in the first place?

MORAL CREDIBILITY AS CRIME CONTROL

We tend to think of criminals as a distinct class of people. This image is reinforced by reports that one group of offenders is responsible for a disproportionately large share of crimes. If we could only do something with these criminal types in our society, the logic goes, we could solve our crime problem. And then the standard punishment-versus-prevention debate is off and running: should we keep more of these folks in prison, or should we target this group for more social services, or should we strike some balance between the two?

Some offenders truly are career criminals. But the greater truth is that no offenders, except for a small group of the mentally ill, are irrevocably driven to crime. For nearly any criminal, whatever the person's age, race, social background, or economic status, one can identify hundreds of thousands of people with essentially the same characteristics who have chosen to act differently and to remain law-abiding.

People who commit crimes are people like us who have chosen to do bad things. The study *Ordinary People and Extraordinary Evil* (1993), by the sociologist Fred Katz, shows how ordinary people in the course of everyday choices can come step by step to undertake serious wrongdoing—even horrendous acts like those of the Nazi Holocaust and the My Lai massacre.

Asking "How should we deal with our criminal class?" distracts us from the positive inquiry "Why do people obey the law?" Why, even in difficult situations of need and temptation, and even when they are unlikely to be caught and punished, do the vast majority of people remain law-abiding? Perhaps if we better understood what makes a person choose not to commit a crime, even when temptation and opportunity present themselves, we could develop and enlarge that influence.

SOCIAL DISAPPROVAL Here is what preliminary social-science research hints at: beyond the threat of legal punishment, people obey the law because they fear the disapproval of their social group and because they generally see themselves as moral beings who want to do the right thing as they perceive it. In a 1980 study the sociologists Harold Grasmick and Donald Green concluded, "Each of the three independent variables [threat of legal punishment, social disapproval, and personal moral commitment] makes a significant, independent contribution to the explained variance [the rate of criminal behavior]."

As to social disapproval specifically, the sociologists Robert Meier and Weldon Johnson found in a 1977 study that "despite contemporary predisposition toward the importance of legal sanctions, our findings are . . . consistent with the accumulated literature concerning the primacy of interpersonal influence [that is, social disapproval]" over legal sanction.

As to moral commitment specifically, the social psychologist Tom Tyler concluded in *Why People Obey the Law* (1990) that "the most important incremental contribution is made by personal morality."

> This high level of normative commitment to obeying the law offers an important basis for the effective exercise of authority by legal officials. People clearly have a strong predisposition toward following the law. If authorities can tap into such feelings, their decisions will be more widely followed.

Can legal authorities tap into these powerful forces for compliance? If they can, the potential benefits are enormous. First, as the studies quoted above suggest, both the fear of social disapproval by one's group and one's own moral commitment have strong effects on compliance—stronger than the present deterrent threat of legal punishment.

Second, unlike the threat of legal punishment, these sources of compliance do not require the likelihood of being arrested, convicted, and imprisoned to be high. A person's family or friends may suspect that he is committing crimes even if the authorities do not, or cannot prove it. In any case, *the person* always knows about his crimes. Thus reinforcing the compliance powers of the social group and personal morality could reduce crime even if policing and prosecuting functions cannot be made more effective.

Finally, neither of these sources of compliance is as staggeringly expensive as large-scale incarceration is. Nor do they require the increased intrusions on privacy that more-effective crime investigation would require, or the increased errors in adjudication that easier rules of prosecution might cause. In other words, they offer the best of both worlds—significantly better compliance at lower cost.

But one key condition must exist if personal moral commitment and the power of social disapproval are to be harnessed: criminal law must be seen by the potential offender and by the potential offender's social group as an authoritative source of what is moral, of what is right—much as, within a functional family, a parent may be seen as such an authoritative source. More specifically, the social-science studies suggest, the extent of the law's power to gain compliance depends upon the extent of the law's moral credibility.

MORAL CREDIBILITY

By "moral credibility" and "moral authority" I mean criminal law's reputation for punishing those who deserve it, under rules perceived as just; protecting from punishment those who do not deserve it; and where punishment is deserved, imposing the amount deserved—no more and no less. I do not underestimate how complex a matter it is to determine liability rules that will be perceived as just. But, as John Darley and I show in our new book, *Justice, Liability, and Blame: Community Views and the Criminal Law,* shared community intuitions on morally just principles of punishment can be determined and articulated.

I would argue that people in our present society do not see the criminal-justice system as having a moral authority even loosely comparable to that which operates within, say, a typical functional family, or within a voluntary association. The criminal-justice system has been shaped over the years by forces that have little to do with moral desert or, sometimes, common sense, and everything to do with legal abstractions, procedural expediency, and the criminological theory of the day. The result is a system in which the dynamic of moral authority that works in successful families and small groups is sadly lacking.

What can we do to increase the moral authority of the criminal-justice system? What current rules and practices undercut the system's moral credibility? Full answers would require a detailed review, but in this brief space I can at least touch upon the highlights.

First a caveat. Some failures of the system are inevitable. Less-than-perfect clearance rates by the police, for example, admittedly limit the system's ability to do justice. But most people understand that not every offender can be caught and punished, that policing and prosecution have practical limits. Failures of the system due to these limits may be frustrating in the individual case, but over time they are not likely to hurt the system's credibility. What can hurt is failures of justice that are avoidable.

AVOIDABLE FAILURES OF JUSTICE

Does the system regularly fail to impose deserved punishment when it has the power to do so? Does it sometimes appear to have *chosen* a course that frustrates justice? Let me suggest five instances in which the answer is yes.

First, the American criminal-justice system routinely excludes reliable evidence under what is called the exclusionary rule. This suggests a system less strongly committed to doing justice than to discouraging overreaching by the police. But one may ask, If that discouraging hurts the system's moral credibility and therefore its power to encourage compliance, can't police overreaching be discouraged by other means? Why not discourage police misconduct by making officers directly liable or by helping victims to get compensation from municipalities? If limiting overreaching by the police is such an important goal, why not attack it head-on rather than "punishing" the offending officers by letting the criminal go free—which punishes society rather than the officers?

Plea bargaining is a second practice seen by many as illustrating the system's moral poverty: an offender who gets a "bargain" does not get justice. Some plea bargains reflect genuine disputes over the facts, but in many cases—the vast majority in some jurisdictions—plea bargains are struck for reasons of expediency. If we are willing to spend an additional $30 billion to fight crime, why not spend a small portion of the money to fight crime by doing justice?

Arbitrary limits on police power are a third reason why the system lacks credibility. Police power is properly limited in the name of individual freedoms. But many will argue that in a democracy the majority ought to be free to choose, for example, less privacy in exchange for less crime. If a majority of residents in a public-housing project want periodic gun sweeps of their building, should their preference be frustrated by the courts? Why not at least allow those who prefer gun sweeps to live together in a building where sweeps are permitted, leaving those who oppose sweeps to live together and to bear the burden of their choice?

Fourth, the law recognizes non-exculpatory defenses. Diplomatic immunity, the statute of limitations, and the entrapment defense, for example, allow blameworthy offenders to remain exempt from criminal liability. Efforts to reduce the scope of diplomatic immunity face practical obstacles. For one thing, diplomatic immunity is mandated by international treaty. But no such obstacles prevent our lengthening the periods of limitation or restricting the entrapment defense to instances of duress (for which a separate defense already exists) or to instances of unconstitutional police conduct (which, like exclusionary-rule violations, might better be deterred by methods other than letting criminals go free).

One more feature of the system which undermines its moral credibility is sentences that are perceived as soft or as no punishment at all—probation, for example. When properly and selectively applied, non-incarcerative sanctions can be a source of real punishment that costs much less than prison. But to many reformers, the intermediate-sanctions movement, as it is called, is just another opportunity to avoid imposing earned punishment. If non-incarcerative sanctions are to succeed, the total punitive bite of the sanctions—as the community perceives it—must match the amount of punishment the offender deserves.

AVOIDABLE INJUSTICE

But doing justice is only half of earning moral authority. As important, if not more so, is that the system does not do injustice. Does the system sometimes seem to have chosen to permit injustice? Here are five instances.

First, American jurisdictions have increasingly defined as criminal actions that do not require proof of a defendant's culpable state of mind. Criminal liability can be imposed for an honest and reasonable mistake or an unavoidable accident. A person can be criminally liable for killing migratory birds even if the person has done everything possible to prevent their death. One can be criminally liable for statutory rape even if any reasonable person would similarly have thought the partner was of legal age. In the same spirit, almost no American jurisdiction recognizes as a defense one's reasonable mistake in understanding the law. Liability without culpability may ease the burden for prosecutors, but it also dilutes the moral significance of a successful prosecution. Every criminal conviction without a showing of blameworthiness increases the likelihood that subsequent criminal convictions will fail to inspire moral condemnation.

Second, and similarly, some states have abolished their insanity defense, others are moving in that direction, and still others have achieved de facto abolition by allowing a verdict of "guilty but mentally ill," which encourages juries to convict even when an offender is insane. Abolition of the insanity defense is touted as necessary to keep dangerous mentally ill people incarcerated, given the limitations imposed by courts upon their civil commitment. But if limitations on civil commitment are the problem, those limitations ought to be attacked directly. Abolition is also fueled by high profile insanity acquittals in controversial cases—for example, the acquittal of John Hinckley for the attempted assassination of President Ronald Reagan. But such acquittals could be avoided simply by narrowing the scope of the defense or by shifting the burden of proof. Instead of giving the prosecution the burden of proving sanity beyond a reasonable doubt, as it had in the Hinckley case, the defendant could be given the burden of proving insanity by a preponderance of the evidence. The number of insane offenders is too small for abolition of the defense to lead to large-scale injustice, but the effect of the abolition trend is to create the impression that the system does not care whether an offender is blameworthy or not.

REGULATORY OFFENSES

Third, criminal law is increasingly used against purely regulatory offenses, such as those involving the activities permitted in public parks, the maintenance procedures at warehouses, and the foodstuffs that may be imported into a state. The move is understandable: reformers seek to enlist the moral force implicit in criminal conviction for the sake of deterrence—a force that civil liability does not carry. But the use of criminal conviction in the absence of serious criminal harm that deserves moral condemnation weakens that very force. As the label "criminal" is increasingly applied to minor violations of a merely civil nature, criminal liability will increasingly become indistinct from civil and will lose its particular stigma.

A similar effect occurs when purely legal entities are criminally "convicted." Legal fictions like corporations cannot make immoral choices; only the human beings within them can. To criminally convict a legal fiction is to undercut the claim that criminal conviction ought to bring moral condemnation.

A fourth source of damage to the system's moral credibility is the current state of correctional facilities. When made a prisoner, a person is stripped of the ability to defend himself and to avoid places and situations of danger. Prison authorities take complete control and, with it, responsibility for protection. Given this responsibility, and given the considerable authority granted to officials to meet it, a single assault on a prisoner by another prisoner is objectionable.

Currently more than 15,000 prisoners are assaulted each year in our prisons.

The criminologist Robert Johnson, in *Hard Time* (1987), wrote, "From the mid-60's to the present, a new prison type has emerged. It is defined by the climate of violence and predation on the part of the prisoners that often marks its yards and other public areas." The trend is borne out by statistics. In California in 1973, for example, 289 assaults on inmates were reported. By 1983 the prison population had approximately doubled, and the number of assaults had nearly quintupled, to 1,438. In Texas in 1973 there were 130 prison assaults. In 1982 the prison population was a bit more than twice as large, and the number had grown to 887—a tripling of the assault rate in less than ten years. The next year in Texas 3,411 assaults were reported: one in ten prisoners in Texas was the victim of an officially reported assault. Imagine the daily fear that these statistics suggest. Imagine those prisoners' views of the system's moral authority.

One final damaging practice, and one of the most pervasive, is a point touched on earlier—setting punishment according to the perceived dangerousness of an offender rather than according to the offender's deserts. Under the assumption that a prior offense proves long-term dangerousness, prior offenses are widely used to increase the term of imprisonment under so-called recidivist statutes, including the "three strikes and you're out" rules of current reforms. The same rationale is used by parole boards in setting release policy and by sentencing commissions in setting guidelines. The United States Supreme Court has approved such practices as constitutional. In *Rummel* v. *Estelle*, for example, it approved a life term for a third fraud conviction, for passing a bad check for $120.75 (the two previous offenses involved an $80 credit-card fraud and a forged check for $28.36).

PERCEIVED DANGEROUSNESS

Even assuming that past offenses are a good predictor of future dangerousness, one simply cannot deserve punishment for an offense not yet committed—for an act that others only think will be done. This is why the law requires, for example, that a person must perform some act before he or she can be held liable for even an offense like attempt. Thinking about committing a crime, we have said since criminal law existed, is not enough to establish criminal liability, because moral lapse occurs only when one chooses to act upon the intention. Yet under recidivist statutes we routinely punish people for offenses they have not yet even thought of.

Certainly society must be able to protect itself from dangerous people, but to criminally commit a person because of a predicted future offense is to undercut the law's moral authority. If we feel we must incarcerate people to protect ourselves against crimes not yet committed, civil rather than criminal commitment ought to be used, just as we civilly commit the mentally ill and persons with contagious diseases when they pose a threat. Civil commitment has requirements that criminal commitment does not. First, because commitment is based on present dangerousness rather than a past offense, periodic reviews test for continuing dangerousness. Second, because commitment is for our protection rather than for deserved punishment, its conditions are nonpunitive in nature. The detainee's liberty is restricted only to the extent required for our protection.

Last year a *New York Times* op-ed piece criticized a jury's death verdict that jurors justified on the grounds that a life sentence would have allowed for the possibility of release. The writer was much offended that the jury could return a death verdict without concluding that the offender actually deserved the death penalty. But the logic of the verdict is entirely consistent with the increasingly common practice of American criminal justice. If we are offended because the death penalty is imposed on the basis of dangerousness rather than deserts, then we ought also to be offended by the hundreds of cases resolved each day in which prison terms are set according to dangerousness rather than deserts. Indeed, the argument against basing sentences on dangerousness is stronger with regard to imprisonment. Incarceration under civil commitment provides society with protection identical to that available through criminal commitment, whereas the death penalty provides a level of protection that civil law cannot match.

We have lost much ground in the past forty years in fighting crime. Ironically, that same period has been one of significant efforts to revolutionize the fight against crime. Our recent insights into the law's moral authority as a force for compliance may help explain our past failures. By setting sentences that would best rehabilitate offenders or would best deter other potential offenders or would best incapacitate dangerous offenders, each of our past programs distributed punishment in a way that could be seriously disproportionate to an offender's blameworthiness. The cumulative effect of these policies has been to divert the criminal-justice system from doing justice, and public perception of that shift has undercut the system's moral authority. Our past crime-control reforms may well have increased rather than decreased crime.

The research is incomplete. We do not yet fully understand the interaction between the system's moral credibility and crime. How much decrease in credibility causes how much increase in crime? Is the relationship a continuous one, or can we find credibility trigger points below which crime increases dramatically? Will research confirm my speculations about the practices that most undercut the system's moral authority?

We do know that human beings share a desire for justice, and giving it to them seems to carry little risk. If further research supports the conclusions of the preliminary studies, the search for effective crime control as well as for justice will demand that we re-examine every practice that contributes to the moral poverty of the American criminal-justice system.

Russian Organized Crime— A Worldwide Problem

The Honorable Ronald K. Noble,

Undersecretary for Enforcement,

U.S. Department of the Treasury, Washington, D.C.

The following article is excerpted from remarks given by the Honorable Ronald K. Noble, Treasury's undersecretary for enforcement, at the Russian Organized Crime Conference held in fall 1994 in Vienna, Virginia. Sponsored by the Financial Crimes Enforcement Network and the National Drug Intelligence Center, this conference brought together more than 300 U.S. federal, state and local government officials, as well as more than 50 representatives of the police services of other nations, including five speakers and participants from Russia.

On the morning of June 26, a cashier and a bank clerk drove through St. Petersburg with two policemen and five soldiers. They were carrying millions of dollars' worth of rubles in a physical inter-bank transfer. But 10 persons were waiting to rob the vehicle in Erivan Square, acting on information from corrupt government officials that the bank transfer was to occur.

The robbers' leader, dressed as an Army officer, created turmoil in the square by warning people that violence was expected. When the bankers and their escort arrived, they were intercepted by the conspirators, using explosives and weapons, and the currency was stolen.

The stolen currency was hidden in a government building in the Caucasus until it was smuggled across the border into Germany a month after the robbery. Then, five months later, the gang sought to launder the currency by placing it in small amounts—we'd call it smurfing—in banks across northern Europe on a single day. At that point, the launderers and at least some of the ringleaders were arrested on information supplied by a German undercover officer to German police and shared with Russian police.

Unless you listen very closely, this story could be of the sort that crosses your desks or appears in Tass almost daily—violent robbery, corruption, smuggling of currency, money laundering. In fact, the events I've described took place in June of 1907. They were part of what has been called "the most famous of all revolutionary robberies," and were staged by the Bolsheviks before 1917.

Organized crime in the states of the former Soviet Union has rightly become a source of growing concern since 1990. This conference itself, with its standing-room-only audience, testifies to the strength of our concerns. But if purposeful, continuing, criminal enterprise—"organized crime"—is not new, in Russia or anywhere else, why is this new phenomenon different, and how should law enforcement officials respond?

Nothing I could say to you about the problems of Russian organized crime would be a surprise. However, many others still need to be reminded of how serious the problems are. I can only provide today a short summary of what we're facing:

• Since the breakup of the Soviet Union, there has been a steep rise in the level of organized criminal activity in Russia and in the other newly independent states, as well as in former Warsaw pact nations.

• The activity is highly organized, often along ethnic lines, and involves individuals who are accustomed to operating in ways that thwart detection. They are also accustomed to dealing with the risk of detection by either corruption or shocking violence.

• The activity is highly entrepreneurial—it is designed to create what might be called "parallel" profit-making centers by people used to a sort of market discipline and operation through their experiences in the "black" market—people who know how to "trade" and grab market opportunities through the most aggressive tactics.

• The activity seeps into every area of society; as markets have opened up, organized criminals have moved in. The cash available to the Russian "mob" organizations gives them an extraordinary opportunity to dominate fledgling sectors of the legitimate economy, as few legitimate firms or business people can.

• Finally, Russian crime is a major export commodity. The topics at this conference include money laundering, import-export fraud, drug trafficking, weapons trafficking and excise tax evasion, as well as case examples of Russian organized crime in the United Kingdom, Germany and virtually every region of the United States. As you have heard, the "international" outlook of the Russian groups reportedly extends to the building of trading relationships and alliances with other organized criminal groups throughout the world.

We have encountered some of these phenomena before. The highly businesslike organization, the tightly knit cell structure and the propensity for violence remind one of classic organized crime groups, such as La Cosa Nostra or, more recently, the cocaine cartels. But the stage on which Russian mobsters and corrupt officials or businessmen operate is larger and more important than that for other groups. The Treasury, in particular, has a number of reasons to be extremely concerned about these developments.

First, these activities, if unchecked, could be extremely destabilizing for political and economic reform in the countries involved. To the extent that organized criminal activity threatens stability in Russia, it threatens the international economic and political settlements on whose continuance American prosperity depends.

I am not only concerned about the possible domination of sectors of the Russian economy by criminal groups. I am equally concerned that the example of the criminal groups, who are operating openly and notoriously at present, will lessen compliance with the law by Russians generally. Tax collection, for example, always depends to a significant degree on voluntary compliance: a nation that cannot reasonably expect a certain level of economic activity to generate a certain level of government revenue cannot hope to balance its budget or strengthen its currency.

Second, of course, the United States and its financial partners, as well as the international organizations to which they contribute heavily, have committed billions of dollars of immediate and long-term aid to Russia and the other states of the former Soviet Union. Organized crime diverts funds and blunts the effectiveness of those that aren't diverted. It hampers the health and competitive ability of honest enterprises funded by international efforts. There is a genuine concern that the rate of foreign investment in the newly independent states will drop significantly if the long-term perception is that one's investment means carrying on business either in competition with or by paying ''protection fees'' to criminal syndicates.

Third, the Russian-dominated groups are engaging in sophisticated financial schemes that strike at the heart of Treasury's interests. Income and excise tax fraud, evasion of customs duties, counterfeiting and credit card fraud are all crimes that affect the stability of the international financial system.

Finally, Russian organized crime groups arise at a particularly crucial time. Much of the world is finally moving in the direction of free markets and democracy, as we have long hoped. But those developments depend, as history has time and again shown us, on a solvent and honest financial system. And the very developments that we have sought, combined with unprecedented changes in banking and communications technology, have given criminals strong levers to try to turn what should be positive change to their own negative interests.

As we all know, however, the Russian crime problem is part of a larger international outbreak of crime. In response, Treasury is committed to an international approach to dealing with financial crime—not only as a matter of policy but as a matter of necessity. We have come to the realization that there is an international *criminal* economy that mirrors—and often abuses—the international economy generally.

This is a crucial point. The final communiqué of this year's G-7 meeting, attended by President Clinton, Treasury Secretary Lloyd Bentsen, and the leaders and finance ministers of the United Kingdom, France, Germany, Italy and Canada, states plainly that: "Organized transnational crime, including money laundering . . . *and the use of illicit proceeds to take control of legitimate business* . . . is a worldwide problem."

Although we are talking today about Russia and Eastern Europe, our concerns with stable financial systems free of criminal influence extend to rebuilding nations around the globe. Russia remains a special case because of its size, location and history. But the Russian challenge is important for what it portends for our ability to meet the task of free development worldwide.

How should we react? Our experience with the cocaine cartels shows us that a purely local strategy—a ''buy-bust'' tactic alone—can never hope to be effective. I think we need to put together several interlocking strategies.

First, we need better information and understanding, as exemplified by this conference. We must patiently attempt to piece together the activities, methods, organization and tactics of Russian organized crime groups. We have to build our information base *now*, and it must include answers to the following questions:

• Who are the leaders of the groups involved?

Treasury is committed to an international approach to dealing with financial crime — not only as a matter of policy but as a matter of necessity. We have come to the realization that there is an international <u>criminal</u> economy that mirrors — and often abuses — the international economy generally.

• How do they operate?
• What are the trademarks or fingerprints that their operations leave?
• Where is the threat the greatest?

The simple fact that so many specialists are gathered together here is encouraging.

Second, we need better intelligence sharing. General understanding must be complemented by intelligence sharing between police forces throughout the United States, and between U.S. police and police in other nations. Determined and combined action is critical.

Third, we have to frame a "problem-oriented" approach. We cannot succeed if we simply work on individual cases together. We must also work together from the beginning to limit the ability of these groups to operate at the same time that we mount creative and forceful investigative operations against them.

I testified earlier this week that an effective anti-money-laundering strategy had to combine prevention, detection and enforcement. I think the same is true of our deployment of resources against Russian groups and others in the international arena.

Many of you will see in this triad a movement toward what might be called "financial community policing," with a nod toward recent developments in local police forces. Without stretching the analogy too far, we also think that simple enforcement after the fact can never hope to do the job.

We also must recognize that Russia is not simply building from the ground up, but it is trying to substitute a free system for a command and control system. A habit of ignoring the "rules" at all levels has become deeply ingrained. The journalist David Remnick recorded the comments of a small businessman, himself operating at the margins of the developing system, who has just been "shaken down" for protection money. According to the businessman: "Ninety-nine percent of the businessmen in town—me included—violate a lot of rules. Taxes, hard currency restrictions, the laws on hiring people. We have to break the law if we want to get anything done. And so the racketeers know we can't resist."

But if the present situation in Russia presents an opportunity for lawlessness, it also presents an opportunity for constructive action to deal with the problem. As the Group of 7's Financial Action Task Force has noted, "[T]he reform and restructuring of the eastern European financial sector presents an ideal opportunity for these states to take measures that would help them to protect themselves. . . ."

The way Russia will ultimately deal with these questions depends on far more than law enforcement, of course. Crucial sectors include tax administration, banking regulation, customs regulation and, of course, the development of a generally understood and observed system of commercial law and practice.

In all of these areas, enforcement professionals have much to consider and much to offer. What can we do specifically, and immediately?

First, technical assistance. Budgets are tight, but it is in our own interest to work wherever we can, in local forces and in cooperation with other nations, to upgrade the training and potential of developing police authorities in Russia. If we want to make a difference, we must devote time to building the ability of investigators within Russia to instill respect for the rule of law.

Second, inter-agency cooperation. We have to encourage such cooperation, wherever appropriate and with reasonable safeguards, on regulatory and investigative matters. The Justice/Treasury trip to Russia last July is one such example. This conference is another example.

Third, upgrading the attention our own forces pay to the issues raised by Russian criminals operating through emigres or financial institutions here. When we turn to Russian organized crime operating within our borders, we must not expect a unified picture to emerge. To develop that picture, as I've already indicated, we must work among ourselves to understand the stages through which Russia and Russian government organizations are passing. Again, the lessons of the fight against drugs apply. We can succeed domestically only if we continually share information, work cases jointly and bring regulators and other agencies, where appropriate, into our planning and investigative process.

Finally, I think that the problems we are grappling with today should remind us all of something quite basic—that enforcement is government's quality control function.

Rules that cannot be enforced or administered are obviously faulty, but without active coordination among enforcement, poli-

cy making and regulation, we lose a vital guarantor of the effectiveness of our policies. Rules that ignore the fact that their realization requires conscious choices of hundreds of thousands of citizens lose their effectiveness. A failure to keep enforcement agencies in good repair is fatal to the respect for law and private property on which democratic systems with free economies depend.

Similarly, the issues that Russian organized crime brings to the fore remind us as enforcement officers that enforcement is not simply a matter of individual prosecutions or investigations; it is at the core of the implementation of policy—and it must be viewed as the continuation of policy.

The risks involved in failing to appreciate these issues as we deal with Russia are great. The journalist Stephen Handleman, writing in *Foreign Affairs* last spring, noted that part of the rapid growth of the Russian Mafia was due to Russia's "seeking to develop a free market before constructing a civil society in which such a market could safely operate."

Louise Shelly, another speaker at this conference, has wondered if the result may be the substitution of the controls of organized crime for the controls of state planning, with all the threat of backlash that such developments would create.

I do not believe we should expect such a result. But we also cannot expect quick or easy progress on many of these issues. Russia is a complex society undergoing a transformation that has few parallels in modern history. But we will be blamed, rightly, if we fail to recognize the risks and to contribute what we as enforcement officers have to offer to address the Russian organized crime problem.

The considerations discussed during this week's meetings must be constant points of reference as the work of rebuilding Russia goes forward. If we work together along the lines I have outlined and this conference has considered, I believe we will have contributed a great deal to the strength of our own societies and to the rebuilding of Russia and the other newly independent states.

Color Blinded?

Race Seems to Play an Increasing Role in Many Jury Verdicts

Blacks Express Skepticism of the Justice System; Acquittals in the Bronx

The Issue of 'Nullification'

Wall Street Journal staff reporters Benjamin A. Holden in Los Angeles, Laurie P. Cohen in New York and Eleena de Lisser in Atlanta.

The evidence against Davon Neverdon seemed overwhelming.

Four eyewitnesses testified that they saw him kill a man in a robbery attempt. Two others said he told them he committed the crime. Even Mr. Neverdon was expecting to be convicted: He had offered to plead guilty in exchange for a 40-year sentence, a deal the prosecutor had rejected at the request of the victim's family.

But that wasn't how the Baltimore jury, which included 11 African-Americans, saw it. After 11 hours of deliberation, they acquitted the defendant, who is black. A note from the jury room before the July 28 verdict suggested an explanation for the contrarian result: "Race," the lone Asian-American juror informed the judge, "may be playing some part" in the jury's decision-making.

Commentators have warned during the yearlong ordeal of the O.J. Simpson case—which ended in not-guilty verdicts yesterday—that a juror's race doesn't dictate his or her verdict, and that evidence matters more than skin color.

But, increasingly, jury watchers are concluding that, as in the Neverdon case, race plays a far more significant role in jury verdicts than many people involved in the justice system prefer to acknowledge. And rather than condemn this influence, some legal scholars argue that it fits neatly into a tradition of political activism by U.S. juries.

The case of Darryl Smith in 1990 is a less celebrated, but perhaps more telling, example of how race can affect a criminal trial. After an all-black jury in Washington acquitted Mr. Smith of murder in March 1990, a letter from an anonymous juror

arrived at the superior court there. The letter said that while most jurors in the case believed Mr. Smith was guilty, the majority bowed to holdouts who "didn't want to send anymore Young Black Men to Jail."

With as many as half of young black men under the supervision of the criminal-justice system in some cities, "African-American jurors are doing a cost-benefit analysis," says Paul Butler, a black criminal-law professor at George Washington University. Many black jurors have determined, he adds, that "defendants are better off out of jail, even though they're clearly guilty."

The phenomenon of race-based verdicts isn't limited to blacks, of course. In past years, all-white juries, particularly in the South, nearly always convicted blacks accused of crimes against whites, regardless of the evidence—while whites who raped or lynched blacks went free. In death-penalty cases, white jurors frequently refused to send whites to death row for murdering blacks. When Los Angeles police officers charged in the videotaped beating of Rodney King were acquitted Simi Valley, Calif., in 1992, many observers attributed the verdict to the fact that 10 of the jurors were white and none were black.

EMERGING PHENOMENON

But the willingness of many blacks, in particular, to side with African-American defendants against a mostly white-dominated justice system is a relatively new phenomenon with specific roots and ramifications, according to researchers who have analyzed recent jury verdicts.

At the simplest level, they say, minority jurors are merely drawing on their own life experiences, as jurors are expected to do, in evaluating evidence. Based on such experiences, they are quicker than whites to suspect racism on the part of police and prosecutors and thus more likely than whites to distrust the evidence they present. Indeed, a recent USA Today/CNN/Gallup Poll found that 66% of blacks believe the criminal-justice system is racist, compared with 37% of whites. This disparity inevitably affects deliberations.

But some black jurors are quietly taking a further, much more significant step: They are choosing to disregard the evidence, however powerful, because they seek to protest racial injustice and to refrain from adding to the already large number of blacks behind bars.

HIGH ACQUITTAL RATES

Most black jurors "understand how fine the line is between doing well and being on trial," says Thomas I. Atkins, a defense lawyer who is former general counsel of the National Association for the Advancement of Colored People. For many blacks, he says, "It's not enough to merely conclude that the right person is on trial and that the evidence is sufficient. You also have to prove that the right thing to come out of this trial is a conviction."

The race factor seems particularly evident in such urban environments as the New York City borough of the Bronx, where juries are more than 80% black and Hispanic. There, black defendants are acquitted in felony cases 47.6% of the time—nearly three times the national acquittal rate of 17% for all races. Hispanics are acquitted 37.6% of the time. This is so even though the majority of crime victims in the Bronx are black or Hispanic.

Although other jurisdictions generally don't break down conviction rates by race, overall figures for heavily black urban areas suggest that the Bronx phenomenon extends elsewhere. In Washington, D.C., where more than 95% of defendants and 70% of jurors are black, 28.7% of all felony trials ended in acquittals last year, significantly above the national average. In Wayne County, Mich., which includes mostly black Detroit, 30% of felony defendants were acquitted in 1993, the last year for which statistics were available.

Jury watchers point to a number of high-profile cases in recent years in which urban juries acquitted black defendants, despite what appeared to many observers to be strong evidence for conviction. These include the 1990 case of Washington Mayor Marion Barry, who was acquitted on all but one of 14 counts against him stemming from a sting operation in which the FBI and police videotaped him smoking crack cocaine; the string of acquittals of defendants charged with beating Reginald Denny during the Los Angeles riots in 1992; and the November 1988 Bronx acquittal of Larry Davis on charges of attempting to murder nine police officers.

After the verdict, Mr. Davis's lawyer, the late William Kunstler, acknowledge that there was "no question" that race influenced the jurors. But he said this had led to a just, rather than an unjust, verdict.

Some black lawyers and scholars argue that any defiance of what blacks perceive as a racist system falls within the tradition of so-called jury nullification—the rejection of the law in favor of the jurors' own views of justice. They note that this controversial power, which the U.S. Supreme Court explicitly affirmed 100 years ago, has played an important role at key times in U.S. history—and may be doing so again today.

During colonial times, for instance, jurors used the power to acquit colonial defendants of political crimes against the Crown. In the mid-19th century, Northern jurors kept the tradition alive by acquitting people who harbored runaway slaves, even though the law explicitly made this a crime. The constitutional prohibition against trying a person twice for the same crime protects the defendant in all such circumstances from having an acquittal overturned because the jurors didn't follow the law.

NATIONAL CRISIS?

Some jury-nullification advocates now say blacks are justified in using their jury-room vote to fight what they perceive as a national crisis: a justice system that is skewed against them by courts, prosecutors and racist police such as former Los Angeles Detective Mark Fuhrman.

"Jury nullification is power that black people have right now and not something Congress has to give them," Mr. Butler says. In a forthcoming law-review article, Mr. Butler even argues that in nonviolent crimes, black jurors should "presume in favor of nullification."

"Black people," he writes, "have a community that needs building, and children who need rescuing, and as long as a person will not hurt anyone, the community needs him there to help."

Not surprisingly, prosecutors vehemently disagree with such reasoning, which they see as undermining the rule of law. "It's terrible and sad that juries will base their opinions on race bias rather than the facts, but it happens every day," says Ahmet Hisim, the assistant state's attorney in Baltimore who lost the Neverdon case. "It's very bad for justice," he adds.

Mr. Hisim blames much of the problem on defense lawyers, whose "main ploy is to nullify juries for racial reasons," he says.

'MONEY AND SURVIVAL'

But some defendants are adopting race-based defense tactics themselves. Representing himself in an Atlanta trial last summer, Erick Bozeman openly pleaded with a jury to acquit him of serious federal drug charges because he is black. In his opening statement, he told jurors that the U.S. war on drugs was part of the same war on black people that "has existed in one way or another since African prisoners arrived in 1619 as slaves." He described his birthplace as "the urban war zone of South Central Los Angeles where the real law is money and survival" and his profession as that of a drug middleman, "a broker, just like Michael Milken and Ivan Boesky."

The case ended in a hung jury on the central charge, that Mr. Bozeman was a drug "kingpin," a crime punishable by life in prison. All three voting to acquit were black. Afterward, Judge Clarence Cooper, who is also black, privately told the jurors he was disappointed with the verdict, and he questioned their common sense.

As in the Neverdon case, the black jurors denied race was a factor in the verdict. Ulysses Garror, one of the jurors who voted for acquittal, says only, "There wasn't enough there to convict." But a white juror, Russell Snellgrove, now says, "These people, I hate to say this, it could have been a racial thing. They didn't come out and say it, but their arguments were such that it was apparent."

More prevalent than outright jury nullification is the greater tendency of many blacks to believe that police will falsify evidence and lie on the witness stand—factors that became major elements in the Simpson case. In this regard, African-American jurors are concentrating on the evidence, but filtering it, as any juror must, through their own perspectives.

'NOT JUST RACE'

Robert E. Kalunian, assistant public defender for Los Angeles Country, while agreeing that "race does affect jury deliberations," adds, "It's not just race. It's life experiences. Blacks are more likely to have been jacked by the police, and less likely to view police testimony with quite the same pristine validity as a white male from the suburbs."

Defense lawyers in urban areas with large black populations routinely attribute acquittals they have won to distrust of the police. "African-American jurors who live in communities where cops are the enemy don't have to be educated that police lie," explains Peter Kirscheimer, a onetime Bronx legal aid attorney who is now a federal defender in Brooklyn.

Many times, of course, a verdict may stem in part from jurors' evaluation of the evidence and in part from a broader, racially influenced desire to see certain defendants acquitted because circumstances make a conviction appear unfair to them.

This mix seemed to be at play in a gun-possession case in September in the same courthouse where the Simpson trial was in progress.

The stakes in the case were particularly high because defendant Byron Carter, 22 years old and black, had two prior convictions, and a conviction here would mean life in prison. Because it was a gun-possession case, the defense appeared to have an instant advantage. Jurors living in dangerous urban ares, recognizing a need to be armed in self-defense, are known to be particularly reluctant to convict for gun possession. Indeed, in the Bronx, 75% of such cases end in acquittals.

CONFLICTING CAMPS

Deliberating after a six-day trial, the jury of five blacks, three Hispanic-Americans, two whites and two Asian-Americans split instantly into two conflicting camps. Leading one side was Howard Anderson, the black 34-year-old jury foreman, who believed certain statements made by the two white arresting officers were transparently false. On the other side were Asian-Americans Ken Chan, 27, and Paul Wong, 35, who felt the police were more believable than the defendant, since he was a convicted felon. One of the two white jurors says he felt Mr. Carter was guilty but came to believe the evidence was sufficient.

The main issue for the panel was whether a young, urban black man would ever confess, as the police claimed that, "I'd rather be caught in this neighborhood by the police with a gun than caught otherwise without one." The two arresting officers, who didn't record the statement or obtain Mr. Carter's signature on a written version of it, claimed he had made the confession after they confronted him in a van that was parked too far away from the curb.

Mr. Carter testified at trial that he actually said: "Everybody and their mamma in this neighborhood got a gun." But he said he told the police that the weapon in question wasn't his. He also said the van was legally parked.

All of the black members of the jury immediately agreed that Mr. Carter's version of the statement was more consistent with urban slang than the police's, which was submitted as part of the alleged confession. After an initial discussion, the first ballot was 10–2 to acquit—with only Messrs. Chan and Wong seeking a conviction.

LITTLE AGREEMENT

The dissenters ultimately gave in, but not a lot of convincing was done: "We reached a unanimous verdict, but we still don't agree on the facts," Mr. Chan says.

The jury experience "showed me the reason so many people are being locked away," Mr. Anderson says. Jurors without experience dealing with inner-city black defendants "just sit there and look on them as criminals before the trial even starts."

After the verdict, several black jurors talked openly about the illogic of sending another young black man away to spend his life in jail for what they considered the "victimless" crime of possessing a .22-caliber handgun. But was this jury prepared to defy the law? Not quite, says black juror Troy Richardson.

The thought of voting to acquit regardless of the evidence "did enter my mind," says Mr. Richardson, "but I decided if the evidence says he's guilty, I'm going to send him away."

Victimology

For many years, crime victims were not considered an important topic for criminological study. Now, however, criminologists consider focusing on victims and victimization essential to understanding the phenomenon of crime. The popularity of this area of study can be attributed to the early work of Hans von Hentig and the later work of Stephen Schafer. These writers were the first to assert that crime victims play an integral role in the criminal event, that their actions may actually precipitate crime, and that unless the victim's role is considered, the study of crime is not complete.

In recent years a growing number of criminologists have devoted increasing attention to the victim's role in the criminal justice process. Generally, areas of particular interest include calculating costs of crime to victims, taking surveys of victims to measure the nature and extent of criminal behavior, establishing probabilities of victimization risks, studying victim precipitation of crime and culpability, and designing services expressly for victims of crime. As more criminologists focus their attention on the victim's role in the criminal process, victimology will take on even greater importance.

Articles in this unit provide sharp focus on key issues. From the lead report, "Criminal Victimization 1993," we learn that there were 43.6 million criminal victimizations, of which 10.9 million were rapes, robberies, or assaults. In spite of that frightening picture, the next article, "True Crime," asserts that a careful examination of the data reveals that much fear among citizens is misplaced. It is true, however, that the worst crimes are increasing and that it is particularly dangerous to live in certain regions of the country. "Stopping Terrorism at Home" provides the reader with a model to consider for combating domestic violence. The promise of this program appears to spring from coordinating the efforts of criminal justice agencies and other organizations.

Two theoretical perspectives that dominate domestic violence research are discussed in "Responding to Domestic Violence against Women." In his essay, "Towards the Institutionalization of a New Kind of Justice Professional: The Victim Advocate," Andrew Karmen argues that jurisdictions throughout the United States should offer all complainants (victims) the services of advocates, free of charge, through mechanisms parallel to those that provide indigent defendants with lawyers.

Ronald Getz, in "Protecting Our Seniors," focuses on victimization of the elderly, manifested in abuse and neglect. The police are networking with social agencies in order to improve the quality of life for seniors.

The unit closes with "Computer Technology Comes to Aid of Crime Victims." Robert Davis describes how a computer-based system of victim notification in Louisville, Kentucky, saves lives and helps victims keep on top of their cases.

Looking Ahead: Challenge Questions

What lifestyle changes might you consider to avoid becoming victimized?

How successful are crime victims when they fight their assailants?

According to "Criminal Victimization 1993," how many crime victims are there in the United States? What are the trends and patterns in victimization?

What can be done to help solve abuse and neglect to seniors?

Does marital status influence victimization risk? Defend your answer.

Criminal

Victimization 1993

Lisa Bastian
BJS Statistician

In 1993 U.S. residents age 12 or older experienced a total of 43.6 million crimes — nearly 11 million violent victimizations and over 32 million property crimes. Expressed as the number of crimes per 1,000 persons or households, crime rates indicate that there were 52 violent victimizations per 1,000 persons and 322 property crimes per 1,000 households.

Violent crimes, a quarter of the total that victims described, include rape and sexual assault, robbery, and both aggravated and simple assault, from the victimization survey, and homicide, from crimes reported to police (see page 50). Property crimes are comprised of burglaries, motor vehicle thefts, and thefts of other property. About 4 in 10 of the violent crimes estimated by the victimization survey, and about 3 in 10 of the property crimes, were reported to the police. For both violent and property crimes, blacks were more likely than whites — and urban residents more likely than rural residents — to be victimized.

Highlights

Of the 43.6 million criminal victimizations that victims described in 1993, 10.9 million were rapes, robberies, or assaults.

Among the almost 100 million households in the United States, there were over 32 million property crimes in 1993.

• Violent victimization rates, the number of crimes during 1993 per 1,000 persons age 12 or older, included —

   2 rapes or attempted rapes
   1 sexual assault
   4 robberies with property taken
   3 assaults with serious injury.

• Victims sustained a rape or some other non-rape injury in over 2.6 million incidents in 1993; about 29% of the robberies involved injury.

• Males, blacks, and the young were more likely than others to experience violent crime:
   — 1 in 16 males and 1 in 23 females
   — 1 in 15 blacks and 1 in 20 whites
   — 1 in 8 persons age 12 to 15 and 1 in 179 persons age 65 or older.

• Persons in households with an income below $7,500 a year were over twice as likely as those from households with $75,000 or more to be victims of violence.

• City dwellers were robbed at more than 3 times the rate of rural residents.

• The households of city dwellers were victimized by motor vehicle theft at almost 5 times the rate of rural households.

• An estimated 35% of the crimes described by victims were reported to law enforcement authorities. Violent victimizations had the highest reporting rate, 42%, compared to 27% of personal thefts and 33% of household property crimes.

From the *Bureau of Justice Statistics Bulletin,* May 1995, pp. 1-6. Reprinted by permission of the U.S. Department of Justice, Bureau of Justice Statistics.

10.9 million violent crimes in 1993

Victims sustained 10.9 million violent crimes. These crimes included almost a half million rapes and sexual assaults, 1.3 million robberies, over 2.5 million aggravated assaults, 6.5 million simple assaults, and 24,526 murders (table 1 and the box on page 50).

In terms of crime rates per 1,000 persons age 12 or older, during 1993 there were 2 rapes or attempted rapes, 1 sexual assault, 6 completed or attempted robberies, 12 aggravated assaults, and 31 simple assaults. Murders were the least frequent violent victimizations — in 1993 about 1 murder per 10,000 persons.

In over 70% of all violent crime incidents, the crime was attempted but not completed. Such incidents ranged from attempts to rape or rob to threats of violence, which may or may not have included a weapon.

Over 2.6 million incidents, nearly a quarter of the violent crimes, resulted in injury to the victim.[1] About 29% of all the robberies occurring that year involved injury to the victim.

Burglaries, motor vehicle thefts, and household thefts

Most crimes sustained in 1993 were property crimes. Nearly three-quarters of all victimizations studied by the survey, or 32 million victimizations, were burglaries, motor vehicle thefts, or thefts.

About 6 million household burglaries occurred in 1993. Almost a third of the total, 1.9 million victimizations, were forcible entries. Three million were unlawful entries without force, and 1.2 million were attempts to enter using force.

There were close to 2 million car thefts and an additional 24 million property thefts. The largest share of the property thefts, 9.6 million or 40%, involved a loss of property valued at less than $50 by the victim. In about 18%, or 4.3 million, the loss was estimated to be at least $250. There were also 1.2 million theft attempts.

Expressed as a property crime rate, there were 60 burglaries, 20 motor vehicle thefts, and 243 property thefts per 1,000 households in 1993.

Victimizations reported to law enforcement authorities

Overall, 42% of the violent crimes committed in 1993 were reported to the police (table 2). Thirty-four percent of all rapes were reported, while 19% of sexual assaults were brought to the attention of law enforcement authorities. Fifty-six percent of robberies, 53% of aggravated assaults, and 35% of simple assaults were reported to the police.

About a third of all the property crimes that victims recalled to NCVS were reported to the police. However, motor vehicle thefts were more likely than

Table 1. Criminal victimizations and victimization rates, 1992-93: Estimates from the redesigned National Crime Victimization Survey

Type of crime	Number of victimizations (1,000's) 1992[a]	1993	Victimization rates (per 1,000 persons age 12 or older) 1992[a]	1993
All crimes	42,912	43,622	...	...
Personal crimes[b]	10,692	11,409	51.1	53.9
Crimes of violence	10,317	10,896	49.3	51.5
Completed violence	3,311	3,226	15.8	15.3
Attempted/threatened violence	7,006	7,670	33.5	36.3
Rape/Sexual assault	607	485	2.9	2.3
Rape/attempted rape	374	313	1.8	1.5
Rape	175	160	.8	.8
Attempted rape	200	152	1.0	.7
Sexual assault	233	173	1.1	.8
Robbery	1,293	1,307	6.2	6.2
Completed/property taken	862	826	4.1	3.9
With injury	310	276	1.5	1.3
Without injury	552	549	2.6	2.6
Attempted to take property	431	481	2.1	2.3
With injury	81	100	.4	.5
Without injury	350	381	1.7	1.8
Assault	8,416	9,104	40.2	43.0
Aggravated	2,317	2,578	11.1	12.2
With injury	671	713	3.2	3.4
Threatened with weapon	1,646	1,865	7.9	8.8
Simple	6,099	6,525	29.1	30.8
With minor injury	1,445	1,358	6.9	6.4
Without injury	4,655	5,167	22.2	24.4
Property crimes	32,220	32,213	325.3	322.4
Household burglary	5,815	5,995	58.7	60.0
Completed	4,756	4,835	48.0	48.4
Forcible entry	1,845	1,858	18.6	18.6
Unlawful entry without force	2,911	2,977	29.4	29.8
Attempted forcible entry	1,059	1,160	10.7	11.6
Motor vehicle theft	1,838	1,967	18.6	19.7
Completed	1,203	1,297	12.1	13.0
Attempted	635	670	6.4	6.7
Theft	24,568	24,250	248.0	242.7
Completed[c]	23,474	23,033	237.0	230.5
Less than $50	10,313	9,642	104.1	96.5
$50-$249	7,976	7,688	80.5	76.9
$250 or more	4,144	4,264	41.8	42.7
Attempted	1,094	1,217	11.0	12.2

Note: These data are preliminary and may vary slightly from the final estimates. Completed violent crimes include completed rape, sexual assault, completed robbery with and without injury, aggravated assault with injury, and simple assault with minor injury. The total population age 12 or older was 209,352,860 in 1992; in 1993 it was 211,524,770. The total number of households in 1992 was 99,046,200; in 1993 it was 99,926,400.
...Not applicable.
[a]These 1992 estimates are based on a half sample of data from the redesigned National Crime Victimization Survey and are not directly comparable with figures previously published for 1992, which were estimated under the previous, and now superseded, survey design.
[b]The victimization survey cannot measure murder because of the inability to question the victim. Personal crimes include purse snatching and pocket picking, not shown separately.
[c]Includes thefts in which the amount taken was not ascertained.

[1]Rapes are included as injuries.

any other crime to be reported; the police were informed in 78% of all motor vehicle thefts or attempted thefts. Compared to personal thefts or household property thefts, violent victimizations had the highest reporting rate. Victims may cite many reasons for reporting or not reporting particular crimes to law enforcement authorities.[2]

When victims report violent incidents to the police, a common reason they give is that they wanted to prevent future crimes from being committed against them by the offender or offenders. Victims also reported incidents because they thought it was the right thing to do. Among victims who chose not to report a violent crime, many indicated that they felt the matter was private or personal in nature.

Victims of personal and property thefts frequently reported the incidents to recover their stolen property, or chose not to report because they had been

---

Murder in the United States, 1993

In its annual compilation of local police agency statistics for 1993, the FBI reported 24,526 murders or non-negligent manslaughters — a 3% increase over the previous year. The national murder rate was 10 per 100,000 inhabitants.

The FBI defines murders in its annual report *Crime in the United States* as the willful (nonnegligent) killing of one human being by another. The incidence of murder varies by U.S. region, and characteristics of murder victims vary according to sex, race, and age.

In 1993 Southern States accounted for 41% of the homicides but 35% of the Nation's population. The West, which held 22% of the population, accounted for 23% of the murders. The Midwest reported 19% of the murders, and the Northeast, 17%.

Supplemental demographic information was available for 23,271 murder victims. About 51% of these victims were black, 46% were white, and more than 2%, of some other racial identity.

Victims were likely to be male and relatively young: 77% were male, and nearly 50% were between ages 20 and 34. About 12% were under age 18.

In 1993, 47% of murder victims were known to be either related to (12%) or acquainted with (35%) their assailants. Fourteen percent of victims were murdered by strangers, while 39% of victims had an unknown relationship to their murderer.

Table 2. Victimizations reported to the police, 1992-93: Estimates from the redesigned National Crime Victimization Survey

Type of crime	Number of victimizations reported (1,000's) 1992[a]	1993	Percent of victimizations reported to the police 1992[a]	1993
All crimes	15,433	15,345	36.0%	35.2%
Personal crimes[b]	4,527	4,670	42.3%	40.9%
Crimes of violence	4,425	4,534	42.9	41.6
Completed violence	1,867	1,732	56.4	53.7
Attempted/threatened violence	2,558	2,802	36.5	36.5
Rape/Sexual assault	196	140	32.2	28.8
Rape/attempted rape	121	106	32.2	34.0
Rape	40	56	22.9	34.7
Attempted rape	81	51	40.4	33.4
Sexual assault	75	33	32.2	19.4
Robbery	755	733	58.4	56.1
Completed/property taken	577	558	66.9	67.5
With injury	213	191	68.9	69.2
Without injury	363	366	65.8	66.7
Attempted to take property	178	176	41.3	36.6
With injury	63	49	77.1	48.8
Without injury	115	127	32.9	33.3
Assault	3,474	3,661	41.3	40.2
Aggravated	1,268	1,367	54.7	53.0
With injury	477	414	71.2	58.0
Threatened with weapon	791	953	48.0	51.1
Simple	2,206	2,294	36.2	35.2
With minor injury	722	674	50.0	49.6
Without injury	1,484	1,620	31.9	31.4
Property crimes	10,906	10,675	33.8%	33.1%
Household burglary	2,952	2,931	50.8	48.9
Completed	2,582	2,496	54.3	51.6
Forcible entry	1,468	1,393	79.5	75.0
Unlawful entry without force	1,114	1,103	38.3	37.1
Attempted forcible entry	371	435	35.0	37.4
Motor vehicle theft	1,405	1,530	76.5	77.8
Completed	1,119	1,212	93.0	93.5
Attempted	287	317	45.1	47.4
Theft	6,549	6,215	26.7	25.6
Completed[c]	6,288	5,864	26.8	25.5
Less than $50	1,375	1,147	13.3	11.9
$50-$249	2,121	1,989	26.6	25.9
$250 or more	2,574	2,429	62.1	57.0
Attempted	260	350	23.8	28.8

Note: These data are preliminary and may vary slightly from the final estimates. Completed violent crimes include completed rape, sexual assault, completed robbery with and without injury, aggravated assault with injury, and simple assault with minor injury.
[a]These 1992 estimates are based on a half sample of data from the redesigned National Crime Victimization Survey and are not directly comparable with figures previously published for 1992, which were estimated under the previous, and now superseded, survey design.
[b]The victimization survey cannot measure murder because of the inability to question the victim. Personal crimes include purse snatching and pocket picking, not shown separately.
[c]Includes thefts in which the amount taken was not ascertained.

---

[2]For analyses of reasons why victims reported or did not report crimes, see *Criminal Victimization in the United States, 1992,* BJS, NCJ-145125, March 1994.

able to recover their property or the theft attempt had been unsuccessful.

Characteristics of victims

Research by BJS has shown a relationship between certain demographic characteristics and the risk of crime victimization.[3] Males, young persons, blacks, Hispanics, residents of central cities, and the poor tend to have higher rates of victimization than persons who do not possess these characteristics (table 3).

For every violent crime category but rape and sexual assault, victimization rates were significantly higher for males than females. Males were twice as likely as females to experience robbery and aggravated assault. However, there were 4 rapes or sexual assaults per 1,000 females age 12 or older and 0.4 rapes per 1,000 males.

Except for rape/sexual assault and simple assault, blacks were more likely than whites or persons of other races, such as Asians or Native Americans, to be victims of crime. For instance, in 1993 there were 19 aggravated assaults per 1,000 black persons, 11.4 per 1,000 whites, and 8.8 per 1,000 persons in other racial categories. The victimization rates for rape and sexual assault were not significantly different among the three racial groups.

Victimization rates generally decline with age. Persons under age 25 had higher victimization rates than older persons. Those 65 or older generally had the lowest victimization rates. The rate of assault, for example, was 98.1 per 1,000 persons age 16 to 19 and 4.1 per 1,000 persons 65 or older.

Hispanics and non-Hispanics had similar victimization rates for the crimes of rape/sexual assault, simple assault, and personal theft. However, Hispanics had significantly higher rates for all other personal crimes, especially robbery, with a rate twice that of non-Hispanics (10.8 versus 5.8).

Victimization rates generally decline with increases in family income. Compared to persons in higher income groups, members of households with an income under $7,500 had signifi-

cantly higher rates of rape and sexual assault and of aggravated assault. For personal crimes of theft, however, this pattern did not hold.

Residents of urban areas had higher victimization rates for all personal crimes than did suburbanites or residents of rural areas. In fact, urban residents were robbed at greater than 3 times the rate of residents of rural areas (10.9 versus 3.0) and raped or sexually assaulted at twice the rate of suburban residents (3.4 versus 1.7).

Higher property crime victimization rates in 1993: households of blacks, Hispanics, the poor, urban dwellers, and renters

As occurred with personal crimes, certain demographic groups had higher property victimization rates than others (table 4). Blacks had a significantly

higher rate of property crime than whites. Compared to non-Hispanics, Hispanics had a higher rate for each of the property crimes.

In general, households with higher annual family incomes were victimized by household property crimes at greater rates than the lowest income households. However, households earning under $7,500 a year sustained burglaries at almost twice the rate of households with the highest annual earnings.

As with personal crimes, place of residence was related to a household's risk of victimization. For each type of property crime in the survey, urban residents had consistently higher rates than suburban or rural residents. For example, households in urban areas were burglarized at 1.5 times the rate of rural households (84.4 versus 53.6).

Table 3. Victimization rates for persons age 12 or older, by type of crime, sex, age, race, ethnicity, income, and locality of residence of victims, 1993

	Victimizations per 1,000 persons age 12 or older							
		Crimes of violence						
			Rape/		Assault			
			Sexual			Aggra-		Personal
Characteristics	Total	Total	assault	Robbery	Total	vated	Simple	theft
Sex								
Male	63.3	61.0	.4	8.5	52.1	16.3	35.8	2.3
Female	45.2	42.6	4.0	4.0	34.5	8.3	26.2	2.5
Age								
12-15	125.3	120.8	4.5	13.6	102.6	23.3	79.3	4.5
16-19	120.7	117.0	7.2	11.7	98.1	30.0	68.1	3.7
20-24	97.7	93.6	5.7	10.5	77.4	27.1	50.3	4.1
25-34	61.2	58.8	2.4	7.4	49.1	15.0	34.1	2.3
35-49	44.9	43.0	1.6	5.1	36.2	8.8	27.5	1.9
50-64	18.3	17.1	.2*	3.0	13.9	4.0	10.0	1.1
65 or older	7.9	5.6	.3*	1.3	4.1	1.1	3.0	2.2
Race								
White	51.8	49.8	2.3	5.1	42.4	11.4	31.1	2.0
Black	72.6	67.0	2.7	13.0	51.3	19.0	32.3	5.6
Other	41.9	39.7	2.0*	8.2	29.5	8.8	20.8	2.2*
Ethnicity								
Hispanic	62.5	59.1	2.1	10.8	46.2	17.2	29.0	3.4
Non-Hispanic	53.2	50.9	2.3	5.8	42.8	11.8	31.0	2.3
Family income								
Less than $7,500	93.5	89.5	5.5	12.2	71.8	23.0	48.8	4.0
$7,500-$14,999	59.4	57.5	2.7	8.9	45.9	14.4	31.5	1.9
$15,000-$24,999	53.5	50.5	2.5	5.9	42.2	13.0	29.2	3.0
$25,000-$34,999	51.9	50.2	2.3	4.7	43.3	11.6	31.7	1.7
$35,000-$49,999	51.5	49.2	1.9	5.0	42.3	11.8	30.6	2.3
$50,000-$74,999	47.6	45.9	1.1	4.6	40.2	8.7	31.4	1.7
$75,000 or more	40.9	38.2	1.9	4.2	32.1	6.4	25.7	2.7
Residence								
Urban	73.8	69.2	3.4	10.9	54.8	15.2	39.6	4.6
Suburban	47.8	46.0	1.7	5.1	39.3	11.2	28.1	1.7
Rural	43.4	42.1	2.2	3.0	36.9	10.6	26.2	1.3

Note: These data are preliminary and may vary slightly from the final estimates.
The victimization survey cannot measure murder because of the inability to question the victim.
*Estimate is based on about 10 or fewer sample cases.

[3]Highlights from 20 Years of Surveying Crime Victims, BJS report, NCJ-144525, October 1993.

2. VICTIMOLOGY

Households that rented their residence had significantly higher victimization rates than households that owned. Households that rented sustained motor vehicle thefts at more than 1.5 times the rate of households that owned their residence, with 26.6 thefts per 1,000 households versus 15.8.

Recent trends

In recent years, a pattern could be discerned in which levels of certain completed violent crimes had been declining or holding steady while levels of attempted victimizations had generally been on the increase.

Data from the redesigned survey comparing victimization levels and rates between 1992 and 1993, however, show little change. Among the major crime categories, there were no statistically significant differences in the numbers of victimizations between the two years (table 5). Because estimates for 1992 are based on a half sample of data from the redesigned survey, larger increases or decreases than usual may be required to indicate statistically significant change between the two years.

The rate at which victims reported their incidents to the police was also generally stable between 1992 and 1993.

Characteristics of sexual assault and domestic violence: new data from the redesigned victimization survey

The redesign effort has increased reporting and improved estimates of some of the most difficult-to-measure crimes, like rape, sexual assault, and domestic violence. These new data permit the analysis of relationships and patterns that the NCVS could not previously detect:

• There were almost a half million rapes and sexual assaults in 1993 — 2 rapes or attempts per 1,000 persons age 12 or older and 1 sexual assault per 1,000.

• Males were the victims in 7% of all rapes and over 13% of the sexual assaults.

• Persons age 12 to 15 experienced 12% of all rapes and 17% of sexual assaults measured by the victimization survey.

• Offenders committed over 1 million violent crimes against victims to whom they were related; in well over half of these, the offender was the victim's spouse or ex-spouse.

• Females were victimized by relatives at 4 times the rate of males (8 violent victimizations per 1,000 females versus 2 per 1,000 males).

• Offenders committed over a half million violent crimes against a spouse or ex-spouse. Of these, 9% were rapes or sexual assaults, 6% were robberies, 14% were aggravated assaults, and 71% were simple assaults.

A comprehensive tabulation of 1993 victimization data from the redesigned NCVS is forthcoming in the publication *Criminal Victimization in the United States, 1993.*

Table 4. Property victimization rates, by type of crime, race, ethnicity, income, residence, and form of tenure of head of household, 1993

| | Victimizations per 1,000 households | | | |
Characteristics	Total	Burglary	Motor vehicle theft	Theft
Race				
White	315.0	56.7	17.2	241.1
Black	369.9	85.8	33.9	250.2
Other	344.3	51.9	33.8	258.7
Ethnicity				
Hispanic	444.7	87.8	36.8	320.2
Non-Hispanic	313.3	58.0	18.5	236.9
Family income				
Less than $7,500	314.4	97.5	14.1	202.8
$7,500-$14,999	299.3	67.1	19.2	213.0
$15,000-$24,999	311.2	58.2	18.8	234.2
$25,000-$34,999	335.9	50.8	21.2	263.9
$35,000-$49,999	340.8	54.1	18.6	268.1
$50,000-$74,999	370.9	49.7	22.4	298.8
$75,000 or more	392.2	51.2	26.4	314.6
Residence				
Urban	411.6	84.4	34.3	292.9
Suburban	304.6	46.8	17.2	240.6
Rural	250.3	53.6	7.2	189.5
Form of tenure				
Home owned	286.3	50.0	15.8	220.5
Home rented	386.4	77.7	26.6	282.1

Note: These data are preliminary and may vary slightly from the final estimates.

Table 5. Comparison of numbers of victimizations experienced and reported to the police, 1992-93

| | Victimizations | | | | | |
| | Number (1,000's) | | | Percent reported to the police | | |
Type of crime	1992	1993	Percent change, 1992-93	1992	1993	Difference between percents, 1993-92
All crimes	42,912	43,622	1.7%	36.0%	35.2%	- .8
Personal crimes	10,692	11,409	6.7	42.3	40.9	-1.4
Crimes of violence	10,317	10,896	5.6	42.9	41.6	-1.3
Rape/Sexual assault	607	485	-20.1	32.2	28.8	-3.4
Robbery	1,293	1,307	1.0	58.4	56.1	-2.3
Assault	8,416	9,104	8.2	41.3	40.2	-1.1
Property crimes	32,220	32,213	0	33.8%	33.1%	- .7
Household burglary	5,815	5,995	3.1	50.8	48.9	-1.9
Motor vehicle theft	1,838	1,967	7.0	76.5	77.8	1.3
Theft	24,568	24,250	-1.3	26.7	25.6	-1.1

Note: These data are preliminary and may vary slightly from the final estimates. None of the percent changes in the data collected using the redesigned survey was statistically significant for the summary categories shown. Estimates for 1992 are based on a half sample of data from the redesigned NCVS. As a result, the magnitude of the percent change required to pass a test for statistical significance may be larger than that required given a full sample of data.

TRUE CRIME

SUMMARY

The media and safety-conscious baby boomers fuel an overwhelming public fear of crime. A close look at the data shows that much of the fear is misplaced. Yet the worst crimes are increasing, and life can be especially dangerous in southern and smaller metros. In the next decade, more criminals and a less tolerant public will transform Americans' lives.

Cheryl Russell

Cheryl Russell is author of The Official Guide to the American Marketplace *(New Strategist, 1995) and editor-in-chief of New Strategist Publications in Ithaca, New York.*

The hour is late. The city street lies dark and empty. Solitary footsteps echo on the pavement. Ahead, an ominous shape lurks in a storefront. Suddenly you're face to face with a gun-wielding, homicidal maniac. You panic. Is it time to run, or time to turn off the TV?

Crime in America has come home. Ask anyone; they can tick off the names, dates, and grisly details from the Oklahoma bombing, the O.J. Simpson double-murder trial, the kidnapping and murder of Polly Klaas, the drowning of Susan Smith's children, the roadside slaying of Michael Jordan's father, the Long Island Railroad massacre, the never-ending string of post office shootings, and on and on. Crime was the number-one issue of concern to the public in 1994, according to the Conference Board. Ninety percent of Americans say that crime is a "serious" problem.

No one escapes the repercussions of Americans' obsession with crime. Some segments of the economy even profit from it. Forty-three percent of Americans have had special locks installed on their doors, and 18 percent have burglar alarms, according to a 1993 Gallup Poll. Half of American households own guns, and sales of personal-security devices such as mace and pepper spray have been brisk in recent years.

More businesses are hurt than helped by the fear of crime. Downtown areas lose shoppers to suburban shopping malls, while tourists and homebuyers shy away from areas where the media have publicized particularly heinous offenses.

Not only do Americans think crime is a terrible problem; they believe it's getting worse. Nearly nine in ten say there was more crime in 1993 in the U.S. than there was a year before, according to a Gallup poll. This perspective accounts for the popularity of a get-tough attitude toward criminals, from stiffer penalties for juvenile offenders to three-strikes-you're-out life terms for repeat felony criminals. Support for the death penalty has grown from just under 50 percent in the early 1960s to 80 percent in 1994.

But is crime really overwhelming America? The public says yes, but crime statistics are contradictory—and so are the experts. Separating the myths from the facts is the best way to understand the current mood of the public. And when you take a close look, one thing becomes clear. Every organization should position itself for a future in which fear of crime is likely to play a major role.

FUEL FOR FEAR

Crime has become a hot issue for a number of reasons, beginning with the

The Books on Crime

The two sets of government crime statistics are contradictory, but both agree that violent crime is increasing.

WHAT POLICE REPORTS SAY

(crimes reported to police per 100,000 population in 1992, 1984, and 1974, by type of crime, and percent change in crime rate, 1984-92 and 1974-92)

	1992	1984	1974	percent change 1984-92	percent change 1974-92
violent crime, total	757.5	539.2	461.1	40.5%	64.3%
rape	42.8	35.7	26.2	19.9	63.4
robbery	263.6	205.4	209.3	28.3	25.9
aggravated assault	441.8	290.2	215.8	52.2	104.7
property crime, total	4,902.7	4,492.1	4,389.3	9.1	11.7
burglary	1,168.2	1,263.7	1,437.7	-7.6	-18.7
larceny	3,103.0	2,791.3	2,489.5	11.2	24.6
motor-vehicle theft	631.5	437.1	462.2	44.5	36.6

WHAT CRIME VICTIMS SAY

(victimizations per 100,000 people aged 12 or older or per 100,000 households, in 1992, 1984, and 1974, and percent change in victimization rate, 1984-92 and 1974-92)

	1992	1984	1974	percent change 1984-92	percent change 1974-92
violent crime, total	3,210	3,140	3,300	2.2%	-2.7%
rape	70	90	100	-27.3	-30.0
robbery	590	570	720	4.0	-17.3
aggravated assault	900	900	1,040	-0.5	-13.8
property crime, total	15,220	17,870	23,570	-14.8	-35.4
burglary	4,890	6,410	9,310	-23.7	-47.5
larceny	8,320	9,940	12,380	-16.3	-32.8
motor-vehicle theft	2,010	1,520	1,880	32.2	6.9

Source: Federal Bureau of Investigation, Uniform Crime Reports 1993; and Bureau of Justice Statistics Bulletin, Criminal Victimization 1992, October 1993

media. The public's concern with crime rises and falls in lockstep with media reporting about the issue. High-profile crimes create sensational news coverage. And the greater the news coverage, the larger the proportion of Americans who cite crime as the most important problem facing the country, according to a 1994 analysis in *The Public Perspective* by Jeffrey D. Alderman, director of polling for ABC News. Public concern with crime follows news coverage of crimes with an exactness that proves the importance of the media in shaping public opinion.

In 1994, a *Los Angeles Times* poll asked Americans whether their feel-ings about crime were based on what they read or saw in the media, or on what they had personally experienced. While 65 percent named the media, only 21 percent named personal experience, and 13 percent said both.

Another reason for the public's heightened concern about crime is the expansion of the middle-aged population. People in the huge baby-boom generation, now aged 31 to 49, are more concerned than young adults about crime. Baby boomers are also more active in protecting themselves from crime. People aged 30 to 49 are more likely than those younger or older to have installed special locks, to have a dog for protection, to have bought a gun, to carry a weapon, or to have a burglar alarm.

In 1995, 38 percent of all American adults are in the 35-to-54 age group, a larger proportion than at any time since the 1950s. The share in this age group will rise to 40 percent by 2000. The middle-aged population is struggling to protect its homes, careers, financial assets, and especially its children. No wonder crime is one of its top concerns.

There is some evidence that the public's fear of crime is driven by a burgeoning population of parents and the crime-crazy media, but not by the facts. Overall crime rates are lower today than they were in the early 1980s. At that time, baby boomers were crime-prone young adults who drove the rates up. And while

> **Sixty-one percent of Americans say they feel "very safe" at home.**

most Americans believe the crime problem is severe, they think it is much worse elsewhere than it is in their community. Seventy-nine percent of Americans think crime is one of the nation's biggest problems, but only 14 percent name crime as one of the biggest problems in their neighborhood. Sixty-one percent of Americans say they feel "very safe" at home. And most Americans say they are not afraid to walk alone at night near their home.

The average American's fear of crime may be a fear for the future. Forty-three percent say that crime in their local area is increasing. While most Americans feel safe in their home and neighborhood, many do not feel secure in their community or when traveling elsewhere. These feelings will intensify in the years ahead, because those most afraid of crime are a growing segment of the population. Moreover, the worst crime does appear to be on the rise.

A LOOK AT THE DATA

How bad is the crime scene? The answer isn't easy to find, because the United

The Most Violent Metros

Many smaller metropolitan areas have higher rates of violent crime than the bigger metros Americans fear the most.

(50 metropolitan areas with the largest number of violent crimes* per 100,000 population,1993)

rank	metropolitan area	violent crime rate	rank	metropolitan area	violent crime rate
1	Miami, FL	2,136.2	26	Orlando, FL	1,118.2
2	New York, NY	1,865.5	27	Memphis,TN-AR-MS	1,109.3
3	Alexandria, LA	1,833.0	28	Nashville, TN	1,098.7
4	Los Angeles-Long Beach, CA	1,682.4	29	Stockton-Lodi, CA	1,091.6
5	Tallahassee, FL	1,546.0	30	Riverside-San Bernardino, CA	1,089.8
6	Baton Rouge, LA	1,510.7	31	San Francisco, CA	1,088.1
7	Little Rock-North Little Rock, AR	1,453.1	32	Fresno, CA	1,084.6
8	Jacksonville, FL	1,419.9	33	Greenville-Spartanburg-Anderson, SC	1,080.0
9	Pueblo, CO	1,403.9	34	Fayetteville, NC	1,076.5
10	Baltimore, MD	1,356.1	35	Pine Bluff, AR	1,058.8
11	Gainesville, FL	1,328.6	36	Waco, TX	1,052.6
12	New Orleans, LA	1,312.6	37	Florence, SC	1,045.8
13	Jackson, TN	1,294.7	38	El Paso, TX	1,031.0
14	Albuquerque, NM	1,273.6	39	Newark, NJ	1,030.9
15	Tampa-St. Petersburg-Clearwater, FL	1,223.4	40	Tuscaloosa, AL	1,009.3
16	Charlotte-Gastonia-Rock Hill, NC-SC	1,204.4	41	Fort Lauderdale, FL	1,005.4
17	Anniston, AL	1,183.6	42	Modesto, CA	992.1
18	Sumter, SC	1,179.1	43	Albany, GA	990.0
19	Gadsden, AL	1,177.5	44	Shreveport-Bossier City, LA	987.9
20	Birmingham, AL	1,146.8	45	Lakeland-Winter Haven, FL	984.3
21	Jersey City, NJ	1,144.1	46	Lake Charles, LA	977.7
22	Ocala, FL	1,141.7	47	Greenville, NC	975.5
23	Oakland, CA	1,137.5	48	Monroe, LA	973.5
24	Sioux City, IA-NE	1,133.8	49	Las Vegas, NV-AZ	959.5
25	Columbia, SC	1,129.1	50	Vineland-Millville-Bridgeton, NJ	953.2

* Murder, rape, robbery, aggravated assault

Source: Crime in the United States, *1993, Federal Bureau of Investigation, 1994*

States keeps two sets of books on crime. One, the FBI's Uniform Crime Reports (UCR), is an annual collection of reported crime in over 16,000 communities across the country. The figures are voluntarily submitted to the FBI by police agencies in those communities. Overall, 95 percent

> **The public's willingness to report crime varies by type of crime.**

of the population is covered by the police agencies that submit their crime data to the FBI, including 97 percent of the metropolitan population and 86 percent of nonmetro residents.

The second data set on crime is the Justice Department's national survey of households, called the National Crime Victimization Survey. In this survey, interviewers ask respondents whether anyone in the household has been a crime victim in the past year. Because many crimes are never reported to police, the National Crime Victimization Survey uncovers much more crime than the police report to the FBI.* By comparing these two data sets, analysts can estimate the amount of crime reported to police.

In 1992, only 39 percent of what the Justice Department refers to as "victimizations" were reported to police. Yet the public's willingness to report crime varies by type of crime. In 1992, the public re-

* *The FBI collects statistics on murder and non-negligent manslaughter, forcible rape, robbery, aggravated assault, burglary, larceny, motor-vehicle theft, and arson. The National Crime Victimization Survey covers all but murder/nonnegligent manslaughter and arson.*

ported 53 percent of rapes, 51 percent of robberies, 49 percent of assaults, 41 percent of household theft, and 30 percent of personal theft. Motor-vehicle theft is most likely to be reported to the police—75 percent in 1992—because such thefts must be reported to make claims on auto insurance.

Over time, the gap between actual and reported crime has narrowed as Americans have become increasingly willing to complain of misdeeds. The 39 percent reporting level of 1992 was up from 32 percent in 1973. The proportion of aggravated assaults reported to the police increased from 52 percent to 62 percent during those years. The proportion of personal theft reported to police rose from 22 to 30 percent. Today's older, better-educated public is more comfortable interacting with authorities than was the

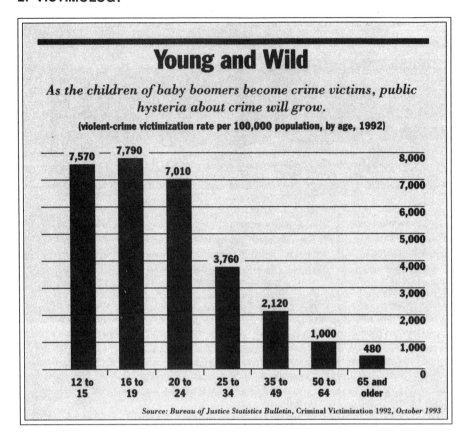

Young and Wild

As the children of baby boomers become crime victims, public hysteria about crime will grow.

(violent-crime victimization rate per 100,000 population, by age, 1992)

Age	Rate
12 to 15	7,570
16 to 19	7,790
20 to 24	7,010
25 to 34	3,760
35 to 49	2,120
50 to 64	1,000
65 and older	480

Source: Bureau of Justice Statistics Bulletin, Criminal Victimization 1992, *October 1993*

public of two decades ago. This increases the likelihood of reporting crime. In addition, the introduction of 911 emergency phone services makes it easier for people to report crime.

The two databases on crime seem to contradict each other in many cases. The Uniform Crime Reports show crime rising over the past 20 years, while the National Crime Victimization Survey shows crime falling. The total crime rate rose from 4,850 offenses per 100,000 population in 1974 to 5,660 per 100,000 in 1992, a 17 percent increase, then dropping slightly to 5,483 per 100,000 in 1993, according to the UCR. In contrast, the household survey shows the percentage of households "touched" by crime falling from 32 to 23 percent from 1975 to 1992. The exclusion of murder and arson from the household survey cannot explain this contradiction, because the two datasets show crime rates moving in opposite directions even for specific types of crime. For example, the UCR statistics show the rate of aggravated assault rising from 2.16 to 4.42

assaults per 1,000 people between 1974 and 1992, a 105 percent increase. In contrast, the victimization survey shows the aggravated assault rate falling from 10.4 to 9.0 assaults per 1,000 people aged 12 or older during those years.

The trends revealed by the two datasets agree in only two areas. Both show

> **The introduction of 911 emergency phone services makes it easier for people to report crime.**

burglary declining and motor-vehicle theft rising. But while the FBI finds that the burglary rate fell 19 percent between 1974 and 1992, the household survey says it fell 48 percent. And while the FBI reports that motor-vehicle theft is up 37 percent, the household survey says just 7 percent.

Which dataset is right? The public finds the FBI's rising crime rates most believable, because it is closer to the carnage

they see on TV. But most experts believe that the trends revealed in the victimization survey are more accurate because of changes in Americans' propensity to report crime. As people report a larger proportion of crime to police, then the UCR statistics will show an increase even if crime rates remain the same. For example, the fact that a larger proportion of aggravated assaults was reported to police in 1993 than in 1974 could account for much of the increase in aggravated assault reported in the UCR.

The trends in the UCR statistics are questionable because of reporting problems. Yet the trends revealed by the victimization survey may not be completely accurate because they are affected by changes in household size, household location, and the age structure of the population. Single-person households are less likely to be victimized by crime than are larger households. Households in central cities are more likely to be victimized than those in suburban areas. If household size declines and an increasing share of households are located in the suburbs, as in the past 20 years, the proportion of households victimized by crime will decline while crime rates remain unchanged.

The Justice Department reports that if households in 1992 were the same size as those in 1975, the proportion "touched" by crime would have been 23.7 percent in 1992 rather than 22.6 percent. But it would still fall far below the 32 percent of 1975. Adjusting for changes in household location would raise it even further, because it turns out that most of the decline in the proportion of households touched by crime is due to the drop in property crime rather than violent crime. The victimization survey shows the burglary rate dropping by 47 percent between 1973 and 1992, household larceny falling by 22 percent, and personal theft down 35 percent. Violent crime rates, on the other hand, have barely budged.

The changing age structure of the population also affects the crime trends revealed by the victimization survey.

SAFETY ZONES

City-dwellers on both coasts tend to think that nothing happens in the Midwest. Although Wisconsinites and Minnesotans may resent having their homes portrayed as boring, they can also have the last laugh. One of the things that isn't happening in the Midwest is crime.

Of the ten metropolitan areas with the lowest assault rates, eight are in Wisconsin and Minnesota, according to the 1993 Federal Bureau of Investigation's Uniform Crime Reports. Bangor, Maine, and Provo-Orem, Utah, are the other two. Four Wisconsin metros rank at the bottom of the list for violent crimes in general.

Wausau, Wisconsin, may be the safest metropolitan area in the country. It has the lowest assault and rape rates, second-lowest burglary rate, third-lowest car-theft rate, fourth-lowest murder rate, and ninth-lowest property-crime rate. Its combined violent crime rate in 1993 was 67 per 100,000 people, versus 2,136 in top-ranked Miami. Other Wisconsin metros also rank tops for lack of crime. Appleton-Oshkosh-Neenah, Sheboygan, and La Crosse each appear on three bottom-ten lists, and Eau Claire appears on two.

Wausau's Deputy Police Chief Paul Luoma modestly declines the credit for his town's low crime rates. "We try to be pro-active, and you have to be visible, but I don't think law enforcement can take credit,"Luoma says. "We have a high employment rate—people don't have a lot of time on their hands. The general values of the community and strong education system keep the crime rate low, too."

But even Wausau has an increasing problem with small-gang activity. "It depends on what you call a gang," says Luoma. "Gangs in a small community could be five to ten individuals causing vandalism." The minority population in Wausau has increased tenfold within the last decade, and it con-sists largely of Hmong and Laotian immigrants who sometimes don't get along. He says the kids band together to create self-assurance. "They put tattoos on their arms, wear their hats a different way, and it's all because they want to be recognized. They're saying 'Hey, I'm a person.'" Luoma acknowledges that there's no short-term solution to these problems.

Sergeant John Roach of Bangor says it's difficult to say why the Maine metro places second-lowest in assault rates, but he attributes some of it to an aggressive pursuit of abusers in domestic assault cases. "We count domestic assaults the same as assaults," Roach says. "If there is any sort of evidence of abuse, the abuser is automatically arrested." He says this is true for the entire state of Maine, not just Bangor.

Outside of the Midwest, metros with older residents and low mobility rates have lower-than-average crime rates. Johnstown, Pennsylvania, has the country's largest share of householders who have not moved since 1959—24 percent—and it also has the nation's lowest property-crime and larceny rates, third-lowest burglary rate, and ninth-lowest car-theft rate. One in five householders in Steubenville-Weirton, Ohio-West Virginia, has stayed put for more than 30 years. The metro has the nation's second-lowest property-crime and larceny rates, fifth-lowest rape and burglary rates, and sixth-lowest car-theft rate.

One expects smaller and more out-of-the-way metros such as Lewiston-Auburn, Maine, and Florence, Alabama, to see less crime than New York and Los Angeles. But one of the country's biggest cities also has relatively low crime rates.Pittsburgh ranks no higher than 81st place out of 245 (see "The Most Violent Metros") metro areas for any of the seven types of crimes studied, and it ranks seventh from the bottom for larceny.

SAFE HAVENS

Cooler climates seem to put violence on ice.

(metros with the lowest violent crime rate per 100,000 people, 1993)

rank	metropolitan area	violent crime rate
1	Wausau, WI	66.5
2	Eau Claire, WI	91.4
3	Appleton-Oshkosh-Neenah, WI	106.4
4	Sheboygan, WI	116.1
5	Bangor, ME	125.7
6	Provo-Orem, UT	141.9
7	Bismarck, ND	175.2
8	Williamsport, PA	176.9
9	Lewiston-Auburn, ME	183.5
10	Fayetteville-Springdale-Rogers, AR	196.0

Source: Crime in the United States, 1993, Federal Bureau of Investigation, 1994

—Jennifer Fulkerson

2. VICTIMOLOGY

Adults are much more likely to be victimized by crime than are older people. Even if crime rates remain unchanged, the overall crime rate should have dropped over the past two decades due to the aging of the population. The fact that the victimization survey shows no significant decline despite the aging of the population suggests that the age-adjusted rate of violent crime is actually on the rise.

Both datasets show violent crime increasing as a proportion of all crime. In the UCR, violent crime grew from 10 to 14 percent of all reported crime from 1974 to 1993. The victimization survey shows the same trend, with violent crime growing from 15 to 20 percent of all crime during those years. This trend alone is enough to alarm the public, since a larger share of the crime around them is of the most-feared type—the random act of violence committed by a stranger.

The UCR shows the rate of violent crime rising fairly steadily since the mid-1970s, peaking in 1992, and standing just below that peak in 1993. The household survey shows the rate of violent crime rising through the early 1980s, falling slightly, then rising again in the early 1990s. The latest statistics from both surveys show violent crime rates today to be close to their all-time high. No wonder people are alarmed.

The trend in violent crime is especially ominous, because the young-adult population—the segment most likely to commit acts of violence—is currently at a low point, due to the small baby-bust generation. As the young-adult population expands with the children of the baby boom in the next decade or so, we can expect a significant increase in violent crime simply because of demographic change.

SMALL, SOUTHERN, AND DANGEROUS

Crime may be pervasive, but each crime is local. This adds another layer of confusion to the crime story. The media's obsessive reporting of every gory detail has increased the public's fear of crime in areas where well-publicized crimes occur. Because the largest number of crimes oc-

---

Demogram

Peter Tyler

Age: 26

Occupation: Police officer in a small city

Why he's a police officer: "It's just go, go, go. I like the variety of calls. You see rich and poor, young and old. You'll go from breaking up a fight to untangling an automobile accident to rescuing an animal. It's never boring."

How to avoid being mugged: "Use common sense. Don't go in dark unlit areas. Don't walk through bad areas alone. Don't display your money, like counting it at an ATM. Assume that people are always watching you. If it happens, do what you're told and don't try to be a hero. Try to get a good description. When it's over, get to the phone."

How to avoid a burglary: "If the bad guys really want to get in, they will. So if there's something you really value, take it with you or put it in storage. And this is so obvious, but do lock your windows and doors. When I do saturation detail in areas where a lot of young people live, I can't believe how many places we can get into."

The root of all evil: In his experience, drugs and alcohol are directly involved in the vast majority of robberies and assaults by strangers. "I see zombies walking around strung out at 4 a.m., needing a rock of crack, and I know they'll do anything to get the money."

Crime and the young black officer: "When I'm in plain clothes, I do get the feeling, often, that people are wary of me. Race is sort of the baseline. But a lot depends on how you act and what you wear, so I'm careful not to provoke people. It used to bother me, but at this point it's more amusing than anything else. I'll walk into a store and the clerk will run over to me-'can I help you?'-and then keep an eye on me until I leave. All the time I'm thinking, 'You don't know who I am, and you'd sure be embarrassed if you did.'"

> **We can expect a significant increase in violent crime simply because of demographic change.**

cur in the most populous metropolitan areas, many people have an exaggerated sense of danger in these places. At the same time, they feel safe in smaller metropolitan areas that may be more dangerous than some big cities. This public confusion is documented in a 1993 Gallup poll that

asked Americans to rank cities according to their danger of crime. Out of a list of 15 cities, Americans correctly ranked Miami and New York as first and second in crime danger. UCR statistics show that the metropolitan area with the highest violent crime rate is Miami, with 2,136 per 100,000 people.* Second is New York, with 1,866. The public ranked Washington, D.C., as the 4th most dangerous city, with two-thirds saying Washington, D.C. is

---

* *The National Crime Victimization Survey is not large enough to supply data for metropolitan areas, so the Uniform Crime Reports are the only source of local data on crime.*

Crime Central

The violent crime rate is dropping in the most violent metros' central cities

(violent crime rate per 100,000 in central cities of the 10 most violent metropolitan areas, 1993, 1994, and percent change 1993-94)

central city	1993	1994	percent change 1993-94
Miami, FL	3,900	3,400	−12.3%
New York, NY	2,100	1,900	−11.0
Alexandria, LA	**	**	**
Los Angeles, CA	2,400	2,100	−13.3
Tallahassee, FL	2,000	1,700	−14.8
Baton Rouge, LA	3,000	2,400	−19.0
Little Rock, AR	3,300	3,000	−10.2
Jacksonville, FL	1,700	1,500	−10.5
Pueblo, CO	1,700	1,400	−17.3
Baltimore, MD	3,000	2,800	−5.3

*See table, p. 25
**Data not available.

Source: Federal Bureau of Investigation

the list, such as Charlotte-Gastonia, North Carolina (16) and Las Vegas (49). These popular metropolitan areas—many touted as wonderful retirement and recreation areas—have much higher crime rates than the cities Americans fear, such as Atlanta (54th in its rate of violent crime), Boston (85), Washington, D.C. (88), and Philadelphia (114).

The FBI's local crime rates are often criticized by civic leaders in crime-prone cities. And in fact, many variables can skew these data. If fewer robberies are reported in New York City than in Tallahassee, for example, New York's rate will look too low, while Tallahassee's will look too high. When Tallahassee launched an aggressive campaign against sex crimes in the mid-1980s, the number of reported rapes increased three times faster than the overall crime rate. Wherever police are aggressive against criminals but approachable to the public, a high proportion of total crimes will be reported.

Still, the FBI data are the only source of information on local crime rates. And the same regional patterns show up in the crime most difficult to hide: murder. New York ranks 5th and Washington, D.C. ranks 28th among the 255 metropolitan areas that supplied their 1993 murder statistics to the FBI. But the nation's highest murder rate is in New Orleans, followed by Shreveport-Bossier City, Louisiana; Jackson, Mississippi; and Jackson, Tennessee. Of the ten metropolitan areas with the highest murder rates,

a dangerous place to live or visit. But its violent crime rate (771 per 100,000 people) places it 88th among the 245 metro areas reporting violent crimes to the FBI in 1993. This rate is far below that of San Francisco or Dallas. Yet only 42 percent of the public think San Francisco is dangerous, and just 24 percent think Dallas is dangerous.

The metropolitan area with the third-highest rate of violent crime is one most Americans have never heard of: Alexandria, Louisiana. The fourth is no sur-

> **The rate of violent crime peaks in July and August, when hot weather shortens tempers.**

prise—Los Angeles-Long Beach. Fifth is Tallahassee, Florida. Other lesser-known cities on the top-ten list are Baton Rouge,

Louisiana; Little Rock, Arkansas; Jacksonville, Florida; and Pueblo, Colorado.

The UCR statistics show that the South is a region plagued by crime. Of the ten metros with the highest rates of violent crime, seven are in the South. Of the top 20, 16 are in the South. Of the top 50, 35 are in the South. Several factors account for the South's high rate of crime. One is the warm climate, which allows people to get out and into trouble year-round. The rate of violent crime peaks in July and August, when hot weather shortens tempers, according to the FBI.

Another reason for the South's high rate of violent crime may be the rapid growth of many of the region's metropolitan areas. The list of the nation's fastest-growing metros looks very similar to the list of the most dangerous. Florida alone is home to 9 of the 50 metropolitan areas with the highest rates of violent crime: Miami (1), Tallahassee (5), Jacksonville (8), Gainesville (11), Tampa (15), Ocala (22), Orlando (26), Fort Lauderdale (41), and Lakeland (45). Other fast-growing metros are also on

> **Of the ten metropolitan areas with the highest murder rates, seven are in the South.**

seven are in the South. Among the top 20, 17 are in the South. Among the top 50, 38 are in the South.

Murder is not included in the Justice Department's victimization survey. But the UCR statistics show that 24,530 Americans were murdered in 1993, or 9.5 murders per 100,000 people. This rate is up 20 percent from a low of 7.9 in 1984 and 1985. This is cause for concern, because the increase occurred despite the shrinking size of the crime-prone young-adult population.

THE NEXT DECADE OF CRIME

The experts agree that violent crime will increase in the years ahead, for demographic reasons alone. The number of Americans aged 15 to 24 is projected to rise 14 percent between 1995 and 2005. Those most likely to commit crime or to be victimized by crime are teenagers and young adults. What's more, crime-prone age groups are getting wilder in the 1990s. The violent crime victimization rate for 16-to-19-year-olds rose from 73.8 to 77.9 per 1,000 between 1989 and 1992, according to the Justice Department's

survey. The rate for 12-to-15-year-olds rose from 62.9 to 75.7, and the rate among 20-to-24-year-olds rose from 57.8 to 70.1. Young black men are now so vulnerable to crime that homicide is the leading cause of death for black men aged 15 to 24.

Violent crime may also increase as people's sense of community dwindles. The emergence of highly individualistic generations in the U.S. and other countries has weakened community standards and eroded public trust. The percentage of Americans who think most people can be trusted fell from 55 percent in 1960 to 36 percent in 1993. The emergence of a highly individualistic population that is indifferent toward public judgment has disturbing consequences that ripple through society. One of the consequences is an increase in violence at society's margins.

As violent crime increases in the next decade, the powerful baby-boom generation will have children entering the age

group most likely to be victimized by crime. These converging trends will probably increase public hysteria over crime in years to come. Specifically:

• Expect middle-aged Americans to demand more protection for their children, whether they are toddlers in day care or young adults in college. Institutions of higher education are likely to discover that the old-fashioned policy of *in loco parentis* has powerful advantages as a marketing tool. Strict on-campus discipline will appeal to fearful parents who are unwilling to grant their children inde-

> **When the baby-boom generation retires, it may retreat behind the walls of a gated community.**

T A K I N G   I T   F U R T H E R

ONLINE

Many of the data analyses used to create this article are available online and free to *American Demographics* subscribers. These data are posted as spreadsheets in DBF and WKS formats and are available through our site on the World Wide Web; point your Web browser to http://www.marketingtools.com. If you don't have internet access, dial our electronic bulletin board, modem access number (607) 273-5579.

Our Web site and electronic bulletin board allow you to download rankings of crime rates per 100,000 population based on the FBI's Uniform Crime Reports for 1993. We offer nine tables that cover all metropolitan areas that reported crimes to the FBI. The tables describe the following crimes: overall violent crimes, murder, aggravated assault, rape, robbery, overall property crimes, car theft, burglary, and larceny.

In addition, 1993 and 1994 data are available for these crimes as reported in 194 cities with more than 100,000 population. Please note that 46 metros did not report crime data to the FBI, and an additional 23 are missing some information. These data will be updated on our online services when the 1994 metro data are published in October 1995.

HARDCOPY

To obtain a printed copy of the FBI's Uniform Crime Reports, *Crime in the United States 1993*, call the Superintendent of Documents, U.S. Government Printing Office; telephone (202) 783-3238. A variety of reports analyzing data from the National Crime Victimization Survey are available from the Bureau of Justice Statistics. These include *Crime and the Nation's Households, 1992; Criminal Victimization 1993*; and *Highlights from 20 years of Surveying Crime Victims: The National Crime Victimization Survey, 1973-92*. In addition, the *Sourcebook of Criminal Justice Statistics*, published annually, includes data from both the UCR and the victimization survey. To order these reports, call the Justice Department at (800) 732-3277. Single copies of reports are free.

For more information about international crime statistics, see *Understanding Crime: Experiences of Crime and Crime Control*, edited by Anna Alvazzi del Frate, Ugljesa Zvekic, and Jan J.M. van Dijk, United Nations Interregional Crime and Justice Research Institute, United Nations Publication No. 49, Rome, August 1993, available for $45 from United Nations Publications, telephone (800) 253-9646.

Most Murderous Metros

Most of the metropolitan areas with the highest murder rates are located in the South.

(50 metropolitan areas with the largest number of murders per 100,000 population, 1993)

rank	metropolitan area	murder rate	rank	metropolitan area	murder rate
1	New Orleans, LA	37.7	26	Monroe, LA	15.8
2	Shreveport-Bossier City, LA	25.8	27	Rocky Mount, NC	15.8
3	Jackson, MS	25.2	28	Washington, DC-MD-VA-WV	15.8
4	Jackson, TN	23.3	29	Galveston-Texas City, TX	15.5
5	New York, NY	23.2	30	Danville, VA	15.3
6	Memphis,TN-AR-MS	21.9	31	Jacksonville, FL	15.1
7	Fayetteville, NC	21.7	32	Vineland-Millville-Bridgeton, NJ	15.0
8	Los Angeles-Long Beach, CA	21.3	33	Montgomery, AL	14.9
9	Gary-Hammond, IN	20.2	34	Dallas,TX	14.6
10	Little Rock-North Little Rock, AR	20.1	35	Riverside-San Bernardino, CA	14.6
11	Alexandria, LA	19.8	36	Savannah, GA	14.6
12	Pine Bluff, AR	19.7	37	Anniston, AL	14.4
13	Birmingham, AL	19.3	38	Oakland, CA	14.4
14	Baton Rouge, LA	19.1	39	Florence, SC	14.2
15	Albany, GA	18.7	40	Laredo, TX	13.9
16	San Antonio, TX	18.6	41	Columbus, GA-AL	13.7
17	Miami, FL	18.1	42	Las Vegas, NV-AZ	13.1
18	Richmond-Petersburg, VA	17.4	43	Mobile, AL	13.0
19	Baltimore, MD	17.2	44	Gadsden, AL	12.9
20	Texarkana, TX-AR	17.1	45	Augusta-Aiken, GA-SC	12.8
21	Fresno, CA	16.9	46	Stockton-Lodi, CA	12.8
22	Charlotte-Gastonia-Rock Hill, NC-SC	16.6	47	Bakersfield, CA	12.5
23	Waco, TX	16.4	48	Flint, MI	12.4
24	Houston, TX	15.9	49	Atlanta, GA	12.2
25	Detroit, MI	15.8	50	Norfolk-Virginia Beach-Newport News, VA-NC	12.1

Source: Crime in the United States, 1993, *Federal Bureau of Investigation, 1994*

pendence at the vulnerable age of 18.

• The public's fear of crime will ensure an ongoing fascination with true crime stories. In this respect, the O.J. Simpson trial is just a harbinger of things to come. Expect at least one major crime story to be at the top of the news at all times from now on.

• The public will shy away from gratuitous fictional violence, because they are so afraid of the real thing. Audiences will demand happy endings from their fiction because there are so many tragedies in real life.

• The personal-security industry will offer increasingly creative high-tech ways to protect oneself, from alarms and security cards to hidden cameras. A growing number of crimes will be captured on videotape and fed to the suppliers of 24-hour news.

• The gun lobby will lose power as an older, educated public demands reasonable compromise in the gun control debate. A growing number of politicians will advocate gun control as their constituents tire of random violence.

• Retailers, restaurateurs, shopping malls, office buildings, train stations, and other public places will offer more visible security. Expect growing demand for guards, metal detectors, and escorts. Even neighborhoods will become more security-conscious. When the baby-boom generation retires, it may retreat behind the walls of a gated community.

Protecting Our Seniors

Elder abuse and neglect [are] coming out of the closet as police network with social agencies to improve the quality of life for senior citizens.

Ronald J. Getz

Ronald J. Getz is a free-lance writer based in Largo, Fla.

Unlike spouses or children, they're often voiceless and abandoned by their families. These victims of elder abuse and neglect are usually terribly vulnerable, isolated and dependent on others. It's a national tragedy; yet it's considered a low priority among many segments of society—including some law enforcement agencies.

"Society treats dogs and animals —and protects them—better than we do some of our own elderly parents and grandparents," said Lt. Rick Duran of the Tampa (Fla.) Police Department, who instructs cops on how to recognize indicators of abuse and neglect of the elderly.

"Elder abuse and neglect is the nation's hidden problem," he said. "It's like child or spousal abuse was 20 years ago."

Abuse is an all-inclusive term encompassing physical, emotional and psychological abuse, financial victimization, neglect by another person and self-neglect. The violence ranges from rape and homicide to a case where a son withheld insulin from his diabetic mother "because it cost too much."

In fact, most elderly victims are abused or neglected in their own homes by family members or paid caregivers—not necessarily by strangers in long-term care facilities.

The following are some typical examples of the more than one million cases of elder abuse and neglect

that occur in this country each year:

■ A deputy found an elderly man abandoned by his children with no heat or hot water in his home. The bed was saturated with urine, and the man was covered with his own excrement. His body was a mass of lesions and sores that were infested with maggots. A foot had to be amputated.

■ A home health aide—previously convicted of dealing in stolen property and grand theft—was assigned by a hospital in Sun City, Fla., to care for an 86-year-old man after open heart surgery. The woman and her husband systematically drained his assets to buy cars and gamble, took out a $22,000 mortgage on his home, and attempted to divert his direct deposit checks to their use before they were finally caught. The bank threatened foreclosure, but—after public pressure—announced that "no further actions will be taken for 30 days."

■ Officials closed down the Riverside Nursing Home in Tampa and removed 19 residents on stretchers after the administrators ignored repeated citations and scores of deficiencies. One resident restricted to soft foods died from choking on a hot dog. Another was treated for dehydration and malnutrition after not being fed for five days.

As the population gets older and social services are reduced, cases like these are expected to escalate.

"Police administrators should plan now for the changing demographics of tomorrow," said Dr. Wilbur L. Rykert, director of the National Crime Prevention Institute at the University of Louisville in Kentucky.

Rykert calls law enforcement officers "the first line of defense" for victims of neglect and abuse. "In the past, law enforcement addressed youth crimes by creating specialized juvenile units," he said. "Now, law enforcement administrators must make similar contributions to the overall good of America by specifically addressing the crime problems of our aging society." (See "The Graying of America".)

An Alliance for Change

Take, for example, Hillsborough County, Fla., which encompasses the city of Tampa and has a larger senior population (350,000) than 16 individuals states. The Tampa Bay P.D. receives about 3,000 calls each year reporting cases of elder abuse and neglect, and there are 20,000 cases statewide.

Nonetheless, not one law enforcement agency had a formal program or systematic training in place to deal with this lethal and rapidly growing problem—until now.

In Tampa Bay, an alliance of law enforcement, social service agencies and members of the aging network launched a unique program focusing on "first responders"—usually cops on the streets—who have first contact with the elderly. Initiated in Hillsborough County in 1992, the First Responder's Program has received recognition for excellence by the National Center on Elder Abuse.

At the time, Joe Breen, who helped launch the program, was serving as a supervisor of Adult Protective Services for Florida's Department of Health and Rehabilitative Services.

"What I found was that my investigators were explaining the laws dealing with elder abuse and neglect to law enforcement," said Breen, who is now a program manager of Mental Health-Care Inc. "The officers just weren't that knowledgeable of the Florida statutes. Moreover, they were inappropriately 'Baker Acting' everybody."

In other words, they were using Florida's Baker Act to get court orders to commit an elderly person to a ward for mental health treatment against the person's wishes when the person was mentally competent.

Breen realized that there had to be a better way to educate police about elder laws. That was the catalyst for earning a federal grant to underwrite "A First Responder's Guide to Abuse, Neglect, and Exploitation of the Elderly and Disabled Adult" with the support of the West Central Florida Area Agency on Aging (AAA).

An advisory team was then formed, consisting of law enforcement —including Lt. Duran and Dpty. Georgia Veitch of the Hillsborough County Sheriff's Office (HCSO)—social service agencies, and emergency medical services to advise West Central Florida AAA on what first responders needed to know when dealing with the elderly and disabled.

"First we created the training manual," said Leslee Boykin of AAA. "Then we distilled the manual into a handy pamphlet, because the officers on the street told us they wanted something easy to understand that they could throw in the glove compartment of the squad car or carry that would give them information in a hurry."

Linking the Pieces

What the team ended up with was actually a package consisting of three modules: the First Responder's Guide

with basic information and vital resources, the training manual and a videotape. The latter, hosted by news anchor Kelly Ring of the Fox Network, was intended to stimulate discussion during training sessions by showing actual cases of at-risk seniors in abusive relationships.

The package is now being updated for release in 1996 to incorporate feedback from law enforcement and to make it even more user-friendly.

The guide also provides a concise overview of the elderly population, types of abuse, neglect and exploitation, a primer on the law and a list of resources. It includes a directory of agencies describing their services and phone numbers.

"We needed something unique for the elderly, because many of the problems law enforcement deals with are not criminal in nature," Duran said. "For instance, many are simply self-neglect.

"Then there are family situations that are legally defined as elder abuse, and we arrest the perpetrator. But just locking people up wasn't the solution either," Duran continued. "Our idea was to link up law enforcement with the social services network so that we can direct the elderly to the part of the system where they belong."

If the elderly person was being abused, for instance, then law enforcement could step in. But with the First Responder's program, the officer has a full array of options.

"Maybe the older person needs Meals on Wheels," Duran said, "or counseling for the family to defuse a violent situation.

"It could be someone in the early stages of Alzheimer's who we connect with the Alzheimer's Wanderer's Identification Program."

According to Duran, police officers want systems in place that *work,* so officers can direct a person to the appropriate services—as long as it's not a criminal justice matter—and then "get them out of there." That's the reason First Responder's has been so invaluable to cops on the streets.

"You get an officer on the street at three in the morning and there's no social services support," said Duran. "That officer's got to make life-and-

death decisions pretty much on his own. Besides that, the social services network is so confusing and hard to navigate (that) an officer just doesn't have the time to figure it all out."

The training component of the First Responder's package has been equally useful.

"We were the first in Florida to develop a curriculum for law enforcement dealing with elder abuse and neglect," Boykin said. "It really took off. As a result of this program, other Area Agencies on Aging have developed similar courses, and personnel in five counties have been trained."

A Three-Way Street

One organization that has been instrumental in improving the quality of life for seniors is TRIAD, which represents the combined forces of the sheriff, the chiefs of police within the county and senior citizens. The group's mission is to reduce the criminal victimization of the elderly and improve law enforcement services to older persons.

The group gets input from an advisory group known as Seniors and Law Enforcement Together (SALT), which evaluates its activities, supports training for law enforcement and community awareness programs, and is an advocacy group that supports law enforcement and legislation affecting senior citizens.

In 1993, the first law enforcement agencies in Florida to organize a TRIAD included the Hillsborough Sheriff's Office, as well as the Tampa, Temple Terrace and Plant City Police Departments. That same year, HCSO was the first law enforcement agency in the Tampa Bay area to establish a Crimes Against the Elderly Unit (CATE).

"Law enforcement has to make a commitment to the elderly and back that up with resources," said Hillsborough County Sheriff Cal Henderson.

"Law enforcement agencies throughout the nation are now recognizing the importance of community policing. What we're doing with our crimes against seniors program is a natural extension of that philosophy," he added. "It makes sense to take advantage of the willingness of seniors and social agencies that want to work with us to improve the quality of life for our elderly."

Working Out the Details

According to Veitch, who heads the CATE unit for the Hillsborough Sheriff's Office, there has to be at least one officer who is designated as the lead person in dealing with crimes against the elderly.

"When there isn't someone responsible for a particular law enforcement responsibility, then nobody is. And normally nothing gets done. Right now most departments don't have even one deputy or officer responsible for crimes against seniors, and that has to change," Veitch said.

One of the first steps the sheriff's office undertook was to initiate in-service training so that all certified personnel would have two hours of instruction on the First Responder's Guide. HCSO conducted a three-day specialized school to familiarize every one of its 900 deputies with the Florida statutes covering crimes against the elderly.

In conjunction with the training, Veitch developed a slide presentation—with support of the Florida Health and Rehabilitative Services Department—to graphically show officers what the at-risk population must endure.

"Cops can get jaded because they've just about seen it all," said Veitch. "Unless you get their attention, they're just going to blow it off because it doesn't mean anything to them. Believe me, I got their attention by showing (cops) elderly victims with burns, battered seniors, bed sores infested with larvae, malnutrition and roaches in food."

Veitch has trained seven deputies who are certified as elder abuse investigators and can assume training responsibilities throughout the agency.

"Ultimately, every squad will have a designated person to handle elder abuse cases," Veitch said. "Each of these elder abuse investigators will have specialized training in dealing with abuse and know how to prepare and handle reports."

Lobbying for Support

Later this year, Veitch will lead a two-day school for HCSO investigators. The training will cover such subjects as financial exploitation, the protocol for emergency removal of an at-risk senior and an update on Florida statutes.

Meanwhile, the Hillsborough County TRIAD is lobbying the Florida Department of Law Enforcement to have a mandated statewide curriculum on crimes against the elderly. HCSO is also joining forces with the Fort Myers P.D. and other agencies to develop a statewide curriculum on elder abuse, which will be completed in 1996 under another federal grant.

In addition, the TRIAD is collaborating with senior groups and social service agencies to change the Florida statutes, so the laws dealing with elder abuse and neglect are consistent, provide for appropriate punishment, are enforceable and result in convictions. Too often, law enforcement representatives nationwide find that cases are thrown out—or not even prosecuted—because the statutes are vague or are ruled unconstitutional.

Early this year, HCSO sponsored a conference on aging sanctioned by the White House entitled "Seniors Impacted By Violence."

The conference, which featured experts from law enforcement, government, universities and the private sector, served as a forum to raise the visibility of crimes against the elderly and encourage greater support of senior abuse and neglect initiatives.

Findings and information from the conference formed the basis for proposals presented by Veitch, who was selected as one of a handful of law enforcement delegates to participate in a recent White House Conference on Aging.

The Graying of America

Take one look at the demographics of America and it's evident why concern about violence and the elderly is very real. America is getting older—and fast. The total population of the United States has tripled in this century, but now there are 10 times as many people 65 years and over; that group has increased from about three million in 1900 to more than 31 million in 1990. And it could reach 70 million by the middle of the next century.

Another way of illustrating the rapidly aging face of America is to note that one in eight Americans were elderly in 1900. Today, the number is one in five. This is the fastest growing demographic group in America.

The sheer mass of the elderly population is one aspect of the challenge facing law enforcement. But there's also the unsettling scale of the violence and hurt inflicted on the elderly. Crime statistics are notoriously unreliable when it comes to determining the incidence of abuse. But most experts now believe that at least one million elderly are abused every year. And the number may be much higher.

Given the prevalence of elder abuse, it would seem that this is an issue that would scream out for attention, headlines and tabloid television. Hardly.

Early this year, "Parade Magazine"—which is distributed as an insert in newspapers to 33 million homes—ran a Special Intelligence Report entitled "Let's Try a Week Without Violence." The magazine registered its dismay and shock over the 2.5 million women who are victims of violent crime and the 2.7 million cases of suspected child abuse. Conspicuously absent was any mention of elders.

—Ronald J. Getz

Assessing At-Risk Elders

Another priority for law enforcement here was to develop a simple information system deputies could use to report and assess calls involving elders at risk.

"For example we found that we have multiple 9-1-1 calls involving the same person," Veitch said, "so officers on three shifts would be responding and filling out paperwork on the same call. That meant a lot of duplication and wasted effort."

Veitch created an Elder Referral Card System (ERCS)—a simple three-by-five card—that deputies complete when they find a senior at risk or in need of services. To reinforce the card referral system, Veitch went to every roll call to explain how the cards worked.

"We told the deputies that if they found a senior that was endangered or was just lonesome and calling 9-1-1, we needed a referral card," she said. "We didn't care if it was a barking dog call or a homicide, or whether or not they filed a report. In addition, we gave them an incentive, because we told them they could get credit for community-oriented policing by turning in a referral card."

The CATE unit now receives about 60 referral cards each month. Once referrals are made to the appropriate agencies, the card is copied and sent to the deputies, so they can see the results and find out what happened to the person in question.

Information from ERCS is then inputted into a computer as part of a database that investigators can draw on for statistical information and data on crimes against the elderly. The information can also be used to assess successes and serve as a guide for program changes.

Connecting with Senior Citizens

Duran emphasizes that the elder program is a way for law enforcement to build bridges with important constituencies in the community. He asserts that it's not only the right thing to do, but it's also politically smart. As a group, seniors volunteer more often than any other single segment of the population, and they have the highest turnout during elections.

"Not only does this system serve our senior citizens, but it's practical," Duran said. "So it's something police departments should initiate in their own self-interest."

Moreover, he said, the First Responder program cuts down on wasted time and unnecessary emergency calls.

"We get people off the 9-1-1 line by plugging them into the telephone reassurance center at the Suicide Prevention Center, where they have volunteers that can call the seniors once a day and talk to them ... Then there's the cases we discover (where there's a) dire need."

A case in point is the experience of Hillsborough County Dpty. Kevin Sowers, who responded when neighbors called to voice their concern about an elderly woman they'd not seen for some time.

When Sowers arrived at her home, he found the woman living in filth, malnourished, dehydrated, with no hot water and too weak to even operate the dial on her rotary telephone.

"Inside—and outside—the place was a mess," Sowers recalls.

The house was entangled in overgrown trees and shrubs, debris was strewn inside and out, there were piles of unwashed clothes and filth throughout the living areas. Sowers called an ambulance, and the woman was dispatched to a hospital's emergency room.

"Some people may think this isn't a law enforcement function, but it is," Sowers said. "Left vacant, that woman's home would have become an easy target for vandals or burglars," Sowers said. "Its deterioration would have led to neighborhood decay, which kills property values and breeds crime."

And, most importantly, the woman might have died or been permanently impaired.

Sowers could have left the matter in the hands of health care professionals. But when he called Florida's Health and Rehabilitative Services Department, he discovered the woman would be forced to go to a nursing home unless her home could be made habitable.

"I said if all we need to do is a massive clean up, I could get it done," Sowers said.

Sowers organized a task force, including himself and five other deputies, who volunteered to clean up the residence. When the deputies were finished with their rehab project, they hauled away two dump-truck loads and an industrial trash bin loaded with garbage and waste.

"Being in law enforcement, we tend to see the worst of people every day," Sowers said. "It's easy to get negative. But this has really charged us up."

Taking a Proactive Approach

Veitch believes that law enforcement needs to be out front in combatting crimes against the elderly with this kind of proactive attitude. And the TRIAD and SALT groups are an effective way to energize society and raise awareness.

But generally, society still doesn't understand the range of violence the elderly face. For example, Florida has an elder abuse hotline, and it's a felony not to report physical abuse, neglect or exploitation of the elderly. But, Veitch admits, not many people know about the hotline.

That's one reason the First Responder's Program is so important.

"Crimes against the elderly in Hillsborough County are taken seriously by our officers, and now we follow up on complaints," Veitch added.

"We know that some of these abuse charges can't be substantiated, and many cases aren't prosecuted because of ambiguities in the law or other circumstances," she continued, "but it's worth investigating every single case—regardless of whether a crime is prosecuted or not—to protect the thousands of seniors in our community who are being victimized, neglected and abused. In many cases, we're the first—and only—line of defense for these older Americans."

Stopping TERRORISM at home

A Massachusetts community shows it can save battered women's lives when the system cares enough.

ANN H. CROWE

Ann H. Crowe is with CSG's Center for Law and Justice.

N o woman has died as a result of domestic violence in more than a decade in Quincy, Mass. Considering that some 1,500 women were killed by intimates in the United States in 1992, Quincy's success in curbing domestic violence attracted coverage by CBS' News show "60 Minutes."

An abused woman told reporter Ed Bradley in the show broadcast Feb. 7, 1993, that she was lucky that when her husband tried to kill her, he did it in Quincy. The court gave her the protection and assistance she needed.

Quincy was one of the first communities to develop a coordinated response to domestic violence by criminal justice agencies and other organizations. And while communities across the United States are start-

ing to follow Quincy's example, state action also is needed in the battle against violence in the home. The 1994 federal Violence Against Women Act charges states with developing and helping communities implement programs to stop domestic abuse. States might look to Quincy as they seek the newly available federal funds to strengthen their efforts.

A lot is at stake. In addition to injuries and deaths suffered by battered women, violence in the home has other consequences. Children from violent homes are more likely to use drugs, become delinquent and have learning problems and difficulties forming relationships. They often grow up to become violent themselves. Domestic violence also costs society in terms of medical treatment for victims and criminal justice spending.

States and communities can do much to curb the violence.

Domestic violence is a serious, violent crime. State laws should reflect

this. Too often, however, abuse of women by their partners is considered a private family matter. If someone assaults a stranger, a neighbor or a co-worker, laws allow for appropriate responses by the criminal justice system. States should do no less for battered women.

The National Council of Juvenile and Family Court Judges has developed a *Model Code* on Domestic and Family Violence. It advocates criminal penalties and procedures for domestic violence crimes and for violations of protective orders. Among other recommendations, it calls for legislation that mandates arrest of perpetrators of domestic abuse and those violating protection orders, weapons seizure, pretrial release conditions and many other provisions that give the criminal justice system needed tools.

Some lessons from Quincy's experience are included in these recommendations:

Forceful law enforcement

Law enforcement protocols and training should prepare police to take a proactive approach to domestic violence. For example, police should give priority to emergency calls made by victims of domestic violence and should have a policy of arresting batterers for probable cause.

"60 Minutes" showed how Quincy police followed up on a woman with visible bruises who came to the police station on an unrelated matter. When questioned by police, she did not want to press charges against her husband for the injuries. The police and prosecutor's office made follow-up calls to her for eight months. She wanted police to leave the situation alone, but Detective Bob Curtis told reporter Bradley, "You can't. People

---

Sarah Buel, an assistant district attorney in Quincy:

"We will enforce the laws of this state the same way for victims in their homes as we will for victims in the street."

A sheriff arrests a man who committed violence against family members. Photo: Jeri Manning, Maricopa County Sheriff's Office, © Sheriff magazine, National Sheriffs' Association.

will wind up dead if you leave it alone." The woman later told Bradley, "I think that if I had not been in Quincy with the help that I had, that I really might be dead now."

Police can help victims in many ways: transporting them for medical treatment or to safety in a shelter, providing information about community services and helping them develop a safety plan. Police also can help victims obtain restraining orders, which should be available 24 hours a day.

Law enforcement also collects evidence and investigates cases of domestic violence for prosecution. Often victims do not want to or are afraid to cooperate with prosecutors. However, if police conduct a thorough investi-

gation, cases can be prosecuted without the victim's cooperation. Police should be trained to document victims' injuries and statements at the scene. Police can gather such evidence as records of a history of violence, copies of 911 tapes, photographs of victims and the scene, and copies of restraining orders.

The Quincy Sheriff's Department protects victims' safety by employing a full-time victim coordinator who flags domestic violence cases as high risk. Staff ensure that batterers are not released from jail until the victim is warned.

Emergency health care

Battered women often are brought by their batterers to public and private health-care facilities for treatment. Medical personnel need to be trained to identify suspicious cases. Just as all states require medical personnel to report suspected child abuse, laws should call for reporting

partner abuse. In addition, medical providers can collect evidence and document injuries that may assist in criminal prosecution, and they can help victims access community services.

Aggressive prosecution

Sarah Buel, an assistant district attorney in Quincy, was once a battered woman. "Our job is public safety," she said on "60 Minutes." "We will enforce the laws of this state the same way for victims in their homes as we will for victims in the street. That's my standard. It's nothing more and nothing less."

In Quincy, unless it would further endanger the victim, all incidents of domestic violence are prosecuted, whether the victim cooperates or not. When victims say they will not testify, Buel said, "we need to hear that as a plea to stay alive. That's not a failure to cooperate."

Quincy prosecutors view domestic violence as a crime against the state and see it as the state's duty to prosecute just as they would in a murder case in which the victim cannot testify. Because of the highly trained and cooperative police in Quincy, the state's case does not rest on the victim's testimony. The prosecution uses evidence such as photographs, 911 tapes, medical records, and carefully documented statements of those at the scene.

The Quincy district attorney's office has a special unit for domestic abuse. Its staff reviews copies of all police reports of family disturbances each day. Counselors attempt to reach each victim by phone or letter and tell victims how to obtain restraining orders and community services.

Every morning Quincy court holds a briefing session for victims seeking restraining orders. The court process is explained, and the victims are advised about what may happen in the courtroom. They also are counseled about safety plans and what to do if their abuser violates a restraining order. They are encouraged to file criminal complaints and obtain restraining orders.

Victims' advocates in the prosecutor's office inform victims of all actions concerning their cases. The counselors also conduct a six-week education program for abused women, and the women can join a support group. The prosecution tries to empower women to take control of their situations and better ensure their own safety.

Friendly but firm courts

Both civil and criminal state courts are involved in domestic violence cases. Civil courts issue restraining or protective orders.

In Quincy, a special office handles only restraining orders. Well-trained clerks and volunteers assist women in completing the restraining order applications. They escort victims to the courtrooms and help them through the process. They also provide referrals to shelters, legal services and counseling and education programs. Twice each day — at 9:30 a.m. and

1:30 p.m. — judges hear only requests for restraining orders. They also will interrupt proceedings at other times to consider these petitions. These practices minimize the time victims must wait. Special sessions for restraining orders also mean the woman does not have to discuss her abuse in open court.

Quincy judges use fully the restrictions allowed by Massachusetts statutes in restraining orders. They often require defendants to refrain from further abuse, have no contact with the victim, stay away from the victim's residence and workplace, surrender custody of children, compensate the victim for damaged property or medical expenses, make temporary support payments and maintain health insurance for the children. In addition, they order the temporary surrender or confiscation of firearms.

Court bailiffs also are trained to be sensitive to victims' fears. To avoid confrontations between victims and defendants, they watch the special waiting area victims use. They often escort victims and their children to and from their cars. And inside the courtroom, they position themselves between defendants and victims.

Finally, judges make it clear to defendants that the court is now in control of cases. If batterers do not abide by the conditions of the restraining order, they will be arrested.

The criminal court in Quincy allows an accused batterer out on release prior to trial only under specific conditions that protect the victim's safety. Domestic violence cases are given priority scheduling for speedy hearings. In Massachusetts, violation of a restraining order is a criminal offense, and batterers who violate them may be fined up to $5,000 and sentenced to a maximum of $2\frac{1}{2}$ years in jail.

Although courts have traditionally been considered neutral and unbiased, special considerations are warranted for domestic violence victims' safety. Retired Judge Albert Kramer in Quincy told an offender on the "60 Minutes" program, "You believe that because you're bigger than she is, because you're married to her, that

you're entitled to settle an argument by the way you want, by using force and abuse on her."

He said, "The offender of domestic violence is probably the most tenacious in the pursuit and relentless persecution of victims."

Domestic violence offenders are accustomed to exerting their power and taking control to get what they want. Many continue to do so, and openly flout the court's orders.

Victims of domestic violence have experienced repeated physical and psychological domination by their abusers. Husbands who batter often threaten to take away their children if the wife attempts to take legal action. Batterers commonly threaten physical harm or legal reprisals.

Many courts are lenient with domestic abusers who violate a restraining order or conditions of release, giving no consequences for infractions. The court's intentions may be to give offenders a second chance to reform and to reduce burdens on the justice system, but this custom may have unintended consequences for the victim.

In most cases involving domestic violence, the victim has suffered many incidents of abuse before she requests a restraining order. She often turns to the court for protection only when she fears for her life or the safety of her children. Thus, the offender already has had several "second chances" before the court becomes involved. The next incident of abuse might be the one that kills the victim.

Corrections

Domestic violence offenders found guilty of criminal acts may be sentenced to jail or probation, or a combination of the two, and some will be released from incarceration for parole supervision. Except in extreme cases, they usually will be supervised in the community.

Quincy intensively supervises batterers. Probation officers have smaller specialized caseloads so they can protect victims and compel batterers to change their behaviors. Probation officers prepare presentence reports and request that judges impose strict conditions on offenders.

Conditions of probation may fall into four categories:

• *Victim protection* includes no contact, intensive probation supervision, forfeiture of weapons and supervised child visitation.

• *Offender rehabilitation* includes mandatory attendance at a batterer's intervention group and substance abuse testing and treatment, if needed.

• *Offender punishment* may include periods of incarceration, fines and community service.

• *Offender financial obligations* often require payment of restitution to the victim, family support and other costs incurred by the victims or the criminal justice system.

In Quincy, probation officers working with domestic violence offenders maintain regular contact with victims. Officers continue the groundwork begun by police and prosecutors by helping victims develop safety plans and referring them to community agencies for education and other services.

The Probation Department in Quincy also takes swift and firm action against offenders who violate conditions of probation. "We see our role as protecting the woman first," said Chief Probation Officer Andrew Klein on "60 Minutes." "If they [the batterers] are told to have no contact with that woman, we won't tolerate a postcard. We won't tolerate a phone call, not even roses being sent to the woman, because it's all part of the continuing manipulation."

Treatment for batterers

In Quincy, domestic batterers are required to attend a group intervention program that meets once a week for 52 weeks. If they do not attend or do not participate fully in the program, their probation can be revoked. The offenders also are required to pay for their treatment using a sliding fee based on income.

Quincy's experience shows that treatment programs need to address the specific offense, provide a group setting, use a cognitive or psychoeducational approach, hold the offender responsible for his behavior, place a priority on protecting victims and hold victims blameless.

Research shows that many batterers have histories of abusing drugs, alcohol or both. The Probation Department in Quincy enforces probation conditions of abstinence, and offenders are required to undergo random weekly urine tests. Drug or alcohol abusers are required to receive treatment.

Shelters and victims advocates

Many shelter programs are becoming full-service agencies for abused women and their children. Among the services provided by the DOVE shelter in Quincy are: emergency housing, 24-hour crisis hotlines, legal advocacy services, support groups and activities for women and children, and community awareness and education activities. The shelter staff works closely with criminal justice agencies on behalf of battered women.

Community coordination

It is not enough to have all the important players in a community doing their jobs well. There needs to be a mechanism for coordinating their efforts. Quincy considers the team effort a vital part of its approach.

Prosecutor Buel said coordination is the focus of the program. "It's not that any one of us does such an extraordinary job," she said on "60 Minutes," "but that together we can better protect battered women."

CSG resources

The Center for Law and Justice at The Council of State Governments has emphasized family violence, including domestic abuse, for the past 18 months. Through grant support and private contracts, staff and consultants have provided training and technical assistance to several states and communities. For additional information about technical assistance or training fees and availability, contact: Ann H. Crowe, Center for Law and Justice, CSG, P.O. Box 11910, Lexington, Ky. 40578-1910, (606) 244-8211, fax (606) 244-8001.

Responding to Domestic Violence Against Women

Loretta J. Stalans

Assistant Professor, Department of Criminal Justice, Loyola University.

Arthur J. Lurigio

Associate Professor, Department of Criminal Justice, Loyola University.

This year, the public is reminded that domestic violence against women has no racial or social class boundaries. Nicole Brown Simpson knew firsthand that wealthy Caucasian women are beaten and psychologically abused. The O. J. Simpson trial dramatically portrays the terror of a battered woman's life and considers the question of whether Nicole Brown Simpson is yet another victim of domestic murder—a fatal consequence that happens all too often in America. According to the National Crime Victimization Survey (NCVS), women are 10 times more likely than men to be victims of violence inflicted by their intimate partners (Zawitz 1994). Based on a national survey of reported incidents of violence (from slapping to choking or using a weapon), Straus (1991) estimated that "over 6 million women are beaten every year in the United States. This is a lower bound estimate and the true figure easily could be double that" (p. 30). About 1.8 million women experience at least one of the more serious forms of violence, such as being kicked, punched, choked, or attacked with a weapon. These numbers, of course, are just estimates because all data sources either underestimate or overestimate certain forms of violence. Women experience similar risks of violence in urban, suburban, and rural areas. Ethnic or racial background is unrelated to rates of violence in the home, but age and social class do place women at a higher risk for violent attacks: younger women with less education and lower incomes have much higher rates of victimizations by intimates than do older women and women with more education and higher incomes (Zawitz 1994).

Women are more likely than men to be seriously injured in domestic violence incidents, as documented by police records (Bell and Bell 1991) and victimization surveys such as Brush's (1993) nationwide survey of 5,474 U.S. households in 1988. Brush asked males and females in married couples the following: "Have you ever been cut, bruised, or seriously injured in a fight with your partner?" "Has your partner ever been cut, bruised, or seriously injured?" Women reported that they were hurt more often than their partners. Moreover, in situations where both partners were violent, women were more likely to be seriously injured (also see Straus 1991). Data from emergency rooms, police reports, and court records also support the conclusion that in domestic disputes women receive more serious injuries than men (for a review, see Kurz 1993). However, men are less likely to report victimization experiences, and many incidents of domestic violence, whether women or men are victims, never come to the attention of police or physicians.

As the above findings clearly suggest, women are susceptible to repeat victimizations in the home and may become hopelessly entangled in abusive relationships. They fear not only the consequences of staying but also, and even more, the consequences of leaving those relationships (Barnett and LaViolette 1993). In the NCVS, 20% of women reported that they had been victims of intimate violence at least three times in the prior 6 months (Zawitz 1994). Many women do not react passively and helplessly when faced with repeat abuse. Most seek help from family, friends, or government agencies (Frieze and Browne 1989). In the NCVS, about 80% attempted to defend themselves: 40% reasoned with the offenders and 40% used physical force (Zawitz 1994). More than one half of the women who attempted to protect themselves thought that their tactics had helped, whereas one fourth believed that their tactics had worsened the situations (Zawitz 1994). Faced with repeated abuse, women often begin to anticipate the next violent episode and may engage in behaviors to actually trigger the violence; for them, the anticipation of abuse is often worse than the abuse itself. Victims of violent street crimes typically do not

From *Crime & Delinquency*, October 1995, pp. 387-398. © 1995 by Sage Publications, Inc. Reprinted by permission.

have contact with offenders after the crime; in contrast, domestic violence victims and their perpetrators often share children, property, insurance, and homes. Even if victims leave their homes, courts often force them to allow offenders to visit their children. Victims of domestic violence are particularly vulnerable to repeat abuse because their children make it difficult to sever all contacts with offenders.

The most fatal consequence of domestic violence frequently happens after escalating incidents of repeat violence (see Frieze and Browne 1989). The exact number of homicides that occur because of the actions of intimates is difficult to estimate because the nature of the relationships between victims and offenders is often unknown (e.g., 39% of the relationships were unknown in FBI data for 1992; see Zawitz 1994). Based on FBI data from 1977 to 1992, an estimated 1,432 women and 657 men were killed by intimates in 1992 (Zawitz 1994). The ratio of women to men who kill their intimate partners varies by race. In 1977, a greater number of African American women killed their husbands compared to African American men who killed their wives, but by 1992 a greater number of African American men killed their wives. "Among Whites, wives have always outnumbered husbands as victims of intimate murder" (Zawitz 1994, p. 3). More than half of the victims and offenders were drinking alcohol at the time of the murders (Zawitz 1994). Several studies report that in instances where wives killed their husbands, the husbands were the first to use physical force or to threaten the use of a weapon (see Frieze and Browne 1989). In 1991, 70% of women prisoners incarcerated for intimate violence were first-time offenders, compared to only 30% of men incarcerated for intimate violence. Of those incarcerated for intimate violence, men with previous convictions for violent crimes outnumbered women almost 3 to 1 (Zawitz 1994).

TWO PERSPECTIVES ON DOMESTIC VIOLENCE

Why does domestic violence occur and what can society and the criminal justice system do about it? Kurz (1993) described two theoretical perspectives that have dominated domestic violence research: the family violence perspective (e.g., Straus, Gelles, and Steinmetz 1980) and the feminist perspective (e.g., Dobash and Dobash 1979; Hanmer, Radford, and Stanko 1989). For the family violence perspective, the unit of analysis is the family (Kurz 1993). For the feminist perspective, the unit of analysis is the relationship between men and women; it encompasses all forms of violence against women from sexual harassment in the workplace to physical, verbal, and sexual abuse in the home (Kurz 1993). Both perspectives urge the legal system to focus on violence against women, but they do so for different reasons, which lead to different solutions to the problem.

The family violence perspective maintains that women and men are equally likely to engage in violence, as evidenced by survey data showing that women and men report similar incidences of physical violence against their partners (Straus et al. 1980). Straus and colleagues (1980) found that about 12% of men and women in their study sample engaged in violence and that in 49% of the homes where violence occurred, both men and women were perpetrators. Other surveys have replicated the finding that men and women report similar levels of violence (Brush 1993; for a review, see Straus 1991). Feminists criticize these results by pointing out that many of women's acts of physical aggression are actually attempts to defend themselves from men's attacks (Dobash and Dobash 1979). According to NCVS data, twice as many women physically attacked intimate assailants to protect themselves than attacked stranger assailants for self-protection (40% vs. 20%, respectively; see Zawitz 1994). Feminists point to the higher percentages of women victims of violence (as opposed to women perpetrators) in police and court records, emergency room data, and victimization surveys to underscore the fact that women are much more likely to be victims of domestic violence.

The family violence perspective suggests that women and men learn from childhood experiences and from media portrayals and societal norms that violence is an acceptable way to resolve disputes. In the family violence perspective, therefore, domestic violence is no different from other forms of violence such as stranger-on-stranger violence and violence against children, the elderly, and other social groups—all of which are seen to result from faulty socialization. The family violence perspective focuses on women victims because men engage in more dangerous forms of violence that lead to more serious injuries (Straus et al. 1980).

Feminists argue that male dominance is a central component in understanding why domestic violence occurs and in finding solutions to it, Feminists assert that men and women do not have equal positions in society. Men have had privileged positions in society for centuries and have acquired and maintained these positions by keeping women subordinate (see Dobash and Dobash 1979). According to this viewpoint, organized religion has perpetuated the attitudes and beliefs that lead to violence against women and children (Dobash and Dobash 1979). As Kurz (1993) observed:

> Feminists believe that the decontextualized family violence perspective denies a central element of women's experience by deflecting attention from one of the key places where women's oppression occurs—in the family. For feminists, family violence is a direct outcome of men's attempt to maintain control over the powerless members of the family—women and children. (pp. 262–3)

Because it ignores variables such as social structure and gender, the family violence perspective places great importance on psychological problems of individuals and families. Fine (1993) discussed the implications of concentrating on individuals rather than on the gender-based nature of violence:

> To focus on the individual . . . contributes to a discourse that finally blames individual survivors, for the source of social inequity is sought inside their and minds. Not only does such an approach decontextualize a woman from her political, social, and personal worlds, but it systematically renders oblique the structure of patriarchy, racism, and classism, and advanced capitalism that have sculpted what appear to be the "conditions" or "choices" of her life. (pp. 280–1)

HISTORICAL TREATMENT OF DOMESTIC VIOLENCE

History supports the feminists' position that laws and community norms perpetuate violence against women. The U.S. Constitution declares that "all men are created equal," but did not extend human and civil rights to women until several decades after its passage. In the 17th and 18th centuries, women were property that could be bought and sold, and they were disciplined through physical punishment. Women did not have the right to own property, to vote, or to manage their wages:

> Married women had always been controlled and abused by legal loss of their property upon marriage and by the husband's right to exploit their labor and to appropriate their wages, but the Married Women's Property Act of 1857 forbade a husband to "seize his wife's earnings and neglect her and allowed her to keep her own wages after the desertion of her lord." (Dobash and Dobash 1979, pp. 67–8)

Until the 19th century, husbands who beat their wives could use the defense of chastisement (Dobash and Dobash 1979). In the latter part of the 19th century, domestic violence was considered a crime and laws were created to punish offenders at the whipping post. "Courts declared that 'the rule of love superseded the rule of force' and 'the moral sense of the community revolts at the idea that the husband may inflict personal chastisement upon his wife, even for the most outrageous conduct.'" (Dobash and Dobash 1979, p. 63) These laws, however, were rarely enforced.

At the turn of the 20th century, domestic violence was viewed once again as a "private matter" that should be kept out of public view. Many states created statutes that did not allow police officers to arrest perpetrators for domestic violence misdemeanors where a neutral third party did not witness the episode. Courts and prosecutors believed that formal prosecution was not appropriate and that rehabilitation was the goal (Buzawa and Buzawa 1990). Historically, legal statutes, criminal justice authorities, and community members have regarded violence against women in the home as a "private matter of the family," best handled through advice or mediation.

CHANGES WITHIN THE LEGAL SYSTEM TO HANDLE DOMESTIC VIOLENCE

During the last two decades, the legal system has faced inside and outside pressure to protect women from violence. The women's movement in the 1970s focused on violence against women and characterized the problem as a public concern. Civil liability suits filed against police departments for failing to provide equal protection to women injured in domestic violence incidents signaled to all law enforcement agencies that ignoring battered women can lead to litigation and financial losses. Academic research (for a review, see Buzawa and Buzawa 1990) also called attention to the problems of existing domestic violence policies. For example, research shows that the likelihood of future domestic violence is lower when police arrest batterers in domestic disputes (Sherman and Berk 1984); however, other research suggests that the effectiveness of arrest is contingent on a number of situational factors and batterer characteristics. Together, feminism, court cases, and empirical findings have helped to change state laws to give police officers more power to arrest suspects in domestic violence incidents.

Several states have changed their laws to allow police officers to arrest suspects without victims' consent when there is probable cause (Hirschel and Hutchison 1991). Despite these statutory changes, only a few states actually require officers to arrest suspects under specific circumstances, such as when there are injured victims (Hirschel and Hutchison 1991). Officers still exercise a lot of discretion when deciding to arrest suspects, even in states with laws mandating arrest, because the concept of probable cause is quite ambiguous (Ferraro 1993). Officers have especially difficult times interpreting domestic violence situations where the wife and husband offer conflicting accounts of how the injuries occurred. To handle these situations, some states have passed laws requiring officers to determine who is the primary aggressor in an incident. In one state with a primary aggressor clause, experienced officers are rarely able to untangle the past to assess blameworthiness; instead, they base their decisions to arrest on the respective credibility and dangerousness of wives and husbands. Their "disinterested objectivity," however, has still created a bias toward less formal processing of cases involving women who violate social norms by exhibiting symptoms of mental illness or alcoholism (Stalans and Finn 1995). Moreover, mandatory and presumptive arrest policies have not resulted in equal protection under the law (e.g., Ferraro 1989).

Early evaluations of how legislative changes influenced local criminal justice practices suggested that gatekeepers (i.e., police officers and prosecutors) often fail to process domestic violence cases through the formal criminal justice system and prefer alternatives such as court-ordered mediation. Moreover, evaluations showing higher rates of arrest after the implementation of presumptive arrest policies (see Hirschel and Hutchison 1991) did not examine several key issues, for example, victims' satisfaction with how the police and system treated them, whether certain groups of women obtained less protection, whether states' attorneys lessened or dropped the charges, and how the courts deal with convicted batterers.

Preferred arrest policies do result in significantly more arrests when they are part of a coordinated response involving the legal system and community agencies (for a review, see Hirschel and Hutchison 1991). Key criminal justice institutions (i.e., police, the prosecutor's office, courts, and defense attorneys), community services (i.e., battered women's shelters, children's services, welfare agencies, and mental health services), and public support can change officers' decisions about using arrest as a solution to domestic violence incidents.

Researchers have paid relatively little attention to how domestic violence cases are prosecuted (Cahn and Lerman 1991; Ford and Regoli 1993). In the past, prosecutors typically required victims of domestic violence to sign complaints against batterers, whereas prosecutors themselves signed complaints in other crimes. Prosecutors' offices are changing their procedures so that they now sign complaints against defendants, and victims serve as key witnesses in those cases; this change sends the message that domestic violence is a crime against the state (Cahn and Lerman 1991). Prosecutors' offices also have adopted policies to prevent victims from dropping charges and regularly use subpoena power to force victims to appear in court. Subpoena power may prevent victims from becoming targets of retaliatory violence because victims can show that they were forced to participate in court proceedings (Cahn and Lerman 1991). Prosecutors also have been successful at prosecuting cases without the participation of victims (Cahn and Lerman 1991).

Research on the effectiveness of different prosecution strategies has been sparse. Ford and Regoli (1993) concluded that

> the limited evidence on the effectiveness of alternative prosecution policies for preventing wife assault suggests that no single policy commonly advocated is better than another. The chance of a man assaulting his partner again in the short term is essentially unaffected by whether he is prosecuted under policies calling for harsh punishment or for rehabilitative treatment. What matters is that he faces treatment. (p. 157)

When victims initiate complaints, they are less likely to be harmed by offenders when prosecutors allow the victims to drop charges than when other strategies such as diversion or "no-drop" policies are used (Ford and Regoli 1993). This effectiveness, however, remains to be documented more thoroughly and may not generalize to police-initiated charges.

Many jurisdictions, thanks largely to the feminist perspective, have created victims' programs that help victims with their decisions to participate in the legal process and to leave domestic batterers. Several studies have found that these programs increase victims' willingness to participate in the criminal justice process as well as increase their satisfaction with the process (Cahn and Lerman 1991). Few studies, however, have examined whether victim advocate programs reduce the risk that victims will experience retaliatory violence, increase their knowledge about the system and community-based programs, and empower them to take control over their lives. Research is sorely needed to better understand how interventions can assist victims' recovery and readjustment. In addressing these issues, researchers should explore the independent and combined effects of victims' programs, civil protection orders, and prosecution and sentencing strategies on victims' satisfaction, safety, recovery, and control over their lives.

The family violence perspective is more likely than the feminist perspective to pay attention to the perpetrators of domestic violence. The family violence perspective, for example, encourages researchers to classify offenders into different profiles based on backgrounds and personality characteristics. Saunders (1993) identified three prominent risk factors for wife assault. Men are more likely to batter women if the men were abused as children. The risk of wife assault increases when both partners were abused or witnessed abuse as children. Alcohol abuse and low income are also prominent risk factors. Other risk factors include offender deficits in communication skills, rigid stereotypes of male and female roles, personality disorders, and problems with anger control. These risk factors have been used to customize treatments for batterers. Many criminal justice systems now impose court-mandated treatment at both pre- and postsentencing (Hamberger and Hastings 1993). In pretrial diversion programs, for example, offenders who successfully complete treatment have their arrest records cleared. Court-mandated treatment also can be part of sentences for convicted offenders.

CHANGES WITHIN THE COMMUNITY TO HANDLE DOMESTIC VIOLENCE

A variety of community services and treatment programs exist to assist victims of domestic violence and to treat domestic violence offenders. Feminists have focused on the task of empowering women to control their own lives and have created social services that allow women with limited financial means to leave abusive partners and to find havens from retaliatory violence. Feminists were volunteers for the first battered women's shelters and have fought to limit the amount of funds that are diverted away from abused women to treat abusive men (Ferraro 1989). Shelters provide a safe place to live and offer supportive counseling, child care, and advocacy services (Dutton-Douglas and Dionne 1991). The number of shelters has grown from 0 in 1970 to more than 1,300 in 1989 (Ferraro 1989); nonetheless, there are not enough shelters to meet the demand for services.

The effectiveness of shelters as a means of allowing women to leave violent relationships is uncertain. Research indicates that each additional step that a victim takes to seek help reduces the number of subsequent victimization incidents (for a review, see Dutton-Douglas and Dionne 1991). Battered women can also receive counseling services from outpatient community mental health treatment programs, clergy, private counseling agencies, and women's groups, the latter of which battered women rate as more effective than the other types of counseling services (Dutton-Douglas and Dionne 1991). . . .

REFERENCES

Barnett, Ola W. and Alyce D. LaViolette. 1993. *It Could Happen to Anyone: Why Battered Women Stay.* Newbury Park, CA: Sage.

Bell, Daniel J. and Susan L. Bell. 1991. "The Victim Offender Relationship as a Determinant in Police Dispositions of Family Violence Incidents: A Replication Study." *Policing and Society* 1:225–34.

Brush, Lisa D. 1993. "Violent Acts and Injurious Outcomes in Married Couples: Methodological Issues in the National Survey of Families and Households." Pp. 237–51 in *Violence Against Women: The Bloody Footprints,* edited by P. B. Bart and E. G. Moran. Newbury Park, CA: Sage.

Buzawa, Eva S. and Carl G. Buzawa. 1990. *Domestic Violence: The Criminal Justice Response.* Newbury Park: Sage.

Cahn, Naomi R. and Lisa G. Lerman. 1991. "Prosecuting Woman Abuse." Pp. 95–112 in *Woman Battering: Policy Responses,* edited by M. Steinman. Cincinnati, OH: Anderson.

Dobash, R. Emerson and Russell Dobash. 1979. *Violence Against Wives.* New York: Macmillan.

Dutton-Douglas, Mary Anne and Dorothy Dionne. 1991. "Counseling and Shelter Services for Battered Women." Pp. 113–30 in *Woman Battering: Policy Responses,* edited by M. Steinman. Cincinnati, OH: Anderson.

Ferraro, Kathleen J. 1989. "The Legal Response to Woman Battering in the United States." Pp. 155–84 in *Women, Policing, and Male Violence,* edited by J. Hanmer, J. Radford, and E. A. Stanko. New York: Routledge.

– –. 1993. "Cops, Courts, and Woman Battering." Pp. 278–87 in *Violence Against Women: The Bloody Footprints,* edited by P. B. Bart and E. G. Moran. Newbury Park, CA: Sage.

Fine, Michelle. 1993. "The Politics of Research and Activism: Violence Against Women." Pp. 278–87 in *Violence Against Women: The Bloody Footprints,* edited by P. B. Bart and E. G. Moran. Newbury Park, CA: Sage.

Ford, David A. and Mary Jean Regoli. 1993. "The Criminal Prosecution of Wife Assaults: Process, Problems, and Effects." Pp. 163–218 in *Legal Responses to Wife Assault: Current Trends and Evaluations,* edited by N. Z. Hilton. Newbury Park, CA: Sage.

Frieze, Irene Hanson and Angela Browne. 1989. "Violence in Marriage." Pp. 163–218 in *Family Violence,* edited by L. Ohlin and M. Tonry. Chicago: University of Chicago Press.

Hamberger, L. Kevin and James E. Hastings. 1993. "Court-Mandated Treatment of Men Who Assault Their Partner." Pp. 188–229 in *Legal Responses to Wife Assault: Current Trends and Evaluations,* edited by N. Z. Hilton. Newbury Park, CA: Sage.

Hanmer, Jalna, Jill Radford, and Elizabeth A. Stanko. 1989. "Policing Men's Violence: An Introduction." Pp. 1–12 in *Women, Policing, and Male Violence,* edited by J. Hanmer, J. Radford, and E. A. Stanko. New York: Routledge.

Hirschel, David J. and Ira Hutchison. 1991. "Police-Preferred Arrest Policies." Pp. 49–72 in *Woman Battering: Policy Responses,* edited by M. Steinman. Cincinnati, OH: Anderson.

Kurz, Demie. 1993. "Social Science Perspectives on Wife Abuse: Current Debates and Future Directions." Pp. 252–69 in *Violence Against Women: The Bloody Footprints,* edited by P. B. Bart and E. G. Moran. Newbury Park, CA: Sage.

Saunders, Daniel G. 1993. "Husbands Who Assault: Multiple Profiles Requiring Multiple Responses." Pp. 9–34 in *Legal Responses to Wife Assault: Current Trends and Evaluation,* edited by N. Z. Hilton. Newbury Park, CA: Sage.

Sherman, Lawrence W. and Richard A. Berk. 1994. "The Specific Deterrent Effects of Arrest for Domestic Assault." *American Sociological Review* 49:261–72.

Stalans, Loretta J. and Mary A. Finn. 1995. "How Novice and Experienced Officers Interpret Wife Assaults: Normative and Efficiency Frames." *Law & Society Review* 29:301–55.

Straus, Murray. 1991. "Conceptualization and Measurement of Battering: Implications for Public Policy." Pp. 19–47 in *Woman Battering: Policy Responses,* edited by M. Steinman. Cincinnati, OH: Anderson.

Straus, Murray, Richard Gelles, and S. Steinmetz. 1980. *Behind Closed Doors: Violence in the American Family.* Garden City, NY: Doubleday.

Zawitz, Marianne W. 1994. "Violence Between Intimates." *Bureau of Justice Statistics Selected Findings,* NCJ-149259. Washington, DC: U.S. Government Printing Office.

"Towards the Institutionalization of a New Kind of Justice Professional: The Victim Advocate"

Andrew Karmen, Ph.D.

ABSTRACT

Advocates look after the interests of crime victims in shelters for battered women, rape crisis centers, prosecutors, victim/witness assistance units, family courts (guardians-ad-litem), in self-help support groups, and in victims' rights organizations. But no jurisdiction in the United States has yet taken the next logical step, which is to offer all complainants the services of advocates, free of charge, through mechanisms that are parallel to the way indigent defendants are provided with lawyers.

The result might be a reduction in the "differential handling" of victims of varying social status, and a more vigorous implementation of victims' rights.

AN IDEA WHOSE TIME HAS COME

One of the driving forces that has spurred on activists in the victims' rights movement, since its emergence in the early 1970s, is their belief that the scales of justice are "tilted" in ways that work to the disadvantage of the injured parties whom the legal system ostensibly serves. An overriding goal of the movement has been to correct this "imbalance" in the direction of "equity" or "parity" by devising mechanisms to defend and advance the rights of the accuser without infringing upon the Constitutional rights of the accused.

One way to empower victims so that they can pursue what they perceive to be their own best interests would be to offer all of them the services of knowledgeable consultants. Providing an advocate to every person harmed by a crime would be as great a reform as was furnishing a lawyer to every person accused of a crime. At the moment of first contact, when complainants formally ask that the machinery of criminal justice be set into motion in their behalf, officers would immediately read them their rights:

To the complainant:
You have a right to remain vocal, to make statements to be used in your favor, and to further your own interests in all criminal justice proceedings.
You have the right to have an advocate present during all proceedings, and to regularly consult with this victim advocate.
If you cannot afford an advocate, one will be provided to you for free.

Even though the victims' movement is poised on the brink of achieving this historic breakthrough, as yet there have been no such explicit demands for institutionalized universal advocacy. This article advances arguments in favor of providing all victims with advocates, and is intended to provoke discussion of the pros and cons of this dramatic reform. The sections that follow describe how advocacy is already offered to some but certainly not all who could benefit from it; outline the kinds of services these consultants would perform for their clients; explain why advocates must be as independent as possible; propose the kinds of preparation advocates might need; project how they could be supplied and paid for; and speculate about how routinized advocacy might affect the criminal justice process.

OVERVIEW OF ADVOCACY TODAY

A trend towards institutionalizing victim advocacy is already underway, but the next logical and decisive step remains to be taken. Right now, scattered individuals and organizations inside and outside the criminal justice system assume certain advocacy tasks. They do work that is necessary but not sufficient; focused and segmented, but not across-the-board; and particular and selective but not as yet general and universal. Today's advocates have fragmented roles, serve specialized functions, and are provided by groups with inadequate resources, and by agencies with limited jurisdictions and responsibilities. They are brought into some cases but not others. They see to it that the problems of certain kinds of victims are addressed to some degree, but not that the needs and wants of all victims are attended to along all possible fronts. Having a victim advocate to consult with is a privilege enjoyed by some victims, but it is not as yet a right exercised by all victims.

At this stage in the evolutionary process, six types of advocacy organizations can be distinguished: those that are 1) private non-profit organizations committed to advancing the cause of victims in general; 2) private non-profit organizations focusing their efforts towards representing the interests of particular types of victims; 3) private law firms representing specific clients in civil cases; 4) self-help networks that offer mutual support and direct aid to specific participants; 5) governmental agencies serving all victims; and 6) governmental agencies protecting and assisting some victims. (See the typology in Chart One.)

Private non-profit organizations engaged in independent general advocacy are dedicated to the cause of alleviating the suffering of all sorts of people harmed by criminals. They lobby Congress and state legislatures for new laws and more funding, run information clearinghouses, devise training programs to sensitize professionals who deal with victims, carry out or contract out research, hold conferences, and undertake educational campaigns to raise public consciousness. Their politicking is "collective" or "class action" in the sense that these umbrella groups agitate for improvements in the way all kinds of victims of interpersonal violence and theft are handled by criminal justice and social service agencies. They rarely get involved in behalf of a victim in any specific case, but endeavor to learn lessons and make changes so that other individuals facing a similar plight in the future will have greater options and will fare better. The National Victim Center and the National Organization For Victim Assistance are the oldest and most prominent examples of non-profit, independent general advocacy groups.

Non-profit groups trying to represent the interests of particular kinds of victims are the most familiar and have the highest profiles because of their public outreach campaigns. Although many of these groups originally received foundation grants and seed money to cover start-up costs from government sources, they now depend mostly upon fund-raising activities and donations. The best known is Mothers Against Drunk Driving (MADD), which successfully campaigned to make sure that drivers, passengers, and pedestrians crashed into by vehicles driven by intoxicated persons are accorded the additional rights and privileges that are granted to crime victims but are denied to accident victims. Other examples of focused advocacy groups are the National Center For Missing And Exploited Children, the National Center On Child Abuse And Neglect, the National Coalition Against Sexual Assault, the National Clearinghouse On Marital and Date Rape, the Gay and Lesbian Anti-Violence Project, Security on Campus (that lobbies to compel university administrations to better protect college students) and Concerns of Police Survivors (that looks after the needs of widows and

orphans of law enforcement officers killed in the line-of-duty). In addition, there are the many locally based child search organizations looking for missing children; small legal clinics offering advice about trial strategies and lawsuits (like the National Battered Women's Law Project and the New Jersey Crime Victims Law Center), and the many ethnically-based civil rights organizations that rally to the defense of victims of hate-motivated bias crimes.

Self-help support groups are the third type of advocacy organizations. They may take part in outreach efforts, but their primary function is to provide direct therapeutic benefits to their members in distress. They offer emotional solace, crisis intervention, and social solidarity to people afflicted by devastating after-effects. Support groups for parents of murdered children and for survivors of childhood incest exemplify this type of self-help approach, in which members who have first-hand experience comfort and look after those who are first undergoing the ordeal. Former victims who led group counseling sessions at shelters for battered women and rape crisis centers pioneered this type of direct, applied, concrete, case-specific advocacy.

Private, for-profit law firms are the

fourth kind of victim advocacy organizations. Since private prosecution in criminal matters is not permitted, attorneys can directly advocate in behalf of the victims who hire them only in civil lawsuits. They become involved in cases, usually on a contingency fee basis, whenever victims might win substantial financial judgments in civil court by suing their offenders, or grossly negligent third parties (businesses or criminal justice agencies) who put these offenders in a position to harm their clients. Since the firms' clients may have been murdered, assaulted, robbed, raped, or otherwise physically, mentally, or financially harmed, their advocacy can be classified as "general" (serving a range of victims) rather than "focused" (even though their assistance is limited to civil lawsuits).

Government-run and taxpayer funded entities, usually connected to either criminal justice or social service functions, can be either general or focused in scope.

General governmental entities try to promote the interests of a wide variety of street crime victims. On the federal level, there is a National Victims Resource Center funded by the Office for Victims of Crime of the U.S. Department of Justice. In many areas, the state Attorney

Chart One		
A Typology of Existing Advocacy Groups		
Type of Advocacy Group	**Kind of Advocacy**	**Examples**
General Independent Non-profit	public awareness, lobbying, training, needs assessment, evaluations, information clearinghouse	National Victims Center, National Organization for Victim Assistance
Focused Independent Non-profit	public awareness, lobbying, information clearinghouse	Mothers Against Drunk Driving
Self-help Group	mutual support, practical advice, direct aid, outreach	Parents of Murdered Children
Private For-profit	representation in civil lawsuits	law firms
General Governmental	data collection, information clearinghouse, public awareness, direct aid, referrals	Office For Victims Of Crime, victim-witness assistance programs
Focused Governmental	direct aid, referrals, public awareness	child protection agencies, battered women's shelters, rape crisis centers

General runs an office of victim-witness advocacy. On the county and municipal level, district attorneys operate victim-witness assistance programs (VWAPS) in which people with job titles like "victim-witness coordinator" offer tangible aid and supportive services to those who testify in behalf of the prosecution. In New York City, the Victim Services Agency offers many forms of assistance to a wide range of residents, commuters, and tourists harmed by street criminals.

Focused governmental agencies channel their energies towards aiding clearly defined groups of victims. On the state and local level, there are child welfare and child protection units that collaborate with court-appointed guardians-ad litem (who look after the best interests of children physically and sexually abused by their own parents); counselors at rape crisis centers; and staff members at domestic violence projects that shelter and assist battered women.

The typology that appears in Chart One shows that case advocacy is available from self-help support groups, private law firms handling civil suits, certain general governmental organizations (prosecutors' victim-witness assistance programs), and some focused governmental organizations (child protection agencies, shelters for battered women, rape crisis centers). But many organizations involved in advocacy operate on a political plane and do not directly intervene on a case-by-case basis. The practice of offering victims the services of knowledgeable consultants has not yet been institutionalized—provided routinely to all who want help, as a legal right (for all victims, not just a select few), from start-to-finish (beginning with the initial filing of a complaint with the police, and ending when the victim is satisfied that justice has been done, or that all reasonable options have been tried and exhausted). The institutionalization of case advocacy would not and should not eliminate the need for any of the general or focused non-profit, profit, or governmental organizations described above; it would supplement their activities by implementing the legacy of their accomplishments on a daily basis.

SCOPE OF THE RESPONSIBILITIES OF A VICTIM ADVOCATE

As a consequence of the movement's many victories, victims increasingly need

to be referred to knowledgeable professionals who are familiar with the complexities of new regulations and service-providers. Victims need to consult with experts concerned about their well-being before they start to interact with the long list of participants in the criminal justice process: the offenders (suspects, defendants, ultimately convicts) whom they accuse of harming them; police officers and detectives who investigate their complaints; assistant district attorneys who prosecute their cases; defense attorneys who attempt to undermine their credibility; judges who determine the conditions of bail and impose sentences; probation officers who prepare pre-sentence investigation reports that incorporate their views and recommendations; and corrections officials (including probation and parole officers and parole board members) who supervise the activities of convicts who may seek revenge or may be compelled to pay restitution. Victims must also deal with people who are not part of the criminal justice system per se, such as reporters who cover their cases; lawyers who pursue their civil lawsuits for damages; insurance company agents who handle their claims; state compensation boards that innocent victims of violent crimes who suffer out-of-pocket losses for medical bills and missed work turn to for reimbursement; and social service agencies that process applications for benefits and counseling.

The cause of victim empowerment has made substantial progress in recent years, in terms of reforming the laws of criminal procedure. For example, in 14 states, legislatures have passed a "Victims' Bill of Rights" either as constitutional amendments or as packages of new statutes. Victims are now entitled to find out about progress in their cases in 22 states, and are allowed to present their views at sentencing hearings in 37 states and at parole board meetings in 36 states. When convicts escape, the victims who helped send them to prison have a right to be notified of the potential danger they face in 29 states (National Victim Center, 1993).

The task of advocates will be to make sure that these recently enacted rights are taken seriously and put into practice in a systematic manner. Advocates will serve their clients in a number of ways: by explaining proceedings in layperson's terms; by monitoring developments in their cases; by asking for timely notification about optional and required appear-

ances at arraignments, evidentiary hearings, trials, sentencing hearings, and parole board meetings; by assisting victims who want to have input (in person or in writing) into the decision-making process regarding bail, sentencing, and parole; by arranging for all forms of assistance and services to which injured parties are entitled; by pursuing different strategies for recovering losses (through court-ordered restitution, state compensation, civil suits against offenders, lawsuits against grossly negligent third parties, and lawsuits against convicts who profit from their notoriety); and by helping to fill out and file complaints, requests for orders of protection, impact statements, insurance claims, and other applications; and by seeking to expedite the return of recovered stolen property held as evidence. Advocates will also attempt to arrange for stepped-up police protection from harassment, intimidation, or reprisals; and will try to fend off improper intrusions by the news media into their clients' personal privacy. The kinds of interventions in the victims' behalf that advocates will undertake are presented in Chart Two.

CONDITIONS NECESSITATING THE INSTITUTIONALIZATION OF VICTIM ADVOCACY

Advocacy must be institutionalized because a gap is growing between what ought to be happening and what is actually taking place within the criminal justice process. In theory, justice professionals working in law enforcement, adjudication, and corrections are supposed to be observing recently promulgated standards for fair treatment. In reality, there are reasons to suspect that many individuals harmed by offenders are not receiving the services, privileges, opportunities, and considerations to which they are entitled [although the degree to which victims' rights are actually being implemented has not yet been the subject of rigorous, systematic evaluations by victimologists and criminologists (see Karmen, 1990b)].

At present, the overwhelming majority of victims are not served by the existing networks of advocacy groups, according to the National Crime Victimization Survey. For example, only 3% of the respondents who reported the offenses committed against them to the police told interviewers that they received help or advice from some office or agency that deals with crime victims in 1991 (Dawson, Smith, and DeFrances, 1993).

Being informed is the simple, basic prerequisite for taking any actions and exercising any rights. But notification rights are often undermined by a hidden "catch-22." In most jurisdictions, victims must be aware that they must file specific requests that they want to be notified. [For example, in order to be informed about the final disposition or to be alerted that an inmate has escaped or has been released, victims are obliged to register with the proper authorities in New York State (see Cuomo, 1992)]. Evidence is accumulating that many victims are never informed of their right to be informed (see Gegan and Rodriguez, 1992). For instance, researchers who carried out a survey of correctional agencies in 1986 discovered that roughly half did not publicize notification rights; victims had to somehow find out on their own (National Victim Center, 1990). Lack of information might explain why most victims fail to attend sentencing hearings (Forer, 1980; Villmore and Neto, 1987); why many eligible victims do not express their views via victim impact statements in presentence investigation reports prepared by probation departments (Wells, 1990); and why only about 8% of all potentially eligible victims of violent crimes apply for state compensation (McCormack, 1989). People working in victim assistance programs recognize this problem: Over 75% reported that procedures needed to be improved in the areas of notifying victims about the status of police investigations; the defendant's bail; the official charges; the outcome of plea negotiations; court dates and schedule changes; and parole hearings and board decisions (Webster, 1988). Apparently, many eligible victims are not being "read their rights" by justice professionals, and thus need the services of advocates.

There is some evidence that prosecutors' offices are not relaying all the information they have to victims who may need to know about these developments, according to the findings of the National Prosecutor Survey. Whereas only 5% of prosecutors' offices failed to routinely notify victims when they had to appear in court, and only 3% didn't regularly inform victims of the disposition of felony cases concerning them, as many as 27% of the offices in the sample failed to

notify victims about the release of the felons they helped to incarcerate (Dawson, 1992; Dawson, Smith, and DeFrances, 1993). Again, the services of advocates might improve the flow of information to interested victims.

Similar arguments can be made that many victims are not taking full advantage of their rights to try to influence key decisions, their chances to receive reimbursement, their entitlements to enhanced protection from reprisals, and their opportunities to safeguard their privacy.

Institutionalizing advocacy appears to be the best solution.

One pressing problem surrounding the implementation of victims rights is that there are no remedies for the aggrieved parties when officials and agencies fail to meet these standards for fair treatment. Victims have no constitutional standing for a cause of action, cannot nullify decisions made in their absence and without their knowledge, and can't sue for monetary damage when they are ignored or overlooked (Gewurz and Mercurio,

Chart Two
An Overview of The Responsibilities of Advocates

Contacts With	Concerning These Issues
Police Department	Complaints about officers' insensitivity; Requests to keep investigation open; Inquiries about progress in the case; Requests for the return of recovered stolen property; Requests for protection from harassment, reprisals.
Prosecutor's Office	Complaints about ADA's behavior; Requests for the return of recovered stolen property held as evidence; Desires about pressing or dropping charges; Demands for input into plea negotiations; Recommendations about retribution and/or restitution, offender rehabilitation, mutual reconciliation; Requests for protection from harassment, reprisals; Requests for intercession with creditors, employers; Calls for assistance to facilitate court appearances; Requests for speedy resolution of the case; Orientation in anticipation of testifying.
Judges	Requests that "no contact" be a condition of granting bail; Obtaining an order of protection; Attempts to influence the sentence via an impact statement or allocution; recommendations concerning retribution, restitution, offender rehabilitation, mutual reconciliation.
Probation Department	Completion of victim impact statement; Inclusion of views into pre-sentence report; Complaints about probationer's harassment; Complaints about probationer's failure to pay restitution.
Corrections Department	Inquiries about prisoner's whereabouts; Complaints about telephone harassment.
Parole Department	Notice of upcoming parole hearings; Presentation of views to parole board; Complaints about parolee's harassment; Complaints about parolee's failure to pay restitution.
State Compensation Board	Assistance in filing an application; Obtaining of emergency loans; Appeal over the amount of restitution.
Civil Court	Referral to a lawyer specializing in civil lawsuits; Assistance in the prepartion of a case for small claims court; Assistance in collection of a judgment.
Social Service Agencies	Referrals to counseling, support groups; Securing all benefits and entitlements; Appeals of decisions.
News Media	Complaints about violations of privacy; Complaints about inaccuracies in coverage.

1992). Focusing again on the issue of notification, only 18 adult state corrections departments, 13 juvenile state corrections departments, and 18 state parole departments had adopted formal procedures for handling victims' complaints about notification and participation rights, according to a 1991 survey (National Victim Center, 1991). Since victims have little or no recourse once their rights are violated, prevention is the best solution, and institutionalizing advocacy is the best means of preventing the need for redress of grievances.

Without advocates "in their corner" to vigorously defend their rights, more and more victims may come to believe the scathing and cynical, but possibly accurate and realistic denunciations voiced by skeptics and critics. Pronouncements that victims' rights will be scrupulously observed by officials have been dismissed by critics as "paper promises" without any real substance that deceptively feed a fallacy of victim empowerment; as simply "cosmetic" changes by legislators looking to placate constituents who are demanding that something be done; as a mere "genuflection to ritualistic legalism" which may have a "placebo value;" and as manipulative exercises in "symbolic politics," which actually leave victims "all dressed up with no place to go" (see Elias, 1983; 1990; 1993; Gegan and Rodriguez, 1992; and Walsh, 1992).

THE NEED FOR INDEPENDENCE

In order to faithfully serve their clients, advocates must be independent of any compromising affiliations with branches of government that have their own agendas.

Some criminal justice agencies already provide victims with advocates. About 34% of all police departments, 38% of all sheriffs' departments, and 77% of all prosecutors' offices report that they have established victim assistance programs, according to a national survey carried out in 1986 (Webster, 1988). Some county and state corrections departments are adding victim advocates to their staffs as well (National Victims Center, 1990; "Corrections Victim Services Director Named," 1993). These advocates are undoubtedly dedicated people, but they face an unavoidable conflict of interests. They must carry out the directives of the agency that employs them, even at the expense of the wants and needs of the victims they are supposed to represent. This is an untenable and compromising

position to be in, once the potential for differing interests and a falling out between victims and criminal justice agencies is recognized (see Karmen, 1992).

To defend and advance what their clients define as their own best interests, advocates must be independent of police departments and sheriffs' offices for the following reasons. Victims can be dissatisfied with the performance of their ostensible allies whenever law enforcement agencies fail to live up to their motto of "to protect and serve." Specifically, victims might be angered or upset if police don't respond quickly enough, don't act professionally, don't believe their versions of events, don't make arrests, close investigations prematurely, fail to locate stolen property, and obtain evidence improperly so that it can't be used in court. Given fairly high non-reporting rates for certain crimes, disappointingly low clearance rates, and abysmally low stolen property recovery rates (see Karmen, 1990a), many dissatisfied victims will want the help of independent advocates to intercede in their behalf with law enforcement authorities.

Effective advocates must be independent of district attorneys as well. First of all, most victims cannot avail themselves of the services of advocates provided by prosecutors' offices because their cases will never reach the adjudication stage: the crimes are not solved, or charges leveled at the time of arrest are later dismissed or dropped. In cases that are pursued, these star witnesses for the state want protection from further harm, progress reports about important developments, consultation before key decisions are made, and information afterwards. But victims can become embroiled in disagreements with "their" lawyers, furnished for free by offices that portray themselves as "the publics' law firm," over being excluded and lost opportunities because of dropped charges, bargained-down convictions, or unwanted trials. Well-meaning "in-house" advocates working for prosecutor-based victim-witness units can find themselves torn between representing the vested interests of the "state" in general and their offices and supervisors in particular, and attending to the wants and needs of their "clients" for retribution, or offender rehabilitation, or restitution and mutual reconciliation.

A proposed "code of ethics" has been developed by the general, independent National Organization For Victim Assis-

tance (NOVA). Advocates are urged to foster "maximum self-determination" and "act on behalf of the victim's stated needs, without regard to personal convictions and within the social and legal parameters of the agency" and "without concern about personal gain" (NOVA Standards And Ethics Committee, 1993:4). These prescriptions will be very difficult to observe for those who are employed by police departments or prosecutors' offices; advocates working for an agency independent of the state in the adversary system will have less problems in living up to these ideals.

In sum, victims need independent advocates because the police and the prosecution are really not "on their side" despite their strategic alliance within the adversary system.

ANTICIPATING HOW ADVOCATES WILL BE PROVIDED AND FUNDED

Complainants can be provided with advocates, free of charge, as soon as they enter police stations, just like attorneys are made available to indigent defendants. Advocates could be furnished by an independent government agency (comparable to the public defender's office), or supplied by a non-profit organization largely funded by charitable donations (similar to New York City's Legal Aid Society). Top notch advocates will have their own private practices, like defense attorneys, private investigators, forensic scientists, or jury consultants, and will be retained for a fee by those who can afford their services. In some jurisdictions, their services will be offered to indigents on a contract basis, just like lawyers are drafted to do pro-bono work or appointed to participate in an "assigned counsel plan." The competition that arises from supplying advocates from a number of sources might work to the advantage of victims, just as furnishing lawyers to indigents in several ways provides flexibility and facilitates correcting malpractice and abuse (see Fritsch, 1994).

If victim advocacy can be entirely financed by funds generated by civil forfeitures (for instance, of drug dealers' assets) in conjunction with penalty assessments levied against convicts, that will put to rest one inevitable objection: creating a new fiscal burden for taxpayers. Congress established a Crime

Victims Fund to help pay for advocacy and assistance programs with money raised from fines and fees imposed on convicts in federal courts, as part of the Victims Of Crime Act passed in 1984 (Finn and Lee, 1988). (In fact, Congress has passed major legislation furthering victim assistance and advocacy at the end of its session in every even-numbered election year (Stein, 1991). Currently, money raised largely from fines and surcharges against offenders and traffic law violators, among other sources, pays for domestic violence intervention programs in 48 states, for county victim-witness assistance programs in 34 states, and for rape crisis centers in 25 states (Roberts, 1990).

EDUCATING PEOPLE TO BECOME PROFESSIONAL ADVOCATES

Today, some of the most dedicated advocates are volunteers who know from bitter, first-hand experience about the depth of suffering criminals can inflict. While there is no substitute for the sensitizing effects of being victimized, advocacy draws upon a much wider range of skills that require formal instruction, advanced education, and special preparation. Professionalization will enable advocates to command greater respect from their criminal justice colleagues, exercise more authority to influence proceedings in behalf of their clients, and meet uniform standards for employment and accountability imposed by federal and state funding sources (Young, 1993a). Today, most of the dedicated volunteers, student interns, and paraprofessionals hired as advocates by service providers are engaged in some form of counseling (see Young, 1993b).

Advocates have to understand basic forensic psychology (about such matters as the "battered woman's syndrome" or the "rape crisis trauma"), to refer distraught persons to appropriate experts, and to exercise crisis intervention skills, but they need not be certified social workers or therapists. Advocates need to understand their state's criminal codes and regulations governing criminal procedure, but they need not be law school graduates or practicing attorneys. Advocates must understand how the criminal justice system is supposed to operate as well as how it actually functions, but they need not have backgrounds as practi-

tioners. A bachelor's degree with a major in criminal justice (including a course in victimology), coupled with a minor in counseling or government or public administration, would be desirable for entry level positions. Supervisors could be former practitioners, lawyers, and social workers.

Institutionalizing victim advocacy will stimulate the growth of criminal justice education by introducing a new career path for humanistically oriented students. The creation of a large number of jobs in the field should open up meaningful opportunities for groups of people who have traditionally been under-represented in criminal justice professions but overrepresented in the ranks of victims: minorities, the urban poor, women, recent immigrants who speak foreign languages fluently, and individuals with special sensitivities (to the plight of incest survivors, abused elders, battered women, and targets of bias-motivated hate crimes, for example). Advocates would presumably have better rapport and be more effective if they resembled the people who were harmed, in terms of age, gender, race/ethnicity, and other characteristics, whenever possible.

THE POTENTIAL SOCIAL IMPACT OF VICTIM ADVOCACY

Institutionalizing victim advocacy may have contradictory effects on what has been called the "differential handling" of cases, or a "double standard" or "dual system" of justice. In the not-too-distant past, before the victims' plight was rediscovered, the needs and wants of nearly all victims were routinely overlooked. Today, some victims get "first class," "V.I.P.," or "red carpet" treatment, but most others continue to get "second class" service within the criminal justice process. How the case is handled depends upon a complex web of factors largely influenced by the social status of the victim as well as the offender, and the nature of the prior relationship (if any) between them. Researchers have documented how those who are underprivileged and disadvantaged generally receive less consideration and less satisfactory handling from justice professionals and agencies (see Karmen, 1990a). It is suspected that the victims who are most effective in exercising their rights are people of higher social status (for instance, in terms of their impact statements

influencing sentencing, see Abramovsky, 1992). Victims with powerful connections, who know how to access the system and negotiate with its key personnel, and who personify important test cases are now finding lawyers to advocate in their behalf (especially during the sentencing phase—see Rowland, 1992). But the kinds of people who suffer the most often, statistically speaking, are those at the other end of the social spectrum. For example, according to the National Crime Victimization Survey, females who face the highest risks of being harmed by a crime of violence like robbery, assault, or rape tend to be black or hispanic, in their late teens or early twenties, unmarried, poor, with limited educational achievements, who reside in central cities (Bachman, 1994). It is likely that these victims are not being provided with all the information they need to know, and all the forms of assistance to which they may be entitled. Therefore, the current situation of "differential access to justice" is quickly becoming more and more unfair, violating notions of "equal protection under law." Access to the system's services and benefits should not be determined by the victims' social standing and financial position. Providing victims from all walks of life with advocates potentially contributes to an equalization of the way everyone's cases are handled.

However, all advocates will not be of equal caliber, and due to varying caseloads, won't be able to devote as much time to some clients as to others. The evolving situation is analogous to providing defendants with legal representation. Lawyers provided for free are better than no lawyers at all, but are not as seasoned, skilled, well-connected, persuasive, and effective as private attorneys in prestigious law firms who can devote more effort and resources to clients who pay high fees. Similarly, providing most victims with publicly supplied advocates while permitting a fortunate few to select the services of high priced professional advocates in private practice may allow glaring inequalities in case handling to re-emerge.

One more consideration merits attention. Institutionalizing advocacy might undermine the spirit of commitment and degree of dedication that inspires most people who identify themselves as part of the victims' movement and are currently engaged in outreach, lobbying, and support activities. Many feel part of a "cause" or "mission" or even "crusade" to advance victims' rights, which means their work is more than just a job or career or even a profession. Again, the closest analogy is with the procedural safeguards and due process guarantees accorded to defendants. The public defender system that arose out of judicial interpretations of the right of indigents to legal counsel within the adversary system never lived up to the equalizing potential that its proponents predicted—but it also did not undermine case processing the way its opponents feared (see Barak, 1980). In the field of victim advocacy, parallel developments are evident, especially in the battered women's movement and the anti-rape movement. The pioneers of advocacy at the first rape crisis centers and shelters for battered women tended to be ardent feminists who had been assaulted themselves. Interpreting rapes and beatings as symbolic of male aggression and female oppression, they set up grass-roots community-based projects stressing self-help, peer support, consciousness-raising and political mobilization (especially challenges to the male-dominated justice system). As the years passed, more pragmatic and less ideological staff members began to reject the non-hierarchical, "unprofessional," and anti-governmental stance of the original advocates. Avoiding radical critiques, the second wave of advocates stressed securing government funding, gaining referrals from hospitals and the police, and cultivating good working relationships with law enforcement agencies and prosecutors' offices. To the founders of rape crisis centers and shelters for battered women, the new emphasis on providing enhanced services signalled a retreat from the original mission of empowering victimized females to become agents for fundamental social change (Amir and Amir, 1979; Schecter, 1982). Therefore, this reform of the system, like all others, is subject to cooptation. Goal displacement always occurs when dramatic changes are institutionalized and the pioneering efforts of charismatic leaders and dedicated followers are routinized and bureaucratized.

Institutionalizing victim advocacy can contribute to the realization of one of the system's stated purposes, delivering justice to victims, in the sense of helping to restore them to the condition they were in before the crime occurred (to the extent that that is possible). Advocates can pressure officials and agencies to be more responsive and accountable for their actions, and can make decision-making more individualized, and less rigid, unimaginative, and beyond community control. Victims supported by advocates might be able to nudge the system towards providing real protection to society, meaningful rehabilitation to offenders, genuine opportunities to convicts to receive job training and job placement so they can make restitution, and more experimental programs designed to try to bring about victim-offender reconciliation and to restore harmony to strife-torn, crime-ridden communities.

The potential for balancing the scales of justice embodied in the original impetus towards advocacy may never be fully realized. And yet, institutionalized universal advocacy is clearly an idea whose time has come. Recruiting people to become a new kind of justice professional is a step in the right direction, in pursuit of the elusive ideals of "fair treatment" and "equal protection under law."

BIBLIOGRAPHY

Abramovsky, A. 1992. "Victim impact statements: Adversely impacting upon judicial fairness." *St. John's Journal of Legal Commentary,* 8, 1 (Fall): 21-35.

Amir, D. and Amir, M. 1979. "Rape crisis centers: An arena for ideological conflicts." *Victimology,* 4, 2: 247-257.

Bachman, R. 1994. Violence Against Women: A National Crime Victimization Report. Bureau of Justice Statistics. Washington, D.C.: U.S. Department of Justice.

Barak, G. 1980. *In Defense Of Whom: A Critique Of Criminal Justice Reform.* Cincinnati: Anderson.

"Corrections victim services director named." 1993. *Crime Victims Digest,* 10, 9 (September): 5.

Cuomo, M. 1992. "The crime victim in a system of criminal justice." *St. John's Journal of Legal Commentary,* 8, 1 (Fall): 1-20.

Dawson, J. 1992. Prosecutors In State Courts, 1990. Bureau of Justice Statistics Bulletin. Washington, D.C.: U.S. Department Of Justice.

Dawson, J. Smith, S., and DeFrances, C. 1993. Prosecutors In State Courts, 1992. Bureau of Justice Statistics Bulletin. Washington, D.C.: U.S. Department Of Justice.

Elias, R. 1983. "The symbolic politics of victim compensation." *Victimology,* 8, 103–112.

—— 1986. *The Politics Of Victimization: Victims, Victimology, And Human Rights.* New York: Oxford University Press.

—— 1990. "Which victim movement?" Pp. 226–251 in A. Lurigio, W. Skogan and R. Davis (eds.), *Victims of Crime.* Newbury Park, Ca.: Sage.

—– 1993. *Victims Still: The Political Manipulation Of Crime Victims.* Newbury Park, Ca.: Sage.

Finn, P. and Lee, B. 1988. *Establishing And Expanding Victim-Witness Assistance Programs.* National Institute Of Justice, Research In Action. Washington, D.C.: U.S. Department of Justice.

Fritsch, J. 1994. "Legal Aid is given bigger court role." *New York Times,* June 14, pp. A1, B3.

Forer, L. 1980. *Criminals And Victims: A Trial Judge Reflects On Crime And Punishment.* New York: Norton.

Gegan, S. and Rodriguez, N. 1992. "Victims' roles in the criminal justice system: A fallacy of empowerment." *St. John's Journal of Legal Commentary,* 8, 1 (Fall): 225-250.

Gewurz, D. and Mercurio, M. 1992. "The victims' bill of rights: Are victims all dressed up with no place to go?" *St. John's Journal of Legal Commentary,* 8, 1 (Fall): 225-250.

Karmen, A. 1990a. *Crime Victims: An Introduction To Victimology.* Second Edition. Belmont, Ca.: Wadsworth.

—— 1990b. "The implementation of victims' rights: A challenge for criminal justice professionals." Pp. 46-57 in R. Muraskin (ed.), *Issues In Justice: Exploring Policy Issues In The Criminal Justice System.* Bristol, In.: Wyndham Hall.

—— 1992. "Who's against victims' rights? The nature of the opposition to pro-victim initiatives in criminal justice." *St. John's Journal Of Legal Commentary,* 8, 1 (Fall): 157-176.

McCormack, R. 1989. *A Perspective On United States Crime Victim Assistance.* Paper presented at the annual meeting of the Academy Of Criminal Justice Sciences, Washington, D.C.

National Victim Center. 1991. National Victim Services Survey Of Adult And Juvenile Corrections And Parole Agencies. Final Report. Fort Worth, Tx.: National Victim Center.

—— 1993. Crime And Victimization In America: Statistical Overview. Fort Worth, Tx.: National Victim Center.

NOVA Standards and Ethics Committee. 1993. "Proposed Ethics Code For Victim Advocates. *NOVA* Newsletter, 16, 9: 4.

Roberts, A. 1990. *Helping Crime Victims: Research, Policy, and Practice.* Newbury Park, Ca.: Sage.

Rowland, J. 1992. "Illusion of justice: Who represents the victim?" *St. John's Journal of Legal Commentary,* 8, 1 (Fall): 177-196.

Schechter, S. 1982. Women And Male Violence. Boston: South End Press.

Stein, J. 1993. "Congress kills VOCA's spending cap; Clinton pledges 'Advocate' in OVC post." *NOVA* Newsletter, 16, 1:1-2.

Young, M. 1993a. "Victim services as a profession." *NOVA* Newsletter, 16, 3: 1-10.

—— 1993b. "Supportive counseling and advocacy." *NOVA* Newsletter, 16, 5: 1-13.

Villmore, E. and Neto, V. 1987. Victim Appearances At Sentencing Under California's Victims' Bill Of Rights. National Institute of Justice Research In Brief. Washington, D.C.: U.S. Department of Justice.

Walsh, A. 1992. "Placebo justice: Victim recommendations and offender sentences in sexual assault cases." Pp. 295–311 in E. Fattah (ed.), *Toward A Critical Victimology.* New York: St. Martin's Press.

Webster, B. 1988. Victim Assistance Programs Report Increased Workloads. National Institute of Justice, Research In Action. Washington, D.C.: U.S. Department of Justice.

Wells, R. 1990. "Considering victim impact— The role of probation." *Federal Probation* (September): 26-29.

Computer Technology Comes to Aid of Crime Victims

Robert Davis

USA TODAY

The day after Mary Byron's boyfriend posted bail on a charge of raping her, he shot her seven times and left her body slumped in her car on top of a balloon and bouquet of flowers.

Police had promised to warn Byron when Donavan Harris was released. But even they didn't know he was out hunting for her on her 21st birthday.

Now, a computerized victim notification system inspired by Byron's death is being copied across the nation. And Kentucky Gov. Brereton Jones has announced plans to expand the Louisville-based system—Victim Information Notification Everyday, or VINE—statewide.

"You'd think being in jail would cool somebody off, but they really do go right back home and right to the victim," says Betsy Carter Helm, Jefferson County Corrections Department systems manager. "It's amazing . . . the cycle of violence."

After Byron's murder, county officials gathered to see if they could stop the cycle. Helm focused everyone's attention on the computerized process of releasing inmates. Before somebody can be released, jail officials type information the court orders into a computer. In January, they programmed the system to also call a victim as soon as check-out begins.

The computer keeps calling until somebody answers, and a taped message warns victims that their accused attackers are about to be freed. In most cases, calls are made before suspects leave jail.

"The victim needs to be notified the instant somebody is released," says Marcia Roth, executive director of the Jefferson County Office for Women. "Time is the key."

Across the nation, 34 states have laws requiring officials to notify victims when suspects are released from jail before trial. Others have laws requiring victims of sex offenders to be notified when their attackers are released.

Louisville system: Anyone can call for updates on inmates

The victim notification system in Louisville is computer based.

When somebody wants to follow the status of an inmate in the county jail, he can call the computer system. By spelling out the person's name, the caller can:

► Check the inmate's location and arrest number.

► Find out when the next hearing is scheduled for the inmate and when the inmate is scheduled for release.

► Register to be called when the inmate is released.

The inmate never knows who is calling about the case. And only information that is available to the public is released on the system.

When paperwork arrives from the court ordering the inmate's release, jail staffers begin typing the information into the computer.

As soon as the computer recognizes the inmate is to be released, it begins calling anyone registered for notification.

Anyone can be registered to be notified of a release.

The computer calls repeatedly until somebody answers. Jail staffers monitor the calls by watching printed lists.

—Robert Davis

Victim notification is not a new concept. Prison officials have routinely notified victims when offenders are about to finish serving time. But those are often made by mail and can come years after an offense.

Louisville and other local officials say their goal is to protect people, especially victims of domestic violence, who have put their attackers in jail days or weeks earlier.

But in the bureaucracy of most justice systems, such simple tasks can be delayed by already overextended workers.

"If you've got somebody on a coffee break, you've lost that valuable lead time," Roth says.

Computers never rest.

"We think technology needs to be utilized a lot more in order to protect crime victims," says Aileen Adams of the U.S. Justice Department's Office for Victims of Crime.

► In New Jersey, Passaic County officials will have a system similar to Kentucky's running next month. Officials expect to notify about 1,000 victims a year in their county of 456,100. They're using money confiscated from criminals to launch the system. They're considering expanding the system to notify the victims of every crime.

If nobody answers the computer's bilingual call, an officer is sent to post a notice at the victim's home.

► In Memphis, officials are grappling with how to pay for the technology. The Louisville system costs $55,000 to start and $57,000 a year to run. But, "when you're talking about one human life, how much is that worth," asks Linda Miller of the Shelby County Government Victim Assistance Center in Memphis. "It's a tough call."

One criticism of computer notification is that mere machines are delivering a wrenching message.

"It's conveying a message that's very frightening and there's no person for the

Notification of the victim

Most states have some kind of law requiring officials to notify victims of violent crimes when the suspect or inmate is about to be released from custody.

State	Type of release			Who is given sex offender information
	Bail	Parole	Other	
Ala.		✔		Police
Alaska		✔		Public
Ariz.	✔	✔	✔	Police
Ark.		✔		Police
Calif.		✔		Police
Colo.	✔		✔	Police
Conn.	✔	✔	✔	Police
Del.		✔		Police; employers of children
D.C.				No law
Fla.	✔	✔	✔	Police
Ga.		✔		Public
Hawaii	✔	✔		Criminal Justice Center
Idaho	✔	✔	✔	Police; on request
Ill.	✔	✔	✔	Police
Ind.		✔		Schools; employers of children
Iowa	✔	✔		No law
Kan.		✔	✔	Public
Ky.	✔		✔	Police
La.	✔	✔	✔	Public[1]
Maine		✔	✔	No law
Md.		✔	✔	No law
Mass.	✔	✔	✔	No law
Mich.	✔	✔	✔	Police
Minn.		✔	✔	Police
Miss.		✔	✔	Police
Mo.	✔	✔	✔	Courts, police
Mont.	✔	✔	✔	No law
Neb.		✔		No law
Nev.	✔	✔	✔	Police
N.H.		✔	✔	Police
N.J.		✔	✔	Police
N.M.		✔	✔	No law
N.Y.	✔	✔	✔	No law
N.C.	✔	✔	✔	No law
N.D.	✔	✔	✔	Public
Ohio		✔	✔	No law
Okla.		✔		Police
Ore.		✔		Criminal Justice agencies
Pa.		✔		No law
R.I.	✔	✔	✔	No law
S.C.	✔	✔	✔	Courts, police
S.D.	✔	✔	✔	DNA database
Tenn.		✔		Police, district attorneys
Texas		✔	✔	Police
Utah		✔	✔	Police, schools
Vt.	✔	✔	✔	No law
Va.		✔		No law
Wash.		✔	✔	Public[1]
W.Va.	✔	✔	✔	Police
Wis.		✔		Police
Wyo.	✔	✔	✔	No law

1–If necessary for public protection
Sources: National Victim Center, National Clearinghouse on Child Abuse and Neglect Information

victim to talk to," she says. "The message that's conveyed needs to be victim-friendly."

What victims do when they get the call ranges from hiding to arming themselves.

One Louisville woman got the message that her abuser was back on the street and went to get a gun. She returned home to find her knife-wielding husband hiding in her closet. She held him at gunpoint while her son dialed 911. He was arrested.

Says Byron's father, John Byron: "Had we known the assailant was out, our daughter would not have been working that day, probably not even within the state."

A jury convicted Harris last month. He's scheduled to be sentenced for rape and murder Oct. 2.

A lawsuit the Byron family filed against police was dismissed by a local judge and is being considered by an appeals court.

VINE "is a system that probably would have saved her life," John Byron says.

Beyond saving lives, Louisville officials say the system has given crime victims a way to stay involved with the case.

One woman learned from the system that her abusive husband's lawyer had quietly changed a court appearance.

"When his lawyer told the judge he was no danger, she stood and said 'I'm here and I am in danger,' " Roth says. "She can find out every single day, every hour of the day where he is."

The knowledge lets victims live without feeling like they have to constantly look over their shoulders for trouble.

"Basically, with this system, we're saying to the victim, this is not just your burden. It's a crime against the community," says Roth. "This is all of our problem."

The Police

The recent O. J. Simpson trial, and the role in it of police officer Mark Fuhrman, did little to help the image of the American police. Many people, though, believe that the problems presented by this case are not universal. The police can help themselves improve their status by striving to achieve professionalism. "Police and the Quest for Professionalism" presents a short overview of the problems that police face and supports community policing as one step toward reaching that goal. Community policing is also the topic of the interviews presented in "Officers from Rural, Suburban, and Urban Jurisdictions Share Views." The article "Police Work from a Woman's Perspective" explores the problems still present as women assume a greater role in policing.

An interesting interview by *Law Enforcement News* with a renowned expert in policing, Professor Carl Klock-

ars of the University of Delaware, covers subjects ranging from community policing to scholarly research. Then, "The Crooked Blue Line" discusses some of the issues raised by the Mark Fuhrman allegations, such as corruption and brutality, and offers corrective measures. In this unit's concluding article, "The Thin White Line," the problems in trying to increase minority representation in the police ranks are discussed.

Looking Ahead: Challenge Questions

There is "community policing" in your area, how well is it working?

What can the police do to help recover from the negative impact of the Mark Fuhrman incidents?

How can the racial mix in the population be more reflected in police forces?

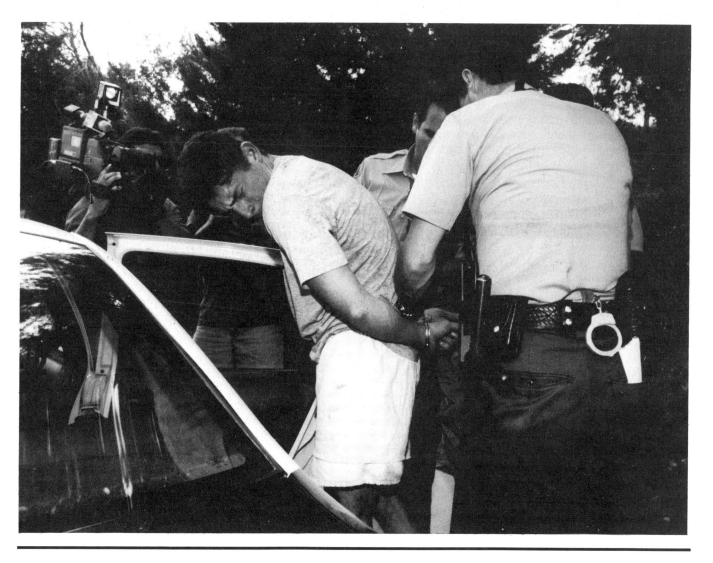

Police & the Quest for Professionalism

Barbara Raffel Price

Barbara Raffel Price is the Dean of Graduate Studies and a professor of criminal justice at John Jay College of Criminal Justice.

Since the early 1900's, under the leadership of August Vollmer, the father of American policing, law enforcement has been fascinated by the possibilities of professionalism. For the police in those early years, professionalism meant control of their work world with an end to interference from corrupt politicians who appointed unqualified patrolmen and interfered with or controlled hiring, firing and assignment. For Vollmer, professionalism also held a loftier meaning – something he called "scientific policing," which emphasized a style of policing that was detached, objective and, especially, adopted techniques that took advantage of the latest scientific advances in detecting and solving crimes and in approaches to patrolling a community.

Soon after Vollmer appeared on the scene, the police incorporated the term "professionalism" into their public rhetoric. However, policing remained an occupation that had far to go before it would be considered a profession. The principal barrier to professionalism, then as now, is the fact that policing is in one fundamental way unlike any other field striving to professionalize: It has the duty and the right to use coercion, an act that fosters a work culture antithetical to professionalism (which is usually understood to mean service to the client).

Professionalism normally entails:

- A transmittable body of knowledge which is constantly growing and being refined;
- A code of ethics defining relations between members of the profession and the public, including an obligation to render services exclusive of any other considerations;
- High standards for membership, often including higher education and formal training;
- Accountability through peer review and, therefore, continuous evaluation and improvement through research of professional practices;

- At some point in the evolution of the occupation, acknowledgement from outsiders that the occupation is a profession.

Although these demanding criteria arguably present significant obstacles to efficient policing, many continue to believe in and work toward the professionalization of law enforcement. Central to that effort over the years – dating back at least to the Wickersham Commission in 1931 – has been an insistence that educational levels of police be raised. More recently, in 1973, the National Commission on Criminal Justice Standards and Goals urged that by 1982, every police department in the United States require four years of college education. In 1995, however, only a relative handful of departments require recruits to have a college degree. It bears mentioning, too, that most police unions have vehemently opposed education for recruits, as they have other components of professionalization, including peer review and accountability.

> *"If there is a future to the professionalization of policing, many believe it rests in pursuing community policing. Others insist that it is an impossible dream."*

Why is professionalism a goal of law enforcement? The most basic answer is that public confidence in the police is essential for order maintenance and stability in the community. When the police are distrusted, government itself is undermined. Professionalism instills confidence and respect because it means to the public that the practitioners have internalized values of service, even altruism, self-control and commitment to high ideals of behavior. Further, professionalism implies higher education. Many have argued that higher education will help police gain an understanding of their role in a democratic society and a fuller comprehension of the responsibilities that come with police power. The President's Crime Commission in 1967 observed that the complexities of policing "dictate that officers possess a high degree of intelligence, education, tact and judgment" and said it was "essential . . . that the requirements to serve in law enforcement reflect the awesome responsibility" facing the personnel selected.

Since the 1960s, when the Federal Government began to assume a major role in upgrading the quality of law enforcement, significant progress has been made, notwithstanding that policing remains fraught with problems. Police are better educated today. Departments are more representative of the communities and populations they serve. Police are more restrained in the use of deadly force. Research on policing, virtually nonexistent in the 1950s, has expanded to a considerable volume generated by universities, private research institutes, nonprofit foundations and Federal agencies. Much more of it is needed.

With the introduction of the patrol car and the two-way radio, the hallmarks of police professionalism were efficiency, as measured by clearance rates, and speed in response to calls. Following the widespread urban unrest of the mid- to late 1960s, law enforcement developed a strategy of community relations that stressed police sensitivity to diverse needs and cultures within the community.

For the past few years, the focus within policing has been directed toward a new, comprehensive strategy called, variously, community policing or problem-oriented policing. In order to work, community policing requires professional police who have acquired nontraditional police skills so that they can involve the community as a co-participant in the control of crime and maintenance of order. Community policing also requires that communities develop consensus as to what steps should be taken to prevent or reduce crime and it requires cooperation and follow-through by the police and the community.

The question arises as to whether a level of trust sufficient to work with the police exists in those communities that are most crime-ridden. Community policing also raises questions as to whether police have the requisite community organization skills, problem-solving skills, and the ability to mobilize scarce community resources to solve problems.

If there is a future to the professionalization of policing, many in law enforcement believe it rests in pursuing community policing. But others insist that it is an impossible dream—from the community's standpoint there is too little cohesion or ability to respond to police initiatives; from the police standpoint, the requisite skills are difficult to obtain and require midmanagement support and facilitation that has, to date, been notably lacking. And then there is the question of availability of resources in the community and their efficacy for solving problems.

About the same time that community policing was taking root around the country, the beating of Rodney King by Los Angeles police was recorded on home video and broadcast worldwide. Other similar incidents of police violence have been noted as well. Public support and trust of the police eroded substantially in the wake of such episodes. Moreover, some have noted the irony of this happening even as advancing professionalism on a variety of fronts (education, organizational structure, accountability and technology) has altered some agencies dramatically within the past decade.

The loss of confidence in the police is due, in part, to the steady increase in the high visibility of crime, including drug abuse, youth gangs, organized crime, and terrorism, and the sense—almost certainly false—that we now have a more disorderly and violent society than at any time in our history. Certainly with the abandonment of President Lyndon Johnson's "war on poverty," socioeconomic divisions have widened, and racism continues to be a major source of tension. In this context, the prognosis for community policing, which has been hailed by the police themselves as "smarter policing" and as the best hope yet for the professionalization of policing, is guarded at best.

With police brutality still a significant factor in 1995, it is difficult to claim that professionalism has taken hold in law enforcement. Eradicating the excessive use of force and the scourge of police corruption are the most critical internal issues police face if they are to continue on the long and arduous course toward professionalism. There have been many successes of late for law enforcement, especially in communications technology, forensics, information systems, interagency cooperation, and the development of a commitment to their peers, if not to professional conduct. But until attitudes of the police toward those they serve can be changed, they will continue to make their own jobs more difficult and more dangerous—and professionalism for the police will not come to pass.

Police Work From a Woman's Perspective

James M. Daum, Ph.D., Police Psychologist, Lippert, Daum and Associates; and Lieutenant Cindy M. Johns, Cincinnati Police Division

Since women have joined the ranks, much attention has been paid to their impact on the police organization and the community. However, comparatively little research has been conducted to determine how the police organization and the community have affected the female police officer. Common wisdom might lead one to believe that becoming a police officer would bring about a more radical change in a woman's life than in a man's. Police work remains a predominantly male occupation, and there is still a remnant of the traditional belief that assertiveness, aggressiveness, physical capability and emotional toughness are "male" characteristics necessary to perform competently as a police officer. When a woman displays these very same characteristics, she is often perceived as "cold," "pushy" or somehow in violation of the role socially prescribed for her gender.

For a man, a career in law enforcement is an option he can select without question. To become an officer, he must demonstrate that he possesses the knowledge, skills and abilities to do the job. In contrast, a woman aspiring to become a police officer is often viewed as unusual. This makes her "different" from other women. In order to become an officer, she must not only prove that she has the "KSAs", but also deal with the obstacles posed by being a true minority. Rather than proving that she can be as good as any other officer, she has to prove that she is as good as any *male* officer. In other words, there is pressure for her to be what she is not—which is male.

She also faces the problem of not being taken seriously as an officer. Although this lack of respect occurs most frequently among her fellow (male) officers, she sometimes encounters this same problem in the community, from citizens who request a male officer after she responds to the call. Although legal and formal organizational barriers no longer exist, a woman is still subjected to the stereotype of being one of "the weaker sex" and therefore not as capable as a man. As such, she must fight a steep uphill battle to gain acceptance as an officer.

What type of impact might such barriers and pressures have upon the female police officer? One might expect a high stress level, along with such side effects as undesirable changes in personality, health, job performance and home life. However, it could also be argued that working to combat stereotypes and gain acceptance has reward value, and that job success might provide a greater feeling of accomplishment. All that can be stated with certainty is that for women, being socialized into a police organization presents a considerable challenge.

Procedure

Eighty-one of the 122 female police officers of a metropolitan police department completed surveys while attending a one-day workshop that addressed issues of women in policing. Participation in this workshop was voluntary, so 41 of these police women did not attend. Thus, the survey results do not represent all of the female members of the department. However, it can be asserted that those who filled out the surveys have an interest in women's issues in policing, and are therefore probably aware of gender-related problems facing female officers.

Of the 12 supervisors and 69 officers who responded, 51 worked in patrol, with the remaining 30 serving in a non-patrol capacity. Eighteen respondents had been with the department for two or fewer years, 23 had been police officers for three to five years, 12 had been officers for six to 10 years and the remaining 27 had been with the division for more than 10 years. Fifty-two respondents were white, 28 were African-American and one was Hispanic.

Results

It is important to note that these findings represent the perceptions of the women who completed the surveys. Their opinions were not verified by consulting outside sources of information, such as performance evaluations, disciplinary records or other documentation. The focus of this study is not on the police department itself, but rather the perceptions, attitudes and behaviors developed among female officers through their exposure to police work.

Acceptance

Asked whether they felt accepted by other officers, supervisors, civilian city employees and the public, very few reported having difficulty being accepted by civilian employees (7 percent) or the public (10 percent). Likewise, there was general agreement that they were accepted by other female officers, as well as by female supervisors. However, 42 percent did not feel accepted by male officers, and 55 percent expressed the opinion that male supervisors did not accept them.

To assess the female officers' confidence on the job, they were asked to compare their job performance with that of male officers. The vast majority (76 percent) felt that they perform the job as well as male officers. It is significant to note, however, that almost one-fourth (24 percent) expressed the opinion that they do a better job than do male officers.

More than two-thirds (68 percent) of the female officers surveyed felt that they had to do a lot more work to receive the same credit as their male counterparts; only 30 percent believed that they were given just as much credit for their work as their male counterparts.

Asked to compare the code of conduct for male and female officers, only 4 percent felt that male officers had a stricter code of conduct, whereas 58 percent believed female officers faced tougher standards; 38 percent saw no difference. Some respondents expressed the opinion that grooming standards were stricter for females, and that their behavior was more closely scrutinized than that of males.

Another issue related to acceptance is the attitude of the recruit's field training officer (FTO). Respondents were split fairly evenly on this question, with slightly over half (52 percent) reporting that they experienced no reluctance on the part of the FTO and the remaining 48 percent reporting having sensed some displeasure about having a female as a partner.

Although the majority (57 percent) saw no difference in morale between male and female officers, a substantial percentage (35 percent) felt that morale was lower among female officers. Several respondents noted that, since the majority of officers are men and they prefer to work and socialize with each other, women tend to be left out and feel disenfranchised from the organization; others observed that there are more "men-only" outings among male officers.

Many respondents expressed the need for the department to realize that female officers have different needs and to adjust its thinking accordingly; others stressed the need for official recognition that women do the job just as well, albeit differently. There were also comments about not wanting to be pampered or given the "quiet beats."

A number of respondents expressed the desire to be treated as equals and receive more support, as well as appreciation for doing a good job. "Just let me feel good about being a female cop," noted one respondent, perhaps summarizing what most female officers felt.

Changes in Attitude and Behavior

Ninety-seven percent of the female officers surveyed firmly agreed that becoming a police officer has changed them in significant ways. Although most of the group were generally pleased with these changes, there were a substantial number who were displeased. Some like feeling more self-confident and less naive. Others mentioned having more distrust of others. Being able to relate more easily to people was listed as a desirable change, whereas being colder, more skeptical and less tolerant were mentioned as undesirable changes. Common themes were that the job produces a negative outlook, less patience, more forcefulness and greater irritability. Overall, there seemed to be a general awareness that exposure to life's harsher realities has significantly changed perceptions and attitudes.

Asked if being a police officer has affected relationships outside the police department, many of these officers reported feeling set apart from others and subjected to stereotypes put forth by the media. Others mentioned that the shifts they work afford little time for relationships, or that it is more difficult to start a relationship because a potential date is uncomfortable with a "cop."

It might be expected that a stressful job would have an impact on the officer's tendency to curse, smoke or use alcohol. Respondents reported the following changes in these behaviors:

	Never Have	More	Less	Same	Quit
Smoking	57%	6%	5%	13%	19%
Drinking	16%	13%	29%	35%	7%
Cursing	3%	63%	8%	24%	2%

It could be said that becoming a police officer appears to have had some positive impact in the areas of smoking and drinking, in that 24 percent have either quit smoking or smoke less than previously, and a total of 36 percent have either decreased their alcohol intake or quit altogether. It is obvious that most of these women find that they curse more now than they did before.

These officers also noted unpleasant changes in sleeping and eating habits, as well as attitude. Changes in sleeping or eating habits were usually attributed to shift work and the corresponding need to alter one's daily schedule. A negative eating habit mentioned by several officers is having to eat more "fast food" instead of home-cooked meals.

Sixty-five percent of respondents reported regularly engaging in one or more stress-reducing activities, including playing team and individual sports, walking, reading, spending time with family, bike riding and doing aerobics. Also mentioned were tending to animals (household pets, horses), exercising, talking out problems and enjoying outdoor activities.

Sexual Harassment

Respondents considered several behaviors to be part and parcel of sexual harassment, including jokes, inappropriate touching, requests for sex, sexually degrading comments or gestures and other threatening behaviors. Some respondents also mentioned being treated differently because of their sex.

Sixty-two percent of the survey respondents had experienced some form of sexual harassment (as defined above)

from a co-worker or supervisor. Of these, one-third confronted the offender, and 6 percent talked to their supervisors about it. A few contacted a representative of the EEOC, but 21 percent took no action at all. Very few took strong measures to address the problem.

Job Goals

Given the difficulties facing female police officers, one might expect discouragement and disenchantment. However, 80 percent stated that they plan to work for the department until retirement. There were very few with definite plans to leave within the foreseeable future, although some mentioned getting another position after finishing college. Only one respondent stated that she sees better opportunities for advancement and promotion outside of a police career. Fifty-six percent of the patrol officers planned on working toward promotion, and 31 percent were seeking a specialized assignment. Only 13 percent preferred to stay on as patrol officers.

There was substantial confidence among female officers that they will be able to succeed in garnering a promotion or preferred assignment—implying either that no major organizational obstacles are perceived or that female officers have confidence in their ability to surmount whatever obstacles there might be. Such confidence may also result from the department's policy of encouraging placement of minorities in preferred assignments.

Seventy-one percent reported that if they had to start over again, they would still become police officers. Therefore, most felt that they had made the right choice and were receiving enough reward and satisfaction from their careers. The 29 percent who would have pursued another career stated that they have remained on the job primarily due to the salary, benefits and job security. A few said they have continued as police officers because they were taught to "tough it out," or that they enjoyed the status that comes with the profession.

Summary

The results of this survey suggest that female police officers continue to struggle to gain acceptance from their male counterparts. The prevailing opinion among respondents to this survey is that they do not receive equal credit for their job performance, even though they believe that they are as capable as male officers. They also sense some degree of ostracism from the male social network, which has a negative impact on their morale. They feel a need to be accepted as female officers, rather than being evaluated according to "male" criteria. Many have experienced some form of sexual harassment from co-workers and supervisors, but did not assertively address the problem.

Exposure to police work produces a change in social attitudes for female officers. Some become more confident, more socially comfortable and less naive, but others become colder, less trusting and less tolerant of others. Most of the officers who responded to the survey regularly engage in healthy activities to relieve stress. Many have decreased their smoking and use of alcohol. Their sleeping and eating habits are adversely affected because of lifestyle adjustments to shift work.

Despite these problems, most do not regret the decision to become a police officer. They plan to continue with the job and are optimistic about career advancement. For these officers, the career is worth the struggle, and although they have yet to gain full acceptance, they see themselves as making valuable contributions to their departments and communities.

Officers from Rural, Suburban and Urban Jurisdictions Share Views

Officer James W. Calhoun
Atlanta Police Department
Population: 500,000
Law Enforcement Experience: 8 years

Officer Vernon Pare
Easthampton Police Department
Population: 16,000
Law Enforcement Experience: 20 years

Deputy Lissah Norcross
Mesa County Sheriff's Department
Unincorporated Population: 60,000
(3,300 Sq. Miles)
Law Enforcement Experience: 8 years

Officer Allen Wolf
Wichita Police Department
Population: 300,000
Law Enforcement Experience: 14 years

Giving Voice interviews informally report the opinions of law enforcement practitioners about developments in community policing. Described are the real-life challenges, successes and solutions faced daily by those who work in this field.

The following questions were asked of four officers representing diverse regions and populations in the United States.

Q1. How integral are sergeants in your department to the implementation of community policing?

Q2. How do you know if community policing is effective in your jurisdiction?

Officer Calhoun

A1. [Big laugh.] How important are sergeants?—very important. Let's put it this way, if your supervisor doesn't support what you're doing out here then the program doesn't work. In my zone, I'm fortunate. I'm expected to go out and meet people and do community policing, but that's a direct reflection of my supervisor. In other zones, that's not the case. There are supervisors in our department who think that the most important thing is arresting criminals and putting them in jail. Getting involved with citizens and doing drop-ins is very secondary in their view.

Also, my supervisor gives me a lot of leeway in decision making. As a beat officer I've got certain rules to

abide by, and as long as I'm doing the right thing then there's no problem. But if I run into something that looks kindof iffy, my supervisor is there and is completely open to me calling him at any time. Basically, my supervisor is there to back me up and support me.

A2. One example I can give you about its [community policing's] effectiveness concerns a cocaine dealer who we arrested 18 times since 1991. I could get this guy arrested but then he'd get a good lawyer and be right back out on the street. One day when I was doing a drop-in, the business owner I was talking to asked me why this guy kept getting off the hook. After giving him all the details about how

the dealer would use a different alias every time he'd go to court, but no one knew it because no one was following up on this guy, this citizen decided that he'd get personally involved. So he enlisted the help of a couple of community leaders and they went down to the D.A.'s office and said 'here's the problem, now what are you going to do about it.' They made this D.A. accountable for this case. See, citizens and community leaders can step on toes and get results, but if an officer did that, it would be career damaging. The end result was [that] the D.A. personally prosecuted this case and the dealer is now spending the next 17 years in jail. But this never would have happened if we weren't able to be out

From the *Community Policing Exchange*, July/August 1995, pp. 6-7. Reprinted by permission of *Community Policing Exchange*, a publication of the Community Policing Consortium, administered and funded by the U.S. Department of Justice. For more information about the Consortium, call 1-800-833-3085.

here and get to know and work with citizens.

Officer Pare

A1. Sergeants in my department, as is true in most, are more administrative. However, our sergeants do come on the road with us, and they do understand the philosophy of community policing. At first, some of our sergeants were resistant to community policing; they thought it was just a fad and would die out within a year. Some thought that this wasn't "real" police work. Now our sergeants are in full support of community officers. A couple of the things I really like about being in this position is that I have a lot more leeway in how to handle my area and also a lot more freedom in what decisions to make. Also, my hours have been made more flexible so

"Hey, if community policing is a bad idea like some say it is, then why are so many people, both citizens and employees, so anxious to be a part of it?"

DEPUTY LISSAH NORCROSS

that I'm better able to service my citizens. The sergeants have no problem with any of this.

A2. The amount of support our department now gets from citizens in our three community policing areas tells me community policing is effective. Calls received from citizens have doubled, as have the number of our arrests. Citizens are no longer afraid to come out of their homes at night and walk through their neighborhoods. I have 613 homes and 1,700 people in my area. Since we started our community policing program last June, there have been no home invasions and only one car broken into. I believe

these stats prove that the program is working. The people in my area are so accustomed to having me around that if I even take a day off, they want to know where I've been. The citizens are extremely happy to have their "own" police officers. We're also seeing the department finally get the support it deserves when override questions appear on election ballots. Because citizens now have a positive attitude about us, the department is able to hire more officers.

Deputy Norcross

A1. In the beginning, sergeants were very much left out. When we first started community policing, we had three line officers answering directly to a captain; the sergeants were just left out of the loop. Needless to say, it was easy for me to see they had a real negative attitude about community policing. I could see it because they were not willing to listen or be open minded about new ideas. The department recognized that had to change and now the sergeants are a positive, integral part of the process. The department provided them with some training by outside supervisors who could directly relate to what they were thinking. At this point, we still have some that are bean-counters, not facilitators. And even for the ones that are facilitators, problem-solving strategies are not necessarily the first ideas that pop into their minds. But I can see a change in how they're thinking and believe they now feel like they're a part of what's going on. For sergeants here now, most of their problem-solving experiences have been internally related. Applying these principles internally has allowed them to see that yeah, this does work and it gives them the ability to positively change things. That experience just needs to be expanded to external issues. Where most of our sergeants are lacking is that they don't have a lot of problem-oriented policing knowledge about how to handle problems out in the community in the same way they've learned to internally. They

haven't had the training I was lucky enough to get; therefore, they can't call on those experiences to apply to situations. Ideally, we should be able to go to our supervisors and ask for community-policing based suggestions. They aren't there yet, but they're getting there.

A2. I know it's effective by all of the small but significant changes that I've seen in my target area over the last year and a half. My first target neighborhood was a very high rental area with little to no investment from the residents. My first assignment there was for 40 hours a week for nine months. I worked very closely with property managers and other citizens. One of the initial problems in the area was several groups of obnoxious kids who caused some major problems in the neighborhood. Residents were very afraid of them. These groups would break into houses and cars, beat up other kids and so on. So I helped these residents get a Neighborhood Watch going. Now they do their own patrolling and with absolutely no direction from me, and they don't step over the line either. How do I know community policing is working? When one of these same 14-year-old kids tells me that 'Nothing ever happens in this neighborhood anymore. It's boring and it's no fun to come here 'cause someone's always watching us,' that's when I know it's working. Now when there's a problem, people in the area call me with information. This helps me to solve more cases. The calls also help me to intervene more often before the problem has a chance to explode.

Another thing I realized was that if you're going to change kids' attitudes towards cops, you've got to do it early. I spent a year going to one elementary school. I'd go to different classes and read books, do math problems, basically I'd do anything whether it was police-related or not. This let the kids see that I

was a real person, just like them. So now when I drive down their streets, they wave at me with all five fingers, not just one. They talk to me when I'm in their neighborhood. It's these little things that show me community policing works.

We also have a citizens' academy that is extremely popular. We always have twice as many citizens trying to get into the program as there is space. It shows me that when you share your information openly, people understand and want to get involved. Hey, if community policing is a bad idea like some say it is, then why are so many people, both citizens and employees, so anxious to be a part of it?

Officer Wolf

A1. In Wichita, our first-line supervisors are lieutenants, and I think they play a vital role in the community policing concept. They're the ones who allow front-line officers the time and opportunity to make decisions on their own and to problem solve. It was tough at first, deciding who should be able to talk to the media. Naturally, there was some concern about giving officers the freedom to speak publicly about issues

"...you need to have supervisors who have enough confidence in their line officers to allow them this kind of responsibility." *OFFICER ALLEN WOLF*

involving our neighborhood. Because basically, when we talk to the media, we represent not only our department, but our city and state as well. Obviously, you need to have supervisors who have enough confidence in their line officers to allow them this kind of responsibility. Supervisors these days aren't just disseminating tasks and seeing that they're done in a certain way and by a certain time. Now, they have to motivate us [line officers] as we go out and attack problems in the community.

A2. The effectiveness of community policing varies from target area to target area. My area has had a major problem with prostitution and drug activity. Since we've been doing community policing, we have seen a noticeable decrease in foot traffic. We developed a strategic plan to deal with this foot traffic, and it's working. One of our supervisors went to a training seminar in San Diego and brought back some ideas about a plan that had been used in St. Petersburg, Fla. We decided that we would modify their plan for our purposes.

From the very beginning, we went to the community and made sure that they were included in the process. After the plan was developed, we took it to the city council and they approved what we recommended. We also publicized the plan through the media—like putting up billboards

"Calls received from citizens have doubled, as have the number of our arrests. Citizens are no longer afraid to come out of their homes at night and walk through their neighborhoods."

OFFICER VERNON PARE

in our area letting the "johns" know that our neighborhood people are watching them and noting their tag numbers. We also work hand-in-hand with city code inspectors and the county health department to monitor the activity of the low-budget motels that are frequented. There's definitely a sense with our neighborhood people that the plan is working. We don't get nearly as many complaints about prostitution activity. That's not to say that it's totally gone, because this problem is one that has been entrenched in this particular area of Wichita for decades. But there's a general sense among citizens that things are better [and] cleaner, and that the police department is addressing their concerns.

A *LEN interview with*

Prof. Carl Klockars of the University of Delaware

"The police have been extraordinarily open to researchers. Police are anxious for input when they become convinced that the people working with them are sincere and are not there to do some kind of hatchet job."

Law Enforcement News Interview by Marie Simonetti Rosen

LAW ENFORCEMENT NEWS: You've been thinking about crime for about two decades now. What changes, if any, do you see in the role of police now compared to the past?

KLOCKARS: My entire perspective on police stems from a single fundamental observation, namely that what distinguishes police from every other domestic institution is that they exercise a general right to use coercive force. That general right to use coercive force is exactly what makes them so valuable to us in society. It's what makes them able to handle situations which no other institution can. That central core of the police role is constant and it always will be; it's what defines police and what makes them worth having in society. So in that way the role of the police is the same.

Now the question becomes, why does society need an institution with that general right to use coercive force? The answer is that there are a whole bunch of situations which ought not to be happening, and about which something ought to be done now, either it's a car that has to be moved from the street after an accident, or people standing in the way when a fire truck is trying to get to a fire. Those are situations that can't await a later resolution. If the people won't move or the motorists won't move their vehicles, we need someone with the right to use coercive force to attend to that situation and move those people or those vehicles out of the way. We invest no other institution in society with that responsibility. And it's an awesome responsibility because essentially what it says is you have

this right to use coercive force in virtually any situation that you see needing it, and no one has the right to resist your use of force when you think it's appropriate. So we invest police with a tremendous and awesome responsibility and one that is absolutely necessary in a democratic society, but fundamentally different from the right we give to any other institution.

LEN: Does society expect something different from police now than it did in the past?

KLOCKARS: I think that what society expects from police is, to a great extent, influenced by what police encourage them to expect. If police promote themselves as engaged in a war on crime, if they take credit when the crime rate goes down, the public's expectation is that police will do something to prevent crime. If they go to city councils asking for more police officers or money in their budgets in an effort to control crime, then the public's expectation is going to be that they do it.

There's a long history of claims that have been made as to why we need police and what police can do—that police make us safe, that they will prevent crime, that they will do various kinds of things. In the United States, certainly, the public has come to accept that a defining role of police is to do something about crime. Unfortunately, criminologists like myself have found only very rare occasions, on which police can make much difference at all in the actual levels of crime in the community. Police can respond to crime when it happens, and they are more or less successful in making arrests when crimes occur. But I know of very few studies which show that police can have any kind of sizable impact on the reduction of crime, no matter what they do—the rare exceptions being extremely high-intensity crackdowns in very small areas, which produce temporary reductions and probably a displacement. Short of that, even though the major mandate and the basis on which the police have sold themselves and the public expectation for police has been to do something about crime, to stop crime, or to wage a war on crime, the evidence is pretty strong that they only make a marginal difference in that effort.

LEN: One of the newest wrinkles has been community policing, with its almost inherent promise that it will make a locality safer. Given what you've just said about the police and their inability to prevent crime, how do you think this new approach stacks up?

KLOCKARS: Actually, the people who have written as advocates of community policing have been very cautious about claims to reduce crime. If you look at the work by Skolnick and Bailey, Mark Moore, George Kelling, Trojanowicz and others, what you'll find is that they're very, very cautious on any kinds of promises to control crime. They say the goal of community policing is crime prevention. But, of course, prevention is one of those strange things; it's very hard to know what prevents something because the idea of preventing is that something

---

"The police won't reduce crime. More prisons are probably not going to reduce crime. The types of things that cause the levels of crime that we have in society are not situations that we'll be able to control by more gun legislation or by punishing more people."

---

doesn't happen. So they've been very cautious about making those promises to reduce crime, probably because we found such rare occasions on which police can do so. I don't blame the police for that failure; it's simply that the kinds of things which determine whether or not there will be more or less crime in society at any time are things over which the police have very little control. For example, the age distribution of the population—how many males in their late teens do you have? If you have a lot of them, you're going to have more crime. There's the level of freedom that we accord people, the extent to which moral, cultural and religious restraints prevail in a population, the status of the economy—all of those things, any criminologist will tell you, are the big-ticket items which determine whether or not we have more or less crime in society at any time. The police at best are a small and marginal influence on the level of crime, and no criminologist I know has much faith that the institution of police is going to be able to change things. We don't give police the means to change those things, and we wouldn't.

DESPERATE MEASURES

LEN: If, as you point out, proponents of community policing hedge their best when it comes to crime reduction,

why do you think so many police executives and politicians have embraced community policing so thoroughly?

KLOCKARS: Politicians—and I include police chiefs in that group—are absolutely desperate to show people who are unhappy with the current crime situation that they are doing something about it. It almost doesn't matter whether that something is actually having an effect; in the face of a public demand that you do something, if you don't know what to do, then you ought to do something anyway simply to satisfy that public. Just look at the dozens of things that are going on that no criminologist I know of would maintain would have any impact on crime, yet they get an enormous amount of political play: gun buyback programs—absolutely no effect; the attempts to introduce more and more gun-control legislation—there's tons of evidence that those kinds of things simply are not going to make an impact in any way on the crime rate. The politicians are desperate and the public is clamoring for it. The police won't reduce crime. More prisons are probably not going to reduce crime. The types of things that cause the levels of crime that we have in society are not going to be situations that we'll be able to control by more gun legislation or by punishing more people.

LEN: If there were fewer weapons in the hands of civilians—a measure that goes further than the Brady Law—might that have a potential for reducing crime?

KLOCKARS: If tomorrow we could snap our fingers and all weapons would vaporize, then I think there would be an effect, probably a dramatic effect, in the reduction of use of handguns in crimes. But we probably have more weapons than people in this country. It is literally impossible to take those away. Any effort to take those away will result in largely the law-abiding citizens surrendering their weapons. Certainly the last people to give them up will be people who intend to use them in crimes. The laws that we have already, such as prohibiting people from doing things like committing armed robberies, don't deter armed robbers, even with extraordinarily severe penalties. Why should we believe that an additional law which says that they can't have handguns would deter them any more? We have 20,000 gun laws on the books. A new handgun comes off the assembly line every 10 seconds, and we have programs in which politicians and police chiefs get their pictures on the front page of the paper because for a couple of weeks they had people turn in 200 weapons. It's sheer political imagery, which will have no impact whatsoever on crime.

WHAT DOES WORK?

LEN: So what *do* you think would reduce crime?

KLOCKARS: There are many ways to answer that question. There are many conditions which encourage a society to have more or less crime: the quality of education in society, the quality of moral education at home, family stability, the amount that society moves around and is dislocated, whether the ethos of society is one that finds citizens subordinated to authorities, to manners, to respect for people, versus a society that celebrates self-expression and individualism. That kind of society is more likely to be criminogenic.

The causes of crime are a densely packed collection of many, many things. You can't pull one out and say this is a cause; it's a product of our entire culture. One of the ironies is that among the things which cause crime are lots of good things that we don't want to give up—like individual freedom, values of self-expression, resistance to authority. Crime may be one of the prices we pay for the individualism that we have in this society and for the type of culture that we have. I'm not going to tell you if you want to stop crime, do X or Y; it's far more complicated than that, although I think that a lot has to do with the moral education of children, and the quality of home life that children experience. The major criminal element in our society is males in their late teens to early 20's. I think what you do is look largely toward their adolescent experience and pre-adolescent experience and you ask, what is it that's going to change that level of behavior?

It is very important to understand that the level of crime we have today, by the best estimates of the social sciences, has been relatively stable. To listen to politicians talk, it looks like we're undergoing a massive boom in violent crime. But in fact, from National Crime Survey data, which is the best that we have, our level of violent crime has been going down gradually, and it's been relatively stable. What has happened is that you have an absolute media explosion in the coverage of crime. The thesis for the evening news is: If it bleeds, it leads. Every day you and I can watch some murder or other terrible crime, and in a society with 240 million people, with the kinds of communication that we have, it's certainly possible to give us a diet of a new murder every day. Just the other night I watched a program on child abduction and we find a legislator in New York introducing legislation to make it mandatory in the schools to teach children how to avoid being abducted. We have between 50 and 100 of those abductions totally each year in the United States. The chance of a child being abducted and murdered in the United States is far less than winning the state lottery jackpot. One of the great things about modern media is that it allows us sitting in our homes in Delaware or New York to worry about a child in South Dakota, another one in California, another one in Maine, another one in upstate New York, as if they were part of our community. In fact, those experiences are extraordinarily rare.

"I'm an advocate of accountability for tax dollars. There's an enormous role in criminal justice for finding out whether the strategies used by police have any effect whatsoever."

LEN: In a number of localities over the past several years, when police chiefs and politicians sell the public on "doing something" about crime it has entailed levying new taxes specifically for crime-control efforts. These higher taxes would seem to mean higher expectations as well. Do you think there could be any backlash if heightened expectations go unfulfilled?

KLOCKARS: The issue always is whether or not we have the capacity to measure if that money has somehow paid off. As I look at the criminal justice system, I see enormous expenditures in all sorts of different ways, for which we have no idea whether or not those expenditures are in any way effective. We go to the citizenry to ask for more police officers, and there's no evaluation of whether it makes any difference on crime. Look at the billions and billions of dollars we have spent on the war on drugs. On the face of it, drug use has been absolutely immune to the multibillion-dollar enforcement and incarceration effort; it's as if it made no difference whatsoever. I'm an advocate of accountability for tax dollars. If some government institution or some politician tells me that he wants my tax dollars to make something happen, I want to see an evaluation to know whether or not that's money well spent. Very often there's either no evaluation made whatsoever, or if there is any kind of evaluation, it falls into the hands of people who have a vested interest in saying how successful it was. I think there's an enormous role in criminal justice for simply finding out whether or not the strategies that are used by police have any effect whatsoever.

EXHAUSTED BY CHANGE

LEN: In an earlier article, you observed that the prevailing wisdom in police management warns the successful administrator of organizational resistance to change. You went on to surmise that it's not so much resistance to change as it is the fact that police may be exhausted by it. Could you explain?

KLOCKARS: There are many myths associated with police, and one of the greatest is that the police are resistant to change. In fact, police agencies are one of the most rapidly changing institutions. They certainly have changed in many ways much faster than, say, colleges and universities have changed. They probably change faster than many contemporary businesses have changed, although I don't have any data to back me up. If you look at how quickly police have shifted from things like team policing, into foot patrol, into community policing, you find that police agencies are enormously open. They're enormously receptive in many, many respects to citizen input. They respond differently in different neighborhoods as those neighborhoods change. They're certainly receptive to all sorts of technological changes. I mean police departments have undergone dramatic computerization in many aspects; they've undergone civilianization radically in many respects. It's part of the nature of policing to be in a sort of constant exchange with the communities they police. That's a very good thing. And police departments very often are not given credit for the amount of change they do engage in.

Twenty years ago, the assumption was that any criminologist studying police was studying one of two things: corruption or brutality. And there was a kind of enmity between criminologists and police. Today, virtually all top quality research on police is research *with* police. It's researchers and police working together. They're finding problems together; the police have been extraordinarily open to researchers, far more than virtually any other industry I can think of. Police are willing and anxious for input when they become convinced that the people working with them are sincere and are not there to do some kind of hatchet job. Many of the people who run police agencies these days are my students! They ought to be receptive to research because many of them have backgrounds in which they have been educated in the importance of research, and have come out of very serious and good criminal justice training.

A SHERIFF'S VIRTUES

LEN: You've been working with sheriffs lately. Given the fact that sheriffs are elected, do you believe they have more insight into the needs of a community?

KLOCKARS: I had no experience with sheriff's departments, and frankly I had harbored the impression that the sheriff system was a kind of an antiquated way of doing police business, and that the really progressive way to get policing done was with a department with an appointed professional chief. I've come to realize over the last five years that the sheriff system has a lot of virtues to it, and many of them are quite in line with things that have been said about community policing. Sheriffs are inherently interested in the community that they serve. They're interested in keeping communications open with as many sectors of the community as possible. They're interested in serving the community and seeing that the community believes itself to be well served. Those things spring directly from the fact that the sheriff is an elected figure. I find in sheriffs' offices a very attractive attitude toward the public because it's widely understood by the sheriff—and that attitude trickles down through the troops—that the people out there are the ones that are going to determine whether or not that sheriff stays in office. As a result, there is a level of responsiveness, a level of involvement with the community in many informal ways that to me characterizes the sheriff's departments. They are virtues of the sheriff's system which, as far as I am concerned, make it a very attractive system.

LEN: In the last year of elected officials' terms, they're often too busy campaigning to be an effective presence in office. On top of that, there is the whole issue of campaign financing and what that can entail. How do sheriffs fare in that particular arena?

KLOCKARS: I think sheriffs get public support not so much by campaigning, but by doing a job day in and day out that pleases the public, and dealing in a responsive way with complaints that the public has. The sheriff system, it seems to me, is a kind of the-buck-stops-where-it-ought-to system. In a normal municipal or county government, the police are but one part of a large bureaucracy, and citizens don't really have the opportunity to evaluate that part independently. You can kick out the mayor, but that's not an evaluation of the police function. The sheriff system makes it possible for citizens to evaluate their police service independently of other government services. So you may have a sheriff who is doing a good job in a county in which the trash removal is terrible and the schools have problems and the rest of government is falling apart and deserves to be kicked out. It gives the citizens an opportunity to selectively make that evaluation of police services, and I think that's a good thing. But the thing that most impresses me about it, again, is a kind of tone within the sheriff system in which the politics are very well known, and that politics says, "We want to keep the citizens happy; we want to make them believe that they are getting a good quality service." Any sheriff with any salt is going to see to it that that attitude prevails, because that's the kind of thing that gets a sheriff re-elected.

NO EXPERIENCE NECESSARY

LEN: Sheriff's don't necessarily have to have any kind of law enforcement background to be run for or hold office. Is that necessarily a good thing?

KLOCKARS: It's a mixed thing, and let me elaborate. I don't think it's a fault that most people we send to our legislatures, or who occupy executive positions, don't have degrees in political science. I think a police chief, depending upon the size of the agency, is a person who is heavily a policy-maker. And a sheriff who is elected can summon about himself or herself whatever professional and technical expertise is necessary. Most sheriffs who are elected come to that post with police experience of one kind or another, but on those occasions when someone is elected with little police experience, you certainly can hire people who have that experience. What people want in a police chief and in a sheriff is leadership, a commitment to integrity, a person who can communicate with the community, and a person who is able to administer a police agency, or at least surround himself or herself with competent administrators. I think the head of a police agency is a very important political figure, and the difference between sheriffs and police chiefs is that, in the case of sheriffs, that politics is largely public, whereas for police chiefs the politics is much more difficult to understand because it happens inside the bowels of government bureaucracies, rather than out there in front of the people.

LEN: Look at the issue another way, then. Do you think police chiefs ought to be elected?

KLOCKARS: I don't want to take a position either way. I think that there are lots of virtues to the sheriff system, and the distinguishing feature of the sheriff system is that the sheriff is an elected official. That could be a very, very good thing. We also have, of course, absolutely superb police chiefs who are appointed. I don't think either situation guarantees a high-quality department. However, I do think there are a lot of things to recommend the sheriff's system.

A QUESTION OF FORCE

LEN: In a 1992 article for LEN on police use of force, you suggested that changes were needed to establish standards

that go beyond—as you put it—conduct that is criminal, civilly liable, or scandalous. Could you describe a model policy for police departments that wish to go one step beyond the norm?

KLOCKARS: Right now, police agencies have three standards that control their use of force, and that society has to control police use of force: the criminal law, the civil law, and the fear of scandal. By and large these are the major mechanisms that we have to set the standards for controlling excessive force by police. In no other occupation would we set the standards so low. If I told you I was looking for a doctor, and you said, "I recommend Dr. Jones because he's never been arrested for anything and he's never been sued and he's never done medicine so badly that it caused a scandal," I'd hardly be satisfied with Dr. Jones. The only place any profession like police can go to set the standards for the use of that thing which distinguishes them as a profession is into the profession itself.

So if you want to define the problem of excessive force in policing, you have to look to the skills of policing to set that standard. What I've done in a number of pieces I've written is argue for a standard that defines excessive force as any more force than a highly skilled police officer would find necessary to use. And I set this as a standard for police agencies to work to achieve, not a standard beneath which policemen should be punished.

LEN: Could you elaborate?

KLOCKARS: Every one of the approaches that police now have for defining excessive force is one that says, "If you use more force than this, you're going to be punished for it." Either you'll be punished criminally, or you'll be punished by being sued along with your agency, or you're going to be punished because it's caused a scandal. Well, as long as you define the problem of excessive force in this punitive way, you're going to be forced to define excessive force at the lowest possible level, because anything that falls beneath it is going to merit punishment.

It seems to me that the proper approach to the idea of excessive force is to ask, what does really skilled policing consist of? What does policing by the most skilled officer imaginable consist of? Let's try to direct police work toward that standard, rather than constantly engaging in cover-your-ass behavior, or all those kinds of defensive responses that police engage in to avoid the lowest standard. The whole problem in police agencies is that their approach toward the use of force is largely punitive, largely focused toward keeping police officers from violating those low standards, rather than encouraging them to work in ways that highly skilled police officers do to minimize the use of force.

GREAT EXPECTATIONS

LEN: An increasing number of departments have established civilian review boards. Does the approach you suggest necessarily preclude civilian involvement?

KLOCKARS: It does, but perhaps for exactly the wrong reason that you're suspecting. We have a fair amount of

research now which shows that civilian review boards are less demanding of police than are other police officers. The problem with civilian review boards is that they don't know enough about police to expect more of them. It would be like me trying to evaluate the behavior of a physician. I don't know enough about medicine to distinguish between highly skilled medicine and medicine which is unskilled. The people who really know the difference between good and bad policing, between highly skilled policing and less than highly skilled policing, are other police officers. The trick in police administration is to find ways to get police officers to mobilize the expectations of high police skill on themselves and others. For a whole variety of reasons, police departments don't do that. Police officers are reluctant to demand those skills from fellow officers. They're reluctant to speak out critically. Actually it all has to do with the fact that the police approach to the control of excessive force is largely punitive. Consequently, there's this defensive mentality that grows up, quite reasonably so on the part of police officers, vis-a-vis the administration in the area of use of force.

"The ATF handling of the [Waco] situation was a catastrophe. The ATF made mistake after mistake in handling that situation, and it's just unforgivable. The behavior of the FBI was even more offensive to anyone who is concerned about the use of force."

INSULT & INJURY

LEN: Last year's debacle in Waco has been characterized by some as the most extreme application of deadly force in recent times, and many police say privately that the siege and the subsequent Justice Department investigation were thoroughly mishandled. Would you agree with those assessments?

KLOCKARS: There were of course, two police events in Waco. The first was the ATF handling of the situation. It was a catastrophe, and one of an almost typical police kind; that is, it involved poor planning. I don't think police are generally very good at those kinds of mass assaults. Police are not like the military in pulling off an assault like that; policing is to a great extent an individual occupation, with police as solitary workers. The ATF just made mistake after mistake after mistake in handling that situation, and it's just unforgivable.

To my way of thinking, though, the behavior of the FBI was even more offensive to anyone who is a student of policing, and to anybody who is concerned about the use of force. The FBI had all the time in the world to make the decision that it did. It seems to me that what the FBI managed to do in that situation is, for a variety and political and organizational reasons, simply talk or think its way out of the value of the lives of those children who were hostages there. The only way that the FBI could come to conclude that the strategy they used to assault that building would be acceptable is to simply discount the potential harm to those children. There is no way in the world that if Chelsea Clinton were one of those hostages, or if a child of any one of those members of the FBI team were in that building, they would have proceeded in that fashion. It was an assault to maximize the danger to the hostages; it minimized the danger to police, but the price of it, as we see, is that something like 26 perfectly innocent children ended up getting killed. How Janet Reno can justify that, and how Bill Clinton could stand behind that decision is simply incomprehensible to me.

On top of that, I am absolutely appalled by the investigation or evaluation which was done of that subsequently by Ed Dennis. It is a whitewash of a catastrophic incident that never should have happened. The whole idea of policing is to accomplish what needs to be accomplished in ways that minimize the use of force. The FBI did not use the skill that it should have, and the consequence was that it resulted in the death of absolutely innocent children. In any hostage situation the rule that you should use to decide whether or not you ought to do something—and hostage people will tell you this—is, would I do this if it were my child or my wife or my spouse that was being held hostage? There's no way they could have reconciled that behavior if it was a person of value like that?

LEN: How else might the evaluation have been handled?

KLOCKARS: A really fascinating study of this incident would have been one that tried to answer the question of how the best and brightest most highly trained police we have—the FBI—came to devalue the lives of those children so much that they could entertain this strategy. What organization dynamics, what political dynamics, what pressures were present that brought about that transformation? We could have learned a great deal, it seems to me, from a careful study of the Waco incident over time, but I doubt that that would be possible at this date.

LEN: One would guess that the Department of Justice would not be eager to give you the money for a study like that.

KLOCKARS: Oh, no. They're already done their studies, and the tragedy is, they didn't learn anything from them. Their studies came out and vindicated the FBI and they vindicated Janet Reno, and they concluded that David Koresh was a bad guy. What they didn't take out was the question of how these highly trained, highly educated police officers could have made such a catastrophic decision. As a criminologist, and as an expert on police and police use of force, I'd like to understand that whole process of what went on in the organization, what went on in the minds of the people there that let them reach these extraordinary conclusions about what they ought to do.

FERTILE GROUND FOR RESEARCH

LEN: A moment ago, in discussing criminal justice research, you mentioned that such research now tends to be conducted *with* police. What areas do you think offer the most fertile ground for research at this time?

KLOCKARS: My own particular interest is in the use of force, and one of the things that I'd like to do is give police agencies a capacity to analyze their own use of force. Most police agencies in this country can't tell you whether they have more force this year than last. They have no capacity to analyze the incidents in which they have used force; there's no capacity to compare the levels of the use of force in the Los Angeles Police Department with Philadelphia, with New York, with Baltimore County. That is, there's no capacity to do any interagency comparisons because the way those departments record and analyze and handle the record-keeping on use of force makes those comparisons utterly impossible. A major area in which police departments can advance for research purposes is in the analysis of the use of force. From that kind of analysis we can learn, for example, that certain approaches to handling certain types of situations will over the long run produce less injury to citizens and less injury to police officers.

Let me also reiterate an important distinction that I made in a previous writing and is now, I think, having some influence. It's the difference between the use of excessive force—that phrase—and the excessive use of force. You can have excessive use of force, even though you have no use of excessive force. Let me explain what I mean. You can pursue a strategy of handling, let's say, domestic violence incidents. Let's say that you allow officers to handle those complaints singlehandedly—that is, you allow a single officer to handle domestic-violence complaints. One of the things you may find as a consequence is that those officers find themselves in lots of use-of-force situations. Now, they may perfectly justify those individual officers in using force in those situations—they may use it in self-defense, for example—but what you find is that if you assign two officers to those domestic-violence complaints, those officers may not have to use force at all. So it's possible to discover ways of handling situations so as to avoid having to use force. That's what we call the problem of excessive *use* of force, though not a use of *excessive* force. There are probably lots of opportunities in policing for police agencies to discover that handling certain types of situations in certain types of ways will reduce the need to use force. but it's only when you're able to collect data on use-of-force incidents over time that you begin to see these problems.

LEN: The Police Foundation recently published a study of use of force, and the IACP, which was involved in the study, voiced some concern about precisely the use of the phrase "excessive force." Their concern was that you can't really analyze the available data and make comparisons from department to department because you don't know how they interpret that phrase. Should the Federal Government get more involved in this area, in a sense of trying to come up with standardization of terms?

KLOCKARS: What I would like to see the Federal Government support is a uniform force-reporting system. That is, I would like to see the Federal Government develop—with the cooperation, let's say of a small group of police agencies to start out with—a way of recording use-of-force incidents that would be standard across police agencies. The whole idea of this is not to pick on any police agency; there could be very good reasons why one police agency uses force at a higher rate than another. I don't have any problem with that. But if we're going to learn about use of force by police, then we have to have some mechanism of recording those incidents and allowing the analysis of those incidents to occur. If you have all sorts of different reporting systems, with different definitions and rules, you simply can't do that analysis. So I'd like to see the Federal Government involved in creating a kind of model system for record and analyzing use-of-force incidents. That would be a great help to police. You see, it's exactly the same thing as medical researchers in evaluating the use of surgery, and whether or not one surgical procedure is more effective than another. If medical science is to advance, it has to have that kind of information on the outcomes of its practices, and the same is absolutely true of police.

THE POLITICS OF RESEARCH

LEN: Based on your long involvement with criminal justice research, to what extent do you think politics plays a role in the allocation of Federal research funds?

"We have to have some mechanism of recording [use-of-force] incidents and allowing the analysis of those incidents to occur. If you have all sorts of different reporting systems, definitions and rules, you simply can't do that analysis."

KLOCKARS: Most of my experience has been in working with the National Institute of Justice, and for that agency I have reviewed grant proposals of one kind or another in various program areas for probably 20 years I'm only one of four or five people who reviews grants for police, and my experience on those grant-review panels has left me extraordinarily impressed with the quality of work that the reviewers put in, with the sincerity of the reviewers' comments and evaluations, and with that part of the peer-review process.

Beyond that, there is a substantial amount of politics that affects the awarding of grants. That is, peer review is one part of the process, and an advisory one at that. Political considerations govern to a substantial extent the setting of the NIJ agenda.

At the core of Carl B. Klockars's two decades of studying law enforcement is a single fundamental observation—a central principle that he says applies to police "everywhere and at all times." It is that "what distinguishes police from every other domestic institution is that they exercise a general right to use coercive force." The problem, he says, is that the three standards currently used to define and control excessive force—the criminal law, the civil law and the fear of scandal—are set too low to be particularly useful.

What Klockars advocates is "a standard that defines excessive force as any more force than a highly skilled police officer would find necessary to use." It would then fall to capable police leaders "to find ways to get police officers to mobilize the expectations of high police skill on themselves and others." But because the control of excessive police force is "largely punitive," a defensive mentality exists that prevents a higher standard from being achieved.

While Klockars is considered to be one of the country's leading experts on police use of force, his scholarly research and writings cover a wide spectrum of areas. One of his earliest works, "The Professional Fence," was the result of 18 months of observing and interviewing a fence—a stolen-property broker, not a real-property marker. This book, based on a doctoral dissertation that earned him a Ph.D. from the University of Pennsylvania in 1973, was selected as one of the "outstanding academic books" of 1975, and to this day it continues to sell more than 1,000 copies annually. Since then Klockars has written several other well-received books, in-

cluding "The Idea of Police" and "Thinking about Police"—considered to be touchstones in police literature—and scores of articles and research reports. In addition to his writing and teaching at the University of Delaware, where he has been a member of the faculty since 1976, Klockars also reviews grants for the National Institute of Justice.

Of late, Klockars's scholarly interests have come to include the sheriffs' departments of the United States—a system that, he says, "has a lot of virtues to it and many of them are in line with a lot of things that have been said about community policing." One such virtue that he particularly likes is that the position is an elected one. This fundamental difference between sheriffs and police chiefs leads to a different type of political environment, says Klockars. For sheriffs, "that politics is largely public, whereas for police chiefs the politics is much more difficult to understand because it happens inside the bowels of government bureaucracies, rather than out there in front of the people." The community's evaluation of public safety efforts, in the case of sheriff's departments, takes place in the form of casting a ballot.

The ever-precise, often-controversial Klockars puts a good deal of emphasis on evaluation—or to be specific, the lack of it in the criminal justice system. He opines, "I see enormous expenditures in all sorts of different ways, for which we have no idea whether or not those expenditures are in any way effective." And when it comes to money, Klockars is firm: Throwing it hand-over-fist at crime problems just won't work.

There are also relationships that grow up between the National Institute of Justice and groups like the Police Executive Research Forum and the Police Foundation, who are regular recipients of NIJ grants. In defense of those agencies, though, they're right there in Washington, they're geared up for it, they have research staffs that are focused on those issues, and we can expect a high degree of success by institutions of that kind in grant-getting in the areas in which they are specialized. If the agency is good at it, and produces—well, nothing succeeds like success. If I were the NIJ director, I don't know that I would do anything different.

LEN: If you were given a blank check, any amount of money you'd care to write in, and were told you could do with it anything in policing that you wanted to, what would you do?

KLOCKARS: I'd tell you to hold your check. The problem with policing is not money. Crime is not going to go away or get better if we throw more money at it. It's not going to go away buying more police, or more police cars, or more computers. So I'd tell you to keep your money.

THE CROOKED BLUE LINE

The allegations concerning Mark Fuhrman help focus attention on charges of seemingly intractable corruption and brutality in America's police departments

Elizabeth Gleick

[My partner] is so hung up on the rules and stuff. I get pissed sometimes and go, "You just don't even [expletive] understand. This job is not rules. This is a feeling. [Expletive] the rules; we'll make them up later."—Former Los Angeles police detective Mark Fuhrman in a tape-recorded conversation

On Nov. 22, 1988, a police officer obtained a routine warrant to search Joseph Morris' Philadelphia steak house by claiming he had watched a teenager sell marijuana outside a local high school, had followed him into the restaurant and had seen him hand a roll of cash to Morris. The officer said he saw Morris hand back a brown paper bag. The officer said he then followed the teen to the street and bought some marijuana, which the teen pulled out of the bag. After breaking down the door of the steak house with a sledgehammer, officers said they found marijuana there and arrested Morris. Based on the sworn testimony of officer Steven Brown, Morris was convicted of drug trafficking and sentenced to three years in prison.

But Brown's testimony was a skein of lies. There was no teenager, no exchange of cash or drugs inside the shop, no brown paper bag and no drug buy. Last March, Brown, a 13-year veteran on the force, pleaded guilty to federal charges involving 25 cases, including the illegal search of Morris' steak house. After nearly 2¹/₂ years in prison, Morris was released. While he has his freedom, peace of mind is a little harder to come by. "It takes a lot away from you," says the 53-year-old father of five, now a self-employed carpenter. "I can't understand why these people can do anything they want and get away with it."

It is the best of times, it is the worst of times for police departments and the citizens they are sworn to protect. News of declines in the rates of violent crime nationwide has been drowned out by the sound of Mark Fuhrman's voice filling a Los Angeles courtroom—swaggering and all too believable as the former cop describes the brutalizing of suspects, fabrication of evidence and abuse of minorities. Although the O.J. Simpson jury will hear only two small snippets of the Fuhrman screed, to the rest of America the tapes provide a profane voice-over to real-life police corruption and brutality dramas that have been playing out not only in Los Angeles—where last Friday two officers were implicated in evidence tampering in a murder case—but also in New York City, Philadelphia, New Orleans, Minneapolis, Detroit and Washington.

The surprise here is not that police corruption exists or that there are, to use law-enforcement officials' favorite metaphor, always "a few bad apples." The question is why police departments appear locked in a perpetual cycle of scandal, repentance, pledges of reform and fresh scandal, seemingly unwilling or unable to police themselves. The answer in part lies in the way departments are set up and managed, and also within the hearts of the officers themselves. "The people in a position to do something about brutality and racism are products of the system," explains James Fyfe, a former New York City cop who teaches criminal justice at Temple University. "There's a sense that their loyalty should be to the department, not to the public."

As offensive as Fuhrman's words may be, they are nothing when compared with the scandal in Philadelphia. To date, along with Brown, five other cops have pleaded guilty to such charges as setting up innocent victims, selling drugs and beating and threatening people, primarily poor blacks in the 39th District. As a result, 46 of their criminal convictions have been overturned, with many more still to come. Last week federal investigators expanded their search to include the Highway Patrol, subpoenaing logs of as many as 100,000 arrests over 10 years. "It's nothing new," says Jerry Day, sitting on the steps of a house a few blocks from the 39th District headquarters. Day, who is African American, claims that he has been falsely arrested and released and that he and the rest of the neighborhood have known for years about the crooked cops. Day and his neighbors never complained, he says, because they felt there was no one they could trust. "Cops lock you up, beat you up and then dump you off at the hospital," he says. "They just lock you up to make their quota."

In the 1980s, more than 30 Philadelphia cops were convicted for shaking down drug dealers. Police Commissioner Willie Williams—now chief of the Los Angeles Police Department—held a press conference in which he vowed to supervise officers more closely. But defense attorneys say no significant reforms occurred. "Unless the institutions change, having prosecutions every five years is not going to be the answer," says David Rudovsky, a civil rights attorney and a University of Pennsylvania law professor. "You can't wait until somebody complains. You have to be pro-active, and every good police department knows that."

The citizens of Los Angeles too did not need Fuhrman to illustrate how vows of absolution are followed by disillusionment. In the wake of the 1991 Rodney King beating, then Mayor Tom Bradley established the Christopher Commission, a blue-ribbon panel entrusted with the job of recommending police reforms. Chief Daryl Gates, who was frequently criticized for closing ranks with his officers rather than being accountable to the public, retired under pressure, and Williams was brought in. Still, 3½ years later, many of the Christopher Commission's recommendations exist only on paper. For instance, the commission identified 44 "problem" officers, all of whom had a history of six or more excessive-force cases during the five years before the King beating; until recently 33 of them remained on the force, with 19 still on the streets dealing with the public. One of the 44 was Andrew Teague, who confessed to forging a key document in a murder case and last week, along with his supervisor, turned in his badge. And in July, another of those 44 officers, Michael Falvo, shot and killed a 14-year-old Latino boy in the Lincoln Heights section of Los Angeles. The police version is that the boy, José Antonio Gutierrez, pointed a TEC-9 pistol at Falvo as the officer arrived, responding to a report of teens with a shotgun. Witnesses insist Gutierrez had already thrown his gun over a fence when the police approached and was holding a flashlight. Falvo has been temporarily assigned to a desk job.

Some Angelenos are outraged that these cops with their histories were still on the job at all. "There are very simple things that could have been done to build a relationship back up with the members of the public in the Latino and African American communities who really felt repressed by the L.A.P.D.," says Rabbi Gary Greenebaum, former president of the Los Angeles Police Commission, which oversees the police department. "And one way of doing that was to see that those 44 officers never saw the streets again."

Los Angeles is not unique. In departments around the country, say many experts, the bad apples are left to rot on the job rather than tossed out as so much garbage. "In every department there's a small group of officers who claim a huge percentage of the complaints," says Samuel Walker, professor of criminal justice at the University of Nebraska and the author of several books on policing. "These are officers who can't seem to control themselves in high-pressure situations. If you had a subpoena, you could walk into any department in the country and find those officers." Fuhrman, who had a history of problems on the job and whose attempts to receive a stress-related disability pension failed, appears to have been one such officer.

To purge a department, however, requires an almost wholesale change of police culture, breaking down officers' instinctive tendency to protect their own. "The thing about the Fuhrman tapes is everybody says,

'What a bad guy Mark Fuhrman is,'" notes Ramona Ripston, executive director of the Southern California branch of the American Civil Liberties Union. "But he worked with other police officers. This code of silence is still very much in existence because [none of them] seem to have come forward and complained about Mark Fuhrman." Although the Christopher Commission recommended a frequent rotation of partners to help loosen personal bonds, no such rotation has yet been established.

Given the power of the police fraternity, many experts believe the single most important tool in keeping police departments on the up and up is a strong, independent civilian review board. Internal-affairs units, while not entirely ineffective, are also not sufficient. Among the findings last year by the Mollen Commission, which convened in New York City in 1993 to look into a Brooklyn corruption case that was reported to the Internal Affairs Bureau 13 times, was the profound inability of internal-affairs departments to conduct effective investigations.

This is clearly the case in the New Orleans police department, which has been riddled with corruption for decades. When New Orleans officer Len Davis, who has been indicted for arranging the murder of a woman who had lodged a brutality complaint against him, came under investigation during an FBI sting, he allegedly learned within hours from someone within internal affairs that he was being investigated. (Davis is in jail pending trial.) The new chief of the New Orleans police, Richard Pennington, who has begun reforming with a vengeance, has since brought in the FBI to help police the newly named "Public Integrity Unit." He also moved the unit out of headquarters to a independent location.

Civilian review boards, however, are relatively rare, with only 65 police forces in the U.S. using them. Even in cities that have some form of independent monitor, however, it is hard to untangle professional loyalties. Chicago's Office of Professional Standards feels the heat from both sides. "OPS takes complaints from anybody, no matter how farfetched," says Bill Nolan, president of Chicago's Fraternal Order of Police. But others say that the OPS investigators are mediocre and that when cases are sustained, there is never any action when the recommendation is returned to the police chief. "I have never had a case that was investigated by OPS and a finding by the administrative body that the officer did something wrong, even after we get jury verdicts and large settlements," says lawyer Edward T. Stein. "Do you think the city pays $1 million to settle cases because they think the officer has done nothing wrong?"

In Philadelphia calls for an independent review board have been largely dis-

missed. For one thing, as Mayor Ed Rendell points out, the current charges arose after an investigation initiated by the police department led to an investigation by a joint anticorruption task force, which to his mind means that his officers are capable of policing themselves. For another, says district attorney Lynne Abraham, a special commission cannot control the force anyway. "Commissions come and go, and then when everybody folds their tent, there is a tendency to slip back again."

There is also a great deal of resistance among the rank and file to outside controls. Los Angeles will finally put in place the Christopher Commission's recommendation for an inspector general later this year. Says a 20-year L.A.P.D. veteran who is disgusted with this and other pledged reforms: "Daryl Gates, even when he made mistakes, he connected with the cops on the street. He remembered people's names. He stood up for you. Now you know you're gonna be second-guessed and have some board review you, no matter what you do. It's not worth it."

Making the job worth their while is in fact an essential issue to cops, who feel they are the brutalized, not the brutalizers. Many cops feel that much of what they do, even if it crosses some line, is justified by the stresses of the street and the need to protect the public. "A lot of times you're arresting people who are out-and-out cold, hard criminals, and they're out on the street on bail before you've done your paperwork," says Jim McDevitt, vice president of the Fraternal Order of Police in Philadelphia. "That gets very, very frustrating." What can be done to ease these frustrations? According to New Orleans chief Pennington, pay cops more and train them better. He recently handed his officers their first pay raise in eight years.

Naturally, officers around the country last week expressed frustration that they were all being unfairly tarred by the Fuhrman brush. That, doubtless, is mostly true. But when people are afraid to report their complaints, when officers work alongside acknowledged racists or miscreants in silence, when news of the latest police scandal is met with a "So what?" by jaded citizens, the system has gone awry. "It can be hard to keep your compassion," says L.A.P.D. sergeant Mike Albanese. "But we need to find a way to help people who have a problem get out of this system. It's not just an L.A.P.D. problem. It's a problem for everybody."

—Reported by Sharon E. Epperson/Philadephia, Julie Grace/Chicago, S.C. Gwynne/New Orleans, Elaine Lafferty and Sylvester Monroe/Los Angeles and Sarah Tippit/New York

The thin white line

City agencies struggle to mix standardized testing and racial balance

When Democrats last week officially chose Chicago for their 1996 presidential convention, they were hoping to bury some painful images from the last Chicago convention in 1968, when Mayor Richard J. Daley's police force beat up antiwar demonstrators on national television. Yet even as the ink was drying on the convention agreement, new troubles were brewing in the Chicago police department that throw an embarrassing spotlight on a vexing social problem: the disparate scores blacks and whites achieve on standardized tests.

The trouble began late last month, when the department announced the scores on a recent exam taken by candidates vying to become police sergeants. Of 500 officers who scored high enough to win promotion, only 40 were black

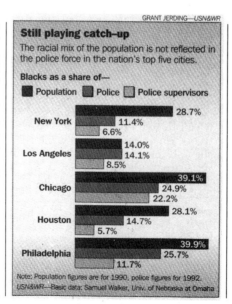

GRANT JERDING—*USN&WR*

Still playing catch–up

The racial mix of the population is not reflected in the police force in the nation's top five cities.

Blacks as a share of—
■ Population ▨ Police ▢ Police supervisors

New York
28.7%
11.4%
6.6%

Los Angeles
14.0%
14.1%
8.5%

Chicago
39.1%
24.9%
22.2%

Houston
28.1%
14.7%
5.7%

Philadelphia
39.9%
25.7%
11.7%

Note: Population figures are for 1990, police figures for 1992.
USN&WR—Basic data: Samuel Walker, Univ. of Nebraska at Omaha

and 22 Hispanic—this in a city that is 39 percent African-American and 19.6 percent Hispanic. Almost immediately, some African-American politicians denounced the test as racially biased, even though the actual test questions have not been publicly released. "Structurally the test was biased, structurally it was racist, structurally it wasn't meant to promote African-Americans," fumed U.S. Rep. Bobby Rush at a church rally in his South Side congressional district.

The furor in Chicago erupted because the police department dropped a past practice known as "race norming" test scores. Previously, when municipal hiring and promotion exams resulted in disproportionately low scores for minorities, city departments often reworked test scores using various statistical techniques. Chicago adjusted the results of its 1985 sergeants' exam, for instance, by giving minority test takers extra points. Other cities, such as Detroit, put black and white test takers into separate categories and compared them by rank order rather than score. Whatever the technique, the results of race norming were the same: More minorities were hired or promoted, often ahead of whites with higher scores. Those who defend affirmative-action hiring argue that having racially diverse police departments helps ameliorate racial tensions. And there are clearly some jobs that white officers can't do as well, such as infiltrating black street gangs.

Under fire. Yet Congress specifically banned race norming in the 1991 Civil Rights Restoration Act, and many cities dropped the practice, often under pressure from lawyers representing predominantly white police and fire fighters. Chicago is the first to feel the full political impact of administering tests without the race-norming safety net. But other cities are likely to follow.

To avoid charges of racial bias or favoritism, Chicago followed the recommendations of a blue-ribbon commission and paid $5 million to consulting firms to devise a series of bias-free, multiple-choice tests. When the test results still showed significant racial disparity, a politically embarrassed Mayor Richard M. Daley—son of the late Richard J.—quickly announced that the city and the U.S. Justice Department would investigate.

While racial bias remains a possible culprit in the low scores—some white officers may have gotten hold of study materials that closely matched the test format—the likelihood is that Chicago and other cities are having to face an uncomfortable fact: On the vast majority of paper-and-pencil tests devised to measure knowledge or aptitude, African-Americans score lower on average than whites. While a few academics such as the American Enterprise Institute's Charles Murray suggest that test differences between races may have some genetic basis, a larger group maintains that cultural bias is the problem. "Any test is grounded in the culture of those who make it," insists Robert Schaeffer of FairTest, a nonprofit advocacy group. Patricia Hill, president of

Chicago's African-American Police League, complains that the test forces "everyone to meet European cultural standards in order to be sanctified."

White cultural bias, however, doesn't explain why Hispanics scored higher on the Chicago sergeants' exam than blacks, or why Asians had higher mean scores than whites. The more plausible explanation for the relatively low black

> *"The conspiracy is to put non-minorities into supervisory positions who will be in place years from now. That's institutional racism."*
>
> **REP. BOBBY RUSH**

scores, say most experts, is that blacks often attend poorer-quality schools and learn less rigorous study habits. "Pencil-and-paper tests tend to reward people who grew up in educationally oriented cultures," notes journalist Nicholas Lemann, who is writing a book on meritocracy in the United States. Winfred Arthur, an African-born psychologist who wrote many of the test questions in the Chicago police exam for Barrett & Associates, agrees: "Tests like these are just capturing the effects of other social issues."

> *"I flunked the bar exam twice.... I had to keep studying harder and harder and harder. I passed it the third time.... That's it. Study harder."*
>
> **MAYOR RICHARD M. DALEY**

A more fundamental question is whether such tests realistically measure the skills police must have to do their jobs effectively. Firms like Barrett craft their test questions by interviewing a department's officers and reading its rule books. Yet concerns over the relevance of written tests have led more and more departments and consulting firms to turn to alternative types of tests in which candidates perform tasks they would actually do if promoted: handling memos, performing roll calls, responding to simulated citizen complaints. Minorities tend to score much closer to whites in such performance tests, which suggests that many minorities have real abilities that traditional written tests don't capture.

But performance tests have their own problems. They are far more expensive—a serious issue for cash-strapped municipalities—and harder to administer, especially in large cities, where thousands of applicants take the test on the same day. And because they are scored by people rather than by machines, performance tests are often seen as less objective. Indeed, black police officers in Chicago fought the use of performance tests, even though they tend to do better on them, out of fear that white supervisors would doctor the results in order to promote their friends.

Most testing experts now recommend a Solomonic compromise: basing promotions on a mix of written and performance tests. Other ways for departments to boost minority supervisory ranks in the post-race-norming era include beefing up recruiting to attract higher-quality officers and rigorous training programs for those seeking promotions. Such training is expensive, but it has been key to the U.S. military's ability to promote large numbers of blacks to high rank without diluting standards.

Yet even with all these measures, it is probably too much to expect racial disparities in testing and hiring to disappear any time soon, notes Temple University criminologist James Fyfe, because "you're asking police departments to deal with the consequences of an inequitable society."

BY PAUL GLASTRIS IN CHICAGO

The Judicial System

The American people really got an inside look at the American judicial system in the past year, as hour upon hour the television screen was filled with scenes from the O. J. Simpson trial. The various players in the system, the police, judges, prosecutors, and defense lawyers, were constantly scrutinized. Some of the articles in this section deal with the roles of these players. "Abuse of Power in the Prosecutor's Office" is a critical analysis of the prosecutor's position. It is offered, not as an indictment of all prosecutors, but to stimulate discussion of possible areas of abuse. This is followed by the essay, "The Trials of The Public Defender," which presents a sympathetic view of the problems faced by this overworked professional.

In "Suspect Confessions," Richard Jerome raises a disturbing issue in reporting on the findings of a social psychologist who alleges that false confessions account for a large number of wrongful convictions. Then, the impact of the O. J. Simpson trial itself is explored in "A Trial for Our Times: An Ugly End to It All." Lance Morrow provides an introduction to Richard Lacayo's essay on the trial and its dramatic impact on the criminal justice system.

J. R. Spencer, in "Justice English Style," presents an interesting discussion of the way a case such as the O. J. Simpson trial would be handled in the English courts. According to Spencer, the differences between the systems are so great that the Simpson trial, if it took place in England, would be entirely dissimilar.

The final unit article, "Jury Consultants: Boon or Bane?" presents the pros and cons of a growing technique of selecting jurors.

Looking Ahead: Challenge Questions

Discuss whether or not there is too much television coverage of high-profile criminal cases.

Do you think that jury nullification is a problem? Why or why not?

What, if anything, in the English approach to a criminal trial should be adopted in the American system?

What is your opinion regarding the use of jury consultants?

ABUSE OF POWER IN THE PROSECUTOR'S OFFICE

Bennett L. Gershman

Bennett L. Gershman is professor of law at Pace University. He is the author of Prosecutorial Misconduct *and several articles on law dealing with such topics as entrapment and police and prosecutorial ethics. For ten years, he was a prosecutor in New York.*

The prosecutor is the most dominant figure in the American criminal justice system. As the Supreme Court recently observed, "Between the private life of the citizen and the public glare of criminal accusation stands the prosecutor. [The prosecutor has] the power to employ the full machinery of the State in scrutinizing any given individual." Thus, the prosecutor decides whether or not to bring criminal charges; whom to charge; what charges to bring; whether a defendant will stand trial, plead guilty, or enter a correctional program in lieu of criminal charges; and whether to confer immunity from prosecution. In jurisdictions that authorize capital punishment, the prosecutor literally decides who shall live and who shall die. Moreover, in carrying out these broad functions, the prosecutor enjoys considerable independence from the courts, administrative superiors, and the public. A prosecutor cannot be forced to bring criminal charges, or be prevented from bringing them. Needless to say, the awesome power that prosecutors exercise is susceptible to

abuse. Such abuses most frequently occur in connection with the prosecutor's power to bring charges; to control the information used to convict those on trial; and to influence juries.

The prosecutor's charging power includes the virtually unfettered discretion to invoke or deny punishment, and therefore the power to control and destroy people's lives. Such prosecutorial discretion has been called "tyrannical," "lawless," and "most dangerous." Prosecutors may not unfairly select which persons to prosecute. But this rule is difficult to enforce, and the courts almost always defer to the prosecutor's discretion. In one recent case, for example, a prosecutor targeted for prosecution a vocal opponent of the Selective Service system who refused to register, rather than any of nearly a million nonvocal persons who did not register. The proof showed that the defendant clearly was selected for prosecution not because he failed to register but because he exercised his First Amendment rights. This was a legally impermissible basis for prosecution. Nevertheless, the courts refused to disturb the prosecutor's decision, because there was no clear proof of prosecutorial bad faith. Many other disturbing examples exist of improper selection based on race, sex, religion, and the exercise of constitutional rights. These cases invariably are decided in the prosecutor's favor. The reasoning is circular. The courts presume that prosecutors act in good faith, and that the prosecutor's expertise, law enforcement plans, and priorities are ill suited to judicial review.

Unfair selectivity is one of the principal areas of discretionary abuse. Another is prosecutorial retaliation in the form of increased charges after defendants raise statutory or constitutional claims. Prosecutors are not allowed to be vindictive in response to a defendant's exercise of rights. Nevertheless, proving vindictiveness, as with selectiveness, is virtually impossible. Courts simply do not probe the prosecutor's state of mind. For example, prosecutors often respond to a defendant's unwillingness to plead guilty to a crime by bringing higher charges. In one recent case, a defendant charged with a petty offense refused to plead guilty despite prosecutorial threats to bring much higher charges. The prosecutor carried out his threat and brought new charges carrying a sentence of life imprisonment. The court found the prosecutor's conduct allowable. Although the prosecutor behaved in a clearly retaliatory fashion, the court nevertheless believed that the prosecutor needed this leverage to make the system work. If the prosecutor could not threaten defendants by "upping the ante," so the court reasoned, there would be fewer guilty pleas and the system would collapse.

Finally, some prosecutions are instituted for illegitimate personal objectives as opposed to ostensibly valid law enforcement objectives. Such prosecutions can be labeled demagogic and usually reveal actual prosecutorial malice or evil intent. Telltale signs of demagoguery often include the appearance of personal vendettas, political crusades, and witch hunts. Examples of this base practice abound. They have involved prosecutions based on racial or political hostility; prosecutions motivated by personal and political gain; and prosecutions to discourage or coerce the exercise of constitutional rights. One notorious example was New Orleans District Attorney James Garrison's prosecution of Clay Shaw for the Kennedy assassination. Other examples have included the prosecutions of labor leader James Hoffa, New York attorney Roy Cohn, and civil rights leader Dr. Martin Luther King.

HIDING EVIDENCE

A prosecutor's misuse of power also occurs in connection with legal proof. In the course of an investigation, in pretrial preparation, or even during a trial, prosecutors often become aware of information that might exonerate a defendant. It is not unusual for the prosecutor to have such proof, in view of the acknowledged superiority of law enforcement's investigative resources and its early access to crucial evidence. The adversary system relies on a fair balance of opposing forces. But one of the greatest threats to rational and fair fact-finding in criminal cases comes from the prosecutor's hiding evidence that might prove a defendant's innocence. Examples of prosecutorial suppression of exculpatory evidence are numerous. Such conduct is pernicious for several reasons: It skews the ability of the adversary system to function properly by denying to the defense crucial proof; it undermines the public's respect for and confidence in the public prosecutor's office; and it has resulted in many defendants being unjustly convicted, with the consequent loss of their liberty or even their lives.

Consider the following recent examples. Murder convictions of Randall Dale Adams in Texas, James Richardson and Joseph Brown in Florida, and Eric Jackson in New York all were vacated because the prosecutors hid crucial evidence that would have proved these defendants' innocence. The Adams case—popularized by the film *The Thin Blue Line*—depicts Texas "justice" at its worst. Adams was convicted in 1977 of murdering a policeman and sentenced to die largely on the testimony of a juvenile with a long criminal record who made a secret deal with the prosecutor to implicate Adams, and the testimony of two eyewitnesses to the killing. The juvenile actually murdered the policeman, as he later acknowledged. At Adams' trial, however, the prosecutor suppressed information about the deal and successfully kept from the jury the juvenile's lengthy record.

The prosecutor also withheld evidence that the two purported eyewitnesses had failed to identify Adams in a line-up, and permitted these witnesses to testify that they had made a positive identification of Adams. A Texas court recently freed Adams, finding that the prosecutor suborned perjury and knowingly suppressed evidence.

Richardson—whose case was memorialized in the book *Arcadia* was condemned to die for poisoning to death his

tor misrepresented to the jury that ballistics evidence proved the defendant's guilt, when in fact the prosecutor knew that the ballistics report showed that the bullet that killed the deceased could not have been fired from the defendant's weapon.

Eric Jackson was convicted of murder in 1980 for starting a fire at Waldbaum's supermarket in Brooklyn in which a roof collapsed and six firefighters died. Years later, the attorney who repre-

---

Abuses most frequently occur in connection with the prosecutor's power to bring charges, to control the information used to convict those on trial, and to influence juries.

---

seven children in 1967. The prosecutor claimed that Richardson, a penniless farm worker, killed his children to collect insurance. A state judge last year overturned the murder conviction, finding that the prosecutor had suppressed evidence that would have shown Richardson's innocence. The undisclosed evidence included a sworn statement from the children's babysitter that she had killed the youngsters; a sworn statement from a cellmate of Richardson's that the cellmate had been beaten by a sheriff's deputy into fabricating his story implicating Richardson; statements from other inmates contradicting their claims that Richardson confessed to them; and proof that Richardson had never purchased any insurance.

Brown's murder conviction recently was reversed by the Eleventh Circuit. Brown was only hours away from being electrocuted when his execution was stayed. That court found that the prosecutor "knowingly allowed material false testimony to be introduced at trial, failed to step forward and make the falsity known, and knowingly exploited the false testimony in its closing argument to the jury." The subornation of perjury related to the testimony of a key prosecution witness who falsely denied that a deal had been made with the prosecutor, and the prosecutor's misrepresentation of that fact to the court. In addition, the prosecu-

sented the families of the deceased firemen in a tort action discovered that one of the prosecutor's expert witnesses at the trial had informed the prosecutor that the fire was not arson related, but was caused by an electrical malfunction. At a hearing in the fall of 1988, the prosecutor consistently maintained that nothing had been suppressed and offered to disclose pertinent documents. The judge rejected the offer and personally inspected the prosecutor's file. The judge found in that file two internal memoranda from two different assistant district attorneys to an executive in the prosecutor's office. Each memorandum stated that the expert witness had concluded that the fire had resulted from an electrical malfunction and had not been deliberately set—and that the expert's conclusion presented a major problem for the prosecution. None of this information was ever revealed to the defense. On the basis of the above, the court vacated the conviction and ordered the defendant's immediate release.

To be sure, disclosure is the one area above all else that relies on the prosecutor's good faith and integrity. If the prosecutor hides evidence, it is likely that nobody will ever know. The information will lay buried forever in the prosecutor's files. Moreover, most prosecutors, if they are candid, will concede that their inclination in this area is not to reveal information that might damage his or her case. Ironically, in this important area in which the prosecutor's fairness, integrity, and good faith are so dramatically put to the test, the courts have defaulted. According to the courts, the prosecutor's good or bad faith in secreting evidence is irrelevant. It is the character of the evidence that counts, not the character of the prosecutor. Thus, even if a violation is deliberate, and with an intent to harm the defendant, the courts will not order relief unless the evidence is so crucial that it would have changed the verdict. Thus, there is no real incentive for prosecutors to disclose such evidence.

Hopefully, in light of the recent disclosures of prosecutorial misconduct, courts, bar associations, and even legislatures will wake up to the quagmire in criminal justice. These bodies should act vigorously and aggressively to deter and punish the kinds of violations that recur all too frequently. Thus, reversals should be required automatically for deliberate suppression of evidence, and the standards for reversal for nondeliberate suppression relaxed; disciplinary action against prosecutors should be the rule rather than the exception; and legislation should be enacted making it a crime for prosecutors to willfully suppress evidence resulting in a defendant's conviction.

MISBEHAVING IN THE COURTROOM TO SWAY THE JURY

Finally, the prosecutor's trial obligations often are violated. The duties of the prosecuting attorney during a trial were well stated in a classic opinion fifty years ago. The interest of the prosecutor, the court wrote, "is not that it shall win a case, but that justice shall be done. As such, he is in a peculiar and very definite sense the servant of the law, the twofold aim of which is that guilt shall not escape or innocence suffer. He may prosecute with earnestness and vigor—indeed, he should do so. But, while he may strike hard blows, he is not at liberty to strike a foul one."

Despite this admonition, prosecutors continually strike "foul blows." In one leading case of outrageous conduct, a prosecutor concealed from the jury in a murder case the fact that a pair of undershorts

with red stains on it, a crucial piece of evidence, was stained not by blood but by paint. In another recent case, a prosecutor, in his summation, characterized the defendant as an "animal," told the jury that "the only guarantee against his future crimes would be to execute him," and that he should have "his face blown away by a shotgun." In another case, the prosecutor argued that the defendant's attorney knew the defendant was guilty; otherwise he would have put the defendant on the witness stand.

The above examples are illustrative of common practices today, and the main reason such misconduct occurs is quite simple: It works. Indeed, several studies have shown the importance of oral advocacy in the courtroom, as well as the effect produced by such conduct. For example, a student of trial advocacy often is told of the importance of the opening statement. Prosecutors would undoubtedly agree that the opening statement is indeed crucial. In a University of Kansas study, the importance of the opening statement was confirmed. From this study, the authors concluded that in the course of any given trial, the jurors were affected most by the first strong presentation that they saw. This finding leads to the conclusion that if a prosecutor were to present a particularly strong opening argument, the jury would favor the prosecution throughout the trial. Alternatively, if the prosecutor were to provide a weak opening statement, followed by a strong opening statement by the defense, then, according to the authors, the jury would favor the defense during the trial. It thus becomes evident that the prosecutor will be best served by making the strongest opening argument possible, thereby assisting the jury in gaining a better insight into what they are about to hear and see. The opportunity for the prosecutor to influence the jury at this point in the trial is considerable, and many prosecutors use this opportunity to their advantage, even if the circumstances do not call for lengthy or dramatic opening remarks.

An additional aspect of the prosecutor's power over the jury is suggested in a University of North Carolina study, which found that the more arguments counsel raises to support the different substantive arguments offered, the more the jury will believe in that party's case. Moreover, this study found that there is not necessarily a correlation between the amount of objective information in the argument and the persuasiveness of the presentation.

For the trial attorney, then, this study clearly points to the advantage of raising as many issues as possible at trial. For the prosecutor, the two studies taken together would dictate an "action-packed" opening statement, containing as many arguments as can be mustered, even those that might be irrelevant or unnecessary to convince the jury of the defendant's guilt. The second study would also dictate the same strategy for the closing argument. Consequently, a prosecutor who through use of these techniques attempts to assure that the jury knows his case may, despite violating ethical standards to seek justice, be "rewarded" with a guilty verdict. Thus, one begins to perceive the incentive that leads the prosecutor to misbehave in the courtroom.

Similar incentives can be seen with respect to the complex problem of controlling evidence to which the jury may have access. It is common knowledge that in the course of any trial, statements fre-

dence on the decisions of jurors. The authors of the test designed a variety of scenarios whereby some jurors heard about an incriminating piece of evidence while other jurors did not. The study found that the effect of the inadmissible evidence was directly correlated to the strength of the prosecutor's case. The authors of the study reported that when the prosecutor presented a weak case, the inadmissible evidence did in fact prejudice the jurors. Furthermore, the judge's admonition to the jurors to disregard certain evidence did not have the same effect as when the evidence had not been mentioned at all. It had a prejudicial impact anyway.

However, the study also indicated that when there was a strong prosecution case, the inadmissible evidence had little, if any, effect. Nonetheless, the most significant conclusion from the study is that inadmissible evidence had its most prejudicial impact when there was little other evidence upon which the jury could base a decision. In this situation, "the controversial evidence becomes quite salient in the jurors' minds."

Finally, with respect to inadmissible evidence and stricken testimony, even if

---

In one leading case of outrageous conduct, a prosecutor concealed from the jury in a murder case the fact that a pair of undershorts with red stains on it, a crucial piece of evidence, was stained not by blood but by paint.

---

quently are made by the attorneys or witnesses despite the fact that these statements may not be admissible as evidence. Following such a statement, the trial judge may, at the request of opposing counsel, instruct the jury to disregard what they have heard. Most trial lawyers, if they are candid, will agree that it is virtually impossible for jurors realistically to disregard these inadmissible statements. Studies here again demonstrate that our intuition is correct and that this evidence often is considered by jurors in reaching a verdict.

For example, an interesting study conducted at the University of Washington tested the effects of inadmissible evi-

one were to reject all of the studies discussed, it is still clear that although "stricken testimony may tend to be rejected in open discussion, it does have an impact, perhaps even an unconscious one, on the individual juror's judgment." As with previously discussed points, this factor—the unconscious effect of stricken testimony or evidence—will generally not be lost on the prosecutor who is in tune with the psychology of the jury.

The applicability of these studies to the issue of prosecutorial misconduct, then, is quite clear. Faced with a difficult case in which there may be a problem of proof, a prosecutor might be tempted to try to sway the jury by adverting to a matter that might be highly prejudicial. In this connection, another study has suggested that the jury will more likely consider inadmissible evidence that favors conviction.

Despite this factor of "defense favoritism," it is again evident that a prosecutor may find it rewarding to misconduct himself or herself in the courtroom. Of course, a prosecutor who adopts the unethical norm and improperly allows jurors to hear inadmissible proof runs the risk of jeopardizing any resulting conviction. In a situation where the prosecutor feels that he has a weak case, however, a subsequent reversal is not a particularly effective sanction when a conviction might have been difficult to achieve in the first place. Consequently, an unethical courtroom "trick" can be a very attractive idea to the prosecutor who feels he must win. Additionally, there is always the possibility of another conviction even after an appellate reversal. Indeed, while a large number of cases are dismissed following remand by an appellate court, nearly one-half of reversals still result in some type of conviction. Therefore, a pros-

moral standards, the problem of courtroom misconduct will inevitably be tolerated by the public.

Moreover, when considering the problems facing the prosecutor, one also must consider the tremendous stress under which the prosecutor labors on a daily basis. Besides the stressful conditions faced by the ordinary courtroom litigator, prosecuting attorneys, particularly those in large metropolitan areas, are faced with huge and very demanding caseloads. As a result of case volume and time demands, prosecutors may not be able to take advantage of opportunities to relax and recover from the constant onslaught their emotions face every day in the courtroom.

Under these highly stressful conditions, it is understandable that a prosecutor occasionally may find it difficult to face these everyday pressures and to resist temptations to behave unethically. It is not unreasonable to suggest that the conditions under which the prosecutor works can have a profound effect on his attempt to maintain high moral and ethical standards. Having established this hy-

---

An unethical courtroom "trick" can be a very attractive idea to the prosecutor who feels he must win.

---

ecutor can still succeed in obtaining a conviction even after his misconduct led to a reversal.

An additional problem in the area of prosecutor-jury interaction is the prosecutor's prestige; since the prosecutor represents the "government," jurors are more likely to believe him. Put simply, prosecutors are the "good guys" of the legal system, and because they have such glamor, they often may be tempted to use this advantage in an unethical manner. This presents a problem in that the average citizen may often forgive prosecutors for ethical indiscretions, because conviction of criminals certainly justifies in the public eye any means necessary. Consequently, unless the prosecutor is a person of high integrity and able to uphold the highest

pothesis, we see yet another reason why courtroom misconduct may occur.

WHY PROSECUTORIAL MISCONDUCT PERSISTS

Although courtroom misconduct may in many instances be highly effective, why do such practices continue in our judicial system? A number of reasons may account for this phenomenon, perhaps the most significant of which is the harmless error doctrine. Under this doctrine, an appellate court can affirm a conviction despite the presence of serious misconduct during the trial. As one judge stated, the "practical objective of tests of harmless error is to conserve judicial resources by enabling appellate courts to cleanse the judicial process of prejudicial error without becoming mired in harmless error."

Although this definition portrays harmless error as having a most desirable consequence, this desirability is undermined when the prosecutor is able to misconduct himself without fear of sanction. Additionally, since every case is different, what constitutes harmless error in one case may be reversible error in another case. Consequently, harmless error determinations do not offer any significant precedents by which prosecutors can judge the status of their behavior. Moreover, harmless error determinations are essentially absurd. In order to apply the harmless error rule, appellate judges attempt to evaluate how various evidentiary items or instances of prosecutorial misconduct may have affected the jury's verdict. Although it may be relatively simple in some cases to determine whether improper conduct during a trial was harmless, there are many instances when such an analysis cannot be properly made but nevertheless is made. There are numerous instances in which appellate courts are deeply divided over whether or not a given error was harmless. The implications of these contradictory decisions are significant, for they demonstrate the utter failure of appellate courts to provide incentives for the prosecutor to control his behavior. If misconduct can be excused even when reasonable judges differ as to the extent of harm caused by such misbehavior, then very little guidance is given to a prosecutor to assist him in determining the propriety of his actions. Clearly, without such guidance, the potential for misconduct significantly increases.

A final point when analyzing why prosecutorial misconduct persists is the unavailability or inadequacy of penalties visited upon the prosecutor personally in the event of misconduct. Punishment in our legal system comes in varying degrees. An appellate court can punish a prosecutor by simply cautioning him not

to act in the same manner again, reversing his case, or, in some cases, identifying by name the prosecutor who misconducted himself. Even these punishments, however, may not be sufficient to dissuade prosecutors from acting improperly. One noteworthy case describes a prosecutor who appeared before the appellate court on a misconduct issue for the third time, each instance in a different case.

Perhaps the ultimate reason for the ineffectiveness of the judicial system in curbing prosecutorial misconduct is that prosecutors are not personally liable for their misconduct. During the course of a trial, the prosecutor is absolutely shielded from any civil liability that might arise due to his or her misconduct, even if that misconduct was performed with malice. To be sure, there is clearly a necessary level of immunity accorded all government officials. Without such immunity, much of what is normally done by officials in authority might not be performed, out of fear that their practices would later be deemed harmful or improper. Granting prosecutors a certain level of immunity is reasonable. Allowing prosecutors to be completely shielded from civil liability in the event of misconduct, however, provides no deterrent to courtroom misconduct.

For the prosecutor, the temptation to cross over the allowable ethical limit must often be tremendous, because of the distinct advantages that such misconduct creates with respect to assisting the prosecutor to win his case by effectively influencing the jury. Most prosecutors must inevitably be subject to this temptation. It takes a constant effort on the part of every prosecutor to maintain the high moral standards necessary to avoid such temptations. Despite the frequent occurrences of courtroom misconduct, appellate courts have not provided significant incentives to deter it. Inroads will not be made in the effort to end prosecutorial misconduct until the courts decide to take a stricter, more consistent approach to this problem.

THE TRIALS OF THE
Public
Defender

Overworked and underpaid lawyers serve up a brand of justice that is not always in their clients' best interests

JILL SMOLOWE

EVERY DAY, AS HE AMBLES through the cobwebbed halls of the New Orleans criminal court building, public defender Richard Teissier feels he violates his clients' constitutional rights. The Sixth Amendment established, and the landmark *Gideon* Supreme Court case affirmed, the right of poor people to legal counsel. At any given moment, when Teissier is representing some 90 accused murderers, rapists and robbers, his office has no money to hire experts or track down witnesses; its law library consists of a set of lawbooks spirited away from a dead judge's chambers.

With so many clients and so few resources, Teissier decided he could not possibly do justice to them all. So he filed suit against himself. He demanded that the court judge his work inadequate, and find more money for more lawyers. A judge agreed and declared the state's indigent-defense system unconstitutional. The ruling is now on appeal before the Louisiana Supreme Court. "This is a test of whether there is justice in the United States," Teissier says. "If you're only going to pay it lip service then get rid of *Gideon*."

Thirty years ago last week, the Supreme Court unanimously voted in favor of Clarence Earl Gideon, an uneducated gambler and petty thief who insisted on his right to legal counsel. "Any person

haled into court who is too poor to hire a lawyer cannot be assured a fair trial unless counsel is provided for him," wrote Justice Hugo Black. "This seems to us to be an obvious truth." Over the next two decades the court expanded the protection to apply to all criminal cases and stressed that the representation must be "effective." But today, as defenders of indigents handle a flood of cases with meager resources, the debate rages on whether the promise of *Gideon* has been fulfilled.

Most public defenders think not. In Memphis, lawyers lament the plead-'em-and-speed-'em-through pace. "It reminds me of the old country song we have here in Tennessee: 'We're not making love, we're just keeping score,' " says chief public defender AC Wharton. Across the country, lawyers watch with frustration as the bulk of criminal-justice funds goes to police protection, prisons and prosecutors, leaving just 2.3% for public defense services. "We aren't being given the same weapons," says Mary Broderick of the National Legal Aid and Defender Association. "It's like trying to deal with smart bombs when all you've got is a couple of cap pistols."

During the war on crime of the '70s and the war on drugs of the '80s, funneling money to defend suspects was a low priority. Meanwhile, the ranks of police and prosecutors were beefed up, leading to

more arrests, more trials and more work for public defenders. "Indigent defense is a cause without a constituency," says Stephen Bright, director of the Southern Center for Human Rights. Over the years, states have unenthusiastically devised three strategies to handle indigent cases: public defender offices, court-appointed lawyers and contract systems. In all cases, the emphasis is on holding costs down. Justice—and sometimes people's lives—can get lost in the mix.

PUBLIC DEFENDERS: NO RESPECT

"Felonies worry you to death, misdemeanors work you to death," says Mel Tennenbaum, a division chief in the Los Angeles public defenders' office. "We're underappreciated and misunderstood." L.A. lawyer David Carleton had his teeth loosened by a client who didn't like his plea arrangement. Manhattan's Judith White needs all seven days of the week to handle her load of drug cases—a task she continues to tackle even since a crack addict murdered her father four years ago. When Lynne Borsuk filed a motion with Georgia's Fulton County Superior Court seeking to reduce her load of 122 open cases, she was demoted to juvenile court. She was lucky; others have been fired for similar actions.

Across the country, the lawyers who staff big-city public defender offices strike a common note: they get no respect. "Clients figure if we were really good, we'd be out there making big money," says Maria Cavalluzzi, a Los Angeles public defender. In courthouse waiting areas—known variously as the Tombs, the Pits, the Tank—defendants cavalierly dismiss their free counselors as "dump trucks," a term that reflects their view that public defenders are more interested in dumping cases than mounting rigorous defenses.

The typical public defender is underpaid and overwhelmed. When Jacquelyn Robins was appointed New Mexico's state public defender in 1985, there were six lawyers in Albuquerque's Metro court to handle the annual load of 13,000 misdemeanor cases. Three years later Robins persuaded state legislators to put up funds for three more lawyers. Even then, lawyers could manage only cursory conferences with clients just 30 minutes before their court appearance. In 1991 Robins again went begging for dollars. When she was accused of having a "management problem," she quit. The move caused such a furor that the Governor promised additional funds. Albuquerque's chief public defender, Kelly Knight, now has 16 lawyers, but the pace is still grueling. "I'm 34, not married, and I have no children," Knight says. "But I'm really, really burned out." She plans to take a sabbatical next year—whether she is granted one or not.

In Los Angeles, which boasts one of the best public defender programs in the country, salaries start at $42,000 and go as high as $97,000. A staff of 570 lawyers juggles roughly 80,000 cases a year. The work is often thankless, but every so often a case upholds the promise of *Gideon*. Earlier this month Frank White, 36, a tall, muscular man covered with tattoos, landed in L.A. County court, accused of murdering a tiny Korean woman with his bare fists. White, diagnosed as a paranoid schizophrenic, refused to take his medication and grew angry when the deputies would not remove his handcuffs. White glared as he stalked into the courtroom and dropped heavily into the seat beside public defender Mark Windham. Without a word, Windham slid his chair closer to his explosive client until they were touching shoulders. And there he stayed throughout the proceeding. "Male bonding," a sheriff's deputy quipped. But to everyone's astonishment, White quieted down. "I did it to make him and everyone else in the room feel better," Windham explained.

Seasoned defense lawyers know the value of the small gesture. And the large. Anticipating the guilty verdict returned by the jury two weeks ago, Windham built a parallel argument that White was not guilty by reason of insanity. If the jury agrees, White will be locked up in a hospital instead of being imprisoned.

ASSIGNED ATTORNEYS: NO EXPERIENCE

In smaller cities, defendants are usually assigned attorneys by the court. Often these lawyers, who tend to be young and inexperienced or old and tired, receive only $20 to $25 an hour. Capital cases go for as little as $400. At Detroit's Recorder's Court, lawyers are paid a flat fee: $1,400 for first-degree murder, $750 for lesser offenses that carry up to a life sentence. "The more time you spend on a case, the less money you make," says attorney David Steingold, a 14-year veteran. Hence lawyers have learned to plead cases quickly and forgo time-consuming motions, a phenomenon known among lawyers as the "plea mill."

Slapdash pleas are sometimes less brutal than the farcical trials that can result when ill-prepared lawyers are thrown in over their heads. In 1983 a man named Victor Roberts and an accomplice stole a car and drove to an Atlanta suburb hunting for a house to burglarize. Posing as insurance salesmen, they entered the home of Mary Jo Jenkins. A skirmish ensued and a gun went off, shooting Jenkins through the heart. H. Geoffrey Slade, a lawyer for 13 years, was assigned to handle the capital case. When he realized he was in over his head and requested co-counsel, the court appointed Jim Hamilton, 75, who had almost no criminal experience.

Their efforts, while well intended, served no one's interests. They conducted no investigation. They interviewed no witnesses in person. They never visited the crime scene. During the trial they introduced no evidence in Roberts' defense. The prosecution, meanwhile, trotted out gory photographs of Jenkins—taken after she had been autopsied. Slade knew enough to object, but he was overruled. The jury deliberated only 45 minutes; Roberts found himself on death row. A federal judge subsequently ordered a new trial, on the ground that the first had been "fundamentally unfair," in part because Roberts' lawyers had failed to "adequately and effectively investigate" the crime. Pretrial proceedings are scheduled to get under way this month—10 years after Roberts' arrest.

CONTRACT LAWYERS: NO SATISFACTION

A variation on court-appointed attorneys, popular in rural areas, is a contract system under which lawyers re-ceive a flat rate. The fee is usually so meager that these attorneys maintain a private practice on the side. Such a system, says Bright, results in "lawyers who view their responsibilities as unwanted burdens, have no inclination to help the client and have no incentive to learn or to develop criminal trial skills." When expenses mount, they economize by refusing the collect calls of their jailed clients. Under a contract system, says L.A.'s Tennenbaum, "you don't investigate, you don't ask for continuances, you plead at the earliest possible moment."

Or worse. In Indiana's Marion County, which includes Indianapolis, reform was sparked after a 1991 study documented abuses in a system where the six superior court judges hired defense lawyers for $20,800 a year to handle the area's indigent work on a part-time basis. Bobby Lee Houston, a truck driver, hired a private counselor whom he couldn't afford when he was arrested in 1989 on charges of child molestation. The lawyer urged him to plead guilty and serve five years; Houston insisted he was innocent. He wrote to a judge complaining of delays and, after 14 months, was assigned David Sexson, one of the contract lawyers. Sexson suggested that Houston plead guilty and get off with time served. Houston was firm: no dice.

One month later, Houston's case was dismissed—but no one bothered to tell him. It would be four more months before Houston learned that he was a free man. After 19 pointless months in a jail cell, Houston has his own bottom line: "Justice is a money thing."

That is precisely what Clarence Earl Gideon complained of in 1962 when he put pencil to lined paper in his Florida cell and and wrote the Supreme Court: "The question is very simple. I requested the court to appoint me attorney and the court refused." Since then, lawyers and judges have stated and restated Gideon's assertion of a fundamental right to adequate representation. Chief Justice Harold Clarke of the Georgia Supreme Court warned state legislators earlier this year, "We need to remember that if the state can deny justice to the poor, it has within its grasp the power to deny justice to anybody." Richard Teissier and his fellow public defenders surely would agree with Judge Clarke: Justice on the cheap is no justice at all.   **—Reported by Julie Johnson/ Washington, Michael Riley/New Orleans and James Willwerth/Los Angeles**

SUSPECT
CONFESSIONS

He's made mincemeat of false memories.
But the social psychologist Richard Ofshe has a more pressing
question: Why do innocent people admit to crimes
they didn't commit?

Richard Jerome

Richard Jerome is a senior writer at People *magazine.*

THROUGH A THICKENING FOG, RICHARD J. OFSHE WINDS his white BMW homeward into the Oakland hills, leaving behind the University of California at Berkeley, where he is a professor of social psychology. In florid tones refined by 30 years at the lectern, Ofshe is expounding on his latest area of interest, the ways in which police interrogations can elicit false confessions. Specifically, he is bemoaning the case of Jessie Lloyd Misskelley Jr., a teen-ager from a squalid Arkansas trailer park who confessed—falsely, Ofshe maintains—to taking part in the ghastly murder of three 8-year-old boys. In spite of Ofshe's voluminous expert testimony on his behalf, Misskelley, who has an I.Q. in the 70's, was sentenced to life plus 40 years in prison.

"It was like walking straight into 'Deliverance,'" Ofshe says, casually veering around another hairpin turn. "The trial was a travesty. The conduct of the judge was outrageous."

At 54, Ofshe has acquired a muted celebrity for his work on extreme influence tactics and thought control. He shared in the 1979 Pulitzer Prize in public service after assisting The Point Reyes (Calif.) Light in its exposé of Synanon, a Bay Area drug rehabilitation group that evolved into an armed cult. More recently, Ofshe has been an aggressive and influential debunker of "recovered memory," the theory whereby long-repressed traumas are retrieved by patients undergoing what Ofshe calls exceedingly manipulative psycho-

therapy. As such, Ofshe is a vivid figure in "Remembering Satan," Lawrence Wright's book about the case of Paul Ingram, a former Olympia, Wash., sheriff's deputy now serving 20 years in prison primarily because he became convinced that the accusations of one of his daughters, who claimed that he had indulged in a 17-year binge of satanism, incest and infanticide, were true. Ofshe, a champion of Ingram, dissects the affair in his recent book, "Making Monsters: False Memories, Psychotherapy and Sexual Hysteria," written with Ethan Watters.

But for the most part, Ofshe has set aside violent cults and overzealous shrinks and is fixated on the third of his bêtes noires: false confessions. According to Ofshe and a considerable body of literature, modern interrogation tactics are so subtly powerful that police can—entirely unwittingly—coerce innocent suspects into admitting to the most heinous crimes. Sometimes, Ofshe says, a suspect admits guilt simply to escape the stress of the interrogation. More rarely, a suspect comes to believe that he actually committed the crime in question, though he has no memory of it.

For Ofshe, exorcising both kinds of false confession from the American justice system has become an almost obsessive quest. All told, he has consulted or testified in more than 80 criminal cases involving suspects from whom, he concluded, confessions were coerced; in most of these cases, the physical evidence strongly suggested innocence. Although he makes money at it overall—$40,000 in 1993—he sometimes works pro bono. With dark, disdaining eyes set against a shock of gray curls and a swirling beard, Ofshe looks vaguely sinister—a wily Renaissance pol, perhaps, or Claudius in a road company of Hamlet. Confession, he points out, is the anchor of a trial in which there is no hard evidence. "And <u>false confession</u>," he says, "<u>ranks third after perjury and eyewitness error as a</u> <u>cause of wrongful convictions in American homi-</u> <u>cide cases.</u>"

His numbers are based on several studies, most recently work by the sociologist Michael L. Radelet of the University of Florida, Hugo Adam Bedau, professor of philosophy at Tufts University, and Constance E. Putnam, a Boston-based writer. In their 1992 book, "In Spite of Innocence," the authors review more than 400 cases in which innocent people were convicted of capital crimes in the United States. Fourteen percent were caused by false confession. "If it happened just one-half of 1 percent of the time," Ofshe says, "it still means that hundreds, or perhaps thousands, of people each year are being unjustly imprisoned. Even if one innocent man or woman is convicted, it's too many. And it's unnecessary because this is a fixable problem"—fixable, he adds, if only police interrogations were electronically recorded, a requirement now only in Alaska and Minnesota.

"Now I don't think for one second," Ofshe stresses, "that the detectives and prosecutors in cases of false confessions want to bring about that result. But because they don't understand the mistake as it is being made, the case moves forward and takes everyone along with it."

THE BMW IS NOW TUCKED SAFELY UNder Ofshe's red Ferrari, which sits on a raised hoist in the garage of his hillside home, a quasi-Mediterranean mix of stone and stucco. Inside, rock music from a new stereo system tumbles down the coiled stairs of a three-and-a-half-story central rotunda, into a cherry-paneled library where Ofshe, propped like a pasha on a brown leather couch, surveys his domain with a reverent sigh: "I never thought I'd ever get to have a house like this."

It mirrors its inhabitant: spare, opulent, imposing yet accessible. One can well appreciate that Ofshe's fondest boyhood memory is of the austere charms of the Frick Collection mansion. His father, a dress designer, moved the family from the Bronx to Queens when Ofshe was a child. Ofshe attended Queens College, then went to graduate school at Stanford. "I honestly can't tell you now what led me to psychology," he says. "I suppose I'm a watcher. I'm comfortable observing people and lecturing at them — but I am absolutely incapable of making small talk, a gift I consider one of the great mysteries of life."

During graduate school, Ofshe was married briefly and then, as he puts it, "got un-married." (He married his present wife, Bonnie Blair, a successful designer of sweaters, in 1981.) Ofshe gravitated toward social psychology; his work on cults grew out of a study of utopian societies

he undertook in the early 1970's. One such community was Synanon, begun as a drug treatment center by Charles Dederich. But by 1978, Dederich had accumulated a substantial arsenal, as well as a large cadre of loyal followers. By this time, The Point Reyes Light, a weekly based near Ofshe's summer home, had begun an investigative series on Synanon, on which Ofshe collaborated. As a result of the media exposure, Synanon lost its tax-exempt status and disintegrated. Dederich sued Ofshe three times unsuccessfully for libel, prompting him to retaliate with a malicious prosecution suit. " 'When this is over, I'll be the one driving the red Ferrari,' " Ofshe says he told people at the time. The Ferrari, he now confides, "accounts for a small percentage of my settlement. A very small percentage."

Material success aside, Ofshe seems to revel most in the validation of his work by respected media outlets. It takes little prodding for him to express his glee at Lawrence Wright's description of him as "Zeus-like" in "Remembering Satan" — which first appeared as an article in The New Yorker, a magazine Ofshe clearly reveres. And he is quick to point out that the television movie of Wright's book, currently being filmed, features him as the central character — as played by William Devane.

What saves this self-absorption from being insufferable is Ofshe's interest in helping people he considers innocent. He first focused on police interrogation in 1987, after a phone call from Joseph G. Donahey Jr., a veteran Florida attorney. Donahey was representing Thomas F. Sawyer, a Clearwater golf course groundskeeper who in 1986, after an uncommonly grueling 16-hour interrogation, confessed to the brutal murder of a neighbor; the police convinced Sawyer that he'd lost all memory of the incident during an alcoholic blackout. (Sawyer, against whom there was no physical evidence, had quickly recanted.) "Donahey realized something was terribly wrong with Tom's confession," Ofshe says. "At first I was skeptical. But once I read the transcript of the interrogation, it became obvious what had happened to Tom."

Ofshe spent 300 hours analyzing the Sawyer interrogation — which, by a lucky quirk, was taped in its entirety — and concluded it was "a tour de force of psychological coercion." Sawyer's police interrogators, Peter Fire and John Dean, invited Sawyer to the station house on the premise that he was being asked to "assist" with their investigation. Then, Ofshe says, they flattered him into providing his own hypothetical murder scenario. The detectives then used leading questions to shape the groundskeeper's responses, eventually tossing his answers back as evidence of his guilt. Consider the following dialogue, slightly condensed, on the position of the victim's body:

FIRE: And he would put her in the bed how? Like she's doing what?

SAWYER: Sleeping.
FIRE: O.K. What would you put her on? Her. . . .
SAWYER: On her back.
FIRE: Put her on her back? . . .
SAWYER: I'd put her on her back sleeping.
FIRE: Put her on her back, sleeping?
SAWYER: Don't you sleep on your back?
FIRE: No. . . .
SAWYER: I don't sleep on my side.
FIRE: Well, what other way could you put her?
SAWYER: Face down.
FIRE: O.K. Face down. . . .
SAWYER: I'd put her on her stomach. . . .
FIRE: You hit the nail on the head. You put her on her stomach.

Deception, typically by lying about the presence of witnesses or physical evidence or about polygraph results, is a common interrogation tactic, Ofshe says, and it was used baldly against Sawyer. ("We found a lot of hairs and fibers on her body," Fire insisted at one point. "We have your hair. . . . There's a lot of evidence. There's a lot of evidence. A lot of evidence.")

"If you're dealing with middle-class types," Ofshe says, "or at least middle-class types socialized by my mother, they're hearing: 'It's inevitable that you'll be caught and punished to the max.' I have no interest in stripping police of tactics that make perfect sense — when those tactics are supported by compelling physical evidence. But the same things that can convince a guilty person that he's been caught can convince someone who's innocent that he's caught."

Under this intense barrage, Sawyer, who for hours steadfastly maintained his innocence, exhibited his first trace of self-doubt: "I honestly believe that I didn't do it. . . . I don't remember doing it. If I did, and I don't think I did. . . . You almost got me convinced I did, but. . . . "

"He went from straight denial to 'I couldn't have done something like this,' " Ofshe says. "And finally, when he confessed, it was so beautiful, so perfect in the way he verbalized it: 'I guess all the evidence is in, I guess I must have done it.' "

Strong evidence of a false confession, Ofshe says, is when the narrative is at odds with the known facts of the case or has been clearly fed to the suspect, however inadvertently, by the police themselves. "Sawyer was wrong about almost everything," Ofshe says, "except for several details" — like the position of the victim's body — "that were clearly introduced by Fire and Dean."

Ultimately, Ofshe's testimony helped exonerate Sawyer, whose confession was suppressed in 1989 after the groundskeeper had spent 14 months in jail awaiting trial. Shortly thereafter, Ofshe — by now increasingly sought by desperate defense attorneys — helped free Mark Nunez, Leo Bruce and Dante Parker, who, fingered by a psychiatric patient and subjected to a highly coercive interrogation, had falsely confessed to killing nine people

at a Buddhist temple outside Phoenix. In Flagstaff, Ofshe was instrumental in winning the 1988 acquittal of George Abney, a graduate student with a history of depression, who had admitted to the ritualistic murder of a Navajo woman. In the Phoenix case, the real murderer was eventually caught and prosecuted.

"WHAT SOME OF THE PSYCHOLOGISTS SAY IS I put you in a room, you're all emotional and at the end of five or six hours, I've fed you everything," Lieut. Ralph M. Lacer is saying in his Oakland police office, several miles from Ofshe's home. "Well, if I was on the jury, I'd be rolling my eyes saying: 'Who is the dumb [expletive] who thinks this is gonna go over?' "

Fiftyish, ruddy and blond, the bespectacled Lacer was one of the interrogating officers in the high-profile case of Bradley Page, a handsome Berkeley student who had admitted — falsely, so Page and his attorneys maintained — to murdering his girlfriend, Roberta (BiBi) Lee, in a fit of anger in 1984. After two trials, the second of which Ofshe consulted on, Page was convicted of manslaughter. (He was released, after serving part of a six-year sentence, in February.)

Only part of the Page interrogation was recorded. From 11:50 A.M. to 1:10 P.M. on Dec. 10, 1984, Lacer and his partner, Sgt. Jerry Harris, taped Page as he gave them a firm, lucid account of his movements during the time since Lee had disappeared a month before — none of which included bludgeoning her to death. Then the detectives shut off the machine until 7:07 P.M., by which time Page was highly emotional, confessing to murder, albeit in vague, halting language peppered with "might haves," "would haves" and other subjunctive phrases that left Ofshe highly suspicious. Lacer freely acknowledges that Page's admission of guilt, made in the absence of hard evidence, was the heart and soul of the case against him. "If we hadn't gotten the confession," Lacer says, "Brad would've walked."

I raise Ofshe's argument, that taping interrogations in full might resolve any ambiguities.

"First of all, a tape is inhibiting," Lacer counters. "It's hard to get at the truth. And say we go for 10 hours — we have 10 hours of tape that maybe boil down to 15 or 20 minutes of you saying, 'Yes, I killed Johnny Jones.' You bet the public defender's going to have the jury listen to all 10 hours of that tape and by that time the jury won't remember what it's all about."

According to Lacer, the craft of interrogation is learned through experience. "Every day when you stop someone on the street, you're interrogating them," he says. " 'Where do you live? Where you headed to?' We definitely try to establish rapport — basically, I want to get you to talk to me. But when we bring a suspect in, we keep the room bare, a table and two or three chairs, a locked door."

I glance around, aware for the first time that the

interview is unfolding in the ideal interrogation setting. I ask Lacer what would happen if a person being questioned invokes his constitutional right of silence or, if he is not under arrest, his right to simply walk out the door.

"Well, that would be the end of the situation," he says. "But many times it won't happen, and here's why: I see you've got a wedding ring on, Rich. Well, say Mrs. Rich ends up dead in the house. We call you down and you say, 'I don't think I want to talk to you guys, I'm out of here.' Well, the thing is, your in-laws find out that you took that route and they know right away who killed your wife.

"Now most of the time, the suspect will set up barriers. Like you got your legs crossed — that's kind of a psychological barrier. And I lean forward, violate your personal space, get closer and closer and pretty soon we're nose to nose." As Lacer edges toward me, his eyes, though still genial, bear into mine.

"Now remember, I'm just talking, not yelling or bullying," he says. "It's not going to help matters if I suddenly say '[Expletive], that's a [expletive] black sweater you have on — I threw away the last black sweater I had like that!' You can maybe bully a little bit verbally by saying: 'Rich, that last story was [expletive]. Let's not even go into that again.'" Lacer's eyes turn caustic through his aviator glasses.

"Now as far as yelling," he says, chummy again, "about the only time we do it here in Oakland is if someone's talking over you or if they're going off on a tangent, and I'd say, 'Hey Rich, let's get back to the *subject!*'" His voice slices through the claustrophobia of the room — a ferocity all the more unnerving because it booms from Lacer's amiable shell.

"We've been in a room together for a while, Rich," he says, chuckling. "Do you feel like confessing to anything?"

"LACER RATIONALIZES THAT SOMEONE LIKE Bradley Page — or you and I — cannot be made to confess," Ofshe says on the day after my encounter with the Oakland lieutenant. "Because it is in many ways one of the worst professional errors you can make — like a physician amputating the wrong arm."

Prevention, he adds, is surprisingly simple: "Above all, no confession ought be accepted unless it has been corroborated with clear-cut and powerful evidence. And you must never instigate a high-pressure, accusatory interrogation unless you have a good and sound reason to do it." Another safeguard, Ofshe reiterates, is to record interrogations. Early last year, the professor helped win a significant victory in the same Clearwater courthouse where the Sawyer case was heard. Relying substantially on Ofshe's testimony, Judge Claire K. Luten formed a forceful opinion that the confession of Francis Dupont, an alcoholic drifter who had admitted to murdering a friend, was psychologically coerced. Moreover, Luten ruled that the failure to tape the interrogation of Dupont was in direct violation of due process.

"I'd be content to devote myself to that issue until I am too old to work on it," Ofshe says.

In a sense, this is Ofshe's moment, for never has the nation been more attuned to what happens in a courtroom. Yet for the plain citizen — the juror — he is also a problematic figure, a bearded academic speaking in tones of unassailable authority about social psychology, a discipline that resounds with squishy inexactitude. Ofshe's theories about false confession, however well researched, risk being perceived as just another set of legal loopholes. And his "one innocent man or woman" might well be shrugged off — probably not worth the trouble and surely not worth the risk.

For which reason Ofshe emphasizes the most basic preventive to false confession: if you find yourself being questioned about a crime you know you did not commit, resist at all costs the impulse to be helpful, no matter how charming or forbidding the interrogator might be.

"I tell my classes," Ofshe says, "that if they ever find themselves in that situation, remember the four magic words of the criminal justice system: 'I want a lawyer.'"

A TRIAL FOR OUR TIMES

Lance Morrow

The easiest meaning of the trial is that we live in a golden age of high trash, an Elizabethan epoch of lowest-common-denominator, everything-is-entertainment daytime drama that in Judge Ito's courtroom composed, day by day, its masterpiece—its soap, Santa Monica Othello.

But the Simpson trial has a deeper geography. Sometimes a trial plays out like a culture's collective dream—a vivid, edgy, distorted story that casts up images and characters from the realm of instinct and has them act out the society's deepest passions: its fears, prejudices and desires.

Courtroom as religious rite: Apollo—the law—sifts through the disorders of Dionysus—human nature in the wild, where Medea's children and Orestes' mother and Nicole Brown Simpson and Ron Goldman all are murdered. To re-establish order, the rational takes the irrational to court. Sometimes the result is itself irrational, but in the drama, you may see for a moment into the society's heart.

Is that what the Simpson trial amounts to? A strange, garish X ray of American society, circa 1994–95?

In the 1920s the Scopes trial enacted the collision between the moral universe of older, agricultural America, where the Bible held authority, and the new urban, secular-humanist nation wherein H.L. Mencken was God. The Sacco-Vanzetti trial stirred up all of America's agitations about immigration, anarchy and the Red Menace.

And so on, through the decades. The 1930s' Scottsboro Boys (race, sex, the myth of endangered white female virtue, which was always the Southern white man's reverse rape projection). The 1940s' Alger Hiss case (emergent cold war and its anxieties of communist infiltration). In the 1960s, the Chicago Seven trial (Vietnam, the crisis of American authority); in the 1970s, Watergate. In the 1980s, insider trading.

Now the defining trial of the 1990s. The Simpson case offhand seems an unbeatably lurid end-of-the-millennium American omnium-gatherum of race (the nation's oldest, most durable inflammmation of the psyche), sex, celebrity, media hype, justice and injustice. . . . A perfect demonstration of how the American tendency to moralize has gone into partnership with the American appetite for trash—the superego and the id so nicely morphed that they are indistinguishable.

Events have two kinds of meanings: 1) what really happened, the facts, and 2) what people believe happened, the immense tapestry of folklore and conviction and myth that surrounds an event like the Simpson-Goldman murders. Category No. 1 addresses the needs of justice and history. But category No. 2 is important and fascinating in its own way. In category No. 2, the Simpson trial became a vivid shadow play of race in America. The defense's evocations of race in the trial may have been only an inflaming diversion. But on the subject of race, America is tinder dry this season.

AN UGLY END TO IT ALL

Escalating racial rhetoric, inside and outside the courtroom, dominates the trial's final days and sets the stage for a divisive verdict.

RICHARD LACAYO

THE IMPOSSIBLY TANGLED ISSUES of the O.J. Simpson trial could best be understood last week by paying attention to the tears. Prosecutor Marcia Clark finished her summation with the chilling sounds of Nicole Brown Simpson's pleading 911 calls to police. While a screen flashed pictures of Nicole's bruised face, followed by her and Ronald Goldman in death, the families of the victims wept. But what may make more of a difference to the verdict is what happened when defense attorney Johnnie Cochran Jr. gave his summation a day earlier. When he reminded the mostly black jury of how often African Americans have been mistreated by racist police, one of the black jurors seemed on the verge of tears.

The Simpson trial was probably destined to come down to race, though maybe it didn't have to come down quite so hard. By the time the case went to the jury last week, careening into its final and most heart-stopping stage, blacks and whites, who often live in separate neighborhoods, were living in separate worlds on the subject of O.J. His trial has generated two utterly opposed views of who is guilty: Simpson for murder, or the Los Angeles police for tainting the evidence against him. That both views might be true is a possibility that threatened to get swept away by the emotions stirred up by the trial.

In her final arguments Clark urged the jurors to ignore "the sideshows." But when it came to the toxic racial elements of the case, there were no clear lines anymore between what was a distraction and what was essential to a fair judgment. It would be

From *Time*, October 9, 1995, pp. 28, 30-35, 38-39. © 1995 by Time Inc. Magazine Company. Reprinted by permission.

OPEN THE WINDOWS. LET IN THE LIGHT. WHEN YOU LOOK AT THE WHOLE PICTURE, YOU SEE THE TRUTH.

—MARCIA CLARK, prosecutor

complicated enough if Simpson were just a wealthy and charming athlete accused of murdering his wife. But from the start there was more to it: he was black, his wife was white and the police department was the same one that brought the world the beating of Rodney King.

That gave Cochran the opening to put at the center of his case Mark Fuhrman, the Los Angeles police detective who played a critical role in collecting evidence at the crime scenes—and whose mind, judging from the taped monologues he made for a would-be screenwriter, is a storm of racial fury. But Cochran set off his own kind of racial tempest when he used his closing arguments to call Fuhrman and another Los Angeles officer, Philip Vannatter, "twin devils" and to compare Fuhrman to Adolf Hitler. More than that, he urged the jurors to see a not-guilty verdict as an opportunity to send a message against racism and police misconduct. "Fuhrman is a nightmare, but he's America's nightmare, not just black people's nightmare," Cochran told TIME last week. "And everybody needs to understand that."

Even before the verdict, it was plain just how passionately the Simpson case pressed upon the sore spots of the American racial psyche. On Thursday Bill Clinton said he was "concerned" about Cochran's play to racial feeling in his final arguments: "I hope the American people will not let this become some symbol of the larger racial issue in our country."

But it already had. In a case in which Fuhrman's racist monologues could have provided a voice-over for the Rodney King beating tape, it wasn't possible to forget race. "The best thing that could come out of this trial is O.J.'s being found not guilty because the jury believes that there was some type of frame-up," says Anthony Taylor, 36, a black Chicago paralegal who carpools to work with a white woman and often discusses the case during their ride. "It

would shed light on the racial problems not only in various police departments but in the general population as a whole."

That outcome would appall Larry Miller, a white man who owns a Chicago hot-dog stand. "If white people yell racism, we're bigots. If a black person yells it, it has to be true. I've never known racism to be an excuse for murder."

> Escalating racial rhetoric, inside and outside the courtroom, dominates the trial's final days and sets the stage for a divisive verdict

There may be no verdict that can reconcile feelings so sharply polarized. Never mind that the jury has nine African Americans—a guilty verdict will infuriate many blacks outside the courtroom. An NBC poll last week showed just 2% of blacks would convict Simpson of first-degree murder, which requires proof of premeditation and could send him to prison for life without parole. Only 15% would support even a second-degree verdict, the one appropriate to killings that might be called crimes of passion, which in California would carry a prison term of 15 years to life. Fifty-nine percent believe he should be acquitted.

Acquitted? For the majority of white Americans who think Simpson did it, a cynical reading of that verdict—and cynical readings would be common—would mean that a millionaire jock who beats his wife, then butchers her and another man, can still walk, provided he buys the best lawyers around and they play the race card. For that majority, an acquittal would be the mirror image of the outcome in the

first Rodney King beating trial, in which a mostly white jury acquitted four white police officers of what looked to most people like a blatant act of brutality.

As for a hung jury? If it should emerge that it was split largely along racial lines, it would leave most Americans with the impression that black jurors could not bring themselves to convict a black defendant so dear to them as O.J. It would also probably mean another trial, and thanks to a year of saturated publicity, the search for a dozen unbiased jurors is certain to be more difficult than it was the first time. Los Angeles district attorney Gil Garcetti has promised to retry Simpson even if the jury votes 11 to 1 for acquittal. The seminars on DNA evidence. The bloody glove. Mark Fuhrman. Kato Kaelin. Could there be anyone, anywhere, who would want to go through that again?

As it awaits the verdict, Los Angeles has been gloomily revisiting some of its worst memories, the ones formed during the riots that followed the first Rodney King trial. The L.A.P.D., which was accused of responding too slowly to the first disturbances that followed the King verdict, will be on low-level alert on O.J.'s verdict day. After Cochran's summation, police chief Willie Williams declared he would hold the entire defense team responsible for heightening tensions in his city: "When this trial is over, they're going to go back to their homes. [But] we're going to have to live with the bile spewed out these last few days."

N FACT, THOUGH, THERE WILL BE NO place in America where the fallout of the Simpson case will not be felt, especially after the explosive events of last week. There were signs as early as Tuesday, when Cochran showed up at the courthouse surrounded by a crew of muscle in bow ties from Louis Farrakhan's Nation of Islam. Cochran says he took up their offer to act as his bodyguards because he had received death threats, including one faxed to the courtroom during his sum-

STOP THIS COVER-UP! STOP THIS COVER-UP! IF YOU DON'T STOP IT, THEN WHO?

—JOHNNIE COCHRAN JR., defense attorney

mation. "We do get threats, so we have to have protection," Cochran shrugs. "It's just one of those things." But given Farrakhan's reputation for antiwhite and anti-Semitic invective, Cochran's decision could not help but heighten tensions around the court.

Cochran says he has visited Yad Vashem, the memorial in Jerusalem to the victims of the Holocaust. "I understand that no particular race has a corner on misery," he told TIME last week. Simpson lawyer Robert Shapiro told a friend he was unhappy about playing up the race issue. But Alan Dershowitz, famously sensitive to anti-Semitism, insists that for putting Fuhrman on the stand in the first place, "the prosecution is entirely to blame for introducing race into this case."

Clark, who has won 20 felony cases and

would take him to the airport. The defense presented witnesses—some less credible than others—who said that at 10:15 all was well around Nicole's house. Clark ridiculed the idea that so many witnesses could have been in the same vicinity at the same time without being aware of one another.

The prosecution is on stronger ground with its testimony from Allan Park, the limo driver who went to Simpson's residence to drive him to the airport. He reported that no one answered when he rang at 10:42 p.m., a time verified by a phone call he then made to his boss. During the call, he says, he saw a black person about six feet tall enter the house—after which O.J. answered the intercom to say he had been sleeping. That contradicts the defense contention that O.J. had been hitting golf balls

the blood as he had earlier testified. It was probably less, he said.

THE BLOODY SOCKS The defense produced a police videotape of Simpson's bedroom with an automatic time mark of 4:13 p.m. It shows no socks. But the work logs of police investigators Andrea Mazzola and Dennis Fung show that they collected the socks there slightly later. The defense suggests that the socks were put on the floor after the video was taken. Neither Clark nor deputy district attorney Chris Darden explained that discrepancy in their final arguments. They did raise the point that even corrupt cops would have no reason to plant socks without blood on them—the defense charges the blood was applied later.

THE GLOVES For prosecutors, the glove found at Simpson's estate is key. It

---

HE IS ONE OF THE MOST DISGUSTING HUMAN BEINGS I HAVE EVER HAD TO LISTEN TO IN MY LIFE.
—FRED GOLDMAN, father of Ronald Goldman, referring to defense lawyer Johnnie Cochran

---

has not lost one in almost 10 years, says the evidence against Simpson is as strong as any she has argued. But it took her too long to understand that Fuhrman's virulent racism, which she recognized early, could poison the entire prosecution case. "Marcia knew Fuhrman was a bad cop, but she felt certain he hadn't planted evidence," says a deputy district attorney in her office. "They felt they could use Fuhrman anyway. Well, you can't use a racist cop. If you know you got a bad cop on your case, you drop him."

Clark dropped Fuhrman hard in her closing remarks when she vehemently rejected him as a racist who had lied on the stand. But it may have been too late to save her case. For his part, Cochran denies that in his summation he was urging "jury nullification"—proposing that jurors set aside the evidence to make their decision on another basis. "What we said is that in this case, where there is such a reasonable doubt, for the prosecution to prevail each link in the chain of things has to be proved beyond a reasonable doubt," he explains. "They didn't do that."

WHAT THE JURY WILL BEGIN TO MULL OVER this week are two versions of events that are in many respects utterly irreconcilable. Some of the main points they must discuss:
THE TIME FRAME The prosecution asserts that the killings occurred at around 10:15 p.m., when neighbors say they heard the cries of Nicole's dog. That would give Simpson enough time—about an hour—to get from his house to Nicole's, commit the murders and return home for the limo that

in his yard around that time—an alibi no witness ever confirmed.
THE BLOOD Prosecutors contend that O.J. left blood—his own and that of his victims—around the crime scene, in his car and at his home. Defense attorneys say the blood was either contaminated by police incompetence, making DNA tests unreliable, or planted by Fuhrman and Vannatter. To support the latter claim, they point out that blood disappeared from the lab sample taken from Simpson's arm for comparison purposes in the DNA tests. A nurse originally testified that the sample contained around 8 cc of blood on June 13, but according to defense testimony it lost 1.5 cc of blood during the police investigation. The defense postulates—but without evidence—that Vannatter took the vial of blood in an unsealed envelope and brought it to Simpson's residence, where it was planted on the socks in O.J.'s bedroom—along with some of Nicole's blood. Later, they say, some was also planted on her back gate. In a video taken at his home, the nurse, who was ailing and couldn't testify in court, said he was not really as precise in measuring out

matches the one found at the murder scene. A glove expert testified that the pair is the kind Simpson is seen wearing on TV broadcasts, and credit-card records show that Nicole bought him such gloves. The one found at Simpson's house has both victims' blood on it.

But these are also the gloves that seemed too small for O.J. when Darden asked him to put them on in court. Will the jury care that O.J. was putting them on over latex lab gloves that would have hampered the fit? More important, it was Mark Fuhrman who found the glove in Simpson's yard. More than once, the jury heard excerpts from the letter by Kathleen Bell, a Fuhrman acquaintance, who said he told her if he wanted to arrest an interracial couple, he would invent a charge if necessary.

A second set of DNA tests, done in a lab not affiliated with the L.A.P.D., also showed the blood of O.J., Ron and Nicole in the Bronco. But the defense explains that by saying Fuhrman rubbed the bloody glove around the car. They offer no physical evidence to support their claims, but to the mind of the jurors they may not need to.

YOU CAN'T ERADICATE RACISM WITHIN THE LAPD...OR WITHIN THE NATION AS A WHOLE BY DELIVERING A VERDICT OF NOT GUILTY.
—CHRISTOPHER DARDEN, deputy district attorney, during rebuttal

---

Their allegations exist in a context of public anger over the L.A.P.D.'s problems with race relations, to say nothing of Fuhrman's.

In the end, it may be that no particular court exhibit will sway the jury. What may matter most is whether the larger notion of a police conspiracy is more compelling than the preponderance of evidence.

Those are the dueling narratives that will be examined by a jury that has spent nine months in captivity—a record for sequestration. During that time, the Simpson 12 (plus two remaining alternates) have been subjected to something like sensory deprivation. Contact with family and friends has been limited to a nightly 15-minute phone call, monitored by sheriff's deputies, and the five-hour conjugal visits on Saturdays. The deputies collect the jurors' room keys each night and routinely search their belongings for diaries or other forbidden items. When a juror got permission to celebrate her wedding anniversary by having dinner with her husband in the hotel restaurant, two security guards watched over them throughout the meal.

THE SIMPSON JURORS HAVE BEEN given no counseling to help them through an ordeal that psychologists warn can induce unique and even dangerous forms of stress. Tracy Kennedy, a juror dismissed in March, attempted suicide two months later with an overdose of sedatives. Tracy Hampton, a flight attendant cut on May 1, struggled with depression so severe that she was hospitalized by the end of the

month. After court adjourned on Wednesday, one juror could be seen at her hotel window with an exhausted look on her face, her forehead pressed against the glass pane. "I'm really worried about some of the people still there," says Francine Florio-Bunten, a juror dismissed at the end of May. "Some of them are really on the edge."

> WE'RE GOING TO HAVE TO LIVE WITH THE BILE SPEWED OUT THESE LAST FEW DAYS.
>
> —WILLIE WILLIAMS, Los Angeles police chief

Meanwhile, most of the lawyers are already thinking about life after Simpson. Darden, who has looked solemn and unhappy much of the time, was asked last week what would be next for him. "Me?" he said with an apparent straight face. "This is my last case." Shapiro, who plans "to reacquaint myself with my family," will also soon be joining a large Los Angeles law firm as a senior partner, dissolving his own. But Johnnie Cochran swears that if O.J. is retried, he will still be beside him. "Despite the fact that I'll probably be in bankruptcy, I'll stay with it until the end."

It may be a favorable sign of the jury's mood that it took the panel only a few minutes last Friday to chose a foreman. Or

forewoman—some ex-jurors say that before they left the panel, a black female juror, 50, had emerged as a leader within the group. There is no telling whether their cooperative mood will last for long. Still, the Simpson case, which has inspired so much division, has also offered some scenes of unexpected harmony. There was a remarkable one on the last day of the trial. During the 15-minute morning break, Simpson's mother Eunice, who uses a wheelchair, could be seen next to Nicole Brown's mother Juditha, who was sitting on a hallway bench next to Arnelle Simpson, the defendant's daughter. Dominique Brown, Nicole's sister, knelt by Eunice. All four women were talking and touching each other. If they can find common ground, maybe there is hope for the jury. And the rest of us too.

—Reported by Elaine Lafferty, Jack E. White and James Willwerth/Los Angeles, with other bureaus

DIVIDING LINE
Jack E. White

A DOUBLE STRAND OF PARANOIA

OF ALL THE JOLTING TWISTS AND TURNS IN THE SIMPSON trial, none was more startling than the defendant's rebirth as a black man. What we tend to forget is that before June 12, 1994, the Juice was no hero to African Americans. His postfootball success was largely due to his ability to make whites comfortable as he played golf with CEOs at country clubs from which other blacks were excluded or shucked and jived his way through goofy movies like some modern Stepin Fetchit. Never one to speak out about civil rights, he seemed to shed his racial identity, crossing over into a sort of colorless minor celebrity as easily as he escaped from tacklers—or from the

black wife he traded in for a white teenager. By trial time Simpson wasn't exactly white, but he wasn't exactly black either.

Yet now O.J. has become black again, thanks to Mark Fuhrman, who treated him like a "nigger," and Johnnie Cochran, who made sure nobody forgot it. Once again, blacks and whites are glaring at each other across the color line in mutual incomprehension as yet another trial of American race relations unfolds in the City of Angels. To whites, the central issue is whether Simpson is a murderer, while to blacks it is whether the process that brought him to trial was fatally contaminated by racial bias. Simpson is still no hero to most blacks, but he has become an indelible symbol of their mistreatment by white authority. "We always reach out to another black person we perceive as being mistreated by whites because it has happened to so many of us," says Darlene Powell Hopson, a black clinical psychologist. Says political scientist Andrew Hacker, author of *Two Nations: Black and White, Separate, Hostile, Unequal:* "I hear a lot of anger from even middle-class and professional blacks about this. They believe that the police, the prosecutors, the whole criminal justice system are out to tear down black men, especially successful black men."

What we have here are two mutually reinforcing strains of paranoia. On one hand, blacks are so suspicious of whites that many seriously believe AIDS is a genocidal plague cooked up by the CIA. That is the flip side of the fear that makes many white women clutch their purses when a black man in a business suit gets on the elevator. Perhaps because of their minority status, most blacks who live with these grim realities have learned to keep their fears in perspective most of the time. They know their justified rage can be exploited, and have schooled themselves to distinguish between cynical appeals to their sense of racial injustice and valid pleas for the unjustly accused. What infuriates them is that whites often fail to make equivalent distinctions, dismissing blacks' protests against racist mistreatment as a tactic without bothering to investigate the mistreatment itself. And that is why the Simpson case is so divisive. Until blacks are convinced that the cops and the prosecutors are dealing fairly with them, they won't listen to anything else.

Blacks seethe when Cochran's attack on Detective Fuhrman is denigrated in the white-controlled media as merely "playing the race card." Such a tactic could hardly have been avoided in a case that, in Hacker's phrase, "was dripping with race" from the start. How could it have been otherwise when a black man stood accused of cutting the throats of two white people in a city that exploded just 3½ years ago after four white cops who beat Rodney King were set free by a jury from which blacks were conspicuously absent? Few would disagree with Thelma Golden, curator of a controversial 1994 exhibition on black males in contemporary culture, that "if Nicole had been black, this case would have been a cover on *Jet* magazine [the black newsweekly] and not much more."

Moreover, Simpson's choice of Johnnie Cochran as his lead lawyer made the race factor inevitable. Cochran's career was built around suing the L.A.P.D. for racially inspired misconduct—some of it even more horrendous than that revealed in the Simpson trial—and he is no fool. Still, prosecutors, knowing Fuhrman's history, decided to have the detective testify. That gave Cochran the opening to cast the trial in racial terms, which worked because Simpson was wealthy enough to hire lawyers and investigators to dig up proof of racially motivated police misconduct. It is no more unethical for Simpson's team to employ such a strategy that it was for Clarence Thomas to claim he was being subjected to a "high-tech lynching" during his Supreme Court confirmation hearings. As Cochran explained to me last week, "any lawyer who didn't go after that would be guilty of malpractice."

Moreover, as inflammatory and cynical as Cochran's tactics may seem to whites, there is little proof that black jurors go easy on black defendants solely due to race. In heavily black jurisdictions such as Washington, mostly black juries routinely send African-American defendants to prison when the evidence merits it. History shows that from Mississippi during the civil rights era to Simi Valley in the '90s, it is all-white juries that tend to exonerate defendants of their own race despite the evidence.

Which is not to say Simpson's lawyers have not crossed the line into cynical exploitation of blacks' sense of racial aggrievement. Case in point: Cochran's acceptance of security guards from the Nation of Islam, which strikes many as being like a white lawyer's taking on bodyguards from the Ku Klux Klan. Cochran and I have been friends for years, but we never discussed the Simpson case until it went to the jury last week. That was in part because I think the evidence points to Simpson's guilt, as well as to police corruption—and I'm not alone, even among blacks. "I think it's possible for the Los Angeles police department to be corrupt and racist and for Simpson to still be guilty," says Julianne Malveaux, the African-American host of a radio show in Washington. "The evidence has clearly shown you can be a clean-cut cop like Fuhrman and still be a racist liar, or be a nice guy like O.J. who smiles all the time and still beat the hell out of women." The cops may have tried to frame a guilty man.

But if the polls can be trusted, most Americans consider those possibilities to be mutually exclusive—dismal proof, as if more were needed, that most of us continue to view race relations as a zero-sum game in which every gain by blacks is a loss for whites and vice versa. It is up to the white majority, I'm afraid, to take the first step in breaking this cycle, because only they have the power to do it. Remove the Fuhrmans from authority. Back laws that make police misconduct a serious crime with serious penalties, and give civilian complaint review boards the power to punish cops who flout them. Raise police salaries to attract better recruits, and make sure that lots of them come from the minority neighborhoods where crime is most serious and relationships between police and citizens are most in need of repair.

Most of all, realize that it is the persistence of racism itself that makes it possible for suspects like Simpson to play the race card. Just as the Simpson case was going to the jury, news broke of another tape of vile racist invective—this time by a member of the Dallas school board, who among other things referred to students as "little niggers." Blacks know Fuhrman is not an aberration. And as long as his brand of bigotry is at large in the land, it may sometimes engender the further injustice that a guilty man goes free.

JUSTICE ENGLISH STYLE

J.R. Spencer

J. R. Spencer is professor of law at Selwyn College, Cambridge University, England.

American law grew out of English law, and American criminal procedure grew out of English criminal procedure. In broad outline, both still look very similar. In both, there are two types of procedure: a rapid one, leading to a reduced sentence, for those who will plead guilty, and a slow and cumbersome one for those who deny their guilt.

If the defendant pleads not guilty, the prosecution must establish his guilt by means of oral evidence. The witnesses are called, examined, and cross-examined adversarially by the parties, not inquisitorially by the court. The defendant has a right of silence. Unlike in France, where the trial starts off with the judge examining the accused about the charges, no one asks the Anglo-American defendant any questions at the trial unless he chooses to give evidence; if he does give evidence, he only does so after the close of the prosecution case.

In both systems, the judge acts as an umpire rather than as an inquisitor. In a serious case, the question of guilt or innocence will be decided by a jury of twelve lay people, who will be told that they must not convict unless they are satisfied of the defendant's guilt beyond a reasonable doubt.

Yet between the American and the English trial there are differences of detail, and these go far beyond the immediately obvious one, which is that in an English Crown Court trial, the judge and barristers wear wigs. These differences of detail are so many and so great that if the O.J. Simpson trial were taking place in England, it would probably seem to be happening in an entirely different legal world.

MAJOR DIFFERENCES

The first big difference between English and American criminal procedure concerns selection of the jury. In England, there is no voir dire. The prosecution and defense are not permitted to ask potential jurors questions, in order to decide whether to challenge them. Thus, the days or even weeks that are sometimes spent in American courts while the opposing lawyers try to mold a jury favorable to their case are quite unknown. In an English court, selecting the jury never takes more than a few minutes.

The defense can challenge jurors, and until 1988 it had a right of peremptory challenge. That is, the defense could challenge without giving any reasons. As long as only householders were eligible for jury service, peremptory challenges were rare: Most jurors were middle-class white males, and the person you peremptorily challenged was likely to be replaced by someone rather like him. When jury service became universal in the 1970s, however, challenging jurors became common. Eventually it turned into something of a scandal, because it was repeatedly asserted that in fraud trials, defense counsel tended to challenge any juror who looked as if he might be numerate, or even intelligent.

In consequence, Parliament in 1988 abolished the defendant's right of peremptory challenge. The defense still has the right to challenge for cause, which means it can challenge a juror if it is able to say why it thinks that he is unsuitable. But as the defense is given no information about the jurors, apart from their name and address, and is not allowed to get it by asking them questions, this is something it rarely can do.

Surprisingly, perhaps, it is not the practice for the judge or court officials to ask questions of potential jurors, either. This means, unfortunately, that in practice no serious attempt is made to eliminate people who are obviously unfit to serve. Sometimes, there are scandals when it emerges that a jury contained some completely unsuitable people: individuals who are deaf, or unable to understand English, or sometimes impersonators—people, usually out of work, who illegally stand in for someone who wishes to avoid doing his jury service.

Some of those who do appear for jury service behave less than responsibly. Several years ago, a fraud trial had to be abandoned when a couple of jurors went to a pub during the lunch break, and a woman juror, rather drunk, started making sexual advances to the foreman of the jury during prosecuting counsel's closing submissions. Last year, the Court of Appeal heard one appeal brought on the ground that a juror had spent part of her time in the jury box writing love letters to one of the barristers, another on the

---

In England, there is no voir dire. The prosecution and defense are not permitted to ask potential jurors questions, in order to decide whether to challenge them.

The article originally appeared in *The World & I,* August 1995, pp. 315-323. Reprinted by permission of *The World & I,* a publication of The Washington Times Corporation. © 1995.

ground that the jury in a murder case had tried to solve the mystery of "who done it" by using a Ouija board.

If potential jurors were routinely questioned about their attitude toward jury service, some of these irresponsible characters would presumably have been kept out of the jury box. But such is our fear of the weeklong voir dires we hear of on the other side of the Atlantic that most English lawyers would rather endure the ill than undergo the cure.

A second difference between an American and an English trial, again to do with jurors, concerns the "secrecy of the jury room." In England, unlike in the United States, it is a criminal offense for jurors to disclose what went on in the jury room, and if they break the law and do so, it is also a criminal offense for the person who received the information to publish it.

Breaking the secrecy of the jury room was made a criminal offense in 1981, partly in response to what had happened after the trial of Jeremy Thorpe—a cause célèbre that attracted nearly as much attention in England as the Simpson trial has attracted in the United States. Thorpe, member of Parliament and former leader of the Liberal Party, was tried and acquitted for incitement and conspiracy to murder one Norman Scott, his former homosexual lover, who had been trying to blackmail him. After Thorpe's acquittal, a juror gave an interview with a magazine in which he stated—to the outrage of Thorpe's defense lawyers—that he and his fellow jurors had believed there was indeed a plot to do something bad to Scott, but that they were not sure beyond reasonable doubt that the intention was to murder him. This sort of disclosure, it was felt, must stop, and Parliament promptly turned it into a criminal offense.

LIMITS ON THE MEDIA

Another significant difference between a criminal trial in England and the United States is that in England there is strict control over what the media can print or broadcast about the case ahead of trial. Once criminal proceedings have been launched, anyone who publishes anything about the case that might affect the ultimate fairness of the trial, in particular by prejudicing the minds of potential jurors, is deemed guilty of the criminal offense of "contempt of court."

The classic example of the offense is where, in a sensational case, the newspapers start discussing the evidence, or reveal the alleged fact that the defendant has committed a series of other offenses in addition to the one or ones for which he is on trial. But it would equally be a contempt of court for the defense to mount a press campaign in the defendant's favor, by trying to discredit the prosecution case.

This law of contempt of court is strict, and on the whole the media stand in awe of it. For one thing, it is punishable summarily. The attorney general does not have to prosecute the defendant before the ordinary criminal courts but has the option—which he generally takes—of instituting proceedings in the High Court. Although this is a civil court, it has the power to summon the person allegedly guilty of contempt to appear before it and to punish him by imprisonment or fine. When it sits to do this, it sits without a jury.

The punishments imposed are sometimes quite severe. In a famous case in 1949, for example, the editor of the *Daily Mirror* was sent to prison for three months and the company fined ten thousand pounds—in those days an astronomical sum—for what they published about Hague, the defendant in a high-profile murder case. Hague had been accused of a series of murders, the victims of which he had allegedly shot and dissolved in an acid bath. The *Daily Mirror's* offense was to publish an article describing him as a "vampire" and saying that he was responsible for a series of other deaths as well.

How strong a sanction is the law on contempt of court was vividly described by the journalist Rebecca West—who, unlike most journalists, actually approved of it—when she wrote the following in *A Train of Powder*.

The legal restrictions on crime-reporting in Great Britain excite the wonder of other nations. They are admirable and it should be our pride to obey them, for

they go far to preventing trial by prejudiced juries. If a gentleman were arrested carrying a lady's severed head in his arms and wearing her large intestine as a garland round his neck and crying aloud that he and he alone had been responsible for her reduction from a whole to parts, it would still be an offense for any newspaper to suggest that he might have had any connection with her demise until he had been convicted of this offense by a jury, and sentenced by a judge.

So severe a restriction was the law of contempt—and so much wonder did it indeed excite among other nations—that in 1981 it caused the United Kingdom to be condemned by the European Court of Human Rights in Strasbourg for a breach of the provision of the European Convention on Human Rights relating to free speech. Afterward, it was necessary for Parliament to amend the law by imposing various limits on the offense, notably section 5 of the Contempt of Court Act of 1981, which provides that

a publication made as or as part of a discussion in good faith of public affairs or other matters of general public interest is not to be treated without more as contempt of court . . . if the risk of impediment or prejudice to particular legal proceedings is merely incidental to the discussion.

In certain other respects, however, the law relating to what the media may report about pending criminal cases has been tightened in recent years rather than relaxed. At one time, the media were completely free to publish all or any of the evidence that was heard in open court in the course of any proceedings preliminary to the trial, such as committal proceedings or, until they were abolished, proceedings before the grand jury. This was thought to be potentially unfair to defendants, because it could result in

---

In England, a criminal trial does not turn into a major public spectacle by becoming televised. Indeed, televising court proceedings is a criminal offense.

potential jurors getting a prejudiced view of the case ahead of trial.

In the famous case of Bodkin Adams—the Eastbourne doctor accused of murdering his patients in 1957—the prosecution gave evidence at the committal proceedings about the deaths of various patients, about whose deaths no evidence was presented at trial. In 1967, Parliament responded to this problem by enacting a law making it an offense to publish anything about committal proceedings other than the bare factual details of who was accused, of what, and where they were sent to trial.

The law, in its original form, provided that this restriction on reporting had to be lifted if the accused, or any one of them, requested it. This led to problems in the Jeremy Thorpe case, when Thorpe and most of his coaccused did not want the restriction lifted, but one of them—allegedly paid to make the request by one of our less scrupulous newspapers—requested it. As a result, the newspapers were able to report, in full sordid detail, all the evidence against Thorpe as it was first called at the committal proceedings, giving their readers second helpings of it all at his eventual trial the following year. Following this, the law was changed, giving the court discretion about lifting the ban when one defendant wants it lifted and his codefendant does not.

In England, furthermore, a criminal trial does not turn into a major public spectacle by becoming televised. Indeed, televising court proceedings is a criminal offense. The Criminal Justice Act of 1925 actually makes it an offense to

take or attempt to take in any court any photograph, or with a view to publication make or attempt to make in any court any portrait or sketch of any person, being a judge of the court or a juror or a witness in or a party to any proceedings before the court, whether criminal or civil.

The only kind of physical representation this law does not forbid is sketches of the court proceedings that artists later draw from memory, an art form that sometimes does appear in the English press.

Recently, there has been some discussion in England about the possibility of televising court proceedings. In Scotland, which has its own separate legal system and different laws, an experiment recently took place. A series of fairly run-of-the-mill criminal trials was televised, and edited versions of them were then broadcast, in England as well as in Scotland, complete with commentary and interviews with the various parties involved.

This experiment has led to something of a public debate. On the one hand, the fear has been expressed that an edited version of a criminal trial, in which the bulk of the evidence is suppressed, must necessarily give a misleading account. On the other hand, neither lawyers nor television companies seem to think there is any future in televising complete criminal trials. If I were a betting man, I would wager that the ban on television cameras in English criminal trials will remain in place.

ROLE OF JUDGE

Another thing which gives an English criminal trial its distinctive flavor is the dominant position of the judge. Compared with a judge in France or Germany, the English judge plays a passive role, but he still dominates the trial to a much greater extent than does his American counterpart. This is shown, in a symbolic way, in the elaborately formal courtesy with which English barristers invariably address the bench.

Behind the symbol is a reality. An English judge can be expected to cut counsel short if he thinks the barrister is wasting the court's time by calling irrelevant evidence or asking irrelevant questions. At the end of the case, furthermore, the English judge—unlike judges in most jurisdictions in the United States—gives the jury a direction, which includes his own personal views on the weight of the evidence. "Members of the jury, it is a matter for you, but you may think that. . . ." In most parts of the United States, the judge who did this would be criticized for usurping what is properly the jury's function.

The comparatively less dominant position of the American judge came about as a result of American politics in colonial days and immediately after the Revolution. In the colonial era, the judges were appointed—as they still are in England—by the Crown. They saw themselves as representatives of the king, and like many English judges of that period they thought it was their duty to exert pressure in favor of the Crown in cases that had political overtones: a tendency that juries tended to react against. This experience gave Americans both a deep and lasting distrust of dominant judges and a corresponding tendency to magnify the role of juries and, to some extent, of the lawyers for the parties.

The less dominant position of the American judge is also a consequence, to some extent, of the sort of people who become judges and the way in which they are appointed to the bench. In the United States, judges are often chosen by election, a process that may give them democratic respectability but that certainly does not ensure that the lawyers who appear before them will have any deep respect for their legal knowledge or forensic skills.

English judges—or at any rate, the sort of judges who preside in Crown Court trials in serious cases—are still appointed, in colonial fashion, by the queen. They hold office for life or until retirement age. They are—and have to be—lawyers with many years of experience behind them. If the newspaper caricature of the English judge is a rather crabby, elderly man, the judge who presides in a serious case is usually someone whose knowledge and experience give him real credibility with the lawyers who appear in front of him.

The position of the English judge, as compared with that of the American, is neatly shown by the use of a common phrase: *trying a case*. In the United States, it will be the attorney who tells you that he is "trying" O.J. Simpson. In England, a barrister would tell you he was "prosecuting" or "defending" him. "Trying" the case is the expression used by the judge, not by counsel.

The relationship between bench and bar in England is more complicated than this, however. A judgeship is a desirable and coveted position, judges are almost exclusively appointed from the upper levels of the bar, and—although no barrister would publicly admit it—what many English barristers want, even more than to get rich, is to become a High Court judge.

Judges are chosen by the queen according to a rather arcane process, which depends in part on information from existing judges. If you ever want to be a judge, you must therefore take care, when prosecuting or defending cases, to play the game according to certain unwrit-

Behind the symbol is a reality. An English judge can be expected to cut counsel short if he thinks the barrister is wasting the court's time by calling irrelevant evidence or asking irrelevant questions.

ten rules—one of which is that there are limits to how far it is proper to exploit the rules of criminal procedure and evidence in order to win your client's case.

Among English barristers and judges, there is a derogatory expression, "a spoiler," which means a lawyer who will put any and every spanner in the works and adopt any time-wasting strategy to achieve the objects of his client. No counsel with a reputation as a "spoiler" is likely to be appointed to the bench. This fact, taken with the unspoken desire of most barristers to end their career as judges, limits the amount of "spoiling" that takes place.

A further matter makes criminal trials in England less adversarial than they are in the United States. This is the absence of any clear professional division between lawyers who prosecute for a living and lawyers who defend. At the Crown Court level—where serious cases are heard—not only the defendant but also the Crown Prosecution Service must be represented by an independent barrister. The barrister who prosecutes today is likely to be someone who, the previous week, appeared for a defendant.

The fact that the Crown Prosecution Service must hand any serious evidence in the case over to a barrister is often criticized, and in some ways it is certainly inefficient. On the other hand, it does mean that the British bar can under-

stand that there is a need for the guilty to be convicted as well as a need for the innocent to be acquitted.

No American who reads this should think that everything in English criminal procedure is perfect. A criticism sometimes heard in England is the one that Americans often make of it: class bias. In England, there is a close connection between accent and social class. With few exceptions, those who go to the bar in England have, or rapidly acquire, accents popularly identified as upper class; judges, who are usually ex-barristers, usually talk in the same way. Partly because of this, perhaps, a recurrent theme in the popular press is that "the judges are out of touch." This theme is played loudly and often when, as sometimes happens, a judge makes a particularly unfortunate remark—as when, some years ago, a High Court judge observed when sentencing a man who had kicked his wife, "If you had been a miner in South Wales, I might have overlooked it. But you are a cultured gentleman living in a respectable part of the country."

For myself, I do not share the view that because judges often talk with upper-class accents, our criminal courts are biased. If our judges do tend to be rather upper class, they also tend to be well-educated and intelligent; they have the wit to recognize the risk of bias and to guard against it. But whatever the real position

may be concerning bias, it certainly does not improve the credibility of our higher judiciary among half of the population that almost all of it is male.

English criminal procedure is also often criticized for the same reasons that American criminal procedure is criticized: It is too slow, too costly, and too much of a game. In right-wing circles, it has long been said that English criminal procedure is too soft and that it makes it too easy for the guilty to be wrongly acquitted. But then, in 1991, we had the Birmingham Six cases, which raised the opposite concern. Here, some sixteen years after they had been sent to prison for killing a large number of people in a terrorist bomb outrage, it was eventually revealed that the six Irish defendants had been convicted on evidence that was seriously unreliable.

Sadly, there have been a series of other cases like it. In response to these, the government appointed a Royal Commission on Criminal Justice, which in 1993 produced a long string of recommended changes. But then the government, by now thoroughly alarmed about law and order, hurriedly forced through Parliament an act that, broadly speaking, put into effect proposals that were favorable to the prosecution, or cheap. It largely ignored ones that favored the defense and—for good measure—made a serious inroad on the defendant's right of silence. So controversy about English criminal procedure still abounds.

When they look at what happens in some trials—like O.J. Simpson's—on the other side of the Atlantic, English lawyers do feel some reassurance. If some things in criminal justice are not good here, at least, somewhere else in the common-law world, some things actually seem to be done worse.

When they look at what happens in some trials—like O.J. Simpson's—on the other side of the Atlantic, English lawyers do feel some reassurance.

Jury Consultants: Boon or Bane?

Communication Is Lawyer's Art, A Litigator Says . . .

The National Law Journal asked two prominent attorneys, one a trial lawyer and the other a jury consultant, for their views on the use of jury consultants. Both have been successful in highly publicized cases. But, as their answers show, that is where the similarly ends.

Frederick P. Furth

Frederick P. Furth is the senior partner of San Francisco's Furth, Fahrner & Mason, which specializes in antitrust litigation. Among recent cases, he represented former New England Patriots owner William Sullivan in his suit against the national Football League, convincing a jury that the NFL had broken antitrust laws in preventing Mr. Sullivan from trying to sell stock in the team. An outspoken jury-consultant critic, Mr. Furth told the Wall Street Journal *that a client said to him about jury consultants: "I thought that's what I pay you for."*

Q: You have been quoted in the past as having a rather dim view of jury consultants. Why?

MR. FURTH: Trial attorneys are using jury consultants as crutches, especially those attorneys who have not had a great deal of real-life experience. They, the attorneys, are insecure and are scared to tell their clients what they think. The attorneys are afraid that if they lose a case and didn't use a jury consultant, it will be discussed in a seminar somewhere as an example of why you should use a consultant.

Why do I want to hire someone who has a Ph.D. in jury consulting or jury research to tell me how to communicate? That's what you hire a trial attorney for. Knowledge of the law is something every lawyer has. When you hire an attorney, hopefully you're hiring someone who has been through life's ups and downs as well.

The ultimate trial is a communion between the attorney and the jury. You don't want that violated. Jury consultants tend to violate that by getting between you and your jury. I don't want someone with a degree in social studies looking over my shoulder.

Q: What about those cases in which a seasoned attorney uses a jury consultant? Does the "crutch" theory apply even then?

MR. FURTH: I don't know. Even experienced attorneys may have emotional problems and need a cheering section. If they're that weak, they can call me. I'll try the case for them and they can stay in Palm Beach.

Q: Have you ever used a jury consultant?

MR. FURTH: Yes, but my experiences with them has led to what I believe. I tried it; it's interesting. You go into analysis every night with your jury consultant. It's like having therapy.

But even if the consultant is a pleasant member of the opposite sex, it is a distraction at the end of a long day to the preparation of your case. They always tell you the good things first, but then follow it

with criticisms. They may say, "The jury really enjoyed when you said this or that, but stop picking your nose."

Q: Can you ever envision a case in which you *would* use a jury consultant again?

MR. FURTH: Yes, but it would be a very minor role. If you have a complicated or very technical case, and you're concerned about the jury understanding it, you could use a small issues panel to see how they would react to certain elements. Or you could do it with your wife and kids. They would be just as good.

Q: Do you think that the use of jury consultants helped in such publicized cases as William Kennedy Smith, the Rodney King officers, the Menendez brothers or the Branch Davidians?

MR. FURTH: I just can't say. I'm sure they all had outstanding lawyers, which probably had more to do with the results.

Q: Do you feel that jury selection has become more complicated as the result of recent decisions, such as the U.S. Supreme Court decision in *J.E.B. v. Alabama ex rel. T.B.,* and may that ultimately change your mind about the use of jury consultants?

MR. FURTH: If I was in the jury selection business, I would say yes. Guess what? I then sell more jury consulting. But no, I don't see how those cases are going to make the selection process any more difficult and I would challenge these jury consultants to tell me how it would make it tougher to pick a jury.

. . . But a Trial Consultant May Bring a Fresh Approach

Robert B. Hirschhorn

Robert B. Hirschhorn, a former trial lawyer, is lead consultant at Galveston, Texas' Cathy E. Bennett & Associates, a trial consulting firm. His high-profile clients have included William Kennedy Smith; Branch Davidian sect members who survived the burning of their Waco, Texas, compound; and U.S. Sen. Kay Bailey Hutchison, R-Texas, whose prosecution for alleged misuse of state funds was dismissed before trial. Mr. Hirschhorn is a member of the faculty of the National Criminal Defense College at Mercer Law School in Maco, Ga.

Q: Why use a jury consultant?

MR. HIRSCHHORN: A competent jury consultant is the eyes and ears of the lawyer. A lawyer cannot develop a rapport with the jury, take notes and observe the jury all at the same time.

The main reason is that when lawyers go to law school, they have a "lawbotomy." When they come out, they talk differently, dress differently and act differently. You therefore don't want to use another lawyer as your eyes and ears, because he or she had the same lawbotomy. You need someone with a clean, fresh and open-minded approach.

Q: There seems to be a growing feeling that jury consultants are losing some of the appeal they enjoyed in the 1980s. What do you attribute this to?

MR. HIRSCHHORN: The bad ones are getting weeded out, and I'm glad of that. But I'm booking trials for January of 1995. At our firm we could hire five more associates and still couldn't handle all of the cases. We reject four out of five cases. I predict in 20 years every major case will have a jury consultant—on both sides.

Q: Should attorneys use jury consultants in every complicated case, or are there instances when an attorney's own experience would be as good or better?

MR. HIRSCHHORN: The only time you should hire a jury consultant is when you want to win. If an attorney is committed to using every resource, a jury consultant should be part of it.

Q: In your most memorable cases—William Kennedy Smith, the Branch Davidians, Sen. Hutchison—would you say the result would have been the same if you had not been brought in as a consultant?

MR. HIRSCHHORN: I'm convinced that Smith would have been found not guilty with or without us. But there might have been very different results in the others if we had not been involved.

Q: Are you stacking the deck by bringing in jury consultants?

MR. HIRSCHHORN: Absolutely not. In all of the cases we've handled, we're 10 yards behind. In the William Kennedy Smith and Branch Davidians cases, everyone thought our clients were guilty. We just want to bring the client up to an equal point on the starting line.

Q: Do you see the use of jury consultants as the province only of wealthy defendants?

MR. HIRSCHHORN: No. Consulting services at our firm are available to anyone on the socioeconomic scale. If I believe in the case, I'll take it. In fact, 25 percent of our work is pro bono. We use the old Robin Hood technique of billing from those who can most afford it so we can help those who can't. Most downtrodden people accused of crimes should have the same shot as those with money.

Q: One trial attorney says that jury consultants are nothing more than "crutches" for inexperienced attorneys who have not had a great deal of real-life experience. How do you respond to that?

MR. HIRSCHHORN: I'll bet he didn't like fax machines either when they first came out. It sounds like he had a couple of bad experiences—either bad results or was overcharged.

I've spent a great deal of time with some of the greatest civil and criminal lawyers in this country. They didn't need crutches. They just wanted to win their cases.

Q: Are there any recent court decisions, such as *J.E.B.*, that will have an impact on your profession in either a positive or negative manner?

MR. HIRSCHHORN: Yes. Lawyers will now have to give gender-neutral and race-neutral reasons for their peremptory strikes. You're seeing the beginning of the end of peremptory challenges.

Lawyers are to blame for this because they brought their own prejudices into the jury selection process. People were getting struck for the color of their skin. *J.E.B.* has blown the lid off the Pandora's box of peremptory challenges.

Q: Should jury consultants be licensed in some manner?

MR. HIRSCHHORN: No, that pushes it into being an elite club. If jury consultants were required to have a Ph.D., for example, that would have excluded the godmother of this profession, our founder, the late Cat Bennett.

The number of degrees has no bearing on how good someone will be as a trial consultant. Some of the best consultants I've ever seen had only high school diplomas and some of the worst have had Ph.D. after their names.

Juvenile Justice

Although there were variations within specific offense categories, the overall arrest rate for juvenile violent crime remained relatively constant for several decades. Then, in the late 1980s something changed, bringing more and more juveniles charged with a violent offense into the justice system. The juvenile justice system is a twentieth-century response to the problems of dealing with children in trouble with the law or children who need society's protection. Juvenile court procedure differs from the procedure in adult courts because juvenile courts were based on the philosophy that their function was to treat and to help, not to punish and to abandon, the offender.

Recently, operations of the juvenile court have received criticism, and a number of significant Supreme Court decisions have changed the way the courts must approach the rights of children. In spite of these changes, however, the major thrust of the juvenile justice system remains one of diversion and treatment rather than adjudication and incarceration, although there is a trend toward dealing more punitively with serious juvenile offenders.

This unit's opening essay, "Rethinking the Sanctioning Function in Juvenile Court: Retributive or Restorative Responses to Youth Crime," asserts that a restorative sanctioning model could provide clear alternatives to punishment-centered sanctioning approaches now dominant in juvenile justice and could ultimately redefine the sanctioning function.

Mark Curriden, in "Hard Times for Bad Kids," tells how the juvenile justice system is turning to get-tough measures to halt a new generation of crime. What factors enter into the decisions a family court judge makes in dealing with dysfunctional families? The article "Judge Hayden's Family Values" discusses how one family court judge deals with society's most personal decisions.

The next essay, "Violence by Young People: Why the Deadly Nexus?" tells of the upward surge since the mid-1980s in the rate of homicides committed by young people, the number of homicides they committed with guns, and the arrest rate of nonwhite juveniles for drug offenses.

David Hawkins advocates using the public health model to curb violence in his article "Controlling Crime before It Happens: Risk-Focused Prevention." He maintains that it is essential to identify and then eliminate the factors that put youth at risk for violence. The unit closes with "Everyday School Violence: How Disorder Fuels It" by Jackson Toby. It concentrates on identifying causes of this violence and ways to reduce it.

Looking Ahead: Challenge Questions

What types of reform efforts are the juvenile justice system currently experiencing?

Why, according to Mark Curriden, doesn't the "get-tough" policy work?

What are some recent trends in juvenile delinquency? In what ways will the juvenile justice system be affected by these trends?

Tell why (or why not) departure of the juvenile justice system from its original purpose is warranted.

Rethinking the Sanctioning Function in Juvenile Court: Retributive or Restorative Responses to Youth Crime

Gordon Bazemore and
Mark Umbreit

Gordon Bazemore: Associate Professor, School of Public Administration, Florida Atlantic University.
Mark Umbreit: Associate Professor, School of Social Work, University of Minnesota.

Although juvenile courts have always administered punishment to youthful offenders, parens patriae *and the individual treatment mission have historically assigned an ambivalent role to sanctioning. In the absence of a coherent sanctioning framework, a punitive model has recently gained dominance over dispositional decision making in juvenile court. This article examines the limitations of sanctioning choices presented by both the individual treatment mission and what some have referred to as a "retributive justice" paradigm. We then consider the implications of an alternative model—restorative justice—as a framework for a new approach to sanctioning consistent with a revitalized juvenile justice mandate.*

INTRODUCTION

The juvenile court is under the most severe attack it has experienced in the 95 years since its birth in 1899. For example, recent legislative changes mandating fixed sentences in adult prisons for youths meeting minimum age requirements (or no age requirements) in Georgia, Florida, Tennessee, and Oregon (Lemov

1994) challenge the viability of a separate court and justice system for young persons. Such changes represent only the most recent and extreme round of legislative assault on the jurisdiction of the juvenile court in more than a decade of transformation in policy and procedure. Although policymakers in some states have been more cautious in moves to abolish or dismantle their juvenile justice systems, what remains today in most jurisdictions can best be described as a "criminalized" or "punitive juvenile court" (Feld 1990) that has moved further away from its original goal of providing treatment in the "best interests" of youth.

In response, some have argued that the best hope for preserving the juvenile justice system is by "reaffirming" or "revitalizing" the individual treatment mission (Krisberg 1988; McHardy 1990; McAllair 1993). Others have argued that even a revitalized treatment mission is insufficient to sustain, or regain, public support for a separate and distinct juvenile justice system (Feld 1993). Whereas much of this debate has focused on the relative effectiveness of treatment, the need to improve assessment and classification, and the need for greater attention to due process in the juvenile court, other public and policymaker concerns have been largely ignored. Prominent among these concerns has been the absence of a clear and coherent sanctioning framework for juvenile offenders.

As coercive measures taken to enforce societal standards, criminal justice *sanctions,* depending on intent, may be directed toward rehabilitative, educative, regulatory, and/or compensatory ends—as well as retribution or deterrence (Packer 1968; Garland 1990). In the absence of a framework that incorporates and gives priority to such nonpunitive objectives, however, juvenile justice policymakers have adopted a one-dimensional approach to sanctioning based on what some have referred to as a *retributive justice* paradigm (Zehr 1990;

The authors wish to thank Ted Rubin and Martha Schiff for comments on an earlier version of this article. Don Gibbons provided helpful suggestions and extensive assistance with revisions on the final draft.

Umbreit 1994). In this article, retributive justice refers to a broad ideological framework that gives priority to punishment and lesser emphasis to rehabilitative goals, places central focus on "desert" as the primary rationale for decision making, and expands the role of formal, adversarial, adjudicatory, and dispositional processes (Feld 1990, 1993).[1] Although this perspective is incompatible with the rationale for a separate and distinct justice system for juveniles based on their special developmental status and a concern with rehabilitative objectives (Feld 1990), the retributive approach to sanctioning has gained popularity because, in the minds of policymakers and the public, punitive sanctions serve to affirm community disapproval of proscribed behavior, denounce crime, and provide consequences to the lawbreaker.

In contrast, the traditional individual treatment mission clearly fails to accomplish these functions. Rather, treatment appears to be unrelated to the offense, to be related solely to the needs of juvenile lawbreakers, and to require nothing of offenders beyond participation in counseling or remedial services. It is difficult to convince most citizens that treatment programs provide anything other than benefits to offenders (e.g., services, recreational activities), and there is little in the message of the treatment response that attempts to communicate to an offender that he or she has harmed someone and should take action to repair damages wreaked upon the victim(s).

Should we give up entirely on the juvenile court? We stand with those who believe that abolition or dismemberment of the juvenile court, as well as the continued expansion of retributive sanctioning policies, represent extreme response to the internal contradictions that have been the source of much criticism leveled at the juvenile justice system. However, the punitive model and the traditional treatment model are not the only options for the juvenile court. Because neither provides an appropriate means of meeting the needs of communities to sanction youth crime, it is important to broaden the debate to consider alternative frameworks.

This article outlines the principles of one such alternative framework that could expand the limited range of available options, prioritize new objectives for sanctioning, and ensure that the use of sanctions is also consistent with other goals of juvenile justice intervention (e.g., rehabilitation and public safety). Drawing on recent theoretical developments that emphasize the importance of sanctioning in the control of criminal behavior (Braithwaite 1989; Garland 1990), the *restorative justice* perspective offers a blueprint to policymakers and juvenile justice professionals for developing an alternative to the retributive model. A restorative model would expand less punitive, less costly, and less stigmatizing sanctioning methods by involving the community and victims in sanctioning processes, thereby elevating the role of victims and victimized communities and giving priority to reparation, direct offender accountability to victims, and conflict resolution (Zehr 1990; Van Ness 1993; Umbreit 1994).

THE SANCTIONING FUNCTION AND JUVENILE JUSTICE

Sanctioning has always been viewed with ambivalence in the juvenile justice system. Although historically juvenile justice decision makers eschewed sanctioning in favor of providing individualized treatment in the "best interests of the child" (e.g., Mack 1909; Melton 1989), juvenile courts have often disguised punishment as treatment (Rothman 1980; Miller 1991) and have not been reluctant to confine offenders for failure to participate in mandated treatment or to comply with other court requirements (Rothman 1980; Bazemore 1994a). Such responses have been viewed as aberrant departures from the court's central mission, however, and juvenile justice decision makers have typically failed to formally acknowledge the sanctioning function. Rather, viewing sanctioning as an *alternative* to treatment, judges and other juvenile justice professionals often have been inconsistent and extreme in the response to juvenile crime (Thompson and McAnany 1984), foregoing sanctions altogether for many "low-end" or "medium-level" offenders deemed worthy candidates for services or treatment programs. On the other hand, those who have taxed decision makers' patience by repeat offending or noncompliance have often received a clearly punitive response—a response now increasingly likely to be administered in the criminal justice system, where little or no consideration is given to treatment needs (Feld 1990; Butts 1994).

The Rise and Impact of "Retributive Juvenile Justice"

One attempt to bring rationality to the erratic decision making in juvenile court sanctioning was through the application of the "just deserts" philosophy (von Hirsch 1976; Schneider and Schram 1983). Though intended to reduce arbitrary and excessive punitive actions, the "just deserts" policies and practices actually implemented—including mandatory and determinate sentencing, expanded prosecutorial powers, and fewer restrictions on transfer to adult court—resulted instead in an expansion of punishment. Specifically, retributive reforms in various states led to increased incarceration and longer stays in residential and detention facilities (Castellano 1986; McAllair 1993).

In addition, by giving new legitimacy to punishment for its own sake, policymakers sent signals to prosecutors and other decision makers that this was an appropriate and just response to delinquent behavior.[2] Moreover, as some criminologists have suggested, equating sanctioning with punitive measures aimed solely at causing pain and discomfort to the offender may fuel demand for more severe punishments, especially when it becomes apparent that current levels are not achieving the desired effect (Christie 1982; Wilkins 1991). In the juvenile justice context, this demand appears to have accelerated the sorting process through which an expanding group of offenders judged to require a punitive, adult-like response are increasingly distinguished from those viewed as deserving of treatment. Perhaps the most damaging effect of the retributive paradigm on the juvenile justice system has been its tendency to make nonpunitive "alternative sanctions" appear weak and less adequate than incarceration, thereby closing off consideration of inexpensive and less harmful responses to youth crime (Garland 1990; Wilkins 1991).

The Limits of Sanctioning Choices: Beyond Punishment and Treatment

Although few question the inevitability of some punishment or deny that any sanction may be experienced by the *offender* as punitive, it is possible to consider and give priority to different sanctioning objectives in the response to crime. In recent years a number of scholars have challenged the effectiveness of retributive punishment and argued that sanctions may also serve important expressive, educative, and symbolic functions (Braithwaite 1989; Wilkins 1991; Garland 1990). Quoting Durkheim (1961, pp. 181–2), for example, Braithwaite (1989) highlights the role of sanctioning in moral education and underscored the limitations of punishment aimed only at threats and offender suffering:

> Since punishment is reproaching, the best punishment is that which puts the blame . . . in the most expressive but least expensive way possible. . . . It is not a matter of making him suffer . . . or as if the essential thing were to intimidate and terrorize. Rather it is a matter of reaffirming the obligation at the moment when it is violated, to strengthen the sense of duty, both for the guilty party and for those witnessing the offense—those whom the offense tends to demoralize. (p. 178)

From this perspective, expressive sanctioning aimed at communicating value-based messages to offenders and the community and affirming obligations and accountability should be more effective in regulating conduct and more likely to promote community solidarity and peaceful dispute resolution (Griffiths and Belleau 1993; Wilkins 1991). Retributive punishment, on the other hand, may have several counterdeterrent effects on offenders, including stigmatization, humiliation, and isolation, that may minimize prospects for regaining self-respect and the respect of the community (Braithwaite 1989; Makkai and Braithwaite 1994). Punishment may also undermine self-restraint, create adjustment problems by exacerbating risk factors linked to future delinquency (Paternoster and Iovanni 1989),

and weaken conventional community bonds by damaging job prospects and peer, family, and other adult relationships (Zhang and Messner 1994). Moreover, as Durkheim and others have argued, punishment may become less effective the more often it is used, by attenuating feelings of shame or moralistic tendencies of offenders (Durkheim 1961; Garland 1990). Ironically, punishment may encourage lawbreakers to focus on themselves rather than on their victims and the community as they learn to "take the punishment" without taking responsibility for their misbehavior (Wright 1991).

Unfortunately, because it fails to acknowledge the sanctioning function and may even appear to excuse or minimize offender responsibility for crime, the treatment model offers little guidance to policymakers wishing to develop more meaningful and appropriate sanctioning options. As Byrne (1989) has observed in assessing the weaknesses of control/surveillance and treatment models in community corrections, both punishment and treatment responses are practically and conceptually incomplete. Taking a one-dimensional view of the offender, each model operates from a "closed system" logic (see also, Reiss 1986) that targets only offenders for service, punishment, or both and fails to include other parties critical to the resolution of crime. Specifically, victims can rarely count on reparation, assistance, or acknowledgment and typically do not participate in any meaningful way in the juvenile justice process (Galaway and Hudson 1990), and community members are seldom asked for input or informed of their potentially vital role in meeting sanctioning, rehabilitation, and public safety objectives. Both punitive and therapeutic interventions place offenders in a passive role—as the object of treatment or services on the one hand, and punishment and surveillance on the other (Eglash 1975), and few opportunities are provided for lawbreakers to actively make amends for their crimes or to practice productive behavior that might facilitate habilitation and reintegration. As atomized responses to delinquent behavior, neither treatment nor punishment is capable of uniting offender, community, family, and victim (McElrea 1993; Walgrave 1993).

Ultimately, as Wilkins (1991, p. 312) asserts, "it is now generally accepted that the problem of crime cannot be simplified to the problem of the criminal." The emerging interest in restorative justice as an alternative sanctioning model for juvenile justice is based in part on an increasing recognition of the inadequacy of sanctioning choices offered by the individual treatment mission and the retributive paradigm and frustration with the detachment of these models from the real problems of victims, offenders, and communities (Christie 1982). This interest does not presume immediate, clearly articulated solutions to current sanctioning problems in juvenile justice.

Rather, it is based on a perceived need for an alternative "lens" (Zehr 1990) for viewing the problem of crime and a new framework to guide rational movement toward new solutions.

EXPLORING RESTORATIVE JUSTICE

Although it draws on ancient concepts and practices abandoned late in the Middle Ages as formal justice systems emerged and began to define the obligation of offenders as a debt to the king or lord (and later to the state) rather than to victims (Schafer 1970; Davis 1992), modern interest in restorative justice has been influenced by several developments in the 1970s and 1980s. Notably, the reemergence of restorative philosophy and practice grew out of experience with reparative sanctions and processes (e.g., restitution, victim-offender mediation) (Schneider 1985; Galaway and Hudson 1990; Umbreit and Coates 1993), the victims' movement, the rise of informal neighborhood justice and dispute resolution processes (Messmer and Otto 1992), and new thinking on equity and human relationships influenced in part by the women's movement and the peace and social justice movements (Pepinsky and Quinney 1991; Harris 1993).

Whereas retributive justice is focused on determining guilt and delivering appropriate punishment ("just deserts") through an adversarial process, restorative justice is concerned with the broader relationship between offender, victim, and the community (Zehr 1990; Van Ness 1993). Restorative justice differs most clearly from retributive justice (see Table 1) in its view of crime as more than simply lawbreaking—or a violation of government authority. Rather, what is most significant about criminal behavior is the injury to victims, communities, and offenders that is its result.[3]

According to its proponents, restorative justice seeks to respond to crime at the *micro* level by addressing the harm that results when a specific offense is committed, giving first priority to victim reparation, and at the *macro* level by addressing the need to build safer communities. Government and community should play collaborative and complementary roles in this response, with government/criminal justice assigned the responsibility for *order*, and the community the responsibility for restoring and maintaining peace (Van Ness 1993; Zehr 1990). As Table 1 suggests, restorative justice emphasizes the need for active involvement of victims, the community, and offenders in a process focused on denunciation of the offense, offender acceptance of responsibility (accountability), and reparation, followed by resolution of conflict resulting from the criminal act and offender reintegration.

RESTORATIVE SANCTIONING FOR JUVENILE JUSTICE

A restorative sanctioning model could provide clear alternatives to punishment-centered sanctioning approaches now dominant in juvenile justice and could ultimately redefine the sanctioning function. Specifically, by shifting the focus of offender accountability or "debt" from the state to the victim (see Table 1), restorative justice sanctions could meet the need of communities to provide meaningful consequences for crime, confront offenders, denounce delinquent behavior, and relay the message that such behavior is unacceptable—without primary reliance on punishment and incarceration. For this to occur, jurisdictions would need to agree on new priorities for sanctioning based on restorative values. Implementation, expansion, or both of the new policies and practices would then be undertaken to achieve clearly articulated goals and objectives consistent with a justice process that challenges the adversarial emphasis of retributive justice.

Values and Assumptions

The emphasis on victim needs, victim involvement, and elevation of the victim's role in restorative justice (Zehr 1990; Marshall and Merry 1990; Davis 1992; Umbreit 1994) is based in part on a reaction to the current state of affairs in which the quality and quantity of victim involvement is low and is driven by other priorities. Although "victims' rights" has become the watchword of many prosecutors and politicians, victim *needs* are not a major concern (Elias 1993). Rather, in most offender-driven juvenile and criminal justice systems, the interests of prosecutors, judges, defense attorneys, and even treatment program directors (e.g., in winning cases, processing offenders, or securing clients) take precedence over the needs and concerns of victims (Wright 1991; Messmer and Otto 1992). Despite frequent complaints about the inability of offenders to pay victim restitution, for example, many jurisdictions that do a poor job at enforcing restitution orders have been highly successful in the collection of offender fines and fees (Hillsman and Greene 1992). Indeed, in many probation and parole agencies, victim compensation and restitution have taken a back seat to the collection of monies used to support criminal justice agency functions (Shapiro 1990). Moreover, whereas prosecutors appear to spare no expense and effort to gain victim input for efforts to increase the probability of conviction and length of sentence, time and resources for providing victim services, mediation, and reparative programs seem always in short supply (Elias 1993).

Restorative justice is *not*, however, a "victims' rights" approach. Motivated by retributive rather than restorative values, some of the more vocal groups advocating victims' rights have often defined these as an *absence of offender rights* in a zero-sum game and have promoted political efforts to "get tough" with offenders through mandatory and determinate sentencing and other retributive policies (McShane and Williams 1992; Elias 1993). In contrast to such policies, restorative justice proponents promote a "victim-centered" approach that does not require that decision makers "choose sides" between victim and offender (Lawrence 1991).[4] Thus, while it places central emphasis on victim needs and the requirement that offenders are held account-

able to victims, the restorative justice paradigm also responds to the "mutual powerlessness" of offenders *and* victims in the current system and assumes the need for communities to provide opportunities for offender repentance and forgiveness following appropriate sanctioning (Wright 1991; Zehr 1990). Therefore, a core value in restorative justice is to balance the needs of offenders, victims, and community as three "customers" of justice systems. A core assumption is that neither public safety, rehabilitative, nor sanctioning goals can be effectively achieved without involvement of each of these parties in the justice process.

TABLE 1: Current and Restorative Assumptions

Current System	Restorative Justice
Crime is an act against the state, a violation of the law, an abstract idea	Crime is an act against another person and the community
The criminal justice system controls crime	Crime control lies primarily in the community
Offender accountability defined as taking punishment	Accountability defined as assuming responsibility and taking action to repair harm
Crime is an individual act with individual responsibility	Crime has both individual and social dimensions of responsibility
Punishment is effective a. threat of punishment deters crime b. punishment changes behavior	Punishment alone is not effective in changing behavior and is disruptive to community harmony and good relationships
Victims are peripheral to the process	Victims are central to the process of resolving a crime
The offender is defined by deficits	The offender is defined by capacity to make reparation
Focus on establishing blame or guilt, on the past (did he/she do it?)	Focus on problem solving, on liabilities/obligations, on the future (what should be done?)
Emphasis on adversarial relationship	Emphasis on dialogue and negotiation
Imposition of pain to punish and deter/prevent	Restitution as a means of restoring both parties; goal of reconciliation/restoration
Community on sideline, represented abstractly by state	Community as facilitator in restorative process

SOURCE: Adapted from Zehr (1990).

TABLE 2: The "Messages" of Sanctions

	Individual Treatment	Retributive Punishment	Restorative Accountability
Offender	You are "sick" or disturbed and your behavior is not your fault. We will provide treatment or services in your best interest.	You are a bad person who willfully chose to commit an offense. We will punish you with swiftness and severity proportionate to the seriousness of the crime.	Your actions have consequences; you have wronged someone or the community through your offense. You are responsible for your crime and capable of restoring the victim or repaying the damages.
Victim	Our fundamental concern is the needs of the offender.	The first concern of the juvenile system is to make offenders suffer the consequences of their crime. You will benefit because the offender will be punished.	The juvenile justice system believes you are important and will do its best to ensure that the offender repays the debt incurred to you from the crime.
Community	We will do our best to rehabilitate offenders through providing appropriate treatment and services. Highly trained professionals will solve the problem. Leave it to us.	We will do our best to punish offenders to teach them that crime will not be tolerated. Threats are the best way to control behavior.	Requiring offenders to repay victims and the public for their crimes receives highest priority in the juvenile justice system. We need the help of the community. The community is a key player in holding offenders accountable.

SOURCE: Adapted from Schneider (1985).

Sanctioning Goals and Objectives

As suggested earlier, a retributive justice model gives priority to punishment as a *determining goal* (Robinson 1987) in juvenile court sanctioning. In contrast, the determining goal of sanctioning in restorative justice is to hold offenders accountable for reparation of harm caused to victims by their crimes (Walgrave 1993). Neither punitive nor lenient in its focus, restorative justice gauges success in sanctioning not by how much punishment was inflicted or treatment provided but by how much reparation, resolution, and reintegration was achieved.

Primary objectives. Restorative sanctioning objectives thus include behavioral, material, emotional, and cognitive outcomes for victims, offenders, and community members. For victims, success in sanctioning is measured by the degree of reparation of damages, the extent of involvement in the justice process, and the level of satisfaction with the process and its outcomes. For offenders, cognitive objectives emphasize gaining an understanding of the consequences of crime for victims, feelings of remorse, recognition that they have been sanctioned, and (ideally) development of empathy with victims. Positive behavioral outcomes include prompt repayment of victims and completion of community service and other reparative requirements (e.g., facing the victim in mediation). For the community, the most important objectives are overall satisfaction that justice has been served, a sense that offenders have been denounced and held accountable to victims, and a sense of peace and community healing and well being (Pepinsky and Quinney 1991; Yazzie 1994).

Finally, a larger educative objective of restorative sanctioning would be to relay a distinctive "message" to victims, offenders, and the community. Compared to the current message of neglect that characterizes both the retributive and the treatment models (Schneider 1985) (see Table 2), the restorative justice message suggests to victims and the community that the system views them as important and values their involvement. It also is intended to assure the community that promoting restoration and community peace is a top priority of the system (Davis 1992). Similarly, as Table 2 suggests, the message to lawbreakers that they are capable of, and responsible for, making amends for the harm caused by their crimes stands in sharp contrast to the message of "sick" or "evil" offenders with nothing to offer but their liberty (Christie 1982).

Limiting goals. In a restorative justice model, systemic concerns with rehabilitation/reintegration and public safety would receive balanced emphasis with sanctioning goals. Moreover, restorative justice would view rehabilitative and sanctioning goals as mutually compatible in a process in which members of the community reinforce the offender's obligation to redress the harm to victims, but then encourage—and create conditions to facilitate—offender reintegration following the shaming and reparative process (Makkai and Braithwaite 1994; McElrea 1993).

In addition, pursuit of full accountability to victims in sanctioning would be constrained by the *limiting* goals of risk management, fairness, and uniformity. Although restorative justice advocates are concerned that excessive use of secure confinement may limit the ability of offenders to fully repair harm to victims and meet other restorative objectives, all acknowledge that some proportion of the youthful offender population will need to be removed from the community and confined in secure facilities for public safety reasons. The goals of fairness and equity would likewise limit the pursuit of victim restoration when excessive requirements on specific lawbreakers that result from differences in victim needs and demands result in unfair and inappropriate consequences disproportionate to offender culpability (Van Ness 1993).

Restorative Process and Due Process

According to Braithwaite (1989, p. 8), in "low crime" societies, tolerance of deviance has clear limits and community members prefer to be actively involved in the response to lawbreakers by "shaming offenders, and, having shamed them, through concerted participation in integrating the offender back into the community." But whereas Native Americans and other aboriginal peoples, as well as the Japanese, have developed numerous sanctioning rituals for carrying out this *reintegrative shaming* process (Braithwaite 1989; Griffiths and Belleau 1993; McElrea 1993; Yazzie 1994), some have argued that the lack of institutional supports for such informal processes and the power of the formal adversarial system and Western legal processes have limited application and use of informal sanctioning mechanisms (Haley 1989, p. 274).

In contrast to the rule-driven, impersonal procedures of retributive justice focused on defining "winners and losers" and fixing blame (Zehr 1990; Messmer and Otto 1992), the restorative justice process would, however, necessarily rely heavily on informal resolution of un-

derlying problems, conflict reduction through dialogue and mediation, and efforts to achieve mutually satisfactory agreements. Such increased reliance on informal processes seems difficult to envision in a system in which formal rules and procedures are in part intended to protect offenders from the abuses of unrestricted retribution and may be especially troubling to youth advocates concerned about further slippage in current due process protections in juvenile courts (e.g., Feld 1990). Proponents of restorative justice would counter that in most cases the current court process is itself often highly informal rather than truly adversarial (see Eisenstein and Jacob 1991; Hackler 1991), but is based on negotiation and bargaining in the service of the retributive ends of the state (and the professional interests of attorneys) rather than the interests of fairness and due process. Moreover, in contrast to the "individualized" justice of *parens patriae,* restorative justice acknowledges and builds on group and community responsibility for crime (Van Ness 1993; McElrea 1993) rather than simply directing blame—and thus sanctions or treatment—at individual offenders.

Due process protections are also important to restorative justice advocates (e.g., Van Ness 1993; Walgrave 1993), and none has argued that it is necessary or desirable to weaken procedural protections for offenders to ensure restoration of victims or to bring about more rapid implementation of restorative policies (Messmer and Otto 1992). What some restorative justice advocates regard as an "obsession with process" in U.S. criminal and juvenile justice, however, may be due in part to the "high stakes" of being found guilty in a system that punishes with a great deal of severity (Wright 1991; Zehr 1990).[5] Thus the opposition of restorative justice advocates to the adversarial process is in large part due to opposition to the predominant emphasis on retributive punishment.

Practice, Programs, and Implementation

Current juvenile court sanctioning based on retributive justice is built around use of incarceration in its various forms, as well as an emphasis on surveillance, punishment, and control in probation and community supervision programs (Armstrong 1991). Based on the goals, objectives, and alternative processes outlined above, restorative justice sanctioning practices and programs would deemphasize retributive punishment in favor of restitution (Schneider 1985), victim-offender mediation (Umbreit and Coates 1993), restorative community service (Bazemore and Maloney 1994), victim awareness education (English and Crawford 1989), and other victim-oriented services. In addition to these now-familiar approaches, the shaming and reintegrative aspects of restorative sanctioning could be more specifically addressed and directly operationalized. Such offender interventions as community service crews that work with public employees to build homeless shelters or repair windows, doors, and other damage to homes victimized by break-ins; involving juveniles in community organizations where they can learn from their elders; direct service to victims where appropriate following mediation; and arranging for supervised home visits to victims come to mind (McElrea 1993; Bazemore and Maloney 1994).

Despite the strong potential of these and similar interventions, as well as the positive public acceptance and promising evaluation findings from empirical studies of restitution and victim-offender mediation programs (Schneider 1985, 1986; Butts and Snyder 1991; Umbreit and Coates 1993), there are dangers in a primary reliance on innovative programs and practices as the sole basis for reform. In recent years juvenile justice systems have been vulnerable to panaceas and "quick fix" solutions to complex problems (Finckenauer 1982) (e.g., boot camps, "Scared Straight"). Like Goldstein's (1979) profile of police departments obsessed with *tactics* rather than *outcomes* and emphasizing means over ends, systems adopting this "program driven" approach to reform typically fail to consider the fit between new programs and existing values, policies, and bureaucratic constraints of criminal justice agencies (McShane and Williams 1992). Programmatic reform, even when based on coherent, theoretical principles, may therefore lead to a dilution of even the most innovative practices to fit existing management protocols. Alternatively, it may simply add a new layer of progressive practices (e.g., based on restorative justice principles) onto a retributive policy core. In a system based on retributive justice values, programs and practices such as restitution and community service may be used as punitive "add-ons" rather than as primary sanctions directed toward restorative ends (Bazemore and Maloney 1994; Shapiro 1990). Similarly, increased involvement in the justice process is of little benefit to victims if the system uses them only to aid in securing convictions or in increasing the length or severity of punishment.

Specific dangers in simply initiating new restorative programs in the absence of wider systemic changes include the possibility that such programs will simply expand and strengthen social control, either by net widening, or by adding to current requirements imposed on offenders under court supervision (Krisberg and Austin 1981); the possibility of staff resistance to change when casework routines built around individual treatment, surveillance protocols, or both are disrupted (Maupin 1993); and the possibility that these programs will be judged by the performance standards of retributive or bureaucratic justice (e.g., increasing the number of cases handled) rather than by restorative justice outcomes (e.g., peace making, meeting victim needs) (Van Ness 1993). Ultimately, competing priorities of retributive justice and individual treatment may limit resources that can be allocated to pursuit of restorative objectives (e.g., involving victims, enabling offenders to pay restitution), and this limitation may quickly set up restorative programs for failure (Shapiro 1990). Moreover, in the absence of values clarification, reparative sanctions may be used primarily for punitive purposes (Bazemore and Maloney 1994) or as an ancillary component of treatment plans. Likewise, purportedly "victim-oriented" practices such as victim impact statements can be easily directed toward retributive ends (Elias 1993; McShane and Williams 1992).

On the other hand, if motivated by restorative values and viewed as primary sanctions rather than add-ons to other punishments and requirements, reparative sanctions can be effective tools for holding offenders accountable to victims and the community. Similarly, victim impact statements and similar mechanisms could be used effectively to determine the nature and type of reparation, increase victim involvement, and provide a more accurate assessment of victim needs. A restorative value framework could also provide the impetus for integrating now marginal victim-focused and reparative programs into the mainstream juvenile justice process and could provide a conceptual and policy basis for coordinating services of these disparate programs to better serve the needs of victims and communities.

DISCUSSION

Punitive values, goals, and policies will not disappear overnight. Although the juvenile justice system has shown progress in implementing programs consistent with a restorative approach (e.g., Schneider 1985; Umbreit & Coates 1993; Umbreit 1994), only a few juvenile courts have adopted these as prototypes for restructuring the sanctioning process based on a restorative philosophy. For the most part, restorative practices remain on the fringes, and their objectives are viewed as secondary to the concerns of retributive justice, as well as to those of individual treatment. In addition, a dramatic change in policy and management agendas governing juvenile justice systems is implied if these systems are to meet the challenge of restorative justice—for example, to identify and then engage communities and victims in the justice process (Van Ness 1993).

"Seeds" of Restorative Juvenile Justice
Despite these cautions and obstacles, policymakers wishing to move in the direction of a restorative justice approach can build on several inherent strengths of the model and take advantage of several opportunities created by the current crisis in juvenile justice policy.

Movement toward increased formalization notwithstanding, juvenile justice in most jurisdictions retains an informal ethic and is more receptive to restorative approaches (Schneider 1985; Umbreit 1994) than criminal justice. In its contextual emphasis on crime as conflict (e.g., Zehr 1990), restorative justice may be highly compatible with this less formal process and situational approach to dispute resolution.

To move forward with the restorative agenda for juvenile court sanctioning, policymakers could exploit the potential for restorative justice to engage and integrate the interests of nontraditional juvenile justice constituencies (e.g., victims, employers) (Bazemore and Maloney 1994), while also building on innovative programs such as comprehensive restitution, restorative community service, and victim-offender mediation that exemplify the restorative process. Such programs could be used specifically to "pilot" practices and policies as models for entire *systems* rather than as "add-ons" to probation and the formal court process. Promising examples of such restorative sanctioning systems now can be found in several European countries and in Australia and New Zealand (Messmer and Otto 1992; Walgrave 1993; McElrea 1993; Marshall and Merry 1990). In the Australian and New Zealand "family group conference" model, for example, the victim and his/her supporters are given the opportunity to speak about how they have been affected by the crime and to condemn the behavior of young offenders. The offender, his/her family or community surrogates, a trained facilitator/mediator, and the victim then participate in designing appropriate ways for the offender to repair the harm and make amends to the victim and the community. This begins a reintegrative process for the delinquent in which members of the family and community take responsibility for monitoring offender compliance and facilitating victim and community healing (Makkai and Braithwaite 1994; McElrea 1993). U.S. cities are not the same as cities in New Zealand or Europe, and juvenile justice systems are larger, more complex, and more crisis-driven. However, it is possible to implement reforms based on these principles, which similarly challenge the adversarial process as pilot efforts in smaller components of such large systems and, as is most consistent with the restorative model, to do so on a neighborhood basis.[6]

CONCLUSION

As an emerging new paradigm, restorative justice sanctioning does *not* offer complete solutions to all of the complex issues facing juvenile justice policymakers. A meaningful and effective sanctioning model is only one aspect of the comprehensive agenda for reform currently needed in juvenile justice. As a holistic framework focused on a balanced response to the needs of offenders and communities, however, restorative justice also has implications for enhancing and building support for a more empowering, holistic, and effective reintegrative approach to rehabilitation (Bazemore and Maloney 1994) and for defining a new role for juvenile justice professionals in enhancing the safety and security of communities.

In addition, we have suggested that rethinking the way juvenile courts carry out the sanctioning function may be a prerequisite for more comprehensive reform aimed at preserving the juvenile court and a rehabilitative focus for juvenile offenders. The blueprint presented here, based on the principles of restorative justice, prescribes a comprehensive redesign of sanctioning policy. Such redesign would begin with change in values; acknowledgment of new "customers" of the system (i.e., victims and the community); the development of new goals and objectives; change in the justice process; and change in the priority assigned to various practices and programs.

From the vantage point of a retributive system steeped in supportive legal traditions and institutional frameworks, the goals and values of restorative justice are idealistic and utopian. At the same time, however, in the current climate of chaos and reaction in juvenile justice, such idealistic goals may be critical to ensure that balanced reform proceeds in a positive direction:

> Giving priority to reparation rather than retribution calls for a change in social ethics and a different ideology of society. That means a society governed with the aims of individual and collective emancipation, in which autonomy and solidarity are not seen as diametrically opposed, but viewed as mutually reinforcing principles. A society doing its utmost to avoid exclusion of its members, because it is a society which draws its strength not from fear but from the high social ethics by which it is governed. . . . Is this Utopia? Yes, but we need a utopia to motivate us and provide guidance for our actions in society. There is nothing more *practical* than a good utopia. (Walgrave 1993, p. 9)

NOTES

1. The retributive/punitive paradigm that emerged in the juvenile justice system in the 1980s was in no way a pure "just deserts" approach (Thompson and McAnany 1984). Rather, retributive juvenile justice as implemented combines the emphasis on the primacy of punishment philosophy and certain policy trappings (e.g., determinate sentencing guidelines) of "just deserts" with a general concern with deterrence, incapacitation, and more traditional punitive objectives supported by Reagan administration policymakers as part of a more general attack on "leniency" in juvenile court sanctioning (e.g., Regnery 1985). The increased formality and adversarial emphasis has generally *not* meant an increase in due-process protections or better representation for juvenile offenders (Feld 1993).

2. Whereas the pursuit of multiple justice goals characterizes most historical eras, by the late 1980s retributive punishment was well on its way toward becoming a *determining goal* (Robinson 1987) in juvenile court dispositions. Determining goals, which set the overall priority for sanctioning, require that certain presumptive components are always included in a disposition. *Limiting goals* define what must be excluded and restrict the overall inten-

sity of sanctioning; for example, goals such as deterrence have often limited the pursuit of rehabilitative ends in juvenile justice.

3. Van Ness (1993) suggested that the term *restorative justice* was first coined by Albert Eglash (1975) in a paper in which he distinguished between retributive justice based on punishment, distributive justice based on therapeutic treatment, and restorative justice based on restitution. Though still unfamiliar in the United States, the term is widely used in Europe, and restorative justice has been on the agenda of policymakers and researchers for approximately a decade (Davis 1992; Messmer and Otto 1992). Whereas retributive and restorative justice are compatible in their common focus on the *offense act* (Davis 1992) and may be contrasted with the utilitarian focus on the offender, they differ in the emphasis on punishment versus reparation, obligation to the victim versus the state, and the emphasis (in restorative justice) on the future rather than the past (Zehr 1990; Davis 1992).

4. Elias (1993) has distinguished between this "official" retributive victims' movement and a "hidden" victims' movement that has often opposed the status quo—and therefore frequently been marginalized (e.g., Zehr 1990; Pepinsky and Quinney 1991). As McShane and Williams (1992) noted, victims and victims' advocacy groups were to a large extent coopted in various "get tough" prison expansion and mandatory sentencing initiatives in the 1980s.

5. This overemphasis on due process may have a number of unintended consequences according to these observers. For example, juveniles may be detained for longer periods or cases adjourned more frequently for continuances to accommodate the needs of attorneys (Hackler 1991). Whereas the parameters of offender and victim process rights and uniformity in restorative justice have yet to be completely defined (Messmer and Otto 1992), the restorative process should not be judged against an ideal adversarial process that rarely occurs in retributive justice (Elias 1993). In countries where restorative processes are more widely used in juvenile justice, a variety of mechanisms have been devised to protect offender rights and maximize access to nonadversarial options (Messmer and Otto 1992; Davis 1992).

6. The Minnesota Department of Corrections has recently adopted restorative justice as its mission, and other states and local jurisdictions are including restorative principles in their codes, mission, and purpose statements. Several U.S. juvenile systems are experimenting with restorative justice policies and practices by initiating small pilot projects as part of an "action research" demonstration effort funded by the Office of Juvenile Justice and Delinquency Prevention (OJJDP) (Bazemore 1994b). Points of view or opinions expressed in this document are, of course, those of the authors and do not necessarily represent the official position of OJJDP or the U.S. Department of Justice.

REFERENCES

Armstrong, Troy, ed. 1991. *Intensive Interventions With High-Risk Youths: Promising Approaches in Juvenile Probation & Parole.* New York: Criminal Justice Press.

Bazemore, Gordon. 1994a. "Understanding the Response to Reforms Limiting Discretion: Judges' Views of Restrictions on Detention Intake." *Justice Quarterly* 11:429–53.

_____. 1994b. *Balanced and Restorative Justice: Program Summary.* Washington, DC: U.S. Department of Justice, Office of Juvenile Justice and Delinquency Prevention.

Bazemore, Gordon and Dennis Maloney. 1994. "Rehabilitating Community Service: Toward Restorative Service in a Balanced Justice System." *Federal Probation* 58:24–35.

Braithwaite, John. 1989. *Crime, Shame and Reintegration.* New York: Cambridge University Press.

Butts, Jeffrey. 1994. *Offenders in Juvenile Court, 1992.* Washington, DC: U.S. Department of Justice, Office of Juvenile Justice and Delinquency Prevention.

Butts, Jeffrey and Howard Snyder. 1991. *Restitution and Juvenile Recidivism.* Pittsburgh: National Center for Juvenile Justice.

Byrne, James M. 1989. "Reintegrating the Concept of Community Into Community-based Corrections." *Crime & Delinquency* 35:471–99.

Castellano, Thomas. 1986. "The Justice Model in the Juvenile Justice System: Washington State's Experience." *Law and Policy* 8:479–506.

Christie, Nils. 1982. *Limits to Pain.* Oxford: Martin Robertson.

Davis, Gwynn. 1992. *Making Amends: Mediation and Reparation in Criminal Justice.* London: Routledge.

Durkheim, Emile. 1961. *Moral Education: A Study in the Theory and Application of the Sociology of Education,* translated by E. K. Wilson and H. Schnurer. New York: Free Press.

Eglash, Albert. 1975. "Beyond Restitution: Creative Restitution." Pp. 91–101 in *Restitution in Criminal Justice,* edited by J. Hudson and B. Galaway. Lexington, MA: Lexington Books.

Eisenstein, James and Herbert Jacob. 1991. *Felony Justice: An Organizational Analysis of Criminal Courts,* 2nd ed. Boston: Little Brown.

Elias, Robert. 1993. *Victims Still: The Political Manipulation of Crime Victims.* Newbury Park, CA: Sage.

English, Sharon and Michael Crawford. 1989. "Victim Awareness Education Is Basic to Offender Programming" (monograph). Sacramento: California Youth Authority.

Feld, Barry. 1990. "The Punitive Juvenile Court and the Quality of Procedural Justice: Disjunctions Between Rhetoric and Reality." *Crime & Delinquency* 36:443–64.

_____. 1993. "The Criminal Court Alternative to Perpetuating Juvenile [In] Justice." Pp. 3–13 in *The Juvenile Court: Dynamic, Dysfunctional, or Dead?* Philadelphia: Center for the Study of Youth Policy, School of Social Work, University of Pennsylvania.

Finckenauer, James. 1982. *Scared Straight! and the Panacea Phenomena.* Englewood Cliffs, NJ: Prentice-Hall.

Galaway, Burt and Joel Hudson, eds. 1990. *Criminal Justice, Restitution and Reconciliation.* Monsey, NY: Willow Tree Press.

Garland, David. 1990. *Punishment and Modern Society: A Study in Social Theory.* Chicago: University of Chicago Press.

Goldstein, Herman. 1979. "Improving Policing: A Problem-Oriented Approach." *Crime & Delinquency* 25:236–58.

Griffiths, Curt T. and Charlene Belleau. 1993. "Restoration, Reconciliation and Healing–The Revitalization of Culture and Tradition in Addressing Crime and Victimization in Aboriginal Communities." Paper presented at the meeting of the 11th International Congress on Criminology, Budapest, Hungary.

Hackler, James. 1991. "The Possible Overuse of Not Guilty Pleas in Juvenile Justice" (monograph). Edmonton, Alberta: Centre for Criminological Research, University of Alberta.

Haley, John. 1989. "Confession, Repentance, and Absolution." Pp. 195–211 in *Mediation and Criminal Justice: Victims, Offenders and Community,* edited by M. Wright and B. Galaway. London: Sage.

Harris, Kay. 1993. "Moving Into the New Millennium: A Feminist Perspective on Justice Reform." Pp. 166–7 in *Criminology as Peacemaking,* edited by H. E. Pepinsky and R. Quinney. Bloomington: Indiana University Press.

Hillsman, Sally and Judith Greene. 1992. "The Use of Fines as an Intermediate Sanction." Pp. 123–41 in *Smart Sentencing,* edited by J. M. Byrne, A. Lorigio, and J. Petersilia. Newbury Park, CA: Sage.

Krisberg, Barry. 1988. *The Juvenile Court: Reclaiming the Vision.* San Francisco: National Council of Crime and Delinquency.

Krisberg, Barry and James F. Austin. 1981. "Wider, Stronger, and Different Nets: The Dialectics of Criminal Justice Reform." *Journal of Research in Crime and Delinquency* 18:165–96.

Lawrence, Richard. 1991. "Reexamining Community Corrections Models." *Crime & Delinquency* 37:449–64.

Lemov, Penelope. 1994. "The Assault on Juvenile Justice." *Governing* December:26–31.

Mack, Julian. 1909. "The Juvenile Court." *Harvard Law Review* 23:104–22.

Makkai, Tony and John Braithwaite. 1994. "Reintegrative Shaming and Compliance With Regulatory Standards." *Criminology* 32:361–85.

Marshall, Tony and Sally Merry. 1990. *Crime and Accountability.* London: Home Office.

Maupin, James. 1993. "Risk Classification Systems and the Provision of Juvenile Aftercare." *Crime & Delinquency* 39:90–105.

McAllair, Daniel. 1993. "Reaffirming Rehabilitation in Juvenile Justice." *Youth and Society* 25:104–25.

McElrea, Frances W. M. 1993. "A New Model of Justice." Pp. 1–14 in *The Youth Court in New Zealand: A New Model of Justice,* edited by B. J. Brown. Auckland, New Zealand: Legal Research Foundation, Pub. 34.

McHardy, Louis. 1990. "Looking at the Delinquency Problem from the Juvenile Court Bench." *International Review of Criminal Policy* 39/40:113–8.

McShane, Marilyn and Frank Williams IV. 1992. "Radical Victimology: A Critique of the Concept of Victim in Traditional Victimology." *Crime & Delinquency* 38:258–71.

Melton, Gary B. 1989. "Taking Gault Seriously: Toward a New Juvenile Court." *Nebraska Law Review* 68:146–81.

Messmer, Heinz and Hans-Uwe Otto, eds. 1992. *Restorative Justice on Trial: Pitfalls and Potentials of Victim Offender Mediation: International Research Perspectives.* Norwell, MA: Kluwer Academic Publishers.

Miller, Jerome. 1991. *Last One Over the Wall.* Columbus: Ohio State University Press.

Packer, Herbert. 1968. *The Limits of the Criminal Sanction.* Palo Alto, CA: Stanford University Press.

Paternoster, Raymond and Lynn Iovanni. 1989. "The Labeling Perspective and Delinquency: An Elaboration of the Theory and an Assessment of the Evidence." *Justice Quarterly* 6:359–94.

Pepinsky, Harold E. and Richard Quinney, eds. 1991. *Criminology as Peacemaking.* Bloomington: Indiana University Press.

Regnery, Alfred. 1985. "Getting Away With Murder: Why the Juvenile Justice System Needs an Overhaul." *Policy Review* 34:65–8.

Reiss, Albert, Jr. 1986. "Why Are Communities Important in Understanding Crime?" Pp. 1–33 in *Communities and Crime,* edited by A. J. Reiss and M. Tonry. Chicago: University of Chicago Press.

Robinson, Paul. 1987. "Hybrid Principles for the Distribution of Criminal Sanctions." *Northern University Law Review* 19:34–6.

Rothman, David. 1980. *Conscience and Convenience: The Asylum and Its Alternatives in Progressive America.* New York: Harper Collins.

Schafer, Steven. 1970. *Compensation and Restitution to Victims of Crime.* Montclair, NJ: Smith Patterson.

Schneider, Anne, ed. 1985. *Guide to Juvenile Restitution.* Washington, DC: U.S. Department of Justice, Office of Juvenile Justice and Delinquency Prevention.

_____. 1986. "Restitution and Recidivism Rates of Juvenile Offenders: Results From Four Experimental Studies," *Criminology* 24:533–52.

Schneider, Anne and Donna Schram. 1983. A *Justice Philosophy for the Juvenile Court.* Seattle: Urban Policy Research.

Shapiro, Carol. 1990. "Is Restitution Legislation the Chameleon of the Victims' Movement?" Pp. 73–80 in *Criminal Justice, Restitution, and Reconciliation,* edited by B. Galaway and J. Hudson. Monsey, NY: Willow Tree Press.

Thompson, Douglas and Patrick McAnany. 1984. "Punishment and Responsibility in Juvenile Court: Desert-based Probation for Delinquents." Pp. 137–75 in *Probation and Justice: Reconsideration of Mission,* edited by P. D. McAnany, D. Thompson, and D. Fogel. Cambridge, MA: Oelgeschlager, Gunn & Hain.

Umbreit, Mark. 1994. *Victim Meets Offender: The Impact of Restorative Justice and Mediation.* Monsey, NY: Criminal Justice Press.

Umbreit, Mark and Robert Coates. 1993. "Cross-site Analysis of Victim-Offender Mediation in Four States." *Crime & Delinquency* 39:565–85.

Van Ness, Daniel. 1993. "New Wine and Old Wineskins: Four Challenges of Restorative Justice." *Criminal Law Forum* 4:251–76.

von Hirsch, Andrew. 1976. *Doing Justice.* New York: Hill & Wang.

Walgrave, Lode. 1993. "Beyond Retribution and Rehabilitation: Restoration as the Dominant Paradigm in Judicial Intervention Against Juvenile Crime." Paper presented at the International Congress on Criminology, Budapest, Hungary.

Wilkins, Leslie T. 1991. *Punishment, Crime and Market Forces.* Brookfield, VT: Dartmouth Publishing Co.

Wright, Martin. 1991. *Justice for Victims and Offenders.* Buckingham, England: Open University.

Yazzie, Robert. 1994. "'Life Comes From It': Navajo Justice Concepts." *New Mexico Law Review* 24:175–90.

Zehr, Howard. 1990. *Changing Lenses: A New Focus for Crime and Justice.* Scottsdale, PA: Herald Press.

Zhang, Lening and Steven E. Messner. 1994. "The Severity of Official Punishment for Delinquency and Change in Interpersonal Relations in Chinese Society." *Journal of Research in Crime and Delinquency* 31:416–33.

Hard Times for Bad Kids

Numbed by teen-age killers and unable to rehabilitate youthful offenders, the juvenile justice system is turning to get-tough measures to halt a new generation of crime.

MARK CURRIDEN

Mark Curriden writes on legal affairs for the Atlanta Journal-Constitution *and other publications.*

One by one, they parade before the judge. Most are sporting expensive athletic shoes or Army-style boots. A few have pimples. Some are frightened. But most display "a'tude"—giving the impression that they are bored and could not care less about what is happening.

"Why did you steal the car?" the judge asks.

The 16-year-old shrugs his shoulders. This is his third time before the judge. The first was for shoplifting a wallet and gloves; the second was for burglary after a neighbor caught him stealing two cameras. The first appearance resulted in unsupervised probation; the second in six weeks' confinement at an unsecured detention facility.

This time, he will be sent to another Minnesota treatment program for a longer period of time. And if that fails, he will be transferred to another facility—neither of them secured.

"These kids think it's a joke," says William McGee, a former defense attorney and now juvenile court prosecutor in Minneapolis.

"They have no respect for the system. As a society, we have glamorized sex and violence. As a result, we have a generation of children who are simply amoral."

Throughout the nation, the search by cities, counties and states for ways to stop the spread of increasingly more serious and violent crimes among youths is in full swing. Officials argue that the juvenile courts are not equipped to handle the kinds of crimes being committed by today's minors. And many judges feel they are struggling just to keep from drowning, let alone making any progress.

"There's one group of kids out there that, no matter what we do, will end up in maximum-security prisons as adults," says Judge Bertrand Poritsky of the St. Paul, Minn., juvenile court. "There's a second group of kids that, no matter what we do to them, are going to be rocket scientists.

"Then there's the third group —the kids who are headed down the wrong trail, but whose consciences and personalities are still impressionable. That's the group we should be targeting.

"The problem is, we are having to spend all of our time and resources dealing with that first group, and we are losing that third group," Poritsky says.

Few communities have avoided the high-profile violent crimes committed by youths that have ignited public outrage and a demand that something be done. In response, politicians and court officials have been experimenting with many options. Some are major reforms, while others are considered tinkering. Among the efforts are:

• More than 50 cities have enacted nighttime curfews for teenagers.

• California parents must help their child convicted of scrawling graffiti to clean up the damage.

• Philadelphia schools have banned pagers (frequently part of drug trafficking) from school buildings.

• Milwaukee police track youths who wear gang-like clothing or tattoos, or who have been photographed in the presence of known gang members.

• Twenty-one states have lowered the death penalty to age 16 for first-degree murder. Four other states say that 17-year-olds are eligible for capital punishment.

• Several states, including Georgia, Maryland, Tennessee and Virginia, have lowered the age at which minors can be tried as adults. Louisiana has gone so far as to amend its statutes to state that juvenile delinquents are incarcerated not for the traditional reason of rehabilitation, but for public protection.

"Every aspect of the system is under the microscope," says Rich Gabel, director of research at the National Center for Juvenile Justice in Pittsburgh, a national research agency. "Communities are re-examining their approach to youth crime at all levels—the streets, courtrooms, churches, schools and correctional facilities."

While the number of juveniles committing crimes has remained about the same or risen only slightly the past decade, the offenses have become more serious and more deadly, according to statistics from the Office of Juvenile Justice and Delinquency Prevention, a division of the U.S. Department of Justice.

All too frequently, the targets of all that violence are other youths. The delinquency prevention office says 55 percent of crimes committed by people under the age of 19 were committed against other juveniles.

"Throughout the entire decade of the 1980s, we averaged less than three kids a year coming before us in homicides," says Minneapolis Juvenile Court judge Philip Bush. "In the 1990s, we are seeing an average of 16 kids a year up on homicide charges."

This increase in serious crime has resulted in 100,000 juveniles incarcerated in jails and prisons. One-tenth of those are in California.

But the juvenile court system itself is "having an identity crisis," says University of Minnesota law professor Barry Feld. "It was originally intended to be a social welfare system. It was supposed to identify needs and point the child or the family to the appropriate service.

"Today, it is little more than a scaled-down, second-class criminal court. Juvenile courts are procedurally bankrupt. The system was never designed to handle the serious criminal matters coming before it now."

The pendulum began to swing away from rehabilitation toward punitive measures during the mid-1970s. However, statistics show that youth crime during that period remained relatively stable. Between 1978 and 1988, the incarceration rate of juveniles jumped nearly 50 percent, while the crime rate

of those under the age of 19 actually dropped 19 percent.

"Many states have completely shunned rehabilitation; they are simply warehousing kids they deem bad," says Mark Soler, president of the Youth Law Center, a Washington, D.C.-based public-interest law firm that specializes in juvenile justice. "Too many lightweight offenders are being locked up, which takes up space for the more serious offender. We are not putting our resources in the right places."

Whether or not crime numbers among those under the age of 19 are climbing, most experts welcome the increased attention being focused on the juvenile courts.

"The difference between the juvenile crime rate of a few years ago and juvenile crime today is that everyone is talking about it now," says Andrew Shookhoff, a juvenile court judge in Nashville, Tenn., and co-chair of the Juvenile Justice Committee of the American Bar Association's Criminal Justice Section. "The juvenile crime rate is just as unacceptable today as it was a few years ago, but at least we are discussing solutions now."

Unfortunately, there are no model systems for cities and states to duplicate, authorities point out. Changing the juvenile justice system is "still very experimental," says Gabel of the National Center for Juvenile Justice. "We're still in the early stages of trying to discover what works, what doesn't, and why. The answer to all of our troubles may be a program out there somewhere in some small town that we don't know about yet."

Juvenile court experts say there are five basic aspects critical to dealing with youth crime: early prevention and intervention, evaluation of needs, court procedures, programs for those more violent, and reintegration into society.

"Each of these is essential to operating a juvenile court system that works," says John J. Wilson, administrator of the Office of Juvenile Justice and Delinquency Prevention. "Some states are doing one or two of these very well, but are dropping the ball on the others. States need to learn they just cannot focus on one segment and think they can solve their problems."

While officials say there will always be debate over whether there are enough social and community programs fo-

cusing on prevention and intervention, the more immediate concern is deciding which programs really work and which ones are right for which juveniles.

"In Minnesota, we're spending a ton of money on programs that are nothing more than cash cows for the treatment providers," says state Supreme Court Justice Sandra Gardebring.

Tennessee's Shookhoff says there is widespread resistance to conducting thorough studies of individual programs out of fear that many highly touted pet projects may be proven to have little or no effect on reducing delinquency.

"No one wants to be told their innovative program is really a flop," says Shookhoff. "So many officials are simply unwilling to allow their programs to be placed under the microscope to study successes and failures. They would rather have a noneffective program continue than be embarrassed by being told that it doesn't work."

The Office of Juvenile Justice and Delinquency Prevention last October published a 240-page report entitled, "What Works: Promising Interventions in Juvenile Justice." The study reviewed more than 1,100 programs nationwide and selected 425 the office found to have demonstrated successes. The study gives basic details of the programs, including a general description of what they do, what group of offenders they target, and their staff and budget sizes.

"Officials must remember that not every program is going to work in every situation," says Michael Saucier, a lawyer in Portland, Maine, and chairman of the National Coalition for Juvenile Justice, an independent program of the Justice Department. "Every community's needs are different. What works for Maine may not for Florida. What works in the city of Portland is not as effective in a rural part of our state or even in a suburb."

However, there are specific elements that are common in most, if not all, successful programs. The keys are to attempt to treat and rehabilitate youthful offenders in small groups, maintain a clear focus on the objective, and have good case management and intensive staff supervision, according to Soler.

"The juvenile justice system must be a place where kids learn that they must take responsibility for their actions," says Soler. "The programs that work have an educational component that teaches kids that doing destructive acts has consequences."

The problem with many newer programs, such as the increasingly popular boot camps in which youths are subjected to military-style discipline, is the lack of follow-up by authorities, experts say. After 16 to 36 weeks of intensive training and rehabilitation, a teen-ager is typically sent back into the same circumstances from which he or she was arrested.

The result, according to a recent national study of boot camps conducted by the *New York Times,* is that there is no reduction in the recidivism rate among offenders.

Officials in Minnesota say keeping the treatment programs in or near the community where the child comes from is important. For years, youths in the inner cities of Minneapolis and St. Paul were sent to "chop wood" in northern Minnesota.

"We've learned that the kids learned nothing from that experience," says Minneapolis prosecutor McGee. "The kids need to be in programs at their local church or school or community center. They need to be near their families."

A major concern to some experts like Shookhoff is doing the proper evaluation of the juveniles coming into the system and placing them into the appropriate programs.

"In a vast majority of these cases, it's not finding out if the kid did the crime. It's what are we going to do to make sure that the kid doesn't have a miserable life and doesn't make life miserable for the rest of us.

"We need much better methods of evaluating why kids who violate the law do it," Shookhoff says.

Judges say they need to know when the parents of a child are going through a divorce, or if a parent is in prison or has an alcohol problem. Despite this being the information and computer age, judges and probation officers say school officials frequently are not even telling them when a child develops a truancy problem.

"You know when a kid officially becomes a truant? When he misses seven straight days of school," says McGee. "And we don't find out about it until after he has missed 20 or 30 days. Alarms should start

going off after a kid misses three days of school."

The response to truancy by students at most schools, according to Minneapolis juvenile judge Charles A. Porter Jr., is to "throw the kid out of school."

"People ask me, when we have so many serious juvenile offenders, why do we still care about some kid skipping class?" Porter says. "I'll tell you why. If you look at 70 percent, maybe 80 percent, of the kids committing serious crimes today, they were truants five or 10 years earlier.

"If we had dealt with their manageable problems back then, we most likely would not be dealing with destructive ones today."

Minnesota, long known for liberal politics and well-funded social programs, has revamped its juvenile justice system. After 18 months of study and assessment, the state has abandoned the longstanding concept that all youths can be rehabilitated and that no juveniles should be imprisoned. Some will be tried as adults and face the greater likelihood of jail time that goes with it.

As of January, youths involved in first-time or minor offenses would still go through the traditional juvenile court system. Those 14 years old or older who commit more serious felony offenses or who are repeat offenders would be sent to adult court. They would be given a lawyer and afforded all the rights of adult defendants, including a jury trial.

If they are found guilty, they would be sentenced to the appropriate time in prison.

However, a trial judge can suspend the sentence and transfer the youth back to juvenile court for further disposition more in keeping with traditional notions of rehabilitation. A refusal to comply with the juvenile court mandates would send the offender back to adult court.

"Previously, kids knew that we couldn't do anything with them; we had nothing to back up our threats," says Minnesota Supreme Court Chief Justice A.M. "Sandy" Keith. "This lets the kid know we are serious. This allows us to tell a serious juvenile offender, 'This is your last chance. We want to help

Violent kids

The number of juvenile arrests for violent crimes per 100,000 persons under age 18:

Aggravated assault   Robbery   Rape   Murder

SOURCE: U.S. DEPARTMENT OF JUSTICE

CHART BY JEFF DIONISE

*Most recent year

'80 '81 '82 '83 '84 '85 '86 '87 '88 '89 '90 '91 '92*

"Juvenile courts in Minnesota have finally grown up," says Minneapolis judge Bush. "Juvenile judges now have a bigger stick to keep kids in line and a longer leash to help them find the appropriate services." The threat: Certain offenders can be tried in an adult court and face the possibility of jail time.

you, but you must cooperate this time or it's back to adult court.'"

The new system does not go as far as law professor Feld would like. He proposes eliminating juvenile courts altogether but recognizing at sentencing that some offenders are younger than others. "I call it short sentences for short people."

But Feld says Minnesota's blurring of boundaries between juvenile and adult court is "very innovative and a positive alternative to the mindless get-tough rhetoric of demagogues."

More important than court procedures for many Minnesota judges, prosecutors and juvenile court probation officers is the new attitude that is being espoused.

But change is going to take cooperation from all segments of society—judges, lawyers, caseworkers, churches, community leaders and politicians.

"If we are serious about solving this problem, we have to work a little harder," says McGee. "No more eight-hour workdays by lawyers and probation officers. When problems arise, the court needs to react quickly. We need to be there on Saturdays and Sundays and at midnight."

McGee and others say prosecutors and defense attorneys need to be more than advocates. They need to find out why a juvenile committed a crime and work together to find out what programs would be in the long-term best interest of the youth.

"Juvenile judges need to exercise their authority to bring parents into the courtroom and make them take an active role in their kids' problems," McGee says. "Judges need to bring schoolteachers, school counselors, ministers and community activists into the juvenile justice process and make them get involved."

Shookhoff agrees, saying juvenile court judges should be activists—jurists in the true sense of the word. "A juvenile court judge who does nothing but sit on the bench, wear his or her black robe and resolve disputes but who does not get personally involved in the community, is going to fail," he says. "The juvenile court needs to call on community and neighborhood program leaders to help supervise kids.

"Today's juvenile court judge needs to be a community catalyst, helping develop community crime prevention programs, visiting church groups, and saying, 'Here are our problems. We need your help.'"

Judge Hayden's Family Values

As Americans fail at marriage and parenting, and new family configurations require fresh solutions, more people end up surrendering their most intimate decisions to a family court judge.

A month inside the mind of Katharine Sweeney Hayden.

JAN HOFFMAN

Jan Hoffman is the metropolitan legal affairs reporter for The New York Times.

IT HAS TAKEN ALMOST FOUR YEARS TO GET to this afternoon in a muggy Newark courtroom. That's how long the parents have been duking it out over their son, each trying to win the judge over, each saying, Your Honor, *you* decide because we can't. Just let me be the one to keep the child. Yet no matter how she calls the custody fight, Judge Katharine Sweeney Hayden knows that one parent will bless her and the other will curse her. She shrugs. It's not my job to make happy endings, she thinks. If a couple is so anger-locked that they have to ask a stranger to make their most intimate decisions, well, too bad: I'm it, I'm what you've got.

Then she relents a little. She reminds herself that people so desperate that they must turn to an Essex County family court judge have no choice but to trust her. And that is why she often feels protective of them.

But today she's unusually edgy: she still has no idea how she is going to rule. It's already June and the case has a firm deadline, two months away.

During the years the parents have come before her, they have treated the boy like a shuttlecock — one month with the mother, first in Cleveland, more recently in Wilmington, Del.; the next month with the father in a New Jersey suburb. But now their son is 6. In September, he must start first grade in one state or another — and stay there.

The husband's lawyer is summing up. He makes a powerful claim for the father, Carl H., a 30-year-old airline supervisor. The court-appointed psychologist has favored the father — important, thinks the judge, but not a deal maker. A tall, quiet man with two years of college, Carl offers the boy not only his own love but also the love and caretaking of Carl's parents, with whom he lives, as well as the boisterous affection of an extended family.

Hayden, a slim, handsome woman of 53 with a passing resemblance to Sigourney Weaver, listens fixedly, chin cradled in her right palm, unconsciously inching an elbow forward across her desk until the upper half of her body is all but horizontal.

Carl's lawyer now turns on the mother, Amber H. It was she who had an affair and moved out, leaving her husband and son behind in 1991. She changed addresses half a dozen times in four years, landing briefly in a violent relationship.

The judge pauses from her note taking to flex a sore wrist. But why, she wonders, has Carl been driving with a revoked license for two years? And why is a 30-year-old man living with his parents?

Now Amber's lawyer gets to her feet. Sure, her 26-year-old client, an airline ticket agent, made some mistakes. But she's matured since she walked away from a marriage that left her emotionally and, she says, physically bruised. Amber has settled down. In Delaware she has a home, a school, a church ready for her boy.

But how, the judge worries, can Amber justify taking the boy to another state, away from his father and grandparents? This bothers her. A lot.

Finally the lawyer offers Amber's most provocative claim — biology is indeed destiny. Amber was adopted. Her only known blood relation is her son. That argument, thinks the judge, has an emotional pull but not a legal one. But the next point will send her to the law library: paternity tests have proved that Carl is not the boy's biological father.

The baby was born less than a year after they started dating. Carl says he always assumed the child was his. Amber says she told him the truth right away. The judge has to decide who's lying.

Hayden announces she will rule in a few weeks. Then she escapes to her chambers, where she tosses off her black robe and nervously runs her long fingers through her close-cropped hair.

This case is driving her nuts.

ON MOST WEEKDAYS, THE JUDGE GETS up at 5:30 A.M., pushes herself through three miles of race walking and makes a good-faith effort to pull into the court's parking lot by 8:26 A.M. She heads over to the Hall of Records, a gloomy, turn-of-the-century building in a downtown Newark neighborhood that empties out when darkness falls.

Today begins promisingly: one of the main entrance's six elevators is actually working. As she strides down a dimly lighted hallway to her chambers, she sees people of all races waiting for her. Aunts and grandmothers dandling babies. A skinny man with oozing scratches from ear to collarbone. An elderly couple. A couple looking prosperous and deeply annoyed, separated by lawyers. They are residents of Essex County, which includes Newark, one of the country's most ravaged cities, as well as the plush, Manhattan-commuter suburbs of South Orange, Livingston and Short Hills.

Hayden is acutely aware that the people who come before her have no buffer to protect them from how she, a white, affluent, divorced and remarried mother of two, views their case. She is their sole juror — there are no jury trials in family court. Many couples come before her without lawyers and cannot afford to challenge her rulings. A scant fistful of her cases have ever been appealed. So although she doesn't share the glamorous status of those who preside over lurid criminal cases or big-ticket lawsuits, the impact she has on litigants can often be more profound and longer lasting.

But her job, like that of her colleagues, is getting harder, at times seemingly impossible, as the definition of family keeps mutating. When Katharine Hayden was starting law school almost a quarter-century ago, in-vitro fertilization was still half a dozen years away, and the landmark New Jersey family court case about Baby M. and Mary Beth Whitehead, the child's surrogate mother, nearly 15. A father like Carl would almost never have challenged his wife over custody, regardless of blood

ties. That gay and lesbian couples might adopt children was virtually unimaginable.

Bewildered and sometimes genuinely stumped by family dilemmas, she and her fellow judges have become society's gatekeepers, making decisions based on an uneasy mixture of inadequate laws and their own private values. The longer she sits on the bench, the more she realizes she's the interpreter of what society views as right and wrong.

Unlike those in many states, where different types of domestic cases are dispersed throughout the system, New Jersey's family court is a self-contained mini-mall of household horrors. Eventually, almost every modern family problem lands in Hayden's court. Her caseload includes child abuse, spousal violence, divorce, custody disputes among unmarried couples, deadbeat dads and termination of parental rights. (Adoptions and juvenile-delinquency cases are assigned to other judges.) She hears about 75 cases a week.

But in contrast to most of her colleagues around the country, who come to the despised, entry-level "kiddie court" with no background in family law, Hayden was a widely respected matrimonial lawyer. Even though she is to be rotated to the more high-profile criminal bench next year, when that stint is up she wants to return to family court. In a 1993 New Jersey Law Journal survey, for which lawyers rated Essex County's 56 family, equity, criminal and civil Superior Court trial judges on efficiency, knowledge and fairness, she was first overall.

While family court judges tend to cling tightly to confidentiality, Hayden spoke candidly about many of her cases to a reporter, whom she permitted to sit in on her court proceedings and chambers conferences for a month. (For privacy reasons, the parents have been identified in this article by first names or initials; the children's names have been omitted.) So it became possible to see how a family court judge, by questioning, scolding and listening to people for whom love has long since turned rancid and dull-eyed, performs a role that is far more complex than administrator of the law. From Hayden's wooden perch in her dingy four-row courtroom, she is mother, psychologist, preacher.

And to the families whose intimate lives she will reshape for years to come, she can seem like the hand of God. Or, occasionally, the Devil's.

THIS AFTERNOON, THE JUDGE TAKES HER FIRST measure of a difficult domestic violence case. The husband presents his story and the judge hears his rough voice breaking; she particularly notices that as he leans toward his daughter and wife, they stiffen. Contact lenses corrected her poor eyesight years ago, but she noses around new cases like a mole, sensing shapes and body language.

Mr. and Mrs. B. have each filed a domestic violence complaint against the other. Each wants to evict the other from their home. Neither spouse has a lawyer. But Mr. B. has brought a witness — their shy, gangling 12-year-old daughter.

Smiling graciously, the judge immediately tells a court officer to escort the daughter outside. A child shouldn't have to hear her parents' ragged, recriminating tales of a 15-year marriage collapsing in infidelity and shattered pride.

At first, the father seems the more sympathetic figure of the two. Mr. B., a 49-year-old truck driver, says in a tear-soaked voice: "I love my wife. I've tried to do everything to keep our family together."

His story is ancient: he caught his wife with another man. At 2 A.M. their escalating fight culminated with Mrs. B.'s pulling a knife on her husband and locking him out of the house, barefoot. The daughter let him in and later confirmed his story to the police.

The judge squints at him. Something doesn't ring true here. Why didn't he kick her out or pack his things? He's a big guy — he can't possibly be physically afraid of her. So what does he want? To get me to evict her so he can get the house?

Mrs. B., a medical secretary, doesn't exactly deny what happened. But in a voice at once defiant and defensive, she explains that her husband, a recovering alcoholic, is insecure because the two have not had "an intimate relationship" in some time.

She locks eyes with the judge, scrupulously avoiding her husband. "He said he wanted to

She has a strict

rule about post-mortem lashing. One good stinging self-beratement session, but that's it. She cannot afford to let the case haunt her.

purchase a gun and blow my head off. He got my mink coat, along with my cellular phone."

The judge throws her arms in the air. Who's to blame? She will have to call the young witness. But first she cautions the parents: "The one who loses will think it's because your daughter pointed the finger one way or the other. I'm telling you on the record I've made up my mind, but I want to explain it to her first. You have to have faith in this judge that I'm not lying to you."

Warily, the daughter enters the courtroom, craning her neck to watch her parents leave, abandoning

her to this stranger in a black robe. After they have gone, the judge speaks gently to the girl. "I want to ask your mom to leave the house because your dad's case fits the law better than hers. But how do you feel about living with him at home?"

The girl stares at her, dumbfounded. Then, to the judge's dismay, the child bursts into tears.

"I want to go with my mother," she says.

The judge pauses. Stay calm, she tells herself. "I could say I want you with your mother and I want you in the house. Do you mind if I tell your dad?"

The girl shakes her head. "He'll be real mad at me," she sobs. "When I was little, he used to beat me. My older sister told me that when they fought, to go to my room and turn the music up loud."

The judge's face is a mask of sympathetic anguish. "That must be a terrible thing for you."

The girl is warming up. "My sister said he used to hit my mother."

The judge scribbles notes and carefully asks, "When did he start up his drinking again?"

"Oct. 1, 1994," the child promptly replies.

"How do you know that date so well?"

"Because it was my birthday," says the girl. "He said he was happy I was turning 12, but I don't believe it, because he started drinking that day."

The judge massages her aching temples. So the family is in a far more precarious state than she had realized. Why did the father resume drinking? Given that his wife isn't sleeping with him, was he unnerved by his daughter's budding puberty?

The judge sighs and tells the girl that she will let her remain with her mother. "But I'm in a pickle," she adds. "I told your parents I wouldn't let you change my mind, but now you've gone and done it."

Then the judge telephones a lawyer who has a gift with child clients and asks her to represent the daughter. According to the law, Mrs. B. should have to leave because she threatened her husband with a dangerous weapon. But now that the daughter has raised new issues, the judge must consider which outcome will be in the child's best interest.

Meanwhile, the girl waits in the judge's chambers, looking almost chipper. Then she goes into the courtroom to whisper in the judge's ear: can Hayden now help the mother, who fears the father may damage their car, down in the court parking lot?

Damn it, the judge thinks irritably, I extended myself, and now she's taking advantage of me. I'm not going to micromanage their squabbles. Politely but firmly, she dusts the girl off.

The hearing resumes. The girl keeps her eyes on the table as her lawyer speaks. "She loves her dad and doesn't want to hurt him," says the lawyer, "but she would be happier if her dad moved and she could see him as much as possible."

The judge issues no-contact orders against both parents: "You are pushing each other's buttons. But if I say Mrs. B. leaves, then your daughter has to leave the house, too. So I'm asking Mr. B. to leave for two weeks."

The family walks tiredly, even peacefully out of court, wife smiling at husband, father wrapping his arm around his daughter. Hayden steps down from the bench. Good job, Katharine, she thinks.

Fifteen minutes later, Mrs. B. and her daughter race back into court, banging on the door of the judge's chambers. They say that in the elevator, Mr. B. swore he would mess up the house and his wife as well. Then he ran off. Mrs. B. speaks in gasps; her daughter looks crushed. When they got to the parking lot, Mrs. B. saw that her right front tire had been slashed and her antenna snapped. He had apparently attacked the car before he returned to court.

The judge's face goes taut with rage. She orders a sheriff's officer to accompany Mrs. B. and her daughter to a service station. Then, tremulously wishing the two of them the best of luck, the judge has another officer tell the local precinct to send a squad car to meet Mrs. B. at the house.

That night, Hayden sleeps fitfully. One of a family judge's worst nightmares is to make a wrong call on a domestic violence case. At 4 A.M. she wakes herself, scolding: letting the daughter live with her father would have been a stupid, dead-wrong decision.

She shouldn't have dismissed the girl when she asked for help. And she had absolutely misread the couple's smiles. She had thought that the wife was smiling in triumph for having got the house and that the husband was smiling because he had just heard his daughter say she loved him.

But she now sees that Mrs. B. had the nervous smile of a very frightened woman and that Mr. B. had been smiling because he knew what was waiting for his wife in the parking lot. All the while, the judge had had the arrogance to think that she had fixed everything.

She can't go back to sleep. She has a strict rule about post-mortem lashing. One good stinging self-beratement session, but that's it. As dawn breaks, she forces herself out of bed and into her running clothes. She cannot afford to let Mr. and Mrs. B. haunt her. Time to cauterize the case, and move on.

FRIDAY IS DIVORCE DAY. YOU CAN SNIFF THE tension and the money in the air. Not coincidentally, Friday is also the Day of the Lawyers.

Today Hayden wears her favorite earrings, dangling portraits of moon-eyed cows. Too bad if people think they're completely silly. To keep herself happy, a judge has to do what a judge has to do.

She takes the bench, sparring deftly with pin stripe after pin stripe as they bring divorce motions before her, flexing her judicial muscle, earrings swaying. She's almost having too much fun. Bearing down on a battalion of lawyers, her face alight with the slyest of grins, she says: "I don't know

The roughest days in court are those when she goes out on a limb for people: 'Follow me into the wilderness for I am the judge.' Yeah, right.

how you'll be ready for trial in two weeks either. You'll have to cram and it will be horrible."

Who's next? One couple, unencumbered by counsel, raise their hands. Like most family court judges, she hates to be the one to divide up the spoils. "You've settled?" she sings out. "Be still, my heart!"

But while 90 percent of divorce cases do settle, often the judge has to bang heads in her chambers to get there. When tempers get too short, she'll wind up the yellow Power Ranger she keeps on her desk and let it stalk noisily across the floor before the embarrassed lawyers.

One day she keeps stepping off the bench for updates from Howard Danzig and Cary Cheifetz, who represent a suburban couple in their mid-40's. The wife is a Wall Street lawyer who earns $165,000 a year; the husband quit his job with the Internal Revenue Service 15 years ago and has since stayed home to raise their five children.

"We don't know what's happening, judge," says Danzig, looking hapless. "They sent us away and they're sitting in the cafeteria with their laptops."

BY DAY'S END, HAYDEN SETS THE TRIAL FOR THE following week. When they return on that date, Danzig, who represents the husband, announces that negotiations have broken down over alimony his client wants the wife to pay.

The judge is both indignant and trying not to laugh. The couple's youngest child is already in high school; the eldest is already out of the house. "Really, Howard! Your client has to go to work. He can't stay at home anymore!"

Danzig looks nearly apoplectic. "Reverse the sexes, Judge! Imagine he earns $165,000 and she stays home with the kids."

"But he's more employable than his analogue," says Hayden. "And I don't want to barter her future for his alimony."

Cheifetz points out that the wife has already offered to pay not only all child support but also all five college tuitions.

Hayden looks quizzical. "I smell a rat," she says. "Is the wife taking on extra responsibility for the children so she won't have to give him money?"

This piece of information is enough to turn her head around about the case. Ushering the two lawyers to the door, she says: "You're right, Howard. Tell them the judge agrees it's definitely an alimony case. I finally saw what a sexist pig I am."

The next week, the couple settle.

When the judge does have to hand out marital booty, she holds her nose. "Financial decisions are intrusive and awkward forays into how people spend their money," she sputters one Friday morning. She stares at a list of items. "*I hate TV's!*" she shouts. "Why can't people divide up their own toys?"

The judge's first marriage, to a professor of medieval literature, fell apart after nearly 20 years. The dissolution was slow, sad but civilized. Even so, she will never forget the one blowup in their Maplewood kitchen, when he shouted, "I'll get a lawyer!" She was by then a major league divorce lawyer, and yet she still felt as if an earthquake had shaken their home. Lawyers? Judges? Combing through *her* life?

All the trust between her and her husband, the father of her two sons, would have been ripped away by the legal system. Luckily, the two of them worked out an amicable settlement. But the memory of those 10 seconds of panic in a suburban kitchen stays with her still, and she recalls it every time she has to reach into a divorcing couple's private cupboard.

The next hearing is to give a couple in divorce litigation a temporary budget until a final ruling. In addition to the divorce case, the husband and wife have filed domestic violence charges against each other. Both matters are before Hayden. Suzanne Spina, 30, is a Verona homemaker with two little children; Robert Spina, 40, is Police Chief of West Orange, appointed last year by his father, the Mayor. In a few weeks, Hayden's finding that Robert Spina abused his wife will be local front-page news. But right now there are bills to be paid. And Suzanne wants Robert to keep right on paying them.

Like Suzanne's car phone.

"Go on the low monthly end — $50," Hayden says. "You can rob from the food bill if you talk too much. How about $55 for your home phone?"

Ellen Marshall, Suzanne's lawyer, leaps up. "Ma'am," she cries out, "this is a devastated lady! She needs the support of her family," who reside in long-distance area codes and whom Suzanne needs to telephone regularly. A piddling $105 a month?

The judge fixes the lawyer with a deadpan stare. "So put it on her family's dime," she says.

Propping her reading glasses on her nose, the judge marches down the list of operations at the Spina manse, revising expenses for lawn care, utilities, repairs on the Mercedes, the burglar alarm, karate and tennis lessons for the 4-year-old, clean-

ing woman, birthday parties. She informs the Spinas that she doesn't do TV's and VCR's. The couple snipe at each other but eventually strike an accord. Then the judge makes a ruling on the treadmill. She gives it to Robert.

She knows that every divorcing party, consciously or not, draws a line that cannot be crossed. Robert has testified extensively about his exercise routine, and she has a hunch that losing the treadmill would have been the deal killer for him.

Besides, she thinks, the Spinas' health club is a good spot for Suzanne to meet people. Many hard bodies, many fancy treadmills — she laughs, shaking her head — and a regular Peyton Place.

HAYDEN HEARS HUNDREDS OF CASES through June and July. But each dawn as she sets out to race walk through her riverfront town, the battle over Amber and Carl's boy hovers in her head. One morning, Amber wins. Carl, the next. While blocks of brownstones go by, details from the case pluck at her. Why hasn't Carl made getting back his driver's license a priority? What about Amber's overbearing mother back in Washington State? She had heedlessly told her grandson that his daddy wasn't his real father. Amber merely said in court that she couldn't control her. Worrisome?

The truth is, Hayden realizes, that even though state family law seems specific, in close cases she can stack the facts and find legal backing for her decision no matter which way she goes.

A week later, during lunch hour in chambers, she is thinking aloud between bites on a chicken sandwich from the corner truck. Amber's insistence on the paternity test is irking her. By saying to her son, "You're mine but not his," Amber is seeking to remove him from his grandparents and his father, as well as an uncle, aunts and cousins — all the family he grew up with. The judge can't buy that.

Yet today, she is starting to think that Carl should lose. The psychologist said Carl played beautifully with his son, but what does that mean? How much time does Carl spend with him, anyway, compared with the grandparents? By contrast, it is Amber who deals with doctors, sets up play dates, gets calls from school and, in the judge's view, edges out Carl because she does it on her own.

Still, is Amber getting her life together? No. During part of the litigation, Amber made some foolhardy choices that worry the judge: for one, she moved in briefly with a Cleveland boyfriend who beat her.

Hayden nibbles some potato chips. She remains unsure about the violence in Amber and Carl's marriage, a factor she must consider in a custody dispute. The testimony from witnesses was inconclusive. She thinks Carl is soft-pedaling the violence and Amber is overdescribing. If Amber was so afraid of her husband, why did she leave their son with him for six months when she walked out?

All month long, the bulging Amber-and-Carl file sits, unexamined and accusing, on the judge's dining-room table at home, amid half a dozen glowering unpaid bills. The more she worries about a case, the longer she avoids it. She knows herself: she's Queen of the Last Minute and so must give herself a deadline.

Even so, the judge dithers away another week, obsessing now about geography. If only Amber had relocated within New Jersey, this case would be a no-brainer. Amber would win residential custody and Carl would get liberal visitation; the boy would not lose access to his extended family.

She asks her law clerk to search case law to see if she can give Amber custody on the condition that she move back to New Jersey. Or construct a ruling that says Carl gets custody unless Amber returns.

But she's clutching at legal straws. A wasted week. And so another morning, another fast wobble-walk through the streets of her humid, somnolent town. It is now the third week of July. The first day of school is fast approaching and she has to make a decision.

AT THE END OF THE DAY—SOMETIMES 6 P.M., OCCAsionally 7—the judge droops out of the courthouse. The roughest days are those when she ignores her own rule: don't go out on a limb for people. Because every time you say, Follow me into the wilderness for I am the judge. . . . *Yeah, right.*

Sometimes a day closes just when she's in the exasperating middle of trying to solve someone's insoluble problem. Or just after somebody has yelled back and embarrassed her on the bench. Her face gets hot, her neck splotchy, her breathing choppy. She hates that. She hates for people in the courtroom to think she's vulnerable. She wants them to see Olympian perfection in a black robe.

She couldn't have done this job when her kids were small because once she got home, they made demands on her. In court, she lavishes all her maternal instincts on people. She is Judge Big Sister Katharine, eldest of three, who learned to take charge after her adored Wall Street lawyer father died when she was 17. But by the end of the court day, she has nothing left to give.

Her friends ask how she can stand it that her husband, Joe Hayden, a criminal lawyer, doesn't get home sometimes until 10:30 at night, but she thinks, thank God, that's the beauty of her marriage: no demands, the solitude at dusk, the freedom just to be quiet and rebuild herself. She returns to her lemon-yellow 19th-century brick behemoth with the twisting staircases and stained-glass windows, feeds the cats, settles back into her armchair and stares at the wall.

Once in a while her thoughts may stray over the cases she has heard in the last few days—in one July week, she terminated the parental rights of a formerly drug-addicted mother and sent a com-

modities broker to jail until he paid $15,000 in overdue support for his young son and wife. But mostly she tries to make her mind blank. Then she may read. Hardly the stuff of someone with a graduate degree in English literature: detective fiction and serial-murder mysteries.

In her first months on the bench, she'd sometimes nod off at the dinner table to stave off attacks of panic. She'd rip her cuticles, curl up in bed in a fetal position, then lie awake for hours, obsessing. This is fun? she would think.

Gradually the terror slid back into the corner and she took command of her court, her self. And she knows she couldn't do her job if this marriage weren't solid. When you're trying to salvage people from their emotional messes, you have to be in decent shape yourself. The Haydens are well known in a circle of New Jersey lawyers and Federal and state judges. A typical vacation for the couple begins in the car ride to a judicial conference, six hours together, the simple pleasures of talk.

To recharge herself, she goes to Mass every Sunday. She's a modern Catholic—she divorced and signs off on hundreds of divorces a year—but she's not entirely certain that God won't strike her dead if she misses a week at Mass. Sure, half the time she's sitting in church she's thinking up recipes. But she says that if she puts herself in the presence of God, when she needs to call upon Him, either shaking her fist or negotiating hard, she will already have paid her respects.

And it's usually on Sundays that she enters races. Her not-so-well-kept secret is that she is a lousy race walker. For a woman whose puckish sense of humor includes herself as fair game, she is unexpectedly earnest on the topic of her little races, as she calls them. She keeps at them to maintain her mental equilibrium. She is moved and bothered by the power she has over people as a judge. But every time she goes out for a race, she feels terror, the potential for humiliation, which may be something close to how the people who come before her feel.

Although the days wring her out, there has not been a morning yet when she hasn't looked forward to sitting in family court, which is still so much better than being a divorce lawyer. It was wrenching when your clients were so unhappy and all you could do was try to pave the way for less anarchy in their lives.

But as a judge, she can make things happen, in a glacial-pace sort of way. That's the thought that keeps her going, the optimism of being a Catholic: a judge can hold out legal absolution, the promise of a redeemed life.

Coming off the bench after a hearing one day, Hayden wants a reality check. "Miss Bert, what did you think of that methadone mother?" she asks Alberta Gregory, her court clerk.

Gregory, who has lived many of her 61 years in

Newark, arches her brows. "Boss, she lies like a rug!"

Hayden looks taken aback but braces herself to hear more; she's quite aware that she's a white woman who was raised on Manhattan's Upper East Side and educated through college by nuns. She depends on Gregory, who is black, to clue her in about life in Newark's poor neighborhoods. "Judge," says Gregory with a sigh, "let me tell you how methadone goes down in this town."

Hayden's rulings are her own, but in addition to voraciously consulting legal, psychological and social tracts, she turns to a select few people to be her sounding board.

So today, she puts up her long legs and considers questions of great moment with Gregory and Patti Cassidy, her secretary: even though that couple have filed for divorce, are they still sleeping together? Is that why they are taking their sweet time to push the case? "Forbidden sex can be pretty hot," muses the judge.

She often speculates about the sexual dynamics of the couples who come before her. On another day, a suburban wife testified that as part of her husband's continuing emotional abuse, he made love to her one spring morning, then got out of bed and, without a word, packed and walked out. The judge, Cassidy and Gregory shriek, collectively appalled. "That's psychological rape!" says the judge.

"But you know the final insult? When he was asked on the stand about whether he had sex with her that morning, he said, 'I don't recall.' "

And Hayden regularly consults with the other "Cardinals," as the four judges in Essex County family court who hear divorce cases have been anointed by their sardonic boss, Judge Philip M. Freeman. ("More like the four Mouseketeers," mutters Gregory.) The Cardinals—Thomas P. Zampino, Richard C. Camp, Herbert S. Glickman and Hayden—sometimes handle multimillion-dollar divorces. Central to why so many matrimonial lawyers kiss their rings is that the Cardinals can order legal fees paid by the wealthier spouse.

The Cardinals often confer in Hayden's whimsical, who's-in-charge-here? chambers. Cat and cow memorabilia clutter the shelves, as do plastic monsters from the movie "Alien." A poster of her son's fledgling rock band hangs under her law diploma. As the Power Ranger looks on, the Cardinals frequently trade tales about litigants and lawyers. Their gallows humor may be indiscreet, but they say that because they preside daily over fraying lives, they need to blow off steam.

Sometimes the judges talk about how their own marriages affect their decision making. Hayden has her ear cocked for problems that face mothers struggling to re-enter the work force. Her own boys were toddlers and she was 30 when she entered Seton Hall University Law School. She would go on to become a Federal prosecutor, a formidable matrimonial lawyer and a county bar association president, dramatically outearning her first husband, the professor. To this day she credits his flexible schedule and willingness to share child care as critical to her success.

And she'll be sitting on the bench, trying to decide whether custody of a prison mother's newborn should be given to an aunt or to the state, when her own family comes knocking. One morning it's her 82-year-old mother, who is living with her this summer, phoning in a report on how the cats are handling the heat. Then her would-be-rock-star son calls. Then from Los Angeles, a call from the other musician son. Later it's her husband: dinner and a movie tonight? Now Patti Cassidy runs in with another scrawled message: does the judge remember where her mother put the house keys this morning?

ON THURSDAYS, THE JUDGE WAKES AT 4 A.M., PADS OUT to the big armchair in the living room and settles in with the two cats to read two dozen files of child abuse and neglect cases—the basic work of virtually every American family court. She pores over them like paperback mysteries, sometimes anxiously skipping to the end to find out what happened. Almost all the parties are Hispanic or black, yet what distinguishes them in her mind from other litigants is not their color but their poverty. Their life experiences couldn't be more different than hers; even so, she must decide which children must be saved from their parents, which struggling families should be saved from the intrusion of the state.

One morning in early July she opens a thick folder and smiles wearily. A mother known in court papers as M. W. is back: my all-star, thinks the judge, obdurate and durable, my Darryl Strawberry of the lot.

M. W., in her mid-20's, has been before Hayden many times over the past 18 months. She has a bad cocaine habit, four children under 6 in foster care and a 13-year-old son who until now has been staying with an uncle. She recently moved to a Southern state to live with a new boyfriend.

The latest issue involves the teen-ager. His uncle refuses to board him any longer. The Division for Youth and Family Services in New Jersey knows that placing the boy in a foster home is futile, because he will run away to find his mother. But M. W. refuses to undergo regular drug screens and enter treatment. The agency does not want to return the boy to her. But it feels it has no choice.

At the hearing later that morning, the judge's patience is sorely tried. (These proceedings are closed to observers. Hayden allowed a reporter to hear a tape of the case.) M. W. assumes that if she gets clean, all her children will be returned by September, a fantasy the judge struggles to dispel. Finally, the judge tells M. W. the unsweetened truth about the state's promises: "Let me make this clear. You will never, never, never get your kids back unless you kick your drug habit. If you kick your drug habit, you may still not get your kids back."

Hayden tells M. W. that she also has to set up a stable home for the children. "Does your fiancé know about the drug problem? Probably not, because I think one of the reasons you're not going to a program is because you're scared he'll find out."

The judge tells the agency's lawyers that she is inclined to deny the return of the son to his mother. Panicky, M. W. vows to enter a program, immediately go for drug screens, tell her boyfriend.

Hayden is dubious; she tries speaking mother to mother. She is about to make a risky decision, so she explains carefully for the record: "Anyone looking at this case will think I'm insane to send your boy to you. The division is telling me to do it anyway. But your son believes in you and he will walk all the way down South to be with you. If my firstborn felt that close to me, that would be an awfully good reason to try to clean up."

Then the judge talks to M. W.'s son. "I'm very concerned that your mom will have a problem licking her drug problem," she says. "In order to keep you with her, she's got to go into a program. I don't think it's right for me to lay on a kid the responsibility for his mother, but in a way, you've done it many times before." She tells him that his main job is to stay in school, that his mother has to come back to court with his attendance records.

"I think you and your mom are a good team," says the judge. "But I also want you to have a good life and be a kid and play sports and have fun."

But later that day, M. W. flunks her drug test: she is caught trying to dilute her urine sample by pouring toilet water into the cup. In the next two weeks, she doesn't head back to the South and doesn't begin treatment. The son briefly disappears.

At another Thursday hearing, the judge tells the boy that because M. W. has failed him, she is sending him to foster care; she tries to rile him so he will distance himself from his beautiful junkie mother. Hayden wants the boy to know that if he feels his mother is using him, she agrees. She says: if you run away, you run. It's up to you.

The system is powerless now, she thinks. What more can a judge do?

ONE THURSDAY, SHE GIVES HERSELF A FINAL DEADLINE for Amber and Carl's case: next Wednesday, the last in July, 9 A.M., she tells the lawyers.

That Saturday, she opens the file on her dining-room table and puts in order nearly four years of narrative—events, motions, cross-motions, trial testimony, expert reports. On the Sunday afternoon before the decision is due, she dives into the file.

Who lied? Did Amber tell Carl during her pregnancy that the baby wasn't his, as she maintained, or didn't she? Did Carl beat her regularly or didn't he?

Late Sunday night the judge begins dictating notes for her secretary, Patti Cassidy. She's in court all day Monday; that night she continues scribbling thoughts. As a pattern emerges from the file, so does the decision. Tuesday she's back on the bench, and that night she works until 1 A.M., crashes and starts up again at 4 A.M. She sprawls on the living-room carpet, piles of legal pads around her.

On Wednesday morning she drives to work like an automaton, radio off. She silently chants, I just have to do this. She isn't dreading making the announcement, exactly; she's steeling herself.

When she takes the bench, she deliberately avoids eye contact with Amber and Carl, instead fixing her squint on the comfortable blur of the parking lot out the window. Then, walking them through her logic, she speaks for two and a half hours.

First she addresses Amber's claim that biology should trump in a custody dispute. She cites a 1984 New Jersey Supreme Court case, Miller v. Miller, which says that once you put something out there, you can't take it back if the repudiation helps you and hurts others. And that is Amber's problem. She had presented Carl as her boy's father for nearly six years and is now withdrawing the claim: it favors her and harms Carl and the boy.

Amber's lawyer glares at the judge. Amber flinches.

The judge plows on, now turning to the paternity question. State law permits a paternity test to establish a child's inheritance rights. But Amber, says the judge, has refused to contact the boy's biological father and so did not use the test for that purpose. Instead, she has stripped her son of one father, Carl; by not bringing in the unnamed one, she is eviscerating the boy's inheritance and rendering him fatherless.

And the judge concludes that because Carl helped raise the boy and held him out as his own, he stands in the shoes of a father. "How can Carl not be taken seriously as an equal parent?" she says.

So far, Carl has been sitting motionless, as if afraid to breathe. His father, whom the judge praises as a wise and loving grandparent, is in the row behind him, listening just as hard, taking notes, occasionally wiping a tear from under his bifocals.

The judge reviews the experts' evaluations. A psychologist said Carl offered a more secure environment and that Amber tended to confuse her own needs with her son's. But both parents have strengths and weaknesses.

Finally she examines the question that propelled her hunt through the file: credibility. Amber, she concludes, has lied.

At one point Amber had testified that when she learned she was pregnant, she told Carl he wasn't the father. Another time she testified that she broke the news to him three months later after a sonogram showed a fetus too large to have been conceived when the couple starting having sex. Her early court papers, filed before she asked for the paternity tests, are evasive: instead of referring to the boy as "our child," she calls him "the child."

The judge concludes that Carl most likely did not know early on that he was not the father. "Why would he acquiesce only five months into their relationship to take on the public role of Dad?" Hayden says. "Probably because she kept it a secret."

Carl's shoulders lower a good inch; Amber is starting to weep.

From there the judge extrapolates about domestic violence, weighing the weak, contradictory testimony. She decides that Amber will say nearly anything to regain her child, her biological connection to the world, whom she believes to be her property right. Therefore, says the judge, "I do not believe that she was regularly abused by Carl."

Amber's lawyer looks fit to spit.

Finally, Hayden lists the 15 factors the state says she must consider to determine what is in the best interest of the child. Domestic violence, safety of the child, quality of education, fitness of the parent and so forth. The case is a close call, she says, but she has to decide whether is it better for the boy to stay with Carl and the grandparents in the home and the town with the friends, church and schools he has known from birth or to move in with his biological mother, who loves him dearly but whose life is still shaky.

Amber, she says, is a young woman still finding her way. She made choices that were in her best interest but not her son's. Carl, by contrast, put his son first, making the decision to move back in with his parents, who could help raise the child.

And although she says she believes Amber loves her son and so should spend substantial time with him, Hayden awards Carl residential custody. Then she stands and walks out.

Carl and his father rush from the courtroom looking stunned. Amber's lawyer starts cursing furiously. Amber slumps, sobbing, saying over and over: "What trial was she at? What trial was she at?"

Meanwhile, Hayden is back in her chambers. She has taken off her black robe and is seated behind her desk, staring at her hands. It was her decision to place the boy, who is his mother's only known blood relative, with a man to whom the child has no biological connection. The judge looks completely drained.

Will Amber figure out that if she moves back to New Jersey, the custody issue could be reopened, perhaps with a different outcome? she wonders. The judge has a queasy feeling that Amber's loss is greater to her than Carl's win to him. Amber, after all, is a reasonably good mother, she muses. Did she make a wrong ruling?

A poisonously seductive question, for that way lies judicial paralysis. No, the judge tells herself, she decided correctly; her responsibility was not to a sorrowful, desperate mother but to the son.

Patti Cassidy sticks her head in. Would the judge like her usual chicken sandwich? Ah, yes, the best way to put the case behind her: protein on rye, mayo on both slices.

But as Amber and Carl start to recede from her mind, she realizes that her impact on them is only beginning. In the years to come, they will have to struggle with the fallout from her decision, the very thing that they had wanted so badly from her. Hayden sighs. Doubt flickering across her face, the judge picks up the stack of papers her secretary has just dropped on her desk. On top is her calendar of cases. Looks like another busy afternoon.

Violence by Young People: Why the *Deadly* Nexus?

Alfred Blumstein

Alfred Blumstein, Ph.D., is J. Erik Jonsson University Professor of Urban Systems and Operations Research at Carnegie Mellon University's H. John Heinz III School of Public Policy and Management.

D espite evidence that aggregate rates of crime have been leveling off or even declining in the past two decades,[1] there continues to be widespread concern about the issue on the part of policymakers and the public. Indeed, among all issues, crime may be the one perceived by Americans as most pressing.[2] When aggregate crime data are broken down by certain demographic and other variables, however, the otherwise flat trend shows major distinctions, indicating that the concern is understandable. Although gender and race account for much of the differences in crime rates, age is the variable whose effect has been changing significantly in recent years. And while many of the national trends have remained strikingly flat, there has been some dramatic change in violent crime committed by young people.

The rise in juvenile crime

Data gathered from a variety of sources indicate that after a period of

relative stability in the rates of juvenile crime, there was a major turning point in about 1985. Then, within the next seven years, the rate of homicides committed by young people, the number of homicides they committed with guns, and the arrest rate of nonwhite juveniles for drug offenses all doubled. The sudden upward surge in all three of these indicators, beginning with the increased drug trafficking of the mid-1980's, is the topic of this article.

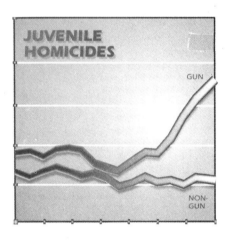

JUVENILE HOMICIDES

GUN

NON-GUN

Particularly relevant to future crime, and to consideration of prevention and intervention strategies, is the size of the current teenage population. The age cohort responsible for much of the recent youth violence is the smallest it has been in recent years. By contrast, the cohort of children ages 5 to 15, who will be moving into the crime-prone ages in the near future, is larger. This suggests that if current age-specific rates do not decline, plan-

ning needs to begin now to address the increase in crime likely to occur as this group grows older.

The age factor

That young people commit crime at a high rate is no revelation. Age is so fundamental to crime rates that its relationship to offending is usually designated as the "age-crime curve." This curve, which for individuals typically peaks in the late teen years, highlights the tendency for crime to be committed during an offender's younger years and to decline as age advances.

For example, figures on rates of robbery and burglary, broken down by age, indicate that for both these crimes, the peak age of offending has been about 17, after which there is a rapid decline as the offender gets older. For burglary, the rate falls to half the peak by age 21, whereas the falloff for robbery is somewhat slower, reaching half the peak rate by age 25. The age-specific patterns are about the same for the most recent year data are available (1992) as they were in 1985.

Young people and murder. The age-specific patterns for murder present quite a different pattern; the trends for this crime have changed appreciably in the past decade. First, the peak is much flatter. For a fairly long period—1965 to 1985—the age at which

From the *National Institute of Justice Journal,* August 1995, pp. 2-9. Reprinted by permission of the U.S. Department of Justice, Office of Justice Programs.

the murder rate was highest remained fairly stable, with a flat peak covering ages 18 to 24. In other words, during this 20-year period, people in this age group were the most likely to commit murder, and it was in the age group of the mid-30's that the rate dropped to half the peak. Then, in 1985, an abrupt change began to take place, with the murder rate moving to a sharp peak at age 18 instead of the more traditional flat peak covering the entire 18-to-24 age group. (See figure 1.)

The change over time in the age-specific murder rate is striking, especially for the peak ages 18 to 24. (See figure 2.) Following an initial increase from 1965 to 1970, the rate remained stable (and about the same for all ages in this group) for about 15 years—from 1970 through 1985. Among people at the older end of this age spectrum—the 24-year-olds—there has been no strong trend since 1970. But beginning shortly around 1985, murder by people under 24 increased, with the rate of increase inversely related to age. For people age 18, the increase was dramatic—it more than doubled.

For people at all ages under age 18, the increase was equally dramatic—it too more than doubled. For 16-year-olds, for example, whose murder rate before 1985 was consistently about half that of the 18-to-24 peak rate, the increase between 1985 and 1992 was 138 percent. By contrast, for ages older than 24, there has been no growth, and even a decline for ages 30 and above.

"Excess" murders committed by young people. The increase in murder by very young people after 1985 has not at all been matched by increases among the older groups (ages 24 and over). Among them murder rates have even declined. Thus, much of the general increase in the aggregate homicide rate (accounting for all ages) in the late 1980's is attributable to the spurt in the murder rate by young people that began in 1985.

One can calculate the "excess" murders attributable to the rise in murder

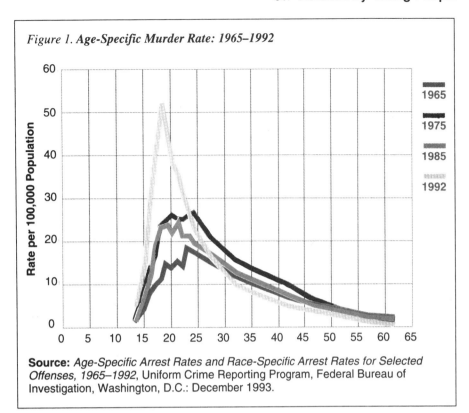

Figure 1. Age-Specific Murder Rate: 1965–1992

Source: *Age-Specific Arrest Rates and Race-Specific Arrest Rates for Selected Offenses, 1965–1992*, Uniform Crime Reporting Program, Federal Bureau of Investigation, Washington, D.C.: December 1993.

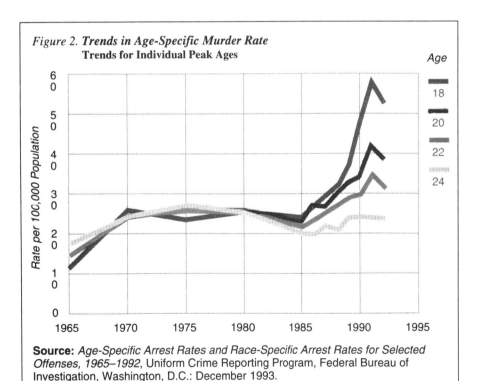

Figure 2. Trends in Age-Specific Murder Rate
Trends for Individual Peak Ages

Source: *Age-Specific Arrest Rates and Race-Specific Arrest Rates for Selected Offenses, 1965–1992*, Uniform Crime Reporting Program, Federal Bureau of Investigation, Washington, D.C.: December 1993.

by young people over and above the average rate that prevailed for each of the young ages in the period 1970–85.

In other words, this figure represents the number of murders that would not have been committed had the youth murder rate remained at its earlier, flat average. For the eight ages, 15 through 22, in the 7 years of 1986 through 1992, the number of "excess" murders is estimated to be 18,600. The number is a significant component of the overall number for that period; it accounts for 12.1 percent of the annual average of about 22,000 murders in those years.

Race

There are important race differences in involvement in murder, both in the rate itself and the change since 1985. Among African-American males ages 14 to 17, murder rates have been about four to five times higher than among white males of the same age group, although for both groups the rates had remained fairly stable from the mid-1970's until the mid-1980's. (See figure 3.) Then, beginning about 1985, the rates rose for both groups, though the growth rate was much faster among blacks. For white males in this age group, their annual rate for murder was 8.1 per 100,000 in the period 1976 to 1987, after which it almost doubled in the next four years (from 7.6 in 1987 to 13.6 in 1991). In those four years, the arrest rate for murder by black males in this age group rose even faster, more than doubling (from 50.4 to 111.8 per 100,000).

Factors generating fear

Strangers. Persistent fear of crime is not caused by reviewing the aggregate rate of homicide and noting the absence of a trend. Rather, distinctive incidents or changing patterns of crime stimulate the anxiety levels. In particular, because young people are generally perceived to be more reckless than their elders, the growth in youth homicide conveys a sense that their killing is random. This is confirmed by the greater extent to which homicide by the young is committed against strangers. When victims seem to be selected at random, vulnerability is heightened: anyone can be a target. For example, the FBI's Supplementary

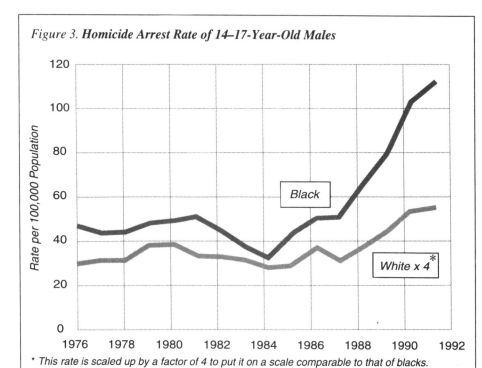

Figure 3. Homicide Arrest Rate of 14–17-Year-Old Males

* *This rate is scaled up by a factor of 4 to put it on a scale comparable to that of blacks.*

Source: The data were generated by Glenn Pierce and James Fox from the FBI's Supplementary Homicide Reports, which are based on reports of individual homicides submitted by the Nation's police departments.

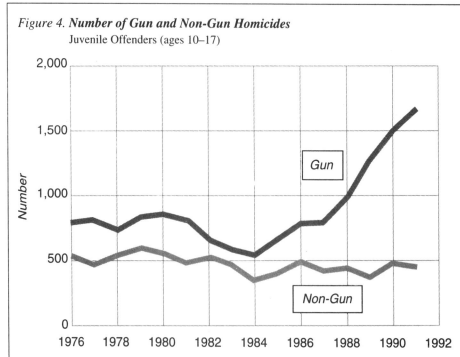

Figure 4. Number of Gun and Non-Gun Homicides
Juvenile Offenders (ages 10–17)

Source: The data were generated by Glenn Pierce and James Fox from the FBI's Supplementary Homicide Reports, which are based on reports of individual homicides submitted by the Nation's police departments.

Homicide Report for 1991 noted that 28 percent of the homicides committed by people under 25 were against strangers, whereas only 18 percent of those committed by offenders age 25 and above were against strangers.

Guns. Also intensifying the fear of crime is the increasing involvement of guns in homicides committed by young people. This factor generates fear because of the recognition that young people are less likely to exercise the restraint necessary to handle dangerous weapons, particularly rapid-fire assault weapons. Data on the use of weapons in homicide reflect the same patterns described above: after a period of stability came an abrupt increase in the mid-1980's. Thus, from 1976 to 1985, a very steady average (59 percent) of homicides committed by juveniles involved a gun. Beginning in 1985, there was steady growth in the use of guns by juveniles in committing murder, leading to a doubling in the number of juvenile murders committed with guns, with no shift in the number of non-gun homicides. (See figure 4.)

Juvenile violence and the drug-crime connection

The public also has a vague sense of a link between the growth in juvenile violence and drugs. In part, this derives from recognition that, especially in the past decade, a major factor affecting many aspects of criminal behavior has been the illicit drug industry and its consequences. Beyond the offenses of drug sale or drug possession, the drug-crime link has been described as taking several forms:

◆ Pharmacologically/psychologically driven crime, induced by the properties of the drug. (The most widely recognized connection is between alcohol and the violence it induces.)

◆ Economic/compulsive crimes, committed by drug users to support their habit.

◆ Systemic crime, which includes the crimes committed as part of the regular means of doing business in the illicit drug industry. (An example is the violence used to resolve disputes between competing traffickers.)[3]

There is a fourth, still broader connection of drugs to crime: the community

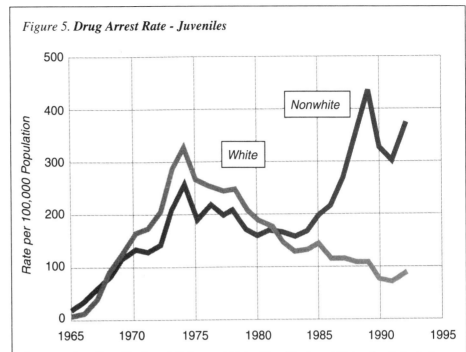

Figure 5. ***Drug Arrest Rate - Juveniles***

Source: *Age-Specific Arrest Rates and Race-Specific Arrest Rates for Selected Offenses, 1965–1992*, Uniform Crime Reporting Program, Federal Bureau of Investigation, Washington, D.C.: December 1993.

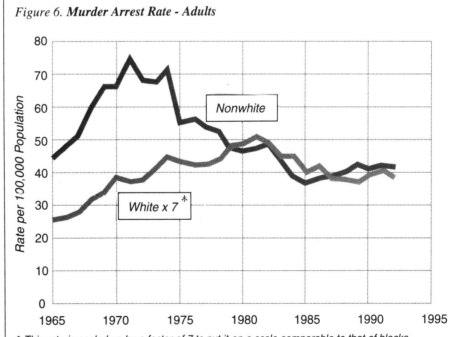

Figure 6. ***Murder Arrest Rate - Adults***

* This rate is scaled up by a factor of 7 to put it on a scale comparable to that of blacks.

Source: *Age-Specific Arrest Rates and Race-Specific Arrest Rates for Selected Offenses, 1965–1992*, Uniform Crime Reporting Program, Federal Bureau of Investigation, Washington, D.C.: December 1993.

disorganization effect of the illicit drug industry and its operations in the larger community. This effect includes

the manner by which the norms and behaviors of the industry, which can become a significant activity in some communities, influence the behavior of people who themselves have no direct connection to drug trafficking. The effect could, for example, include the influence on others of the widespread possession of guns by drug sellers. When guns are so prevalent, people in the community might arm themselves, perhaps for self-defense, perhaps to settle disputes that have nothing to do with drugs, or perhaps just to gain respect. In other words, once guns are used within the illicit drug market, they become more prevalent in the larger community, and used for purposes unrelated to buying and selling drugs. Hence, they add to community disorganization well beyond what happens as a direct result of the drug industry.

Juveniles and illicit drug marketing.

Drug arrest rates, especially for nonwhites, began to move upward in the early 1980's, and then accelerated appreciably after 1985 as the distribution of crack cocaine became widespread, particularly in inner-city areas. Among nonwhite juveniles, drug arrest rates were lower than those of whites in the 1970's, and were also fairly constant, until they began a very rapid acceleration until about 1985, doubling by 1989. This pattern contrasted with that of the 1960's and 1970's, when the rate at which young whites were arrested for drug-related offenses followed the pattern of whites, but stayed somewhat low. The arrest rate of whites then peaked in 1974 and then began a steady decline. (See figure 5.) The acceleration in drug arrests of young nonwhites (primarily blacks) reflected a major recruitment of sellers to market crack, which required many more street transactions. The racial differences in arrest rates indicate the extent to which drug enforcement has focused on blacks more than on whites. The black-white difference is magnified also because black drug sellers tend much more often to operate in the street, where they are vulnerable to arrest, whereas white sellers are much more likely to operate indoors. The amenability of inner-city nonwhite juveniles to recruitment into

the illicit drug industry was undoubtedly enhanced by their pessimism—or perhaps even hopelessness—as they weighed the diminishing opportunities available to them in the legitimate economy.

A proposed hypothesis

This striking array of changes in juvenile crime since 1985—a doubling of the homicide rate, a doubling of the number of homicides committed with guns, and a doubling of the arrest rate of nonwhites for drug offenses, all after a period of relative stability in these rates—cries out for an explanation that will link them all together. The explanation that seems most reasonable can be traced to the rapid growth of the crack markets in the mid-1980's. To service that growth, juveniles were recruited, they were armed with the guns that are standard tools of the drug trade, and these guns then were diffused into the larger community of juveniles.

Recruitment. The process starts with the illicit drug industry, which recruits juveniles partly because they work more cheaply than adults, partly because the sanctions they face are less severe than those imposed by the adult criminal justice system, and partly because they tend to be daring and willing to take risks that more mature adults would eschew. The plight of many urban black juveniles, many of whom see no other comparably satisfactory route to economic sustenance, makes them particularly vulnerable to the lure of the profits of the drug industry. The growth in the drug arrest rate of nonwhite juveniles is evidence of this recruitment.

Guns as a means of self-protection. These juvenile recruits, like all participants in the illicit drug industry, are very likely to carry guns for self-protection, largely because in that industry guns are a major instrument for dispute resolution as well as self-defense. People involved in the drug industry are likely to be carrying a considerable amount of valuable prod-

uct—money or drugs—and are not likely to be able to call on the police if they are robbed.

The diffusion of guns. Since a considerable number of juveniles can be involved in the drug industry in communities where the drug market is active, and since juveniles are tightly "networked," at school or on the street, other juveniles are also likely to arm themselves. Again, the reason is a mixture of self-protection and status-seeking. Thus begins an escalation: as more guns appear in the community, the incentive for any single individual to arm himself increases, and so a local "arms race" develops.

The violent outcome. The recklessness and bravado that often characterize teenage behavior, combined with their lack of skill in settling disputes other than through physical force, transform what once would have been fist fights with outcomes no more serious than a bloody nose into shootings with much more lethal consequences because guns are present. This sequence can be exacerbated by the socialization problems associated with extreme poverty, the high proportion of single-parent households, educational failures, and the pervasive sense of hopelessness about one's economic situation.

It does appear, however, that by the time these young people move beyond their early twenties, they develop a measure of prudence. It may be that the diffusion process is far slower because adults are less tightly networked and less prone to emulate each other's behavior. Even within the drug industry, they appear to act more cautiously when they are armed, and to otherwise display greater restraint. However, there is some concern that the restraint that normally comes with age may not materialize in this particular age group. It is possible that a cohort effect may be occurring, with the possibility that the 18-year-olds currently responsible for the higher homicide rates may continue their recklessness as they get older. This possibility needs to be monitored and explored.

Evidence of the diffusion. The possibility that guns are diffused from drug markets to the larger community through juvenile recruits is further confirmed by the pattern of white and nonwhite arrests for murder. Since 1980, the murder arrest rates for adults, both white and nonwhite, have followed the same downward trend, and have shown no growth since 1985. (See figure 6.) By contrast, among juveniles the murder arrest rates for whites and nonwhites have grown markedly between 1985 and 1992. The increase among nonwhite juveniles was 123 percent (from 7.1 to 15.8 per 100,000). Among white juveniles the murder arrest rate also increased markedly, although by a lesser amount—80 percent (from 1.5 to 2.7 per 100,000). (See figure 7.)

What is notable in these figures is that the murder rate rose among white as well as nonwhite juveniles since 1985, at a time when the drug arrest rate for nonwhites alone began to climb. Thus, the apparent absence of significant involvement of white juveniles in the drug markets during this time (figure 5) has not insulated them from the growth of their involvement in homicide, possibly through the suggested process of the diffusion of guns from drug sellers into the larger community.

When the arrest trends of young nonwhites for homicide and drug offenses are compared (figure 8), it is evident that both rates climbed together from 1985 through 1989, suggesting the relationship between the two. The drug arrest rate declined somewhat after 1989. There was a flattening out, but no corresponding decline in the murder arrest rate. In other words, the continued high rate of murder arrests seems to demonstrate that once guns are diffused into the community, they are much more difficult to purge.

Reversing the trends

If the explanation outlined above is at all valid, it implies the need for solutions, some immediate and others longer range. One immediate approach would involve aggressive steps to confiscate guns from juveniles carrying them on the street. Laws permitting confiscation of guns from juveniles are almost universal, but they require more active and skillful enforcement.

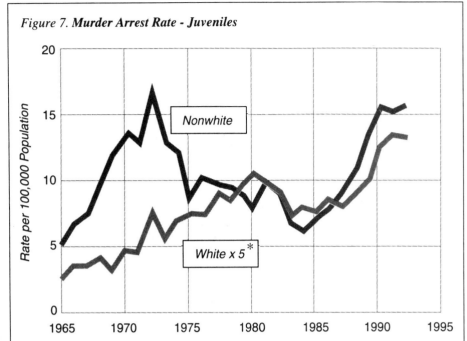

Figure 7. **Murder Arrest Rate - Juveniles**

* This rate is scaled up by a factor of 5 to put it on a scale comparable to that of blacks.

Source: *Age-Specific Arrest Rates and Race-Specific Arrest Rates for Selected Offenses, 1965–1992*, Uniform Crime Reporting Program, Federal Bureau of Investigation, Washington, D.C.: December 1993.

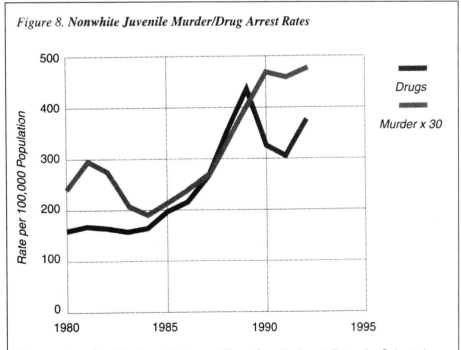

Figure 8. **Nonwhite Juvenile Murder/Drug Arrest Rates**

Source: *Age-Specific Arrest Rates and Race-Specific Arrest Rates for Selected Offenses, 1965–1992*, Uniform Crime Reporting Program, Federal Bureau of Investigation, Washington, D.C.: December 1993.

The need is particularly urgent in communities where homicide rates have risen dramatically, probably co-incident with the appearance of drug markets. James Q. Wilson has made some concrete proposals for pursuing such efforts, including better devices for detecting guns from a distance.[4]

Also, in contrast to the intense pursuit of drug markets by law enforcement over the past 15 years, very little attention has been paid to the illegal gun markets through which guns are distributed to juveniles. This issue clearly needs much greater attention. More complex in its implications for policy are the links among the magnitude of the criminal drug market, the use of guns in drug markets, and the juvenile homicide rate—the subject of this discussion. The presence of guns in drug markets results from the fact that these markets are criminalized. This does not, of course, warrant an immediate call for legalization of drugs. Any policy in the broad spectrum between full prohibition and full legalization involves carefully weighing the costs of criminalization (of which homicide is but one) against the probable consequences of greater use of dangerous drugs. The complexity of this issue prohibits its discussion here. However, if the diffusion hypothesis is correct, the impact on juvenile homicide represents one component of the cost of the current policy.

To the extent that efforts to diminish the size of the illegal drug market could be pursued (through greater investment in treatment, more effective prevention, or other health care initia-tives responsive to addicts' needs), then although illegal markets would continue, the demand for drugs and the volume of drugs sold in the markets would diminish. A cost-benefit comparison of current policies and possible alternatives is needed but has yet to be made. Perhaps concern about the recent rise in the juvenile homicide rate might lend urgency to the issue.[5]

Notes

1. *Criminal Victimization in the United States: 1973–92 Trends—A National Crime Victimization Survey Report*, Washington, D.C.: U.S. Department of Justice, Bureau of Justice Statistics, July 1994:1. In the period 1973–92, the highest rate of violent victimization was 35.3 per 1,000 persons, reported in 1981. That number fell until 1986, then started to climb, reaching 32.1 in 1992 (pp. 1, 9). National Crime Victim Survey data do reveal a 5.6 percent increase between 1992 and 1993 in victimization for violent crime, principally because of a rise in attempted (as opposed to completed) assaults. "Crime Rate Essentially Unchanged Last Year," press release, U. S. Department of Justice, Bureau of Justice Statistics, October 30, 1994. Homicide rates show a flat trend similar to that for violent victimization (homicide figures are not included in the victimization survey). The homicide rate per 100,000 people was 9.5 in 1993, but the historical high occurred in 1980, when the rate was 10.2. *Crime in the United States, 1993: Uniform Crime Reports*, Washington, D.C.: U.S. Department of Jus-tice, Federal Bureau of Investigation, December 4, 1994:13, 283.

2. A New York Times/CBS nation-wide poll reported early in 1994 indicated crime or violence as the leading issue (cited by 19 percent of respondents), followed by health care—the subject of considerable public discussion at the time—with 15 percent. See Richard L. Berke, "Crime Joins Economic Issues as Leading Worry, Poll Says," *New York Times*, January 23, 1994.

3. This taxonomy of the drug-crime connection was developed by Paul Goldstein in "The Drug/Violence Nexus: A Tripartite Conceptual Framework," *Journal of Drug Issues* 15 (1985):493–506.

4. James Q. Wilson, "Just Take the Guns Away," *New York Times*, March 20, 1994. NIJ is now sponsoring research to aid in detecting concealed weapons. See page 35 of this Journal.

5. In my presidential address to the American Society of Criminology in November 1992, I suggested proposing establishment of a Presidential Commission to examine the costs and benefits of our current zero-tolerance policy and to contrast that with various possible alternatives. Such an assessment would require major research support from the National Academy of Sciences. (See Alfred Blumstein, "Making Rationality Relevant," *Criminology* 30:1–16.)

The research reported in this article is being extended with the aid of an NIJ grant on juvenile violence and its relationship to drug markets.

Controlling Crime Before It Happens: Risk-Focused Prevention

J. David Hawkins

Traditionally, the juvenile justice system has employed sanctions, treatment, and rehabilitation to change problem behaviors after they have occurred. Advocates of a prevention-based approach to crime control invite the scorn of critics who believe prevention amounts to little more than "feel-good" activities. Yet the practitioner—the probation officer confronted daily with young people in trouble—is often aware of the need for effective prevention. As a probation officer in the early 1970's working with delinquent teenagers, I found myself asking, "Couldn't we have prevented these youngsters from getting to this point? Couldn't we have interceded before they were criminally referred to the courts?"

Once they have experienced the reinforcing properties of drugs and are convinced of crime's profitability, young people are difficult to turn around. Once invested in the culture of crime, they reject the virtues attributed to school and family, for reasons that are all too clear. For them, school is not a place of attachment and learning, but of alienation and failure; family is not a source of love and support, but of unremitting conflict.

Dealing with these youths as a probation officer, I saw my job as something akin to operating an expensive ambulance service at the bottom of a cliff. The probation staff were the emergency team patching up those who fell over the edge. Many of us who have worked in juvenile corrections have come to realize that to keep young people from falling in the first place, a barrier is needed at the top of the cliff. In short, we believe that prevention is more effective and less costly than treatment after the fact. David Mitchell, chief judge of the juvenile court for Baltimore County, once observed, "It is of no value for the court to work miracles in rehabilitation if there are no opportunities for the child in the community. Until we deal with the environment in which they live, whatever we do in the courts is irrelevant."

Effective prevention based on the public health model

In prevention, where action precedes the commission of crime, it is wise to heed the admonition that guides physicians: "Above all, do no harm." Hard work and good intentions, by themselves, are not enough to ensure that a program to prevent violence or substance abuse will succeed, let alone that it will not make things worse.

Early prevention efforts in the "War on Drugs" serve to illustrate this point. Well-meaning people were concerned about substance abuse and decided to do something about it by introducing prevention programs in the schools. They collected information, pictures, and even samples of illicit drugs, took these materials to the schools, and showed them to students; they talked about the behavioral and health effects of drugs and warned of the risks associated with their use. Contrary to intention and expectation, these drug information programs failed to reduce or eliminate drug use and, in some instances, actually led to its increase.[1] The real lesson learned in the schools was that information, which is neutral, can be employed to the wrong end, producing more harm than good. These early prevention workers had not envisioned drug information in the context of a comprehensive prevention strategy.

Increasingly, the preventive approach used in public health is being recognized as appropriate for use as part of a criminal justice strategy.[2] It is instructive to review an example of how the model has been applied to disease control. Seeking to prevent cardiovascular disease, researchers in the field of public health first identified risk factors; that is, the factors whose presence increased a person's chances of contracting the disease: tobacco use, high-fat diet, sedentary lifestyle, high levels of stress, and family history of heart disease. Equally important, they determined that certain protective factors (e.g., aerobic exercise or relaxation techniques) helped prevent the development of heart problems.

From the *National Institute of Justice Journal*, August 1995, pp. 10-18. Reprinted by permission of the U.S. Department of Justice, Office of Justice Programs.

These public health researchers were concerned with halting the onset of heart disease in order to avoid risky, invasive, and costly interventions, such as angioplasty or bypass surgery, after the disease had taken hold. Their goal was to reduce or counter the identified risk factors for heart disease in the population at large; their strategy was to launch a massive public advocacy campaign, conducted in multiple venues (e.g., the media, government, corporations, schools), aimed at elimination of "at risk" behaviors (and the attitudes supporting them). If risk could not be avoided altogether, the campaign could at least promote those behaviors and attitudes that reduce risk of heart disease. Proof that this two-pronged strategy has been effective is in the numbers: a 45-percent decrease in the incidence of cardiovascular disease, due in large measure to risk-focused prevention.[3] Application of the same prevention principles to reduce the risks associated with problem behaviors in teenagers, including violence, can work as well.

Identifying risk factors for violence

Using the public health model to reduce violence in America's communities calls for first identifying the factors that put young people at risk for violence in order to reduce or eliminate these factors and strengthen the protective factors that buffer the effects of exposure to risk. Over the past few years, longitudinal research (that is, studies that follow youngsters from the early years of their lives into adulthood) has identified factors associated with neighborhoods and communities, the family, the schools, and peer groups, as well as factors residing in the individual that increase the probability of violence during adolescence and young adulthood. These factors, presented in exhibit 1, also have been shown to increase the probability of other health and behavior problems, including substance abuse, delinquency, teen pregnancy, and dropping out of school. It is important to note that only factors identified in *two or more* of these longitudinal studies to increase the probability of the checked health or behavior problem have been included in the exhibit. Although future research may reveal, for example, that alienation and rebelliousness place an individual at risk of violent behavior, consistent evidence does not yet exist to support this hypothesis.

In neighborhoods. Five risk factors arising from the community environment are known to increase the probability that a young person will engage in violence:

◆ *Availability of guns.* The United States has one of the highest rates of criminal violence in the world, and firearms are implicated in a great number of these crimes. In recent years, reports of gun-toting youths in inner-city schools and of violent incidents involving handguns in school environs have created mounting concern. Given the lethality of firearms, the increased likelihood of conflict escalating into homicide when guns are present, and the strong association between availability of firearms and homicide rates, a teenager having ready access to firearms through family, friends, or a source on the street is at increased risk of violence.

◆ *Community laws/norms favorable to crime.* Community norms are communicated through laws, written policies, informal social practices, and adult expectations of young people. Sometimes social practices send conflicting messages: for example, schools and parents may promote "just say no" themes while alcohol and substance abuse are acceptable practices in the community. Community attitudes also influence law enforcement. An example is the enforcement of laws that regulate firearms sales. These laws have reduced violent crime, but the effect is small and diminishes as time passes. A number of studies suggest that the reasons are community norms that include lack of proactive monitoring or enforcement, as well as the availability of firearms from jurisdictions having no legal prohibitions on sales or illegal access. Other laws related to reductions in violent crime, especially crime involving firearms, include laws governing penalties for licensing violations and for using a firearm in the commission of a crime.

◆ *Media portrayals of violence.* The highly charged public debate over whether portrayals of violence in the media adversely affect children continues. Yet research over the past 3 decades demonstrates a clear correlation between depictions of violence and the development of aggressive and violent behavior. Exposure to media violence also teaches violent problem-solving strategies and appears to alter children's attitudes and sensitivity to violence.

◆ *Low neighborhood attachment/community disorganization.* Indifference to cleanliness and orderliness, high rates of vandalism, little surveillance of public places by neighborhood residents, absence of parental involvement in schools, and low rates of voter participation are indicative of low neighborhood attachment. The less homogeneous a community in terms of race, class, religion, or mix of industrial to residential areas, the less connected its residents may feel to the overall community and the more difficult it is to establish clear community goals and identity. Higher rates of drug problems, juvenile delinquency, and violence occur in such places.

◆ *Extreme economic deprivation.* Children who live in deteriorating neighborhoods characterized by extreme poverty are more likely to develop problems with delinquency, teen pregnancy, dropping out of school, and violence. If such children also have behavior and adjustment problems early in life, they are also more likely to have problems with drugs as they mature. The rate of poverty is disproportionately higher for African American, Native American, or Hispanic children than for white children; thus, children are differentially exposed to risk depending on their racial or cultural backgrounds.

In families. Obviously, the home environment, family dynamics, and parental stability play a major role in shaping children. Three risk factors for violence are associated with the family constellation: poor family management practices, including the absence of clear expectations and standards for children's behavior, excessively severe or inconsistent punishment, and parental failure to monitor their children's activities, whereabouts, or friends; family conflict, either between parents or between parents and children, which enhances the risk for all of the problem behaviors; and favorable parental attitudes and involvement in violent behavior, which increases the risk that children witnessing such displays will themselves become violent.

At school. Two indicators of risk for violence are associated with a child's experiences at school. Antisocial behavior of early onset (that is, aggressiveness in grades K–3, sometimes combined with isolation or withdrawal or sometimes combined with hyperactivity or attention-deficit disorder) is more frequently found in boys than girls and places the child at increased risk for problems, including violence, during adolescence. The risk factor also includes persistent antisocial behavior first exhibited in adolescence, such as skipping school, getting into fights, and misbehaving in class. Young people of both genders who engage in these behaviors during early adolescence are at increased risk for drug abuse, juvenile delinquency, violence, dropping out of school, and teen pregnancy. Academic failure, if it occurs in the late elementary grades and beyond, is a second school-related risk factor that is likely to result in violence and other problem behaviors. Specifically, it is the *experience* of failure that appears to escalate the risk, rather than ability per se.

*Exhibit 1. **Risk Factors and Their Association With Behavior Problems in Adolescents***

Risk Factors	Adolescent Problem Behaviors				
	Substance Abuse	Delinquency	Teen Pregnancy	School Drop-Out	Violence
Community					
Availability of Drugs	✓				
Availability of Firearms		✓			✓
Community Laws and Norms Favorable Toward Drug Use, Firearms, and Crime	✓	✓			✓
Media Portrayals of Violence					✓
Transitions and Mobility	✓	✓		✓	
Low Neighborhood Attachment and Community Disorganization	✓	✓			✓
Extreme Economic Deprivation	✓	✓	✓	✓	✓
Family					
Family History of the Problem Behavior	✓	✓	✓	✓	
Family Management Problems	✓	✓	✓	✓	✓
Family Conflict	✓	✓	✓	✓	✓
Favorable Parental Attitudes and Involvement in the Problem Behavior	✓	✓			✓
School					
Early and Persistent Antisocial Behavior	✓	✓	✓	✓	✓
Academic Failure Beginning in Elementary School	✓	✓	✓	✓	✓
Lack of Commitment to School	✓	✓	✓	✓	
Individual/Peer					
Alienation and Rebelliousness	✓	✓		✓	
Friends Who Engage in a Problem Behavior	✓	✓	✓	✓	✓
Favorable Attitudes Toward the Problem Behavior	✓	✓	✓	✓	
Early Initiation of the Problem Behavior	✓	✓	✓	✓	✓
Constitutional Factors	✓	✓			✓

© 1993 Developmental Research and Programs, Inc.

In peer groups and within the individual. If youngsters associate with peers who engage in problem behaviors (for example, drug abuse, delinquency, violence, sexual activity, or dropping out of school), they are much more likely to do the same. Further, the earlier in their lives that young people become involved in these kinds of experiences—or take their first drink of alcohol or smoke their first marijuana cigarette—the greater is the likelihood of prolonged, serious, and chronic involvement in health and behavior problems. Even when a young person comes from a well-managed family and is not burdened with other risk factors, associating with friends who engage in problem behaviors greatly increases the child's risk. In addition, certain constitutional factors—those that may have a biological or physiological basis—appear to increase a young person's risk. Examples of constitutional factors include lack of impulse control, sensation seeking, and low harm avoidance.

Protective factors

It is well known that some youngsters, even though they are exposed to multiple risk factors, do not succumb to violent, antisocial behavior. Research indicates that protective factors reduce the impact of negative risk factors by providing positive ways for an individual to respond to these risks. Three categories of protective factors have been identified:[4]

✦ Individual characteristics: A resilient temperament and positive social orientation.

✦ Bonding: Positive relationships with family members, teachers, or other adults.

✦ Healthy beliefs and clear standards: Beliefs in children's competence to succeed in school and avoid drugs and crime coupled with establishing clear expectations and rules governing their behavior.

Individual characteristics. Youths who seem able to cope more successfully than others with risk factors appear resilient: they are able to bounce back in the face of change or adversity; they experience less frustration in the face of obstacles and do not give up easily. They are also good-natured, enjoy social interaction, and elicit positive attention from others. Gender is another factor. Given equal exposure to risks, girls are less likely than boys to develop violent behavioral problems in adolescence. Finally, intelligence protects against certain problem behaviors, such as delinquency and dropping out of school, although it does not protect against substance abuse. Such individual characteristics enhance the likelihood that children will identify opportunities to make a personal contribution, develop the skills necessary to follow through successfully, and receive recognition for their efforts. However, these individual protective factors—resilient temperament, positive social orientation, gender, and intelligence—are innate and are extremely difficult to change.

Bonding. Several studies have revealed that children raised in environments in which they are exposed to multiple risk factors have nevertheless become productive, contributing members of the community. In interviews with these young people, they invariably note that someone took an interest in them. Some adult in the community—whether a parent, an aunt, a grandmother, a teacher, a youth worker, a minister, a businessperson—established a bond of affection and cared enough to reach out. Research has shown that the protective factor of bonding with positive, prosocial family members, teachers, or other significant adults or peers can be strengthened by preventive intervention.

Healthy beliefs and clear standards. When the adults with whom young people bond have healthy beliefs and well-defined standards of behavior, these serve as protection against the onset of health and behavior problems in those youngsters. Examples of healthy beliefs include believing it is best for children to be free of drugs and crime and to do well in school. Examples of well-defined standards include clear, consistent family prohibitions against drug and alcohol use, demands for good performance in school, and disapproval of problem behaviors. When a young person bonds to those who hold healthy beliefs and set clear standards, the two protective factors are reinforcing; they work in tandem by providing a model on which to base behavior and the motivation to practice approved behavior so that the bond is not jeopardized. Both bonding and healthy beliefs/clear standards mediate the relationship between a young person and the social environment, including community, family, schools, and peer groups; these protective factors can be encouraged and strengthened.

The preconditions of bonding. Bonding may take place with a caregiver, a family member or other significant adult, or it may represent an attachment to a social group. For bonding to occur, however, three conditions must be met. The first is the *opportunity for active involvement*. People become bonded to a family, a school class, or a community because they are given the chance to participate in the life of the group. In a classroom where the teacher calls on only the students in the front who raise their hands, the others are denied an opportunity for active involvement; as a result they may lose their commitment to education. The situation is similar in a family where the 13- or 14-year-old uses the home as a hotel—essentially a place to sleep—but has no responsibilities in the family. Youngsters need to be given the chance to contribute, in ways commensurate with their level of development, to life in the family,

developed and how they influence one another.

Community guidelines for preventive intervention

In designing preventive interventions for the 1990's and beyond, community leaders should keep in mind some key principles. The first is that prevention strategies should focus on *known* risk factors. Once communities identify the risk factors they need to address, the prevention program developed in response should be targeted to reducing those factors and to enhancing protective factors. Another guideline is that intervention should be planned to coincide with the point in a child's development that is optimal for achieving the desired outcome. Thus, prevention interventions need to be geared to the *appropriate developmental stages* of the child. If behavior problems at age 4, 5, and 6 are known to be associated with substance abuse and delinquency later in life, this means all youngsters should be taught in the early elementary grades the skills they need to manage and control their impulses in order to get along with others. .

Allied to the principle of intervention at the appropriate stage is *early intervention*, necessary to prevent behavior problems from stabilizing and becoming entrenched. Ideally, prevention begins before the child is born to ensure that low-income mothers and other adult caregivers have the skills they need to nurture children. These skills will equip them to understand that a crying baby is not a bad baby who needs to be spanked or disciplined. Prenatal care, home visits to low-income single mothers, and caregiver training in nurturing skills can significantly reduce child abuse. Studies show that more than a fourfold reduction in child abuse is achievable by home visitation before birth

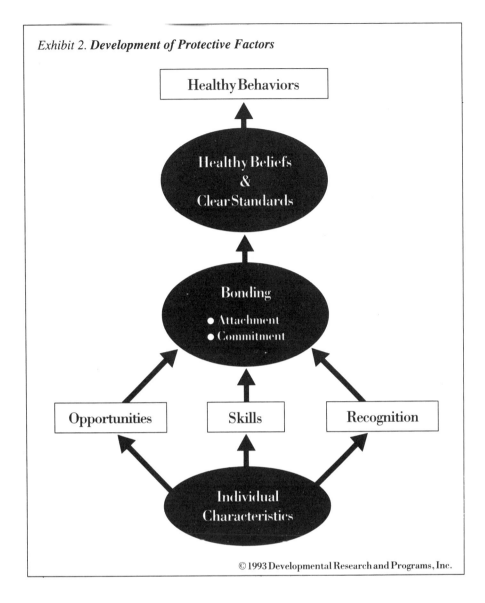

Exhibit 2. Development of Protective Factors

Healthy Behaviors

Healthy Beliefs & Clear Standards

Bonding
- Attachment
- Commitment

Opportunities Skills Recognition

Individual Characteristics

© 1993 Developmental Research and Programs, Inc.

in the classroom, and in the wider community.

The opportunity to become involved is not enough, however. A second condition of effective bonding is *having the skills needed* to succeed once involvement gets underway. Young people need to be taught the skills without which they will be unable to pursue opportunities effectively. Examples of skills that have been shown to protect children include good cognitive skills, such as problem-solving and reading abilities, and good social skills, including communication, assertiveness, and the ability to ask for support. The third condition of bonding is *a consistent system of recognition or reinforcement for skillful perfor-*

mance. Young people often receive little or no recognition for doing the right thing. The focus is on what they have done wrong; much less frequently are their accomplishments acknowledged. The efforts they put forth, the challenges they face, and the contributions they make should be celebrated in personally and culturally accepted ways.

Thus, along with opportunities and access to skills, recognition or appreciation provides an incentive for continued contribution and is a necessary condition for enabling young people to form close attachments to their communities, schools, and families. Exhibit 2 shows how protective factors are

and during the first few months of infancy.[5]

Prevention programs need to reach those who are at high risk by virtue of exposure to *multiple risk factors.* These multiple risks require multiple strategies that also are sensitive to the cultural diversity that characterizes many communities.

Commitment to risk-focused prevention programs arises only when there is buy-in by the community; that is, when the programs are felt to be "owned and operated" by the community. This sense of proprietorship evolves when all the various stakeholders in the community—the key leaders through the grassroots members—come together representing their diverse interests and develop a strategy for how to implement risk-focused prevention. The "Communities That Care" approach is one such strategy.

Implications for criminal justice

The inclusion of prevention as a central element of criminal justice policy and practice is emblematic of a new emphasis reflecting the realization that enforcement alone is not enough to reduce youth violence. This realization reflects the recognition that, in spite of geometrically increasing investments in enforcement, the courts, and corrections, violent crime, especially among young people, has continued to rise over the past decade (see previous article "Violence by Young People: Why the Deadly Nexus?").

For criminal justice, the orientation to prevention means establishing partnerships with other organizations, groups, and agencies in the community to identify and reduce risks for crime and violence and to strengthen protective factors that inhibit violence in the community. Community policing represents a clear example of this shift in criminal justice from an exclusive focus on the "back end"—after the crime has been committed. Integral to the intervention process is the involvement of the community and of social service and other agencies at the "front end"—working in tandem with law enforcement to identify problems and design strategies to solve them. In refining its role, criminal justice is taking on a much greater challenge than in the past, but doing so holds the promise of reducing crime in the long term.

Notes

1. Stuart, R.B., "Teaching Facts About Drugs: Pushing or Preventing?" *Journal of Educational Psychology* 37 (1974): 98–201; and Weaver, S. C. and F. S. Tennant, "Effectiveness of Drug Education Programs for Secondary School Students," *American Journal of Psychiatry* 130 (1973): 812–814.

2. See, for example, William DeJong's *Preventing Interpersonal Violence Among Youth: An Introduction to School, Community, and Mass Media Strategies*, Issues and Practices, Washington, D.C.: U.S. Department of Justice, National Institute of Justice, August 1994: 12–15.

3. From a speech delivered at the National Academy of Sciences in January 1994, by Kenneth I. Shine, M.D., President of the National Institute of Medicine.

4. See Hawkins, J. D., R. F. Catalano, and J. M. Miller, "Risk and Protective Factors for Alcohol and Other Drug Problems in Adolescence and Early Childhood: Implications for Substance Abuse Prevention," *Psychological Bulletin* 112 (1992): 64–105; Werner, E. E. and R. S. Smith, *Overcoming the Odds: High Risk Children From Birth to Adulthood,* New York: Cornell University Press, 1992; and Rutter, M., "Resilience in the Face of Adversity: Protective Factors and Resistance to Psychiatric Disorder," *British Journal of Psychiatry* 147 (1987): 598–611.

5. Olds, David L., C. R. Henderson, Jr., R. Chamberlin, and R. Tatelbaum, "Preventing Child Abuse and Neglect: A Randomized Trial of Nurse Home Visitation," *Pediatrics* 78 (1986): 65–78.

6. For information about the Communities That Care comprehensive community prevention planning approach, contact Developmental Research and Programs, 130 Nickerson Street, Suite 107, Seattle, WA 98109. Phone: (800) 736–2630; Fax: (206) 286–1462.

J. David Hawkins teaches social work at the University of Washington in Seattle and directs the University's Social Development Research Group.

EVERYDAY SCHOOL VIOLENCE: HOW DISORDER FUELS IT

JACKSON TOBY

Jackson Toby, professor of sociology and director of the Institute of Criminological Research at Rutgers University, is writing a book, Everyday Violence at School.

IN JANUARY 1989, an alcoholic drifter named Patrick Purdy walked onto the playground of the Cleveland Elementary School in Stockton, California, and, without warning, began spraying bullets from his AK-47 assault rifle. Five children died and 29 persons were wounded, some critically. In January 1992, two students at Thomas Jefferson High School in Brooklyn, New York, were fatally shot by an angry 15-year-old classmate. In April 1993, three teenagers armed with a baseball bat, a billy club, and a buck knife invaded an American Government class at Dartmouth High School, in Dartmouth, Massachusetts, a small town six miles southwest of New Bedford. They were looking for a boy they had fought with the previous Sunday. When 16-year-old Jason Robinson stood up and asked why they were looking for his friend, one of the youths fatally stabbed him in the stomach. That same month a 17-year-old Long Island high school student who had been reprimanded by her teacher poured nail polish into the teacher's can of soda. The teacher was taken to Good Samaritan Hospital; the student was arrested for second-degree assault.

The public is outraged when dramatic murders and attempted murders—as well as assaults and rapes—in or around schools are widely reported in the press and on television. Parents fear for the safety of their children and for the integrity of the educational process. People ask, "Why is there so much more school violence now than when I was in school?"

School violence is often blamed on a violence-prone society. Some urban schools *are* located—as Thomas Jefferson High School is—in slum neighborhoods where drug sellers routinely kill one another, as well as innocent bystanders, on the streets surrounding the school. More than 50 Thomas Jefferson students died in the past five years, most of them in the neighborhood, a few in the school itself. Some violence erupts inside schools like Thomas Jefferson when intruders import neighborhood violence to the schools or when students—themselves products of the neighborhood—carry knives and guns to school in order "to protect themselves." But the other three violent incidents—in Stockton, California; Dartmouth, Massachusetts; and Deer Park, Long Island—did not occur in particularly violent communities.

The most frightening cases of school violence, those of insanely furious armed intruders such as Patrick Purdy, are, like floods or tornadoes, not easy to predict or to prevent. Although these dramatically violent acts occur at schools, the acts cannot be blamed on anything the schools did or failed to do. Such unusual cases of school violence differ from *everyday* school violence: a group of students beating up a schoolmate, one student forcing another to surrender lunch money or jewelry. Mundane non-lethal, everyday school violence is more common in big-city schools than in suburban and rural ones, but it can be found in these schools as well.

Everyday school violence is more predictable than the sensational incidents that get widespread media attention, because everyday school violence is caused at least in part by educational policies and procedures governing schools and by how those policies are implemented in individual schools. This article addresses the causes of everyday school violence and the educational policies that might be changed to reduce it.

STATISTICAL FACTS ABOUT EVERYDAY SCHOOL VIOLENCE

Partly in response to alarming newspaper, magazine, and television reports of violence and vandalism in American public schools—not just occasionally or in the central cities, but chronically and all over the United States—the 93rd Congress decided in 1974 to require the Department of Health, Education, and Welfare to conduct a survey to determine the extent and seriousness of school crime.

In January 1978, the National Institute of Education published a 350-page report to Congress, *Violent Schools—Safe Schools,* which detailed the findings of an elaborate study. Principals in 4,014 schools in large cities, smaller cities, suburban areas, and rural areas filled out questionnaires. Then, 31,373 students and 23,895 teachers in 642 junior and senior high schools throughout the country were questioned about their experiences with school crime—in particular whether they themselves had been victimized and, if so, how. From among these 31,373 students who filled out anonymous questionnaires, 6,283 were selected randomly for individual interviews on the same subject. Discrepancies between questionnaire reports of victimization and interview reports of victimization were probed to find out exactly what respondents meant when they answered that they had been attacked, robbed, or had property stolen from their desks or lockers. Finally, intensive field studies were conducted in 10 schools that had experienced especially serious crime problems in the past and had made some progress in overcoming them.

The results of this massive study are still worth paying attention to even though the data are nearly 20 years old. Because the study was conducted in schools, it remains the only large-scale national study of school violence that probed a broad range of questions about the school milieu. The other national surveys of school violence, one (McDermott, 1979) based on data collected at about the same time as the Safe Schools study, the other in 1989 (Bastian and Taylor, 1991), were based on a few questions about school victimizations in the interview schedule of the National Crime Survey—too few to throw light on why some schools seemed unable to control violent students.

The statistical picture of crime and violence in public secondary schools that emerged from these three studies placed the sensational media stories in the broader context of everyday school violence.

The report, *Violent Schools—Safe Schools,* was not mainly concerned with mischief or with foul language—although it mentioned in passing that a majority of American junior high school teachers (and about a third of senior high school teachers) were sworn at by their students or were the target of obscene gestures within the month preceding the survey. The report was concerned mainly with illegal acts and with the fear those acts aroused, not with language or gestures. Both on the questionnaires and in personal interviews, students were asked questions designed to provide an estimate of the amount of theft and violence in public secondary schools:

In [the previous month] did anyone steal things of yours from your desk, locker, or other place at school?

Did anyone take money or things directly from you by force, weapons, or threats at school in [the previous month]?

At school in [the previous month] did anyone physically attack and hurt you?

Eleven percent of secondary-school students reported in personal interviews having something worth more than a dollar stolen from them in the past month. A fifth of these nonviolent thefts involved property worth $10 or more. One-half of 1 percent of secondary-school students reported being robbed in a month's time—that is, having property taken from them by force, weapons, or threats. One out of nine of these robberies resulted in physical injuries to the victims. Students also told of being assaulted. One-and-one-third percent of secondary-school students reported being attacked over the course of a month, and two-fifths of these were physically injured. (Only 14 percent of the assaults, however, resulted in injuries serious enough to require medical attention.)

These percentages were based on face-to-face interviews with students. When samples of students were asked the same questions, by means of anonymous questionnaires, the estimates of victimization were about twice as high overall, and in the case of robbery four times as high. Methodological studies conducted by the school-crime researchers convinced them that the interview results were more valid than the questionnaire results for estimating the extent of victimization; some students might have had difficulty reading and understanding the questionnaire.

The report also contained data on the victimization of teachers, which were derived from questionnaires similar to those filled out by students. (There were no teacher interviews, perhaps because teachers were presumed more capable of understanding the questions and replying appropriately.) An appreciable proportion of teachers reported property stolen, but only a tiny proportion of teachers reported robberies and assaults. However, robberies of teachers in inner-city schools were three times as common as in rural schools, and assaults were nine times as common. Even in big-city secondary schools, less than 2 percent of the teachers surveyed cited assaults by students within the past month, but threats were more frequent. Some 36 percent of inner-city junior high school teachers reported that students threatened to hurt them, as did 24 percent of inner-city high school teachers. Understandably, many teachers said they were afraid of their students. Twenty-eight percent of big-city teachers reported hesitating to confront misbehaving students for fear of their own safety, as did 18 percent of smaller-city teachers, 11 percent of suburban teachers, and 7 percent of rural teachers.

Violence against teachers (assaults, rapes, and robberies) is more rare than violence against students. It is an appreciable problem only in a handful of inner-city schools, but, when it occurs, it has enormous symbolic importance. The violent victimization of teachers suggests that they are not in control of the school. In another segment of the Safe Schools study, principals were questioned about a variety of crimes against the school as a community: trespassing, breaking and entering, theft of school property, vandalism, and the like. Based on these reports as well as on data collected by the National Center for Educational Statistics in a survey of vandalism, *Violent Schools—Safe Schools* estimated the monetary cost of replacing damaged or stolen property at $200 million per year. Vandalism, called "malicious mischief" by the legal system, is a nuisance in most schools, not a major threat to the educational process. But vandalism of school property, especially major vandalism and firesetting, is a precursor of school violence because its existence suggests that school authorities are not in control and "anything goes."

Some of the statistics from the two national studies were reassuring. Both the 1978 Safe Schools study and the 1989 School Crime Supplement to the National Crime Survey studies showed that, in the aggregate, school crime consisted mostly of nonviolent larcenies rather than violent attacks or robberies, which were rare. In other words, the bulk of school crime is essentially

What would have been furtive larcenies in a well-ordered school can become robberies when the school authorities do not appear to be in control, just as angry words can turn into blows or stabbings.

furtive misbehavior—theft of unattended property of other students and teachers, fights between students that stop as soon as teachers loom into view, graffiti scrawled secretly on toilet walls. But schools differ in the mix of nonviolent and violent crime: In some schools, violence was appreciable—and frightening—both to students and to teachers. What apparently happens is that what would have been furtive larcenies in a well-ordered school can become robberies when the school authorities do not appear to be in control, just as angry words can turn into blows or stabbings. Under conditions of weak control, students are tempted to employ force or the threat of force to get property they would like or to hurt someone they dislike. Consequently, student-on-student shakedowns (robberies) and attacks occur, infrequently in most schools, fairly often in some inner-city schools.

Thus, school crime partly reflects weak control and is partly the cause of further disorder, which in turn leads to more crime.

HOW DISORDER PROMOTES EVERYDAY SCHOOL VIOLENCE

Everyday school violence is a visible threat to the educational process, but it's only the tip of the iceberg. Under the surface is what criminologist James Q. Wilson calls "disorder" (Wilson, 1985). Professor Wilson argues (in a more general analysis of the relationship between disorder and criminal violence) that neighborhoods ordinarily become vulnerable to the violent street crime that arouses so much fear among city dwellers only *after* they have first become disorderly. What makes a neighborhood "disorderly"? When panhandlers are able to accost passersby, when garbage is not collected often enough, when alcoholics drink in doorways and urinate in the street, when broken windows are not repaired or graffiti removed, when abandoned cars are allowed to disintegrate on the street—a sense of community is lost, even when the rate of statutory crimes is not particularly high. According to Wilson, "disorderly" means the violation of conventional expectations about proper conduct in "public places as well as allowing property to get run down" or broken. Wilson believes that the informal community controls effective in preventing crime cannot survive in a neighborhood where residents believe nobody cares:

[M]any residents will think that crime, especially violent crime, is on the rise, and they will modify their behavior accordingly. They will use the streets less often, and when on the streets will stay apart from their fellows.... For some

residents, this growing atomization will matter little, because the neighborhood is not their "home" but "the place where they live." But it will matter greatly to other people, whose lives derive meaning and satisfaction from local attachments rather than from worldly affairs; for them, the neighborhood will cease to exist except for a few reliable friends whom they arrange to meet.

Such an area is vulnerable to criminal invasion. Though it is not inevitable, it is more likely that here, rather than in places where people are confident they can regulate public behavior by informal controls, drugs will change hands, prostitutes will solicit, and cars will be stripped. Drunks will be robbed by boys who do it as a lark, and the prostitutes' customers will be robbed by men who do it purposefully and perhaps violently. Muggings will occur.

Persuasive as Wilson's thesis is with regard to *neighborhood* crime rates, it seems even more relevant to *school* crime. A school in which students wander the halls during times when they are supposed to be in class, where candy wrappers and empty soft-drink cans have been discarded in the corridors, and where graffiti can be seen on most walls, invites youngsters to test further and further the limits of acceptable behavior. One connection between the inability of school authorities to maintain order and an increasing rate of violence is that—for students who have little faith in the usefulness of the education they are supposed to be getting—challenging rules is part of the fun. When they succeed in littering or in writing on walls, they feel encouraged to challenge other, more sacred, rules like the prohibition against assaulting fellow students. If the process goes far enough, students come to think they can do *anything*. The school has become a jungle.

The Significance of Disorder

Psychologists and sociologists long have recognized that families vary both in their cohesiveness and in their effectiveness at raising children; experts regard "dysfunctional families" as a factor in juvenile delinquency, substance abuse, and the personality pathologies of young people that lead to violence. The concept of "school disorder" suggests that schools, like families, also vary in their cohesiveness and effectiveness. What school disorder means in concrete terms is that one or both of two departures from normality exists: A significant proportion of students do not seem to recognize the legitimacy of the rules governing the school's operation and therefore violate them frequently; and/or a significant proportion of students defy the authority of teachers and other staff members charged with enforcing the rules.

Although disorder is never total, at some point in the deterioration process, students get the impression that the perpetrators of violent behavior will not be detected or, if detected, will not be punished. When that happens, the school is out of control. Even lesser degrees of school disorder demoralize teachers, who make weaker efforts to control student misbehavior, lose enthusiasm for teaching, and take "sick days" when they are not really sick. Some teachers, often the youngest and the most dynamic, consider leaving the profession or transferring to private or suburban schools. A disorderly atmosphere also demoralizes the most academically able students,

Verbal abuse of a teacher, because it prevents a teacher from maintaining classroom authority, or even composure, may interfere with education more than would larceny from a desk or locker.

and they seek escape to academically better, safer schools. For other students, a disorderly atmosphere presents a golden opportunity for class-cutting and absenteeism. The proportions of potentially violent students grow in the disorderly school, and thus the likelihood decreases that violence will meet with an effective response from justifiably fearful teachers.

Disorder leads to violence partly because it prevents meaningful learning from taking place. Thus, an insolent student who responds to his history teacher's classroom question about the Civil War: "I won't tell you, asshole," merely commits an offense against school order, not a criminal offense in the larger society. Nevertheless, verbal abuse of a teacher, because it prevents a teacher from maintaining classroom authority, or even composure, may interfere with education more than would larceny from a desk or locker. The disrespectful student challenges the norm mandating a cooperative relationship between teachers and students to promote education. Under conditions of disorder, a building may look and smell like a school, but an essential ingredient is missing. Punching a teacher is only a further stage on the same road.

SOCIAL TRENDS LEADING TO DISORDERLY SCHOOLS

Part of the explanation for the greater incidence of disorderly schools in central cities is that there is less consensus in inner cities that education is crucially important. Why? Because big cities tend to be the first stop of immigrants from less developed societies where, frequently, formal secular education is less valued. (Toby, 1957; Hawaii Crime Commission, 1980) Consequently, maintaining order is easier in rural and suburban schools than those in central cities. But the problem of school disorder is not solely a problem of central cities. Social trends in American society have tended greatly to reduce the effectiveness of adult controls over students in all public secondary schools. Some of these developments have simultaneously tempted enrolled students to be unruly. It is to these trends that I now turn.

The Separation of School and Community

Historically, the development of American public education increasingly separated the school from students' families and neighborhoods. Even the one-room schoolhouse of rural America represented separation of the educational process from the family. But the consolidated school districts in nonmetropolitan areas and the jumbo schools of the inner city carried separation much further. Large schools developed because the bigger the school, the lower the per capita cost of education; the more feasible it was to hire teachers with academic specialties like art, music, drama, or advanced mathematics; and the more likely that teachers and administrators could operate according to professional standards instead of in response to local sensitivities—for example, in teaching biological evolution or in designing a sex-education curriculum. But the unintended consequence of large schools that operated efficiently by bureaucratic and professional standards was to make them relatively autonomous from the local community. While the advantages of autonomy were immediately obvious, the disadvantages took longer to reveal themselves.

The main disadvantage was that students developed distinctive subcultures only tangentially related to education. Thus, in data collected during the 1950s Professor James Coleman found that American high school students seemed more preoccupied with athletics and personal popularity than with intellectual achievement. Students were doing their own thing, and their thing was not what teachers and principals were mainly concerned about. Presumably, if parents had been more closely involved in the educational process, they would have strengthened the academic influence of teachers. Even in the 1950s, student subcultures at school promoted misbehavior; in New York and other large cities, fights between members of street gangs from different neighborhoods sometimes broke out in secondary schools. However, Soviet achievements in space during the 1950s drew more attention to academic performance than to school crime and misbehavior. Insofar as community adults were brought into schools as teacher aides, they were introduced not to help control student misbehavior but to improve academic performance.

Until the 1960s and 1970s, school administrators did not sufficiently appreciate the potential for disorder when many hundreds of young people come together for congregate instruction. Principals did not like to call in police, preferring to organize their own disciplinary procedures. They did not believe in security guards, preferring to use teachers to monitor behavior in the halls and lunchrooms. They did not tell school architects about the need for what has come to be called "defensible space," and as a result schools were built with too many ways to gain entrance from the outside and too many rooms and corridors where surveillance was difficult. Above all, principals did not consider that they had lost control over potential student misbehavior when parents were kept far away, not knowing how their children were behaving. The focus of PTAs was on the curriculum, and it was the better-educated, middle-class parents who tended to join such groups. In short, the isolation of the school from the local community always meant that, if a large enough proportion of students misbehaved, teachers and principals could not maintain order.

Conceivably, schools can exercise effective control even though parents and neighbors do not reinforce their values through membership in PTAs or through conferences with teachers. But social control is weakened by population mobility, which creates an atmosphere of anonymity. Consider how much moving around there is in the United States. Only 82 percent of persons were living in the same residential unit in 1990 as they were in 1989. Residential mobility was much greater in the central cities of metropolitan areas. Since cities have long been considered places to which people migrate from rural areas, from other cities, and indeed from foreign countries, it may come as no surprise that during a five-year period, a majority of the residents of American central cities move to a different house. Yet the anonymity generated by this atmosphere of impermanence can plausibly explain why American society is not very successful in imposing order in urban neighborhoods. Anonymity is not confined to central cities. High rates of mobility are typical, creating the anonymity that complicates problems of social control. Schools vary of course in their rates of student turnover. In some big-city schools less than half the students complete an academic year; in some small-town schools, on the other hand, the bulk of students are together for four years of high school.

The Relentless Pressure to Keep Children In School Longer

The most important trend underlying school disorder is the rising proportion of the age cohort attending high school in all modern societies. The reason for raising the age of compulsory school attendance is excellent: Children need all the education they can get in order to work at satisfying jobs in an increasingly complex economy and to be able to vote intelligently. However, higher ages of compulsory school attendance mean that some enrolled youngsters hate school and feel like prisoners. Obviously, such youngsters don't respect the rules or the rule-enforcers as much as students who regard education as an opportunity.

Compulsory education laws vary from state to state. But they share an assumption that the state can compel not only school attendance but school achievement. In reality, compulsory education laws are successful only in keeping children *enrolled*, sometimes longer than the nominal age of compulsory school attendance. Parental consent was often written into the law as necessary for withdrawal from school before reaching 17 or 18 or a specified level of educational achievement. Parents have little incentive to consent, partly because they hold unrealistic educational aspirations even for academically marginal students, partly because they recognize the difficulties faced by adolescents in the labor market and do not want their children loitering on the streets, and partly because benefits are available from programs like Aid to Families with Dependent Children for children enrolled in school.

Like their parents, the disengaged students also have incentives to remain enrolled, although not necessarily to attend regularly. In addition to conforming to parental pressure, they are called "students" although they are not necessarily studious, and this status has advantages. The school is more pleasant than the streets in cold or rainy weather—it is an interesting place to be. Friends are visited; enemies attacked; sexual adventures begun; drugs

bought and sold; valuables stolen. There are material advantages also to being an enrolled student, such as bus passes and lunch tickets, which can be sold as well as used. Consequently, many remain enrolled although they are actually occasional or chronic truants. The existence of a large population of enrolled nonattenders blurs the line between intruders and students. School officials understand this all too well, but the compulsory school attendance laws prevent them from doing much about it. (Toby, 1983)

Keeping more children in school who do not want to be there interferes with traditional learning. Consequently, functional illiteracy has spread to more students, resulting not necessarily in the formal withdrawal from school of marginal students but, more usually, in "internal" dropouts. School systems are making strenuous efforts to educate such students whom they would have given up on in a previous generation. Such students used to be described as "lazy," and they were given poor grades for "conduct." It is perhaps not surprising that the public schools have had great difficulty providing satisfaction, not to mention success, to students whose aptitudes or attitudes do not permit them to function within the range of traditional standards of academic performance. One response is to "dumb-down" the curriculum with "relevant," intellectually undemanding courses that increase the proportion of entertainment to work.

The Extension of Civil Rights to Children

A third trend indirectly affecting school order is the increasing sensitivity of public schools to the rights of children. A generation ago it was possible for principals to rule schools autocratically, to suspend or expel students without much regard for procedural niceties. Injustices occurred; children were "pushed out" of schools because they antagonized teachers and principals. But this arbitrariness enabled school administrators to control the situation when serious misbehavior occurred. Student assaults on teachers were punished so swiftly that such assaults were almost unthinkable. Even disrespectful language was unusual. Today, as a result of greater concern for the rights of children, school officials are required to observe due process in handling student discipline. Hearings are necessary. Charges must be specified. Witnesses must confirm suspicions. Appeals are provided for. Greater due process for students accused of misbehavior gives unruly students better protection against teachers and principals; unfortunately, it also gives well-behaved students less protection from their classmates.

Related to the extension of civil rights in the school setting is the decreased ability of schools to get help with discipline problems from the juvenile courts. Like the schools, the juvenile courts also have become more attentive to children's rights. Juvenile courts today are less willing to exile children to a correctional Siberia. More than 20 years ago, the Supreme Court ruled that children could not be sent to juvenile prisons for "rehabilitation" unless proof existed that they had *done* something for which imprisonment was appropriate. The 1967 *Gault* decision set off a revolution in juvenile court procedures. For example, formal hearings with youngsters represented by attorneys became common practice for serious offenses that might result in incarceration.

Furthermore, a number of state legislatures restricted the discretion of juvenile court judges. In New York and New Jersey, for example, juvenile court judges may not commit a youngster to correctional institutions for "status offenses," that is, for behavior that would not be a crime if done by adults. Thus, truancy or ungovernable behavior in school or at home are not grounds for incarceration in these two states. The differentiation of juvenile delinquents from persons in need of supervision (PINS in New York nomenclature, JINS in New Jersey) may have been needed. However, one consequence of this reform is that the public schools can less easily persuade juvenile courts to help with school-discipline problems. In some cases, the juvenile court judge cannot incarcerate because the behavior is a status offense rather than "delinquency." In other cases the alleged behavior, such as slapping or punching a teacher, is indeed delinquency, but many judges will not commit a youngster to a correctional institution for this kind of behavior, because they have to deal with what they perceive as worse juvenile violence on the streets. Thus, for its own very good reasons, the juvenile justice system does not help the schools appreciably in dealing with disorder. Only when disorder results in violence will the juvenile courts intervene; their reponse is too little, too late.

Increased attention to civil rights for students, including students accused of violence, was also an unintended consequence of compulsory school attendance laws. The Supreme Court held in *Goss v. Lopez* not only that schoolchildren were entitled to due process when accused by school authorities of misbehavior and that greater due-process protections were required for students in danger of suspension for more than 10 days or for expulsion, than for students threatened with less severe disciplinary penalties. The Court held also that the state, in enacting a compulsory school attendance law, incurred an *obligation* to educate children until the age specified in the law, which implied greater attention to due process for youngsters still subject to compulsory attendance laws than for youngsters beyond their scope. Boards of education interpreted these requirements to mean that formal hearings were necessary in cases of youngsters in danger of losing the educational benefits the law required them to receive. Such hearings were to be conducted at a higher administrative level than the school itself, and the principals had to document the case and produce witnesses who could be cross-examined.

In Hawaii, for example, which has a compulsory education law extending to age 18, Rule 21, which the Hawaii Department of Education adopted in 1976 to meet the requirement of *Goss v. Lopez,* aroused unanimous dissatisfaction from principals interviewed in the Crime Commission's study of school violence and vandalism. They had three complaints. First, in cases where expulsion or suspension of more than 10 days might be the outcome, the principal was required to gather evidence, to file notices, and to participate in long adversarial hearings at the district superintendent's office in a prosecutorial capacity, which discouraged principals from initiating this procedure in serious cases. Thus principals downgraded serious offenses in order to deal with them expeditiously, by means of informal hearings. Second, Rule 21 forbade principals to impose a series of short suspensions of a student within one semester that cumulatively amounted to more than 10 days unless there was a formal hearing. Although intended to prevent principals from getting around the requirement for formal hearings in serious cases involving long suspensions, what this provision achieved was to prevent principals from imposing any discipline at all on multiple offenders. Once suspended for a total of 10 days in a semester, a student could engage in minor and not-so-minor misbehavior with impunity. Third, the principals complained that their obligation to supply "alternative education" for students expelled or suspended for more than 10 days was unrealistic in terms of available facilities.

The Blurring of the Line Between Disability And Misbehavior

"Special education" serves a heterogeneous group of students, some with physical handicaps, others with behavior problems from which emotional handicaps are inferred without independent psychiatric justification. Inferring personality disturbances from deviant behavior has a long, disreputable history in the criminal courts where defense attorneys have creatively described stealing and fire-setting as "kleptomania" and "pyromania" when the behavior had no intuitively plausible explanation. In 1975 Congress passed Public Law 94-142, the Education for All Handicapped Children Act, which provided "not only that every handicapped child is entitled to a free public education, but that such an education shall be provided *in the least restrictive educational setting.*" (Hewett and Watson, 1979) Thus the philosophy of mainstreaming handicapped children—exceptional children, as they are sometimes called—became national policy. Some of the handicaps are verifiable independent of classroom behavior: deafness, blindness, motor problems, speech pathologies, retardation. But learning disabilities and behavior disorders, especially the latter, are more ambiguous. Does a child who punches other children in his classroom have a behavior disorder for which he should be pitied, or does he deserve punishment for naughtiness?

The state of Hawaii ran into this dilemma in attempting to implement Public Law 94-142. The Hawaii Board of Education promulgated Rule 49.13, which asserted that "handicapped children in special education programs may not be seriously disciplined by suspensions for over 10 days or by dismissal from school for violating any of the school's rules." This meant that there were two standards of behavior, one for ordinary students and one

Part of the reason for the decline of homework in public secondary schools is the erosion of teacher authority.

for "handicapped" students. But students who were classified as handicapped because of a clinical judgment that they were "emotionally disturbed" (usually inferred from "acting out" behavior) seemed to be getting a license to commit disciplinary infractions.

According to a 1980 Hawaii Crime Commission report, *Violence and Vandalism in the Public Schools of Hawaii:*

> [I]t was the consensus of 14 principals from the Leeward and Central School Districts of Oahu that the special disciplinary section under Rule 49 created a "double standard" between regular students who were subject to varying degrees of suspensions and special education students who were not. These principals believe that such an alleged double standard fosters a belief among special education students that they are immune from suspension under regular disciplinary rules and, therefore, can engage in misconduct with impunity.

"Special education" students placed in that category because of supposed emotional disturbance may have violence-prone personalities. On the other hand, they may only be assumed to have such personalities because they have engaged in inexplicably violent behavior. They might be able to control their behavior if they had incentives to do so. In formulating Rule 49.13, the Department of Education of the state of Hawaii has been explicit about denying responsibility to special education youngsters, but the same heightened concern about the special needs of presumed emotionally disturbed students is common in other American public school systems. One result of not holding some children responsible for violent behavior is that they are more likely to engage in violence than they would otherwise be.

The Erosion of Teacher Authority

The social changes that have separated secondary schools from effective family and neighborhood influences and that have made it burdensome for school administrators to expel students guilty of violent behavior or to suspend them for more than 10 days partially explain the eroding authority of teachers. Social changes are not the entire explanation, however. There also have been *cultural* changes undermining the authority of teachers. There was a time when teachers were considered godlike, and their judgments went unquestioned. No more. Doubtless, reduced respect for teachers is part of fundamental cultural changes by which many authority figures—parents, police, government officials have come to have less prestige. In the case of teachers, the general demythologizing was amplified by special ideological criticism. Bestselling books of the 1960s portrayed teachers, especially middle-class teachers, as the villains of education—insensitive, authoritarian, and even racist.

Part of the reason for the decline of homework in public secondary schools is the erosion of teacher authority. When teachers could depend on all but a handful of students to turn in required written homework, they could assign homework and mean it. The slackers could be disciplined. But in schools where teachers could no longer count on a majority of students doing their homework, assigning it became a meaningless ritual, and many teachers gave up. Professor James Coleman and his research team found that private and parochial school sophomores in high school reported doing, on the average, at least two hours more of homework per week than public school sophomores. Many teachers felt they lacked authority to induce students to do *anything* they did not want to do: to attend classes regularly, to keep quiet so orderly recitation could proceed, to refrain from annoying a disliked classmate.

A charismatic teacher can still control a class. But the erosion of teacher authority meant that *run-of-the-mill* teachers are less effective at influencing behavior in their classes, in hallways, and in lunchrooms. What has changed is that the *role* of teacher no longer commands the automatic respect it once did from students and their parents. This means that less forceful, less experienced, or less effective teachers cannot rely on the authority of the role to help them maintain control. They are on their own in a sense that the previous generation was not.

WHAT CAN BE DONE

Faced with the worrisome problem of school violence, Americans look for simple solutions like hiring additional security guards or installing metal detectors. Security guards and metal directors *are* useful, especially in inner-city schools where invading predators from surrounding neighborhoods are a major source of violence. But dealing with *student* sources of everyday school violence requires more effective teacher control over the submerged part of the violence iceberg: disorder.

Teachers, not security guards, already prevent disorder in most American high schools. They do it by expressing approval of some student behavior and disapproval of other student behavior. This is tremendously effective in schools where the majority of students care about what teachers think of them. Expressing approval and disapproval is useless (and sometimes dangerous) in schools where students have contempt for teachers and teachers know it. In such schools, particularly those in inner cities, many teachers are too intimidated to condemn curses, threats, obscenities, drunkenness, and, of course, the neglect of homework and other academic obligations. It would help enormously if all families inculcated moral values before children started school and if all teachers motivated students better in the earliest grades so that they are hooked on education by the time they reach high school. But, unfortunately, many students arrive without these desirable formative experiences.

The problem is how to empower teachers in schools where they are now intimidated by students who are not as receptive to education as we would like them to be. Teachers cannot empower themselves. Ultimately, teachers derive their authority from student respect for education and the people who transmit it. Japan provides a classic illustration of what respect for teachers, inculcated in the family, can accomplish. Japanese high school

The age limit for high school entitlement should be raised from 21, the usual age at present, to 100.

teachers are firmly in control of their high schools without the help of security guards or metal detectors. No Japanese high school teacher is afraid to admonish students who start to misbehave, because the overwhelming majority of students will respond deferentially. Japanese high school teachers know that their students care about the grades they receive at school.

Students have good reason to care. Japanese teachers give grades that employers as well as colleges scrutinize; they also write letters of recommendation that prospective employers take seriously. In short, Japanese high school students are deeply concerned about the favorable attitudes of their teachers. As a result, Japanese teachers can require lots of homework. Homework is a major factor in the superior academic performance of Japanese students in international comparisons. But effective teacher control has consequences for school safety too. Japanese high school teachers never are assaulted by their students; on the contrary, high school students pay attention to their teachers and graduate from high school in greater proportions (93 percent) than American students. They *want* to go to school because they are convinced, correctly, that their occupational futures depend on educational achievement.

It is unlikely that American high school students will ever respect their teachers as much as Japanese students do theirs. Japan's culture is more homogeneous than American culture, and Japan's high schools have a closer connection with employers than American high schools do. Japanese employers as well as Japanese colleges want to see the grades that students receive in high school, and they pay attention to letters of recommendation from teachers. Furthermore, Japan's high schools have the advantage of containing only voluntary students. (Compulsory education ends in junior high school in Japan.) But there are several measures we can take that will greatly enhance teacher control in American high schools.

The first one is to break through the anonymous, impersonal atmosphere of jumbo high schools and junior highs by creating smaller communities of learning within larger structures, where teachers and students can come to know each other well. A number of urban school districts—New York and Philadelphia among them—are already moving ahead with this strategy of schools within schools or "house plans," as they are sometimes called. Such a strategy promotes a sense of community and encourages strong relationships to grow between teachers and students. Destructive student subcultures are less likely to emerge. Problems are caught before they get out of hand; students do not fall between the cracks. And teacher disapproval of student misbehavior carries more sting in schools where students and teachers are close.

The second measure we can take—one that would significantly empower teachers—is to have employers start demanding high school transcripts and make it known to students that the best jobs will go to those whose effort and learning earn them. This idea, which John Bishop and James Rosenbaum have written about, and which Al Shanker has devoted a number of his *New York Times* columns to, is an important one. Employers currently pay little or no attention to high school transcripts. Very few ask for them. They don't know what courses their job applicants took or what grades they got. The only requirement the typical employer has is that the applicant possess a high school diploma. Whether that diploma represents four years of effort, achievement, and good behavior—or four years of seat time and surliness—is a distinction not made.

And the students know it. Rosenbaum describes the consequences:

> Since employers ignore grades, it is not surprising that many work-bound students lack motivation to improve them. While some students work hard in school because of personal standards or parental pressure or real interest in a particular subject, students who lack these motivations have little incentive since schoolwork doesn't affect the jobs they will get after graduation, and it is difficult for them to see how it could affect job possibilities ten years later.
>
> The consequences are far reaching . . . . Many kinds of motivation and discipline problems are widespread: absenteeism, class cutting, tardiness, disruptive behavior, verbal abuse, failure to do homework assignments, and substance abuse. . . .
>
> While employers ask why teachers don't exert their authority in the classroom, they unwittingly undermine teachers' authority over work-bound students. Grades are the main direct sanction that teachers control. When students see that grades don't affect the jobs they will get, teacher authority is severely crippled.

Employers, of course, would have to hold up their end of the bargain: good jobs for good grades. Once the system was credible, significant numbers of students would take heed, and teachers would be re-armed—not with hardware, but with the authority to command serious attention to the work of school.

Third, we should show that American society takes education seriously by insisting that it is not enough for a youngster to be on the school rolls and show up occasionally. Dropout prevention is not an end in itself; perhaps a youngster who does not pay attention in class and do homework *ought* to drop out. Our policy in every high school, including inner-city high schools with traditionally high dropout rates, should be that excellence is not only possible, it is expected. Those who balk at giving prospective dropouts a choice between a more onerous school experience than they now have and leaving school altogether should keep in mind that students would make the choice in consultation with parents or other relatives. Most families, even pretty demoralized ones, would urge children to stay in school when offered a clear choice. The problem today is that many families don't get a clear choice; the schools attended by their children unprotestingly accept tardiness, class cutting, inattention in class, and truancy. A child can drop out of such a school psychologically, unbeknownst to his family, because enrollment doesn't even mean regular attendance. In effect, prospective dropouts choose whether to fool around inside school or outside school. That is why making schools tougher academically, with substantial amounts of homework, might have the paradoxical effect of persuading a higher proportion of families to encourage their kids to opt for an education. Furthermore, education, unlike imprisonment, depends on cooperation from the beneficiaries of the opportunities offered. Keeping internal dropouts in school is an empty victory.

A fourth measure will demonstrate that we really meant it when we said we would welcome dropouts back when they are ready to take education seriously. School boards should encourage community adults to come into high schools, not as teachers, not as aides, not as counselors, not as security guards, but as students. A recent front-page story in the *New York Times* (November 28, 1993) illustrated the practicality of this proposal. Dropouts from an impoverished neighborhood not only hungered for a second chance at a high school education but became role models for younger students. At Chicago's DuSable High School, an all-black school close to a notorious public housing project, a 39-year-old father of six children, a 29-year-old mother of a 14-year-old son, who, like his mother is a freshman at DuSable, a 39-year-old mother of five children—returned to high school. They had come to believe that dropping out a decade or two earlier was a terrible mistake. Some of these adult students are embarrassed to meet their children in the hallways; some of their children are embarrassed that their parents are schoolmates; some of the teachers at the high school were initially skeptical about mixing teenagers and adults in classes. But everyone at DuSable High School agrees that these adult students take education seriously, work harder than the teenage students, and, by their presence, set a good example.

Adult students are not in school to reduce school violence. But an incidental byproduct of their presence is improved order. For example, it is less easy to cut classes or skip school altogether when your mother or even your neighbor is attending the school. The principal at DuSable High School observed one mother marching her son off to gym class, which he had intended to cut. Unfortunately, most school systems do not welcome adult students except in special adult school programs or G.E.D. classes. Such age-segregated programs will continue to enroll most of the high school dropouts who later decide they want a high school diploma because work or childcare responsibilities will keep all but the most deter-

mined in these age-segregated programs. But education laws should not *prevent* persons over 21 from re-enrollment in high school. The age limit for high school entitlement should be raised from 21, the usual age at present, to 100. Especially in inner-city high schools, much can be gained by encouraging even a handful of adult dropouts to return to regular high school classes. Teachers who have an adult student or two in their classes are not alone with a horde of teenagers. They have adult allies during the inevitable confrontations with misbehaving students. Even though the adults say nothing, their presence bolsters the will of teachers to maintain order.

Teenage students who feel a stake in educational achievement and adult students who have lived to regret dropping out and are eager to return to high school both empower teachers in the struggle against disorder. These secret weapons against violence are less expensive—and probably more effective—than additional security guards. Teachers need all the help they can get.

It is important also to remind ourselves that plenty of schools—including ones in the worst crime-ridden neighborhoods—are oases in the midst of despair, where teachers have managed, against all odds, to maintain a good environment for learning. America's goal must be nothing short of making all schools safe havens where children can come to learn and grow.

REFERENCES

Bastian, Lisa D. and Bruce M. Taylor, *School Crime: A National Crime Victimization Survey Report.* Washington: Bureau of Justice Statistics, 1991.

Hawaii Crime Commission, *Violence and Vandalism in the Public Schools of Hawaii. Vol. 1.* Honolulu: Mimeographed Report to the Hawaii State Legislature, September 1980.

Hewett, Frank M. and Philip C. Watson, "Classroom Management and the Exceptional Learner." In *Classroom Management,* Daniel L. Duke, ed. Chicago: University of Chicago Press, 1979.

McDermott, M. Joan, *Criminal Victimization in Urban Schools.* Washington, D.C.: U.S. Government Printing Office, 1979.

Rosenbaum, James, E., "What If Good Jobs Depended on Good Grades?" *American Educator,* Winter 1989.

Toby, Jackson, "Hoodlum or Business Man: An American Dilemma." In *The Jews: Social Patterns of an American Group,* ed. Marshall Sklare, Glencoe, Ill. Free Press, 1957.

Toby, Jackson, "Violence in School," from *Crime and Justice: An Annual Review of Research,* Vol. 4, Michael Tonry and Norval Morris, eds., 1983.

U.S. Department of Health, Education and Welfare, *Violent Schools— Safe Schools: The Safe Schools Report to the Congress.* Washington, D.C.: U.S. Government Printing Office, 1978.

Wilson, James Q., *Thinking About Crime,* pp. 75–89. New York: Vintage, 1985.

Punishment and Corrections

In the American system of criminal justice, the term "corrections" has a special meaning. It designates programs and agencies that have legal authority over the custody or supervision of persons who have been convicted of a criminal act by the courts. The correctional process begins with the sentencing of the convicted offender. The predominant sentencing pattern in the United States encourages maximum judicial discretion and offers a range of alternatives from probation (supervised, conditional freedom within the community) through imprisonment to the death penalty.

Selections in this unit focus on the current condition of the U.S. penal system and the effects that sentencing, probation, imprisonment, and parole have on the rehabilitation of criminals. In the unit's opening essay, "Probation's First 100 Years: Growth through Failure," Charles Lindner asserts that, through the years, probation's ineffectiveness has been linked to inadequate resources available to do the job.

Governments are identifying alternative ways to sentence and rehabilitate offenders, according to Jon Jefferson in "Doing Soft Time." The stimulus for this approach is linked to rising crime rates and declining financial resources.

Laurin Wollan, in "Punishment and Prevention," maintains that an effective approach to fighting crime must include both prevention and control strategies. One without the other is shortsighted, she contends.

According to a national report, "HIV in Prisons and Jails, 1993," HIV-infected inmates were concentrated in relatively few states, with four states—New York, Florida, Texas, and California—having over half of known HIV cases.

Fox Butterfield's article, "More in U.S. Are in Prisons, Report Says," identifies 1994 as the year in which the number of Americans under the control of the criminal justice system reached 5 million, including a record 1.5 million inmates in federal and state prisons and local jails, and 3.5 million convicted criminals on probation and parole.

Can private enterprise make the prison industry more effective? Anthony Ramirez, in "Privatizing America's Prisons, Slowly," states that after a questionable beginning, the future looks good for private prisons.

In "Crime Takes on a Feminine Face," Chi Chi Sileo offers some insight as to why growing numbers of women are turning to crime. The expense of their incarceration is high, but often their children are the biggest losers.

The next report, "Psychiatric Gulag or Wise Safekeeping?" by Rorie Sherman, gives evidence that sex offenders, perhaps unlike any other offenders, are particularly troubling and troublesome to the justice system. Strong public sentiments against sex offenders fuel the problem.

The Rev. Russell Ford, a prison chaplain for 11 years, strives to save the souls of death row inmates. His story is told in "Bringing God to Death Row." David Kaplan, in "Anger and Ambivalence," explores why citizens of this country have mixed feelings about putting people to death. According to a Legal Defense Fund report, "Death Row U.S.A.," there are 40 jurisdictions with capital punishment statutes and over 3,000 inmates on death row.

The unit closes with Robert Johnson's report " 'This Man Has Expired.' " This essay focuses on the executioners themselves as they carry out typical executions.

Looking Ahead: Challenge Questions

What issues and trends are most likely to be faced by corrections administrators in the latter part of the 1990s?

List some of the reasons for overcrowding in our nation's prisons in the past decade. What should be the U.S. strategy for dealing with prison overcrowding in the years ahead?

Why have prisons become so violent and difficult to manage in recent years? What might be done to alleviate this situation?

Discuss reasons for favoring and for opposing the death penalty.

PROBATION'S FIRST 100 YEARS: GROWTH THROUGH FAILURE

Charles J. Lindner, Ph.D

Charles Lindner is a Professor of Law, Police Science and Criminal Justice Administration at the John Jay College of Criminal Justice, where he is coordinator of the Corrections Major. He has a J.D. from Brooklyn Law School and a M.S.W. from Fordham University. He has over 20 years of experience as a practitioner in the field of probation.

Professor Lindner is the author of numerous articles in professional journals, frequently addressing issues related to community-based corrections. He is a training consultant to many law enforcement agencies, including police, probation, and parole departments. Among other awards, Professor Lindner was the recipient of the American Probation and Parole Association's University of Cincinnati Award (1985) for "significant contributions to the probation and parole field."

The author is grateful to Professors Thomas Eich, John Kleinig and Maria Volpe for their constructive criticisms and insightful comments.

With the turn of the century, many of the early probation agencies will be commemorating their 100th anniversary. Over the years, probation has outgrown even the most optimistic expectations of a handful of pioneering reformers and is now the most frequently used sentencing alternative (Dawson, 1990:1). Moreover, while all correctional populations are increasing, during the years of 1982-1990 the number of sentenced offenders placed on probation surpassed any other correctional sentence (U.S. Department of Justice, 1992).

While the questions of probation's success in terms of offender rehabilitation, recidivism rates, and public safety continues to be problematic, its contribution to a perilously overcrowded criminal justice system is critical. Probation serves as a spillway for the overflowing of correctional institutions. Without the option of probation supervision, correctional institutions would be in chaos, local and state governments would be bankrupted by jail and prison costs, and inmates would of necessity be released after serving mere fractions of their sentences.

As probation becomes increasingly essential to the continued functioning of an already besieged justice system, probation agencies throughout the country are similarly facing new challenges never imagined by the early pioneers of this community-based corrections service. The probationer population has dramatically changed, so that caseloads are increasingly populated with "felony probationers" or by offenders who would have, with certainty, been incarcerated in the recent past (Petersilia, 1985; Stewart, 1986). Consistent with societal changes,

substantial numbers of probationers suffer from mental and physical illnesses, including AIDS, and regularly abuse alcohol, drugs, or both. Moreover, long-term increases in violent crimes and a proliferation of firearms on the streets of our cities, including more sophisticated and potent weapons, all contribute to the increased challenges faced by probation.

Ironically, despite the increased reliance of the justice system on probation services and the changed nature of the probationer population, many probation agencies are experiencing budgetary cutbacks. The author of this article contends that the diminution of resources at the time of increased demands upon probation agencies, is consistent with the low esteem in which probation is viewed within the criminal justice system. Moreover, in being compelled unrealistically to "do more with less," probation agencies can never really meet the dual test of increasing public safety through reduced probationer recidivism rates.

THE EARLY YEARS

The voluntary and unofficial contributions of John Augustus, "father of probation," and his small band of followers, to the creation of a probation system have been well chronicled. Based on the seminal work of Augustus, it is not surprising that the first probation law, limited to the criminal courts in the City of Boston, went into effect in the State of Massachusetts in 1878 (Chute & Bell, 1956). Vermont passed a probation law in 1898, followed by Rhode Island in 1899, and by 1910, thirty-seven states and the District of Columbia had enacted probation laws (Chute & Bell, 1956).

In retrospect, probation may have erred early on by justifying its very existence as a "cheap alternative" to other components of the criminal justice system. Augustus (1852: 100) for example made frequent reference to the savings accruable to the municipality through the use of probation as an alternative to incarceration. Unfortunately, through his own and other charitable contributions, he also set the pattern of relieving the State of the costs of probation services. At one point, for example, he bitterly denied accusations that he benefitted from his work, noting that neither the offender, nor the municipality, nor the State relieved him of the financial burdens of his volunteer efforts:

> While it saves the county or State hundreds, and I may say, thousands of dollars, it drains my pockets, instead of

From the *Journal of Probation and Parole*, Spring 1993, pp. 1-7. © 1993 by the New York State Probation Officers Association, Inc. Reprinted by permission.

enriching me. To attempt to make money by bailing poor people would prove an impossibility (1852: 103).

The pattern of equivocating probation services in terms of financial considerations was further demonstrated with the very creation of a formal system of probation. In the Chicago Juvenile Court, for example, despite frequent judicial attributions of probation as the essential ingredient to an effective court system (Schultz, 1973), the original law establishing a juvenile court deliberately avoided the payement of salaries to probation officers, as it was feared that the cost of officer salaries might imperil the passage of such a bill (Bartelme, 1931; Schultz, 1973). To eschew the cost of professional probation officers, the early juvenile court depended upon services from civil servants, including police, court, and truant officers, all of whom were paid by their own Agency, social workers paid by private or religious organizations, and volunteers (Lindner & Savarese, 1984a). This practice was not unique to Illinois, but was also found in other jurisdictions (Linder & Savarese, 1984a), and helps to understand the proliferation of volunteers in early probation (Linder & Savarese, 1984b).

Similarly, over the years, probation was generally touted as a "cheap alternative" to incarceration. Illustrative is an early statement of the NYS Probation Commission (1906; 44-5) which cited the financial advantages, among others, of probation.

> The probation system has also another and important value to the community in its economy. The cost to the community of maintaining prisons and reformatory institutions is large. The actual saving in dollars and cents by reducing the number of persons committed to penal institutions, to be maintained therein at the expense of the public, is no inconsiderable item. The additional saving involved in the wages of men who would otherwise be unproductive is also large. Not infrequently a family has to be supported by charity while the bread winner is imprisoned.

A review of the early literature indicates that cost-savings was traditionally cited as an advantage of probation, both in official reports (NYS Probation Commission, 1907; NYS Probation Commission, 1922; and in academic publications (Morrisson, 1896), and continues to be cited today as a primary advantage of probation.

Accordingly, probation has been traditionally underfunded over the years, with chronically high caseloads from its inception to today (Mack, 1906; NYS Probation Commission, 1912; Flexner and Baldwin, 1914; NYS Probation Commission, 1915; NYS Probation Commission; 1917; Young, 1937; Rothman, 1980). Unlike institutional corrections, where even overcrowded facilities are eventually subject to the finite limitations of steel bars and concrete walls, there are no caps on the size of a probation caseload. And unlike institutional overcrowding, often monitored by court appointed masters, probation caseloads, like watered down soup, always have room for one more. Moreover, unlike the police, probation is not considered primarily as a law enforcement organization in which there is a perception that funding is related to public safety. Finally, unlike public service organizations with a strong public constituency, as in the case of elementary schools, public support for probation services is minimal. Indeed, few lay persons can accurately articulate the difference between probation and parole, and those who are more knowledgeable of probation services, are likely to be critical of probation for being "soft on criminals."

TODAY'S PROBATION

Probation caseloads are far more difficult to manage than in the past years. Today's caseloads tend to be populated with greater numbers of violent offenders, felons, substance abusers, and physically and emotionally ill persons than every before. Moreover, many probation departments also report high numbers of recidivists on the supervision caseload, "who pose a higher risk for failure and, as such, can require more staff resources" (Irish, 1990: 90). Many of today's probationers would have been incarcerated in the recent past, and their placement on probation can be attributed only to the overcrowding of our correctional institutions. As noted by Stewart (1986), "probation departments have become spillways for overflowing prisons — an abuse of the whole probation system."

Traditionally, probation was intended to serve a misdemeanant population, generally first-time offenders who had committed non-violent acts and were believed capable of rehabilitation (Petersilia: 1985). Over the first half century of probation supervision, rarely would the number of convicted felons placed on probation exceed 10% of the total probation population. In New York State, for example, over a 14-year period ending on September 30, 1921, the number of convicted felons on probation amounted to approximately nine percent of the total population (N.Y.S. Probation Commission, 1923: 11, 20). Similarly, Rothman (1980: 108) found that "In a state like New York, a little over 90 percent of probationers in 1914 were misdemeanants and only 10 percent felons; in fact, the percentages did not vary much over the next decades."

With the insatiable demands of our correctional facilities for more space, probation nation-wide was rapidly transformed from a misdemeanant to a felony population, and by the 1980's, the term "felony probation" was popular in the literature. Petersilia (1985: 2) reported that "over one-third of the Nation's adult probation population consists of persons convicted in superior courts of felonies (as opposed to misdemeanors)." Similarly, New York State is illustrative of the dramatic increase of convicted felons under probation supervision:

> "In 1984, 47% of cases under supervision were for felony convictions. By the end of the first quarter of 1989, the felony population had increased to 54% (Seymour et al. 1989: 2).

Predictably, the growth of "felony probation" has been especially pervasive in large urban areas. In New York City, for example, the felony population in 1989 represented 70% of the total caseload, as opposed to 54% statewide (Seymour et al., 1989: 2).

Although it might be argued that "felony probation" does not of necessity pose an increased risk to public safety in that many of the felons placed on probation did not commit crimes of violence, it is in reality only an argument as to the degree of increased risk. While many felons placed under probation supervision may not have been convicted of violent crimes, it is probable that many of those who *were* convicted of violent acts would not have been placed on probation in the recent past. Moreover, a recent study of recidivism among felony probationers during the years of 1986 through 1989 found that:

> Within 3 years of sentencing, while still on probationd, 43% of these felons were rearrested for a felony. Half of the arrests were for a violent crime (murder, rape, robbery, or aggravated assault) or a drug offense (drug trafficking or drug possession) (Langan & Cunniff, 1992: 1).

Not only is supervision more difficult because of the growth of "felony probation," but studies reflect similar increases in special needs offenders. Substance abusers, for example, an especially difficult category to manage, are being placed on probation in unprecedented numbers. Smyley (1989: 34), When Commissioner of the New York City Department of Probation, reflected the concern of many urban probation departments when he estimated that between 9,000 and 13,000 crack abusers were under the supervision of his agency, with possibly as many as 40% of the probationer population "afflicted by one or more forms of chemical dependence." On the opposite coast, Nidord estimated that between 60% and 80% of the Los Angeles County probationers need drug testing and treatment programs for their addictions (Labaton, 1990).

The changed nature of the probationer population is a matter of concern to probation staff. In a nationwide study of probation/parole personnel, it was reported that "at least three-fourths of the respondents believe that the supervision needs of offenders are greater now than in the past. Thus, not only are the numbers larger, the offenders are also a more difficult group to manage." (Guynes, 1988; 8). A suburban probation agency, for example, reported that:

> More difficult offenders continued to enter the supervision program in 1990. The monitoring of undocumented aliens, mentally impaired chemical abusers, HIV positive offenders, and homeless individuals challenged supervising probation officers. The high level of recidivists or repeat offenders presented additional issues for the supervision program, as offenders with prior records pose a higher risk for failure on probation and often require increased staff

resources (Nassau County Probation Department, 1990: 19).

Recent evidence further reflects concerns as to probation officer victimization, especially as related to field activities (Ely, 1989; Holden, 1989; Parsonage, 1989; Serant, 1989; Labaton, 1990; Parsonage & Miller, 1990; Lindner, 1991; Martin, 1991; Pshide, 1991; Lindner & Koehler, 1992). Although some concern during field visits may have always existed, this is not reflected in the early literature (Hussey & Duffee, 1980; Smykla, 1984; Carter et al., 1984). Recent officer concern appears to be related not only to the new "felony probation," but their disquietude is further attributable to having to make visits to high-crime, drug ridden areas in which there is a proliferation of dangerous weapons (Linder & Koehler, 1992). As a result, many officers are reluctant to make field visits, which they view as unusually stressful and an undesirable component of their work (Ely, 1989; Parsonage, 1990; Lindner & Koehler, 1992). Probation officer victimization concerns may also be responsible, at least in part, to an increase in the number of officers carrying firearms (Brown, 1989 and 1990) and radical changes in the fieldwork policies of a number of large probation agencies (N.Y.C. Department of Probation, 1989).

A HABITUAL PAUCITY OF RESOURCES

During the 100 year existence of probation, inadequate resources have frequently been identified as an underlying factor contributing to the ineffectiveness of offender supervision. Inadequate resources are characterized by staff shortages, insufficient funding, and a lack of appropraite probationer services. The underfunding of probation, characteristic of so many of today's agencies, is especially doleful when one considers the chronic nature of the problem, little changed over the years. Moreover, since the truest test of governmental commitment to any of its public services is resource allocation, the historical underfunding of probation agencies is symptomatic of the low status awarded probation. In light of the chronic resource deprivation experienced by so many probation agencies, advocates argue that it is not that probation over the years has failed, but that it never had the opportunity to succeed. Because of chronic underfunding, inadequate resources, excessive caseloads, and policies more often shaped by politics than by reason, probation's true potential remains untested.

The historical underfunding of probation services, generally reflected in excessive caseloads and inadequate services, is well chronicled in the literature (Mack, 1906: 129; N.Y.S. Probation Commission, 1912: 87-93; Flexner & Baldwin, 1914: 116; N.Y.S. Probation Commission, 1915: 217; N.Y.S. Probation Commission: 114; Rothman, 1980). Moreover, over the years, a chronic underfunding of probation services remained the rule, rather than the exception. Lundberg's (1923: 4) contemporaneous plea for greater resources is illustrative of what is perhaps the total probation experience:

the probation staff is deplorably inadequate, both in numbers and in equipment for the work...in very many courts the average number of cases handled by each probation officer runs up to one hundred or even two hundred.

Some fifteen years later, Young (1937: 14) would similarly warn that "most probation officers carry too heavy a load of cases to put into practice the ideals prescribed for them," while Tappan (1960: 552) later cautioned that "much that has been written...has little relevance to practice and little proof of its validity because the staff in most departments carries an overload of work."

In his monumental review of the failed promise of probation, Rothman (1980: 92) recounted the chronic shortage of probation officers, inadequate salaries, and excessive caseloads, and concluded that probation failed quickly and uniformly. Interestingly, it was his contention that probation's failures were related to grandiose promises typical of the Progressive Movement, despite a "flimsy quality of reform theory" (1980: 92). Moreover, Rothman believed that the reformers failed to understand the economic and political realities of probation, in that while probation salaries were paid by local government, the primary beneficiary of diversion from prison was the State. This was because "the state government paid the costs of incarceration in state prisons, but the locality paid the costs of release on probation" (1980: 94). As a result, each case diverted from prison and placed on probation reduced state costs, but at the same time, increased municipal costs. As a result, while probtion was cheaper than incarceration, it was only the state, and not the municipality, which benefited from the diversion to probation supervision.

Finally, and perhaps most importantly, Rothman asserted that despite its many failings, probation survived because it facilitated the "specific interests of those who administered criminal justice: the prosecuting attorneys, the judges, the criminal lawyers" (1980: 98). Basically, it was the promise of a probation sentence that often convinced a defendant to accept a plea bargain, thereby expediating the process for all.

PROBATION: A PROBLEMATIC PROCESS

Whether probation will survive another hundred years is debatable. Probation supervision, as an alternative to incarceration, is ailing, and some believe that it provides neither the necessary controls to insure public safety nor offender services essential to rehabilitation. Byrne (1988: 1) argues that the crowding of probation "poses a more immediate threat to the criminal justice process and to community protection" than does prison crowding, while Lauen (1988: 33), after studying the effectiveness of a number of probation and parole programs, reported that "the evidence that probation and parole are effective correctional treatments is weak..." and we can conclude only that they might "have a marginal effect on some offenders for short periods of time." Morris and Tonry were

especially forceful in rejecting traditional probation supervision, which they concluded "degenerated into ineffectiveness under the pressure of excessive caseloads and inadequate resources" (1990: 6). Similar criticisms of probation effectiveness were recently expressed by other highly respected sources (Silberman, 1978; Forer, 1980; Wilson, 1983; Conrad, 1985). Most painful is the recognition that many of the criticisms of today's probation, is consistent with those expressed in the past (NYS Probation Commission, 1906; NYS Probation Commission, 1912; NYS Probation Commission, 1922; NYS Crime Commission, 1927; Glueck, 1933; Young, 1937; US Attorney General, 1939; Tappan, 1960; President's Commission on Law Enforcement and the Administration of Justice, 1967).

Unfortunately, many of the major studies of probation effectiveness have been equally discouraging. In 1976 the Comptroller General of the United States (74) concluded that "state and county probation systems are not adequately protecting the public." One year later, the Comptroller General, based on a study of five Federal Probation districts, reported a number of serious problems in the supervision of offenders, and concluded that "higher risk offenders are still not getting the required amount of personal supervision" (1977: 9-10).

More recent studies question probation's ability to effectively supervise "felony probationers." Petersilia (1985: 3) found that the emergence of "felony probation" presented "a serious threat to public safety," noting that "as far official records indicate, during the 40-month period following their probationary sentence, 65 percent of the total sample were rearrested and 53 percent had official charges filed against them." Although other studies of the supervision of felony probation caseloads were more positive (Ficter, M., Hirschburgh, P. & McGaha, J. 1987; 9), a very recent study of 79,000 felons sentenced to probation in 1986 and tracked for a 3-year period commencing with the date of sentence, is strongly supportive of the Petersilia research (Langan & Cuniff, 1992). It was found that 43% of the felons, while still on probation, were rearrested for a new felony, almost half of which were for violent crimes or a drug offense (Langan & Cuniff, 1992).

Walker (1985: 176), a critic of probation services, was especially acerbic in stating that:

> Probation supervision, in fact, is essentially a myth. The supervision amounts to little more than bureaucratic paper shuffling. The offender reports to the probation officer once a month and has a brief conversation about work, drugs, alcohol, crime, whatever. The probation officers fills out the required reports and that is that.

While some would take exception to Walker's definition of probation supervision, few would deny that probation is in need of a major overhaul. Rosecrance (1986: 25) perhaps best summarizes the desperate situation faced by probation:

Judicial support for probation services has eroded, public support has diminished; legislative backing has wavered. Probation officers themselves question the efficacy and purposefulness of their actions, while probationers seriously doubt that any good will come from their contacts with probation officials.

FUTURE PROSPECTS FOR PROBATION

The problems facing probation, as outlined above, are serious enough to raise concern as to probation's future. As stated by Conrad (1985; 421), "in the present circumstances the survival of the idea of probation as a service is in jeopardy."

At the very least, it would appear that probation's survival is linked to adequate funding, serving both to insure quality control of the offender's behavior and to provide sufficient services to make rehabilitation viable. Ideally, this would allow for manageable work loads, adequate and competent staffing, and the provision of offender services which are both plentiful and meaningful. While it is recognized that caseload size per se, as is true of the other components of this wish list, are not a guarantee of success (Champion, 1990: 284; McShane & Krause, 1993: 106), excessive caseloads, inadequate staffing, and a lack of offender services are a guarantee of failure.

Future determinations of "adequate funding" should no longer be based on the "cheap alternative" formula which has so long controlled the financing of probation agencies, but must be based on legitimate organizational needs. Obviously, this requires that budgetary decision-makers no longer view probation as an after-thought, whose status is at the very bottom of the correctional scale. Finally, it must be understood that probation costs are of necessity greater than ever, as probation now supervises a higher-risk and higher-needs population.

Unfortunately, recent indiciations, although admittedly limited, lead us to believe that many probation agencies will not only not receive increased funding, but will more likely, experience drastic budgetary reductions. Fiscal cutbacks will be justified on the basis of the financial difficulties experienced by local governments, although, as in the past probation agencies will proportionately suffer more than other criminal justice agencies. As noted by Allen (1985: 196), "in tax shortfall situations and inadequate public resource allocations, there is a tendency to underallocate resources to communuity corrections, particularly probation." Allen believes in addition that probation is considered to be of low-priority in the funding of municipal agencies:

Finally, there is some evidence that elected officials are unwilling to make the necessary hard decisions on community corrections. The easiest escape from conflicting demands is to "fund-out" all resources to meet higher priority needs (police protection, fire, mandated school programs, cost-sharing welfare programs, and so on)...

Similarly, Petersilia (1988) found that the funding of probation agencies has not kept up with the increased number of offenders under probation supervision. She reported that 25 cents of every dollar spent on criminal justice goes to correction, with only three cents of that quarter spent on probation. Most important, she found that whereas most criminal justice agencies on a nationwide basis received increased funding over the past ten years, only probation received fiscal reductions.

Not only did Petersilia (1985: 2) conclude that budget cuts were experienced by probation on a nationwide basis, but she also reported that:

With Proposition 13 and other fiscal constraints, California's probation agencies may have suffered the most severe cuts of all. Since 1975, the state's probation population has risen 15 percent, while the number of probation officers has fallen by 20 percent. In the same time period, the state has spent 30 percent more on criminal justice in general, but 10 percent less on probation."

The Nassau County Probation Department experience further illustrates the funding problems noted by Allen and Petersilia, and experienced by many probation agencies. The civil servants of Nassau County, a comparatively wealthy suburb of New York City, are traditionally well compensated. Nevertheless, when faced with serious budgetary problems in the early 1990s, caused in part by a downturn in tax revenues, the County chose to substantially reduce the probation budget. It was publicly announced that the Agency faced severe staffing cutbacks, including the lay-offs of employees with years of service. These staffing reductions were planned despite increasing caseloads, a felony offender population of 34 percent of the total cases under supervision in 1991 (New York State Division of Probation & Correctional Alternatives, 1991), and the fact that "the increased numbers of high risk offenders has required more stringent standards and the use of intermediate sanctions as special conditions of probation" (Nassau County Probation Department, 1980: 7). Although public pressure caused fewer probation officers to be discharged than originally announced, the trend towards larger caseloads is apparent.:

1990 . . . . . . .75 cases per probation officer.
1991 . . . . . . .85 cases per probation officer.
1992 . . . . . .103 cases per probation officer.

Unfortunately, because of the chronic underfunding of probation departments, even agencies that have not suffered cutbacks, fear the possibility of budget reductions. Rocco A. Pozzi, director of the Westchester County (N.Y.) Department of Probation, for example, stated to the media, that although his Agency had not experienced major cutbacks, "he feared that the final state budget could include huge cuts for probation officers" (1991: 6).

A proposed downsizing of the New York City Department of Probation, if carried out, would be even more extreme. Although not finalized, it is projected that probation officer staffing would be reduced by approximately 25 percent by 1995 (Office of the Mayor of the City of New York). Ironically, these cutbacks will be made by an Agency with a "felony probationer" population of about 70 percent (Seymour, Lockhart & Ely, 1989), and where it is estimated that the under supervision caseload includes between 9,000 and 13,000 crack abusers and "that as much as 40 percent of the probationer population may have been afflicted by one or more forms of chemical dependency" (Smyley, 1989: 34). Moreover, an Agency which has suffered from chronically high caseloads, including undifferentiated adult caseloads of approximately 200 (Lauen, 1988: 31), and where, even in a depressed economic climate, probation turnover rate was approximately 22 percent in the fiscal year ending June 30, 1991 (New York City Department of Probation, 1991). If these proposed staffing reductions come to fruition, then the New York City Department of Probation may become Jacob's classic example of a probation so watered down "that it is widely regarded as providing no punishment or control" (n.d.: 2).

At this time, the chronic underfunding of probation agencies is especially serious because of a nationwide economic downturn. In a 1991 survey of its Executive Committee, Board of Directors, and selected chief probation administrators, the American Probation and Parole Association reported that nearly half of the respondents (30 of 70) "stated that they (or their states or agencies) had experienced or anticipated cutbacks in providing services. Among the services mentioned most often as suffering cutbacks were: intensive supervision, sex offender or substance abuse treatment" (Reeves, 1991: 11).

While othe publicly funded agencies have also experienced budgetary reductions, probation is often among the departments proportionately suffering the most severe cutbacks (Allen, 1985; Petersilia, 1985). Moreover, in many instances, probation is already underfunded, struggling with high caseloads, low salaries, and insufficient programs. Most importantly, today's typical probationer caseload is likely to be populated by higher risk and special needs probationers. These types of offenders are more likely to present a multiplicity of serious problems, and as a result, usually require more intensive controls, experience the greatest likelihood of probation sentences which include intermediate sanctions, and need more extensive and expensive services.

Unfortunately, as we enter the 21st Century, the hope of adequate funding of probation agencies, is understandably pessimistic. Chronic underfunding has so diluted the quality of offender supervision, both in terms of community protection and effective treatment and services, as to debase the promise of probation. A continued diminution of an already diluted probation service may lead to its demise.

REFERENCES

Allen, H.E. (1985). The organization and effectiveness of community corrections in L.E. Travis, 111 (ed). *Probation, Parole, and Community Corrections.* Prospect Heights, Illinois: Waveland: 185-199.

Augustus, J. (1972). *John Augustus: First Probation Officer.* (S. Glueck, Introd.) Montclair, N.J.: Patterson Smith. (Original work published 1852 under the title, "A report of the labors of John Augustus."

Bartelme, M.M. (1931). *Twenty-five years ago and since.* The Yearbook. A record of the 25th Annual Conference of the National Probation Association, Minneapolis, MN, June 12 to 19, 1931. NY: The National Probation Association.

Brown, P.W. (1989). Probation and parole officers up in arms over the gun issue. Corrections Today, 51(2): 194-196.

Brown, P.W. (1990). Guns and probation officers: the unspoken reality. *Federal Probation,* 54(2): 21-25.

Byrne, J.M. (1988). *Probation.* U.S. Department of Justice, National Institute of Justice Crime File. Washington, DC: U.S. Government Printing Office.

Carter, R.N., Glasser, D., & Wilkins, L.T. (1984). *Probation, Parole, and Community Corrections.* (3rd ed.) NY: John Wiley & Sons.

Champion, D.J. (1990). *Probation and Parole in the United States.* Columbus, Ohio: Merrill.

Chute, C.L. & Bell, M. (1956). *Crime, Courts and Probation.* NY: MacMillan.

Comptroller General of the United States, General Accounting Office. (1976). *Report to the Congress: State and County Probation: Systems in Crisis.* Washington, DC: U.S. Government Printing Office.

Comptroller General of the United States, General Accounting Office. (1977). *Report to the Congress: Probation and parole activities need to be better managed.* Washington, DC: U.S. Government Printing Office.

Conrad, J.P. (1985). The penal dilemma and its emergeing solution. *Crime and Delinquency,* 31: 411-422.

Dawson, J.M. (1990). *Felons sentenced to probation in state courts, 1986.* U.S. Department of Justice, Bureau of Justice Statistics, Washington, DC: U.S. Government Printing Office.

Ely, R.E. (1989) *Report on the safety concerns of probation and alternatives to incarceration staff in New York State.* Albany, NY: New York State Division of Probation and Correctional Alternatives.

Fichter, M., Hirschburg, P. and McGaha, J. (1987). Felony probation: A comparative analysis of public risk in two states. *Perspectives.* 11(2): 6-11.

Flexner, B., & Baldwin, R.N. (1916). *Juvenile Courts and Probation.* NY: Century.

Forer, L.G. (1980). *Criminals and victims.* NY: Norton.

Glueck, S. (1933). *The signficance and promise of probation. In S. Glueck (ed.) Probation and criminal justice.* NY: MacMillan.

Guynes, R. (1988). *Difficult clients, large caseloads plague probation, parole agencies.* U.S. Department of Justice, National Institute of Justice, Research in Action. Washington, DC: U.S. Government Printing Office.

Holden, T. (1989). Point and counterpoint: Firearms-Debating the issues for probation and parole. *Perspectives.* 13(3): 6-8

Hussey, F., & Duffee, D.E. (1980). *Probation, parole and community field services.* NY: Harper and Row.

Irish, J.F. (1990) *Crime, criminal justice and probation in 1989.* Mineola, NY: Nassau County Probation Department.

Jacobs, J.B. (n.d.) *Inside Prisons. U.S. Department of Justice, National Institute of Justice Crime File.* Washington, DC: U.S. Government Printing Office.

Labaton, S. (1990). Glutted probation system puts communities in peril. *The New York Times,* A1, A16.

Langan, P.A., and Cunniff, M.A. (1992). *Recidivism of felons on probation, 1986-89.* U.S. Department of Justice: Bureau of Justice Statistics, Special Report. U.S. Government Printing Office.

6. PUNISHMENT AND CORRECTIONS

Lauen, R.J. (1988). *Community managed corrections*. American Correctional Association.

Lindner, C., (1991). The refocused probation home visit: A subtle but revolutionary change. *The Journal of Contemporary Criminal Justice*, 7(2): 115-127.

Lindern, C., & Koehler, R.J. (1992). Probation officer victimization: An emerging concern. *Journal of Criminal Justice*, 20: 53-62.

Lindner, C., & Savarese, M.R. (1984a). The evolution of probation: early salaries, qualifications and hiring practices. *Federal Probation*, 48(1): 3-10.

Lindner, C., & Savarese, M.R. (1984b). The evolution of probation: The historical contribution of the volunteer. *Federal Probation*, 48(2): 3-11.

Lundberg, E.O. (1923). *The probation officer and the community: An address*. Albany, NY: The New York State Probation Commission: 1-8.

McShane, M.D., & Krause, W. (1993). *Community Corrections*. New York, Macmillan.

Mack, J.W. (1906). *The juvenile court: The judge and the probation officer*. Proceedings of the National Conference of Charities and Correction at the Thirty-Third Annual Session. Philadelphia, Pennsylvania: Press of Fred J. Heer.

Martin, D.R. (1991). Probation and parole officer safety: Examining an urgent issue. *Perspectives*, 15(1): 20-25.

Morris, N., & Tonry, M. (1990). *Between prison and probation*. NY: Oxford University Press.

Morrison, W.D., (1975). *Juvenile Offenders*. (J.F. Short, Jr., Introd.). Montclair, N.J.: Patterson Smith. (Original work printed in 1896.)

Nassau County Probation Department. (1991). *Annual Report: 1990*. Nassau County, NY.

New York City Department of Probation. (1989). *Executive policy and procedure 40-1-89: Field activity*, NY

New York City Department of Probation. (1991). *Staffing report as of 6/28/91*. NY.

New York State Crime Commission. (1927). *Report of the Crime Commission* (New York Legislative Document No. 94.) Albany, NY: J.B. Lyon Co., Printers.

N.Y.S. Probation Commission. (1906). *Report of the Temporary State Probation Commission of 1905-6*. Brandow Printing Co., Albany, NY.

N.Y.S. Probation Commission. (1907). *A Study of Probation in Yonkers, N.Y.*, Albany, NY: J.B. Lyon Company, State Printers.

N.Y.S. Probation Commission. (1912). *Fifth annual report*. Albany, NY: J.B. Lyon Company, State Printers.

N.Y.S. Probation Commission. (1915). *Eighth annual report*. Albany, NY: J.B. Lyon Company, State Printers.

N.Y.A. Probation Commission. (1917). *Tenth annual report*. Albany, NY: J.B. Lyon Company, State Printers.

N.Y.S. Probation Commission. (1923). *Sixteenth annual report*. Albany, NY: J.B. Lyon Company, State Printers.

N.Y.S. Division of Probation and Correctional Alternatives. (1991). *All-case report; Client data system*. Albany, NY.

Nidorf, B.J. (1988). Sanction-oriented community corrections: Sales job? Sellout? Or response to reality? *Perspectives*, 12(3): 6-8.

Office of the Mayor of the City of New York. *Mayor's management report for the City of New York*.

Parsonage, W.H. (1989). Worker safety in probation and parole. Washington, DC: U.S. Department of Justice, National Institute of Justice.

Parsonage, W.H., & Miller, J.A. (1990). A study of probation and parole worker safety in the Middle Atlantic region. Middle Atlantic States Correctional Association.

Petersilia, J. (1985). Probation and felony offenders. U.S. Department of Justice, National Institute of Justice Research in Brief. Washington, DC: U.S. Government Printing Office.

Petersilia, J. (1988). Probation reform in J. Scott (ed.), *Controversial Issues in Crime and Justice*. Newbury Park, CA: Sage.

Pozzi, R.A. (1991, March 3). Probation officers adapt to a changing caseload. *The New York Times, Westchester Weekly*, 1, 6.

Pshide, W. (1991). Probation officer field safety in the 90's. *Perspectives*, 15(1): 26-27.

Reeves, R. (1991). A report of the 1991 fiscal survey results: Down, but not out. *Perspectives*, 15(4): 11-12.

Rosecrance, J. (1986). Probation supervision: Mission impossible. *Federal Probation*, 50(1): 25-31.

Rothman, D.J. (1980). *Conscience and convenience: The asylum and its alternatives in progressive America*. Boston, Mass.: Little, Brown.

Schultz, J.L. (1973). The cycle of juvenile court history. *Crime and Delinquency*, 19(4): 457-476.

Seymour, J., Lockhart, P., & Ely, R. (1989). *Felonization of the probation caseload in New York State*. Albany, NY.: N.Y.S. Division of Probation and Correctional Alternatives.

Silberman, C.E. (1978). *Criminal violence, criminal justice*. New York, NY: Random House.

Smykla, J.O. (1984). *Probation and parole: Crime control in the community*, NY: Macmillan.

Smyley, K.T. (1989). The new probation. *Perspectives* 13(2): 34-36.

Stewart, J.K. (1986). Felony probation: An ever increasing risk. *Correction Today*, 48(8): 94-102.

Serant, C. (1989). Dangerous drug visits. *New York Daily News*, 49.

Tappan, P.W. (1960). *Crime, justice and correction*. NY: McGraw-Hill.

The President's Commission on Law Enforcement and Administration of Justice. (1967). *Task force report: Juvenile delinquency and youth crime*. Washington, DC: U.S. Government Printing Office.

U.S. Attorney General. (1939). *Survey of release procedures: Vol. 2: Probation*. Washington, DC: U.S. Government Printing Office.

U.S. Department of Justice. (1992). *National Update*. Office of Justice Programs, Bureau of Justice Statistics. Vol. 1(3), Washington, DC: U.S. Government Printing Office.

Walker, S. (1985). *Sense and Nonsense about Crime*. Monterey, CA: Brooks/Cole.

Young, P. (1937). *Social treatment in probation and delinquency*, NY: McGraw-Hill.

DOING SOFT TIME

Jon Jefferson

Jon Jefferson is a free-lance writer in Knoxville, Tenn.

With 1.25 million people behind bars in the United States, even the law-abiding are prisoners of sorts. Locked into a system that spends more for jails and prisons than for job training, unemployment benefits and medical research combined, society has begun to look for an escape route.

While much of the public debate remains mired in simplistic labels—"soft on crime" or "law-and-order mentality"—more cash-starved governments are seeking new ways to curb their corrections budgets and still mete out the punishment, deterrence and security that the public demands. In New York City, where crime rates and jail crowding have forced the corrections system into the national forefront of alternatives to incarceration, the story of one young offender has an all-too-common beginning. Anthony G. grew up on the edge of Harlem, dropped out of school, and at age 18 faced one to three years in prison for beating and robbing two teen-agers. In the typical version of this story, Anthony would be behind bars.

Instead, he's at large and at "Liberty," literally: Two hundred feet below the statue's golden torch, Anthony works in the bookstore housed in the base of the nation's symbol of freedom. Amid a swarm of tourists—on peak summer days, as many as 16,000 will visit—he stocks shelves, runs the cash register, and answers questions about how the statue was built, how many stairs to the crown or how soon the next ferry leaves.

What has given Anthony's story another twist—and given him another chance—is the alternative program to which a judge sent him instead of prison. For six months, he reported to the program's Harlem office every weekday and met with a caseworker at least once a week; he also took classes, passed a high school equivalency test, learned basic computer skills and practiced interviewing for jobs. By the time he left the program, he had already landed his bookstore job.

For a now 21-year-old with a criminal record, it's a remarkable turnaround. For an overburdened prison system, it's a tiny but noteworthy measure of relief.

The nation's estimated inmate population of 1.25 million is roughly four times what it was in 1973, when a sharp 20-year climb in incarceration began. Most inmates—about 728,000—are in state prisons;

FACED WITH RISING CRIME AND FALLING REVENUES, GOVERNMENTS ARE LOOKING FOR NEW WAYS TO SENTENCE AND REHABILITATE OFFENDERS

the rest are in federal prisons and city and county jails.

The statistics, abstractly impersonal and ungraspably large, represent hundreds of overcrowded facilities, thousands of double-bunked inmates, and dozens of court orders to reduce prison crowding. They also represent the gradual ascent of a get-tough, lock-'em-up philosophy that, over the past two decades, has turned U.S. imprisonment rates into the world's highest.

In addition to those actually confined, another 3 million are on probation or parole, or are awaiting trials or appeals. When the relatively small numbers of incarcerated women, youths and elderly are factored out of the totals, roughly one of every dozen adult males in the United States is being held or watched by the criminal justice system.

"Over a lifetime, it turns out, something like a third of white men will be arrested at some point for a nontrivial crime, and something like 40 percent of black men," said Michael Tonry, a University of Minnesota law professor who also edits the bimonthly newsletter *Overcrowded Times*, which tracks the prison-population crisis and the efforts to solve it.

At an average annual price tag of $30,000 per inmate, prisons and jails now cost the nation $37.5 billion a year to operate. With the public clamoring for even tougher anticrime measures and President Clinton backing so-called three-time-loser legislation for federal offenses, the pressures show no signs of letting up.

The best hope for relief, Tonry contended, lies in alternative sentences—or "intermediate punishments" as he prefers to call them—that mete out punishment without adding to the prison population. In a book entitled "Between Prison and Probation" (Oxford University Press, 1990), Tonry and Norval Morris, a University of Chicago law professor, urged far greater reliance on fines, community service, strictly supervised probation, electronic monitoring and day-reporting programs.

Their clear favorite is the means-based fine, or "day fine," named for the price of a day's freedom from prison. In one version of this system, a day's freedom equals a day's net income; in practice then, a convicted burglar might be fined a year's income instead of spending a year in jail.

Tonry and Morris downplayed concerns that criminals might commit additional crimes to raise cash for their fines: "No doubt some offenders will commit more crimes to pay their fines," they wrote. "If that be a serious risk, then there is merit to adding controls in the community for a period to reduce the risk. ..." They also rejected the argument that fines are unfair to the poor, citing a

Global prisoners

Incarceration rates during 1990/1991 per 100,000 population:

U.S.	455
South Africa	311
Venezuela	177
Hungary	117
Canada	111
China	111
Australia	79
Portugal	77
Czechoslovakia	72
Denmark	71
Albania	55
Netherlands	46
Rep. of Ireland	44
Sweden	44
Japan	42
India	34

Note: Nations from the former Soviet Union were not included in study.

Source: The Sentencing Project "America behind bars: One year later"

ABA Journal research by Joseph Wharton

Source: FBI

1986 analysis of fines in the Staten Island area of New York City, which showed that students and unemployed offenders who had been fined did as well at paying them as others did.

Even if day fines were limited to nonviolent offenders, Tonry explained, they still could ease dramatically the burden on prisons. "In 1991, only 27 percent of the people sent to state or federal prison had been sentenced for a violent crime," he said. "So for the other 73 percent, there's a real possibility we could do something different [impose fines] that wouldn't cost $30,000 a year, wouldn't ruin their lives, and would actually generate revenues."

Day fines are widely used in Europe. In what was West Germany before unification, for example, adoption of fines 25 years ago gradually reduced the number of short prison sentences (six months or less) by three-fourths. In 1968, just before the move to fines began, 184,000 prison sentences were handed down;

by 1989, the number had shrunk to just 48,000. During the same period, the number of criminal convictions in West Germany rose from 573,000 to 609,000.

But in the United States—which relies on the dollar for incentive and disincentive in most other arenas—fines are a form of punishment reserved almost exclusively for traffic offenses and misdemeanors. The reason, Tonry said, is "the idea that no punishment is serious unless it involves imprisonment." But if financial alternatives aren't yet helping relieve prison crowding, the same can't be said of technological ones.

Beep. "John Doe is not at home." Sounds like a message machine and it is, but not the usual sort: A version of this message has just flashed onto a computer screen at Vorec Corp., a New York company that makes electronic monitoring systems for corrections agencies. Nationwide, some 35,000 ankles are currently adorned with electronic "bracelets"; about 10 percent of them wear Vorec's version, which uses a fiber-optic circuit to increase tamper resistance. In New York, the state Department of Correctional Services has about 75 people on bracelets at a time; New York City has a similar number.

Built into the bracelet is a radio-frequency transmitter, explained David Manes, Vorec's president. The transmitter sends signals to a "smart" telephone receiver in the prisoner's home. "Typically, an individual is confined to his home for some periods of the day," Manes said. "At other times he's allowed—in fact, he's expected—to be at work, at counseling, at anger control, and so on."

A schedule of curfews and permitted travel periods is entered into the telephone unit and into the system's computers; if the bracelet moves beyond range of the phone unit during a curfew period, a computer immediately signals an operator, who notifies corrections officers. Vorec also makes a tracking antenna similar to those used to follow radio-collared wildlife that lets officers tell, simply by driving past a workplace or drug-treatment program, whether an inmate is there when required.

With a day of jail now costing $162, electronic monitoring has powerful financial advantages, said Carol Shapiro, New York City's assistant commissioner for alternatives to incarceration. The technology is cheap—

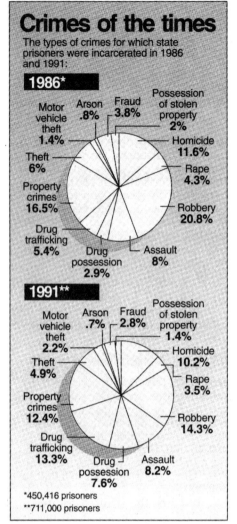

Crimes of the times

The types of crimes for which state prisoners were incarcerated in 1986 and 1991:

1986*

Motor vehicle theft 1.4%
Arson .8%
Fraud 3.8%
Possession of stolen property 2%
Homicide 11.6%
Theft 6%
Rape 4.3%
Property crimes 16.5%
Robbery 20.8%
Drug trafficking 5.4%
Drug possession 2.9%
Assault 8%

1991**

Motor vehicle theft 2.2%
Arson .7%
Fraud 2.8%
Possession of stolen property 1.4%
Theft 4.9%
Homicide 10.2%
Property crimes 12.4%
Rape 3.5%
Drug trafficking 13.3%
Robbery 14.3%
Drug possession 7.6%
Assault 8.2%

*450,416 prisoners
**711,000 prisoners

Source: FBI

"the device itself costs us $2.47 per person per day," said Shapiro—but the program as a whole averages about $75 per day. This is still $87 a day less than jail for every person wearing a bracelet.

"By the end of this year," said Shapiro, "we expect to have 100 to 150 on [electronic monitoring]. By then we'll begin to see some significant cost savings."

Electronic monitoring has another advantage, Shapiro said, as "a real support for the prisoners—we're rooting them in their communities," where they can work, stay with their families, and receive social services such as job training and drug treatment. For Shapiro, who said she believes that in this country "we overuse our capacity for imprisoning people," the community ties allowed by incarceration alternatives seem at least as important as the cost savings. "We only get [offenders] for a blink of a moment. So we really try to work with other programs and services."

In fact, other programs and services outside the corrections department provide the vast majority of New York City's alternatives to incarceration. Last year some 5,000 offenders were sent, either before trial or as part of a sentence or plea bargain, to a community-based incarceration alternative program. Services offered range from drug treatment for addicts to job training for unemployed mothers who have been arrested.

The largest of these programs is the Center for Alternative Sentencing and Employment Services (CASES), which handles more than half the city's participants in alternative programs. With 180 staffers and an annual budget of $8.5 million, the center is practically a mini-corrections system, existing in a sort of parallel corrections universe where alternative sanctions are the rule, prison the exception.

At the milder end of the center's spectrum, its Community Service Sentencing Project took in about 1,800 parole violators and chronic misdemeanants last year. Instead of going back to jail—increasingly the fate of parole violators, as New York parole officers struggle with caseloads of 200 or more—these offenders each spent 70 unpaid hours cleaning playgrounds, painting senior-citizen centers, renovating apartments or planting gardens.

The center estimates the value of this work at about $500,000 a year. That's a couple of million dollars less than the program cost. But by keeping participants out of jail—at least, the 62 percent who fulfilled the program requirements—the community service program saves on jail costs.

The center's other program, the Court Employment Project (CEP), operates at a darker end of the spectrum: prison-bound felony offenders only. When Anthony G. was arrested, for example, it was the Court Employment Project that kept him out of prison, helped him earn a high-school equivalency certificate, and arranged a job interview at the Statue of Liberty.

Begun in 1967, the project now enrolls nearly 1,000 participants a year. Like Anthony, who completed the CEP program two years ago, most are first-time youthful offenders; also like Anthony, most—nearly two-thirds—have committed crimes involving violence or weapons.

"We're clearly the biggest alternative program in New York state," said Oren Root Jr., project director. "We also take much heavier offenders than most programs. Our 'big three' crimes are robberies, including armed robberies; drug sales; and possession of weapons."

The reasons for the project's parameters are simple: Prisons are full, and money talks. "Virtually all our money comes from the city and the state," said Root, "and their principal interest is in creating jail displacements."

At an average cost of about $9,400 per participant, the CEP program costs far less than a year in state prison ($32,000) or in the city's 20,000-bed corrections complex on Rikers Island ($59,000).

In addition—harder to calculate but maybe more valuable—there's the difference between a stint with the center and a stint behind bars. During participants' six months in the CEP program, each spends 20 to 30 hours a week in counseling, classes (at their own schools or at one of CASES' two centers), vocational training and other activities designed to land them on their feet in society.

Some, but Root conceded not enough, get jobs after graduation. Most common (but least rewarding) are fast-food jobs; more promising are the linkages the alternative sentencing center is building with more prestigious employers, including The Nature Company, Limited Express and the Statue of Liberty.

Although it's hard for the center to track the long-term fate of its graduates, Root is convinced that the two-thirds who finish the CEP program have a better shot at going straight than if they had gone to prison. "When you're in prison," he said, "it's a lot easier to learn to be a better criminal than it is to learn to be a law-abiding citizen."

The worst nightmare for an alternative sentencing program like CASES is that a participant commits a violent crime like murder or rape while released to the program's supervision. So far, center officials said, nothing like that has happened.

"We'd be foolish to be unconcerned about the risk of violence," Root said. "But we've carved out a mission of getting the most serious cases we can into the program."

But is the center possibly playing it too safe, working what law professor Tonry called the "Milquetoast" factor?

"If a program has virtually no significant failures," Tonry argued, "what that tells you is not that the program is magically perfect; what that tells you is that they're creaming off incredibly lightweight offend-

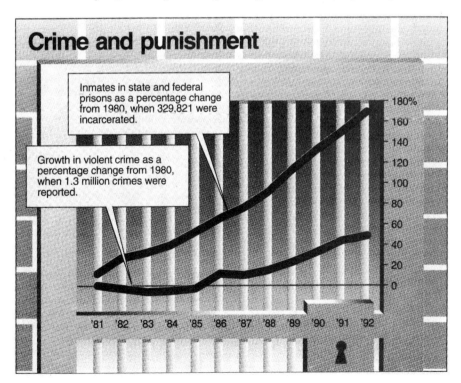

Crime and punishment

Inmates in state and federal prisons as a percentage change from 1980, when 329,821 were incarcerated.

Growth in violent crime as a percentage change from 1980, when 1.3 million crimes were reported.

'81 '82 '83 '84 '85 '86 '87 '88 '89 '90 '91 '92

180%
160
140
120
100
80
60
40
20
0

Source: FBI

ers who should be fined and put on probation instead."

But Root challenged that description of Court Employment Project participants. "These aren't people who would be spending 10 or 20 years in prison," he conceded, "but they are felony offenders, and some are second-felony offenders." (Indeed, their offenses are serious enough to keep many CEP participants out of boot camps—ironic, since CEP participants have relative freedom while New York's boot-camp inmates are guarded 24 hours a day.)

The center's good record stems not from Milquetoast, Root said, but from case managers' intensive supervision of only 15 to 20 individuals at a time and their readiness to act swiftly if a participant shows signs of trouble.

"A third of the people fail the [CEP] program," Root pointed out. "In those instances, we tell the judges why, and tell them we're no longer supervising that person. We've worked out an elaborate system not only to get accurate information to judges, but to get it to them very quickly. We help make it possible for judges to take the risk they're taking in sending these people to us."

In Manhattan Supreme Court, Judge Michael Corriero is taking that risk again. A judge since 1980, Corriero spent four years as a prosecutor and another seven as a defense attorney. He also spent his childhood years on some rough Manhattan streets; a black-and-white photo on his desk shows a youthful Corriero sporting a dangling cigarette and a tough-guy attitude.

Last year about 200 defendants—mostly young men with attitudes as well as crimes—stood before Corriero. He sent a tenth of them to CASES. In his recent risk-taking decision, he sent Deshawn M., a 15-year-old who committed armed robbery and who faced one to three years in prison. "The reason I'm prepared to sentence you to youthful-offender treatment and alternative sentencing is that you're in school," Corriero told him, "and there are what may be called mitigating circumstances." (The main one: The gun was unloaded.)

Having leaned thus far in the direction of compassion with Deshawn, Corriero tilted abruptly back toward toughness: "You put a pistol in a man's back and stole his wallet," he said with an in-your-face intensity. "Don't think for one minute that just because I'm not putting you in jail, I won't put you in jail. Every week, I'm going to check up on you. If you foul up, I'm going to put you in jail for a minimum of two years and a maximum of six."

As if for emphasis, a half-hour later Corriero confronted Charlene E., a 15-year-old he had sent to CASES' Court Employment Project for beating and robbing a woman. "As far as I can tell, nothing has changed," he snapped. "I warned you. Remanded." Handcuffed and returned to jail, Charlene could face two to six years in prison.

Compassion and consequences—justice and just deserts: Like Corriero, the nation's entire criminal justice system teeters between these polarities daily. With the system running on overload—with more than one million persons already behind bars, tens of thousands more on the way this year, and public fears of crime growing—the balance point has become elusive.

Meanwhile, from courtrooms and classrooms and electronic monitoring centers, a message—sometimes hopeful, sometimes desperate—is emerging: There is an alternative.

Punishment and Prevention

Both are needed if crime in America is to be brought under control.

LAURIN A. WOLLAN, JR.

Laurin A. Wollan, Jr., is associate professor of criminology and criminal justice at Florida State University in Tallahassee.

The hard lesson about crime causation is that we the people have failed to do what most of us know is right. We have failed to parent and school our children effectively and to use punishment along the way. We have allowed delinquency, crime, and even violence to increase. The result has been too many children and adults whose offenses could have been prevented who now must be punished severely. We have failed even to provide the prison space for that. Many of us, and especially our children, have been the victims.

Violence, especially among youngsters, has become so alarming that the whole country has concluded that something must be done. Although crime rates in general have declined, according to statistics kept by the Census Bureau, violent crime has increased. Juvenile crime, especially violent crime, has gone up even more.

Recent polls, such as one by the *New York Times*/CBS News, indicate that the public is now as concerned about crime as it is about the economy. Asked what is the single biggest problem facing the nation, 19 percent said "crime or violence," 15 percent said "health care," 14 percent said "the state of the economy." The number who mentioned crime, violence, or guns was up from 2 percent to 20 percent from January 1992.

Our leaders have been similarly affected by the specter of violence. A strategy of punishment-and-prevention has emerged and enchanted them from the attorney general down; it gets repeated in speeches and newspaper columns like a mantra. And it is high time because it is the right response.

But a fundamental truth about policy is this: Prescription rests on diagnosis. Does this mean that the violence afflicting us stems from the *absence* of punishment and prevention? It does. There has been too little of each—too little punishment, too little prevention. But what that means is complex and controversial.

Criminologists of recent decades have argued (at least implicitly) that violence, like delinquency more generally, is *not* the result of the absence of punishment. Indeed, they contend that there has been altogether too much punishment. The corrections system, they have said, is too punitive: Prison sentences are generally too long and too many offenders receive them.

Criminologists have resisted the idea that punishment deters. Twenty years ago, James Q. Wilson, formerly of Harvard and now of UCLA, observed that the leading criminology textbooks of that day simply dismissed the idea of deterrence. Only gradually, and only by a handful, have some criminologists come to appreciate what common sense tells most of us: that the threat of punishment is an important consideration in the choice of actions, provided that it is a credible threat of swift and certain, though not necessarily severe, punishment.

For the most part, criminologists have argued instead for more prevention, but they mean by that a set of strategies that are not what most ordinary citizens have in mind. The citizen would employ more cops on the beat or devices like "the Club" to make crime more dangerous or more difficult for those so inclined. The criminologist, by contrast, would intervene early in the life of "at risk" juveniles to render them disinclined toward delinquency. And so would we all, but not generally in the ways suggested by the theories of criminology.

Modern criminologists have been busy discovering dozens of factors associated with delinquency and inventing at least as many theories to explain the connection. The factors include: age, gender, intelligence, body type, drugs, TV, socioeconomic status, schools, anomie, neighborhood, inequality, housing, peers, mental health, cultural values, discipline, opportunities, self-esteem, employment skills, interpersonal relations, life chances, motivation, family, literacy, class conflict, sexual activity, emotional ties, educational success, role models, to mention only a few—the presence or absence of which (and which?) and the degree (of which?) makes all the difference in the world—or in the science—of delinquency. There are many more factors, of course, and each one—like a carbuncle, a car, or an uncle—has something to do with how we behave, if only on a given occasion.

Theories explaining those connections go by names that only specialists need to know, but the major ones are: the *choice*, *biosocial*, and *psychological* theories, which lodge causation in the individual; the *social disorganization*, *strain*, and *cultural deviance* theories, which lodge it in social structure; *social learning* and *social control* theories, in social process; and *labeling*, *conflict*, and *instrumental theories*, in social reaction. Nearly all theories have subtypes that vary somewhat from each other, such as the theories of differential association, differential rein-

forcement, and neutralization within social learning theory.

Moreover, most of the theories and subtheories have been integrated with others. The permutations and combinations yield dozens of theories. No science has so many theories to explain the same thing. Or as George Homans of Harvard said of sociology, it "sometimes appears to have many theories but no explanations." (For a serious effort to sort it all out, see Larry Siegel and Joseph Senna, *Juvenile Delinquency: Theory, Practice, and Law* 5th ed., West Publishing Company, 1994).

Most criminologists, on the one hand, and the rest of us, on the other hand, could not be much further apart on what to do about crime and, by implication what causes it. (The criminologists are wrong about punishment but right about prevention, at least in citing childhood as the time when preventive measures must begin if they are to work later on in the crime-prone years.) The reason for this division has been suggested by one leading criminologist, Travis Hrischi of the University of Arizona, who has gone against the grain of modern criminology. He says:

The major reason for the neglect of the family is that the explanations of crime that focus on the family are directly contrary to the metaphysics of our age. "Modern" theories of crime accept this metaphysics. They assume that the individual would be noncriminal were it not for the operations of unjust and misguided institutions. "Outdated" theories of crime assume that decent behavior is not part of our native equipment, but is somehow built in by socialization and maintained by the threat of sanctions.

In this welter of theories, few suggest much of a role for punishment, except for the newest one, choice theory, which is also the oldest one. All the others stress prevention, but their prevention strategies involve prolonged and expensive restructuring of society, reallocation of resources, reprocessing of life experience, reshaping of institutions like family and school, and rejiggering of this, that, and many other things as well.

Returning to an older view

The newest theory of crime causation, by contrast, suggests no transformation of society into something new but rather a return to what we seem to have forgotten. Rational-choice theory rests on the idea that people do not merely behave in response to environmental determinants but choose to conduct themselves according to judgments made mindfully that some alternatives are advantageous and others disadvantageous— among which are crime, which brings pleasure, and punishment, which brings pain.

A TWO-TRACK APPROACH TO CONTROL CRIME

Punishment begins with a series of firm measures that parents and teachers must employ so that prisons will be less necessary later on.

Prevention requires more police on patrol and more prison space.

This theory suggests its own strategy. Like the other theories, it calls for a turn from what we have been doing to what we used to do—a return, as it were, to an older view characterized (derisively, one suspects) as classical criminology. Beginning in the eighteenth century, this view held unapologetically that punish-

The Vigilante Society

by Joey Merrill

Society has determined that the government can no longer effectively protect them, and individuals are taking matters into their own hands. The 1993 Gallup Poll on crime indicated this shift to self-protection: 43% had installed special locks, 38% have a guard dog, and for the first time in 35 years, a majority (51%) of households have a gun in the house. A Vermont company that sells Mace reports sales increasing ten-fold in one year. The company that produces a car theft device, the Club, can hardly meet market demand, growing in sales from $22 million to $107 million over two years. Citizens Against Crime reports that each week 15,000 people take their self-protection courses.

People are trying to protect themselves from random violence and from a criminal justice system that often seems to coddle criminals. This move to self-protection was poignantly illustrated during the L.A. riots as Korean business owners held rifles on the roofs of their businesses. Beyond these measures, there is some evidence that a similar backlash to crime is occurring in the judicial system. For example, in 1992 a Bronx jury dismissed attempted murder charges against a man who shot his son's killer on the courthouse steps. The underlying theme of situations such as these is that people are rightly or wrongly taking back control.

Cost of crime

Not only does society now feel the urge to protect itself (apart from dialing 911), we are also literally paying for crime. William Raspberry notes that the threat of becoming a victim to crime has inflicted so much fear that people are increasingly changing the way they live their lives. Working, taking classes, going to school events at night are simply no longer options for many people. These type of changes upset the natural incentives of the American system to improve self and family.

Beyond these indirect costs of crime, there is a very real economic cost of crime. *Business Week* estimates that crime costs America $425 billion every year. The $425 billion in losses are comprised of $90 billion for the criminal justice system, $65 billion for private protection measures, $50 billion in urban decay, $45 billion in property loss, $5 billion in medical care, and $170 billion in indirect costs of crime.

From an economic standpoint, industry must contend with the cost of keeping their businesses safe from crime: a "security tax" is imposed because of crime. The security tax is especially high in inner cities where violent crime rates are from two to seven times higher than in the suburbs—forcing business and jobs out of the inner city. After the killing of the German tourist, some Miami tourism businesses have experienced losses of up to 50%. However, the costs of crime not only have a toll on the inner city, as the manager of a Mobil station which suffered a carjacking in Topanga Canyon, California, explains: "The customers have not come back. Business is down as much as 30%. The people are in shock and they associate what happened with this place. Nothing like this has ever happened here before."

A 1992 Bureau of Alcohol, Tobacco and Firearms study of career criminals found that most commit an average of 160 crimes a year. With an average value of $2,300 per crime (as estimated by the National Institute of Justice), one criminal's habits costs the U.S. about $350,000 a year. A Rand Corporation survey estimated that an average criminal committed even more crimes (187–287 per year)—resulting in even higher costs to society.

Violent crime is especially costly. By using techniques from cost-benefit analysis of safety regulations, economists have determined that a murder costs about $2.4 million. A rape costs approximately $60,000 and assault costs roughly $20,000. *Business Week* reports that violent crime cost the United States $170 billion last year. They note, "The rewards for hard work for the less-educated have fallen, while the payoff for crime has risen." The basic problem is that the incentives have become confused and crime does pay in America.

Reprinted in part from "Personal Security and the Black Community" in Black America 1994: Changing Direction, *published by the National Center for Public Policy Research.*

Joey Merrill is a research analyst at the Hudson Institute in Indianapolis. She serves on the board of directors of Third Millennium, an organization working to raise pertinent generational public-policy issues.

ment is a deterrent to crime—and, of course, it is, difficult as it may be to measure its effects.

But it understood what we have not, that punishment cannot be held in reserve until a misbehaving youngster turns 18, only then to be hammered with a long sentence to a prison cell. Instead, punishments—for the most part of a light-handed sort—must be employed in a sensible regimen of disciplinary measures

Polls indicate that the public is now as concerned about crime as it is about the economy.

starting when a child is a toddler.

Rational-choice theory does not naively suppose that nothing

else matters. Like the other theories, it implicates the family and the school because both institutions are crucial in the teaching of values and discipline. And both have failed, leaving much to be done remedially. This remedial work is not so much along innovative as traditional lines.

When this pre-modern, eighteenth-century view is coupled with the truly ancient view that justice requires doing right (or at least avoiding wrong) and that it can be cultivated by example, the result is a potent mix of policy prescriptions that fit the notions most citizens have of what we ought to be doing about violence.

None of these preventive strategies will produce effects for many years, perhaps a generation. If every parent would begin to read William Bennett's bestseller *The Book of Virtues* to every four-year-old tonight, and if its moral lessons "took" in every case, a decade would pass before any appreciable effects were evident. This does not mean that

any parent should put it off for even one more night. It means only that the preventive measures addressed to the deep-seated wellsprings of human conduct take time to play out.

But there are preventive measures that reach less deeply, that promise some earlier relief, that are employable by government agencies, and that are of use to policymakers—though not to many criminologists because they do not go to root causes of crime. Wilson once noted that the quest for root causes is not helpful to the policymaker, who needs to know what government can do about crime. He wrote

Ultimate causes cannot be the object of policy efforts precisely because, being ultimate, they cannot be changed. . . . Social problems—that is to say, problems occasioned by human behavior rather than mechanical processes—are almost invariably "caused" by factors that cannot be changed easily

---

An Issue of Character

by Charles W. Colson

What we are witnessing in today's chilling headlines is the loss of a generation—criminals who kill without rhyme or reason. To stop crime requires us as a culture to once again learn how to inculcate character in young people—to build conscience.

That begins with secure and stable families. Charles Murray describes illegitimacy as "the single most important social problem of our time—more important than crime, drugs, poverty, illiteracy, welfare, or homelessness." Why? Because illegitimacy "drives everything else." President Clinton, with refreshing candor, has joined the chorus saying Dan Quayle was right. Now the president ought to lead the way with policies that support and encourage traditional two-parent families.

We also ought to demand that schools teach real values, real right and wrong: Pressure the networks and entertainment outlets to develop family-friendly programming. Don't wait for Congress to do this. You and I have to.

If we allow ourselves to be deluded that a bill in Congress will lick the crime problem, it will be at our grave peril. The crime plague will continue to spread, bringing fear in its wake, and people will finally turn to the strong arm of the government.

Ominous signs are already everywhere: calls for the National Guard to patrol the streets; cur-

fews for young people in several states, despite their dubious constitutionality. A recent Miami Herald poll found 71 percent support for police roadblocks to stop drugs, even at the expense of the Fourth Amendment's protection against unreasonable search and seizure.

The dark truth is that people always prefer order to chaos—even when imposed at the cost of freedom. So there is much more at stake here than building prisons and writing new laws. At stake is nothing less than our liberty.

Reprinted in part from "Neither liberal nor conservative nostrums: Crime is an issue of character first of all," *Washington Times*, 31 Jan. 1994.

Charles W. Colson is chairman of Prison Fellowship Ministries, a prison outreach and criminal justice reform organization.

or at all. This is because human behavior ultimately derives from human volition—tastes, attitudes, values, and so on—and these aspects of volition in turn are either formed entirely by choice or the product of biological or social processes that we cannot or will not change.

Certainly they will not be changed by government bureaucracy, whether lean and mean like a police department or fat and philanthropic like a welfare department.

Incarceration works

There are, however, levers government can manipulate that will alter the rate of violence. But they require a willingness to consider a more modest conception of causation. Willie Sutton said he robbed banks because that's where the money is. Why not separate Sutton from the banks? We did that for many years, and in those years he robbed no banks.

So one cause of crime is allowing criminals to get close to their targets. It follows that prevention is keeping them away from their targets. We can make it difficult for criminals to get close to their targets by putting more police on the streets. Crime rates in Los Angeles plummeted after the riots and earthquake because the police were out in extraordinary numbers. Their visibility was much more plainly established than at normal times.

We can make the proximity of criminal to his target not merely more difficult but impossible. Keep the robber from banks, the cutthroat from throats, the rapist from women, the pedophile from children, the graffiti artist from walls, the thief from cars, the burglar from dwellings, the picker from pockets, the snatcher from purses, the lifter from shops—by locking them up. Incarceration

works not only for punishment but also for incapacitation.

It requires attention by the criminologists to establish how to know who should be locked up and for how long—all in light of the costs of the crimes that would otherwise be committed by one no longer able to do so. Studies indicate that the costs of incarceration are significantly less than the costs of the crimes prevented. Some studies suggest that the benefits of incarceration greatly outweigh the costs.

But who among the unimprisoned should be locked up?

■ *L.A. gang:* **To stop crime requires us to once again learn how to inculcate character in young people.**

PETER HOLDEN / THE WORLD & I

The family and the school are crucial in the teaching of values and discipline.

That is not easy to say, and there is good reason to be wary of locking up someone for offenses not yet committed. (And that, it must be understood, is what incapacitation is all about!) But research by the Rand Corporation and others suggests that a policy of selective incapacitation can be carried out on the basis of reasonably accurate predictions (but never completely accurate because the inmates' hypothetical behavior on the outside cannot be observed).

Punishment begins with an array of measures (punitive to be sure, but not brutal) that parents and teachers must be willing to use so that future prisons will be emptier. (But there must be the willingness as well as the capacity to use those prisons later on.) It also means those measures such as more police on patrol and prisons used for incapacitation. This formula is old-fashioned, not easy, and not inexpensive. But when it works, and it usually does, all the guns and drugs and TV violence in the world will have little criminogenic effect.

There are reasons, call them *theory* if theory be necessary, by which we can begin to turn it around. And from it follow these measures:

● Reform the welfare system so that it makes dysfunctional families less likely.

● Empower schools to establish and enforce discipline.

● Remove trouble makers from schools and bus them to special schools (formerly called "reform schools") in Department of Corrections buses, which can be used later in the morning and later in the afternoon to transport prisoners.

● Sentence juveniles over 13 as adults for violent offenses. True enough, we have failed them, but they are too dangerous to be free.

● Develop a range of intermediate sanctions like intensive supervision, electronically monitored "house arrest," and boot camp to punish and somewhat incapacitate those who don't deserve or need prison but do deserve or need more than "walking-around probation."

● Build prisons, as many and as large as necessary to assure that inmates serve 85 percent of their sentence.

● Enact "three strikes and you're in" laws, as New Jersey Gov. Christine Todd Whitman puts it, but not so the inmate is hopeless, therefore dangerous. Better a 70/70 plan so that if a three-time loser goes in at 25, he is eligible for parole 70 percent of the way to age 70, or at age 61 (or 80/80, which would make it 69).

● Put more police on the beat on foot in what is known as community policing, so that small units are responsible for neighborhoods.

Additional Reading

Ronald Akers, *Criminological Theories*, Roxbury Publishing Company, Los Angeles, 1994.

Travis Hirschi and Michael Gottfredson, *A General Theory of Crime*, Stanford University Press, Palo Alto, California, 1990.

James Q. Wilson and Richard Hernnstein, *Crime and Human Nature*, Simon & Schuster, New York, 1985.

James Q. Wilson, *Thinking about Crime,* rev. ed., Basic Books, New York, 1983.

HIV in Prisons and Jails, 1993

Peter M. Brien
Caroline Wolf Harlow, Ph.D.
BJS Statisticians

At yearend 1993, 21,538 of the 880,101 inmates held in U.S. prisons — 2.4% of Federal and State prison inmates — were known to be infected with the human immunodeficiency virus (HIV) that causes AIDS. Of the total prison population, 3,765 inmates, or 0.4%, had AIDS, and 2,312 inmates, or 0.3%, showed lesser symptoms of infection.

On June 30, 1993, 6,711 local jail inmates were infected with HIV, and of these, 1,888 had AIDS and 1,200 had some symptoms. Of local jail inmates in reporting jurisdictions, 1.8% carried HIV, almost 0.5% had confirmed AIDS, and 0.3% had HIV symptoms.

Data sources

Local jail administrators, the departments of corrections of the 50 States and the District of Columbia, and the U.S. Bureau of Prisons provided the data in this report to the Bureau of

Highlights

- State prisons reported that 2.6% of inmates were HIV positive; Federal prisons reported 1.2%.

- Nine States had 500 or more inmates known to be HIV positive at yearend 1993:

State	Number	Percent of custody population
New York	8,000	12.4 %
Florida	1,780	3.4
Texas	1,212	1.7
California	1,048	.9
Connecticut	886	6.6
New Jersey	881	3.7
Maryland	769	3.8
Georgia	745	2.7
Illinois	591	1.7

- The highest percentage of prisoners infected with HIV was in the Northeast (7.4% of all State prisoners in that region), followed by the South (2.1%), Midwest (1.1%), and the West (0.8%).

- After 1991, when the Bureau of Justice Statistics first reported these numbers, HIV cases increased from 17,551 to 21,538 prison inmates — from 2.2% to 2.4% of the prison population.

- In 1993, 4.2% of female prison inmates in reporting States were HIV positive, up from 3.0% in 1991. Among male State prison inmates the percentages were 2.5% in 1993 and 2.2% in 1991.

- At midyear 1993 an estimated 1.8% of all local jail inmates were known to be HIV positive. In the Nation's largest jails, 2.9% of inmates were HIV positive.

- There were 89 AIDS-related deaths per 100,000 State prison inmates during 1993 and 15 such deaths per 100,000 local jail inmates from midyear 1992 to midyear 1993.

- Fifteen States and the Bureau of Prisons tested all inmates for the presence of HIV, either on admission or at release. Two more States and the District of Columbia tested random samples. All other States tested selected inmates, such as high risk groups or those presenting clinical symptoms.

From the *Bureau of Justice Statistics Bulletin,* August 1995, pp. 1, 3. Reprinted by permission of the U.S. Department of Justice, Bureau of Justice Statistics.

6. PUNISHMENT AND CORRECTIONS

Justice Statistics. Jurisdictional testing policies varied. Some policies mandated testing all inmates; some provided for testing of a sample of inmates or established testing under specified conditions. The reported number of cases of known HIV infection in part reflected the jurisdictions' policies for testing for the virus.

Trends in HIV infection in U.S. prisons

In State and Federal prisons at yearend 1993, 21,538 inmates were reported to have the human immunodeficiency virus (HIV) that causes AIDS (table 1). In State prisons 20,579 inmates were HIV positive, and in Federal prisons, 959. In total, 2.4% of prison inmates had HIV — 2.6% of State inmates and 1.2% of Federal inmates.

In 1991, 17,551 Federal and State prisoners were known to be HIV infected, and in 1993, 21,538 — an increase of 3,987 inmates. In 1991 2.2% were HIV positive; in 1993, 2.4%.

At the end of 1991, States had 16,921 inmates infected with HIV. The number grew to 20,579 by yearend 1993, a 22% increase. The Federal Bureau of Prisons had 630 HIV-positive inmates in 1991 and 959 in 1993, a 52% increase.

HIV-infected inmates were concentrated in relatively few States. Four States — New York, Florida, Texas, and California — had over half of known HIV cases. Connecticut, New Jersey, Maryland, Georgia, Illinois, and North Carolina together had another fifth of the cases. Six States reported having fewer than 10 cases.

States reporting the highest percentage of prisoners infected with HIV were New York (12.4%), Connecticut (6.6%), Massachusetts (3.9%), Maryland (3.8%), and New Jersey (3.7%). Twenty-five States reported that less than 1.0% of their inmates were HIV positive.

Table 1. Inmates in custody of State or Federal prison authorities and known to be positive for the human immunodeficiency virus, 1991-93

Jurisdiction	Total known to be HIV positive			HIV/AIDS cases as a percent of total custody population[a]		
	1991	1992	1993	1991	1992	1993
U.S. total[b]	17,551	20,651	21,538	2.2%	2.5%	2.4%
Federal	630	867	959	1.0	1.2	1.2
State	16,921	19,784	20,579	2.3	2.7	2.6
Northeast	10,247	11,422	10,690	8.1%	8.3%	7.4%
Connecticut	574	621	886	5.4	5.6	6.6
Maine	1	21	8	.1	1.4	.6
Massachusetts	484	322	394	5.3	3.2	3.9
New Hampshire	18	26	17	1.2	1.4	.9
New Jersey[c]	756	1,326	881	4.0	5.9	3.7
New York	8,000	8,645	8,000	13.8	14.0	12.4
Pennsylvania	313	338	409	1.3	1.4	1.6
Rhode Island	98	120	89	3.5	4.4	3.4
Vermont	3	3	6	.3	.2	.5
Midwest	1,128	1,392	1,671	.7%	.9%	1.1%
Illinois	299	403	591	1.0	1.3	1.7
Indiana	62	--	--	.5	--	--
Iowa	19	18	11	.5	.4	.2
Kansas	13	20	39	.2	.3	.7
Michigan	390	454	434	1.1	1.2	1.1
Minnesota	14	26	30	.4	.7	.7
Missouri	127	164	136	.8	1.0	.8
Nebraska	11	26	17	.4	1.0	.7
North Dakota	1	1	2	.2	.2	.3
Ohio	152	232	355	.4	.6	.9
South Dakota	--	--	--	--	--	--
Wisconsin	40	48	56	.5	.6	.6
South	4,314	5,659	6,657	1.5%	2.0%	2.1%
Alabama	178	183	194	1.1	1.1	1.1
Arkansas	68	70	80	.9	.9	1.0
Delaware	85	104	113	2.6	2.6	2.7
District of Columbia	--	--	--	--	--	--
Florida	1,105	1,616	1,780	2.4	3.3	3.4
Georgia	807	733	745	3.4	2.9	2.7
Kentucky	27	35	42	.3	.4	.5
Louisiana	100	425	262	.7	2.6	1.6
Maryland	478	666	769	2.5	3.4	3.8
Mississippi	106	--	118	1.3	--	1.4
North Carolina	170	364	485	.9	1.8	2.2
Oklahoma	74	94	102	.7	.8	.8
South Carolina	316	350	452	2.0	2.1	2.7
Tennessee	28	53	88	.3	.5	.8
Texas	615	846	1,212	1.2	1.4	1.7
Virginia	152	112	207	.9	.7	1.1
West Virginia	5	8	8	.3	.5	.4
West	1,232	1,311	1,561	.8%	.8%	.8%
Alaska	9	13	--	.4	.5	--
Arizona	84	78	89	.5	.5	.5
California[d]	786	899	1,048	.8	.9	.9
Colorado	82	52	74	1.0	.6	.8
Hawaii	19	24	21	.8	.9	.7
Idaho	10	20	26	.5	.9	1.0
Montana	7	4	5	.5	.3	.3
Nevada	117	105	163	2.0	1.8	2.6
New Mexico	10	5	11	.3	.2	.3
Oregon	24	21	29	.4	.3	.4
Utah	35	30	26	1.3	1.0	.9
Washington	42	54	63	.5	.5	.6
Wyoming	7	6	6	.6	.6	.5

--Not reported.
[a]The custody population includes only those inmates housed in a jurisdiction's facilities.
[b]Totals exclude inmates in jurisdictions that did not report data on HIV/AIDS.
[c]Percentages for New Jersey were calculated from the 1993 jurisdiction count.
[d]This report reflects updated totals for 1991.

More in U.S. Are in Prisons, Report Says

Number of Inmates at the End of 1994 Has Tripled Since 1980

Fox Butterfield

The number of Americans under the control of the criminal justice system reached 5 million last year, including a record 1.5 million inmates in Federal and state prisons and local jails and 3.5 million convicted criminals on probation and parole, the Justice Department said today in the most comprehensive report ever done on the scope of law-enforcement network.

Will there be more prisoners than students in America?

If the current trend continues—as law-enforcement experts and criminologists interviewed today predicted it would—the number of Americans behind bars or on probation or parole will soon approach the six million students enrolled full-time in four-year colleges and universities nationwide; within a decade the number of people behind bars will exceed the entire New York City population, currently about 7.3 million.

During 1994, the number of inmates in Federal, state and local prisons increased by more than 1,600 a week, and the number of people incarcerated at year's end had tripled since 1980, according to the study, by the Bureau of Justice Statistics, a research arm of the Justice Department.

There are wide divergences among experts on how fast the prison population will grow, with estimates depending both on the crime rate and changes in legislation. This year, for instance, the Republicans' Contract With America calls for providing possibly billions of dollars in Federal financing for state prison construction if states lengthen the required amount of time inmates serve to at least 85 percent of their sentences, a provision that Florida recently met.

Criminologists and politicians today offered conflicting opinions about whether the large increase in the number of Americans behind bars had had any effect on the crime rate. The Federal Bureau of Investigation reported in May that the rate of violent and serious crimes had dropped 3 percent in 1994, the third consecutive year of decline. Some cities, including New York, have reported a significant decrease in homicide.

Representative Bill McCollum, the Florida Republican who is chairman of the House subcommittee on crime, called today's report "encouraging" and said it showed that Congress's efforts to stop crime by lengthening prison sentences and building more prisons were beginning to work.

"If you can get these violent criminals to serve more time, you will inevitably reduce the violent crime rate," Mr. McCollum said. "Anyone who is locked up will not commit a crime."

Alfred Blumstein, a criminologist at Carnegie Mellon University, acknowledged that the increase in imprisonment clearly removed some criminals from the streets and meant that fewer murders would be committed. But he said that since 1985 there had been only a 10 percent reduction in the homicide rate among adults over the age of 24, a disproportionately small gain when measured against the vast increase in the number of prisoners.

"We should think very hard about the trade-off" between the tripling in the prison population and the relatively small decrease in crime, Professor Blumstein said.

Today's report found that there were 95,034 people in Federal prisons at the end of 1994, with 958,704 in state prisons. The total represented an overall increase of 9 percent compared with 1993, which was the second largest yearly increase on record.

Allen J. Beck, an author of the report, said there were another 483,717 people locked up in city and county jails at the end of 1994. Most inmates in local jails at any given time are awaiting trial or have been sentenced to terms of a year or less.

There were widespread variations by region in rates of incarceration, the report found. Southern states had the highest per capita rate of incarceration, 451 per 100,000 residents, while the Northeast had the lowest rate, 285 per 100,000 residents.

During 1994, Texas led the nation in the growth of its state prison population with an increase of 28 percent, followed by Georgia with a 20 percent increase.

The report offered conflicting evidence about whether many of those being arrested are simply drug users instead of serious, violent criminals, as some critics of America's crime policy have charged. The study showed that between 1980 and 1993, the number of people imprisoned for violent offenses grew by 221,200 nationwide, while those convicted on drug charges increased by 167,000.

But at the same time the report found that from 1980 to 1993 the percentage of drug offenders in state prisons rose to 26 percent from 8 percent, while the proportion of drug offenders in Federal prisons soared to 60 percent from 25 percent.

John J. DiIulio Jr., professor of politics and public affairs at Princeton University, said that the report had overlooked an important development: that violent criminals are gradually being made to serve a greater proportion of their sentences. In 1988, he said, violent offenders served only 43 percent of their sentences, compared with 51 percent today.

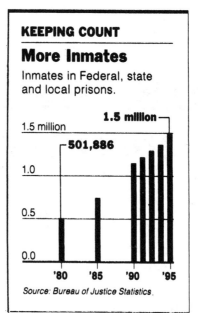

KEEPING COUNT

More Inmates

Inmates in Federal, state and local prisons.

Source: Bureau of Justice Statistics.

The New York Times

"This is good news and will account for tens of millions of serious crimes averted," Professor DiIulio said.

But Jerome G. Miller, the director of the National Center on Institutions and Alternatives, said that today's report was discouraging because it showed that "the percentage of Americans going in and out of jails is phenomenal" and that "as you go down the socio-economic scale the percentage gets much higher." America, Mr. Miller asserted, is relying too heavily on imprisonment as a way to stop crime, and the criminal justice system is turning the majority of impoverished minorities in the inner cities into criminals.

Almost three quarters of the new admissions to prisons are now black or Hispanic, Mr. Miller said, and if present trends continue, he asserted, by 2010, "we will have the absolute majority of all African-American males between age 18 and 40 in prisons and camps."

Today's report, though not addressing the racial breakdown of new admissions to prison, confirms that between 1980 and 1993 the proportion of inmates in state and Federal prisons who were black rose to 50.8 percent from 46.5 percent, while the proportion of prisoners of Hispanic descent almost doubled to 14.3 percent from 7.7 percent.

"The effects of relying so heavily on the criminal justice system have not been looked at," Mr. Miller said, "but it explains a lot of things." When so many poor families have a father, brother, uncle or son who has been arrested at one time or another, Mr. Miller said, "It makes it very hard to organize them against the criminal element."

Privatizing America's Prisons, Slowly

Despite a checkered past, the future is looking brighter
for the private prison industry.

Anthony Ramirez

NASHVILLE

Ernest Anderson, his biceps straining his blue prison fatigues, cocks back his shining bald head and smiles his gap-toothed smile as he talks about crime, punishment and private enterprise.

"I am a career criminal," Mr. Anderson said. Then, the 35-year-old convict goes on to describe the last decade of his life, years filled with gunplay, drug dealing and struggling, often unsuccessfully, with what he calls "my anger problem." He has spent most of those years in prison, five different ones.

Mr. Anderson's story is more or less typical of repeat offenders, and seasoned criminals like him account for the majority of the million people locked up in state and Federal prisons today—five times the number two decades ago.

A typical American prisoner perhaps. But Mr. Anderson is one of a growing number of inmates who are being guarded, fed and put through rehabilitation programs run not by government, but by private companies.

So far, less than 2 percent of inmates are in such facilities and only 13 states, including Texas and Florida, allow private prisons. But this veteran consumer of prison services sounds satisfied. "Until this facility,

with this facility's programs, I have not been given the opportunity to turn my life around," Mr. Anderson said.

His current residence, the Metro-Davidson Detention Facility in Nashville, is managed by the Corrections Corporation of America, the largest company in the business of for-profit prisons.

The private-prison industry has no shortage of critics, from public-sector unions out to protect their jobs to civil liberties advocates who warn that company-run prisons are less accountable.

Private prisons are not new; they date back to colonial times. But by the 1950's, prisoner-abuse scandals at private operations led to the public administration of prisons. The private-prison movement revived in the early 1980's, but grew slowly for years.

But while the private-prison business has critics and a checkered past, its future seems bright. True, the $33 billion crime bill that is stalled, for now, in Congress would have accelerated the industry's growth even more with over $10 billion for prison construction, some of which would have gone to private prisons. Still, the industry's optimism remains unshaken, and it is explained mainly by a familiar, if dreary, litany: the unchecked national problems of crime,

and overcrowded state and Federal prisons. The need to control Government spending makes privately managed prisons look increasingly attractive.

A Better Image, Too

The reputation of the $250 million-a-year private prison business has also improved lately. The industry is still small, with nearly a score of little companies in the field. But the two largest companies, Corrections Corporation of America and Wackenhut Corrections Corporation, which went public last month, hold more than half of the private-prison population. Policy experts say these companies manage a wide range of facilities, and are developing innovative drug-rehabilitation, educational and job-training programs.

Leading the industry's surge is the Corrections Corporation of America, based in Nashville. Its 23 prisons under contract in seven states house about a third of the prisoners in the United States who are now held in private prisons. Last year, the company's profits rose 57 percent to $4 million on revenues of $100 million.

This year, Corrections Corporation's income rose 30 percent during the first half, and analysts predict further growth. Over the next two years, the company's 13,000 beds under contract should increase by 85 percent and profits should more than double, said William Oliver, an analyst at Equitable Securities in Nashville. Corrections Corporation's share price more than doubled in the last year, closing Friday at $15.75.

Equally impressive, the company has been able to win over some former critics with its ability to both cut costs and offer ample prison services. Policy analysts and prisoner advocates worry that private contractors like Corrections Corporation will run bare-bones prisons to maximize profits. After all, they reasoned, private operators are paid a per-day fee for each prisoner.

So far, however, these experts say that Corrections Corporation has surprised them and prompted them to rethink at least the Nashville company's version of prison privatization. William C. La Rowe, director of the Texas Center for Correctional Services, a prisoners' rights group, says he was once an opponent of prison privatization and of Corrections Corporation. But Mr. La Rowe, who has made unannounced visits to Texas prisons for years, likes what he has seen.

"At Corrections Corporation prisons you don't have the atmosphere of impending violence that you have in a state prison," Mr. La Rowe said. "If Corrections Corporation ran more prisons, I am sure you'd see an increase in savings and a decrease in violence."

Even prison experts who remain skeptical about privatization in general seem impressed by Corrections Corporation. "Not everybody is Corrections Corporation," said John J. DiIulio Jr., a professor at Princeton University. "I'm worried about the fly-by-night companies."

The praise is welcome indeed to Doctor R. Crants, the 49-year-old, white-haired chairman and chief executive of Corrections Corporation, who led the often difficult struggle to build the business.

A West Point graduate, Mr. Crants founded Corrections Corporation in 1983 along with Thomas W. Beasley, an insurance executive, and T. Don Hutto, a former Virginia corrections commissioner. Mr. Beasley, the former chairman, is now a director of the firm, and Mr. Hutto is international projects manager, including prison ventures in Australia and Britain.

Its founders and financial backers wanted to bring prisons into the wider movement to "privatize" services that were once the exclusive province of government, including public schools, mass transit systems and municipal hospitals. In fact, Corrections Corporation got some of its venture capital from the Massey Burch Investment Group, which also backed HCA Hospital Corporation of America, the nation's largest for-profit operator of hospitals.

But for years, Corrections Corporation seemed to falter. It underestimated the political resistance to the concept of private prisons, and time needed to create a profitable business. Overreaching, it failed in an ambitious bid to persuade the Tennessee legislature to let the company run the entire state prison system in the mid-1980's. The company went public in 1986 with high hopes, but it did not report a yearly profit until 1989. It lost money again in 1991, recovering steadily thereafter.

Today, however, Mr. Crants sounds confident that Corrections Corporation has fine-tuned its private-prison formula. The company's biggest customers are the United States Marshals Service, which is responsible for Federal prisoners up to their sentencing, and the prison systems of Texas, Tennessee and Louisiana. If the door to private prisons should open nationally, Mr. Crants says, his company is ready to expand.

Perhaps, but Corrections Corporation's growth and profits depend on the company being able to run prisons less expensively than states or the Federal Government. In Texas, for example, where it runs four

prisons, the company's contract specifies that it manage prisons for 10 percent less than those of the state.

Corrections Corporation does own 9 of the 25 prisons it manages or is now building, but in each case the company constructed these smaller operations as a condition of its contract. In short, Corrections Corporation does not risk its money in the construction business. Its profit depends on managing its prisons so that its costs are less than the contracted "per diem" fee it receives for each prisoner. Every contract varies, but last year the company collected just under $40 a day on average for each prisoner.

How does Corrections Corporation cut costs? It pays the prevailing wage in the states where it operates, but its prisons are not unionized. The company offers its 2,300 employees a stock-option program, but it does not have a pension plan. According to union officials, pension costs can add up to 15 percent of compensation costs for public-sector prison workers.

The no-pensions approach saves some, but Corrections Corporation executives and wardens insist that the far larger gains come from changing the unhealthy environment found in so many prisons. Part of the formula is to keep potentially quarrelsome prisoners like Mr. Anderson at Metro-Davidson so busy with drug rehabilitation, recreational and educational programs that trouble will not tempt them. These prisoner programs add to costs at the outset, but company officials believe they more than pay for themselves, though the savings are hard to measure.

It is a truism that there are no perfect days in prison. Yet anything that makes prisoners less dissatisfied reduces the tension between the inmates and prison staff, making costly disturbances less likely. That means attention to detail and quality control in basic services like food and mail delivery to inmates, and communicating regularly with prisoners.

"In this environment, little problems become big monsters real fast," said Jimmy Turner, warden of Metro-Davidson.

"In a state prison," Mr. Turner continued, "if a prisoner said, 'I'm going to tear this cell up if you don't talk to me.' Well, the attitude of the state employee was, 'Go ahead and tear it up. We'll repair that $1,000 commode, but you're not going to threaten us to talk to you.'"

Mr. Turner paused. "I can tell you right now, as a shareholder in this company, if an inmate wants to talk to me, he can talk to me."

In the prison environment, small changes can make a big difference. David Myers, who is now the company's president, was warden at Bay County Jail, a Panama City, Fla., operation taken over by Corrections Corporation in 1985 after a series of disturbances. Once there, Mr. Myers found that the prisoners' breakfast consisted of a hard-boiled egg and a stale piece of bread. He ordered the fare changed the next day to scrambled eggs and bacon. The new breakfast menu helped calm the inmates, and disturbances subsided.

The real day-to-day savings from easing the inmate-staff tension in prison life come from reducing labor costs, which represent up to two-thirds of the cost of running a prison. Though salaries vary widely state by state, corrections officers are not highly paid, with a typical salary estimated at $20,000 or less. But it is a high-stress job, with notoriously high levels of absenteeism, or "blue flu."

That adds to overtime costs, swelling the expense of running a prison. If, for example, one corrections officer calls in sick, he is still paid $10 an hour for his day. But his absence may well mean two other officers have to fill in, working eight hours of straight time and four hours each being paid at time and a half. The salary for those three that day becomes $360, or a 50 percent increase because one person called in sick.

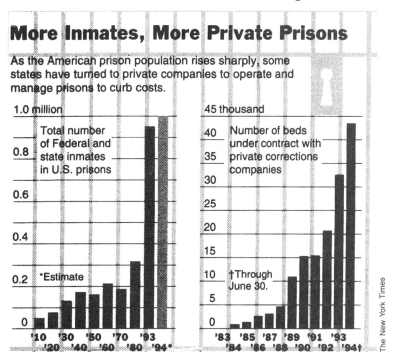

More Inmates, More Private Prisons

As the American prison population rises sharply, some states have turned to private companies to operate and manage prisons to curb costs.

1.0 million — Total number of Federal and state inmates in U.S. prisons — *Estimate — '10 '20 '30 '40 '50 '60 '70 '80 '93 '94*

45 thousand — Number of beds under contract with private corrections companies — †Through June 30. — '83 '84 '85 '86 '87 '88 '89 '90 '91 '92 '93 '94†

The New York Times

Sources: Corrections Corporation of America, Charles W. Thomas/University of Florida at Gainesville

Stress is hard to measure, but it also leads to costly staff turnover and can lead to prison-yard troubles.

"A better work environment means you are less likely to have tired, short-tempered, confrontational people who become violent," said Mr. Crants, the company chairman. "And I am talking about the guards."

And spending more at the outset might save money in the long run. For example, the company buys costly $40 chairs made from hard-to-destroy plastic. In a state-run prison, wardens might be required to buy cheaper wooden chairs or benches.

Cheaper might even be more dangerous. In Texas, prisoners would shatter wooden benches into four-foot-long planks with rusty nails.

The ideal situation for Corrections Corporation is when it can help design and build a prison from scratch as it did with Metro-Davidson, an $18 million, nearly 900-bed facility that opened in February 1992. The prison holds locally sentenced felons serving one to six years.

The prison employs a "wheel-and-spoke design," where one or two corrections officers in an electronic command post constantly monitor prison cells circled around the post. The arrangement reduces blind spots, company officials say.

"What you want to avoid is the telephone-pole design," said Robert Britton, vice-president for operations. "That's the long, traditional cell block you see in old Jimmy Cagney movies. You can't see. It isn't secure for guards or prisoners."

To keep inmates busy and to prepare them for life after prison, Metro-Davidson has an unusually large number of educational and rehabilitation programs for an operation in which the average stay is 12 months. Inmates not only can get a high-school equivalency degree, but also attend programs that teach marketable skills like computer data processing.

An especially innovative program, called Lifeline, is a six-month drug rehabilitation and psychological counseling program designed to bring brooding loners out of their self-destructive cycle of drug addiction and anger. The program, developed by Corrections Corporation, was not a requirement of the state contract.

Yet the company says there is room for improvement—and cost savings—at state prisons it takes over but had no hand in designing.

The Winn Correctional Center in Winn Parish, La., is an example. It is a classic Jimmy Cagney prison out in the middle of rural nowhere. When Corrections Corporation took over management of the 1,300-bed facility in 1990, it became the first privately operated medium-security prison in the United States.

Small things tell. At the commissary, where prisoners can buy personal items like candy bars, the store once opened onto a long corridor. A guard had to stand there and observe the prisoners. By caging the commissary, a guard could now roam the corridor, enhancing security.

Perhaps the biggest innovation at Winn is the continuing experimentation with programs to try to give prisoners marketable skills. Besides the usual computer and "culinary arts" classes, Corrections Corporation is starting a 60-worker garment factory using standard single- and double-needled tailoring machines to make disposable hazardous waste suits. "These are real skills,' said Michael Phillips, assistant warden.

The prisoners show a qualified enthusiasm for the job training. Ricky Temple, 36, is serving a 40-year sentence at Winn for rape and forcible assault. Mr. Temple says he has already learned some things in prison, like "how to be a better burglar, a better bank robber." But, he added, "I want to have a legitimate skill when I get out."

Other inmates, however, are impressed by other advantages that they say the Corrections Corporation prison seems to offer.

"You don't have to sleep with one eye open here," said Jesse Howard, 37, who is serving a 30-year sentence for armed robbery. "You don't have to carry two or three knives with you because the guards are always looking at everybody."

Crime Takes On a Feminine Face

Chi Chi Sileo

Summary: Driven by economic need, self-defense or greed, more women are turning to crime, at a cost beyond the expense of incarceration. Often children are the losers. How should society handle female offenders? Some experts say the solution is in counseling and probation, not jail.

For more and more women, the legend "home sweet home" is being hung on the walls of a prison cell.

The increase in the rate at which women are going to prison has outpaced that of men. Since 1981, the number of men being put behind bars has gone up 112 percent; the number of women, 202 percent. This corresponds neatly with the upward trend in arrest rates; the rate of increase for women is now nearly double that for men.

What's behind these statistics? Are more women being drawn into a life of crime, or is the criminal justice system just getting more adept at catching and sentencing them?

"Both," says Rita Simon, a sociologist at American University in Washington and author of two books on women and crime. "Part of it is that just as women have more opportunities outside the home, they have more opportunities to fall into crime. And it's also true that in the past, judges tended to be more lenient with women, especially when they had children. But now justice is becoming more gender-blind."

The quasi-glamorous phrase "female criminal" conjures up the gun molls, femmes fatales and high-class madams beloved by tabloids and the movies. But the reality of women's criminality has far less to do with these captivating images and far more with the dreary exigencies of petty thievery, low-level drug dealing and small-time grifting. Women's growing presence in jails and prisons is being fueled by changing sentencing laws, a rise in white-collar crime and new legal tactics targeted at prosecuting women (in some cases, for nonexistent crimes).

In actual numbers, men still far outrank women in every type of crime, and even the wildest women don't indulge in the freewheeling activities that some male criminals do. FBI spokesman Kurt Crawford speculates that "there are maybe two" female serial killers at large (compared with estimates of as many as 500 males), and women are barely represented in crimes such as kidnapping, hostage-taking or terrorism. "These are just not female types of crimes," says Harvey Schlossberg, a former police officer and now the chief psychologist for the New York/New Jersey Port Authority. "Women tend to be motivated by economic concerns, while men are motivated by power and control."

Nancy Hollander, a past president of the National Association of Criminal Defense Lawyers, agrees that economics are at the root of women's fall from legal grace. "Women are going to jail for writing bad checks to get out of abusive homes," she asserts.

That's true of certain crimes, according to Simon, but not all: "Look at white-collar criminals; these are not poor women or abused women.

When I tell radical feminists this, they get furious. They believe that women are inherently more moral, that they only steal to feed their children. Well, the data just don't bear that out."

In fact, white-collar crime is where women seem to be flocking. The primary increase in arrests of women is for property offenses: larceny, fraud, embezzlement and forgery. And it isn't happening only in the United States: Reports are surfacing in Europe of female white-collar criminals, and a few years ago the Egyptian newsweekly *October* reported with alarm a rise in "the feminization of fraud."

When women take the money and run, they do so with much smaller amounts (an average of $50,000 compared with the $150,000 average that men take). Ironically, the barriers that hold women back here are the same ones that stall them in more legitimate professions. But as more women enter top executive circles, many experts predict, more of them will develop both the skills and the opportunity to play for larger criminal stakes. "Just give them time," says Simon.

Women who commit white-collar crime almost always act alone, and in this way such crimes stand out from other women's crimes. When a woman breaks the law it is usually through a personal connection — specifically, involvement with a man.

"Most women who are brought in for drug offenses have gotten there through their connection to a man," says Helen Butler, public affairs specialist at the Federal Bureau of Prisons. "Often their criminal involvement is very slight, so in the past judges would look more favorably on giving them things like probation." She adds that recent crime legislation which made drug dealing a federal offense and instituted mandatory minimum sentences has made sentencing stiffer all around, for both men and women. "Judges don't have any choice now. They have to hand down very tough sentences."

The war on drugs is packing prisons and jails with both male and female inmates. In Washington, D.C., for instance, 60 percent of the women held in jail are there for drug-related offenses; in the federal system the percentage is even higher. Most of these women are small-time, low-level accomplices who would have gotten probation or short sentences in the past.

According to Brenda Smith, director of the Women's Prison Project at the National Women's Law Center, women are highly vulnerable to involvement with drugs. "Women historically turn to crime to generate income. And drug dealing is a quick and easy way to do this. Also, because women are more low-level, they're more likely to get caught," says Smith, who has worked with imprisoned women for more than a decade.

In addition to accomplices in drug crimes and theft, there is also what Hollander calls "the most frightening group: women who are accomplices to men who abuse or kill other women or children." Stressing that these are a highly deviant minority of criminal women, Hollander differentiates them from women trapped in abusive relationships who end up abusing their children. In the latter situation, she says, "we have to be careful about assessing blame. . . . After all, these children had two parents. Where was the father? Also, it's possible that in these situations, the women are just so terrorized they can't think straight."

"I have a hard time accepting that," counters Schlossberg. He believes that women might abuse their children as a way of punishing their own abusers. "The child is his, too, and is an easier target. They may not be consciously aware that they're doing it, but at any rate, they still know right from wrong. They know they're harming that child."

Divorced or single mothers may become unwitting accomplices to abuse when they attempt to create a nuclear family. Studies have shown that stepfathers and boyfriends are more likely than natural fathers to abuse and neglect children living in their homes.

Family life in general doesn't seem to keep women out of the law's reach. Violent women rarely attack strangers, usually keeping their violent attacks close to home: Two-thirds of violent female offenders have attacked a family member, compared with 17 percent of violent male inmates. And while fewer than 6 percent of men serving time for homicide have killed a family member, more than 25 percent of women killers turned against what Justice Department statistics call "an intimate" — a lover, spouse, ex-spouse or pimp.

Those numbers have to be taken in context. According to even conservative estimates, about 40 percent of women who are charged with killing an intimate are women who found that deadly force was the only effective counteraction to long-term abuse. "Some of these women truly see no other option," says Smith of the Women's Law Center. "And in a purely technical sense, they are probably right. Think about it this way. A man can overpower a woman without killing her. He can beat her into submission and stop just short of killing her to make her stop doing something. A woman can't usually do that to a man. To stop him, she has to kill him."

Issues about spousal abuse and sticky legalistic questions of self-defense for battered wives are labyrinthine, but here certain facts bear consideration. The majority of women in prison report a history of physical or sexual abuse; almost all crime experts agree that learned violence begets later violence. And while it's true that battered women have more options now, and more awareness of those options, the fact remains that an abused woman's life is most in danger when she decides to leave the relationship.

According to Ann Jones, author of Women Who Kill, "There are cases on record of men still harassing and beating their wives twenty-five years after the wives left them and tried to go into hiding. If researchers were not quite so intent upon assigning the pathological behavior to the women, they might see that the more telling question is not 'Why do the women stay?' but 'Why don't the men let them go?'"

For women, if economic necessity, self-defense, punishing their abuser through their children or choosing to become an embezzler doesn't land them in jail, they might try this: getting pregnant.

A new trend in the war on drugs is accusing pregnant drug addicts of fetal abuse, a notion that is legally unclear. Pregnant women who are turned in by doctors when traces of drug use show up in tests are being hit with charges that range from illegal transport of narcotics (through the umbilical cord), child abuse and even assault with a deadly weapon.

"It's an abuse of prosecutorial power, plain and simple," says Lynn Paltrow, director of special litigation for the Center for Reproductive Law and Policy. "A complete misuse of criminal law. There is not one single state in which this law — fetal abuse — is even on the books." In fact, every challenge to these indictments in lower courts has been won, but the indictments keep coming anyway.

Minority women make up more than 70 percent of the 400 or more women charged with these offenses in cases currently before the courts. "These are the women most likely to use public health facilities instead of going to a private doctor who knows you personally," points out Smith. "If you're a middle-class white woman, your doctor would never even ask a question about drug abuse, certainly never administer a test for it."

Adds Paltrow, "These prosecutors claim that they just want the women to be forced into getting treatment. That's nonsense. There are no drug treatment programs for pregnant or parenting women with drug and alcohol problems."

The trend is particularly disturbing in light of new studies which indicate that while alcohol abuse during pregnancy is very dangerous, crack use actually inflicts limited damage on unborn children. And good prenatal care is universally acknowledged as the best way to ensure the birth of healthy children.

But, Paltrow says, "women are being scared away from both prenatal care and drug treatment because they don't want to be turned in. The fact is, if you care about the health of women or babies, you cannot adopt a punitive approach."

Poverty, drugs and physical abuse are the depressing trinity of women behind bars. The majority of them are mothers, and for many their real problems begin when they get out finding a job and housing and reclaiming children in the care of relatives or foster parents.

Diana Hernandez, the director of counseling for the Fortune Society in

New York, an organization operated by former inmates that helps ex-offenders reintegrate into society, says these are the most difficult problems that many women face when they're released from prison: "Without a job, without a place to live, and a child or two depending on her, what is she supposed to do? Without help and support, chances are she's going to go back."

The impact on society goes beyond the costs of incarceration. The children, raised apart from their mothers and often in unstable conditions, are more likely to grow up with a host of problems—including a higher chance of becoming criminals themselves.

And, Hernandez says, some of the foster families who take care of these children get very attached to them; in some cases, women coming out of jail have lost their children as a result. "In either case, it's traumatic for mother, foster family and child," she says.

Women "getting out," like anyone with a criminal record, have an extremely difficult time finding employment and are more likely to return to crime or end up on welfare. Hernandez notes that just dealing with the bureaucratic red tape of life after imprisonment can be overwhelming.

"These are women whose behavior needs monitoring," Smith says. "But not to be locked up. I mean, they're not killers. What good does prison do them? If they weren't hardcore addicts or criminals when they went in, they sure will be when they get out." Smith, Hollander and other criminologists advocate probation and counseling in place of more-expensive jail terms. Because the majority of nonviolent female offenders (aside from white-collar crooks) do seem driven by economic need, such alternatives would probably be more sensible, they say.

Hollander, who has studied and worked with many child abuse cases, believes that imprisonment is a bad choice, particularly for family abusers — male or female. She cites one of her own cases, in which a year of intensive counseling was offered as an alternative for an abusive family. The family stayed together — without further violence.

"The more people we lock up," she says, "the fewer parents there are. Do we stop caring about 'the family' just because these people are poor and troubled? What's going to happen to those children without their parents? We're going to raise a generation of antisocial outcasts." Counseling does not work in every case, she concedes, but she believes it's worth a try.

"The real truth," Smith says, "is that you can't shut certain things out of your sight. You can't imprison away addiction or poverty or misery."

Psychiatric Gulag or Wise Safekeeping?

Lawmakers use civil commitment to detain sex predators.

Rorie Sherman

National Law Journal *Staff Reporter*

In Washington State, it's called the "Sexual Predator Law." In Minnesota, it's the "Psychopathic Personality Statute." Kansas and Wisconsin have their own versions. But in New Jersey, no matter what formal title the bill receives when enacted, as expected this fall, it will be known as "Megan's Law."

Jesse Timmendequas, previously convicted of sexually assaulting young girls, has admitted he raped, strangled and killed 7-year-old Megan Kanka, his neighbor in Hamilton Township, N.J. Before Mr. Timmendequas, 33, was released from prison in 1988, he told authorities he feared he would strike again. But because he had finished serving six years of his 10-year sentence, authorities say, they were forced to grant him parole.

Outrage at Megan's murder prompted New Jersey legislators to promise a package of legal reforms. A key provision—designed to keep the likes of Mr. Timmedequas off the streets for life—would add New Jersey to a list of at least four other states engaged in a legal experiment so fraught with constitutional questions that it is on appeal to the U.S. Supreme Court in a case from Minnesota. *In Re: Phillip Jay Blodgett, Alleged Psychopathic Personality,* 510 N.W.2d 910 (1994).

These laws target violent rapists and pedophiles who have served their sentences but are deemed by a parole board likely to commit further crimes if released. Under these laws, prosecutors can seek to have them transferred directly from prison to mental institutions, where the odds are they will remain involuntarily committed for the rest of their lives.

Legal observers agree that these measures shakily bridge the criminal justice and mental health systems. "We are pushing the envelope," says James A. Harkness, general counsel to the New Jersey Senate. Says Jim Haney, director of research and information for Wisconsin's attorney general, "It really is on the frontier."

Yet more states are expected to experiment with these laws. Unless appellate courts uniformly strike them down, the Supreme Court, even if it declines to hear *Blodgett,* eventually will have to decide their constitutionality.

The laws pit the public's safety against the liberty interests of individuals deemed likely to strike again. Among the legal objections: The statutes provide for an illegal form of preventive detention, create double jeopardy problems, violate constitutional equal protection and due process rights and operate as ex post facto laws. But two state supreme courts already have rejected these arguments.

CRITICS HORRIFIED

Civil libertarians condemn what they see as the use of the mental health system as a stopgap. According to John Q. La Fond, a professor of both mental health and criminal law at Seattle University School of Law, who has been fighting Washington's sexual predator statute, "We now have a system of lifetime preventive detention in place where we identify in advance who will re-offend and confine them . . . in a psychiatric gulag for what they might do."

Even some prosecutors criticize the civil commitment of dangerous criminals.

Linda Fairstein, chief of the Sex Crimes Prosecution Unit in the Manhattan district attorney's office, says she finds certain aspects of laws like Washington's "attractive" because "we seen an extraordinary amount of recidivist behavior with the stranger rapists and the pedophiles." She suggests that a better answer would be to give these people lengthy criminal sentences and make sure they serve their full term.

Meanwhile, mental health experts who doubt their colleagues' ability to predict dangerousness or cure sexual deviancy say the vast majority of these offenders are simply criminal—not mentally ill. They say only a small subset of sexual offenders actually suffer from an identifiable mental disorder and might benefit from treatment. But many psychiatrists say that they believe even this group can be handled within the criminal justice system, and that treatment must be voluntary to be effective.

HIGH RECIDIVISM

"There are issues of constitutional rights," acknowledges Paul J. Morrison, district attorney of Johnson County, Mo., encompassing Kansas City. "It is hard to make a good argument against doing everything we can to incapacitate violent sex offenders with a high risk of recidivism."

Gregory P. Canova, chief of the criminal division in the Washington attorney general's office, who pushed for the enactment of and helped implement the state's 1990 law, says he's been called for information on it by prosecutors across the United States, as well as from New Zealand and Canada.

Some of the laws have been on the books for years. During the 1960s, Minne-

From *The National Law Journal,* September 5, 1994, pp. A1, A24. © 1994 by the New York Law Publishing Company. Reprinted by permission.

sota prosecutors revived the use of a 1939 law known as the Psychopathic Personality Statute. In a unanimous 1940 opinion authored by then-Chief Justice Charles Evans Hughes, the U.S. Supreme Court found Minnesota's statute not to be unconstitutionally vague. Using a rational basis test, the court also rejected the claim that the statute violated the equal protection clause of the 14th Amendment. *State ex rel Pearson v. Probate Court of Ramsey County,* 287 N.W. 297 (1939); 309 U.S. 270 (1940).

By 1959, a total of 26 states and the District of Columbia had sexual psychopath statutes. Half of them have since repealed these laws, however. In 1989, the American Bar Association Standards for Criminal Justice condemned the statutes and recommended that they be eliminated.

Such professional organizations as the Group for the Advancement of Psychiatry and the President's Commission on Mental Health agreed. The remaining states never followed suit, but they didn't apply the laws either. (Those states include New Jersey, Colorado, Connecticut, Illinois, Massachusetts, Minnesota, Nebraska, Oregon, Tennessee, Utah, Virginia, Washington and the District of Columbia.)

Minnesota seems to be alone in continuing to use its old psychopath law, say mental health law experts. And just this January, its supreme court found that the law as now applied does not violate substantive due process or the equal protection clauses of either the state or U.S. constitutions.

Writing for the majority, now-retired Minnesota Justice John E. Simonett summed up the central question posed by these laws: "Is it better for a person with an uncontrollable sex drive to be given an enhanced prison sentence or to be committed civilly?"

Justice Simonett says, "the safety of the public" must be balanced against "the liberty interests of the individual who acts destructively for reasons not fully understood by our medical, biological and social sciences." In the final analysis, he stated, "It is the moral credibility of the criminal justice system that is at stake. In the present imperfect state of scientific knowledge, where there are no definitive answers, it would seem a state legislature should be allowed, constitutionally, to choose either or both alternatives for dealing with the sexual predator. At the very least, we [will allow this] . . .

until the United States Supreme Court says otherwise."

U.S. SUPREME COURT

Unsurprisingly, the *Blodgett* plaintiffs have appealed to the U.S. Supreme Court and asked it to re-examine the Psychopathic Personality Statute using the strict scrutiny standard the high court has come to employ when a liberty interest is at stake. Among many arguments, the plaintiffs point to the high court's 1992 decision in *Foucha v. Louisiana,* 112 S. Ct. 1780. In that case, the justices struck down, as a violation of substantive due process, a Louisiana civil commitment statute that allowed the continued civil commitment of a man who was no longer mentally ill but might still be considered dangerous.

Minnesota Supreme Court Justice Esther M. Tomljanovich, dissenting in *Blodgett,* essentially agreed with the plaintiffs that *Foucha* invalidates the Minnesota statute. Under the Minnesota law, she said, a person "may be involuntarily committed, without the requirement of a finding that the person suffers from a medically diagnosable and treatable mental illness, to a confinement of indefinite duration until the person proves he is no longer dangerous to the public and no longer in need of inpatient treatment." That, added the judge, "in my view, violates the Due Process and Equal Protection Clauses of the Fourteenth Amendment of the United States Constitution."

Also, the dissenting Minnesota justices said, "The rigor and methodical efficiency with which the Psychopathic Personality Statute is presently being enforced is creating a system of wholesale preventive detention, a concept foreign to our jurisprudence."

Minnesota has 68 such criminals in state psychiatric care; one has been held for treatment since 1965.

CONFINED FOR THREE YEARS

On June 30, two decisions were handed down by the state supreme court ordering the release of two such "patients." Peter Rickmyer was released because the state high court found that the spanking and fondling of children for which he was convicted does not rise to the level of dangerousness envisioned by the statute. Mr. Rickmyer had been sentenced to 30 months in prison, which was reduced

to 21; he served six months and then was sent to a mental hospital, where he was confined for three years—a total of about 42 months' confinement.

Dennis D. Linehan was released because the state had failed to show clear and convincing evidence that he could not control his sexual impulses. Mr. Linehan was sentenced to 40 years for kidnapping; he served 14 years in prison and spent two years civilly committed.

Both men were freed from the hospital Aug. 9, according to their attorney, John E. Gryzbek, a St. Paul sole practitioner. *In re Matter of Peter Rickmyer,* C8-93-523; *In re Matter of Dennis D. Linehan,* C3-93-381. In the wake of these decisions, Minnesota lawmakers called a special legislative session for Aug. 31 to codify the court's standards.

NEW GENERATION OF LAWS

While the standard in Minnesota is "clear and convincing," a more stringent standard is being used in the new generation of sex offender civil commitment laws.

These are modeled on Washington's sexual predator law, whose civil commitment procedure is designed to emulate a criminal trial. The statute requires that the criminal justice evidentiary burden of "beyond a reasonable doubt" be met before sexual predators can be civilly committed. It also entitles respondents to appointed counsel, a trial before 12 jurors and a unanimous verdict.

Since July 1990, when Washington's law went into effect, an end-of-sentence review committee has examined the case of every sexual offender in the state who is about to be paroled.

Some 1,600 to 2,000 offenders have been reviewed, according to Mr. Canova. Of those, 130 criminals were referred to the attorney general's office or local prosecutors to consider filing for civil commitment. Eighteen cases are now pending and 17 criminals have been committed, says Mr. Canova, who notes that every respondent who has gone before a jury has been found to be a sexually violent predator.

Of course no one who is put before a jury under such circumstances will go free, says Seattle's Robert Boruchowitz, director of the King County Public Defender's Association and one of the fiercest opponents of sexual predator laws: "It's a kangaroo court. All a prosecutor has to do is stand up and list the

Psychiatrists Object to Predator Laws

The American Psychiatric Association is expected to take a strong stand against using the mental health system to continue the confinement of convicted sex offenders.

Responding to state legislatures' interest in locking convicted sex offenders in mental institutions and the role of psychiatrists in that effort, the APA has created a special task force to develop an official policy on such civil commitment. A preliminary report is due in September; a final statement should be ready by next year.

But already it's clear the APA will reject the wholesale use of civil commitment for convicted sex offenders. The only question is how strongly the APA will word its objections.

Psychiatrists today insist that most sex offenders are criminals—not mentally ill—and therefore belong in prisons, not mental institutions. Mental health experts say that there is no proven therapy for the subgroup that might be mentally ill, and that court orders confining sex offenders in mental institutions until they are rehabilitated are, in effect, life sentences.

Psychiatrists say stranger rapists—a group targeted by Statutes such as Washington's Sexual Predator Law—are not particularly characterized by mental disorder.

"A crime itself is not a syndrome," asserts Dr. Steven Kenny Hoge, chair of the APA Council on Psychiatry and the Law and an associate professor at the University of Virginia School of Law. To qualify as a mental illness, there must be a biological basis or, as with Post Traumatic Stress, a provable set of symptoms that occur with regularity.

Studies demonstrate that stranger rapists have the highest rate of recidivism; pedophiles are next, with incest offenders having the lowest. Among pedophiles, men who molest boys have a higher rate than those who molest girls.

Recidivism rates for all these categories of offenders generally stay below 50 percent with treatment but can run higher than 50 percent without, says Dr. Judith Becker, president of the Oregon-based Association for the Treatment of Sexual Abusers.

Preliminary results from ongoing studies suggest that the most effective form of treatment may be cognitive behavioral therapy conducted in a group setting. Anti-depressants and drugs that curtail the male sex drive also have had some success.

But, since therapeutic work with sex offenders is a relatively new and still developing field, says Prof. Peter Margulies of St. Thomas University School of Law in Miami, reliance on the mental health system is misplaced. "We are putting our faith in a system that can't possibly yet . . . make dangerous people nondangerous," he says.

Rorie Sherman

guy's crimes, and the jury is frightened into putting him away forever."

Despite Mr. Boruchowitz's objections, Washington's sexual predator law recently survived a state constitutional challenge. In a 6–3 decision, the state supreme court in August 1993 ruled that the law was consistent with *Foucha* and passed muster on equal protection grounds. Additionally, the majority found the law did not, as plaintiffs alleged, constitute a form of ex post facto law or violate the double jeopardy prohibition because the court concluded the commitment process is a civil, not a second criminal, action. *In re Young*, 122 Wash. 2d 1.

A federal challenge to the constitutionality of the Washington law is pending. And on June 3, in yet another action, U.S. Judge William Dwyer of Seattle found that the state's current system of civil commitment for sexual predators fails to provide appropriate treatment. *Young v. Weston*, CN480C; *Turay v. Weston*, C91-994.

SPREADING LIKE WILDFIRE

Wisconsin's law went into effect June 2. Already there have been 16 petitions, with two state district court rulings declaring the law unconstitutional. *State v. Carpenter*, 94-CF-1216 (Dane Co.); *State v. Schmidt*, 94-CF-140 (Sauk Co.). The Kansas law went into effect in April, but the first screening of offenders won't occur until the end of August, according to Mr. Morrison, the Johnson County district attorney.

New Jersey's proposal introduced in reaction to Megan Kanka's death calls for increased penalties and mandatory minimum sentencing for violent sexual crimes, including a life sentence for a violent sexual attack on a child. Lawmakers also want lifetime supervision of those defined as "violent sexual predators" and mandatory life sentences if a second offense is committed while under lifetime supervision.

In addition, the bill requires an end-of-sentence review for every convicted sex offender and allows the attorney general to apply for the civil commitment of those who have demonstrated a pattern of compulsive behavior and pose a danger to others. The bill could be up for a vote on the Senate floor as early as Sept. 19.

Why would civil commitment procedures be needed in New Jersey if the state puts in place a system of lifetime mandatory sentences for habitual child molesters?

Because, state Senate counsel Mr. Harkness explains, civil commitment would allow prosecutors to go after those people already in the criminal system "who will max out [of their sentences] in the next couple of years . . . Obviously, we can't change the terms of their [criminal] sentences. And," he says, "it takes care of those who will slip through the cracks."

Manhattan Special Victims Bureau chief Ms. Fairstein says, "I just don't know how it's going to beat the constitutional challenge." But, she adds, "Good luck!"

Bringing God to Death Row

*The Rev. Russell A. Ford can't save
the lives of the men in his death row congregation.
But he can try to save their souls.*

Erik Brady

USA Today

Boydton, Va.

Russ Ford used to watch when his friends died. He doesn't anymore. Now he watches the faces of other witnesses at Virginia executions.

"I still see the horror," he says softly. "But I see it reflected in the faces of others."

Ford does not look away to avoid the sight of state-sponsored death. He does so because of what he saw in the eyes of child-killer Albert Clozza, just as the switch was pulled to Virginia's oak electric chair.

Words don't fail Ford often. But what he saw four years ago in those other-worldly eyes is hard to say.

Maybe he looked directly into a human soul.

"Bert's eyes were wide open, like windows," Ford says. "I could see deep, deep within. That look was on the other side. I was at a place no man has a right to be."

For 11 years, The Rev. Russell A. Ford has been a chaplain on death row. He has "made the walk" with 20 men. He'll make it with two more before the year is out.

It is a long, hard road from cold-blooded murderer to penitent pilgrim. Ford likens it to the spiritual journey in Dante's *Divine Comedy.* Danta visits souls in hell and purgatory on his way to heaven. Fellow poet Virgil is his guide.

"I see myself as Virgil, a spiritual guide," says Ford, 43, a broad-shouldered Southern Baptist minister. "Virgil doesn't know all the routes and back roads to heaven, but he has traveled enough to know some of the signposts. I help the men on 'row' on their journeys. I can't show them the way. They have to find it for themselves. But I can help."

THE VALLEY OF DEATH

Morris Mason died hard. He was 32 when the state put him to death in 1985. It was Ford's first execution. He had no clue what to do.

"I walked in reading the 23rd Psalm, just like the movies," Ford says. " 'Yea, though I walk through the valley of the shadow of death, I will fear no evil.' It's a beautiful prayer, but it had no meaning for Morris. There was no connection. He died alone and afraid."

Mason's hands raised up as the current surged through him. Those hands, like Clozza's eyes, haunt Ford. That was the night he learned dead men are taken from the chair to a "cooldown" room where sandbags are used to flatten fused joints.

Mason was a farmworker who raped an elderly woman, hit her with an ax, nailed her to a chair and set her house on fire.

"These men are responsible for tragic death, in most cases involving beastly attacks," Ford says. "But Christ died for all of our sins. These men committed terrible sin, but they are not beyond God's love."

It is not a popular position. The Rev. Joseph M. Vought is a Lutheran minister who works with Ford. He says some in his congregation at first questioned his work's worth.

"There is a feeling we should not be giving these men aid and comfort; they gave none to their victims," Vought says. "But the Bible is filled with stories of redemption. No soul is beyond redemption."

That is the cornerstone of Gateway Parish, the non-profit organization through which Ford conducts his ministry of the 58 men now on Virginia's death row.

Ford's first 19 executions were electrocutions. Now the condemned may choose lethal injection instead. Ford sees little difference.

"Lethal injection is thought of as somehow more humane, like putting a dog to

From *USA Today Newspaper,* August 25, 1995, p. 9A. © 1995 by USA Today, a division of Gannett Company, Inc. Reprinted by permission.

sleep," he says. "Killing a healthy body is not humane."

Ford opposes the death penalty, but it's not the point of his ministry. "We take what is, the death penalty, and work within that reality."

THE GATE AND THE WAY

Clozza was the 150th person to die in the United States since the death penalty was reinstated in 1976. The number now is near 300.

Ford wept on the ride home the night Clozza died. Marie Deans, an advocate for death row inmates, was his passenger. "Russ was at that vortex between life and death," she says. "You've got to keep one hand on the lifeline. To do this work, I like to tell Russ, you must be a courageous fool."

That comes at great physical cost. Some nights, Ford can't sleep.

"There is a lot of pain associated with his work," says Ford's wife, Teresa. "But the wisdom he's gained has blessed our relationship."

They live with three teen-age children in Chesterfield, Va., outside Richmond. It is 110 miles to death row at Mecklenburg Correctional Center; 55 miles to the death house at Greensville Correctional Center. Ford visits Mecklenburg in Boydton at least once a week. He talks to men standing at the bars of the common area outside their cells or, more often, through the small pass-through in their solid cell doors.

"I like to see men in their cells," he says. "How they own the space they're in says a lot about them emotionally and spiritually."

Once a man gets an execution date, Ford visits more often. By the time a man is transferred to Greensville, at least 15 days before execution, Ford is with him daily.

Chaplains in other states often are on prison payrolls; in Virginia, churches provide them. Ford appreciates his independence, though he says some prison guards regard him with suspicion, if not disdain, for ministering to murderers.

"I'm sure some people think that," says Ronald Angelone, director of the Virginia Department of Corrections, though he says he doesn't feel that way.

"Russ Ford has a commitment spiritually," Angelone says. "I respect him deeply for that. But states make laws that individuals who commit certain crimes, gruesome murders, face an ultimate penalty."

LOVE YOUR ENEMY

Almost a year ago, a friend gave Ford a copy of *The Chamber*, John Grisham's 1994 best seller.

"I've heard it's pretty accurate in its descriptions of death row," Ford says. "But I can't bring myself to read it. I've lived it."

The chaplain in *The Chamber* is a minor character who shows up on the day the book's protagonist dies. The chaplain does not walk with the condemned to the gas chamber, instead finding a dark corner to cry.

Ford admits he wasn't much more effective at his first execution.

"Morris looked at me and said to tell the boys back at 'row' he'd taken it like a man," Ford says. "I said I would. And then he died—cold and distant. I never reached him."

Ford worked three more executions in the next three years. And each time he felt he had failed the men. Like Mason, they died hard.

Then came Alton Waye, who had stabbed a 61-year-old woman 42 times with a butcher knife. Ford made little progress with Waye in the months before he was taken to the death house, then in Richmond.

Days before Waye's 1989 death, Ford walked in to find him singing spirituals. Ford was stunned. Waye's temperament was considered mean even on death row. But now there was a palpable peace about him.

"I could not believe this was the same man," Ford says. "He'd had a genuine conversion experience."

Waye asked to be baptized the night before he died. Twelve members of the death squad accompanied them to the chapel. There, hands joined, they sang *Amazing Grace* and said the Lord's Prayer.

"You have to understand how unusual this is," Ford says. "The death squad holds the condemned in contempt. They see themselves as representing the victim's family. But this time they saw the change. Alton hugged them. 'Russ,' he said, 'they don't really want to kill me.' He took us all on a journey."

Ford had found another signpost: Love your enemy.

"Jesus didn't teach us to love our enemies for their good," Ford says. "It is for our own good—to keep from becoming the enemy. There is the answer, for all of us."

FORGIVE US OUR TRESPASSES

Greg Beaver was 19 and high on drugs when he shot a Virginia state trooper who pulled him over in a stolen car in 1985. He is 30 now.

"They're going to execute me in the next year or so," he says. "The flesh is nervous. But in my mind, I'm getting prepared—for my day of reckoning, I guess you'd say."

Beaver smiles wanly. He stands behind bars on a cement floor in the common area outside his cell, wearing shorts but no shirt. A fan whirring in the corner is as close as death row gets to air conditioning.

"Most of them here have an innocence claim," Beaver says. "I don't profess to any. I did it. I shot a trooper. I was 19, stupid, scared and made the biggest mistake of my life." He shrugs. "Obviously."

Ford has been working with Beaver for years. The one-on-one will intensify when Beaver gets an execution date. But the rapport is already there. That's part of Ford's method. He is minister, friend, confessor and link to the outside.

"Religion isn't just words with Russ," Beaver says. "Before you can bring salvation to a man, you have to connect on a personal level. Russ does that."

Prayer is usually free-form, but there is sometimes formal prayer, too. The Lord's Prayer contains another signpost on the journey. *Forgive us our trespasses, as we forgive those who trespass against us.*

Ford tells the men he counsels there are two things they must do on the journey. They must forgive themselves for the grievousness of their sins. And they must forgive those who will put them to death.

"For me, I'm finding those two things difficult," Beaver says. "How can I forgive myself when I know that man had a wife and children?"

Yet he also believes the death penalty is immoral. "That's why it's hard not to hold animosity for the people who'll carry it out. But I know if I hang onto my hate I'm doing more harm to me than them."

THOU SHALT NOT KILL

Religion has not often been a large part of these men's lives until Ford begins working with them. Many are men who, if they used the Lord's name, took it in vain.

But this is not the broken commandment that landed them on death row. That would be the fifth one: Thou shalt not kill.

Larry Stout was convicted of stabbing a female dry-cleaning attendant during a 1987 robbery. He's been on death row for eight years.

That's long enough to lose a lot of friends. Virginia has put to death 26 inmates since capital punishment was reinstated. Only Texas and Florida have executed more.

Days before a condemned man is transferred to Greensville, he gives away his worldly goods in a solemn death row ritual.

"It's like a wake for the person who is leaving," Stout says. He has a mother lode of these bequests. He crouches to show them through the tiny pass-through opening in his cell door—Cell No. 90 in C Pod.

Here is a composition notebook from Bert Clozza, a cigar box from Timothy Bunch, a plastic salt shaker from Wayne DeLong.

"On the outside, this stuff is junk," Stout says. "It only means something to us. I cherish these things like diamonds."

The locks and barbed wire bar the men from escape. Ford bars their minds from it. He asks men to face their inner darkness. He calls it dungeon work—slaying the dragons. The work must be done. There is no salvation without it.

"Jesus tells us in John's gospel that men love darkness more than light," Ford says. "We all have a dark side. These men lived on it.

"They must come to grips with what they have done . . . and then come to know God's forgiveness. This is not coddling criminals. It is a painful passage."

THE ENEMY WITHIN

The men on death row are there for a reason. They have committed crimes of the most despicable nature. They belong in jail.

"They are enemies of society," Ford says. "But when we kill them, we are allowing their evil to contaminate us. If someone crawls in my window tonight to harm my family, I would go at them tooth and nail. But should we let that kind of passion dictate public policy? Sometimes we commit evil in the name of justice."

Ford is thinking of the gurney on which men lie with arms extended in the shape of a cross—an irony, he says, that is lost on the state.

"There is less trauma associated with the gurney" than the chair, he says, "but dynamically the men confront the same

issues. The state offers a sedative, but I encourage them not to take it. I challenge them to embrace the moment . . . be alive as long as you can."

The mission is salvation. But Ford also tries to give a man what he calls a "good death experience"—with less fear, more dignity.

Ford finds answers for this in the Bible and beyond. His small library is crammed with books. He is a devotee of Jungian psychology, Joseph Campbell's *Myths to Live By* and C. S. Lewis' *Chronicles of Narnia*. He reads what the world's great religions say about death.

"The best religions in the world," he says, "require self-honesty."

Ford tells many parables, but almost all the men hear the story of the rabbi's son who goes to live for a time in a neighboring town.

When the son returns, his father asks if that town was different. Yes, the son says, there they teach you to love your enemy. We teach the same, the father protests. Yes, but in this town, the son says, they teach you to love the enemy within.

HIS FATHER'S BUSINESS

No man is beyond redemption, but some reject it. Ford takes such losses hard. Souls don't get second chances.

Of the 15 executed men with whom he has worked since Alton Waye, Ford says three refused to face their inner demons. One was Andrew Chabrol, a former Navy officer who in 1991 stalked and strangled a woman who had complained of his advances when she was a petty officer under his command.

Chabrol never showed an ounce of remorse, going to his death believing he'd been right to kill her.

"You could see the killer's look in his eyes," Ford says. "The way his light was lit was bad—all evil and twisted. There was no humanity there. Just the beast, nothing else."

It's how many of us like to think of men on death row. It's easier to execute a man who is seen as a symbol. But Ford finds humanity in most of men. This is why, and how, Ford soldiers on.

"This is my calling," he says. "Christ commanded us to work with the outcast and the condemned."

In high school, Ford attended a religious retreat "because the prettiest girl in the class was going." There, he says, he heard a call.

While in the seminary 20 years ago, he became an intern chaplain. In 1984, he entered death row. He was to rotate the duty with other chaplains, but when he found he had talent for it, he stayed.

Last year, its funding strained by a growing prison population, Chaplain Services of Virginia eliminated Ford's full-time post. It would have been a good time to walk away. He was exhausted at the pace. In his first several years, there had been just one execution a year. Now there were routinely three or four.

But Ford felt he couldn't forsake his friends. He took six months off to launch Gateway Parish. He says he needs $70,000 a year to make it go. He seeks donations from churches and benefactors. It is not an easy sell. Why help murderers?

Ford has a ready answer: "Christ was crucified between two thieves, death row inmates condemned at the hand of the state. Jesus told one, 'Today you will be with me in Paradise.' You see, Christ was the first death row chaplain. He was about His Father's business."

THERE ARE NONE RIGHTEOUS

Albert Clozza abducted a 13-year-old girl as she walked to a bookmobile in 1983. He sodomized her and penetrated her with a tree branch before beating her to death.

How does one forgive oneself for such criminal cowardice? Clozza saw himself as unworthy of God's forgiveness, or his own. He had murdered an innocent child. Hadn't he assured himself a place in hell?

He was the first executed in the new death house at Greensville. Ford worked with him intensively there. Midway through the 15-day countdown, Clozza came to a point where he faced what he had done.

"He took a child; he was heinous with her," Ford says. "But Bert found the courage to look at that. And he found, just maybe, God loves someone like him, a wretched murderer."

Ford says Clozza began to glow. Was it a rush of endorphins—or a physical manifestation of grace?

As with Waye, word got around the death house that Clozza had experienced a spiritual change.

The night before he died, Ford and another chaplain celebrated the Eucharist for Clozza, a Catholic who had gotten into Buddhism.

"Working with men of other faiths has

taught me the empowering nature of the sacraments," Ford says. "We offered everyone Communion. The death squad stepped back, as if someone said, 'Boo!' "

But when Ford asked whether any wished to speak, the death squad captain stepped up. "There are none righteous," the captain said, "No, no one."

"I get chills down my spine just thinking about it," says Steve Northup, one of Clozza's lawyers. "It was one of the most profound religious experiences of my life."

Condemned men are offered a final statement, all part of the death house ritual. Clozza chose not to make one. But he had joked with Ford about leaving these last words: "Anyone coming with me?"

Just before Ford's fateful gaze into Clozza's eyes, the death row chaplain offered his friend a final thought. "You asked who will join you," he said. "All will follow. No one will be left behind."

Clozza said he'd discovered the gift of courage. Then, a moment before the killing current—that look.

What was it? It haunts Ford still.

"Bert was leaving his body. He had an openness of soul. There is a point at which death is a private act, something between you and your Maker. I will be greeted there in my time, but I should not be there before.

"I haven't spent time trying to find words for what I saw. The best I can do is go back to The Divine Comedy. Virgil led Dante through hell and purgatory but he could only go so far. A guide can go only two-thirds of the way.

"He must stay on the shore."

Anger and Ambivalence

Most Americans support capital punishment, yet few inmates are actually executed. Why the country has mixed feelings about putting people to death.

DAVID A. KAPLAN

F IT'S SWIFT PUNISHMENT YOU want, you'll love the case of Giuseppe Zangara. Back on Feb. 15, 1933, in the middle of Miami, this slightly deranged malcontent pulled a gun on President-elect Franklin Roosevelt and fired repeatedly. He missed, but mortally wounded the mayor of Chicago. Thirty-three days later—after arrest, guilty plea and sentence—Zangara was electrocuted in Florida's "Old Sparky." In the good old days of capital punishment, there wasn't even enough time to sign a book deal.

The machinery of capital justice cranks a lot more slowly now. Death row is a growth industry. The rare inmate to die hangs on close to 10 years before meeting the executioner. In Florida, triple-killer Gary Alvord is celebrating his 22d year, still hoping, still appealing. Up the interstate, one quarter of Georgia's 109 death-row prisoners have been there since at least 1980. And in Montana, until May 10, Duncan McKenzie had avoided the lethal needle for 20 years. In fact, he fell just one vote short of gaining his eighth stay of execution. He may have been the cold-blooded murderer of a schoolteacher, but he had chutzpah. His last argument in court: two

decades on death row was itself "cruel and unusual" punishment, and therefore a violation of his constitutional rights. Never mind that McKenzie's lawyers had asked for the prior stays and had helped to create the judicial black hole he found himself in. A federal court didn't buy the claim and within days McKenzie became the first inmate executed in Montana since FDR's third term.

Give or take a few miscreants, there are currently 3,000 inmates on American death rows. That's more by far than at any time in world history. California alone has 407, followed by Texas with 398 and Florida with 342. Yet for each of the last 19 years—ever since the U.S. Supreme Court allowed states to resume capital punishment—no more than about 2 percent of the death-row total has ever been executed. In 1994, the number was 31; this year, the figure might reach 50. Spending a reported annual $90 million on capital cases, California has managed to gas just two inmates—and one of them waived all his appeals.

Capital punishment in America is a paper tiger. Despite tough political bluster and overwhelming poll numbers, the nation is ambivalent about the ultimate penalty. For

many years, legislators, governors, judges and victims'-rights activists have vowed to finally get on with it—to bar endless appeals, sanction mollycoddling defense lawyers, root out of office bleeding-heart governors. Congress passed reforms and cut funding for defense lawyers, the U.S. Supreme Court cracked down, and leaders like New York Gov. Mario Cuomo were voted out. The press, NEWSWEEK included, proclaimed in various aqueous illusions that the floodgates would soon open or that the logjam was about to be broken.

It's never happened. State prosecutors' offices remain understaffed and overwhelmed, courts have hopelessly long backlogs (assuming they can find lawyers for the defendants in the first place) and juries in most states enthusiastically continue to send killers to death row. For every inmate to die, though, there are five new ones to take his (or, in the rare case, her) cell. To clean up the backlog, states would have to execute a killer a day (Christmas and Easter included) through 2021. Even Texas—far and away the nation's death-penalty capital, with a third of all executions since 1976—manages to dispatch only about one in eight condemned inmates.

6. PUNISHMENT AND CORRECTIONS

At the water cooler and in the streets of Union, S.C., people argue about what fate the Susan Smiths of the world deserve. And race and poverty have never gone away in the vexing national debate over the death penalty. But those moral and ideological questions have now been overshadowed by a simpler fact: people sentenced to death nonetheless live on in prison. What's the most frequent cause of death for death-row inmates? As of 1992, according to the U.S. Bureau of Justice Statistics, electrocution and lethal in-

---

Oscar Ortiz III
Age: 19
San Antonio, Texas, July 6.
One death sentence.

Every year, about 260 Americans are sentenced to die—though actual executions are usually delayed for years. Oscar Ortiz III and the men whose profiles follow are among those whose juries, unlike Susan Smith's, gave them the death penalty last month. Ortiz abducted businessman Joe Ince Jr., 38, from an ATM on Jan. 19, 1994. After forcing Ince to divulge his personal identification number, Ortiz drove him, in Ince's truck, to a second ATM. When the PIN worked, Ortiz rolled down the passenger window, presumably to keep blood from splattering the upholstery, and shot Ince in the head. Ortiz drove to three more ATMs, then dumped Ince on a highway. He died 12 hours later.

---

jection were mere runnerups. The No. 1 killer: "Natural Causes." What becomes of a penal policy that on its face is a sham?

Ask Alex Kozinski, one of the country's most outspoken and conservative federal judges who almost always upholds death sentences. "We have constructed a machine that is extremely expensive, chokes our legal institutions, visits repeated trauma on victims' families and ultimately produces nothing like the benefits we would expect from an effective system of capital punishment," he wrote in a recent, controversial op-ed article in The New York Times. "This is surely the worst of all worlds."

The systemic ambivalence about the death penalty is reflected in virtually all the 38 states that have death chambers open for business. During his election campaign last year, South Carolina's new attorney general, Charlie Condon, was so taken with a triple execution in Arkansas that he proposed doing away with his state's electric chair. His reform? An "electric sofa," to juice several inmates at a time. South Carolina's death-row population is 59; its last execution was in 1991. Ambivalence may best be demonstrated by the Smith verdict itself last week. While polls showed

wide support for her execution, it took jurors less than three hours to reach a unanimous verdict to spare her.

NEW YORK, AFTER 20 YEARS OF abolitionist administrations in Albany, this spring became the newest state with capital punishment on the books. When it will post a job listing for executioners is another matter. It typically takes a decade before all courts sign off on a death statute. New York's is so full of procedural safeguards that some wonder if executions will ever resume. "That new law essentially says, 'KICK ME,'" observes law professor Franklin Zimring, of the University of California, Berkeley. "They'll be lucky to have an execution in the 21st century." In a liberal state like New York, that may be the perfect political outcome for Republican Gov. George Pataki. He got the death penalty out of legislative purgatory, but he'll never actually have to deal with administering it.

That may also be the strategy of Bill Clinton. Already his re-election-campaign spots disingenuously boast of adding dozens of new crimes to the federal death statute. And the U.S. government is busily building its own death row in the Midwest, complete with a $300,000 death chamber, even though currently there are only six federal inmates convicted of capital crimes. Trouble is, federal executions, assuming they even get underway this decade, are unlikely to be more than a criminal-justice blip. The new laws contain such everyday offenses as killing a chicken inspector of the Agriculture Department.

Nobody in the capital-punishment system wants to accept blame for the current stalemate. Prosecutors blame judges, who blame courts, who blame the law, which gets passed down by Supreme Court justices, who don't speak, except to Nina Totenberg on occasion. But the primary whipping boys for execution gridlock have long been defense lawyers. It's true that a ferociously dedicated group of abolitionists, among them David Bruck, Smith's counsel, have fought the death penalty in every venue across the land. The fact is, judges are the ones who grant stays of execution, courts come up with incredibly complex rules and prosecutors don't push cases along. In one Indiana case, the state took two years to transcribe the trial record of a case. In most state A.G.s' offices in the death-belt states, appeals sit around because there aren't enough government lawyers to handle the load.

AT THE TOP OF THE SYSTEM, THE U.S. Supreme Court has labored hard to get out of the death-penalty business. But the justices every year get drawn into a few major cases and wind up having to revise doctrine. Worse, while there are no justices anymore like William Brennan

or Thurgood Marshall—who voted against all death sentences all the time—the high court often still splits 5-4 on capital cases, indicating that even the Supremes can't figure things out. That leads to further confusion for lower-court judges, who have enough trouble keeping up with legal changes from two years prior. Chief Judge Gerald Tjoflat of the 11th U.S. Circuit Court of Appeals in Atlanta says that some of his colleagues spend half their time wading through capital cases. "I've been in the judging business for 28 years," Tjoflat says, "and there's nothing harder."

Some judges take an especially long time to make up their minds. In 1986, an Arizona killer named Ruben Zaragoza exhausted his state remedies and appealed to the federal district court in Phoenix. Zaragoza's case hasn't been heard from since. Judge Earl H. Carroll, who has had the case for the last nine years, declined to comment. Two years ago, Arizona Attorney General Grant Woods got so annoyed with slow federal judges in his state that he took an extraordinary step.

Michael Clagett
Age: 34
Virginia Beach, Va., July 13.
Five death sentences.

Michael Clagett liked to hang out at the Witchduck Inn in Virginia Beach, where his girlfriend had once worked as a waitress. So when the couple needed cash for a trip to Oregon, they knew they would find gas money at the "Cheers"-like pub. They arrived shortly before midnight on June 30, 1994, and found four people inside, including the owner, whom Clagett later described as his "buddy." Clagett told everyone to lie on the floor while the girlfriend took $400 from the register. Then he shot them one by one in the head. Although his attorneys attempted various defenses—including blaming the girlfriend—Clagett was his own worst enemy. He gave police a weeping, videotaped confession in which he detailed each grisly shot he fired and told reporters and the police that he deserved to die. After deliberating for five hours, the jury agreed.

Woods asked the Ninth U.S. Circuit Court of Appeals, based in San Francisco, to order the judges to rule on 30 cases that had languished for a decade. The appeals court refused. "That was real smart of Arizona," says a deputy attorney general of one Southern state. "Trying to move a federal judge is like trying to make a pig dance. It doesn't work and it annoys the pig."

The Ninth Circuit itself has come under frequent attack from politicians. That court "is the most liberal of the circuits in the United States," complains California Attorney General Dan Lungren. "Some members appear to have a strong bias against the death penalty." Lungren has in mind the notorious case of Robert Alton Harris in 1992 that embarrassed the entire federal judicial system. Harris had been before both the California and the U.S. Supreme Courts six times in his 13 years on San Quentin's death row. On the eve of his scheduled April 21 appointment with the executioner, the Ninth Circuit kept issuing stays and the justices in Washington kept lifting them—into the predawn hours. Finally, an enraged Supreme Court—citing the Ninth Circuit's "civil disobedience"—ordered the circuit judges to abstain from any further interference. Harris was executed in the gas chamber forthwith. The case continues to haunt all participants in the California system.

Lungren correctly notes that the 24-member Ninth Circuit appeals court does in fact have several judges—from both ends of the political spectrum—who consistently vote against death sentences and thereby slow down the tumbrels. But so what? Of California's 407 death-row inmates, only eight have cases pending before the Ninth Circuit. And what of Lungren's own office? Of the state's 407 condemned prisoners, 120 are totally stalled before the state supreme court because there are no defense lawyers for them. (Constitutional law entitles them to representation.) "We haven't appointed counsel for anyone in 1993, 1994 and 1995," says Robert Reichman, a court administrator.

Douglas Kelly
Age: 37
Van Nuys, Calif.,
July 10.
One death sentence.

Five times over the years, Douglas Kelly had been convicted of sexually or violently assaulting women. But Sara Weir, a woman who befriended Kelly at the health club where he worked as a janitor, didn't know that. On or before Sept. 7, 1993, Kelly lured Weir, 19, to the apartment he shared with his girlfriend and her 10-year-old son. He raped and stabbed Weir 34 times with a pair of sewing scissors, then pushed Weir's body under the boy's bed. He put a plastic bag on Weir's head, a plastic Dodgers helmet on top of that, and stole her Ford Bronco. Though the defense admitted the murder, Kelly said that he did not rape Weir or steal from her—aggravating factors triggering the death penalty. But after four women testified that Kelly had raped them, the jury chose death.

"We're on 1992's cases." In short, that means at least three extra years of life and free meals for California's condemned. Capital punishment is about the only area of litigation where there aren't lawyers climbing over each other to earn a fee.

With his considerable political skills, why doesn't Lungren press the state supreme court to find lawyers, or urge the state bar to get members to take their ethics obligations seriously? Or, as one Ninth Circuit judge asked, why doesn't he simply call a press conference to explain why more than one quarter of California's condemned population is no closer to execution now than three years ago when the Ninth Circuit was being pummeled for its handling of the Harris case? "While this may be an area of legitimate concern," Lungren answered in a prepared statement, "we do not have any direct jurisdiction over it and, at a time when my own department is facing cuts of $10 million, it is questionable how much leverage we would have in achieving funding for court-appointed defense lawyers."

Ambivalence is not limited to judges and prosecutors. Earlier this year, the Florida clemency board voted to defer a decision on Danny Doyle—a mentally impaired murderer who was sentenced 13 years earlier—until the year 2020. He'll remain in death-row lockup, says Joe Bizarro, spokesman for the Florida attorney general. Jurors, too, seem to have mixed feelings. In 1987, Louisiana's electric chair got humming. It claimed four lives in one nine-day period and four more in a five-week period later in the year. In the following 21 months, juries throughout the state imposed only two death sentences. Homicide rates, among the highest in the nation, hadn't changed. Observers suggested that jurors lost their nerve, now that a death sentence was no longer an illusion.

There are really only two political positions to take on the death penalty. You can support it or oppose it. The great irony about American capital punishment, as Zimring says, is that "no one on either side can defend the current system, which is hypocritical and unprincipled." Unless the purpose of the penalty is to create a gruesome illusion, there are just two alternatives. Those who write the statutes can narrow the category of killers eligible for death down to a manageable few, as many advocates of capital punishment are beginning to suggest. Single out the terrorists, mass murderers and contract killers. Use limited resources and political capital to maneuver them into the death chambers. After all, they're the ones—not the liquor-store holdup guy who panicked—that most citizens want dead anyway.

The other choice, of course, is to summon up the political will to commence executions

---

Rogers Lacaze
Age: 18
New Orleans, July 21.
Three death sentences.

On March 4, 1995, at the Kim Anh Vietnamese restaurant in New Orleans, two employees and a police officer moonlighting as a security guard were killed during an armed robbery. At first, Rogers Lacaze claimed he wasn't even in the restaurant. Then he admitted he was there but denied having a gun. His lawyer argued that Lacaze would have been splattered with blood (he wasn't) if, as prosecutors contended, he had shot policeman Ronald Williams at close range. Lacaze even took the witness stand to say, "I didn't pull no trigger, I didn't kill those peoples. Please spare my life, please!" But two eyewitnesses fingered him. Even though Lacaze's father attempted to deflect the blame by testifying he had been absent for most of his son's life, the jury took fewer than four hours to give Lacaze three death sentences.

---

in record numbers—at the very least, more than the nationwide high-water mark of 199 in 1935. That means devoting millions of tax dollars for more prosecutors, and new U.S. Supreme Court policy to give those prosecutors more leeway. In turn, that would mean more tolerance of imperfect justice. "I tell folks that if they want appeals limited to two or three years, some time we'll execute the wrong person," says Georgia Attorney General Michael Bowers. "Of course we will. We're human. But it's a question of will."

Which brings us back to Judge Kozinski, who kindled much of the current debate with his scathing indictment of the modern capital-punishment charade. Kozinski was appointed by President Reagan. Though a judicial independent and freethinker, Kozinski is firmly rooted in the tradition of judging that tries to keep one's personal views out of the courtroom. At times, he's excoriated his colleagues on the Ninth Circuit for not getting on with the death penalty. How would Kozinski feel about a system that produced several hundred executions a year?

"I'd hope it wouldn't affect how I handled cases, but I just don't know," he says. "I just don't know."

With GINNY CARROLL *in Houston,* PETER KATEL *in Miami,* THOMAS HEATH *in Denver,* KAREN SPRINGEN *in Chicago and* ANTHONY DUIGNAN-CABRERA *in New York*

Death Row, U.S.A.

TOTAL NUMBER OF DEATH ROW INMATES KNOWN TO LDF*:

(As of August 31, 1995)

Race of Defendant:

White	1,467	(48.42%)
Black	1,224	(40.42%)
Latino/Latina	234	(7.73%)
Native American	51	(1.68%)
Asian	23	(.76%)
Unknown at this issue	29	(.96%)

Gender: Male	2,978	(98.35%)
Female	50	(1.65%)

DISPOSITIONS SINCE JANUARY 1, 1973:

Executions:	295	
Suicides:	41	
Commutations:	72	(including those by the Governor of Texas resulting from favorable court decisions)

Died of natural causes, or killed while under death sentence: 92
Convictions/Sentences reversed: 1,469

JURISDICTIONS WITH CAPITAL PUNISHMENT STATUTES: 40

(Underlined jurisdictions have statutes but no sentences imposed)

Alabama, Arizona, Arkansas, California, Colorado, Connecticut, Delaware, Florida, Georgia, Idaho, Illinois, Indiana, Kansas, Kentucky, Louisiana, Maryland, Mississippi, Missouri, Montana, Nebraska, Nevada, New Hampshire, New Jersey, New Mexico, New York, North Carolina, Ohio, Oklahoma, Oregon, Pennsylvania, South Carolina, South Dakota, Tennessee, Texas, Utah, Virginia, Washington, Wyoming, U.S. Government, U.S. Military.

JURISDICTIONS WITHOUT CAPITAL PUNISHMENT STATUTES: 13

Alaska, District of Columbia, Hawaii, Iowa, Maine, Massachusetts, Michigan, Minnesota, North Dakota, Rhode Island, Vermont, West Virginia, Wisconsin.

execution update August 31, 1995

Total number of executions since the 1976 reinstatement of capital punishment (there were no executions in 1976): ***295***

'77	'78	'79	'80	'81	'82	'83	'84	'85	'86	'87	'88	'89	'90	'91	'92	'93	'94	'95
1	0	2	0	1	2	5	21	18	18	25	11	16	23	14	31	38	31	38

*NAACP Legal Defense and Educational Fund

gender of defendants executed

total number   295
    Female · 1   (.34%)
    Male · · · · · · · · · · · · · · · · · · 294   (99.66%)

gender of victims

total number   396
    Female · · · · · · · · · · · · · · · · · · 175   (44.19%)
    Male · 221   (54.81%)

race of defendants executed

White · 161   (54.58%)
Black · 117   (39.66%)
Latino · 16   (5.42%)
Native American · · · · · · · · · · · · · · 1   (.34%

race of victims

White · 326   (82.32%)
Black · 51   (12.88%)
Latino · 14   (3.53%)
Asian · 5   (1.26%)

defendant-victim racial combinations

White Defendant and
    White Victim · 223   (56.31%)
    Black Victim · 4   (1.01%)
    Asian Victim · 2   (.50%)
    Latino/a Victim · 5   (.25%)

Black Defendant and
    White Victim · 96   (24.24%)
    Black Victim · 46   (11.62%)
    Asian Victim · 2   (.50%)
    Latino Victim · 1   (.25%)

Latino Defendant and
    White Victim · 8   (2.02%)
    Latino Victim · 7   (1.77%)
    Asian Victim · 1   (.25%)

Native American and
    White Victim · 1   (.25%)

'THIS MAN HAS EXPIRED'

WITNESS TO AN EXECUTION

ROBERT JOHNSON

ROBERT JOHNSON *is professor of justice, law, and society at The American University, Washington, D.C. This article is drawn from a Distinguished Faculty Lecture, given under the auspices of the university's senate last spring.*

The death penalty has made a comeback in recent years. In the late sixties and through most of the seventies, such a thing seemed impossible. There was a moratorium on executions in the U.S., backed by the authority of the Supreme Court. The hiatus lasted roughly a decade. Coming on the heels of a gradual but persistent decline in the use of the death penalty in the Western world, it appeared to some that executions would pass from the American scene [cf. *Commonweal*, January 15, 1988]. Nothing could have been further from the truth.

Beginning with the execution of Gary Gilmore in 1977, over 100 people have been put to death, most of them in the last few years. Some 2,200 prisoners are presently confined on death rows across the nation. The majority of these prisoners have lived under sentence of death for years, in some cases a decade or more, and are running out of legal appeals. It is fair to say that the death penalty is alive and well in America, and that executions will be with us for the foreseeable future.

Gilmore's execution marked the resurrection of the modern death penalty and was big news. It was commemorated in a best-selling tome by Norman Mailer, *The Executioner's Song.* The title was deceptive. Like others who have examined the death penalty, Mailer told us a great deal about the condemned but very little about the executioners. Indeed, if we dwell on Mailer's account, the executioner's story is not only unsung; it is distorted.

Gilmore's execution was quite atypical. His was an instance of state-assisted suicide accompanied by an element of romance and played out against a backdrop of media fanfare. Unrepentant and unafraid, Gilmore refused to appeal his conviction. He dared the state of Utah to take his life, and the media repeated the challenge until it became a taunt that may well have goaded officials to action. A failed suicide pact with his lover staged only days before the execution, using drugs she delivered to him in a visit marked by unusual intimacy, added a hint of melodrama to the proceedings. Gilmore's final words, ''Let's do it,'' seemed to invite the lethal hail of bullets from the firing squad. The nonchalant phrase, at once fatalistic and brazenly rebellious, became Gilmore's epitaph. It clinched his outlaw-hero image, and found its way onto tee shirts that confirmed his celebrity status.

Befitting a celebrity, Gilmore was treated with unusual leniency by prison officials during his confinement on death row. He was, for example, allowed to hold a party the night before his execution, during which he was free to eat, drink, and make merry with his guests until the early morning hours. This is not entirely unprecedented. Notorious English convicts of centuries past would throw farewell balls in prison on the eve of their executions. News accounts of such affairs sometimes included a commentary on the richness of the table and the quality of the dancing. For the record, Gilmore served Tang, Kool-Aid, cookies, and coffee, later supplemented by contraband pizza and an unidentified liquor. Periodically, he gobbled drugs obligingly provided by the prison pharmacy. He played a modest arrangement of rock music albums but refrained from dancing.

Gilmore's execution generally, like his parting fete, was decidedly out of step with the tenor of the modern death penalty. Most condemned prisoners fight to save their lives, not to have them taken. They do not see their fate in romantic terms; there are no farewell parties. Nor are they given medication to ease their anxiety or win their compliance. The subjects of typical executions remain anonymous to the public and even to their keepers. They are very much alone at the end.

In contrast to Mailer's account, the focus of the research I have conducted is on the executioners themselves as they carry out typical executions. In my experience executioners—not

From *Commonweal*, January 13, 1989, pp. 9-15. © 1989 by Commonweal Foundation. Reprinted by permission.

unlike Mailer himself—can be quite voluble, and sometimes quite moving, in expressing themselves. I shall draw upon their words to describe the death work they carry out in our name.

DEATH WORK AND DEATH WORKERS

Executioners are not a popular subject of social research, let alone conversation at the dinner table or cocktail party. We simply don't give the subject much thought. When we think of executioners at all, the imagery runs to individual men of disreputable, or at least questionable, character who work stealthily behind the scenes to carry out their grim labors. We picture hooded men hiding in the shadow of the gallows, or anonymous figures lurking out of sight behind electric chairs, gas chambers, firing blinds, or, more recently, hospital gurneys. We wonder who would do such grisly work and how they sleep at night.

This image of the executioner as a sinister and often solitary character is today misleading. To be sure, a few states hire free-lance executioners and traffic in macabre theatrics. Executioners may be picked up under cover of darkness and some may still wear black hoods. But today, executions are generally the work of a highly disciplined and efficient team of correctional officers.

Broadly speaking, the execution process as it is now practiced starts with the prisoner's confinement on death row, an oppressive prison-within-a-prison where the condemned are housed, sometimes for years, awaiting execution. Death work gains momentum when an execution date draws near and the prisoner is moved to the death house, a short walk from the death chamber. Finally, the process culminates in the death watch, a twenty-four-hour period that ends when the prisoner has been executed.

This final period, the death watch, is generally undertaken by correctional officers who work as a team and report directly to the prison warden. The warden or his representative, in turn, must by law preside over the execution. In many states, it is a member of the death watch or execution team, acting under the warden's authority, who in fact plays the formal role of executioner. Though this officer may technically work alone, his teammates view the execution as a shared responsibility. As one officer on the death watch told me in no uncertain terms: "We all take part in it; we all play 100 percent in it, too. That takes the load off this one individual [who pulls the switch]." The formal executioner concurred. "Everyone on the team can do it, and nobody will tell you I did it. I know my team." I found nothing in my research to dispute these claims.

The officers of these death watch teams are our modern executioners. As part of a larger study of the death work process, I studied one such group. This team, comprised of nine seasoned officers of varying ranks, had carried out five electrocutions at the time I began my research. I interviewed each officer on the team after the fifth execution, then served as an official witness at a sixth electrocution. Later, I served as a behind-the-scenes observer during their seventh execution.

The results of this phase of my research form the substance of this essay.

THE DEATH WATCH TEAM

The death watch or execution team members refer to themselves, with evident pride, as simply "the team." This pride is shared by other correctional officials. The warden at the institution I was observing praised members of the team as solid citizens—in his words, country boys. These country boys, he assured me, could be counted on to do the job and do it well. As a fellow administrator put it, "an execution is something [that] needs to be done and good people, dedicated people who believe in the American system, should do it. And there's a certain amount of feeling, probably one to another, that they're part of that—that when they have to hang tough, they can do it, and they can do it right. And that it's just the right thing to do."

The official view is that an execution is a job that has to be done, and done right. The death penalty is, after all, the law of the land. In this context, the phrase "done right" means that an execution should be a proper, professional, dignified undertaking. In the words of a prison administrator, "We had to be sure that we did it properly, professionally, and [that] we gave as much dignity to the person as we possibly could in the process....If you've gotta do it, it might just as well be done the way it's supposed to be done—without any sensation."

In the language of the prison officials, "proper" refers to procedures that go off smoothly; "professional" means without personal feelings that intrude on the procedures in any way. The desire for executions that take place "without any sensation" no doubt refers to the absence of media sensationalism, particularly if there should be an embarrassing and undignified hitch in the procedures, for example, a prisoner who breaks down or becomes violent and must be forcibly placed in the electric chair as witnesses, some from the media, look on in horror. Still, I can't help but note that this may be a revealing slip of the tongue. For executions are indeed meant to go off without any human feeling, without any sensation. A profound absence of feeling would seem to capture the bureaucratic ideal embodied in the modern execution.

The view of executions held by the execution team members parallels that of correctional administrators but is somewhat more restrained. The officers of the team are closer to the killing and dying, and are less apt to wax abstract or eloquent in describing the process. Listen to one man's observations:

It's a job. I don't take it personally. You know, I don't take it like I'm having a grudge against this person and this person has done something to me. I'm just carrying out a job, doing what I was asked to do....This man has been sentenced to death in the courts. This is the law and he broke this law, and he has to suffer the consequences. And one of the consequences is to put him to death.

I found that few members of the execution team support the death penalty outright or without reservation. Having seen executions close up, many of them have lingering doubts about the justice or wisdom of this sanction. As one officer put it:

I'm not sure the death penalty is the right way. I don't know if there is a right answer. So I look at it like this: if it's gotta be done, at least it can be done in a humane way, if there is such a word for it. . . . The only way it should be done, I feel, is the way we do it. It's done professionally; it's not no horseplaying. Everything is done by documentation. On time. By the book.

Arranging executions that occur "without any sensation" and that go "by the book" is no mean task, but it is a task that is undertaken in earnest by the execution team. The tone of the enterprise is set by the team leader, a man who takes a hard-boiled, no-nonsense approach to correctional work in general and death work in particular. "My style," he says, "is this: if it's a job to do, get it done. Do it and that's it." He seeks out kindred spirits, men who see killing condemned prisoners as a job—a dirty job one does reluctantly, perhaps, but above all a job one carries out dispassionately and in the line of duty.

To make sure that line of duty is a straight and accurate one, the death watch team has been carefully drilled by the team leader in the mechanics of execution. The process has been broken down into simple, discrete tasks and practiced repeatedly. The team leader describes the division of labor in the following exchange:

the execution team is a nine-officer team and each one has certain things to do. When I would train you, maybe you'd buckle a belt, that might be all you'd have to do. . . . And you'd be expected to do one thing and that's all you'd be expected to do. And if everybody does what they were taught, or what they were trained to do, at the end the man would be put in the chair and everything would be complete. It's all come together now.

So it's broken down into very small steps. . . .

Very small, yes. Each person has *one* thing to do.

I see. What's the purpose of breaking it down into such small steps?

So people won't get confused. I've learned it's kind of a tense time. When you're executin' a person, killing a person—you call it killin', executin', whatever you want—the man dies anyway. I find the less you got on your mind, why, the better you'll carry it out. So it's just very simple things. And so far, you know, it's all come together, we haven't had any problems.

This division of labor allows each man on the execution team to become a specialist, a technician with a sense of pride in his work. Said one man,

My assignment is the leg piece. Right leg. I roll his pants leg up, place a piece [electrode] on his leg, strap his leg in. . . . I've got all the moves down pat. We train from different posts; I can do any of them. But that's my main post.

The implication is not that the officers are incapable of performing multiple or complex tasks, but simply that it is more efficient to focus each officer's efforts on one easy task.

An essential part of the training is practice. Practice is meant to produce a confident group, capable of fast and accurate performance under pressure. The rewards of practice are reaped in improved performance. Executions take place with increasing efficiency, and eventually occur with precision. "The first one was grisly," a team member confided to me. He explained that there was a certain amount of fumbling, which made the execution seem interminable. There were technical problems as well: The generator was set too high so the body was badly burned. But that is the past, the officer assured me. "The ones now, we know what we're doing. It's just like clockwork."

THE DEATH WATCH

The death-watch team is deployed during the last twenty-four hours before an execution. In the state under study, the death watch starts at 11 o'clock the night before the execution and ends at 11 o'clock the next night when the execution takes place. At least two officers would be with the prisoner at any given time during that period. Their objective is to keep the prisoner alive and "on schedule." That is, to move him through a series of critical and cumulatively demoralizing junctures that begin with his last meal and end with his last walk. When the time comes, they must deliver the prisoner up for execution as quickly and unobtrusively as possible.

Broadly speaking, the job of the death watch officer, as one man put it, "is to sit and keep the inmate calm for the last twenty-four hours—and get the man ready to go." Keeping a condemned prisoner calm means, in part, serving his immediate needs. It seems paradoxical to think of the death watch officers as providing services to the condemned, but the logistics of the job make service a central obligation of the officers. Here's how one officer made this point:

Well, you can't help but be involved with many of the things that he's involved with. Because if he wants to make a call to his family, well, you'll have to dial the number. And you keep records of whatever calls he makes. If he wants a cigarette, well he's not allowed to keep matches so you light it for him. You've got to pour his coffee, too. So you're aware what he's doing. It's not like you can just ignore him. You've gotta just be with him whether he wants it or not, and cater to his needs.

Officers cater to the condemned because contented inmates are easier to keep under control. To a man, the officers say this is so. But one can never trust even a contented, condemned prisoner.

The death-watch officers see condemned prisoners as men with explosive personalities. "You don't know what, what a man's gonna do," noted one officer. "He's liable to snap, he's liable to pass out. We watch him all the time to prevent him from committing suicide. You've got to be ready—he's liable to do anything." The prisoner is never out of at least one officer's sight. Thus surveillance is constant, and control, for all intents and purposes, is total.

Relations between the officers and their charges during the death watch can be quite intense. Watching and being watched are central to this enterprise, and these are always engaging activities, particularly when the stakes are life and death. These relations are, nevertheless, utterly impersonal; there are no grudges but neither is there compassion or fellow-feeling. Officers are civil but cool; they keep an emotional distance from the men they are about to kill. To do otherwise, they maintain, would make it harder to execute condemned prisoners. The attitude of the officers is that the prisoners arrive as strangers and are easier to kill if they stay that way.

During the last five or six hours, two specific team officers are assigned to guard the prisoner. Unlike their more taciturn and aloof colleagues on earlier shifts, these officers make a conscious effort to talk with the prisoner. In one officer's words, "We keep them right there and keep talking to them—about anything except the chair." The point of these conversations is not merely to pass time; it is to keep tabs on the prisoner's state of mind, and to steer him away from subjects that might depress, anger, or otherwise upset him. Sociability, in other words, quite explicitly serves as a source of social control. Relationships, such as they are, serve purely manipulative ends. This is impersonality at its worst, masquerading as concern for the strangers one hopes to execute with as little trouble as possible.

Generally speaking, as the execution moves closer, the mood becomes more somber and subdued. There is a last meal. Prisoners can order pretty much what they want, but most eat little or nothing at all. At this point, the prisoners may steadfastly maintain that their executions will be stayed. Such bravado is belied by their loss of appetite. "You can see them going down," said one officer. "Food is the last thing they got on their minds."

Next the prisoners must box their meager worldly goods. These are inventoried by the staff, recorded on a one-page checklist form, and marked for disposition to family or friends. Prisoners are visibly saddened, even moved to tears, by this procedure, which at once summarizes their lives and highlights the imminence of death. At this point, said one of the officers, "I really get into him; I watch him real close." The execution schedule, the officer pointed out, is "picking up momentum, and we don't want to lose control of the situation."

This momentum is not lost on the condemned prisoner. Critical milestones have been passed. The prisoner moves in a limbo existence devoid of food or possessions; he has seen the last of such things, unless he receives a stay of execution and rejoins the living. His identity is expropriated as well. The critical juncture in this regard is the shaving of the man's head (including facial hair) and right leg. Hair is shaved to facilitate the electrocution; it reduces physical resistance to electricity and minimizes singeing and burning. But the process has obvious psychological significance as well, adding greatly to the momentum of the execution.

The shaving procedure is quite public and intimidating. The condemned man is taken from his cell and seated in the middle of the tier. His hands and feet are cuffed, and he is dressed only in undershorts. The entire death watch team is assembled around him. They stay at a discrete distance, but it is obvious that they are there to maintain control should he resist in any way or make any untoward move. As a rule, the man is overwhelmed. As one officer told me in blunt terms, "Come eight o'clock, we've got a dead man. Eight o'clock is when we shave the man. We take his identity; it goes with the hair." This taking of identity is indeed a collective process—the team makes a forceful "we," the prisoner their helpless object. The staff is confident that the prisoner's capacity to resist is now compromised. What is left of the man erodes gradually and, according the officers, perceptibly over the remaining three hours before the execution.

After the prisoner has been shaved, he is then made to shower and don a fresh set of clothes for the execution. The clothes are unremarkable in appearance, except that velcro replaces buttons and zippers, to reduce the chance of burning the body. The main significance of the clothes is symbolic: they mark the prisoner as a man who is ready for execution. Now physically "prepped," to quote one team member, the prisoner is placed in an empty tomblike cell, the death cell. All that is left is the wait. During this fateful period, the prisoner is more like an object "without any sensation" than like a flesh-and-blood person on the threshold of death.

For condemned prisoners, like Gilmore, who come to accept and even to relish their impending deaths, a genuine calm seems to prevail. It is as if they can transcend the dehumanizing forces at work around them and go to their deaths in peace. For most condemned prisoners, however, numb resignation rather than peaceful acceptance is the norm. By the account of the death-watch officers, these more typical prisoners are beaten men. Listen to the officers' accounts:

A lot of 'em die in their minds before they go to that chair. I've never known of one or heard of one putting up a fight. . . . By the time they walk to the chair, they've completely faced it. Such a reality most people can't understand. Cause they don't fight it. They don't seem to have anything to say. It's just something like "Get it over with." They may be numb, sort of in a trance.

They go through stages. And, at this stage, they're real humble. Humblest bunch of people I ever seen. Most all of 'em is real, real weak. Most of the time you'd only need one or two people to carry out an execution, as weak and as humble as they are.

These men seem barely human and alive to their keepers. They wait meekly to be escorted to their deaths. The people who come for them are the warden and the remainder of the death watch team, flanked by high-ranking correctional officials. The warden reads the court order, known popularly as a death warrant. This is, as one officer said, "the real deal," and nobody misses its significance. The condemned prisoners then go to their deaths compliantly, captives of the inexorable, irresistible momentum of the situation. As one officer put it, "There's no struggle. . . . They just walk right on in there." So too, do the staff "just walk right on in there," following a routine they have come to know well. Both the condemned and the executioners, it would seem, find a relief of sorts in mindless mechanical conformity to the modern execution drill.

WITNESS TO AN EXECUTION

As the team and administrators prepare to commence the good fight, as they might say, another group, the official witnesses, are also preparing themselves for their role in the execution. Numbering between six and twelve for any given execution, the official witnesses are disinterested citizens in good standing drawn from a cross-section of the state's population. If you will, they are every good or decent person, called upon to represent the community and use their good offices to testify to the propriety of the execution. I served as an official witness at the execution of an inmate.

At eight in the evening, about the time the prisoner is shaved in preparation for the execution, the witnesses are assembled. Eleven in all, we included three newspaper and two television reporters, a state trooper, two police officers, a magistrate, a businessman, and myself. We were picked up in the parking lot behind the main office of the corrections department. There was nothing unusual or even memorable about any of this. Gothic touches were notable by their absence. It wasn't a dark and stormy night; no one emerged from the shadows to lead us to the prison gates.

Mundane considerations prevailed. The van sent for us was missing a few rows of seats so there wasn't enough room for all of us. Obliging prison officials volunteered their cars. Our rather ordinary cavalcade reached the prison but only after getting lost. Once within the prison's walls, we were sequestered for some two hours in a bare and almost shabby administrative conference room. A public information officer was assigned to accompany us and answer our questions. We grilled this official about the prisoner and the execution procedure he would undergo shortly, but little information was to be had. The man confessed ignorance on the most basic points. Disgruntled at this and increasingly anxious, we made small talk and drank coffee.

At 10:40 P.M., roughly two-and-a-half hours after we were assembled and only twenty minutes before the execution was scheduled to occur, the witnesses were taken to the basement of the prison's administrative building, frisked, then led down an alleyway that ran along the exterior of the building. We entered a neighboring cell block and were admitted to a vestibule adjoining the death chamber. Each of us signed a log, and was then led off to the witness area. To our left, around a corner some thirty feet away, the prisoner sat in the condemned cell. He couldn't see us, but I'm quite certain he could hear us. It occurred to me that our arrival was a fateful reminder for the prisoner. The next group would be led by the warden, and it would be coming for him.

We entered the witness area, a room within the death chamber, and took our seats. A picture window covering the front wall of the witness room offered a clear view of the electric chair, which was about twelve feet away from us and well illuminated. The chair, a large, high-back solid oak structure with imposing black straps, dominated the death chamber. Behind it, on the back wall, was an open panel full of coils and lights. Peeling paint hung from the ceiling and walls; water stains from persistent leaks were everywhere in evidence.

Two officers, one a hulking figure weighing some 400 pounds, stood alongside the electric chair. Each had his hands crossed at the lap and wore a forbidding, blank expression on his face. The witnesses gazed at them and the chair, most of us scribbling notes furiously. We did this, I suppose, as much to record the experience as to have a distraction from the growing tension. A correctional officer entered the witness room and announced that a trial run of the machinery would be undertaken. Seconds later, lights flashed on the control panel behind the chair indicating that the chair was in working order. A white curtain, opened for the test, separated the chair and the witness area. After the test, the curtain was drawn. More tests were performed behind the curtain. Afterwards, the curtain was reopened, and would be left open until the execution was over. Then it would be closed to allow the officers to remove the body.

A handful of high-level correctional officials were present in the death chamber, standing just outside the witness area. There were two regional administrators, the director of the Department of Corrections, and the prison warden. The prisoner's chaplain and lawyer were also present. Other than the chaplain's black religious garb, subdued grey pinstripes and bland correctional uniforms prevailed. All parties were quite solemn.

At 10:58 the prisoner entered the death chamber. He was, I knew from my research, a man with a checkered, tragic past. He had been grossly abused as a child, and went on to become grossly abusive of others. I was told he could not describe his life, from childhood on, without talking about confrontations in defense of a precarious sense of self—at home, in school, on the streets, in the prison yard. Belittled by life and choking with rage, he was hungry to be noticed. Paradoxically, he had found his moment in the spotlight, but it was a dim and unflattering light cast before a small and unappreciative audience. "He'd pose for cameras in the chair—for the attention," his counselor had told me earlier in the day. But the truth was that the prisoner wasn't smiling, and there were no cameras.

The prisoner walked quickly and silently toward the chair, an escort of officers in tow. His eyes were turned downward, his expression a bit glazed. Like many before him, the prisoner had threatened to stage a last stand. But that was lifetimes ago, on death row. In the death house, he joined the humble bunch and kept to the executioner's schedule. He appeared to have given up on life before he died in the chair.

En route to the chair, the prisoner stumbled slightly, as if the momentum of the event had overtaken him. Were he not held securely by two officers, one at each elbow, he might have fallen. Were the routine to be broken in this or indeed any other way, the officers believe, the prisoner might faint or panic or become violent, and have to be forcibly placed in the chair. Perhaps as a precaution, when the prisoner reached the chair he did not turn on his own but rather was turned, firmly but without malice, by the officers in his escort. These included the two men at his elbows, and four others who followed behind him. Once the prisoner was seated, again with help, the officers strapped him into the chair.

The execution team worked with machine precision. Like a disciplined swarm, they enveloped him. Arms, legs, stomach, chest, and head were secured in a matter of seconds. Electrodes were attached to the cap holding his head and to the strap holding his exposed right leg. A leather mask was placed over his face. The last officer mopped the prisoner's brow, then touched his hand in a gesture of farewell.

During the brief procession to the electric chair, the prisoner was attended by a chaplain. As the execution team worked feverishly to secure the condemned man's body, the chaplain, who appeared to be upset, leaned over him and placed his forehead in contact with the prisoner's, whispering urgently. The priest might have been praying, but I had the impression he was consoling the man, perhaps assuring him that a forgiving God awaited him in the next life. If he heard the chaplain, I doubt the man comprehended his message. He didn't seem comforted. Rather, he looked stricken and appeared to be in shock. Perhaps the priest's urgent ministrations betrayed his doubts that the prisoner could hold himself together. The chaplain then withdrew at the warden's request, allowing the officers to affix the death mask.

The strapped and masked figure sat before us, utterly alone, waiting to be killed. The cap and mask dominated his face. The cap was nothing more than a sponge encased in a leather shell with a metal piece at the top to accept an electrode. It looked decrepit and resembled a cheap, ill-fitting toupee. The mask, made entirely of leather, appeared soiled and worn. It had two parts. The bottom part covered the chin and mouth, the top the eyes and lower forehead. Only the nose was exposed. The effect of a rigidly restrained body, together with the bizarre cap and the protruding nose, was nothing short of grotesque. A faceless man breathed before us in a tragicomic trance, waiting for a blast of electricity that would extinguish his life. Endless seconds passed. His last act was to swallow, nervously, pathetically, with his Adam's apple bobbing. I was struck by that simple movement then, and can't forget it even now. It told me, as nothing else did, that in the prisoner's restrained body, behind that mask, lurked a fellow human being who, at some level, however primitive, knew or sensed himself to be moments from death.

The condemned man sat perfectly still for what seemed an eternity but was in fact no more than thirty seconds. Finally the electricity hit him. His body stiffened spasmodically, though only briefly. A thin swirl of smoke trailed away from his head and then dissipated quickly. The body remained taut, with the right foot raised slightly at the heel, seemingly frozen

there. A brief pause, then another minute of shock. When it was over, the body was flaccid and inert.

Three minutes passed while the officials let the body cool. (Immediately after the execution, I'm told, the body would be too hot to touch and would blister anyone who did.) All eyes were riveted to the chair; I felt trapped in my witness seat, at once transfixed and yet eager for release. I can't recall any clear thoughts from that moment. One of the death watch officers later volunteered that he shared this experience of staring blankly at the execution scene. Had the prisoner's mind been mercifully blank before the end? I hoped so.

An officer walked up to the body, opened the shirt at chest level, then continued on to get the physician from an adjoining room. The physician listened for a heartbeat. Hearing none, he turned to the warden and said, "This man has expired." The warden, speaking to the director, solemnly intoned: "Mr. Director, the court order has been fulfilled." The curtain was then drawn and the witnesses filed out.

THE MORNING AFTER

As the team prepared the body for the morgue, the witnesses were led to the front door of the prison. On the way, we passed a number of cell blocks. We could hear the normal sounds of prison life, including the occasional catcall and lewd comment hurled at uninvited guests like ourselves. But no trouble came in the wake of the execution. Small protests were going on outside the walls, we were told, but we could not hear them. Soon the media would be gone; the protestors would disperse and head for their homes. The prisoners, already home, had been indifferent to the proceedings, as they always are unless the condemned prisoner had been a figure of some consequence in the convict community. Then there might be tension and maybe even a modest disturbance on a prison tier or two. But few convict luminaries are executed, and the dead man had not been one of them. Our escort officer offered a sad tribute to the prisoner: "The inmates, they didn't care about this guy."

I couldn't help but think they weren't alone in this. The executioners went home and set about their lives. Having taken life, they would savor a bit of life themselves. They showered, ate, made love, slept, then took a day or two off. For some, the prisoner's image would linger for that night. The men who strapped him in remembered what it was like to touch him; they showered as soon as they got home to wash off the feel and smell of death. One official sat up picturing how the prisoner looked at the end. (I had a few drinks myself that night with that same image for company.) There was some talk about delayed reactions to the stress of carrying out executions. Though such concerns seemed remote that evening, I learned later that problems would surface for some of the officers. But no one on the team, then or later, was haunted by the executed man's memory, nor would anyone grieve for him. "When I go home after one of these things," said one man, "I sleep like a rock." His may or may not be the sleep of the just, but one can only marvel at such a thing, and perhaps envy such a man.

——CRIME CLOCK—

1994

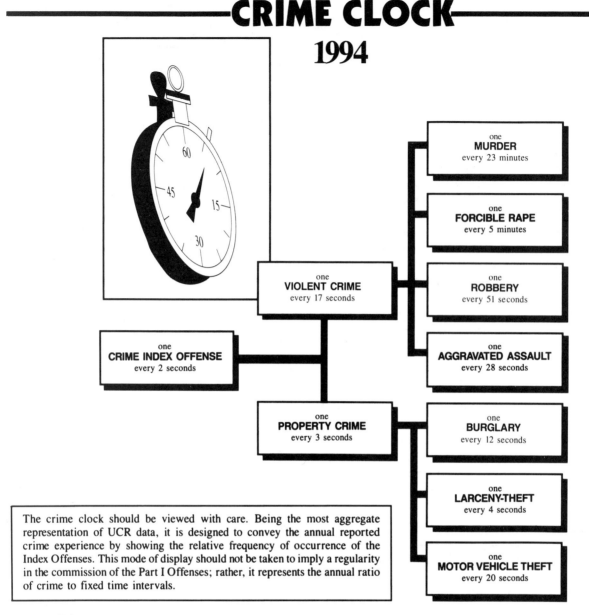

one **VIOLENT CRIME** every 17 seconds	one **MURDER** every 23 minutes
	one **FORCIBLE RAPE** every 5 minutes
	one **ROBBERY** every 51 seconds
	one **AGGRAVATED ASSAULT** every 28 seconds
one **PROPERTY CRIME** every 3 seconds	one **BURGLARY** every 12 seconds
	one **LARCENY-THEFT** every 4 seconds
	one **MOTOR VEHICLE THEFT** every 20 seconds

one **CRIME INDEX OFFENSE** every 2 seconds

The crime clock should be viewed with care. Being the most aggregate representation of UCR data, it is designed to convey the annual reported crime experience by showing the relative frequency of occurrence of the Index Offenses. This mode of display should not be taken to imply a regularity in the commission of the Part I Offenses; rather, it represents the annual ratio of crime to fixed time intervals.

Crime in the United States 1994

The Crime Index total dropped 1 percent to less than 14 million offenses in 1994, the third consecutive year of decline. A 2-percent decrease reported in the Nation's cities collectively was accounted for by the largest cities, those with populations over 25,000. Within this group, the largest decrease, 7 percent, was reported in cities having a million or more inhabitants.

Geographically, the largest volume of Crime Index offenses was reported in the most populous Southern States, which accounted for 38 percent of the total. Following were the Western States with 25 percent, the Midwestern States with 21 percent, and the Northeastern States with 16 percent. The Northeast and South showed Crime Index decreases of 6 and 1 percent, respectively, during 1994 as compared to 1993. In the West, the 1994 Index total showed virtually no change from the 1993 level, while the Midwest's total was up 1 percent.

As in previous years, Crime Index offenses occurred most frequently in August and least often in February.

Rate

Crime rates relate the incidence of crime to population. In 1994, there were an estimated 5,374 Crime Index offenses for each 100,000 in United States population. The Crime Index rate was highest in the Nation's metropolitan areas and lowest in the rural counties. The national 1994 Crime Index rate fell 2 percent from 1993 and 8 percent from the 1990 level. It was 3 percent above the 1985 rate.

Regionally, the Crime Index rates ranged from 6,152 in the West to 4,344 in the Northeast. Two-year percent changes (1994 versus 1993) showed declines of 6 percent in the North-

Table 1.—Index of Crime, United States, 1975-1994

Population[1]	Crime Index total[2]	Modified Crime Index total[3]	Violent crime[4]	Property crime[4]	Murder and non-negligent man-slaughter	Forcible rape	Robbery	Aggra-vated assault	Burglary	Larceny-theft	Motor vehicle theft	Arson[3]
	Number of Offenses											
Population by year:												
1985-238,740,000	12,431,400		1,328,800	11,102,600	18,980	88,670	497,870	723,250	3,073,300	6,926,400	1,102,900	
1986-241,077,000	13,211,900		1,489,170	11,722,700	20,610	91,460	542,780	834,320	3,241,400	7,257,200	1,224,100	
1987-243,400,000	13,508,700		1,484,000	12,024,700	20,100	91,110	517,700	855,090	3,236,200	7,499,900	1,288,700	
1988-245,807,000	13,923,100		1,566,220	12,356,900	20,680	92,490	542,970	910,090	3,218,100	7,705,900	1,432,900	
1989-248,239,000	14,251,400		1,646,040	12,605,400	21,500	94,500	578,330	951,710	3,168,200	7,872,400	1,564,800	
1990-248,709,873	14,475,600		1,820,130	12,655,500	23,440	102,560	639,270	1,054,860	3,073,900	7,945,700	1,635,900	
1991-252,177,000	14,872,900		1,911,770	12,961,100	24,700	106,590	687,730	1,092,740	3,157,200	8,142,200	1,661,700	
1992-255,082,000	14,438,200		1,932,270	12,505,900	23,760	109,060	672,480	1,126,970	2,979,900	7,915,200	1,610,800	
1993-257,908,000[5]	14,144,800		1,926,020	12,218,800	24,530	106,010	659,870	1,135,610	2,834,800	7,820,900	1,563,100	
1994-260,341,000	13,991,700		1,864,170	12,127,500	23,310	102,100	618,820	1,119,950	2,712,200	7,876,300	1,539,100	
Percent change: number of offenses:												
1994/1993	-1.1		-3.2	-.7	-5.0	-3.7	-6.2	-1.4	-4.3	+.7	-1.5	
1994/1990	-3.3		+2.4	-4.2	-.6	-.4	-3.2	+6.2	-11.8	-.9	-5.9	
1994/1985	+12.6		+40.3	+9.2	+22.8	+15.1	+24.3	+54.8	-11.7	+13.7	+39.6	
	Rate per 100,000 Inhabitants											
Year:												
1985........................	5,207.1		556.6	4,650.5	7.9	37.1	208.5	302.9	1,287.3	2,901.2	462.0	
1986........................	5,480.4		617.7	4,862.6	8.6	37.9	225.1	346.1	1,344.6	3,010.3	507.8	
1987........................	5,550.0		609.7	4,940.3	8.3	37.4	212.7	351.3	1,329.6	3,081.3	529.4	
1988........................	5,664.2		637.2	5,027.1	8.4	37.6	220.9	370.2	1,309.2	3,134.9	582.9	
1989........................	5,741.0		663.1	5,077.9	8.7	38.1	233.0	383.4	1,276.3	3,171.3	630.4	
1990........................	5,820.3		731.8	5,088.5	9.4	41.2	257.0	424.1	1,235.9	3,194.8	657.8	
1991........................	5,897.8		758.1	5,139.7	9.8	42.3	272.7	433.3	1,252.0	3,228.8	659.0	
1992........................	5,660.2		757.5	4,902.7	9.3	42.8	263.6	441.8	1,168.2	3,103.0	631.5	
1993........................	5,484.4		746.8	4,737.6	9.5	41.1	255.9	440.3	1,099.2	3,032.4	606.1	
1994[5]......................	5,374.4		716.0	4,658.3	9.0	39.2	237.7	430.2	1,041.8	3,025.4	591.2	
Percent change: rate per 100,000 inhabitants:												
1994/1993	-2.0		-4.1	-1.7	-5.3	-4.6	-7.1	-2.3	-5.2	-.2	-2.5	
1994/1990	-7.7		-2.2	-8.5	-4.3	-4.9	-7.5	+1.4	-15.7	-5.3	-10.1	
1994/1985	+3.2		+28.6	+.2	+13.9	+5.7	+14.0	+42.0	-19.1	+4.3	+28.0	

[1]Populations are Bureau of the Census provisional estimates as of July 1, except 1980 and 1990 which are the decennial census counts.

[2]Because of rounding, the offenses may not add to totals.

[3]Although arson data are included in the trend and clearance tables, sufficient data are not available to estimate totals for this offense.

[4]Violent crimes are offenses of murder, forcible rape, robbery, and aggravated assault. Property crimes are offenses of burglary, larceny-theft, and motor vehicle theft. Data are not included for the property crime of arson.

[5]The forcible rape, robbery, aggravated assault, and motor vehicle theft categories have been adjusted for 1993.

Complete data for 1994 were not available for the states of Illinois, Kansas, and Montana; therefore, it was necessary that their crime counts be estimated.

All rates were calculated on the offenses before rounding.

east; 2 percent in the South; and 1 percent in the West. Virtually no change was reported in the Midwest.

Nature

The Crime Index is composed of violent and property crime categories, and in 1994, 13 percent of the Index offenses reported to law enforcement were violent crimes and 87 percent, property crimes. Larceny-theft was the offense with the highest volume, while murder accounted for the fewest offenses.

Property estimated in value at $15.6 billion was stolen in connection with all Crime Index offenses, with the largest losses due to thefts of motor vehicles; jewelry and precious metals; and televisions, radios, stereos, etc. Law enforcement agencies nationwide recorded a 34-percent recovery rate for dollar losses in connection with stolen property. The highest recovery percentages were for stolen motor vehicles, livestock, consumable goods, clothing and furs, and firearms.

Law Enforcement Response

Law enforcement agencies nationwide recorded a 21-percent clearance rate for the collective Crime Index offenses in 1994 and made an estimated 2.9 million arrests for Index crimes. Crimes can be cleared by arrest or by exceptional means when some element beyond law enforcement control precludes the placing of formal charges against the offender. The arrest of one person may clear several crimes, or several persons may be arrested in connection with the clearance of one offense.

The Index clearance rate has remained relatively stable throughout the past 10-year period. As in 1994, the clearance rate was 21 percent in 1985; it was 22 percent in 1990.

The number of persons arrested for Index crimes increased 1 percent in 1994 when compared to 1993. Juvenile arrests for Index crimes increased 6 percent, while those of adults were down 1 percent. Arrests of females increased 4 percent for the 2-year period, while those of males showed virtually no change.

CRIME INDEX OFFENSES REPORTED

Between 1993 and 1994, the number of persons arrested for the individual offenses comprising the Index increased for arson, 5 percent; aggravated assault, 3 percent; and larceny-theft, 2 percent. Arrest volumes for the remaining Index offenses decreased during the same 2-year period. The declines were 6 percent for murder and forcible rape; 4 percent for burglary; 2 percent for robbery; and 1 percent for motor vehicle theft.

As in past years, larceny-theft accounted for the highest volume of Crime Index arrests at 1.5 million.

MURDER AND NONNEGLIGENT MANSLAUGHTER

DEFINITION

Murder and nonnegligent manslaughter, as defined in the Uniform Crime Reporting Program, is the willful (nonnegligent) killing of one human being by another.

TREND

Year	Number of offenses	Rate per 100,000 inhabitants
1993	24,526	9.5
1994	23,305	9.0
Percent change	−5.0	−5.3

Volume

The number of persons murdered in 1994 was estimated at 23,305, the lowest total since 1989. The 1994 total was 5 percent lower than the 1993 count and 1 percent below the 1990 total. It was, however, 23 percent above the 1985 level.

Monthly figures show that more persons were murdered in the month of August in 1994, while the fewest were killed in February.

The suburban counties recorded a 2-percent decrease in their murder volumes and the rural counties, a 10-percent decline in 1994 from 1993. In the Nation's cities overall, murder decreased 5 percent for the 2-year period. The greatest decrease — 12 percent — was registered in cities with populations of 500,000 to 999,999.

When viewing the four regions of the Nation, the Southern States, the most populous region, accounted for 42 percent of the murders. The Western States reported 23 percent; the Midwestern States, 20 percent; and the Northeastern States, 16 percent. All the regions showed declines in the number of murders reported from 1993 to 1994. The Northeast experienced a 13-percent decrease, the South and West each showed 4-percent declines, and the Midwest showed the smallest decline, 1 percent.

Rate

Down 5 percent from 1993, the national murder rate in 1994 was 9 per 100,000 inhabitants. Five- and 10-year trends showed the 1994 rate was 4 percent lower than in 1990 but 14 percent above the 1985 rate.

Murder by Month, 1990-1994

[Percent distribution]

Months	1990	1991	1992	1993	1994
January	7.9	8.0	8.1	8.1	8.2
February	7.0	7.0	7.5	6.7	7.6
March	8.0	7.7	8.2	7.9	8.8
April	7.4	7.8	8.0	7.6	8.1
May	8.1	8.1	8.5	7.8	8.2
June	8.4	8.6	7.9	8.6	8.3
July	9.6	9.1	9.1	9.3	9.0
August	9.3	9.4	9.1	9.2	9.2
September	9.2	8.8	8.7	8.3	8.3
October	8.8	8.6	8.0	8.4	8.5
November	7.6	7.8	8.1	8.2	7.9
December	8.8	9.0	8.8	9.8	8.0

On a regional basis, the South averaged 11 murders per 100,000 people; the West, 9 per 100,000; the Midwest, 8 per 100,000; and the Northeast, 7 per 100,000. Compared to 1993, murder rates in 1994 declined in all of the four geographic regions, with the Northeast experiencing the largest change, a decrease of 13 percent.

The Nation's metropolitan areas reported a 1994 murder rate of 10 victims per 100,000 inhabitants. In the rural counties and in cities outside metropolitan areas, the rate was 5 per 100,000.

Nature

Supplemental data were provided by contributing agencies for 22,076 of the estimated 23,305 murders in 1994. Submitted monthly, the data consist of the age, sex, and race of both victims and offenders; the types of weapons used; the relationships of victims to the offenders; and the circumstances surrounding the murders.

Based on this information, 79 percent of the murder victims in 1994 were males; and 88 percent were persons 18 years of age or older. Forty-seven percent were aged 20 through 34. Considering victims for whom race was known, 51 percent were black, 47 percent were white, and the remainder were persons of other races.

Supplemental data were also reported for 25,052 murder offenders in 1994. Of those for whom sex and age were reported, 91 percent of the offenders were males, and 84 percent were persons 18 years of age or older. Sixty-nine percent were aged 17 through 34. Of offenders for whom race was known, 56 percent were black, 42 percent were white, and the remainder were persons of other races.

Murder is most often intraracial among victims and offenders. In 1994, data based on incidents involving one victim and one offender showed that 94 percent of the black murder

Murder Victims by Race and Sex, 1994

Race of Victims	Sex of Victims			
	Total	Male	Female	Unknown
Total White Victims	10,191	7,609	2,582	....
Total Black Victims	11,221	9,226	1,995	....
Total Other Race Victims	498	373	125	....
Total Unknown Race	·166	101	37	28
Total Victims[1]	22,076	17,309	4,739	28

[1]Total murder victims for whom supplemental data were received.

victims were slain by black offenders, and 84 percent of the white murder victims were killed by white offenders. Likewise, males were most often slain by males (88 percent in single victim/single offender situations). These same data showed, however, that 9 of every 10 female victims were murdered by males.

FORCIBLE RAPE

DEFINITION

Forcible rape, as defined in the Program, is the carnal knowledge of a female forcibly and against her will. Assaults or attempts to commit rape by force or threat of force are also included; however, statutory rape (without force) and other sex offenses are excluded.

TREND

Year	Number of offenses	Rate per 100,000 inhabitants
1993	106,014	41.1
1994	102,096	39.2
Percent change	−3.7	−4.6

Volume

The 102,096 forcible rapes reported to law enforcement agencies across the Nation during 1994 represented the lowest total since 1989. The 1994 count was 4 percent lower than in 1993.

Geographically, 39 percent of the forcible rape total in 1994 was accounted for by the most populous Southern States, 26 percent by the Midwestern States, 22 percent by the Western States, and 13 percent by the Northeastern States. Two-year trends showed that all regions experienced declines ranging from 2 percent in the South to 7 percent in the Northeast.

As in previous years, monthly totals show most forcible rapes were reported during the summer months of 1994. The lowest volume occurred in December.

Forcible Rape by Month, 1990-1994
[Percent distribution]

Months	1990	1991	1992	1993	1994
January	7.6	7.1	7.0	7.7	7.5
February	6.7	7.0	7.6	6.9	7.3
March	7.9	7.9	8.6	8.5	8.3
April	8.1	8.3	8.5	8.2	8.4
May	9.1	9.2	8.9	8.9	8.9
June	9.0	9.2	8.7	9.2	9.2
July	9.6	9.5	9.4	9.7	9.7
August	9.4	9.7	9.6	9.3	9.6
September	9.1	8.8	8.7	8.3	8.7
October	8.4	8.6	8.4	8.1	8.5
November	7.7	7.8	7.6	7.5	7.3
December	7.4	6.8	7.0	7.7	6.5

Rate

By Uniform Crime Reporting definition, the victims of forcible rape are always female, and in 1994, an estimated 77 of every 100,000 females in the country were reported rape victims. The 1994 female forcible rape rate was 4 percent lower than both the 1993 and 1990 rates.

The highest rate in 1994 was recorded in the Nation's metropolitan areas where it was 80 victims per 100,000 females. In cities outside metropolitan areas, the rate was 77 per 100,000 females, and in rural counties, it was 51 per 100,000 females. Although metropolitan areas record the highest rape rates, they have shown the only rate decline over the past 10 years, 2 percent. During this same time, the rate increased in cities outside metropolitan areas by 88 percent, and rural counties recorded a 46-percent rate rise.

Geographically, in 1994, the highest female rape rate was in the Southern States, which recorded 85 victims per 100,000 females. The Midwestern States followed closely with a rate of 84; the Western States registered 78; and the Northeastern States, 52. Three of the four regions showed rate declines between 1993 and 1994. In the Midwest, however, the female rape rate increased by 1 percent over the 2-year period.

Over the last 10 years, regional decreases in the female forcible rape rate were 8 percent in the West and 7 percent in the Northeast. Rate increases were reported in the Midwest and South, 29 and 10 percent, respectively, for the same timeframe.

Nature

Rapes by force constitute the greatest percentage of total forcible rapes, 87 percent of the 1994 experience. The remainder were attempts or assaults to commit forcible rape. The number of rapes by force decreased 4 percent in 1994 from the 1993 volume, and attempts to rape decreased 5 percent.

As for all other Crime Index offenses, complaints of forcible rape made to law enforcement agencies are sometimes found to be false or baseless. In such cases, law enforcement agencies "unfound" the offenses and exclude them from crime counts. The "unfounded" rate, or percentage of complaints determined through investigation to be false, is higher for forcible rape than for any other Index crime. In 1994, 8 percent of forcible rape complaints were "unfounded," while the average for all Index crimes was 2 percent.

Law Enforcement Response

Over half of the forcible rapes reported to law enforcement nationwide and in cities were cleared by arrest or exceptional means in 1994. Rural and suburban county law enforcement agencies cleared a slightly higher percentage of the offenses brought to their attention than did city law enforcement agencies.

Geographically, forcible rape clearance rates in 1994 were 45 percent in the Midwest, 48 percent in the West, 55 percent in the Northeast, and 57 percent in the South.

Of the total clearances for forcible rape in the country as a whole, 15 percent involved only persons under 18 years of age. The percentage of juvenile involvement varied by community type, ranging from 13 percent in the Nation's cities to 20 percent in suburban counties.

Law enforcement agencies nationwide made an estimated 36,610 arrests for forcible rape in 1994. Of the forcible rape arrestees, about 4 of every 10 were under age 25. Over half of those arrested were white.

The number of arrests for forcible rape fell 6 percent nationwide from 1993 to 1994. A decrease of 7 percent was experienced in the Nation's cities, and 4-percent declines were recorded in the rural and suburban counties.

ROBBERY

DEFINITION
Robbery is the taking or attempting to take anything of value from the care, custody, or control of a person or persons by force or threat of force or violence and/or by putting the victim in fear.

TREND

Year	Number of offenses	Rate per 100,000 inhabitants
1993	659,870	255.9
1994	618,817	237.7
Percent change	−6.2	−7.1

Volume

Estimated at nearly 619,000 offenses, robberies in 1994 accounted for 4 percent of all Index crimes and 33 percent of the violent crimes. During the year, robberies occurred most frequently in August and October and least often in February.

Robbery by Month, 1990-1994
[Percent distribution]

Months	1990	1991	1992	1993	1994
January	8.7	8.7	9.0	8.8	8.7
February	7.3	7.5	8.0	7.1	7.7
March	8.1	8.0	8.1	8.3	8.6
April	7.2	7.4	7.8	7.4	8.0
May	7.7	7.8	7.9	7.5	8.0
June	7.8	7.8	7.9	8.1	8.0
July	8.5	8.4	8.4	8.7	8.5
August	8.8	8.8	8.6	8.8	8.8
September	8.6	8.5	8.3	8.4	8.3
October	8.9	9.2	8.7	9.0	8.8
November	8.7	8.7	8.3	8.5	8.2
December	9.6	9.2	9.0	9.4	8.4

The 1994 robbery volume was down 6 percent from 1993 levels nationally and in the Nation's cities. The largest decline—11 percent—was experienced in cities with a million or more inhabitants. During the same period, the robbery volume dropped 4 percent in the suburban counties but increased 4 percent in the rural counties.

Regionally, the Southern States, the most populous region, accounted for 32 percent of all reported robberies. The Northeastern and Western States each recorded 24 percent; and the Midwest, 20 percent. Two-year trends show the number of robberies in 1994 was down in all regions as compared in 1993. The declines ranged from 10 percent in the Northeast to 1 percent in the Midwest.

In 1994, the number of robbery offenses was 3 percent lower than in 1990 but 24 percent higher than in 1985.

Rate

The national robbery rate in 1994 was 238 per 100,000 people, 7 percent lower than in 1993. In metropolitan areas, the 1994 rate was 288; in cities outside metropolitan areas, it was 75; and in the rural areas, it was 17. With 877 robberies per 100,000 inhabitants, the highest rate was recorded in cities with a million or more inhabitants.

Robbery rates per 100,000 inhabitants declined in all regions from 1993 to 1994. The rates of 291 in the Northeast and 256 in the West were down 10 and 9 percent respectively. The South's rate of 221 was 6 percent lower; and the Midwest's rate of 200 was down 2 percent.

Nature

Losses estimated at $496 million were attributed to robberies during 1994. The value of property stolen averaged $801 per robbery, down from $815 in 1993. Average dollar losses in 1994 ranged from $387 taken during robberies of convenience stores to $3,551 per bank robbery. The impact of this violent crime on its victims cannot be measured in terms of monetary loss alone. While the object of a robbery is to obtain money or property, the crime always involves force or threat of force, and many victims suffer serious personal injury.

Robberies on streets or highways accounted for more than half (55 percent) of the offenses in this category during 1994. Robberies of commercial and financial establishments accounted for an additional 21 percent, and those occurring at residences, 11 percent. The remainder were miscellaneous types. All robbery types declined in 1994 as compared to 1993 totals. The decreases ranged from 25 percent for bank robberies to 1 percent for residential robberies.

Robbery, Percent Distribution, 1994
[By region]

	United States Total	North-eastern States	Mid-western States	Southern States	Western States
Total[1]	100.0	100.0	100.0	100.0	100.0
Street/highway	54.6	61.6	62.1	50.2	49.6
Commercial house	12.3	9.9	9.4	12.5	15.8
Gas or service station	2.2	1.8	2.5	2.2	2.3
Convenience store	5.1	2.7	3.6	7.1	5.7
Residence	10.9	11.0	9.1	13.3	8.3
Bank	1.4	.8	1.2	1.3	2.4
Miscellaneous	13.5	12.1	12.1	13.3	15.8

[1]Because of rounding, percentages may not add to totals.

AGGRAVATED ASSAULT

DEFINITION
Aggravated assault is an unlawful attack by one person upon another for the purpose of inflicting severe or aggravated bodily injury. This type of assault is usually accompanied by the use of a weapon or by means likely to produce death or great bodily harm.

TREND		
Year	Number of offenses	Rate per 100,000 inhabitants
1993	1,135,607	440.3
1994	1,119,950	430.2
Percent change	−1.4	−2.3

Volume

After increasing steadily since 1983, aggravated assaults dropped 1 percent in 1994 to an estimated 1,119,950 offenses. Aggravated assaults in 1994 accounted for 60 percent of the violent crimes.

Geographic distribution figures show that 40 percent of the aggravated assault volume was accounted for by the most populous Southern Region. Following were the Western Region with 25 percent, the Midwestern Region with 19 percent, and the Northeastern Region with 15 percent. Among the regions, only the Midwest registered an increase in the number of reported aggravated assaults.

The 1994 monthly figures show that the greatest number of aggravated assaults was recorded during July, while the lowest volume occurred during February.

Aggravated Assault by Month, 1990-1994
[Percent distribution]

Months	1990	1991	1992	1993	1994
January	7.4	6.9	7.3	7.5	7.2
February	6.7	6.6	7.3	6.5	7.0
March	7.8	7.7	8.0	8.1	8.3
April	8.2	8.1	8.7	8.3	8.5
May	9.0	9.1	9.2	8.9	8.8
June	9.4	9.3	8.9	9.1	8.9
July	10.1	9.7	9.4	9.6	9.5
August	9.3	9.9	9.1	9.2	9.4
September	8.9	9.0	8.6	8.3	8.9
October	8.3	8.6	8.5	8.5	8.7
November	7.4	7.6	7.6	7.4	7.7
December	7.5	7.6	7.4	8.6	7.3

The Nation's cities collectively experienced a decrease of 2 percent in the aggravated assault volume from 1993 to 1994. Percent changes among the city population groupings ranged from a 4-percent decline in cities with populations over 1 million to a 1-percent increase in cities with 10,000 - 24,999 inhabitants. The suburban counties registered a 1-percent increase in the number of aggravated assaults reported, and the rural counties, a 5-percent rise for the 2-year period.

Five- and 10-year trends for the country as a whole showed aggravated assaults 6 percent higher than in 1990 and 55 percent above the 1985 experience.

Rate

There were 430 reported victims of aggravated assault for every 100,000 people nationwide in 1994, the lowest rate since 1990. The rate was 2 percent lower than in 1993, 1 percent higher than in 1990, and 42 percent above the 1985 rate.

Higher than the national average, the rate in metropolitan areas was 472 per 100,000 in 1994. Cities outside metropolitan areas experienced a rate of 382, and rural counties, a rate of 189.

Regionally, the aggravated assault rate was 337 per 100,000 people in the Northeast, 350 in the Midwest, 493 in the South, and 500 in the West. Compared to 1993, 1994 aggravated assault rates were down in all regions except the Midwest, which experienced virtually no change.

Nature

Thirty-two percent of the aggravated assaults in 1994 were committed with blunt objects or other dangerous weapons. Of the remaining weapon categories, personal weapons such as hands, fists, and feet were used in 26 percent of the assaults; firearms in 24 percent; and knives or cutting instruments in the remainder.

Firearms were used in 6 percent fewer assaults in 1994 than in 1993. Assaults with knives or cutting instruments also decreased, 1 percent. Showing increases were assaults with personal weapons (hands, fists, and feet) and those involving blunt objects or other dangerous weapons, both up 2 percent over 1993.

Aggravated Assault, Type of Weapons Used, 1994
[Percent distribution by region]

Region	Total all weapons[1]	Fire-arms	Knives or cutting instru-ments	Other weapons (clubs, blunt objects, etc.)	Personal weapons
Total	100.0	24.0	17.8	32.0	26.2
Northeastern States	100.0	15.9	20.9	33.7	29.5
Midwestern States	100.0	28.5	18.0	34.2	19.2
Southern States	100.0	26.4	19.1	32.8	21.8
Western States	100.0	22.4	13.8	28.3	35.4

[1]Because of rounding, percentages may not add to totals.

BURGLARY

DEFINITION
The Uniform Crime Reporting Program defines burglary as the unlawful entry of a structure to commit a felony or theft. The use of force to gain entry is not required to classify an offense as burglary.

TREND		
Year	Number of offenses	Rate per 100,000 inhabitants
1993	2,834,808	1,099.2
1994	2,712,156	1,041.8
Percent change	−4.3	−5.2

Volume

The estimated 2.7 million burglaries in the United States during 1994 accounted for 19 percent of the Crime Index total and 22 percent of the property crimes. Distribution figures for the regions showed that the highest burglary volume (40 percent) occurred in the most populous Southern States. The Western States followed with 24 percent, the Midwestern States with 20 percent, and the Northeastern States with 15 percent.

The greatest number of burglaries was recorded during August of 1994, while the lowest count was in February.

Burglary by Month, 1990-1994
[Percent distribution]

Months	1990	1991	1992	1993	1994
January	8.8	8.1	8.6	8.3	7.9
February	7.5	7.3	7.7	6.9	7.1
March	8.1	8.1	8.2	8.2	8.2
April	7.8	7.9	7.8	7.7	8.0
May	8.1	8.3	8.2	8.0	8.5
June	7.9	8.2	8.1	8.4	8.3
July	8.9	9.2	9.0	9.0	9.2
August	9.0	9.2	9.0	9.1	9.4
September	8.3	8.6	8.4	8.5	8.6
October	8.5	8.6	8.3	8.4	8.6
November	8.3	8.0	8.2	8.1	8.4
December	8.7	8.6	8.3	9.3	7.9

Nationwide, the burglary volume dropped 4 percent in 1994 from the 1993 total. In the Nation's cities, it decreased 5 percent; in the suburban counties, 3 percent; and in the rural counties, 1 percent.

All four regions of the United States reported decreases in burglary volumes during 1994 as compared to 1993. The Northeastern States experienced an 8-percent decline; the Southern States, a 5-percent decrease; and the Western States, a 3-percent drop. The Midwestern States reported the smallest change, a 1-percent decline.

Longer term national trends show burglary down 12 percent from both the 1990 and 1985 volumes.

Rate

The burglary rate was 1,042 per 100,000 inhabitants nationwide in 1994. The rate was 5 percent lower than in 1993, down 16 percent from 1990, and 19 percent below the 1985 rate. In 1994, for every 100,000 in population, the rate was 1,113 in the metropolitan areas, 965 in the cities outside metropolitan areas, and 632 in the rural counties.

Regionally, the burglary rate was 1,206 in the Southern States, 1,163 in the Western States, 886 in the Midwestern States, and 804 in the Northeastern States. A comparison of 1993 and 1994 rates showed decreases of 8 percent in the Northeast, 6 percent in the South, 5 percent in the West, and 1 percent in the Midwest.

Nature

Two of every 3 burglaries in 1994 were residential in nature. Sixty-seven percent of all burglaries involved forcible entry, 25 percent were unlawful entries (without force), and the remainder were forcible entry attempts. Offenses for which time of occurrence was reported showed that 52 percent of burglaries happened during daytime hours and 48 percent at night. More residential burglaries (59 percent) occurred during the daytime, while 62 percent of nonresidential burglaries occurred during nighttime hours.

The volume of property stolen in burglaries was estimated at $3.6 billion in 1994, and the average dollar loss per burglary was $1,311. The average loss for residential offenses was $1,296 and for nonresidential offenses, $1,341. Compared to 1993, the 1994 average loss for both residential and nonresidential property increased.

Both residential and nonresidential burglary volumes also showed declines from 1993 to 1994, 4 and 6 percent, respectively.

LARCENY-THEFT

DEFINITION

Larceny-theft is the unlawful taking, carrying, leading, or riding away of property from the possession or constructive possession of another. It includes crimes such as shoplifting, pocket-picking, purse-snatching, thefts from motor vehicles, thefts of motor vehicle parts and accessories, bicycle thefts, etc., in which no use of force, violence, or fraud occurs.

TREND

Year	Number of offenses	Rate per 100,000 inhabitants
1993	7,820,909	3,032.4
1994	7,876,254	3,025.4
Percent change	+.7	−.2

Volume

Larceny-theft, estimated at nearly 7.9 million offenses during 1994, comprised 56 percent of the Crime Index total and 65 percent of the property crimes. Similar to the experience in previous years, larceny-thefts were recorded most often during August and least frequently in February.

Larceny-Theft by Month, 1990-1994
[Percent distribution]

Months	1990	1991	1992	1993	1994
January	8.2	7.8	8.2	7.7	7.4
February	7.4	7.5	7.8	6.8	7.1
March	8.2	8.2	8.3	8.0	8.1
April	7.9	8.1	8.1	8.0	8.1
May	8.3	8.4	8.2	8.2	8.5
June	8.3	8.5	8.5	8.7	8.6
July	8.9	9.2	9.1	9.2	9.2
August	9.1	9.3	9.1	9.3	9.5
September	8.2	8.3	8.4	8.3	8.5
October	8.7	8.7	8.6	8.6	8.9
November	8.1	7.9	7.9	8.0	8.3
December	8.4	8.2	8.0	9.1	7.9

Viewed geographically, the Southern States, the most populous region, recorded 38 percent of the larceny-theft total. The

Western States recorded 24 percent; the Midwestern States, 22 percent; and the Northeastern States, 15 percent. (See Table 3.)

The 1994 volume of larceny-thefts was 1 percent higher than the 1993 total. The Nation's cities collectively showed no change for the 2-year period, while increases of 3 percent were experienced in both the rural and suburban counties.

Larceny volumes increased in three of four geographic regions. The West showed a 2-percent rise and the Midwest and the South, both 1-percent increases. In the Northeast, the number of larceny-thefts dropped 3 percent.

The 5- and 10-year national trends indicated larceny was down 1 percent when compared to the 1990 total but 14 percent above the 1985 level.

Rate

Virtually unchanged from 1993, the 1994 larceny-theft rate was 3,025 per 100,000 United States inhabitants. The rate was 5 percent lower than in 1990 but 4 percent above the 1985 rate. The 1994 rate was 3,268 per 100,000 inhabitants of metropolitan areas; 3,623 per 100,000 population in cities outside metropolitan areas; and 1,046 per 100,000 people in the rural counties.

By region, the 1993 larceny-theft rate per 100,000 inhabitants in the Northeast was 2,280, down 3 percent; and the South's rate of 3,329 declined less than 1 percent. Increasing 1 percent were the rates in the West, at 3,384, and the Midwest, at 2,869.

Nature

During 1994, the average value of property stolen due to larceny-theft was $505, up from $504 in 1993. When the average value was applied to the estimated number of larceny-thefts, the loss to victims nationally was $4 billion for the year. This estimated dollar loss is considered conservative since many offenses in the larceny category, particularly if the value of the stolen goods is small, never come to law enforcement attention. Losses in 39 percent of the thefts reported to law enforcement were under $50. Twenty-three percent involved losses ranging from $50 to $200, while in 37 percent, they were over $200.

Losses of goods and property reported stolen as a result of pocket-picking averaged $428; purse-snatching, $279; and shoplifting, $133. Thefts from buildings resulted in an average loss of $851; from motor vehicles, $542; and from coin-operated machines, $228. The average value loss due to thefts of motor vehicle accessories was $312 and for thefts of bicycles, $252.

Thefts of motor vehicle parts, accessories, and contents made up the largest portion of reported larcenies—37 percent. Also contributing to the high volume of thefts were shoplifting, accounting for 15 percent; thefts from buildings, 13 percent; and bicycle thefts, 6 percent. The remainder was distributed among pocket-picking, purse-snatching, thefts from coin-operated machines, and all other types of larceny-thefts.

Larceny Analysis by Region, 1994
[Percent distribution]

	United States Total	North-eastern States	Mid-western States	Southern States	Western States
Total[1]	100.0	100.0	100.0	100.0	100.0
Pocket-picking	.8	2.8	.3	.5	.4
Purse-snatching	.8	1.5	.8	.6	.6
Shoplifting	15.0	14.0	13.6	14.8	16.7
From motor vehicles (except accessories)	23.7	21.4	20.9	21.9	29.7
Motor vehicle accessories	12.9	13.3	13.6	13.5	11.2
Bicycles	6.3	7.3	6.8	5.4	6.8
From buildings	13.0	18.6	16.3	10.1	12.3
From coin-operated machines	.7	.8	.6	.7	.6
All others	26.9	20.2	27.1	32.5	21.8

[1]Because of rounding, percentages may not add to totals.

MOTOR VEHICLE THEFT

DEFINITION

Defined as the theft or attempted theft of a motor vehicle, this offense category includes the stealing of automobiles, trucks, buses, motorcycles, motorscooters, snowmobiles, etc.

TREND

Year	Number of offenses	Rate per 100,000 inhabitants
1993	1,563,060	606.1
1994	1,539,097	591.2
Percent change	−1.5	−2.5

Volume

The over 1.5 million thefts of motor vehicles occurring in the United States during 1994 comprised 13 percent of all property crimes. The regional distribution of thefts showed 32 percent of the volume was in the Southern States, 30 percent in the Western States, 20 percent in the Northeastern States, and 18 percent in the Midwestern States.

The 1994 monthly figures show that the greatest numbers of motor vehicle thefts were recorded during the months of July and August, while the lowest count was in February.

Motor Vehicle Theft by Month, 1990-1994
[Percent distribution]

Months	1990	1991	1992	1993	1994
January	8.5	8.3	8.8	8.5	8.2
February	7.6	7.5	7.9	7.3	7.4
March	8.4	8.2	8.2	8.2	8.5
April	7.9	7.8	7.8	7.8	8.0
May	8.1	8.1	8.1	7.9	8.2
June	8.1	8.2	8.2	8.4	8.3
July	8.8	8.7	8.8	8.9	8.9
August	8.8	8.9	8.9	8.9	9.1
September	8.4	8.3	8.2	8.4	8.4
October	8.8	8.7	8.6	8.6	8.8
November	8.3	8.5	8.3	8.3	8.4
December	8.4	8.8	8.2	8.8	7.8

Motor vehicle thefts declined 2 percent nationally and in the cities overall from 1993 to 1994. Among the city groupings, percent changes ranged from an 8-percent decline in cities with populations of 1 million or more to a 3-percent increase in those with populations from 100,000 to 249,999. During the same 2-year period, increases occurred in the suburban counties, 3 percent, and the rural counties, 6 percent.

Geographically, decreases in motor vehicle thefts were recorded in the Northeast, 10 percent, and in the South, 1 percent. The West and Midwest regions showed increases, 2 and 1 percent, respectively.

The accompanying chart shows that the volume of motor vehicle thefts in 1994 declined 6 percent from the 1990 volume.

Rate

The 1994 national motor vehicle theft rate—591 per 100,000 people—was 2 percent lower in 1993 and 10 percent below the 1990 rate. The 1994 rate was 28 percent above the 1985 rate.

For every 100,000 inhabitants living in metropolitan areas, there were 701 motor vehicle thefts reported in 1994. The rate in cities outside metropolitan areas was 230 and in rural counties, 119. As in previous years, the highest rates were in the Nation's most heavily populated municipalities, indicating that this offense is primarily a large-city problem. For every 100,000 inhabitants in cities with populations over 250,000, the 1994 motor vehicle theft rate was 1,414. The Nation's smallest cities, those with fewer than 10,000 inhabitants, recorded a rate of 244 per 100,000.

Among the regions, the motor vehicle theft rates ranged from 800 per 100,000 people in the Western States to 460 in the Midwestern States. The Northeastern States' rate was 599 and the Southern States' rate, 545. From 1993 to 1994, the Midwest and West registered rate increases of 1 percent. Both the South and Northeast reported decreases of 2 and 10 percent, respectively.

An estimated average of 1 of every 130 registered motor vehicles was stolen nationwide during 1994. Regionally, this rate was greatest in the West where 1 of every 98 motor vehicles registered was stolen. The other three regions reported lesser rates—1 per 179 in the Midwest, 1 per 141 in the South, and 1 per 113 in the Northeast.

Nature

The estimated value of motor vehicles stolen nationwide in 1994 was nearly $7.6 billion. At the time of theft, the average value per vehicle was $4,940. The recovery percentage for the value of vehicles stolen was higher than for any other property type. Relating the value of vehicles stolen to the value of those recovered resulted in a 61-percent recovery rate for 1994.

Seventy-nine percent of all motor vehicles reported stolen during the year were automobiles, 16 percent were trucks or buses, and the remainder were other types.

Motor Vehicle Theft, 1994
[Percent distribution by region]

Region	Total	Autos	Trucks and buses	Other vehicles
Total	100.0	79.0	15.6	5.4
Northeastern States	100.0	92.3	4.5	3.2
Midwestern States	100.0	83.4	11.6	5.0
Southern States	100.0	75.0	18.1	6.9
Western States	100.0	72.3	22.2	5.5

From *Crime in the United States 1994: Uniform Crime Reports,* November 1995. A publication of the U.S. Department of Justice, Federal Bureau of Investigation.

Abet: To encourage another to commit a crime.

Accessory: One who harbors, assists, or protects another person, although he or she knows that person has committed or will commit a crime.

Accomplice: One who knowingly and voluntarily aids another in committing a criminal offense.

Acquit: To free a person legally from an accusation of criminal guilt.

Adjudicatory hearing: The fact-finding process wherein the court determines whether or not there is sufficient evidence to sustain the allegations in a petition.

Admissible: Capable of being admitted; in a trial, such evidence as the judge allows to be introduced into the proceeding.

Affirmance: A pronouncement by a higher court that the case in question was rightly decided by the lower court from which the case was appealed.

Affirmation: Positive declaration or assertion that the witness will tell the truth; not made under oath.

Alias: Any name by which one is known other than his or her true name.

Alibi: A type of defense in a criminal prosecution that proves the accused could not have committed the crime with which he or she is charged, since evidence offered shows the accused was in another place at the time the crime was committed.

Allegation: An assertion of what a party to an action expects to prove.

American Bar Association (ABA): A professional association, comprising attorneys who have been admitted to the bar in any of the 50 states, and a registered lobby.

American Civil Liberties Union (ACLU): Founded in 1920 with the purpose of defending the individual's rights as guaranteed by the U.S. Constitution.

Amnesty: A class or group pardon.

Annulment: The act, by competent authority, of canceling, making void, or depriving of all force.

Appeal: A case carried to a higher court to ask that the decision of the lower court, in which the case originated, be altered or overruled completely.

Appellate court: A court that has jurisdiction to hear cases on appeal; not a trial court.

Arbitrator: The person chosen by parties in a controversy to settle their differences; private judges.

Arraignment: The appearance before the court of a person charged with a crime. He or she is advised of the charges, bail is set, and a plea of "guilty" or "not guilty" is entered.

Arrest: The legal detainment of a person to answer for criminal charges or civil demands.

Autopsy: A postmortem examination of a human body to determine the cause of death.

Bail: Property (usually money) deposited with a court in exchange for the release of a person in custody to assure later appearance.

Bail bond: An obligation signed by the accused and his or her sureties, that ensures his or her presence in court.

Bailiff: An officer of the court who is responsible for keeping order in the court and protecting the security of jury deliberations and court property.

Bench warrant: An order by the court for the apprehension and arrest of a defendant or other person who has failed to appear when so ordered.

Bill of Rights: The first ten amendments to the U.S. Constitution that state certain fundamental rights and privileges that are guaranteed to the people against infringement by the government.

Biocriminology: A relatively new branch of criminology that attempts to explain criminal behavior by referring to biological factors which predispose some individuals to commit criminal acts. *See also* Criminal biology.

Blue laws: Laws in some jurisdictions prohibiting sales or merchandise, athletic contests, and the sale of alcoholic beverages on Sundays.

Booking: A law-enforcement or correctional process officially recording an entry-into-detention after arrest and identifying the person, place, time, reason for the arrest, and the arresting authority.

Breathalizer: A commercial device to test the breath of a suspected drinker and determine that person's blood-alcohol content.

Brief: A summary of the law relating to a case, prepared by the attorneys for both parties and given to the judge.

Bug: To plant a sound sensor or to tap a communication line for the purpose of surreptitious listening or audio monitoring.

Burden of proof: Duty of establishing the existence of fact in a trial.

Calendar: A list of cases to be heard in a trial court, on a specific day, and containing the title of the case, the lawyers involved, and the index number.

Capital crime: Any crime that may be punishable by death or imprisonment for life.

Career criminal: A person having a past record of multiple arrests or convictions for crimes of varying degrees of seriousness. Such criminals are often described as chronic, habitual, repeat, serious, high-rate, or professional offenders.

Case: At the level of police or prosecutorial investigation, a set of circumstances under investigation involving one or more persons.

Case law: Judicial precedent generated as a byproduct of the decisions that courts have made to resolve unique disputes. Case law concerns concrete facts, as distinguished from statutes and constitutions, which are written in the abstract.

Change of venue: The removal of a trial from one jurisdiction to another in order to avoid local prejudice.

Charge: In criminal law, the accusation made against a person. It also refers to the judge's instruction to the jury on legal points.

Circumstantial evidence: Indirect evidence; evidence from which a fact can be reasonably inferred, although not directly proven.

Clemency: The doctrine under which executive or legislative action reduces the severity of or waives legal punishment of one or more individuals, or an individual exempted from prosecution for certain actions.

Code: A compilation, compendium, or revision of laws, arranged into chapters, having a table of contents and index, and promulgated by legislative authority. Criminal code; penal code.

Coercion: The use of force to compel performance of an action; The application of sanctions or the use of force by government to compel observance of law or public policy.

Common law: Judge-made law to assist courts through decision making with traditions, customs, and usage of previous court decisions.

Commutation: A reduction of a sentence originally prescribed by a court.

Complainant: The victim of a crime who brings the facts to the attention of the authorities.

Complaint: Any accusation that a person committed a crime that has originated or been received by a law enforcement agency or court.

Confession: A statement by a person who admits violation of the law.

Confiscation: Government seizure of private property without compensation to the owner.

Conspiracy: An agreement between two or more persons to plan for the purpose of committing a crime or any unlawful act or a lawful act by unlawful or criminal means.

Contempt of court: Intentionally obstructing a court in the administration of justice, acting in a way calculated to lessen its authority or dignity, or failing to obey its lawful order.

Continuance: Postponement or adjournment of a trial granted by the judge, either to a later date or indefinitely.

Contraband: Goods, the possession of which is illegal.

Conviction: A finding by the jury (or by the trial judge in cases tried without a jury) that the accused is guilty of a crime.

Corporal punishment: Physical punishment.

Corpus delicti **(Lat.):** The objective proof that a crime has been committed as distinguished from an accidental death, injury, or loss.

Corrections: Area of criminal justice dealing with convicted offenders in jails, prisons; on probation or parole.

Corroborating evidence: Supplementary evidence that tends to strengthen or confirm other evidence given previously.

Crime: An act injurious to the public, that is prohibited and punishable by law.

Crime Index: A set of numbers indicating the volume, fluctuation, and distribution of crimes reported to local law enforcement agencies for the United States as a whole.

Crime of passion: An unpremeditated murder or assault committed under circumstances of great anger, jealousy, or other emotional stress.

Criminal biology: The scientific study of the relation of hereditary physical traits to criminal character, that is, to innate tendencies to commit crime in general or crimes of any particular type. *See also* Biocriminology.

Criminal insanity: Lack of mental capacity to do or refrain from doing a criminal act; inability to distinguish right from wrong.

Criminal intent: The intent to commit and act, the results of which are a crime or violation of the law.

Criminalistics: Crime laboratory procedures.

Criminology: The scientific study of crime, criminals, corrections, and the operation of the system of criminal justice.

Cross examination: The questioning of a witness by the party who did not produce the witness.

Culpable: At fault or responsible, but not necessarily criminal.

Defamation: Intentional causing, or attempting to cause, damage to the reputation of another by communicating false or distorted information about his or her actions, motives, or character.

Defendant: The person who is being prosecuted.

Deliberation: The action of a jury to determine the guilt or innocence, or the sentence, of a defendant.

Demurrer: Plea for dismissal of a suit on the grounds that, even if true, the statements of the opposition are insufficient to sustain the claim.

Deposition: Sworn testimony obtained outside, rather than in, court.

Deterrence: A theory that swift and sure punishment will discourage others from similar illegal acts.

Dilatory: Law term that describes activity for the purpose of causing a delay or to gain time or postpone a decision.

Direct evidence: Testimony or other proof that expressly or straightforwardly proves the existence of fact.

Direct examination: The first questioning of witnesses by the party who calls them.

Directed verdict: An order or verdict pronounced by a judge during the trial of a criminal case in which the evidence presented by the prosecution clearly fails to show the guilt of the accused.

District attorney: A locally elected state official who represents the state in bringing indictments and prosecuting criminal cases.

Docket: The formal record of court proceedings.

Double jeopardy: To be prosecuted twice for the same offense.

Due process model: A philosophy of criminal justice based on the assumption that an individual is presumed innocent until proven guilty.

Due process of law: A clause in the Fifth and Fourteenth Amendments ensuring that laws are reasonable and that they are applied in a fair and equal manner.

Embracery: An attempt to influence a jury, or a member thereof, in their verdict by any improper means.

Entrapment: Inducing an individual to commit a crime he or she did not contemplate, for the sole purpose of instituting a criminal prosecution against the offender.

Evidence: All the means used to prove or disprove the fact at issue. *See also Corpus delicti.*

Ex post facto **(Lat.):** After the fact. An *ex post facto* law is a criminal law that makes an act unlawful although it was committed prior to the passage of that law. *See also* Grandfather clause.

Exception: A formal objection to the action of the court during a trial. The indication is that the excepting party will seek to reverse the court's actions at some future proceeding.

Exclusionary rule: Legal prohibitions against government prosecution using evidence illegally obtained.

Expert evidence: Testimony by one qualified to speak authoritatively on technical matters because of her or his special training of skill.

Extradition: The surrender by one state to another of an individual accused of a crime.

False arrest: Any unlawful physical restraint of another's freedom of movement; unlawful arrest.

Felony: A criminal offense punishable by death or imprisonment in a penitentiary.

Forensic: Relating to the court. Forensic medicine would refer to legal medicine that applies anatomy, pathology, toxicology, chemistry, and other fields of science in expert testimony in court cases or hearings.

Grandfather clause: A clause attempting to preserve the rights of firms in operation before enactment of a law by exempting these firms from certain provisions of that law. *See also Ex post facto.*

Grand jury: A group of 12 to 23 citizens of a county who examine evidence against the person suspected of a crime and hand down an indictment if there is sufficient evidence. *See also* Petit jury.

Habeas corpus **(Lat.):** A legal device to challenge the detention of a person taken into custody. An individual in custody may demand an evidentiary hearing before a judge to examine the legality of the detention.

Hearsay: Evidence that a witness has learned through others.

Homicide: The killing of a human being; may be murder, negligent or nonnegligent manslaughter, or excusable or justifiable homicide.

Hung jury: A jury which, after long deliberation, is so irreconcilably divided in opinion that it is unable to reach a verdict.

Impanel: The process of selecting the jury that is to try a case.

Imprisonment: A sentence imposed upon the conviction of a crime; the deprivation of liberty in a penal institution; incarceration.

In camera **(Lat.):** A case heard when the doors of the court are closed and only persons concerned in the case are admitted.

Indemnification: Compensation for loss or damage sustained because of improper or illegal action by a public authority.

Indictment: The document prepared by a prosecutor and approved by the grand jury that charges a certain person with a specific crime or crimes for which that person is later to be tried in court.

Injunction: An order by a court prohibiting a defendant from committing an act, or commanding an act be done.

Inquest: A legal inquiry to establish some question of fact; specifically, and inquiry by a coroner and jury into a person's death where accident, foul play, or violence is suspected as the cause.

Instanter: A subpoena issued for the appearance of a hostile witness or person who has failed to appear in answer to a previous subpoena and authorizing a law enforcement officer to bring that person to the court.

Interpol (International Criminal Police Commission): A clearing house for international exchanges of information consisting of a consortium of 126 countries.

Jeopardy: The danger of conviction and punishment that a defendant faces in a criminal trial.

Judge: An officer who presides over and administers the law in a court of justice.

Judicial notice: The rule that a court will accept certain things as common knowledge without proof.

Judicial process: The procedures taken by a court in deciding cases or resolving legal controversies.

Jurisdiction: The territory, subject matter, or persons over which lawful authority may be exercised by a court or other justice agency, as determined by statute or constitution.

Jury: A certain number of persons who are sworn to examine the evidence and determine the truth on the basis of that evidence.

Jury, hung: A trial jury which, after exhaustive deliberations, cannot agree on a unanimous verdict, necessitating an mistrial and a subsequent retrial.

Justice of the peace: A subordinate magistrate, usually without formal legal training, empowered to try petty civil and criminal cases and, in some states, to conduct preliminary hearings for persons accused of a crime, and to fix bail for appearance in court.

Juvenile delinquent: A boy or girl who has not reached the age of criminal liability (varies from state to state) and who commits and act which would be a misdemeanor or felony if he or she were an adult. Delinquents are tried in *Juvenile* Court and confined to separate facilities.

Law Enforcement Agency: A federal, state, or local criminal justice agency or identifiable subunit whose principal functions are the prevention, detection, and investigation of crime and the apprehension of alleged offenders.

Libel and slander: Printed and spoken defamation of character, respectively, or a person or an institution. In a slander action, it is usually necessary to prove specific damages caused by spoken words to recover, but in a case of libel, the damage is assumed to have occurred by publication.

Lie detector: An instrument that measures certain physiological reactions of the human body from which a trained operator may determine whether the subject is telling the truth or lies; polygraph; psychological stress evaluator.

Litigation: A judicial controversy; a contest in a court of justice for the purpose of enforcing a right; any controversy that must be decided upon evidence.

Mala in se (**Lat.**): Evil in itself. Acts that are make crimes because they are, by their nature evil and morally wrong.

Mala fides (**Lat.**): Bad faith, as opposed to *bona fides,* or good faith.

Mala priohibita (**Lat.**): Evil because they are prohibited. Acts that are not wrong in themselves but which, to protect the general welfare, are make crimes by statute.

Malfeasance: The act of a public officer in committing a crime relating to his official duties or powers. Accepting or demanding a bribe.

Malice: An evil intent to vex, annoy, or injure another; intentional evil.

Mandatory sentences: A statutory requirement that a certain penalty shall be set and carried out in all cases upon conviction for a specified offense or series of offenses.

Martial Law: Refers to control of civilian populations by a military commander.

Mediation: Nonbinding third-party intervention in the collective bargaining process.

Mens rea (**Lat.**): Criminal intent.

Miranda Rights: Set of rights that a person accused or suspected of having committed a specific offense has during interrogation and of which he or she must be informed prior to questioning, as stated by the Supreme Court in deciding *Miranda v. Arizona* in 1966 and related cases.

Misdemeanor: Any crime not a felony. Usually, a crime punishable by a fine or imprisonment in the county or other local jail.

Misprison: Failing to reveal a crime.

Mistrial: A trial discontinued before reaching a verdict because of some procedural defect or impediment.

Modus operandi: A characteristic pattern of behavior repeated in a series of offenses that coincides with the pattern evidenced by a particular person or group of persons.

Motion: An oral or written request made to a court at any time before, during, or after court proceedings, asking the court to make a specified finding, decision, or order.

Motive: The reason for committing a crime.

Municipal court: A minor court authorized by municipal charter or state law to enforce local ordinances and exercise the criminal and civil jurisdiction of the peace.

Narc: A widely used slang term for any local or federal law enforcement officer whose duties are focused on preventing or controlling traffic in and the use of illegal drugs.

Negligent: Culpably careless; acting without the due care required by the circumstances.

Neolombrosians: Criminologists who emphasize psychopathological states as causes of crime.

No bill: A phrase used by a Grand jury when they fail to indict.

Nolle prosequi (**Lat.**): A prosecutor's decision not to initiate or continue prosecution.

Nolo contendre (**Lat., lit.**): A pleading, usually used by a defendant in a criminal case, that literally means "I will not contest."

Notary public: A public officer authorized to authenticate and certify documents such as seeds, contracts, and affidavits with his or her signature and seal.

Null: Of no legal or binding force.

Obiter dictum (**Lat.**): A belief or opinion included by a judge in his or her decision in a case.

Objection: The act of taking exception to some statement or procedure in a trial. Used to call the court's attention to some improper evidence or procedure.

Opinion evidence: A witness' belief or opinion about a fact in dispute, as distinguished from personal knowledge of the fact.

Ordinance: A law enacted by the city or municipal government.

Organized crime: An organized, continuing criminal conspiracy that engages in crime as business (e.g., loan sharking, illegal gambling, prostitution, extortion, etc.).

Original jurisdiction: The authority of a court to hear and determine a lawsuit when it is initiated.

Overt act: An open or physical act done to further a plan, conspiracy, or intent, as opposed to a thought or mere intention.

Paralegals: Employees, also know as legal assistants, of law firms, who assist attorneys in the delivery of legal services.

Pardon: There are two kinds of pardons of offenses: the absolute pardon, which fully restores to the individual all rights and privileges of a citizen, setting aside a conviction and penalty, and the conditional pardon, which requires a condition to be met before the pardon is officially granted.

Parole: A conditional, supervised release from prison prior to expiration of sentence.

Penal code: Criminal codes, the purpose of which is to define what acts shall be punished as crimes.

Penology: The study of punishment and corrections.

Peremptory challenge: In the selection of jurors, challenges made by either side to certain jurors without assigning any reason, and which the court must allow.

Perjury: The legal offense of deliberately testifying falsely under oath about a material fact.

Perpetrator: The chief actor in the commission of a crime, that is, the person who directly commits the criminal act.

Petit jury: The ordinary jury composed of 12 persons who hear criminal cases and determines guilt or innocence of the accused. *See also* Grand jury.

Plaintiff: A person who initiates a court action.

Plea-bargaining: A negotiation between the defense attorney and the prosecutor in which the defendant receives a reduced penalty in return for a plea of "guilty."

Police power: The authority to legislate for the protection of the health, morals, safety and welfare of the people.

Postmortem: After death. Commonly applied to an examination of a dead body. *See also* Autopsy.

Precedent: Decision by a court that may serve as an example or authority for similar cases in the future.

Preliminary hearing: The proceeding in front of a lower court to determine if there is sufficient evidence for submitting a felony case to the grand jury.

Premeditation: A design to commit a crime or commit some other act before it is done.

Presumption of fact: An inference as to the truth or falsity of any proposition or fact, make in the absence of actual certainty of its truth or falsity or until such certainty can be attained.

Presumption of innocence: The defendant is presumed to be innocent and the burden is on the state to prove his or her guilt beyond a reasonable doubt.

Presumption of law: A rule of law that courts and judges must draw a particular inference from a particular fact or evidence, unless the inference can be disproved.

Probable cause: A set of facts and circumstances that would induce a reasonably intelligent and prudent person to believe that a particular person had committed a specific crime; reasonable grounds to make or believe an accusation.

Probation: A penalty placing a convicted person under the supervision of a probation officer for a stated time, instead or being confined.

Prosecutor: One who initiates a criminal prosecution against an accused. One who acts as a trial attorney for the governments as the representative of the people.

Public defender: An attorney appointed by a court to represent individuals in criminal proceedings who do not have the resources to hire their own defense council.

Rap sheet: Popularized acronym for record of arrest and prosecution.

Reasonable doubt: That state of mind of jurors when they do not feel a moral certainty about the truth of the charge and when the evidence does no exclude every other reasonable hypothesis except that the defendant is guilty as charged.

Rebutting evidence: When the defense has produced new evidence that the prosecution has not dealt with, the court, at its discretion, may allow the prosecution to give evidence in reply to rebut or contradict it.

Recidivism: The repetition of criminal behavior.

Repeal: The abrogation of a law by the enacting body, either by express declaration or implication by the passage of a later act whose provisions contradict those of the earlier law.

Reprieve: The temporary postponement of the execution of a sentence.

Restitution: A court requirement that an alleged or convicted offender pay money or provide services to the victim of the crime or provide services to the community.

Restraining order: An order, issued by a court of competent jurisdiction, forbidding a named person, or a class of persons, from doing specified acts.

Retribution: A concept that implies that payment of a debt to society and thus the expiation of one's offense. It was codified in the biblical injunction, "and eye for an eye, a tooth for a tooth."

Sanction: A legal penalty assessed for the violation of law. The term also include social methods of obtaining compliance, such as peer pressure and public opinion.

Search warrant: A written order, issued by judicial authority in the name of the state, directing a law enforcement officer to search for personal property and, if found, to bring it before the court.

Selective enforcement: The deploying of police personnel in ways to cope most effectively with existing or anticipated problems.

Self-incrimination: In constitutional terms, the process of becoming involved in or charged with a crime by one's own testimony.

Sentence: The penalty imposed by a court on a person convicted of a crime; the court judgment specifying the penalty; and any disposition of a defendant resulting from a conviction, including the court decision to suspend execution of a sentence.

Small claims court: A special court that provides expeditious, informal, and inexpensive adjudication of small contractual claims. In most jurisdictions, attorneys are not permitted for cases, and claims are limited to a specific amount.

Stare decisis **(Lat.):** To abide by decided cases. The doctrine that once a court has laid down a principle of laws as applicable to certain facts, it will apply it to all future cases when the facts are substantially the same.

State's attorney: An officer, usually locally elected within a county, who represents the state in securing indictments and in prosecuting criminal cases.

State's evidence: Testimony by a participant in the commission of a crime that incriminates others involved, given under the promise of immunity.

Status offense: An act that is declared by statute to be an offense, but only when committed or engaged in by a juvenile, and that can be adjudicated only by a juvenile court.

Statute: A Law enacted by, or with the authority of, a legislature.

Statute of limitations: A term applied to numerous statutes that set a limit on the length of time that may elapse between an event giving rise to a cause of action and the commencement of a suit to enforce that cause.

Stay: A halting of a judicial proceeding by a court order.

Sting operation: The typical sting involves using various undercover methods to control crime.

Subpoena: A court order requiring a witness to attend and testify as a witness in a court proceeding.

Subpoena *duces tecum:* A court order requiring a witness to bring all books, documents, and papers that might affect the outcome of the proceedings.

Summons: A written order issued by a judicial officer requiring a person accused of a criminal offense to appear in a designated court at a specified time to answer the charge(s).

Superior court: A court of record or general trial court, superior to a justice of the peace or magistrate's court. In some states, an intermediate court between the general trial court and the highest appellate court.

Supreme court, state: Usually the highest court in the state judicial system.

Supreme court, U.S.: Heads the judicial branch of the American government and is the nation's highest law court.

Suspect: An adult or juvenile considered by a criminal agency to be one who may have committed a specific criminal offense but who has not yet been arrested or charged.

Testimony: Evidence given by a competent witness, under oath, as distinguished from evidence from writings and other sources.

Tort: The breach of a duty to an individual that results in damage to him or her, for which one may be sued in civil court for damages. Crime, in contrast may be called the breach of duty to the public. Some actions may constitute both torts and crimes.

Uniform Crime Reports (U.C.R.): Annual statistical tabulation of "crimes known to the police" and "crimes cleared by arrest" published by the Federal Bureau of Investigation.

United States claims court: Established in 1982, it serves as the court of original and exclusive jurisdiction over claims brought against the federal government, except for tort claims, which are heard by district courts.

Untied States district courts: Trial courts with original jurisdiction over diversity-of-citizenship cases and cases arising under U.S. criminal, bankruptcy, admiralty, patent, copyright, and postal laws.

Venue: The locality in which a suit may be tried.

Verdict: The decision of a court.

Vice squad: A special detail of police agents, charged with raiding and closing houses of prostitution and gambling resorts.

Victim and Witness Protection Act of 1984: The federal VWP Act and state laws protect crime victims and witnesses against physical and verbal intimidation where such intimidation is designed to discourage reporting or crimes and participation in criminal trials.

Victimology: The study of the psychological and dynamic interrelationships between victims and offenders, with a view toward crime prevention.

Vigilante: An individual or member of a group who undertakes to enforce the law and/or maintain morals without legal authority.

Voir dire **(Fr.):** The examination or questioning of prospective jurors in order to determine his or her qualifications to serve as a juror.

Warrant: A court order directing a police officer to arrest a named person or search a specific premise.

White-collar crime: Nonviolent crime for financial gain committed by means of deception by persons who use their special occupational skills and opportunities.

Witness: Anyone called to testify by either side in a trial. More broadly, a witness is anyone who has observed an event.

Work release (furlough programs): Change in prisoners' status to minimum custody with permission to work outside prison.

World court: Formally known as the International Court of Justice, it deals with disputes involving international law.

SOURCES

The Dictionary of Criminal Justice, Fourth edition, © 1994 by George E. Rush. Published by The Dushkin Publishing Group, Inc., Guilford, CT 06437.

Credits/ Acknowledgments

Cover design by Charles Vitelli

1. Crime and Justice in America
Facing overview—Photo by Pamela Carley.

2. Victimology
Facing overview—United Nations photo by John Isaac.

3. The Police
Facing overview—AP/Wide World photo by Michael Caulfield.

4. The Judicial System
Facing overview—EPA Documerica photo.

5. Juvenile Justice
Facing overview—Photo by Dr. Phillip Zimbardo.

6. Punishment and Corrections
Facing overview—AP/Wide World photo.

PHOTOCOPY THIS PAGE!!!*

ANNUAL EDITIONS ARTICLE REVIEW FORM

■ NAME: _____ DATE: _____

■ TITLE AND NUMBER OF ARTICLE: _____

■ BRIEFLY STATE THE MAIN IDEA OF THIS ARTICLE: _____

_____

■ LIST THREE IMPORTANT FACTS THAT THE AUTHOR USES TO SUPPORT THE MAIN IDEA:

_____

_____

_____

_____

_____

_____

■ WHAT INFORMATION OR IDEAS DISCUSSED IN THIS ARTICLE ARE ALSO DISCUSSED IN YOUR TEXTBOOK OR OTHER READING YOU HAVE DONE? LIST THE TEXTBOOK CHAPTERS AND PAGE NUMBERS:

_____

_____

_____

_____

_____

_____

■ LIST ANY EXAMPLES OF BIAS OR FAULTY REASONING THAT YOU FOUND IN THE ARTICLE:

_____

_____

_____

_____

■ LIST ANY NEW TERMS/CONCEPTS THAT WERE DISCUSSED IN THE ARTICLE AND WRITE A SHORT DEFINITION:

_____

_____

_____

_____

_____

*Your instructor may require you to use this Annual Editions Article Review Form in any number of ways: for articles that are assigned, for extra credit, as a tool to assist in developing assigned papers, or simply for your own reference. Even if it is not required, we encourage you to photocopy and use this page; you'll find that reflecting on the articles will greatly enhance the information from your text.

ANNUAL EDITIONS: CRIMINAL JUSTICE 96/97
Article Rating Form

Here is an opportunity for you to have direct input into the next revision of this volume. We would like you to rate each of the 45 articles listed below, using the following scale:

1. **Excellent: should definitely be retained**
2. **Above average: should probably be retained**
3. **Below average: should probably be deleted**
4. **Poor: should definitely be deleted**

Your ratings will play a vital part in the next revision. So please mail this prepaid form to us just as soon as you complete it.
Thanks for your help!

Annual Editions revisions depend on two major opinion sources: one is our Advisory Board, listed in the front of this volume, which works with us in scanning the thousands of articles published in the public press each year; the other is you—the person actually using the book. Please help us and the users of the next edition by completing the prepaid article rating form on this page and returning it to us. Thank you.

Rating	Article	Rating	Article
	1. An Overview of the Criminal Justice System		22. Abuse of Power in the Prosecutor's Office
	2. The Real Problems in American Justice		23. The Trials of the Public Defender
	3. What to Do about Crime		24. Suspect Confessions
	4. The Decline of the American Mafia		25. A Trial for Our Times: An Ugly End to It All
	5. How Much Crime Is There?		26. Justice English Style
	6. Moral Credibility and Crime: Why People Obey the Law		27. Jury Consultants: Boon or Bane?
	7. Russian Organized Crime—A Worldwide Problem		28. Rethinking the Sanctioning Function in Juvenile Court: Retributive or Restorative Responses to Youth Crime
	8. Color Blinded? Race Seems to Play an Increasing Role in Many Jury Verdicts		29. Hard Times for Bad Kids
	9. Criminal Victimization 1993		30. Judge Hayden's Family Values
	10. True Crime		31. Violence by Young People: Why the *Deadly* Nexus?
	11. Protecting Our Seniors		32. Controlling Crime before It Happens: Risk-Focused Prevention
	12. Stopping Terrorism at Home		33. Everyday School Violence: How Disorder Fuels It
	13. Responding to Domestic Violence against Women		34. Probation's First 100 Years: Growth through Failure
	14. "Towards the Institutionalization of a New Kind of Justice Professional: The Victim Advocate"		35. Doing Soft Time
	15. Computer Technology Comes to Aid of Crime Victims		36. Punishment and Prevention
			37. HIV in Prisons and Jails, 1993
	16. Police and the Quest for Professionalism		38. More in U.S. Are in Prisons, Report Says
	17. Police Work from a Woman's Perspective		39. Privatizing America's Prisons, Slowly
	18. Officers from Rural, Suburban, and Urban Jurisdictions Share Views		40. Crime Takes on a Feminine Face
	19. A LEN Interview with Professor Carl Klockars of the University of Delaware		41. Psychiatric Gulag or Wise Safekeeping?
			42. Bringing God to Death Row
	20. The Crooked Blue Line		43. Anger and Ambivalence
	21. The Thin White Line		44. Death Row, U.S.A
			45. 'This Man Has Expired'

(Continued on next page)

ABOUT YOU

Name _____ Date _____

Are you a teacher? ❑ Or student? ❑

Your School Name _____

Department _____

Address _____

City _____ State _____ Zip _____

School Telephone # _____

YOUR COMMENTS ARE IMPORTANT TO US!

Please fill in the following information:

For which course did you use this book? _____

Did you use a text with this Annual Edition? ❑ yes ❑ no

The title of the text? _____

What are your general reactions to the Annual Editions concept?

Have you read any particular articles recently that you think should be included in the next edition?

Are there any articles you feel should be replaced in the next edition? Why?

Are there other areas that you feel would utilize an Annual Edition?

May we contact you for editorial input?

May we quote you from above?

ANNUAL EDITIONS: CRIMINAL JUSTICE 96/97

BUSINESS REPLY MAIL

First Class   Permit No. 84   Guilford, CT

Postage will be paid by addressee

**Dushkin Publishing Group/
Brown & Benchmark Publishers**
Sluice Dock
Guilford, Connecticut 06437

IIl‖‖‖‖l‖‖‖l‖l‖l‖ll‖‖‖l‖l‖l‖l‖l‖l‖l‖l‖ll‖l‖l